BRITISH VESSELS LOST AT SEA 1914-18

Contents

Publisher's introduction   vi

Section I: Navy Losses
Part I: Warships
I: List of Losses arranged according to Year and Class   3
II: Summary of Losses   7
III: Analysis of Causes of Loss   8
IV: Classified Nominal List of Losses   8
Part II: Auxiliaries on Admiralty Service
V: List of Losses arranged according to Year and Class   9
VI: Summary of Losses   28
VII: Analysis of Causes of Loss   29
VIII: Classified Nominal List of Losses   29
Index to Section I   33

Section II: Merchant Shipping (Losses)
List I: British Merchant Vessels Captured or Destroyed by the Enemy   1
List II: British Fishing Vessels Captured or Destroyed by the Enemy   99
List III: British Merchant Vessels Damaged or Molested by the Enemy but not Sunk   125
Table A: Showing Number and Gross Tonnage of British Merchant Vessels Lost through Enemy Action during each month since Outbreak of War; and number of Lives Lost   162
Table B: Showing Number and Gross Tonnage of British Fishing Vessels Lost through Enemy Action during each month since Outbreak of War; and number of Lives Lost   163
Table C: Showing Number and Gross Tonnage of British Merchant Vessels Damaged or Molested (but not Sunk) by the Enemy during each month since Outbreak of War; and number of Lives Lost   164
Index to Section II   165

Publisher's introduction

In August 1919, less than a year after the First World War ended, His Majesty's Stationery Office issued two important House of Commons papers. One was entitled *Navy Losses* and the other *Merchant Shipping (Losses)*. Not surprisingly, original editions of both these reports are extremely scarce today but, although prepared so soon after the cessation of hostilities, they are still invaluable reference sources for anyone interested in 20th-century military affairs.

Now both these indispensable papers have been combined into one case-bound volume. Apart from a minor alteration in the order of the contents, they are reprinted exactly as they first appeared, but in a smaller, more practical format.

All the information is presented in clear and concise tabular form for ease of reference. Section I, which is devoted to the Royal Navy, gives the following data on warships: class, name, displacement, date of launch, date of completion, date of loss, and how lost and where; while there is also an additional feature on auxiliaries on Admiralty service.

The second section, on merchant and fishing vessels, represents the major part of the book. Here the information given for each vessel includes: name, tons, date, position, cause of loss, how attacked, how sunk, and lives lost. There is also a list of merchant vessels damaged or molested by the enemy but not sunk, together with surveys of total losses during each month of the war.

Judging by the enthusiastic response to *British Vessels Lost at Sea 1939-45*, we are quite sure that this faithful reprint of two rare collectors' items will be eagerly sought after by naval historians and shipping enthusiasts throughout the world.

Acknowledgements
The publishers would like to thank the following for their help and assistance with this reprint: Her Majesty's Stationery Office, London; the Central Library of the Department of Trade and Industry, London (in particular Mr G. Cook); and Mr R. Perry.

Special note
Both sections of this book are separately numbered and indexed, as were the original papers.

Section I
NAVY LOSSES

NAVY LOSSES.

RETURN to an Order of the Honourable the House of Commons,
dated 1 August 1919 ;—*for*,

RETURN " showing the losses of ships of the ROYAL NAVY during the period 4th day of August 1914 to 11th day of November 1918, distinguishing Battleships, Cruisers, Light Cruisers, Torpedo Gunboats, Coast Defence Ships, Monitors, Sloops, River Gunboats, Flotilla Leaders, Torpedo Boat Destroyers, Torpedo Boats, Submarines, Coastal Motor Boats, Patrol Boats, Armed Merchant Cruisers, Minelayers, Aircraft Carriers and Armed Boarding Steamers; to show, as far as is known, Name, Class, Displacement, Date of Launch, Date of Completion, and Date, Place and Method of Loss.

" And showing the losses of AUXILIARY SHIPS of the ROYAL NAVY during the period 4th day of August 1914 to 11th day of November 1918, distinguishing Hospital Ships, Store Carriers, Mine Sweepers, Auxiliary Patrol Paddlers, Mine Carriers, Fleet Messengers, Commissioned Escort Ships, Miscellaneous Craft, Colliers, Oilers, Special Service Ships, Tugs, Yachts, and other Auxiliary Craft; to show, as far as is known, Name, Class, Gross Tonnage, whether or not commissioned, and Date, Place and Method of Loss."

ADMIRALTY,
August, 1919.

O. A. R. MURRAY,
Secretary.

(*Lieutenant-Colonel Burgoyne.*)

Ordered, by The House of Commons, *to be Printed*,
19 *August* 1919.

Losses of H.M. Ships and Auxiliaries during the War from 4th August 1914 to 11th November 1918.

CONTENTS.

	Page.
PART I.—WARSHIPS.	
I.—List of Losses arranged according to Year and Class	3
II.—Summary of Losses	7
III.—Analysis of Causes of Loss	8
IV.—Classified Nominal List of Losses	8
PART II.—AUXILIARIES ON ADMIRALTY SERVICE.	
V.—List of Losses arranged according to Year and Class	9
VI.—Summary of Losses	28
VII.—Analysis of Causes of Loss	29
VIII.—Classified Nominal List of Losses	29
General Index of Warships and Auxiliaries	33

PART I.—WARSHIPS.

I.—List of Losses arranged according to Year and Class.—Warships.

Class.	Name.	Displacement.	Date of Launch.	Date of Completion.	Date of Loss.	How Lost and Where.
		Tons.			**1914.**	
BATTLESHIPS	Audacious	23,000	14 Sept. 1912	Oct. 1913	27 Oct.	Sunk by mine off N. Coast of Ireland.
	Bulwark	15,000	18 Oct. 1899	March 1902	26 Nov.	Internal explosion off Sheerness.
CRUISERS	Aboukir	12,000	16 May 1900	Feb. 1902	22 Sept.	
	Cressy	12,000	4 Dec 1899	May 1901	22 Sept.	Sunk by submarine in North Sea.
	Hogue	12,000	13 Aug. 1900	Sept. 1902	22 Sept.	
	Hawke	7,350	11 March 1891	March 1893	15 Oct.	
	Good Hope	14,100	21 Feb. 1901	Nov. 1902	1 Nov.	Sunk by "Scharnhorst" and "Gneisenau" off Valparaiso.
	Monmouth	9,800	13 Nov. 1901	Nov. 1903	1 Nov.	
LIGHT CRUISERS	Amphion	3,440	4 Dec. 1911	April 1913	6 Aug.	Sunk by mine in North Sea.
	Pathfinder	2,940	16 July 1904	July 1905	5 Sept.	Sunk by submarine in North Sea.
	Pegasus	2,135	4 March 1897	Dec. 1898	20 Sept.	Sunk by "Königsberg" off Zanzibar.
TORPEDO GUNBOATS	Speedy	810	18 May 1893	March 1894	3 Sept.	Sunk by mine off the Humber.
	Niger	810	17 Dec. 1892	July 1893	11 Nov.	Sunk by submarine off Deal.
DESTROYER	Success	385	21 March 1901	May 1902	27 Dec.	Wrecked off Fifeness.
SUBMARINES	A.E. 1	791	18 June 1913	Jan. 1914	19 Sept.	Accident — cause unknown. Lost off Bismarck Archipelago.
	D. 5	620	28 Aug. 1911	Jan. 1912	3 Oct.	Sunk by mine in North Sea.
	E. 3	791	29 Oct. 1912	June 1914	18 Oct.	Sunk in North Sea—cause unknown.
	D. 2	600	25 May 1910	March 1911	25 Nov.	
AIRCRAFT CARRIER	Hermes	5,600	7 April 1898	Oct. 1899	31 Oct.	Sunk by submarine in Straits of Dover.
ARMED MERCHANT CRUISER.	Oceanic	17,274 (gross).	—	Built 1899	8 Sept.	Wrecked off Shetland Islands.
					1915.	
BATTLESHIPS	Formidable	15,000	17 Nov. 1898	Sept. 1901	1 Jan.	Sunk by submarine in the English Channel.
	Irresistible	15,000	15 Dec. 1898	Feb. 1902	18 March	Sunk by mine in the Dardanelles.
	Ocean	12,950	5 July 1898	Feb. 1900	18 March	
	Goliath	12,950	23 March 1898	March 1900	13 May	Sunk by T.B. off Cape Helles.
	Triumph	11,985	15 Jan. 1903	June 1904	25 May	Sunk by submarine off Gaba Tepe.
	Majestic	14,900	31 Jan. 1895	Dec. 1895	27 May	Sunk by submarine off Cape Helles.
CRUISERS	Argyll	10,850	3 March 1904	Dec. 1905	28 Oct.	Wrecked on East Coast of Scotland.
	Natal	13,550	30 Sept. 1905	April 1907	31 Dec.	Internal explosion, Cromarty Firth.
RIVER GUNBOATS	Shaitan		No particulars available.		28 Nov.	Grounded in River Tigris.
	Comet				1 Dec.	
DESTROYERS	Erne	550	14 Jan. 1903	Feb. 1904	6 Feb.	Wrecked off Rattray Head.
	Goldfinch	747	12 July 1910	Feb. 1911	18/19 Feb.	Wrecked off Orkney Islands.
	Recruit	385	22 Aug. 1896	Oct. 1900	1 May	Sunk by submarine off Galloper.
	Maori	1,035	24 May 1909	Nov. 1909	7 May	Sunk by mine in North Sea.
	Lightning	320	10 April 1895	Jan. 1896	30 June	Do. do.
	Lynx	935	20 March 1913	Jan. 1914	9 Aug.	Mined off Moray Firth.
	Velox	420	11 Feb. 1902	Feb. 1904	25 Oct.	Mined off Nab Light Vessel.
	Louis	965	30 Dec. 1913	May 1914	31 Oct.	Wrecked in Suvla Bay.
TORPEDO BOATS	064	87	—	Sept. 1886	21 March	Do. Ægean Sea.
	10	245	13 Feb. 1907	May 1907	10 June	Sunk by submarine in North Sea.
	12	263	15 March 1907	May 1907	10 June	
	96	130	—	April 1896	1 Nov.	Sunk in collision off Gibraltar.
	046	79	—	July 1886	27 Dec.	Wrecked by heavy weather while in tow in Eastern Mediterranean.
SUBMARINES	C. 31	321	2 Sept. 1909	Nov. 1909	4 Jan.	Lost off Belgian coast—cause unknown.
	E. 10	805	29 Dec. 1913	Aug. 1914	18 Jan.	Lost in North Sea—cause unknown.
	E. 15	805	23 April 1914	Oct. 1914	15 April	Wrecked in Dardanelles.
	A.E. 2	791	22 May 1913	Feb. 1914	30 April	Sunk in action in Sea of Marmora.
	C. 33	321	10 May 1910	Aug. 1910	4 Aug.	Lost in North Sea—cause unknown.
	E. 13	791	22 Sept. 1914	Dec. 1914	18 Aug.	Wrecked off Saltholm, and interned.
	C. 29	321	19 June 1909	Sept. 1909	29 Aug.	Sunk by mine in North Sea.
	E. 7	791	2 Oct. 1913	March 1914	4 Sept.	Sunk in Dardanelles.
	E. 20	807	12 June 1915	Aug. 1915	6 Nov.	Sunk by submarine in Dardanelles.
	E. 6	791	12 Nov. 1912	Oct. 1913	26 Dec.	Sunk by mine in North Sea.
MINELAYER	Princess Irene	6,000 (gross)	—	Built 1914	27 May	Internal explosion, Sheerness.
ARMED MERCHANT CRUISERS.	Viknor	5,386 (gross)	—	„ 1888	13 Jan.	Lost off Irish Coast.
	Clan MacNaughton	4,985 (gross)	—	„ 1911	3 Feb.	Believed to have foundered in North Atlantic.
	Bayano	5,948 (gross)	—	„ 1913	11 March	Sunk by submarine off Clyde.
	India	7,940 (gross)	—	„ 1896	8 Aug.	Sunk by submarine off Norwegian Coast.

Class.	Name.	Displacement.	Date of Launch.	Date of Completion.	Date of Loss.	How Lost and Where.
		Tons.			**1915.**	
ARMED BOARDING STEAMERS.	The Ramsey	1,443 (gross)	—	Built 1895	8 Aug.	Sunk by German auxiliary minelayer "Meteor" in North Sea.
	Tara	1,862 (gross)	—	,, 1900	5 Nov.	Sunk by submarine in Eastern Mediterranean.
					1916.	
BATTLESHIPS - -	King Edward VII.	16,350	23 July 1903	Feb. 1905	6 Jan.	Sunk by mine off North of Scotland.
	Russell	14,000	19 Feb. 1901	Feb. 1903	27 April	Sunk by mine off Malta.
BATTLE CRUISERS	Indefatigable	18,750	28 Oct. 1909	April 1911	31 May	
	Invincible	17,250	13 April 1907	March 1909	31 May	
	Queen Mary	27,000	20 March 1912	August 1913	31 May	
CRUISERS - - -	Black Prince	13,550	8 Nov. 1904	March 1906	31 May	Sunk in action in North Sea.
	Defence	14,600	27 April 1907	Feb. 1909	31 May	
	Warrior	13,550	25 Nov. 1905	May 1907	31 May	
	Hampshire	10,850	24 Sept. 1903	Aug. 1905	5 June	Sunk by mine off Orkneys.
LIGHT CRUISERS -	Arethusa	3,500	25 Oct. 1913	Aug. 1914	11 Feb.	Sunk by mine in North Sea.
	Falmouth	5,250	20 Sept. 1910	Sept. 1911	19 Aug.	Sunk by submarine in North Sea.
	Nottingham	5,440	18 April 1913	April 1914	19 Aug.	
MONITOR - - -	M. 30	355	23 June 1915	June 1915	13 May	Sunk in action in Gulf of Smyrna.
SLOOPS - - -	Arabis	1,250	6 Nov. 1915	Dec. 1915	10 Feb.	Sunk by T.B.D. in North Sea.
	Primula	1,250	6 Dec. 1915	Jan. 1916	1 March	Sunk by submarine in Mediterranean.
	Nasturtium	1,250	21 Dec. 1915	Feb. 1916	27 April	Sunk by mine in Mediterranean.
	Genista	1,250	26 Feb. 1916	April 1916	23 Oct.	Sunk by submarine in Atlantic.
FLOTILLA LEADERS	Tipperary	1,737	5 March 1915	May 1915	31 May	Sunk in action in North Sea.
	Hoste	1,666	16 Aug. 1916	Nov. 1916	21 Dec.	Sunk in collision in North Sea.
DESTROYERS - -	Coquette	355	25 Nov. 1897	Nov. 1899	7 March	Sunk by mine in North Sea.
	Medusa	1,007	27 March 1915	June 1915	25 March	Sunk by collision in North Sea.
	Ardent	981	8 Sept. 1913	Feb. 1914	31 May	
	Fortune	1,000	17 May 1913	Dec. 1913	31 May	
	Nestor	1,025	22 Dec. 1915	April 1916	31 May	
	Nomad	1,025	7 Feb. 1916	April 1916	31 May	Sunk in action in North Sea.
	Shark	935	30 July 1912	April 1913	31 May	
	Sparrowhawk	935	12 Oct. 1912	May 1913	31 May	
	Turbulent	1,080	5 Jan. 1916	May 1916	31 May	
?	Eden	540	14 March 1903	June 1904	18 June	Sunk in collision in English Channel.
	Lassoo	1,010	24 Aug. 1915	Oct. 1915	13 Aug.	Sunk by mine in North Sea.
×	Flirt	380	15 May 1897	April 1899	27 Oct.	Sunk in action in Straits of Dover.
	Zulu	1,027	16 Sept. 1909	March 1910	27 Oct.	Damaged in action and afterwards made into one ship named "Zubian."
	Nubian	1,062	20 April 1909	Sept. 1909		
	Negro	1,025	8 March 1916	May 1916	21 Dec.	Sunk by collision in North Sea.
TORPEDO BOATS -	13	270	10 July 1907	May 1908	26 Jan.	
	11	263	29 Jan. 1907	May 1907	7 March	Sunk by mine in North Sea.
	9	247	18 March 1907	June 1907	26 July	Sunk by collision in North Sea.
SUBMARINES - -	E. 17	805	16 Jan. 1915	April 1915	6 Jan.	Wrecked on Dutch Coast.
	H. 6	434	—	June 1915	18 Jan.	Wrecked on Dutch Coast and interned.
	E. 5	791	17 May 1912	June 1913	7 March	Lost in North Sea—cause unknown.
	E. 24	807	9 Dec. 1915	Jan. 1916	24 March	Do. do.
	E. 22	807	27 Aug. 1915	Nov. 1915	25 April	Sunk by submarine in North Sea.
	E. 18	805	4 March 1915	June 1915	24 May	Lost in Baltic—cause unknown.
	E. 26	807	11 Nov. 1915	Dec. 1915	6 July	Lost in North Sea—cause unknown.
	H. 3	434	—	June 1915	15 July	Lost in Adriatic—cause unknown.
	B. 10	316	7 March 1906	May 1906	9 Aug.	Sunk by bomb from aircraft at Venice.
	E. 16	805	23 Sept. 1914	Feb. 1915	22 Aug.	Lost in North Sea—cause unknown.
	E. 30	807	29 June 1915	Dec. 1915	22 Nov.	
	E. 37	807	25 Sept. 1915	March 1916	1 Dec.	
ARMED MERCHANT CRUISER.	Alcantara	15,300 (gross)	—	Built 1913	29 Feb.	Sunk in action in North Sea.
ARMED BOARDING STEAMERS.	Fauvette	2,644 (gross)	—	,, 1912	9 March	Sunk by mine in North Sea.
	Marcella	127 (gross)	—	,, 1887	24 March	Sunk by collision in North Sea.
	Duke of Albany.	1,997 (gross)		,, 1907	25 Aug.	Sunk by submarine in North Sea.
					1917.	
BATTLESHIPS - -	Cornwallis	14,000	17 July 1901	Feb. 1904	11 Jan.	Sunk by submarine off Malta.
	Vanguard	19,250	22 Feb. 1909	Feb. 1910	9 July	Blown up by internal explosion at Scapa.
CRUISER - - -	Drake	14,100	5 March 1901	Jan. 1903	2 Oct.	Sunk by submarine in North Channel.
TORPEDO GUNBOAT	Jason	810	14 May 1892	June 1893	7 April	Sunk by mine off West Coast of Scotland.
MONITOR - - -	M. 15	540	28 April 1915	May 1915	11 Nov.	Sunk by submarine off Coast of Palestine.
SLOOPS - - -	Mignonette	1,250	26 Jan. 1916	March 1916	17 March	Sunk by mine off S.W. Coast of Ireland.
	Alyssum	1,250	5 Nov. 1915	Dec. 1915	18 March	
	*Tulip	1,250	15 July 1916	Sept. 1916	30 April	Sunk by submarine in Atlantic.

* Employed as Special Service Ship.

5

Class.	Name.	Displacement.	Date of Launch.	Date of Completion.	Date of Loss.	How Lost and Where.
		Tons.			**1917.**	
SLOOPS—*continued*	Lavender	1,200	12 June 1915	Aug. 1915	5 May	Sunk by submarine in English Channel.
	*Salvia	1,250	16 June 1916	Oct. 1916	20 June	Sunk by submarine off W. Coast of Ireland.
	Aster	1,200	1 May 1915	June 1915	4 July	Sunk by mine in Mediterranean.
	*Bergamot	1,290	5 May 1917	July 1917	13 Aug.	Sunk by submarine in Atlantic.
	*Begonia	1,200	26 Aug. 1915	Oct. 1915	— Oct.	Probably sunk by submarine in Atlantic.
	*Candytuft	1,290	19 May 1917	Aug. 1917	18 Nov.	Sunk by submarine in Mediterranean.
	*Arbutus	1,290	8 Sept. 1917	Nov. 1917	16 Dec.	Sunk by submarine off Bristol Channel.
DESTROYERS	Simoon	1,072	30 Oct. 1916	Dec. 1916	23 Jan.	Sunk in action in North Sea.
	Ghurka	880	29 April 1907	Dec. 1908	8 Feb.	Sunk by mine in English Channel.
	Pheasant	1,025	23 Oct. 1916	Nov. 1916	1 March	Sunk off Orkneys, apparently by floating mine.
	Foyle	550	25 Feb 1903	March 1904	15 March	Sunk by mine in Dover Straits.
	Paragon	917	21 Feb. 1913	Dec. 1913	18 March	Sunk in action in Dover Straits.
	Laforey	995	22 Aug. 1913	Feb. 1914	23 March	} Sunk by mine in English Channel.
	Myrmidon	370	26 May 1900	May 1901	26 March	
	Derwent	555	14 Feb. 1903	July 1904	2 May	
	Setter	1,040	18 Aug. 1916	Feb. 1917	17 May	Sunk by collision in North Sea.
	Cheerful	370	14 July 1897	Feb. 1900	30 June	Sunk by mine off Shetland Islands.
	Itchen	550	17 March 1903	Jan. 1904	6 July	Sunk by submarine in North Sea.
	Recruit	1,075	9 Dec. 1916	April 1917	9 Aug.	Sunk by mine in North Sea.
	Contest	957	7 Jan. 1913	June 1913	18 Sept.	Sunk by submarine in English Channel.
	Mary Rose	1,017	8 Oct. 1915	March 1916	17 Oct.	} Sunk in action in North Sea.
	Strongbow	898	30 Sept. 1916	Nov. 1916	17 Oct.	
	Marmion	1,029	28 May 1915	Sept. 1915	21 Oct.	Sunk by collision in North Sea.
	Staunch	748	29 Oct. 1910	March 1916	11 Nov.	Sunk by submarine off Coast of Palestine.
	Partridge	1,016	4 March 1916	June 1916	12 Dec.	Sunk in action in North Sea.
	Wolverine	986	15 Jan. 1910	Sept. 1910	12 Dec.	Sunk by collision off Irish Coast.
	Surprise	910	25 Nov. 1916	Jan. 1917	} 23 Dec.	Sunk by mine in North Sea.
	Tornado	1,091	4 Aug. 1917	Nov. 1917		
	Torrent	1,069	26 Nov. 1916	Feb. 1917		
	Attack	785	21 Dec. 1911	May 1912	30 Dec.	Sunk by mine off Alexandria.
TORPEDO BOATS	24	319	19 March 1908	June 1909	28 Jan.	Wrecked off Dover breakwater.
	117	197	18 Feb. 1904	Sept. 1904	10 June	Sunk by collision in English Channel.
SUBMARINE	E. 36	807	16 Sept. 1916	Nov. 1916	19 Jan.	Lost in North Sea—cause unknown.
	E. 49	807	18 Sept. 1916	Dec. 1916	12 March	Mined off Shetland Islands.
	C. 34	321	8 June 1910	Sept. 1910	21 July	Sunk by submarine off Shetland Islands.
	E. 47	807	29 May 1916	Oct. 1916	20 Aug.	Lost in North Sea—cause unknown.
	G. 9	965	15 June 1916	Aug. 1916	16 Sept.	Accidentally sunk in North Sea.
	C. 32	321	29 Sept. 1909	Nov. 1909	24 Oct.	Ran ashore and was blown up in Baltic Sea.
	K. 1	2,650	14 Nov. 1916	April 1917	18 Nov.	Sunk by collision in North Sea.
AIRCRAFT CARRIER	Ben-my-Chree	3,888	—	— 1908	11 Jan.	Sunk in action off Asia Minor.
PATROL BOAT	P. 26	613	22 Dec. 1915	May 1916	10 April	Sunk by mine in English Channel.
MINELAYER	Ariadne	11,000	22 April 1898	Nov. 1899	26 July	Sunk by submarine in English Channel.
ARMED MERCHANT CRUISERS.	Laurentic	14,892 (gross)	—	*Built* 1908	23 Jan.	Sunk by mine off Irish Coast.
	Hilary	6,329 (gross)	—	,, 1908	25 May	Sunk by submarine in Atlantic.
	Avenger	15,000 (gross)	—	,, 1915	14 June	} Sunk by submarine in N. Atlantic.
	Otway	12,077 (gross)	—	,, 1909	23 July	
	Champagne	5,360 (gross)	—	,, 1895	9 Oct.	} Sunk by submarine in Atlantic.
	Orama	12,927 (gross)	—	,, 1911	19 Oct.	
ARMED BOARDING STEAMERS.	Dundee	2,187 (gross)	—	,, 1911	3 Sept.	Sunk by submarine in entrance to English Channel.
	Fiona	1,611 (gross)	—	,, 1905	6 Sept.	Wrecked off Pentland Skerries.
	Stephen Furness.	1,712 (gross)	—	,, 1910	13 Dec.	Sunk by submarine in Irish Sea.
	Grive	2,037 (gross)	—	,, 1905	24 Dec.	Torpedoed in North Sea 8th December and foundered 24th December.
COASTAL MOTOR BOATS.	No. 1	5	—	,, 1916	19 June	Sunk in action off Ostend.
	No. 8	5	—	,, 1916	27 Sept.	Sunk off Belgian Coast to avoid capture.
	No. 11	5	—	,, 1916	2 Nov.	Caught fire in Dover Straits after collision.

* Employed as Special Service Ships.

Class.	Name.	Displacement.	Date of Launch.	Date of Completion.	Date of Loss.	How Lost and Where.
		Tons.			**1918.**	
BATTLESHIPS	Britannia	16,350	10 Dec. 1904	Sept. 1906	9 Nov.	Sunk by submarine off Cape Trafalgar.
LIGHT CRUISERS	Brilliant	3,600	24 June 1891	April 1893	23 April	Sunk as blockship at Ostend.
	Intrepid	3,600	20 June 1891	Nov. 1892	23 April	Sunk as blockship at Zeebrugge.
	Iphigenia	3,600	19 Nov. 1891	May 1893	23 April	Do. do.
	Sirius	3,600	27 Oct. 1890	April 1892	23 April	Sunk as blockship at Ostend.
	Thetis	3,400	13 Dec. 1890	April 1892	23 April	Sunk as blockship at Zeebrugge
	Vindictive	5,750	9 Dec. 1897	Oct. 1898	10 May	Sunk as blockship at Ostend.
TORPEDO GUN-BOATS.	Hazard	1,070	17 Feb. 1894	Sept. 1894	28 Jan.	Sunk by collision in English Channel.
	Seagull	735	31 May 1889	Dec. 1890	30 Sept.	Sunk in collision in Firth of Clyde.
COAST DEFENCE SHIP.	Glatton	5,700	8 Aug. 1914	Sept. 1918	16 Sept.	Sunk by internal explosion in Dover Harbour.
MONITORS	Raglan	6,150	29 April 1915	June 1915	20 Jan.	Sunk at Imbros in action with "Goeben" and "Breslau."
	M. 28	540	28 June 1915	Aug. 1915	20 Jan.	
	M. 21	540	27 May 1915	July 1915	20 Oct.	Mined off Ostend.
SLOOPS	Gaillardia	1,290	19 May 1917	Nov. 1917	22 Mar.	Sunk by mine in North Sea.
	Cowslip	1,290	19 Oct. 1917	Dec. 1917	25 April	Sunk by submarine off Cape Spartel.
	Rhododendron	1,290	15 Oct. 1917	Feb. 1918	5 May	Sunk by submarine in North Sea.
	Anchusa	1,290	21 April 1917	June 1917	16 July	Sunk by submarine off North Coast of Ireland.
FLOTILLA LEADER	Scott	1,801	18 Oct. 1917	Jan. 1918	15 Aug.	Sunk by submarine in North Sea.
DESTROYERS	Racoon	913	15 Feb. 1910	Oct. 1910	9 Jan.	Wrecked on Irish Coast.
	Narbrough	1,010	2 March 1916	April 1916	12 Jan.	Wrecked off Orkneys.
	Opal	1,000	11 Sept. 1915	April 1916	12 Jan.	
	Boxer	280	28 Nov. 1894	June 1895	8 Feb.	Sunk by collision in English Channel.
	Arno	550		June 1915	23 March	Sunk by collision off Dardanelles.
	Kale	545	8 Nov. 1904	Aug. 1905	27 March	Sunk by mine in North Sea.
	Falcon	408	29 Dec. 1899	Dec. 1901	1 April	Sunk by collision in North Sea.
	Bittern	360	1 Feb. 1897	April 1899	4 April	Sunk by collision in English Channel.
	North Star	1,042	9 Nov. 1916	Feb. 1917	23 April	Sunk in action at Zeebrugge.
	Phoenix	765	9 Oct. 1911	May 1912	14 May	Sunk by submarine in Adriatic.
	Fairy	380	29 May 1897	Aug. 1898	31 May	Sunk after ramming and destroying enemy submarine in North Sea.
	Pincher	975	15 March 1910	Sept. 1910	24 July	Wrecked on Seven Stones.
	Vehement	1,300	6 July 1917	Oct. 1917	2 Aug.	Sunk by mine in North Sea.
	Ariel	763	26 Sept. 1911	March 1912	2 Aug.	Do. do.
	Comet	747	23 June 1910	Jan. 1911	6 Aug.	Sunk by submarine in Mediterranean.
	Ulleswater	923	4 Aug. 1917	Sept. 1917	15 Aug.	Sunk by submarine in North Sea.
	Nessus	1,022	24 Aug. 1915	Nov. 1915	8 Sept.	Sunk by collision in North Sea.
	Ulysses	1,090	24 March 1917	June 1917	29 Oct.	Sunk by collision in Firth of Clyde.
TORPEDO BOAT	90	130	—	Nov. 1895	25 April	Capsized and sank in Straits of Gibraltar.
SUBMARINES	G. 8	965	1 May 1916	June 1916	14 Jan.	Lost in North Sea—cause unknown.
	H. 10	434	—	June 1915	19 Jan.	Do. Do.
	E 14	795	7 July 1914	Dec. 1914	28 Jan.	Sunk in action in Dardanelles.
	K. 4	2,650	15 July 1916	Dec. 1916	31 Jan.	Sunk in collision in North Sea.
	K. 17	2,650	10 April 1917	Sept. 1917		
	E. 50	807	14 Nov. 1916	Jan 1917	31 Jan.	Lost in North Sea—cause unknown.
	H. 5	434		June 1915	6 March	Sunk by collision in Irish Sea.
	D. 3	620	17 Oct. 1910	Sept. 1911	15 March	Accidentally sunk in English Channel.
	E. 1	795	9 Nov. 1912	April 1913	3 & 4 April	Destroyed at Helsingfors to avoid capture.
	E. 8	795	30 Oct. 1913	June 1914		
	E. 9	807	29 Nov. 1913	June 1914		
	E. 19	807	13 May 1915	July 1915		
	C. 26	321	20 March 1909	May 1909		
	C. 27	321	22 April 1909	Aug. 1909		
	C. 35	321	2 Nov. 1909	Feb. 1910		
	C. 3	316	3 Oct. 1906	Feb. 1907	23 April	Blown up at Zeebrugge Mole.
	D. 6	620	23 Oct. 1911	April 1912	28 June	Sunk by German submarine off North Coast of Ireland.
	E. 34	807	27 Jan. 1917	March 1917	20 July	Lost in North Sea—cause unknown.
	L. 10	1,070	24 Jan. 1918	June 1918	3-4 Oct.	Sunk in action in North Sea.
	J. 6	1,900	9 Sept. 1915	July 1916	15 Oct.	Accidentally sunk in North Sea.
	G. 7	965	4 March 1916	Aug. 1916	1 Nov.	Lost in North Sea—cause unknown.
AIRCRAFT CARRIER	Campania	18,000	—	April 1915*	5 Nov.	Sunk by collision in Firth of Forth.
PATROL BOAT	P. 12	613	4 Dec. 1915	Feb. 1916	4 Nov.	Sunk by collision in English Channel.
ARMED MERCHANT CRUISERS.	Calgarian	17,515 (gross)	—	*Built* 1914	1 March	Sunk by submarine off Irish Coast.
	Moldavia	9,500 (gross)	—	„ 1903	23 May	Sunk by submarine in English Channel.

* Date of completion of reconstruction as Aircraft Carrier.

Class.	Name.	Displacement.	Date of Launch.	Date of Completion.	Date of Loss.	How Lost and Where.
ARMED MERCHANT CRUISERS—cont.	Patia	Tons. 6,103 (gross)	—	Built 1913	1918. 13 June	Sunk by submarine in Bristol Channel.
	Marmora	10,509 (gross)	—	,, 1903	23 July	Sunk by submarine off South Coast of Ireland.
	Otranto	12,124 (gross)	—	,, 1909	6 Oct.	Wrecked off Islay after collision.
ARMED BOARDING STEAMERS.	Louvain	1,830 (gross)	—	,, 1897	20 Jan.	Sunk by submarine in Mediterranean.
	Tithonus (late Titania)	3,463 (gross)	—	,, 1908	28 March	Sunk by submarine in North Sea.
	Snaefell	1,368 (gross)	—	,, 1910	5 June	} Sunk by submarine in Mediterranean.
	Sarnia	1,498 (gross)	—	,, 1910	12 Sept.	
COASTAL MOTOR BOATS.	No. 18A	10 (disp.)	—	,, 1917	12 April	Sunk by collision off Belgian coast.
	No. 33A	10 (disp.)	—	,, 1918	12 April	Sunk in action off Ostend.
	No. 39B	10 (disp.)	—	,, 1918	28 April	Accidentally burnt at Dunkirk.
	No. 10	5 (disp.)	—	,, 1916	7 May	Accidentally burnt at Dover.
	No. 2	5 (disp.)	—	,, 1916	9 July	Accidentally burnt in Portsmouth Harbour.
	No. 50	5 (disp.)	—	,, 1918	19 July	Sunk in Heligoland Bight to avoid capture.
	No. 40	5 (disp.)	—	,, 1918	11 Aug.	} Sunk in action with aircraft off Frisian Islands.
	No. 42	5 (disp.)	—	,, 1918	11 Aug.	
	No. 47	5 (disp.)	—	,, 1918	11 Aug.	Caught fire during action off Frisian Islands and sank.
	No. 71A	10 (disp.)	—	,, 1918	15 Oct.	Missing, believed foundered off Belgian coast as result of collision.

II.—Summary of Losses.—Warships.

Class.	4 Aug. 1914 to 31 Dec. 1914.	1915.	1916.	1917.	1 Jan. 1918 to 11 Nov. 1918.	Total Number lost.	Total Displacement Tonnage lost (gross tonnage in *italics* is additional).
	No.	No.	No.	No.	No.	No.	Tons.
Battleships	2	6	2	2	1	13	200,735
Battle Cruisers	—	—	3	—	—	3	63,000
Cruisers	6	2	4	1	—	13	158,300
Light Cruisers	3	—	3	—	6†	12†	46,255
Torpedo Gunboats	2	—	—	1	2	5	4,235
River Gunboats	—	2	—	—	—	2	—‡
Coast Defence Ships	—	—	—	—	1	1	5,700
Monitors	—	—	1	1	3	5	8,125
Sloops	—	—	4	10	4	18	22,630
Flotilla Leaders	—	—	2	—	1	3	5,204
Torpedo Boat Destroyers	1	8	14*	23	18	64*	52,045
Torpedo Boats	—	5	3	2	1	11	2,230
Submarines	4	10	12	7	21§	54§	43,649
Aircraft Carriers	1	—	—	1	1	3	27,488
Patrol Boats	—	—	—	1	1	2	1,226
Minelayers	—	1	—	1	—	2	{ 11,000 6,000
Armed Merchant Cruisers	1	4	1	6	5	17	*179,169*
Armed Boarding Steamers	—	2	3	4	4	13	*23,779*
Coastal Motor Boats	—	—	—	3	10	13	85
Total—Nos.	20	40	52	63	79	254	—
Tons Displacement.	124,172	119,890	190,378	103,785	113,682	—	651,907‡
Tons Gross	*17,274*	*33,564*	*20,068*	*74,132*	*63,910*	—	*208,948*

* Including "Zulu" and "Nubian," damaged in action and afterwards made into one ship named "Zubian" (counted as one lost of 1,027 tons displacement).
† Six Light Cruisers sunk as blockships at Zeebrugge and Ostend.
‡ River Gunboats "Comet" and "Shaitan," tonnage uncertain.
§ Including seven destroyed at Helsingfors to avoid capture.

III.—Analysis of Causes of Loss.—Warships.

Class.	Action.	Submarine.	Mine.	Destruction to avoid Capture.	Used as Blockships.	Internal Explosion.	Collision.	Wrecked.	Accident.	Unknown.	Total.
Battleships	1	5	5	—	—	2	—	—	—	—	13
Battle Cruisers	3	—	—	—	—	—	—	—	—	—	3
Cruisers	5	5	1	—	—	1	—	1	—	—	13
Light Cruisers	1	3	2	—	6	—	—	—	—	—	12
Torpedo Gunboats	—	1	2	—	—	—	2	—	—	—	5
River Gunboats	—	—	—	—	—	—	—	2	—	—	2
Coast Defence Ship	—	—	—	—	—	1	—	—	—	—	1
Monitors	3	1	1	—	—	—	—	—	—	—	5
Sloops	1	11	5	—	—	—	—	—	—	1	18
Flotilla Leaders	1	1	—	—	—	—	1	—	—	—	3
Torpedo Boat Destroyers	16*	7	20	—	—	—	12	8	—	1	64*
Torpedo Boats	—	2	1	—	—	—	4	4	—	—	11
Submarines	3	4	4	9	1†	—	4	4	4	21	54
Aircraft Carriers	1	1	—	—	—	—	1	—	—	—	3
Patrol Boats	—	—	1	—	—	—	1	—	—	—	2
Minelayers	—	1	—	—	—	1	—	—	—	—	2
Armed Merchant Cruisers	1	11	1	—	—	—	—	2	—	2	17
Armed Boarding Steamers	1	9	1	—	—	—	1	1	—	—	13
Coastal Motor Boats	5	—	—	2	—	—	2	—	3	1	13
Total	42	62	44	11	7	5	28	22	7	26	254

* "Nubian" and "Zulu" counted as 1. (See Note, p. 7.)
† Blown up at Zeebrugge Mole.

IV.—Classified Nominal List of Losses.—Warships.

BATTLESHIPS.
Audacious.
Britannia.
Bulwark.
Cornwallis.
Formidable.
Goliath.
Irresistible.
King Edward VII.
Majestic.
Ocean.
Russell.
Triumph.
Vanguard.
(13)

BATTLE CRUISERS.
Indefatigable.
Invincible.
Queen Mary.
(3)

CRUISERS.
Aboukir.
Argyll.
Black Prince.
Cressy.
Defence.
Drake.
Good Hope.
Hampshire.
Hawke.
Hogue.
Monmouth.
Natal.
Warrior.
(13)

LIGHT CRUISERS.
Amphion.
Arethusa.
Brilliant.
Falmouth.
Intrepid.
Iphigenia.
Nottingham.
Pathfinder.
Pegasus.
Sirius.
Thetis.
Vindictive.
(12)

TORPEDO GUNBOATS.
Hazard.
Jason.
Niger.
Seagull.
Speedy.
(5)

RIVER GUNBOATS.
Comet.
Shaitan.
(2)

COAST DEFENCE SHIP.
Glatton.

MONITORS.
M. 15.
M. 21.
M. 28.
M. 30.
Raglan.
(5)

SLOOPS.
Alyssum.
Anchusa.
Arabis.
*Arbutus.
Aster.
*Begonia.
*Bergamot.
*Candytuft.
Cowslip.
Gaillardia.
Genista.
Lavender.
Mignonette.
Nasturtium.
Primula.
Rhododendron.
*Salvia.
*Tulip.
(18)

FLOTILLA LEADERS.
Hoste.
Scott.
Tipperary.
(3)

TORPEDO BOAT DESTROYERS.
Ardent.
Ariel.
Arno.
Attack.
Bittern.
Boxer.
Cheerful.
Comet.
Contest.
Coquette.
Derwent.
Eden.
Erne.
Fairy.
Falcon.
Flirt.
Fortune.
Foyle.
Ghurka.
Goldfinch.
Itchen.
Kale.
Laforey.
Lassoo.
Lightning.
Louis.
Lynx.
Maori.
Marmion.
Mary Rose.
Medusa.
Myrmidon.
Narbrough.
Negro.
Nessus.

* Employed as special Service Ships.

TORPEDO BOAT DESTROYERS—cont.

Nestor.
Nomad.
North Star.
*Nubian.
Opal.
Paragon.
Partridge.
Pheasant.
Phœnix.
Pincher.
Racoon.
Recruit (1).
Recruit (2).
Setter.
Shark.
Simoon.
Sparrowhawk.
Staunch.
Strongbow.
Success.
Surprise.
Tornado.
Torrent.
Turbulent.
Ulleswater.
Ulysses.
Vehement.
Velox.
Wolverine.
*Zulu.

(64)*

TORPEDO BOATS.

046.
064.
9.
10.
11.
12.
13.
24.
90.
96.
117.

(11)

SUBMARINES.

A.E. 1.
A.E. 2.
B. 10.
C. 3.
C. 26.
C. 27.
C. 29.
C. 31.
C. 32.
C. 33.
C. 34.
C. 35.
D. 2.
D. 3.
D. 5.
D. 6.
E. 1.
E. 3.
E. 5.
E. 6.
E. 7.
E. 8.
E. 9.
E. 10.
E. 13.
E. 14.
E. 15.
E. 16.
E. 17.
E. 18.
E. 19.
E. 20.
E. 22.
E. 24.
E. 26.
E. 30.
E. 34.
E. 36.
E. 37.
E. 47.
E. 49.
E. 50.
G. 7.
G. 8.
G. 9.
H. 3.
H. 5.

SUBMARINES—cont.

H. 6.
H. 10.
J. 6.
K. 1.
K. 4.
K. 17.
L. 10.

(54)

AIRCRAFT CARRIERS.

Ben-my-Chree.
Campania.
Hermes.

(3)

PATROL BOATS.

P. 12.
P. 26.

(2)

MINELAYERS.

Ariadne.
Princess Irene.

(2)

ARMED MERCHANT CRUISERS.

Alcantara.
Avenger.
Bayano.
Calgarian.
Champagne.
Clan MacNaughton.
Hilary.
India.

ARMED MERCHANT CRUISERS—cont.

Laurentic.
Marmora.
Moldavia.
Oceanic.
Orama.
Otranto.
Otway.
Patia.
Viknor.

(17)

ARMED BOARDING STEAMERS.

Duke of Albany.
Dundee.
Fauvette.
Fiona.
Grive.
Louvain.
Marcella.
Sarnia.
Snaefell.
Stephen Furness.
Tara.
The Ramsey.
Tithonus.

(13)

COASTAL MOTOR BOATS.

No. 1.
No. 2.
No. 8.
No. 10.
No. 11.
No. 18A.
No. 33A.
No. 39B.
No. 40.
No. 42.
No. 47.
No. 50.
No. 71A.

(13)

* "Nubian" and "Zulu" counted as 1. (*See* Note, p. 7.)

PART II.—AUXILIARIES ON ADMIRALTY SERVICE.
V.—List of Losses arranged according to Year and Class.—Auxiliaries.

From 4th August 1914 to 11th November 1918, comprising the following classes:—

Hospital Ships.
Store Carriers.
Minesweepers.
Auxiliary Patrol Paddlers.
Mine Carriers.

Fleet Messengers.
Commissioned Escort Ships.
Miscellaneous Craft.
Colliers.
Oilers.

Special Service Ships.
Tugs.
Yachts.
Other Auxiliary Patrol Craft.

Class.	Name.	Gross Tonnage.	Date Lost.	How Lost and Where.	C = Commissioned. NC = Not Commiss[d].
				1914.	
Hospital Ship -	Rohilla - -	7,891	30.10.14	Wrecked off Whitby - - -	NC
Colliers - -	Buresk - -	4,337	27.9.14	Captured by "Emden" and sunk by H.M.A.S. "Sydney," 9.11.14, at Cocos Isles.	NC
	North Wales -	3,691	16.11.14	Sunk by "Dresden" 360 miles S.W. ¼ W. (true) from Valparaiso.	NC
Admiralty Trawler.	Spider - -	271	21.11.14	Wrecked at Lowestoft - - -	C

Class.	Name.	Gross Tonnage.	Date Lost.	How Lost and Where.	C = Commissioned. NC = Not Commiss[d].
			1914.		
Hired Trawlers	Thomas W. Irvin	201	27.8.14	} Sunk by mine off River Tyne	C
	Crathie	210	27.8.14		
	Princess Beatrice	214	5.10.14	} Sunk by mine off Belgian coast	C
	Drumoak	208	5.10.14		
	Ivanhoe	190	3.11.14	Wrecked in Firth of Forth	C
	Mary	256	5.11.14	Sunk by mine off Yarmouth	C
	Condor	227	22.11.14	Wrecked off Lowestoft	C
	Lorenzo	173	17.12.14	Wrecked at Hoy Sound	C
	Orianda	273	19.12.14		
	Garmo	203	20.12.14	} Sunk by mine off Scarborough	C
	Night Hawk	287	25.12.14		
	Tom Tit	169	26.12.14	Wrecked at Peterhead	C
	Fair Isle	192	26.12.14	Wrecked at Sinclair Bay	C
Hired Drifters	Eyrie	84	2.9.14	} Sunk by mine off Outer Dowsing	C
	Lindsell	88	3.9.14		
			1915.		
Ammunition Ship.	Combe	2,030	12.10.15	Lost on voyage from United Kingdom to Archangel—cause not recorded.	NC
Store Carrier	Immingham	2,083	6.6.15	Sunk in collision off Mudros	NC
Minesweepers	Roedean (ex Roebuck).	1,094	13.1.15	Sunk at Longhope—cause not recorded.	C
	Brighton Queen	553	6.10.15	Sunk by mine off Nieuport	C
	Hythe	509	28.10.15	Sunk by collision with "Sarnia" near Cape Helles.	C
	Duchess of Hamilton.	553	29.11.15	Sunk by mine near Galloper	C
	Lady Ismay	495	21.12.15	Sunk by mine near Longsand Light Vessel.	C
Fleet Messengers.	Nugget	405	31.7.15	Sunk by submarine 45 miles S.W. from Scilly Isles.	C
	Turquoise	486	31.7.15	Sunk by submarine 60 miles S.W. from Scilly Isles.	C
	Portia	494	2.8.15	Sunk by submarine 70 miles South from Scilly Isles.	C
Colliers	Ben Cruachan	3,092	30.1.15	Sunk by submarine 15 miles N.W. of Morecambe Light.	NC
	Oakby	1,976	23.2.15	Sunk by submarine 4 miles E. by N. from Royal Sovereign Light Vessel.	NC
	Branksome Chine	2,026	23.2.15	Sunk by submarine 6 miles E. by S. ¾ S. from Beachy Head.	NC
	Bengrove	3,840	7.3.15	Sunk by submarine 5 miles N.N.E. from Ilfracombe.	NC
	Invergyle	1,794	12.3.15	Sunk by submarine 12 miles N.N.E. from Tyne,	NC
	Lochwood	2,042	2.4.15	Sunk by submarine 25 miles S.W. from Start Point.	NC
	Mobile	1,950	28.4.15	Sunk by submarine 25 miles N.W. from Butt of Lewis.	NC
	Cherbury	3,220	29.4.15	Sunk by submarine 27 miles W.N.W. from Eagle Island, Co. Mayo.	NC
	Fulgent	2,008	30.4.15	Sunk by submarine 20 miles W.N.W. from Blaskets.	NC
	Don	939	8.5.15	Sunk by submarine 7 miles E. from Coquet Isle.	NC
	Spennymoor	2,733	28.5.15	Sunk by submarine 50 miles S.W. ¼ W. from Start Point.	NC
	Strathcarron	4,347	8.6.15	Sunk by submarine 60 miles W. of Lundy Island.	NC
	Inglemoor	4,331	1.7.15	Sunk by submarine 75 miles S.W. by W. from the Lizard.	NC
	African Monarch	4,003	6.7.15	Sunk by mine entrance White Sea.	NC
	Glenby	2,196	17.8.15	Sunk by submarine 30 miles N. from the Smalls.	NC
	The Queen	557	17.8.15	Sunk by submarine 40 miles N.N.E. from the Smalls.	NC

Class.	Name.	Gross Tonnage.	Date Lost.	How Lost and Where.	C = Commissioned. NC = Not Commiss^d.
				1915.	
Colliers—cont.	Kirkby	3,034	17.8.15	Sunk by submarine 23 miles W. by S. from Bardsey Isle.	NC
	Ben Vrackie	3,908	19.8.15	Sunk by submarine 55 miles N.W. by N. from Scilly Isles.	NC
	Churston	2,470	3.9.15	Sunk by mine 2½ miles S. from Orfordness.	NC
	Linkmoor	4,306	20.9.15	Sunk by submarine 50 miles W. from Cape Matapan.	NC
	Craigston	2,617	4.10.15	Sunk by submarine 35 miles W. from Ovo Island.	NC
	Burrsfield	4,037	5.10.15	Sunk by submarine 70 miles W. from Cape Matapan.	NC
	Thorpwood	3,184	8.10.15	Sunk by submarine 122 miles S. from Cape Martello, Crete.	NC
	Apollo	3,774	9.10.15	Sunk by submarine 63 miles S. from Gavdo Island, Crete.	NC
	Monitoria	1,904	21.10.15	Sunk by mine 1¾ miles N. by E. ¾ E. from Sunk Head Buoy.	NC
	Cape Antibes	2,549	21.10.15	Sunk by mine entrance to White Sea.	NC
	Enosis	3,409	18.11.15	Sunk by submarine 150 miles E.S.E. from Malta.	NC
	Hallamshire	4,420	19.11.15	Sunk by submarine 20 miles S.W. by S. from Cerigotto Island.	NC
	Lemnos	1,530	16.12.15	Wrecked at entrance to River Tees	NC
	Knarsdale	1,641	21.12.15	Sunk by mine 2¾ miles E. by S. of Orfordness.	NC
	Lady Iveagh	2,286	24.12.15	Wrecked at entrance to St. Valery of Cayaux.	NC
	Satrap	2,234	31.12.15	Left Barry—not since heard of	NC
	Tynemouth	2,222	31.12.15	Left Cardiff—not since heard of	NC
Oilers	Desabla	6,047	12.6.15	Sunk by submarine 12 miles E. from Tod Head.	NC
	Caucasian	4,656	1.7.15	Sunk by submarine 80 miles S. from the Lizard.	NC
	Silvia	5,268	23.8.15	Sunk by submarine 47 miles W. from the Fastnet.	NC
	Cymbeline	4,505	4.9.15	Sunk by submarine 96 miles W. by S. from the Fastnet.	NC
	Balakani	3,696	9.9.15	Sunk by mine ½ mile S.W. from S. Longsand Buoy.	NC
	H. C. Henry	4,219	28.9.15	Sunk by submarine 59 miles S. ½ E. from Cape Matapan.	NC
	Lumina	5,950	6.11.15	Sunk by submarine 120 miles S. by E. from Cape Martello, Crete.	NC
	El Zorro	5,989	28.12.15	Sunk by submarine 10 miles S. from Old Head of Kinsale.	NC
Tugs	Char (ex Stranton)	149	16.1.15	Sunk by collision in the Downs	C
	Alexandra	168	28.10.15	Wrecked, Hoxa Sound	C
	Marsden	131	1.11.15	Stranded at Suvla Bay	C
Yachts	Rhiannon	137	20.7.15	Sunk by mine off Longsand	C
	Clementina	625	5.8.15	Beached after collision off Tor Cor Point. Salvage abandoned.	C
	Sanda	351	25.9.15	Sunk by gunfire off Belgian coast	C
	Aries	268	31.10.15	Sunk by mine off Leathercoat	C
	Resource II.	1,000	12.11.15	Destroyed by fire in Southampton Harbour.	C
Admiralty Trawlers.	Jasper	221	26.8.15	Sunk by mine in Moray Forth	C
	Javelin	205	17.10.15	Sunk by mine off Longsand	C
Hired Trawlers	Banyers	448	6.1.15	Do. do. Scarborough	C
	Bedouin	188	13.2.15	Do. do. Tory Island	C
	Blakedown	207	19.2.15	Wrecked at Crudensgeir	C
	Corcyra	225	20.2.15	Do. Bacton	C
	Tern	199	23.2.15	Do. Loch Erribol	C
	Rondo	117	3.3.15	Wrecked, Shetland Islands	C
	John Sherburn	244	6.3.15	Wrecked near Dover	C
	Okino	241	8.3.15	Sunk by mine in Dardanelles	C
	Manx Hero	221	10.3.15	Sunk by mine in Mediterranean	C
	Orlando	276	14.3.15	Wrecked at Stornoway	C
	Trygon	289	30.3.15	Sunk by collision in Clyde	C
	Rhodesia	155	19.4.15	Wrecked at Stornoway	C

Class.	Name.	Gross Tonnage.	Date Lost.	How Lost and Where.	C = Commissioned. NC = Not Commiss^d.
				1915.	
Hired Trawlers —cont.	Balmedie	205	27.4.15	Sunk after collision in Dardanelles	C
	Columbia	266	1.5.15	Torpedoed by enemy T.B.D. off Foreness.	C
	Berkshire	133	15.5.15	Sunk after collision off Red Bay	C
	Rolulo	170	27.5.15	Wrecked on Obb Rock, Isle of Lewis.	C
	Schiehallion	198	9.6.15	Sunk by mine in Mediterranean	C
	Quail III.	162	23.6.15	Sunk after collision off Portland	C
	Edison	196	6.7.15	Wrecked, Isle of Lewis	C
	Strathgarry	202	6.7.15	Sunk after collision at Scapa	C
	Agamemnon II.	225	15.7.15	Sunk by mine off Shipwash	C
	Briton	196	21.7.15	Do. do. Longsand	C
	Leandros	276	6.8.15	Do. do. North Knock	C
	Ben Ardna	187	8.8.15	Sunk by mine near Elbow Buoy	C
	Worsley	309	14.8.15	Do. off Aldeburgh	C
	Japan	205	16.8.15	Do. off the Shipwash	C
	Lundy	188	16.8.15	Sunk by collision in Suvla Bay	C
	Poonah	171	18.8.15	Sunk by collision	
	Miura	257	23.8.15	Sunk by mine off Yarmouth	C
	Dane	265	28.8.15	Do. do. Aldeburgh	C
	Nadine	150	1.9.15	Do. do. N. Shipwash Buoy	C
	Malta	138	1.9.15	Do. do. N. Shipwash Buoy	C
	City of Dundee	269	14.9.15	Sunk after collision off Folkestone	C
	Lydian	244	18.9.15	Sunk by mine off South Foreland	C
	Erin II.	181	19.10.15	Do. do. Nab	C
	Scott	288	22.10.15	Do. do. Tongue	C
	Lord Denman	309	22.10.15	Sunk after collision in White Sea	C
	Bonar Law	284	27.10.15	Do. do. off S. Goodwin	C
	Othello II.	206	31.10.15	Sunk by mine off Leathercoat	C
	John G. Watson	196	31.10.15	Sunk after collision at Stornoway	C
	Princess Victoria	272	7.11.15	Do. do. near Ushant	C
	Xerxes	243	16.11.15	Do. do. off Girdleness	C
	Falmouth III.	198	19.11.15	Sunk by mine off Dover	C
	Ruby	198	24.11.15	Wrecked in Grandes Bay, Crete	C
	William Morrison	211	28.11.15	Sunk by mine near Sunk Head Buoy.	C
	Etoile Polaire	278	3.12.15	Sunk by mine off S. Goodwin	C
	Carilon	226	24.12.15	Do. do. near Margate	C
	Resono	230	26.12.15	Do. do. near Sunk Light	C
	Speeton	205	31.12.15	Do. do. off Lowestoft	C
	Responso	228	31.12.15	Wrecked at Sanday Island	C
Hired Drifters	G.M.V.	94	13.3.15	Sunk after collision off Larne	C
	Thistle IV.	71	30.6.15	Sunk after collision off Great Orme's Head.	C
	Waterlily	82	23.7.15	Sunk after collision off St. Alban's Head.	C
	Great Heart	78	24.9.15	Sunk off Dover. Cause unknown (probably explosion own mine).	C
	Restore	93	12.10.15	Sunk by submarine in Adriatic	C
	Frons Oliviae	98	12.10.15	Sunk by mine off Elbow Buoy	C
	Star of Buchan	81	20.10.15	Do. do. Nab	C
	Charity	102	24.10.15	Disappeared on passage from Great Yarmouth to Poole.	C
	Silvery Wave	96	13.11.15	Wrecked in Crow Sound	C
	Susanna	83	14.12.15	Foundered off Milford	C
	Lottie Leask	94	18.12.15	Sunk by submarine off Saseno Island.	C
	Ladysmith	89	27.12.15	Disappeared in gale off Milford	C
	Ferndale	75	27.12.15	Wrecked on St. Ann's Head	C
Motor Boats	Dorothea	33	21.7.15	Destroyed by fire in E. Mediterranean.	C
	Dolores	12	28.8.15	Destroyed by fire, Douglas Harbour, Isle of Man.	C
	Nita Pita	—	2.12.15	Destroyed by fire at Poole	C
				1916.	
Store Carrier	Leicester	1,001	12.2.16	Sunk by mine 2½ miles S.E. by E. from Folkestone Pier.	NC

Class.	Name.	Gross Tonnage.	Date Lost.	How Lost and Where.	C = Commissioned. NC = Not Commiss^d.
				1916.	
Minesweepers -	Clacton - -	820	3.8.16	Sunk by submarine at Chai Aghizi	C
	Fair Maid -	430	9.11.16	Sunk by mine near Cross Sand Buoy.	C
	Ludlow - -	810†	29.12.16	Sunk by mine off Shipwash Light Vessel.	C
Auxy. Patrol Paddlers.	Majestic II. -	408	28.7.16	Sprang a leak and sank near Oran -	C
	Stirling Castle -	271	26.9.16	Sunk by explosion, cause unknown, off West Coast of Malta.	C
Fleet Messenger	Clifford - -	487	16.5.16	Sunk by submarine in Lat. 34° 2' N., Long. 27° 32' E.	C
Colliers - -	Dromonby -	3,627	13.1.16	Sunk by raider " Möwe " 220 miles W. (true) from Lisbon.	NC
	Larchwood -	689	14.1.16	Sunk in collision off Bull Point -	NC
	Ashby - -	1,947	15.2.16	Wrecked off Ushant - - -	NC
	Wilston - -	2,611	15.2.16	Sunk by mine 20 miles E.N.E from Wick.	NC
	Duckbridge -	1,491	22.2.16	Sunk by mine 6 miles N. from Straithie Point.	NC
	Kilbride - -	3,712	1.3.16	Sunk by submarine 30 miles E. from Galita Islands, Tunis.	NC
	Rio Tiete - -	7,464	28.3.16	Sunk by submarine 140 miles W. from Ushant.	NC
	Sneaton - -	3,470	3.4.16	Sunk by submarine 35 miles N.N.E. from Cap de Garde. Tunis.	NC
	Adamton - -	2,304	8.4.16	Sunk by submarine 15 miles S. from Skerryvore.	NC
	Zafra - -	3,578	8.4.16	Sunk by submarine 44 miles N. from Oran.	NC
	Margam Abbey -	4,471	10.4.16	Sunk by submarine 55 miles S.W. ¼ S. from the Lizard.	NC
	Ribston - -	3,048	23.4.16	Sunk by submarine 66 miles W. by S. from Ushant.	NC
	Trunkby - -	2,635	27.5.16	Sunk by submarine 50 miles S. by E. from Port Mahon, Minorca.	NC
	Lincairn - -	3,638	27.5.16	Sunk by mine 8 miles N. by E. of the Shipwash.	NC
	Silverton - -	2,682	13.7.16	Sunk by submarine 14 miles N.E. from Canae Rocks.	NC
	Swift Wings -	4,465	1.9.16	Sunk by submarine 18 miles E. from Cape Bengut, Algeria.	NC
	Butetown - -	3,789	8.9.16	Sunk by submarine 55 miles W.S.W. from Cape Matapan.	NC
	Inververbie -	4,309	14.9.16	Sunk by submarine 17 miles S. by W. from Cape Rizzuto, Italy.	NC
	Etton - -	2,831	20.9.16	Sunk by mine in entrance to White Sea.	NC
	St. Gothard -	2,788	26.9.16	Sunk by submarine 12 miles N. by W. from Fair Isle.	NC
	Lotusmere -	3,911	2.10.16	Sunk by submarine 48 miles N.N.E. from Teriberski Lighthouse.	NC
	J. Y. Short -	2,193	4.10.16	Sunk by submarine 80 miles E. from Vardo.	NC
	Iolo - - -	3,903	11.10.16	Sunk by submarine 153 miles N. from Vardo.	NC
	Ethel Duncan -	2,510	18.10.16	Sunk by submarine 40 miles W.N.W. from Noop Head, Orkneys,	NC
	Penylan - -	3,875	19.10.16	Sunk by submarine 5 miles W. by N. from Cape Bougaroni.	NC
	Polruan - -	3,692	25.10.16	Foundered off Whitby - - -	NC
	Oola - -	2,494	26.10.16	Sunk by submarine 22 miles N.E. by N. from North Cape.	NC
	Adriatic - -	3,028	31.10.16	Left Newport (Mon.)—not since heard of.	NC
	Kilellan - -	1,971	8.11.16	Sunk by submarine 17 miles S.W. by S. ¼ S. from Colbart Light Vessel.	NC
	Sarah Radcliffe -	3,333	11.11.16	Sunk by submarine 170 miles S.W. from Ushant.	NC

† Displacement tonnage.

Class.	Name.	Gross Tonnage.	Date Lost	How Lost and Where.	C = Commissioned. NC = Not Commiss[d].
				1916.	
Colliers—*cont.*	Lady Carrington	3,269	12.11.16	Sunk by submarine 98 miles N. by W. from Cape Ortegal.	NC
	Corinth	3,669	13.11.16	Sunk by submarine 28 miles S. 3/4 E. from Flamborough Head.	NC
	F. Matarazzo	2,823	15.11.16	Sunk by submarine 26 miles E.N.E. from Linosa Island.	NC
	Canganian	1,142	17.11.16	Left Methil for Scapa—not since heard of.	NC
	Mansuri	3,227	17.11.16	Left S. Shields for St. Nazaire—not since heard of.	NC
	Reapwell	3,417	27.11.16	Sunk by submarine 148 miles N.W. by N. from Alexandria.	NC
	Luciston	2,948	29.11.16	Sunk by mine 4 miles E. from Dellamara Point, Malta.	NC
	Zoroaster	3,803	29.12.16	Sunk by mine 1 3/4 miles E.N.E. from Sunk Light Vessel, Harwich.	NC
Oilers	Prudentia	2,781	12.1.16	Sunk in collision with s.s. "Hermione" of Scapa.	NC
	Goldmouth	7,446	31.3.16	Sunk by submarine 60 miles W.N.W. from Ushant.	NC
	Elax	3,980	10.10.16	Sunk by submarine 70 miles W.S.W. from Cape Matapan.	NC
	Clearfield	4,229	21.10.16	Left Invergordon for Hampton Roads—not since heard of.	NC
	● Ponus	5,077	3.11.16	Wrecked in Falmouth Bay	NC
	Murex	3,564	21.12.16	Sunk by submarine 94 miles N.W. from Port Said.	NC
Special Service Ships.	King Stephen	162	25.4.16	Sunk by submarine in North Sea	C
	Remembrance	3,660	14.8.16	Do. do. in Mediterranean	C
	Fame	22 (net)	19.11.16	Sunk by collision in North Sea	C
	Perugia	4,348	3.12.16	Sunk by submarine in Gulf of Genoa.	C
	Kent County	86	8.12.16	Sunk by mine off Cross Sand, Lowestoft.	C
Yachts	Hersilia	454	6.1.16	Wrecked on Eilean Chuai, Hebrides	C
	Mekong	899	12.3.16	Do. Christthorpe Cliff	C
	Ægusa	1,242	28.4.16	Sunk by mine or submarine near Malta.	C
	Zaida	350	17.8.16	Sunk by submarine in Gulf of Alexandretta.	C
	Conqueror II.	526	26.9.16	Sunk by submarine N. of Fair Isle.	C
Admiralty Trawlers.	Crownsin (prize)	137	4.5.16	Probably sunk by mine near Malta	C
	Carbineer	276	18.5.16	Wrecked on Crebawethan Point	C
Hired Trawlers	Mediator	178	2.1.16	Sunk by mine off Hornsea	C
	Courtier	181	6.1.16	Do. do. Kilnsea	C
	● Albion II.	240	13.1.16	Sunk by mine off St. Catherine's Point.	C
	Rosy Morn	181	13.1.16	Sunk by mine near Dogger Bank	C
	Fulmar	231	17.1.16	Disappeared off Gulf of Sollum. Probably sunk by British mine.	C
	● De la Pole	255	4.2.16	Wrecked on Goodwin Sands	C
	● Carlton	266	21.2.16	Sunk by mine off Folkestone	C
	● Angelus	304	28.2.16	Do. do. Dover	C
	● Weigelia	262	28.2.16	Do. do. Dover	C
	Chester II.	143	29.2.16	Sunk after collision in Firth of Forth.	C
	Manx Queen	234	1.3.16	Wrecked on Filey Brig	C
	● Flicker	192	4.3.16	Sunk by mine off Dover	C
	Calliope II.	240	5.3.16	Sunk after collision off Butt of Lewis.	C
	Ameer	216	18.3.16	Sunk by mine off Felixstowe	C
	Valpa	230	19.3.16	Sunk by mine off Spurn Head	C
	● Corona	212	23.3.16	Sunk by mine near Ramsgate	C
	● Saxon Prince	237	28.3.16	Disappeared in storm off Dover	C
	Commandant	207	2.4.16	Sunk by mine off Sunk Light	C
	Alberta	209	14.4.16	Sunk by mine off Grimsby	C
	Orcades	270	14.4.16	Sunk by mine off Grimsby	C
	Lena Melling	274	23.4.16	Sunk by mine near Elbow Light Buoy.	C

Class.	Name.	Gross. Tonnage.	Date Lost.	How Lost and Where.	C = Commissioned. NC = Not Commiss^d.
			1916.		
Hired Trawlers —cont.	Klondyke	155	4.6.16	Sunk after collision near Owers Light Vessel.	C
	Kaphreda -	245	8.6.16	Sunk by mine near Corton Light Vessel.	C
	Tugela -	233	26.6.16	Sunk by mine off Lowestoft - -	C
	Hirose -	275	29.6.16	Sunk by mine off Aldborough Napes	C
	Whooper -	302	30.6.16	Sunk by mine off Lowestoft - -	C
	Onward -	266	11.7.16	⎫	
	Nellie Nutten -	184	11.7.16	⎬ Sunk by submarines off Aberdeen	C
	Era - - -	168	11.7.16	⎭	
	John High -	228	7.8.16	Sunk by mine off Mt. Sozonova, White Sea.	C
	Irawadi - -	238	10.8.16	Wrecked on Tigani Rocks, E. Mediterranean.	C
	Neath Castle -	225	14.8.16	Sank after collision with Dutch steamship off Orkneys.	C
	Birch - -	215	23.8.16	Sunk by mine off Yarmouth - -	C
	Italy - -	145	3.9.16	Sunk after collision off Sunderland	C
	Jessie Nutten -	187	4.9.16	Sunk by mine off Lowestoft - -	C
	Loch Garry -	176	13.9.16	Foundered at her moorings at Kirkwall.	C
	Loch Shiel -	216	26.9.16	Sunk by mine off Milford Haven -	C
	Sarah Alice -	299	26.9.16	Sunk by submarine north of Fair Isle.	C
	Orsino - -	172	28.9.16	Sunk by submarine between Loch Erribol and Stromness.	C
	Filey - -	226	2.10.16	Wrecked at Camusmore Bay, Tory Island.	C
	Lord Roberts -	293	26.10.16	Sunk by mine off the Shipwash -	C
	Bradford - -	163	28.10.16	Foundered in gale near Old Head of Kinsale.	C
	Glenprosen -	224	3.11.16	Sunk by mine off Cross Sand Light Vessel.	C
	Knot - -	168	5.11.16	Wrecked on North Carr Rock -	C
	Cantatrice -	302	5.11.16	Sunk by mine near Yarmouth -	C
	Benton Castle -	283	10.11.16	Sunk by mine off Dartmouth -	C
	Anthony Hope -	288	16.11.16	Sunk by mine off Havre - -	C
	Dhoon - -	275	24.11.16	Sunk by mine near Newarp Light Vessel, Great Yarmouth.	C
	Burnley - -	275	25.11.16	Sunk by mine off Orfordness - -	C
	Narval - -	211	26.11.16	Disappeared between Grimsby and Harwich.	C
	Lord Airedale -	215	29.11.16	Sunk by mine near Sunk Light Vessel, Harwich.	C
	Remarko - -	245	3.12.16	Sunk by mine off Lowestoft - -	C
	Tervani - -	457	5.12.16	Sunk by mine off Orfordness - -	C
	Dagon - -	250	8.12.16	Sunk by mine off Royal Sovereign Light Vessel.	C
	Crathie - -	225	16.12.16	Wrecked on Nizam Point, Barra Head.	C
	St. Ives - -	325	21.12.16	Sunk by mine off St. Anthony, Falmouth.	C
	Abelard - -	187	24.12.16	Wrecked off Plymouth Breakwater	C
	Relevo - -	176	30.12.16	Wrecked off El Arish - - -	C
Hired Drifters	Freuchny - -	84	8.1.16	⎫ Sunk by mine off Brindisi - -	
	Morning Star -	97	8.1.16	⎭	C
	Everard - -	82	15.1.16	Sunk after collision off Tuskar -	C
	Chance - -	92	26.1.16	Sunk in collision off Orkneys -	C
	Persistive -	82	9.2.16	Sunk by mine off Dover - -	C
	Gavenwood -	88	20.2.16	Sunk by mine off Brindisi - -	C
	Lily Reaich -	88	26.2.16	Sunk by mine off Durazzo - -	C
	Boy Harold -	74	3.3.16	⎫ Sunk by mine off Brindisi - -	
	Enterprise II. -	84	8.3.16	⎭	C
	Grateful - -	107	25.3.16	Wrecked off Torr Head - -	C
	Hilary II. -	78	25.3.16	Sunk by mine near Spit Buoy -	C
	Lerwick - -	86	27.3.16	Wrecked in Yarmouth Roads -	C
	Pecheur - -	67	3.4.16	Sunk after collision off Smalls Light	C
	Clover Bank -	78	24.4.16	Sunk in action off Zeebrugge -	C
	Au Fait - -	83	25.4.16	Captured by German T.B.D. off Zeebrugge.	C
	Beneficent -	80	1.6.16	Sunk by gunfire near Sarnichey Light Vessel, Adriatic.	C

Class.	Name.	Gross Tonnage.	Date Lost.	How Lost and Where.	C = Commissioned. NC = Not Commiss[d].
				1916.	
Hired Drifters —cont.	Laurel Crown	81	2.6.16	Sunk by mine west of Orkneys	C
	Astrum Spei	82	9.7.16	} Sunk by enemy in Adriatic	C
	Clavis	87	9.7.16		C
	White Rose	79	26.7.16	Sunk after collision off Dover	C
	Rooke	84	3.8.16	Sunk after collision off Deal	C
	Rosie	84	26.8.16	Sunk by bomb from enemy seaplane in Adriatic.	C
	Ocean Plough	99	27.8.16	} Sunk by mine off Lowestoft	C
	Tuberose	67	31.8.16		
	Manzanita	93	6.9.16	Wrecked on Ugenti Rocks, Adriatic	C
	Girl Eva	76	2.10.16	Sunk by mine off Elbow Light Buoy.	C
	Fame	68	22.10.16	Wrecked on Hook Sand, Poole	C
	Waveney II.	58	27.10.16	Disabled by German T.B.D.'s in Dover Straits and subsequently sank.	C
	Ajax II.	81	27.10.16		
	Datum	90	27.10.16		
	Gleaner of the Sea.	91	27.10.16	} Sunk by German T.B.D.'s in Dover Straits.	C
	Launch Out	67	27.10.16		
	Roburn	83	27.10.16		
	Spotless Prince	85	27.10.16		
	Speedwell V.	92	28.10.16	Stranded on Splaugh Rock near Greenore Point.	C
	Michaelmas Daisy	99	26.11.16	Sunk by mine near Santa Maria di Leuca, Mediterranean.	C
	Finross	78	26.11.16	Wrecked near Gallipoli, Adriatic	C
	Pelagia	84	28.11.16	Sunk by mine off Nab Light Vessel.	C
	Eskburn	90	30.11.16	Sunk after collision off Dover	C
	Adequate	90*	2.12.16	Sunk after collision off Kirkabista Light.	C
Motor Launches	M.L. 19	25	31.1.16	Destroyed by fire at Harwich	C
	M.L. 40	25	18.5.16	Destroyed by fire, Suez Canal	C
	M.L. 149	37	10.9.16	Destroyed by fire at Taranto	C
	M.L. 230	37	14.9.16		
	M.L. 253	37	14.9.16	} Sunk in Gulf of Squillace when "Inververbie" was torpedoed.	C
	M.L. 255	37	14.9.16		
Motor Boats	Allegro	7	8.9.16	} Lost when "Achaia" was torpedoed outside Oran.	C
	Doreen	9	8.9.16		
	Griffin	—	8.9.16		
				1917.	
Store Carriers	Charles Goodanew.	791	17.4.17	Sunk by mine 3½ miles E.N.E. from Rattray Head.	NC
	Hebble	904	6.5.17	Sunk by mine 1½ miles E. from Roker Pier, Sunderland.	NC
Minesweepers	Duchess of Montrose.	322	18.3.17	Sunk by mine off Dunkirk	C
	Nepaulin	314	20.4.17	Sunk by mine near Dyck Light Vessel, Dunkirk.	C
	Kempton	810†	24.6.17	} Sunk by mine off Dover	C
	Redcar	810†	24.6.17		
	Newmarket	833	16.7.17	Proceeded to sea (E. Mediterranean). Not heard of since.	C
	Queen of the North.	590	20.7.17	Sunk by mine off Orfordness	C
	Marsa	317	18.11.17	Sunk by collision at entrance to Harwich Harbour.	C
Fleet Messengers.	Princess Alberta	1,586	21.2.17	Sunk by mine en route from Stavros to Mudros.	C
	Redbreast	1,313	15.7.17	Sunk by submarine in Mediterranean.	C
	Ermine	1,777	2.8.17	Sunk by mine or submarine in Ægean Sea.	C
	Osmanieh	4,041	31.12.17	Sunk by mine in entrance to Alexandria.	C

* Estimated. † Displacement tonnage.

Class.	Name.	Gross Tonnage.	Date Lost.	How Lost and Where.	C = Commissioned. NC = Not Commiss'd.
				1917.	
Commissioned Escort Ships.	Quernmore	7,302	31.7.17	Sunk by submarine 160 miles W. by N. ¾ N. from Tory Island.	C
	Bostonian	5,736	10.10.17	Sunk by submarine 34 miles S. by E. ½ E. from Start Point.	C
Miscellaneous -	White Head	1,172	15.10.17	Sunk by submarine 40 miles N.N.E. from Suda Bay.	C
Colliers - -	Lynfield -	3,023	8.1.17	Sunk by submarine 32 miles S.E. by S. from Malta.	NC
	Minieh	3,806	9.1.17	Sunk by raider " Möwe " 170 miles E.N.E. (true) from Pernambuco.	NC
	Excellent -	1,944	9.1.17	Sunk by submarine 40 miles N.W. from Noop Head, Orkneys.	NC
	Garfield -	3,838	15.1.17	Sunk by submarine 60 miles N.E. by N. ½ N. from Alexandria.	NC
	Artist	3,570	27.1.17	Sunk by submarine 58 miles W. ½ S. from the Smalls.	NC
	Eavestone	1,858	3.2.17	Sunk by submarine 95 miles W. from the Fastnet.	NC
	Cliftonian	4,303	6.2.17	Sunk by submarine 4½ miles S. ¾ E. from Galley Head.	NC
	Lullington	2,816	8.2.17	Sunk by mine 3 miles E. from Royal Sovereign Light Vessel.	NC
	Foreland -	1,960	12.2.17	Sunk by mine 6 miles S. ¾ W. from Shipwash Light Vessel.	NC
	Cilicia	3,750	12.2.17	Sunk by mine 5 miles S. from Dassen Island, Cape of Good Hope.	NC
	Lucent	1,409	12.2.17	Sunk by submarine 20 miles E. from the Lizard.	NC
	Okement -	4,349	17.2.17	Sunk by submarine 140 miles S.E. by S. from Malta.	NC
	Romsdalen	2,548	17.2.17	Sunk by submarine 10 miles S.W. from Portland Bill,	NC
	Iser -	2,160	23.2.17	Sunk by submarine 14 miles N.W. from Belle Ile.	NC
	Burnby -	3,665	26.2.17	Sunk by submarine 20 miles N. from Cape Falcone.	NC
	Munificent	3,270	1.3.17	Sunk by submarine 3½ miles N.N.W. from Cape Gris Nez.	NC
	Meldon -	2,514	3.3.17	Sunk by mine, Firth of Lorne -	NC
	Craigendoran	2,789	3.3.17	Sunk by submarine 6 miles E. from Cape Sigli, Algeria.	NC
	River Forth	4,421	3.3.17	Sunk by submarine 60 miles S. by E. from Malta.	NC
	Kincardine	4,108	3.3.17	Sunk by submarine 20 miles N.E. from Tearagh Island.	NC
	Tandil -	2,897	12.3.17	Sunk by submarine 20 miles W. by N. ½ N. from Portland.	NC
	Bilswood -	3,097	12.3.17	Sunk by mine 8 miles N.W. from Alexandria.	NC
	Ambient -	1,517	12.3.17	Sunk by mine off Aldeburgh - -	NC
	Rose Lea -	2,830	14.3.17	Sunk by submarine 230 miles W. from Bishop Rock.	NC
	Pola	3,061	18.3.17	Sunk by submarine 280 miles W.N.W. from Ushant.	NC
	Trevose -	3,112	18.3.17	Sunk by submarine 230 miles W. by N. ½ N. from Ushant.	NC
	Vellore -	4,926	25.3.17	Sunk by submarine 21 miles N.W. by N. from Alexandria.	NC
	Don Benito	3,749	27.3.17	Sunk by collision in Lat. 49° 35' N., Long. 6° 44' W.	NC
	Wychwood	1,985	28.3.17	Sunk by submarine 4 miles S.S.W. from S. Arklow Light Vessel.	NC
	Zambesi -	3,759	1.4.17	Sunk by submarine 15 miles N. by W. from Alexandria.	NC
	Margit -	2,490	4.4.17	Sunk by submarine 80 miles S.W. ½ W. from Cape Matapan.	NC
	Trefusis -	2,642	7.4.17	Sunk by submarine 30 miles S.E. from Cape Pula, Sardinia.	NC
	Lowdale -	2,660	20.4.17	Sunk by submarine 90 miles W. by N. from Gibraltar.	NC
	Plutus -	1,189	24.4.17	Sunk by submarine 9 miles N.N.W. from Trevose Head.	NC

Class.	Name.	Gross Tonnage.	Date Lost.	How Lost and Where.	C = Commissioned. NC = Not Commiss^d.
Colliers—*cont.*				1917.	
	Chertsey	3,264	26.4.17	Sunk by submarine 4 miles N. from Algiers.	NC
	Beemah	4,750	27.4.17	Sunk by submarine 30 miles S.W. by S. from Bishop Rock.	NC
	Alfalfa	2,993	27(?)4.17	Sunk by submarine, position not known.	NC
	Hurlford	444	29.4.17	Wrecked on south coast of Tiree	NC
	Gena	2,784	1.5.17	Sunk by enemy seaplane off Southwold.	NC
	Herrington	1,258	4.5.17	Sunk by mine ¾ mile E.S.E. from Red Head, Forfar.	NC
	Repton	2,881	7.5.17	Sunk by submarine 45 miles S.S.E. from Cape Matapan.	NC
	● Broomhill	1,392	10.5.17	Sunk by submarine 9 miles S.W. from Portland Bill.	NC
	Lady Charlotte	3,593	11.5.17	Wrecked off Scilly Isles	NC
	Millicent Knight	3,563	18.5.17	Sunk by submarine 130 miles E. by S. ½ S. from Malta.	NC
	● Porthkerry	1,920	20.5.17	Sunk by submarine 16 miles W. by S. from Beachy Head.	NC
	Ampleforth	3,873	21.5.17	Sunk by submarine 15 miles W.S.W. from Gozo.	NC
	Milo	1,475	22.5.17	Foundered 10 miles S. from St. Albans Head.	NC
	England	3,798	23.5.17	Sunk by submarine 40 miles S. by E. from Cape Bon.	NC
	Holmesbank	3,051	26.5.17	Sunk by submarine 90 miles N. by W. from Alexandria.	NC
	Boldwell	3,118	27.5.17	Sunk by submarine 35 miles N.E. from Linosa Island.	NC
	Islandmore	3,046	3.6.17	Sunk by submarine 20 miles N.W. from Cape Falcon, Algeria.	NC
	New Zealand Transport.	4,481	14.6.17	Sunk by submarine 8 miles S.E. from Serpho Pulo, Ægean.	NC
	Longbenton	924	27.6.17	Sunk by submarine 12 miles S. by W. from Flamborough Head.	NC
	Southina	3,506	7.7.17	Sunk by submarine 6 miles W.N.W. from Cape Sigli, Algeria.	NC
	Calliope	2,883	14(?)7.17	Sunk by submarine in Atlantic	NC
	Valentia	3,242	16.7.17	Sunk by submarine 70 miles W. ½ S. from Bishop Rock.	NC
	Clan McLachlan	4,729	19.7.17	Sunk by collision near Gibraltar	NC
	Huelva	4,867	23.7.17	Sunk by submarine 270 miles S.W. from the Fastnet.	NC
	Purley	4,500	25.7.17	Sunk by submarine 210 miles S.W. ¼ S. from the Fastnet.	NC
	Monkstone	3,097	25.7.17	Sunk by submarine 240 miles W. from Scilly Isles.	NC
	Bestwood	2,248	29.7.17	Sunk by collision when on passage from Cardiff to Loch Ewe.	NC
	Snowdonian	3,870	31.7.17	Sunk by submarine 245 miles S. by E. from Sta. Maria, Azores.	NC
	Maston	3,881	13.8.17	Sunk by submarine 35 miles E.N.E. from Cape Spartivento, Italy.	NC
	● Glocliffe	2,211	19.8.17	Sunk by submarine 9 miles E.N.E. from Berry Head.	NC
	Norhilda	1,175	21.8.17	Sunk by submarine 5 miles S.E. from Scarborough.	NC
	Winlaton	3,270	23.8.17	Sunk by submarine 25 miles W. from Cape Spartel.	NC
	Kilwinning	3,071	24.8.17	Sunk by submarine 94 miles E.S.E. from Malta.	NC
	Mountpark	1,376	21.8.17	Sunk by collision 1½ miles N. of Lundy Island.	NC
	Heatherside	2,767	24(?)8.17	Probably sunk by submarine in Atlantic.	NC
	Nairn	3,627	27.8.17	Sunk by submarine 125 miles N. by W. ¼ W. from Ben Ghazi.	NC
	Westbury	3,097	31.8.17	Sunk by submarine 8 miles S.S.E. from the Fastnet.	NC
	Clan Ferguson	4,808	6.9.17	Sunk by submarine 15 miles N.W. from Cape Spartel.	NC

Class.	Name.	Gross Tonnage.	Date Lost.	How Lost and Where.	C = Commissioned. NC = Not Commiss^d.
				1917.	
Colliers—*cont.*	Hunsbridge -	3,424	7.9.17	Sunk by submarine 60 miles S.W. by W. ¾ W. from Cape Spartel.	NC
	Hockwold -	1,472	9.9.17	Sunk by collision off the Lizard -	NC
	Sandsend - -	3,814	16.9.17	Sunk by submarine 6 miles S.E. by E. from Mine Head.	NC
	Polar Prince -	3,611	18.9.17	Sunk by submarine 8 miles W. by S. from Cape Spartel.	NC
	Etal Manor -	1,875	19.9.17	Sunk by submarine 7 miles S. by W. from Hook Point, Waterford.	NC
	Kurdistan - -	3,720	20.9.17	Sunk by submarine 27 miles E.S.E. from Pantellaria.	NC
	Rosehill - -	2,788	23.9.17	Sunk by submarine 5 miles S.W. by S. from Fowey.	NC
	Cydonia - -	3,085	27.9.17	Wrecked when on passage from Methil to Brest.	NC
	Nuceria - -	4,702	2.10.17	Sunk by submarine 120 miles W. ½ N. from Cape Spartel.	NC
	Ellerslie - -	299	3.10.17	Wrecked - - - - -	NC
	Bedale - -	2,116	6.10.17	Sunk by submarine 25 miles S.E. by S. from Mine Head.	NC
	Poldown - -	1,370	9.10.17	Sunk by mine 2 miles W.S.W. from Trevose Head.	NC
	Eskmere - -	2,293	13.10.17	Sunk by submarine 15 miles W.N.W. from South Stack.	NC
	Elsiston - -	2,908	19.10.17	Sunk by submarine 150 miles E. by S. ½ S. from Malta.	NC
	Pera - -	7,635	19.10.17	Sunk by submarine 105 miles E. ¾ N. from Marsa Susa.	NC
	Collegian - -	7,520	20.10.17	Sunk by submarine 100 miles N.W. by N. ¼ N. from Alexandria.	NC
	Seistan - -	4,238	23.10.17	Sunk by submarine 3½ miles N. by W. ¼ W. from Flamborough Head.	NC
	Euston - -	2,841	24.10.17	Sunk by submarine 37 miles S.W. from Cape Matapan.	NC
	Redesmere -	2,123	28.10.17	Sunk by submarine 6 miles W.S.W. from St. Catherine's Point.	NC
	Axminster -	1,905	13.11.17	Sunk by submarine off Pakefield Gat.	NC
	Trowbridge -	3,712	14.11.17	Sunk by submarine 12 miles S.E. from Cape de Gata.	NC
	Prophet - -	3,230	14.11.17	Sunk by submarine 3 miles S.E. from Antikithera Island.	NC
	Gasconia - -	3,801	16.11.17	Sunk by submarine 12 miles N.E. ½ E. from Shershel.	NC
	Western Coast -	1,394	17.11.17	Sunk by submarine 10 miles W.S.W. from the Eddystone.	NC
	Gisella - -	2,502	18.11.17	Sunk by submarine 2 miles S.W. by S. from Skokham Island.	NC
	Bilbster - -	4,478	21.11.17	Sunk by collision in Lat. 43° 30′ N., Long. 13° 24′ W.	NC
	Eastfield - -	2,145	27.11.17	Sunk by submarine 7 miles E.S.E. from Dedman Point.	NC
	Groeswen -	3,570	27.11.17	Sunk by mine 3 miles N.E. ½ E. from Sunk Light Vessel, Harwich.	NC
	Bleamoor - -	3,755	27.11.17	Sunk by submarine 4 miles S.S.E. from Berry Head.	NC
	Jane Radcliffe -	4,074	28.11.17	Sunk by submarine 2 miles S.W. from Antimilo.	NC
	Ilvington Court	4,217	6.12.17	Sunk by submarine 8 miles N.W. by N. from Shershel.	NC
	Venetia - -	3,596	9.12.17	Sunk by submarine 3 miles N.N.W. from Whitby Rock buoy.	NC
	Persier - -	3,874	11.12.17	Sunk by submarine 50 miles E. from Cape Spartivento, Italy.	NC
	Charleston -	1,866	12.12.17	Sunk by submarine 30 miles W. from the Smalls.	NC
	Bangarth - -	1,872	13.12.17	Sunk by submarine 13 miles N.N.E. from the Tyne.	NC
	Arnewood -	2,259	13.12.17	Sunk by mine 4 miles E.S.E. from Sleat Point, Skye.	NC
	Greenhill - -	1,900	16.12.17	Sunk by collision off Long Sand -	NC

Class.	Name.	Gross Tonnage.	Date Lost.	How Lost and Where.	C = Commissioned. NC = Not Commiss⁴.
				1917.	
Colliers—cont.	Argo	3,071	24.12.17	Sunk by submarine 18 miles N.W. from Cape Tenez.	NC
	Turnbridge	2,874	24.12.17	Sunk by submarine 34 miles N.E. by N. from Cape Ivi.	NC
	Cliftondale	3,811	25.12.17	Sunk by submarine 36 miles E. by N. ½ N. from Cape Tenez.	NC
	Lord Derby	3,757	28.12.17	Sunk by submarine 7 miles S.W. by S. from St. Ann's Head.	NC
	Clara	2,425	28.12.17	Sunk by submarine 1½ miles S.S.W. from the Runnelstone.	NC
	Hercules	1,295	30.12.17	Sunk by submarine 3 miles E.N.E. from Whitby.	NC
Oilers	El Toro	5,958	2.1.17	Wrecked on Blasket Island	NC
	Palmleaf	5,489	4.2.17	Sunk by submarine 230 miles W. from the Fastnet.	NC
	Turritella	5,528	27.2.17	Captured by raider "Wolf." Scuttled 4.4.17 Indian Ocean.	NC
	Gafsa	3,974	28.3.17	Sunk by submarine 10 miles S.E. ½ S. from Kinsale Head.	NC
	Rosalind	6,535	6.4.17	Sunk by submarine 180 miles W.N.W. from the Fastnet.	NC
	Powhatan	6,117	6.4.17	Sunk by submarine 25 miles N. by W. from N. Rona.	NC
	Telena	4,778	21.4.17	Sunk by submarine 170 miles W.N.W. from the Fastnet.	NC
	Bullmouth	4,018	28.4.17	Sunk by submarine 125 miles N.W. by N. from Tory Island.	NC
	Teakwood	5,315	28.4.17	Sunk by submarine 26 miles S.W. by W. from Sapienza Island.	NC
	British Sun	5,565	1.5.17	Sunk by submarine 230 miles E.S.E. from Malta.	NC
	Sebastian	3,110	10.5.17	Lost by fire off Nantucket	NC
	San Onofre	9,717	12.5.17	Sunk by submarine 64 miles N.W. ½ N. from the Skelligs.	NC
	Ashleaf	5,768	29.5.17	Sunk by submarine 150 miles W. from Bishop Rock.	NC
	Wapello	5,576	15.6.17	Sunk by submarine 14 miles W.S.W. from Owers Light Vessel.	NC
	Fornebo	4,259	17.6.17	Sunk by submarine 4 miles N. from Cape Wrath.	NC
	Batoum	4,054	19.6.17	Sunk by submarine 6 miles S. from the Fastnet.	NC
	Oakleaf	8,106	25.7.17	Sunk by submarine 64 miles N.W. ¼ N. from Butt of Lewis.	NC
	Bulysses	6,127	20.8.17	Sunk by submarine 145 miles W.N.W. from the Butt of Lewis.	NC
	Echunga	6,285	5.9.17	Sunk by submarine 40 miles N. by E. from Ushant.	NC
	Mira	3,700	11.10.17	Sunk by mine 4 miles S.W. ½ W. from Beachy Head.	NC
	Derbent	3,178	30.11.17	Sunk by submarine 6 miles N E. by E. from Lynas Point.	NC
Special Service Ships.	Lady Olive	701	19.2.17	Sunk by submarine in English Channel.	C
	Warner	1,273	13.3.17	Sunk by submarine off West Coast of Ireland.	C
	Lady Patricia	1,372	20.5.17	Sunk by submarine in Atlantic	C
	Zylpha	2,917	15.6.17	Sunk by submarine off S.W. of Ireland.	C
	Bayard	220	29.6.17	Sunk by collision in English Channel.	C
	Mona	Not known	4.7.17	Blown up to avoid capture in Mediterranean off Cape Passaro.	C
	Asama	284	16.7.17	Sunk by submarine west of Ushant	C
	Bracondale	2,095	7.8.17	Sunk by submarine in Atlantic	C
	Dunraven	3,117	10.8.17	Torpedoed by submarine, then sunk in tow at entrance to English Channel.	C
	Else	227	14.8.17	Sunk by submarine in Atlantic	C
	Ethel and Millie	Not known	15.8.17	Sunk by submarine in North Sea	C
	Nelson	34	15.8.17	Sunk by submarine in North Sea	C
	Bradford City	3,683	16.8.17	Sunk by submarine in Straits of Messina.	C

Class.	Name.	Gross Tonnage.	Date Lost.	How Lost and Where.	C = Commissioned. NC = Not Commiss[d].
Special Service Ships—*cont.*				1917.	
	Vala	1,016	21.8.17	Probably sunk by submarine; last reported Lat. 47° N., Long. 9° 32' W.	C
	Glenfoyle	1,680	18.9.17	Sunk by submarine in Atlantic	C
	Peveril	1,459	6.11.17	Sunk by submarine outside Straits of Gibraltar.	C
	Penshurst	1,191	25.12.17	Sunk by submarine off Bristol Channel.	C
Tug	Jack	360	9.8.17	Stranded off River Tyne	C
Yachts	Verona	437	24.2.17	Sunk by mine off Portmahomack	C
	Zarefah	279	8.5.17	Sunk by mine off Mull Head, Deer Ness.	C
	Kethailes	611	11.10.17	Sunk after collision off Blackwater Lightship.	C
Admiralty Trawlers.	Charles Astie	295	26.6.17	Sunk by mine off Fanad Point, Lough Swilly.	C
	Benjamin Stevenson.	255	18.8.17	Sunk by submarine 40 miles E. of Fetlar, Shetlands.	C
	James Seckar	255	25.9.17	Disappeared at sea; last seen Lat. 46° 30' N., Long. 12° 00' W	C
	Charlsin (prize)	241	30.9.17	Sunk by submarine 8 miles N. of Marsa Matruh, Mediterranean.	C
Hired Trawlers	Sapper	276	29.12.17	Disappeared off Owers Light Vessel	C
	Teal	165	2.1.17	Wrecked off Buckie	C
	Donside	182	7.1.17	Sunk by mine off Lowestoft	C
	Amplify	342	17.1.17	Wrecked at Skeirascape, Castlebay	C
	New Comet	177	20.1.17	Sunk by mine off Orfordness	C
	Jacamar	293	28.1.17	Sunk after collision off Folkestone Southgate Light Vessel.	C
	Holdene	274	2.2.17	Sunk by mine off Orfordness	C
	Cotsmuir	242	2.2.17	Disappeared on passage from Tyne to Humber.	
	Longset	275	6.2.17	Sunk by mine off Nells Point	C
	Yesso	229	9.2.17	Sunk by mine off Aberdeen	C
	Euston	209	12.2.17	Sunk by mine off Hartlepool	C
	Sisters Melville	260	13.2.17	Sunk by mine near Aldeburgh	C
	Recepto	245	16.2.17	Sunk by mine off Longscar Buoy, Tees Bay.	C
	Clifton	242	18.2.17	Sunk by mine off Daunt Light Vessel.	C
	Hawk	243	17.2.17	Sunk by submarine 120 miles S.E. of Malta.	C
	Picton Castle	245	19.2.17	Sunk by mine off Dartmouth Harbour.	C
	Evadne	189	27.2.17	Sunk by mine off Owers Light Vessel	C
	Northumbria	211	3.3.17	Sunk by mine near May Island, Firth of Forth.	C
	Vivanti	226	7.3.17	Foundered off Fairlight, Hastings	C
	Caledonia	161	17.3.17	Sunk by submarine off Newton, Northumberland.	NC
	Evangel	197	25.3.17	Sunk by mine off Milford Haven	C
	Christopher	316	30.3.17	Sunk by mine off Southwold	C
	Strathrannoch	215	6.4.17	Sunk by mine off St. Abbs Head	C
	Orthos	218	9.4.17	Sunk by mine off Lowestoft	C
	Amy	270	11.4.17	Sunk by mine off Havre	C
	Pitstruan	206	13.4.17	Sunk by mine off Nosshead Lighthouse, Wick.	C
	Star of Freedom	258	19.4.17	Sunk by mine off Trevose Head	C
	Lobelia II.	184	19.4.17	Sunk by mine off Fanad Point, Lough Swilly.	C
	Loch Eye	225	20.4.17	Sunk by mine off Dunmore	C
	Othonna	180	20.4.17	Sunk by mine off Fife Ness	C
	Ruthin Castle	275	21.4.17	Sunk by mine off Skinningrove, Yorkshire.	C
	Rose II.	213	23.4.17	Sunk by mine in Belfast Lough	C
	Margate	161	24.4.17	Sunk by submarine off Spurn Point	C
	Repro	230	26.4.17	Sunk by mine off Tod Head	C
	Agile	246	27.4.17	Sunk by mine off Sunk Head Light Vessel, Harwich.	C
	Arfon	227	30.4.17	Sunk by mine off St. Albans Head	C
	Lord Salisbury	285	4.5.17	Sunk by mine off Eros Island, Salonika.	C

Class.	Name.	Gross Tonnage.	Date Lost.	How Lost and Where.	C = Commissioned. NC = Not Commiss[d].
				1917.	
Hired Trawlers —cont.	Lord Ridley	215	10.5.17	Sunk by mine off Whitby	C
	Bracklyn	303	11.5.17	Sunk by mine off Yarmouth	C
	Lucknow	171	18.5.17	Sunk by mine off Portsmouth	C
	Senator	211	21.5.17	Sunk by mine off Tory Island	C
	Epworth	223	22.5.17	Sunk after collision off East Coast	C
	Merse	296	22.5.17	Sunk by mine off Garroch Head, Bute.	C
	Tettenhall	227	23.5.17	Sunk by mine off Lowestoft	C
	Ina William	337	30.5.17	Sunk by mine off Bull Light, Berehaven.	C
	Carew Castle	256	12.6.17	Sunk by mine off Hartland Point	C
	Towhee	199	15.6.17	Disappeared while on escort duty in English Channel.	C
	Fraser	310	17.6.17	Sunk by mine off Boulogne	C
	Bega	318	18.6.17	Sunk by submarine 40 miles N. of Muckle Flugga.	C
	Borneo	211	18.6.17	Sunk by mine off Beachy Head	C
	Corientes	280	23.6.17	Sunk by mine off Malin Head	C
	Taipo	247	24.6.17	Sunk by mine off Royal Sovereign Light Vessel.	C
	Gelsina	227	25.6.17	Sunk by mine off Girdleness	C
	Drake II.	207	3.7.17	Wrecked in Garinish Bay, Kenmare River.	C
	Kelvin	322	7.7.17	Sunk by mine off Harwich	C
	Vale of Leven	223	10.7.17	Sunk after collision off Worthing	C
	George Milburn	235	12.7.17	Sunk by mine off Dunmore	C
	Robert Smith	211	20.7.17	Disappeared in Lat. 59° 14′ N., Long. 9° 40′ W. (approx.).	C
	Orphesia	273	22.7.17	Sank after striking submerged wreck off Alexandria.	C
	Bovic	162	5.8.17	Sunk after collision 3 miles S.E. of Souter Point.	C
	Jay	144	11.8.17	Sunk by submarine off Southwold	C
	Kirkland	224	20.8.17	Sunk by mine off Fugla Skerry, Papastour, Shetlands.	C
	Sophron	195	22.8.17	Sunk by mine off Firth of Tay	C
	Eros	286	5.9.17	Sunk by mine off Felixstowe	C
	Helgian	220	6.9.17	Sunk by mine in Gulf of Ruphani, Ægean Sea.	C
	By George	225	7.9.17	Sunk by mine in Gulf of Ruphani, Ægean Sea.	C
	Loch Ard	225	10.9.17	Sunk by mine off Lowestoft	C
	Asia	309	12.9.17	Sunk by mine off Bressay Islands, Shetlands.	C
	Ben Heilem	196	8.10.17	Wrecked off Berwick	C
	Waltham	161	10.10.17	Disappeared off Isle of Man (presumed sunk by submarine).	C
	Clyde	146	14.10.17	Sunk after collision off Sidmouth	C
	Ruby	251	17.10.17	Sunk by submarine off Ushant	C
	Vitality	262	20.10.17	Sunk by mine off Orfordness	C
	Thomas Stratten	309	20.10.17	Sunk by mine off Butt of Lewis	C
	Earl Lennox	226	23.10.17	Sunk by mine off entrance to Sound of Islay.	
	Strymon	198	27.10.17	Sunk by mine off Shipwash Light Vessel.	C
	Thuringia	297	11.11.17	Blown up off Youghal (presumed torpedoed).	C
	Newbridge	228	19.11.17	Sunk after collision off Prawle Point.	C
	Morococola	265	19.11.17	Sunk by mine off Daunt Rock Light Vessel.	C
	Lord Grey	215	2.12.17	Wrecked on La Barrier Shoal, Cape Gris Nez.	C
	Apley	250	6.2.17	Sunk by mine off E. end of Isle of Wight.	C
	Commander Fullerton.	227	12.12.17	⎱ Sunk by enemy destroyer in North Sea.	C
	Livingstone	213	12.12.17		
	Lord Alverstone	247	12.12.17		
	Tokio	295	12.12.17	⎰	
	Duster	192	17.12.17	Wrecked off Scratten Cove near Portreath.	C

Class.	Name.	Gross Tonnage.	Date Lost.	How Lost and Where.	C = Commissioned. NC = Not Commiss^d.
				1917.	
Hired Trawlers —cont.	Ocean Scout I. -	200	21.12.17	Sunk after collision off Inisheer Light, W. Coast of Ireland.	C
Hired Drifters -	Cape Colony -	82	8.1.17	Sunk by mine off Harwich - -	C
	G. S. P. - -	100	2.2.17	Sunk after collision 6 miles south of Owers Light Vessel.	C
	Aivern - -	72	8.2.17	Foundered in English Channel while on passage from Mediterranean.	C
	Gracie - -	83	10.2.17	Sunk after collision off Tongue Light Vessel.	C
	Campania II. -	90	5.3.17	Disappeared in gale off St. Abbs Head.	C
	Energy - -	45	5.3.17	Wrecked in Peterhead Bay - -	NC
	Protect - -	98	16.3.17	Sunk by mine off Dover - -	C
	Gowan - -	45	17.3.17	Sunk by submarine off Newton, Northumberland.	NC
	Forward III. -	89	31.3.17	Sunk by mine off the Shipwash -	C
	Plantin - -	84	26.4.17	Sunk by mine off Staudfast Point -	C
	Admirable -	90	15.5.17	⎫	C
	Avondale - -	80	15.5.17	⎪	C
	Coral Haven -	82	15.5.17	⎪	C
	Craignoon -	77	15.5.17	⎪	C
	Felicitas - -	67	15.5.17	⎪	C
	Girl Gracie -	95	15.5.17	⎪	C
	Girl Rose - -	86	15.5.17	⎬ Lost in action in Adriatic - -	C
	Helenora - -	88	15.5.17	⎪	C
	Quarry Knowe -	98	15.5.17	⎪	C
	Selby - -	75	15.5.17	⎪	C
	Serene - -	86	15.5.17	⎪	C
	Taits - -	93	15.5.17	⎪	C
	Transit - -	83	15.5.17	⎪	C
	Young Linnett -	93	15.5.17	⎭	C
	Rosevine - -	100	24.5.17	Sunk after collision off Great Yarmouth.	C
	George V. -	67	3.6.17	Sunk after E.C. mine explosion near Dover.	C
	Southesk - -	93	7.7.17	Sunk by mine in Auskerry Sound -	C
	Betsy Sim -	53	18.7.17	Sunk after collision near Haisboro' Light Vessel.	C
	Nina - -	83	2.8.17	Sunk after explosion off Prawle Point.	C
	Dewey - -	83	12.8.17	Sunk after collision off Royal Sovereign Light Vessel.	C
	Ocean's Gift II.	50	30.8.17	Destroyed by fire off the Wash -	C
	Hastfen - -	77	24.9.17	Sunk by mine off Longsand - -	C
	Ocean Star -	92	26.9.17	Disappeared off the Nab Light (presumed mined).	C
	Active III. -	81	15.10.17	Sunk by mine off Milford Haven -	C
	Jean - -	94	17.10.17	Sunk by mine off Cape Santa Maria di Leuca.	C
	Comrades - -	63	18.10.17	Sunk by mine off Cape d'Antifer -	C
	Deliverer - -	79	3.11.17	Disappeared outside Dublin Bay (presumed sunk by submarine).	C
	John Mitchell -	89	14.11.17	Sunk after collision off St. Albans Head.	C
	Bounteous -	63	4.12.17	Wrecked on North Shore, Rhum -	C
	Helen Wilson -	44	5.12.17	Destroyed by fire at Oban - -	C
	Annie - -	94	19.12.17	Destroyed after grounding off Enos	C
	Piscatorial II. -	93	29.12.17	Disappeared off Newhaven - -	C
Motor Launches	M.L. 197 - -	37	31.1.17	Wrecked near Ballincourty Lighthouse.	C
	M.L. 534 - -	37	13.4.17	Destroyed by fire at Taranto - -	C
	M.L. 431 - -	37	22.4.17	Destroyed by fire at Poole - -	C
	M.L. 540 - -	37	8.6.17	⎫ Lost in " Hunstrick," which was ⎬ torpedoed by submarine off	C
	M.L. 541 - -	37	8.6.17	⎭ Tangier.	
	M.L. 474 - -	37	23.7.17	Destroyed by fire after being struck by enemy shell near Chios.	C
	M.L. 52 - -	37	29.11.17	Destroyed by fire in Sandown Bay	

Class.	Name.	Gross Tonnage.	Date Lost.	How Lost and Where.	C = Commissioned. NC = Not Commiss^d.
				1918.	
Hospital Ship -	Rewa - -	7,308	4.1.18	Sunk by submarine W. ¼ S. from Hartland Point.	NC
Frozen Meat Ship.	Romeo - -	1,730	3.3.18	Sunk by submarine 7 miles S. from Mull of Galloway.	NC
Mine Carriers -	●Eleanor - -	1,980	12.2.18	Sunk by submarine 9 miles W. by S. ½ S. from St. Catherine's Point.	C
	Lady Cory-Wright.	2,516	26.3.18	Sunk by submarine 14 miles S.S.W. from the Lizard.	C
Minesweepers -	St. Seiriol -	928	25.4.18	Sunk by mine off the Shipwash -	C
	Blackmorevale -	750*	1.5.18	Sunk by mine off Montrose -	C
	Ascot - -	810*	10.11.18	Blown up off Farn Islands (presumed torpedoed).	C
Fleet Messenger	Chesterfield -	1,013	18.5.18	Sunk by submarine 42 miles N.E. by E. ½ E. from Malta.	C
Commissioned Escort Ship.	●Mechanician -	9,044	20.1.18	Sunk by submarine 8 miles W. from St. Catherine's Point.	C
Miscellaneous -	Lowtyne - -	3,231	10.6.18	Sunk by submarine 3½ miles E.S.E. from Whitby.	C
	Puruni - -	295	29.8.18	Wrecked off W. point of Mayers Islands, Grenadines.	C
Colliers - -	Birchwood -	2,756	3.1.18	Sunk by submarine 25 miles E. from Blackwater Light Vessel.	NC
	●Gartland - -	2,613	3.1.18	Sunk by submarine 5 miles E.S.E. from Owers Light Vessel.	NC
	Steelville - -	3,649	3.1.18	} Sunk by submarine 20 miles N. from Cape Bon.	} NC
	Allanton - -	4,253	3.1.18		
	Birtley - -	1,438	4.1.18	Sunk by submarine (?) 8 miles N. from Flamborough Head.	NC
	Knightsgarth -	2,889	5.1.18	Sunk by submarine 5 miles W.N.W. from Bull Point, Rathlin Island.	NC
	Rose Marie -	2,220	5.1.18	Sunk by submarine 13 miles S.E. from N. Arklow Light Vessel.	NC
	Taiyabi - -	3,157	9.1.18	Foundered when on passage from Cardiff to Malta.	NC
	West Wales -	4,331	21.1.18	Sunk by submarine 140 miles S.E. ¾ S. from Malta.	NC
	Hartley - -	1,150	26.1.18	Sunk by submarine 2 miles N.E. from Skinningrove, Yorkshire.	NC
	Butetown - -	1,829	29.1.18	Sunk by submarine 1½ miles S. from Dodman Point.	NC
	Towneley - -	2,476	31.1.18	Sunk by submarine 18 miles N.E. ¼ E. from Trevose Head.	NC
	Standish Hall -	3,996	4.2.18	Sunk by submarine 38 miles W. by N. from Alexandria.	NC
	●Lydie - -	2,599	9.2.18	Sunk by submarine 1 mile E. by S. from Manacles Buoy.	NC
	Dorisbrook -	3,431	9.2.18	Sunk by collision in South Pacific -	NC
	Pinewood -	2,219	17.2.18	Sunk by submarine 15 miles S. from Mine Head.	NC
	●Northville . -	2,472	17.2.18	Sunk by submarine 3½ miles S.E. by E. from Berry Head.	NC
	Remus - -	1,079	23.2.18	Sunk by submarine 6 miles S.S.W. from Copinsay, Orkneys.	NC
	Rubio - -	2,395	25.2.18	Sunk by mine 4 miles N. ½ E. from Shipwash Light Vessel.	NC
	Maltby - -	3,977	26.2.18	Sunk by submarine 10 miles S.W. by S. from Pantellaria.	NC
	Greavesash -	1,263	26.2.18	Sunk by submarine 10 miles N.E. from Cape Barfleur.	NC
	Dalewood -	2,420	26.2.18	Sunk by submarine 10 miles S.W. from the Isle of Man.	NC
	Largo - -	1,764	27.2.18	Sunk by submarine 12 miles W. from Calf of Man.	NC
	Northfield -	2,099	3.3.18	Sunk by submarine 25 miles S.W. from Lundy Island.	NC
	Castle Eden -	1,949	4.3.18	Sunk by submarine 4 miles S.S.E. from Inistrahull Lighthouse.	NC
	Intent - -	1,564	8.3.18	Sunk by submarine 4 miles E. by N. from Seaham.	NC
	●Tweed - -	1,025	13.3.18	Sunk by submarine 10 miles S. by W. ¼ W. from St. Catherine's Pt.	NC

* Displacement tonnage.

Class.	Name.	Gross Tonnage.	Date Lost.	How Lost and Where.	C = Commissioned. NC = Not Commiss⁴.
				1918.	
Colliers—*cont.*	Ardandearg	3,237	14.3.18	Sunk by submarine 86 miles E. ¼ N. from Malta.	NC
	Ellaston	3,192	16.3.18	Sunk by submarine 180 miles W. by S. (true) from Palma, Canary Islands.	NC
	Burnstone	2,340	19.3.18	Sunk by submarine 44 miles N. from Farn Islands.	NC
	Begonia	3,070	21.3.18	Sunk by submarine 44 miles S. by W. from Wolf Rock.	NC
	Boscastle	2,346	7.4.18	Sunk by submarine 14 miles N.N.W. from Strumble Head.	NC
	Marstonmoor	2,744	14.4.18	Sunk by submarine 55 miles N.N.E. from Cape Wrath.	NC
	Gregynog	1,701	18.4.18	Sunk by submarine 16 miles S.W. from Hartland Point.	NC
	Bellview	3,567	21.4.18	Sunk by submarine 16 miles E.N.E. from Cape Bon.	NC
	Eric Calvert	1,862	22.4.18	Sunk by submarine 4 miles S.S.W. from St. Anthony Point.	NC
	Dronning Maud	2,663	22.4.18	Sunk by submarine 65 miles N. by E. ¾ E. from Cape Sigli, Algeria.	NC
	Llwyngwair	1,304	26.4.18	Sunk by submarine 5 miles S.S.E. from Seaham Harbour.	NC
	Ellis Sayer	2,549	29.4.18	Sunk by submarine 15 miles E. by N. from Royal Sovereign Light Vessel.	NC
	Baron Ailsa	1,836	9.5.18	Sunk by submarine 18 miles W.N.W. from the Smalls.	NC
	Heron Bridge	2,420	16.5.18	Sunk by submarine 320 miles E. by N. (true) from San Miguel, Azores.	NC
	Mavisbrook	3,152	17.5.18	Sunk by submarine 50 miles S.E. by S. ½ S. from Cape de Gata.	NC
	Snowdon	3,189	19.5.18	Sunk by submarine 84 miles S. ½ W. from Malta.	NC
	Clan Forbes	3,946	9.6.18	Sunk by submarine 115 miles W.N.W. from Alexandria.	NC
	Waitemata	5,432	14.7.18	Sunk by submarine 100 miles E. ¾ N. from Marsa Susa.	NC
	Marie Suzanne	3,106	19.8.18	Sunk by submarine 47 miles W. ¾ S. from Mudros Bay.	NC
	Boscawen	1,936	21.8.18	Sunk by submarine 23 miles W.N.W. from Bardsey Isle.	NC
	Milly	2,964	6.9.18	Sunk by submarine 2¼ miles W. ¾ S. from Tintagel Head.	NC
	Madryn	2,244	16.9.18	Sunk by submarine 5 miles N.N.E. from Trevose Head.	NC
	Lord Stewart	1,445	16.9.18	Sunk by submarine 6 miles E. ½ N. from Hope's Nose.	NC
	Muriel	1,831	17.9.18	Sunk by submarine 3½ miles N.E. from Peterhead.	NC
	John O'Scott	1,235	18.9.18	Sunk by submarine 9 miles W. by N. from Trevose Head.	NC
	Gorsemore	3,079	22.9.18	Sunk by submarine 44 miles S.E. ½ E. from Cape Colonne.	NC
	Hebburn	1,938	25.9.18	Sunk by submarine 14 miles S. from Mine Head.	NC
	Westwood	1,968	3.10.18	Sunk by submarine 5 miles S.W. ½ W. from the Lizard.	NC
	War Council	5,875	16.10.18	Sunk by submarine 85 miles W.S.W. from Cape Matapan.	NC
Oilers	Trocas	4,129	19.1.18	Sunk by submarine 10 miles N.E. from Skyros Lighthouse.	NC
	Baku Standard	3,708	11.2.18	Sunk by submarine 5 miles S. by W. ½ W. from Tod Head.	NC
	Beacon Light	2,768	19.2.18	Sunk by submarine 15 miles S.E. from Butt of Lewis.	NC
	British Viscount	3,287	23.2.18	Sunk by submarine off Holyhead	NC
	Oilfield	4,000	16.3.18	Sunk by submarine 15 miles N.W. from Cape Wrath.	NC
	Samoset	5,251	20.3.18	Sunk by submarine 50 miles N. by E. ¾ E. from Port Said.	NC

Class.	Name.	Gross Tonnage.	Date Lost.	How Lost and Where.	C = Commissioned. NC = Not Commiss^d.
				1918.	
Oilers—*cont.*	Waneta	1,683	30.5.18	Sunk by submarine 42 miles S.S.E. from Kinsale Head.	NC
	Tatarrax	6,216	11.8.18	Sunk by internal explosion off Alexandria.	NC
	Arca	4,839	2.10.18	Sunk by submarine 40 miles N.W. by W. from Tory Island.	NC
Special Service Ships.	●Wellholme	113	30.1.18	Sunk by submarine in English Channel.	C
	Westphalia	1,467	11.2.18	Sunk by submarine in Irish Sea	C
	●Brown Mouse	42	28.2.18	Caught fire and blew up in Lyme Bay.	C
	Willow Branch	3,314	25.4.18	Sunk by submarine probably off W. Coast of Africa, E. of Cape Verde.	C
	Ocean Fisher	96	16.6.18	Sunk by mine in North Sea	C
	●Stockforce	732	30.7.18	Sunk by submarine in English Channel.	C
	M. J. Hedley	449	4.10.18	Capsized and sank while coaling in Barry Docks, Cardiff.	C
Tugs	Blackcock	253	18.1.18	Wrecked in White Sea	C
	Desire	165	24.1.18	Sunk by submarine off Yorkshire Coast.	NC
	Guiana	166	29.1.18	Sunk by collision off East Coast	C
	Ludgate	165	15.2.18	Stranded in Wigtown Bay	C
	Thames	32	16.2.18	Foundered off E. Coast of Scotland	C
	David Gillies	375	5.5.18	Stranded in Mediterranean	C
	Dalkeith	741	18.5.18	Sunk by enemy action in Mediterranean.	C
	Oceana	337	18.10.18	Stranded at Scapa	C
	George R. Gray	268	27.10.18	Stranded at Farn Islands	C
	Blazer	283	9.11.18	Stranded at Scilly Islands	C
Whalers	Hirpa	110	2.1.18	Wrecked near Buckie	C
	Blackwhale	237	3.1.18	Sunk by mine off Fife Ness	C
Admiralty Trawlers.	Nathaniel Cole	275	6.2.18	Sprung a leak off Buncrana	C
	●James Pond	275	15.2.18	Lost in action off Dover	C
	Thos. Collard	215	1.3.18	Sunk by submarine N. of Rathlin Island.	C
	Antares II.	275*	2.5.18	Sunk by gunfire after collision off Gibraltar.	C
	●Lancer II.	275*	18.7.18	Sunk after collision off Brighton Light Vessel.	C
	●Michael Clements	324	8.8.18	Sunk after collision off St. Catharine's Point.	C
	Thos. Cornwall	324	29.10.18	Sunk after collision off Flamborough Head.	C
	Charles Hammond	324	2.11.18	Sunk after collision with H.M.S. "Marksman" off Kirkcaldy.	C
Hired Trawlers	Miranda III.	173	14.1.18	Wrecked in Pelwick Bay	C
	John E. Lewis	253	16.1.18	Sunk by mine off Cork Light Vessel, Harwich.	C
	●Gambri	274	18.1.18	Sunk by mine off Royal Sovereign Light Vessel.	C
	●Drumtochty	211	29.1.18	Sunk by mine off Dover	C
	●Cleon	266	1.2.18	Sunk by mine off Folkestone Gate Buoy.	C
	●Remindo	256	2.2.18	Lost off Portland. Cause unknown	C
	Idena	270	5.2.18	Abandoned and sunk by gunfire, Lat. 71° N., Long. 17° E.	C
	Sardius II.	206	13.2.18	Wrecked in Pendower Cove (near Tolpenden Penwith).	C
	Marion	128	23.2.18	Sunk by mine off Malta	C
	Nerissa II.	173	28.2.18	Wrecked off end of Valanidhi Shoal, Lemnos.	C
	Princess Alice	225	6.3.18	Sunk after collision off Alexandria	C
	Columba	138	10.3.18	Sunk by mine off May Island	C
	Endeavour	156	10.3.18	Sunk after collision at Kirkwall Boom.	C
	Adrian	199	13.3.18	Sunk after collision off Harwich	C
	●Agate	248	14.3.18	Sunk by mine off Royal Sovereign Light Vessel.	C
	Vulture II.	190	16.3.18	Sunk after collision in Eriboll wreck.	C

* Approximate.

Class.	Name.	Gross Tonnage	Date Lost.	How Lost and Where.	C = Commissioned. NC = Not Commiss[d].
				1918.	
Hired Trawlers —cont.	Swallow	243	29.3.18	Sunk after collision off Whitby	C
	Lord Hardinge	212	9.4.18	Sunk after collision off Daunt Light Vessel.	C
	Numitor	242	20.4.18	Sunk by mine off Orfordness	C
	Plethos	210	23.4.18	Sunk by mine off Montrose	C
	Emley	223	28.4.18	Sunk by mine off May Island	C
	Loch Naver	216	13.5.18	Sunk by mine near Mandili Point Ægean Sea.	C
	Balfour	285	13.5.18	Sunk after collision off Royal Sovereign Light Vessel.	C
	Gabir	219	24.5.18	} Sunk by mine off Lowestoft	C
	Yucca	198	24.5.18		
	Dirk	181	28.5.18	Sunk by submarine off Flamborough Head.	C
	St. John's	208	3.6.18	Sunk by submarine 45 miles N. of Tory Island.	C
	Princess Olga	245	14.6.18	Sunk by mine off Havre	C
	Achilles II.	225	26.6.18	Sunk by mine off Shipwash Light Vessel.	C
	Loch Tummel	228	14.7.18	Foundered in Mediterranean, Lat. 33° 35' N., Long. 21° 45' E. Cause unknown.	C
	Speedwell II.	273	15.7.18	Ran ashore in Mounts Bay and broke up.	C
	Ijuim	257	22.7.18	Sunk by gunfire of enemy submarine.	C
	Lochiel	241	24.7.18	Sunk by mine or torpedo off Whitby.	C
	Elise	239	22.9.18	Blown up 2 miles N.E. of St. Mary's Lighthouse, Blyth (presumed torpedoed).	C
	Sealark II.	182	30.9.18	Sunk after collision off St. John's Point.	C
	Kalmia	189	7.10.18	Destroyed by fire at Stavros	C
	Neptunian	315	27.10.18	Sunk after collision 5 miles N.N.W. of Albacarry Lighthouse.	C
	Riparvo	230	2.11.18	Sunk after collision, Lat. 35° 08' N., Long. 18° 54' E.	C
	Renarro	230	10.11.18	Sunk by mine in Dardanelles	C
Hired Drifters	Golden Sunset	85	4.1.18	Sunk after collision off Shambles Light Vessel.	C
	Ethnee	86	15.1.18	Wrecked on Goodwin Sands	C
	Christina Craig	86	15.2.18		
	Clover Bank	92	15.2.18		
	Cosmos	91	15.2.18		
	Jeannie Murray	90	15.2.18	} Lost in action off Dover	C
	Silver Queen	84	15.2.18		
	Veracity	96	15.2.18		
	W. Elliott	60	15.2.18		
	William Tennant	93	5.3.18	Sunk after collision off Humber	C
	Frigate Bird	84	11.3.18	Sunk after collision off Marsa Scirocco, Mediterranean.	C
	Nexus	86	13.3.18	Sunk by mine in Thames Estuary	C
	J. C. P.	73	22.3.18	Sunk after collision off Green Flash Buoy.	C
	New Dawn	93	23.3.18	Sunk by mine at entrance to Needles Channel.	C
	Border Lads	86	25.3.18	Blown up off Tyne (believed torpedoed).	C
	J. and A.	98	4.4.18	Sunk after collision off Scarborough	C
	Annie Smith	84	9.4.18	Sunk after collision off Lundy Island.	C
	Select	74	16.4.18	Sunk after collision off St. Govans Light Buoy.	C
	Sunbeam I.	75	16.4.18	Sunk after collision at Inchkeith	NC
	Pursuit	79	22.4.18	Sunk after collision at Penzance	C
	Holly III.	93	11.5.18	Sunk after collision off Lands End	C
	Silvery Harvest	86	16.5.18	Sunk after collision off Berry Head	C
	Clara and Alice	79	26.5.18	Sprang a leak off Palermo	C
	City of Liverpool	88	31.7.18	Believed sunk by mine off South Foreland.	C
	Scania	88	2.8.18	Sunk by collision in Dover Straits	C

Class.	Name.	Gross Tonnage.	Date Lost.	How Lost and Where.	C = Commissioned. NC = Not Commiss[d].
				1918.	
Hired Drifters —cont.	Strathmore	56	20.8.18	Destroyed by fire off Buncrana	C
	Tulip II.	88	23.8.18	Sunk after collision off St. Anthony	C
	Guide Me II.	100	29.8.18	Sunk after collision off the Muglins	C
	Lustring	71	3.10.18	Sunk after collision off Hellier Holm.	C
	Coleus	102	4.10.18	Sunk by mine off Dover	C
	Ocean Foam	90	7.10.18	Sunk after collision in Penzance Bay.	C
	Calceolaria	92	27.10.18	Sunk by mine off Elbow Light Buoy.	C
	Falkirk	56	29.10.18	Sunk in collision off Kinnaird Head	C
Motor Launches	M.L. 278	37	15.1.18	Wrecked on Dunkirk Pier	C
	M.L. 55	37	28.1.18	Destroyed by fire at yard of Messrs. Wills and Packham, Sittingbourne.	C
	M.L. 421	37	6.4.18	Wrecked in Seaford Bay	C
	M.L. 356	37	11.4.18	Sunk after collision off Dover	C
	M.L. 110	37	23.4.18	Lost in action off Zeebrugge	C
	M.L. 424	37	23.4.18	Lost in action off Zeebrugge	C
	M.L. 254	37	10.5.18	Sunk off Ostend to avoid capture	C
	M.L. 64	37	10.6.18	Destroyed by fire in Granton Harbour.	C
	M.L. 403	37	22.8.18	Blown up in Runswick Bay while endeavouring to salve German torpedo.	C
	M.L. 247	37	29.9.18	Wrecked on Oar Rock, West of Clodgy Point, St. Ives.	C
	M.L. 561	37	21.10.18	Sunk by mine off Ostend.	

VI.—Summary of Losses of Auxiliary Vessels.

Class.	4 Aug. 1914 to 31 Dec. 1914.	1915.	1916.	1917.	1 Jan. 1918 to 11 Nov. 1918.	Total Number lost.	Total Tonnage lost (Gross Tonnage in *italics*, Displacement Tonnage in ordinary type).
	No.	No.	No.	No.	No.	No.	Tons.
Hospital Ships	1	—	—	—	1	2	*15,199*
Frozen Meat Ship	—	—	—	—	1	1	*1,730*
Store Carriers	—	1	1	2	—	4	*4,779*
Ammunition Ship	—	1	—	—	—	1	*2,030*
Mine Carriers	—	—	—	—	2	2	*4,496*
Minesweepers	—	5	3	7	3	5 / 13	3,990 / *7,758*
Auxiliary Patrol Paddlers	—	—	2	—	—	2	*679*
Fleet Messengers	—	3	1	4	1	9	*11,602*
Commissioned Escort Ships.	—	—	—	2	1	3	22,082
Miscellaneous	—	—	—	1	2	3	*4,698*
Colliers	2	33	38	115	56	244	*714,613*
Oilers	—	8	6	21	9	44	*216,445*
Special Service Ships	—	—	5	17	7	29	*35,760*
Tugs	—	3	—	1	10	14	*3,593*
Yachts	—	5	5	3	—	13	*7,179*
Whalers	—	—	—	—	2	2	*347*
Admiralty Trawlers	1	2	2	5	8	18	*4,719*
Hired Trawlers	13	50	58	86	39	246	*56,300*
Hired Drifters	2	13	40	42	33	130	*10,809*
Motor Launches	—	—	6	7	11	24	*864*
Motor Boats	—	3	3	—	—	6	*61*
Total { Nos.	19	127	170	313	186	815	—
Tons Displacement.	—	—	810	1,620	1,560	—	3,990
Tons Gross.	19,165	155,222	180,444	538,322	232,590	—	*1,125,743**

* Excluding two Motor Boats and two Special Service Ships whose Tonnage is uncertain.

VII.—Analysis of Causes of Loss—Auxiliary Vessels.

Class.	Action.	Submarine.	Mine.	Destruction to avoid Capture.	Fire.	Collision.	Wrecked.	Various.	Unknown.	Total.
Hospital Ships	—	1	—	—	—	—	1	—	—	2
Frozen Meat Ships	—	1	—	—	—	—	—	—	—	1
Store Carriers	—	—	3	—	—	1	—	—	—	4
Ammunition Ships	—	—	—	—	—	—	—	—	1	1
Mine Carriers	—	2	—	—	—	—	—	—	—	2
Minesweepers	—	1	12	—	—	2	—	2	1	18
Auxiliary Patrol Paddlers	—	—	—	—	—	—	—	2	—	2
Fleet Messengers	—	6	2	—	—	—	—	1	—	9
Commissioned Escort Ships	—	3	—	—	—	—	—	—	—	3
Miscellaneous	—	2	—	—	—	—	1	—	—	3
Colliers	—	193	22	—	—	9	10	5	5	244
Oilers	—	35	2	—	1	1	2	1	2	44
Special Service Ships	—	22	2	1	1	2	—	1	—	29
Tugs	1	1	—	—	—	2	9	1	—	14
Yachts	1	2	4	—	1	2	2	1	—	13
Whalers	—	—	1	—	—	—	1	—	—	2
Admiralty Trawlers	1	3	4	—	—	5	2	1	2	18
Hired Trawlers	5	14	140	—	1	35	34	9	8	246
Hired Drifters	32	3	32	—	3	33	11	8	8	130
Motor Launches	3	—	1	—	8	1	4	7	—	24
Motor Boats	—	—	—	—	3	—	—	3	—	6
Total	43	289	225	1	18	93	77	38	31	815

VIII.—Classified Nominal List of Losses—Auxiliary Ships.

AMMUNITION SHIP.

Combe.
(1)

AUXILIARY PATROL PADDLERS.

Majestic II.
Stirling Castle.
(2)

COLLIERS.

Adamton.
Adriatic.
African Monarch.
Alfalfa.
Allanton.
Ambient.
Ampleforth.
Apollo.
Ardandearg.
Argo.
Arnewood.
Artist.
Ashby.
Axminster.
Baron Ailsa.
Bedale.
Beemah.
Begonia.
Bellview.
Ben Cruachan.
Bengarth.
Bengrove.
Ben Vrackie.
Bestwood.
Bilbster.

COLLIERS—continued.

Bilswood.
Birchwood.
Birtley.
Bleamoor.
Boldwell.
Boscastle.
Boscawen.
Branksome Chine.
Broomhill.
Buresk.
Burnby.
Burnstone.
Burrsfield.
Butetown (1).
Butetown (2).
Calliope.
Canganian.
Cape Antibes.
Castle Eden.
Charleston.
Cherbury.
Chertsey.
Churston.
Cilicia.
Clan Ferguson.
Clan Forbes.
Clan McLachlan.
Clara.
Cliftondale.
Cliftonian.
Collegian.
Corinth.
Craigendoran.
Craigston.
Cydonia.
Dalewood.
Don.

COLLIERS—continued.

Don Benito.
Dorisbrook.
Dromonby.
Dronning Maud.
Duckbridge.
Eastfield.
Eavestone.
Ella Sayers.
Ellaston.
Ellerslie.
Elsiston.
England.
Enosis.
Eric Calvert.
Eskmere.
Etal Manor.
Ethel Duncan.
Etton.
Euston.
Excellent.
F. Matarazzo.
Foreland.
Fulgent.
Garfield.
Gartland.
Gasconia.
Gena.
Gisella.
Glenby.
Glocliffe.
Gorsemore.
Greavesash.
Greenhill.
Gregynog.
Groeswen.
Hallamshire.
Hartley.

COLLIERS—continued.

Heatherside.
Hebburn.
Hercules.
Heron Bridge.
Herrington.
Hockwold.
Holmesbank.
Huelva.
Hunsbridge.
Hurlford.
Ilvington Court.
Inglemoor.
Intent.
Invergyle.
Inververbie.
Iolo.
Iser.
Islandmore.
Jane Radcliffe.
John O'Scott.
J. Y. Short.
Kilbride.
Kilellan.
Kilwinning.
Kincardine.
Kirkby.
Knarsdale.
Knightgarth.
Kurdistan.
Lady Carrington.
Lady Charlotte.
Lady Iveagh.
Larchwood.
Largo.
Lemnos.
Lincairn.
Linkmoor.

30

COLLIERS—continued.

Llwyngwair.
Lochwood.
Longbenton.
Lord Derby.
Lord Stewart.
Lotusmere.
Lowdale.
Lucent.
Luciston.
Lullington.
Lydie.
Lynfield.
Madryn.
Maltby.
Mansuri.
Margam Abbey.
Margit.
Marie Suzanne.
Marstonmoor.
Maston.
Mavisbrook.
Meldon.
Millicent Knight.
Milly.
Milo.
Minieh.
Mobile.
Monitoria.
Monkstone.
Mountpark.
Munificent.
Muriel.
Nairn.
New Zealand Transport.
Norhilda.
Northfield.
Northville.
North Wales.
Nuceria.
Oakby.
Okement.
Oola.
Penylan.
Pera.
Persier.
Pinewood.
Plutus.
Pola.
Polar Prince.
Poldown.
Polruan.
Porthkerry.
Prophet.
Purley.
Reapwell.
Redesmere.
Remus.
Repton.
Ribston.
Rio Tiete.
River Forth.
Romsdalen.
Rosehill.
Rose Lea.
Rose Marie.
Rubio.
St. Gothard.
Sandsend.
Sarah Radcliffe.
Satrap.
Seistan.
Silverton.
Sneaton.
Snowdon.
Snowdonian.
Southina.
Spennymoor.

COLLIERS—continued.

Standish Hall.
Steelville.
Strathcarron.
Swift Wings.
Taiyabi.
Tandil.
The Queen.
Thorpwood.
Towneley.
Trefusis.
Trevose.
Trowbridge.
Trunkby.
Turnbridge.
Tweed.
Tynemouth.
Valentia.
Vellore.
Venetia.
Waitemata.
War Council.
Westbury.
Western Coast.
West Wales.
Westwood.
Wilston.
Winlaton.
Wychwood.
Zafra.
Zambesi.
Zoroaster.

(244)

COMMISSIONED ESCORT SHIPS.

Bostonian.
Mechanician.
Quernmore.

(3)

DRIFTERS (HIRED).

Active III.
Adequate.
Admirable.
Aivern.
Ajax II.
Annie.
Annie Smith.
Astrum Spei.
Au Fait.
Avondale.
Beneficent.
Betsy Sim.
Border Lads.
Bounteous.
Boy Harold.
Calceolaria.
Campania II.
Cape Colony
Chance.
Charity.
Christina Craig.
City of Liverpool.
Clara and Alice.
Clavis.
Clover Bank (1).
Clover Bank (2).
Coleus.
Comrades.
Coral Haven.
Cosmos.
Craignoon.
Datum.
Deliverer.
Dewey.

DRIFTERS (HIRED)—continued.

Energy.
Enterprise.
Eskburn.
Ethnee.
Everard.
Eyrie.
Falkirk.
Fame.
Felicitas.
Ferndale.
Finrose.
Forward III.
Freuchny.
Frigate Bird.
Frons Oliviae.
Gavenwood.
George V.
Girl Eva.
Girl Gracie.
Girl Rose.
Gleaner of the Sea.
G.M.V.
Golden Sunset.
Gowan.
Gracie.
Grateful.
Great Heart.
G.S.P.
Guide Me II.
Hastfen.
Helenora.
Helen Wilson.
Hilary II.
Holly III.
J. and A.
J.C.P.
Jean.
Jeannie Murray.
John Mitchell.
Ladysmith.
Launch Out.
Laurel Crown.
Lerwick.
Lily Reaich.
Lindsell.
Lottie Leask.
Lustring.
Manzanita.
Michaelmas Daisy.
Morning Star.
New Dawn.
Nexus.
Nina.
Ocean Foam.
Ocean Plough.
Ocean Gift II.
Ocean Star.
Pecheur.
Pelagia.
Persistive.
Piscatorial II.
Plantin.
Protect.
Pursuit.
Quarry Knowe.
Restore.
Roburn.
Rooke.
Rosevine.
Rosie.
Scania.
Selby.
Select.
Serene.
Silver Queen.
Silvery Harvest.

DRIFTERS (HIRED)—continued.

Silvery Wave.
Southesk.
Speedwell V.
Spotless Prince.
Star of Buchan.
Strathmore.
Sunbeam I.
Susanna.
Taits.
Thistle IV.
Transit.
Tuberose.
Tulip II.
Veracity.
Waterlily.
Waveney II.
W. Elliott.
White Rose.
William Tennant.
Young Linnett.

(130)

FLEET MESSENGERS.

Chesterfield.
Clifford.
Ermine.
Nugget.
Osmanieh.
Portia.
Princess Alberta.
Redbreast.
Turquoise.

(9)

FROZEN MEAT SHIPS.

Romeo.

(1)

HOSPITAL SHIPS.

Rewa.
Rohilla.

(2)

MINE CARRIERS.

Eleanor.
Lady Cory-Wright.

(2)

MINESWEEPERS.

Ascot.
Blackmorevale.
Brighton Queen.
Clacton.
Duchess of Hamilton.
Duchess of Montrose.
Fair Maid.
Hythe.
Kempton.
Lady Ismay.
Ludlow.
Marsa.
Nepaulin.
Newmarket.
Queen of the North.
Redcar.
Roedean (ex Roebuck).
St. Seiriol.

(18)

31

MISCELLANEOUS.
Lowtyne.
Puruni.
White Head.
(3)

MOTOR BOATS.
Allegro.
Dolores.
Doreen.
Dorothea.
Griffin.
Nita Pita.
(6)

MOTOR LAUNCHES.
M.L. 19.
M.L. 40.
M.L. 52.
M.L. 55.
M.L. 64.
M.L. 110.
M.L. 149.
M.L. 197.
M.L. 230.
M.L. 247.
M.L. 253.
M.L. 254.
M.L. 255.
M.L. 278.
M.L. 356.
M.L. 403.
M.L. 421.
M.L. 424.
M.L. 431.
M.L. 474.
M.L. 534.
M.L. 540.
M.L. 541.
M.L. 561.
(24)

OILERS.
Arca.
Ashleaf.
Baku Standard.
Balakani.
Batoum.
Beacon Light.
British Sun.
British Viscount.
Bullmouth.
Bulysses.
Caucasian.
Clearfield.
Cymbeline.
Derbent.
Desabla.
Echunga.
Elax.
El Toro.
El Zorro.
Fornebo.
Gafsa.
Goldmouth.
H. C. Henry.
Lumina.
Mira.
Murex.
Oakleaf.
Oilfield.
Palmleaf.
Ponus.
Powhatan.
Prudentia.

OILERS—continued.
Rosalind.
Samoset.
San Onofre.
Sebastian.
Silvia.
Tatarrax.
Teakwood.
Telena.
Trocas.
Turritella.
Waneta.
Wapello.
(44)

SPECIAL SERVICE SHIPS.
Asama.
Bayard.
Bracondale.
Bradford City.
Brown Mouse.
Dunraven.
Else.
Ethel and Millie.
Fame.
Glenfoyle.
Kent County.
King Stephen.
Lady Olive.
Lady Patricia.
M. J. Hedley.
Mona.
Nelson.
Ocean Fisher.
Penshurst.
Perugia.
Peveril.
Remembrance.
Stockforce.
Vala.
Warner.
Wellholme.
Westphalia.
Willow Branch.
Zylpha.
(29)

STORE CARRIERS.
Charles Goodanew.
Hebble.
Immingham.
Leicester.
(4)

TRAWLERS (ADMIRALTY).
Antares II.
Benjamin Stevenson.
Carbineer.
Charles Astie.
Charles Hammond.
Charlsin.
Crownsin.
James Pond.
James Seckar.
Jasper.
Javelin.
Lancer II.
Michael Clements.
Nathaniel Cole.
Sapper.
Spider.
Thos. Collard.
Thos. Cornwall.
(18)

TRAWLERS (HIRED).
Abelard.
Achilles II.
Adrian.
Agamemnon II.
Agate.
Agile.
Alberta.
Albion II.
Ameer.
Amplify.
Amy.
Angelus.
Anthony Hope.
Apley.
Arfon.
Asia.
Balfour.
Balmedie.
Banyers.
Bedouin.
Bega.
Ben Ardna.
Ben Heilen.
Benton Castle.
Berkshire.
Birch.
Blakedown.
Bonar Law.
Borneo.
Bovic.
Bracklyn.
Bradford.
Briton.
Burnley.
By George.
Caledonia.
Calliope II.
Cantatrice.
Carew Castle,
Carilon.
Carlton.
Chester II.
Christopher.
City of Dundee.
Cleon.
Clifton.
Clyde.
Columba.
Columbia.
Commandant.
Commander Fullerton.
Condor.
Corcyra.
Corientes.
Corona.
Cotsmuir.
Courtier.
Crathie (1).
Crathie (2).
Dagon.
Dane.
De la Pole.
Dhoon.
Dirk.
Donside.
Drake II.
Drumoak.
Drumtochty.
Duster.
Earl Lennox.
Edison.
Elise.
Emley.
Endeavour.
Epworth.
Era.
Erin II.

TRAWLERS (HIRED)—continued.
Eros.
Etoile Polaire.
Euston.
Evadne.
Evangel.
Fair Isle.
Falmouth III.
Filey.
Flicker.
Fraser.
Fulmar.
Gabir.
Gambri.
Garmo.
Gersina.
George Milburn.
Glenprosen.
Hawke.
Helgian.
Hirose.
Holdene.
Idena.
Ijuin.
Ina William.
Irawadi.
Italy.
Ivanhoe.
Jacamar.
Japan.
Jay.
Jessie Nutten.
John E. Lewis.
John G. Watson.
John High.
John Sherburn.
Kalmia.
Kaphreda.
Kelvin.
Kirkland.
Klondyke.
Knot.
Leandros.
Lena Melling.
Livingstone.
Lobelia II.
Loch Ard.
Loch Eye.
Loch Garry.
Lochiel.
Loch Naver.
Loch Shiel.
Loch Tummel.
Longset.
Lord Airedale.
Lord Alverstone.
Lord Denman.
Lord Grey.
Lord Hardinge.
Lord Ridley.
Lord Roberts.
Lord Salisbury.
Lorenzo.
Lucknow.
Lundy.
Lydian.
Malta.
Manx Hero.
Manx Queen.
Margate.
Marion.
Mary.
Mediator.
Merse.
Miranda III.
Miura.
Morococola.

TRAWLERS (HIRED)—continued.

Nadine.
Narval.
Neath Castle.
Nellie Nutten.
Neptunian.
Nerissa II.
Newbridge.
New Comet.
Night Hawk.
Northumbria.
Numitor.
Ocean Scout I.
Okino.
Onward.
Orcades.
Orianda.
Orlando.
Orphesia.
Orsino.
Orthos.
Othello II.
Othonna.
Picton Castle.
Pitsruan.
Plethos.
Poonah.
Princess Alice.
Princess Beatrice.
Princess Olga.
Princess Victoria.
Quail III.
Recepto.
Relevo.
Remarko.

TRAWLERS (HIRED)—continued.

Remindo.
Renarro.
Repro.
Resono.
Responso.
Rhodesia.
Riparvo.
Robert Smith.
Rolulo.
Rondo.
Rose II.
Rosy Morn.
Ruby (1).
Ruby (2).
Ruthin Castle.
St. Ives.
St. Johns.
Sarah Alice.
Sardius II.
Saxon Prince.
Schiehallion.
Scott.
Sealark II.
Senator.
Sisters Melville.
Sophron.
Speedwell II.
Speeton.
Star of Freedom.
Strathgarry.
Strathrannoch.
Strymon.
Swallow.
Taipo.

TRAWLERS (HIRED)—continued.

Teal.
Tern.
Tervant.
Tettenhall.
Thomas Stretton.
Thomas W. Irvin.
Thuringia.
Tokio.
Tom Tit.
Towhee.
Trygon.
Tugela.
Vale of Leven.
Valpa.
Vitality.
Vivanti.
Vulture II.
Waltham.
Weigelia.
Whooper.
William Morrison.
Worsley.
Xerxes.
Yesso.
Yucca.
(246)

TUGS.

Alexandra.
Blackcock.
Blazer.
Char (ex Stranton).
Dalkeith.

TUGS—continued.

David Gillies.
Desire.
George R. Gray.
Guiana.
Jack.
Ludgate.
Marsden.
Oceana.
Thames.
(14)

WHALERS.

Blackwhale.
Hirpa.
(2)

YACHTS.

Ægusa.
Aries.
Clementina.
Conqueror II.
Hersilia.
Kethailes.
Mekong.
Resource II.
Rhiannon.
Sanda.
Verona.
Zaida.
Zarefah.
(13)

INDEX.

Black type = **Warships.**

Ordinary type = Auxiliary Vessels.

A.

	Page.
Abelard	15
Aboukir	**3**
Achilles II	27
Active III.	23
Adamton	13
Adequate	16
Admirable	23
Adrian	26
Adriatic	13
A.E. 1	**3**
A.E. 2	**3**
Ægusa	14
African Monarch	10
Agamemnon II.	12
●Agate	26
Agile	21
●Aivern	23
●Ajax II.	16
Alberta	14
●Albion II.	14
Alcantara	**4**
Alexandra	11
Alfalfa	18
Allanton	24
Allegro	16
Alyssum	**4**
Ambient	17
Ameer	14
Amphion	**3**
Ampleforth	18
Amplify	21
Amy	21
Anchusa	**6**
●Angelus	14
Annie	23
Annie Smith	27
Antares II.	26
Anthony Hope	15
●Apley	22
Apollo	11
Arabis	**4**
Arbutus	**5**
Arca	26
Ardandearg	25
Ardent	**4**
Arethusa	**4**
Arfon	21
Argo	20
Argyll	**3**
●**Ariadne**	**5**
Ariel	**6**
Aries	11
Arnewood	19
Arno	**6**
Artist	17
Asama	20
Ascot	24
Ashby	13
Ashleaf	20
Asia	22
Aster	**5**
Astrum Spei	16
Attack	**5**
Audacious	**3**
Au Fait	15
Avenger	**5**
Avondale	23
Axminster	19

B.

	Page.
B. 10	**4**
Baku Standard	25
Balakani	11
●Balfour	27
Balmedie	12
Bangarth	19
Banyers	11
Baron Ailsa	25
Batoum	20
●Bayard	20
Bayano	**3**
Beacon Light	25
Bedale	19
Bedouin	11
Beemah	18
Bega	22
Begonia (Sloop)	**5**
Begonia (Collier)	25
Bellview	25
Ben Ardna	12
Ben Cruachan	10
Beneficent	15
Bengrove	10
Ben Heilem	22
Benjamin Stevenson	21
Ben-my-Chree	**5**
●Benton Castle	15
Ben Vrackie	11
Bergamot	**5**
Berkshire	12
Bestwood	18
Betsy Sim	23
Bilbster	19
Bilswood	17
Birch	15
Birchwood	24
Birtley	24
●**Bittern**	**6**
Blackcock	26
Blackmorevale	24
Black Prince	**4**
Blackwhale	26
Blakedown	11
Blazer	26
●Bleamoor	19
Boldwell	18
Bonar Law	12
Border Lads	27
●Borneo	22
Boscastle	25
Boscawen	25
Bostonian	17
Bounteous	23
Bovic	22
●**Boxer**	**6**
Boy Harold	15
Bracklyn	22
Bracondale	20
Bradford	15
Bradford City	20
●Branksome Chine	10
Brighton Queen	10
Brilliant	**6**
Britannia	**6**
British Sun	20
British Viscount	25
Briton	12
●Broomhill	18
●Brown Mouse	26

	Page.
Bullmouth	20
Bulwark	**3**
Bulysses	20
Buresk	9
Burnby	17
Burnley	15
Burnstone	25
Burrsfield	11
Butetown (1) (Collier)	13
Butetown (2) (Collier)	24
By George	22

C.

	Page.
C. 3	**6**
C. 26	**6**
C. 27	**6**
C. 29	**3**
C. 31	**3**
C. 32	**5**
C. 33	**3**
C. 34	**5**
C. 35	**6**
Calceolaria	28
Caledonia	21
Calgarian	**6**
Calliope (Collier)	18
Calliope II. (Trawler)	14
Campania (Air-craft Carrier)	**6**
Campania II. (Drifter)	23
Candytuft	**5**
Canganian	14
Cantatrice	15
Cape Antibes	11
Cape Colony	23
Carbineer	14
Carew Castle	22
●Carilon	12
●Carlton	14
Castle Eden	24
Caucasian	11
Champagne	**5**
Chance	15
●Char (ex Stranton)	11
●Charity	12
Charles Astie	21
Charles Goodanew	16
Charles Hammond	26
Charleston	19
Charlsin	21
Cheerful	**5**
Cherbury	10
Chertsey	18
Chester II	14
Chesterfield	24
●Christain Craig	27
Christopher	21
Churston	11
Cilicia	17
City of Dundee	12
City of Liverpool	27
Clacton	13
Clan Ferguson	18
Clan Forbes	25
Clan McLachlan	18
Clan MacNaughton	**3**
Clara	20
Clara and Alice	27
Clavis	16
Clearfield	14

	Page.
Clementina	11
●Cleon	26
Clifford	13
Clifton	21
Cliftondale	20
Cliftonian	17
Clover Bank (1) (Drifter)	15
●Clover Bank (2) (Drifter)	27
Clyde	22
Coastal Motor Boats—	
No. 1	**5**
No. 8	**5**
No. 11	**5**
No. 18a	**7**
No. 33a	**7**
No. 39b	**7**
No. 16	**7**
No. 2	**7**
No. 50	**7**
No. 40	**7**
No. 42	**7**
No. 47	**7**
No. 71a	**7**
●Coleus	28
Collegian	19
Columba	26
Columbia	12
Commandant	14
Commander Fullerton	22
Combe	10
Comet (T.B.D.)	**6**
Comet (River Gunboat)	**3**
Comrades	23
Condor	10
Conqueror II.	14
●**Contest**	**5**
Coquette	**4**
Coral Haven	23
Corcyra	11
Corientes	22
Corinth	14
Cornwallis	**4**
●Corona	14
●Cosmos	27
Cotsmuir	21
Courtier	14
Cowslip	**6**
Craigendoran	17
Craignoon	23
Craigston	11
Crathie (1) (Trawler)	10
Crathie (2) (Trawler)	15
Cressy	**3**
Crownsin	14
Cydonia	19
Cymbeline	11

D.

	Page.
D. 2	**3**
D. 3	**6**
D. 5	**3**
D. 6	**6**
●Dagon	15
Dalewood	24
Dalkeith	26
Dane	12
Datum	16
David Gillies	26

	Page.		Page.		Page.		Page.
Defence	4	Eric Calvert	25	Glenby	10	Iser	17
De la Pole	14	Erin II.	12	Glenfoyle	21	Islandmore	18
Deliverer	23	Ermine	16	Glenprosen	15	Italy	15
Derbent	20	**Erne**	3	Gloclifie	18	**Itchen**	5
Derwent	5	Eros	22	G. M. V.	12	Ivanhoe	10
Desabla	11	Eskburn	16	Golden Sunset	27		
Desire	26	Eskmere	19	**Goldfinch**	3	**J.**	
Dewey	23	Etal Manor	19	Goldmouth	14		
Dhoon	15	Ethel Duncan	13	**Goliath**	3	**J. 6**	6
Dirk	27	Ethel and Millie	20	**Good Hope**	3	J. & A.	27
Dolores	12	Ethnee	27	Gorsemore	25	Jacamar	21
Don	10	Etoile Polaire	12	Gowan	23	Jack	21
Don Benito	17	Etton	13	Gracie	23	James Pond	26
Donside	21	Euston (Collier)	19	Grateful	15	James Seckar	21
Doreen	16	Euston (Trawler)	21	Great Heart	12	Jane Radcliffe	19
Dorisbrook	24	Evadne	21	Greavesash	24	Japan	12
Dorothea	12	Evangel	21	Greenhill	19	**Jason**	4
Drake (Cruiser)	4	Everard	15	Gregynog	25	Jasper	11
Drake II. (Trawler)	22	Excellent	17	Griffin	16	Javelin	11
Dromonby	13	Eyrie	10	**Grive**	5	Jay	22
Dronning Maud	25			Groeswen	19	J. C. P.	27
Drumoak	10	**F.**		G. S. P.	23	Jean	23
Druntochty	26			Guiana	26	Jeannie Murray	27
Duchess of Hamilton	10	Fair Isle	10	Guide Me II.	28	Jessie Nutten	15
Duchess of Montrose	16	Fair Maid	13			John E. Lewis	26
Duckbridge	13	**Fairy**	6	**H.**		John G. Watson	12
Duke of Albany	4	Falcon	6			John High	15
Dundee	5	Falkirk	28	H. 3	4	John Mitchell	23
Dunraven	20	Falmouth (Light		H. 5	6	John O'Scott	25
Duster	22	Cruiser)	4	H. 6	4	John Sherburn	11
		Falmouth III.		H. 10	6	J. Y. Short	13
		(Trawler)	12	Hallamshire	11		
E.		Fame (Special Service		**Hampshire**	4	**K.**	
		Ship)	14	Hartley	24		
E. 1	6	Fame (Drifter)	16	Hastfen	23	K. 1	5
E. 3	3	**Fauvette**	4	Hawk	21	K. 4	6
E. 5	4	Felicitas	23	**Hawke**	3	K. 17	6
E. 6	3	Ferndale	12	**Hazard**	6	Kale	6
E. 7	3	Filey	15	H. C. Henry	11	Kalmia	27
E. 8	6	Finross	16	Heatherside	18	Kaphreda	15
E. 9	6	**Fiona**	5	Hebble	16	Kelvin	22
E. 10	3	Flicker	14	Hebburn	25	Kempton	16
E. 13	3	**Flirt**	4	Helenora	23	Kent County	14
E. 14	6	F. Matarazzo	14	Helen Wilson	23	Kethailes	21
E. 15	3	Foreland	17	Helgian	22	Kilbride	13
E. 16	4	**Formidable**	3	Hercules	20	Kilellan	13
E. 17	4	Fornebo	20	**Hermes**	3	Kilwinning	18
E. 18	4	**Fortune**	4	Heron Bridge	25	Kincardine	17
E. 19	6	Forward III.	23	Herrington	18	**King Edward VII.**	4
E. 20	3	**Foyle**	5	Hersilia	14	King Stephen	14
E. 22	4	Fraser	22	Hilary (A.M.C.)	5	Kirkby	11
E. 24	4	Freuchny	15	Hilary II. (Drifter)	15	Kirkland	22
E. 26	4	Frigate Bird	27	Hirose	15	Klondyke	15
E. 30	4	Frons Oliviae	12	Hirpa	26	Knarsdale	11
E. 34	6	Fulgent	10	Hockwold	19	Knightgarth	24
E. 36	5	Fulmar	14	**Hogue**	3	Knot	15
E. 37	4			Holdene	21	Kurdistan	19
E. 47	5	**G.**		Holly III.	27		
E. 49	5			Holmesbank	18	**L.**	
E. 50	6	G. 7	6	Hoste	4	L.10	6
Earl Lennox	22	G. 8	6	Huelva	18	**Lady Carrington**	14
Eastfield	19	G. 9	5	Hunsbridge	19	Lady Charlotte	18
Eavestone	17	Gabir	27	Hurlford	18	Lady Cory-Wright	24
Echunga	20	Gafsa	20	Hythe	10	Lady Ismay	10
Eden	4	Gaillardia	6			Lady Iveagh	11
Edison	12	Gambri	26	**I.**		Lady Olive	20
Elax	14	Garfield	17			Lady Patricia	20
Eleanor	24	Garmo	10	Idena	26	Ladysmith	12
Elise	27	Gartland	24	Ijuin	27	**Laforey**	5
Ella Sayer	25	Gasconia	19	Ilvington Court	19	Lancer II.	26
Ellaston	25	Gavenwood	15	Immingham	10	Larchwood	13
Ellerslie	19	Gelsina	22	Ina William	22	Largo	24
Else	20	Gena	18	**Indefatigable**	4	**Lassoo**	4
Elsiston	19	**Genista**	4	**India**	3	Launch Out	16
El Toro	20	George V.	23	Inglemoor	10	Laurel Crown	16
El Zorro	11	George Milburn	22	Intent	24	**Laurentic**	5
Emley	27	George R. Gray	26	**Intrepid**	6	**Lavender**	5
Endeavour	26	**Ghurka**	5	Invergyle	10	Leandros	12
Energy	23	Girl Eva	16	Inververbie	13	Leicester	12
England	18	Girl Gracie	23	**Invincible**	4	Lemnos	11
Enosis	11	Girl Rose	23	Iolo	13	Lena Melling	14
Enterprise II.	15	Gisella	19	**Iphigenia**	6	Lerwick	15
Epworth	22	**Glatton**	6	Irawadi	15	**Lightning**	3
Era	15	Gleaner of the Sea	16	**Irresistible**	3	Lilly Reaich	15

Lincairn	13	●Michæl Clements	26	North Wales	9	Prophet	19
Lindsell	10	Michælmas Daisy	16	**Nottingham**	4	●Protect	23
Linkmoor	11	**Mignonette**	4	**Nubian**	4	Prudentia	14
Livingstone	22	Millicent Knight	18	Nuceria	19	Purley	18
Llwyngwair	25	Milly	25	Nugget	10	Pursuit	27
Lobelia II.	21	Milo	18	Numitor	27	Puruni	24
Loch Ard	22	Minieh	17				
Loch Eye	21	●Mira	20	**O.**		**Q.**	
Loch Garry	15	Miranda III.	26				
Lochiel	27	Miura	12	●Oakby	10	●Quail III.	12
Loch Naver	27	M. J. Hedley	26	Oakleaf	20	Quarry Knowe	23
Loch Shiel	15	M.L. 19	16	**Ocean**	3	**Queen Mary**	4
Loch Tummel	27	M.L. 40	16	Oceana	26	Queen of the North	16
Lochwood	10	●M.L. 52	23	Ocean Fisher	26	Quernmore	17
Longbenton	18	M.L. 55	28	Ocean Foam	28		
Longset	21	M.L. 64	28	**Oceanic**	3	**R.**	
Lord Airedaile	15	M.L. 110	28	Ocean Plough	16		
Lord Alverstone	22	M.L. 149	16	Ocean Scout I.	23	**Racoon**	6
Lord Denman	12	M.L. 197	23	Ocean's Gift II.	23	**Raglan**	6
Lord Derby	20	M.L. 230	16	●Ocean Star	23	Reapwell	14
Lord Grey	22	M.L. 247	28	Oilfield	25	Recepto	21
Lord Hardinge	27	M.L. 253	16	Okement	17	**Recruit 1** (T.B.D.)	3
Lord Ridley	22	M.L. 254	28	Okino	11	**Recruit 2** (T.B.D.)	5
Lord Roberts	15	M.L. 255	16	Onward	15	Redreast	16
Lord Salisbury	21	M.L. 278	28	Oola	13	●Redcar	16
Lord Stewart	25	●M.L. 356	28	**Opal**	6	●Redesmere	19
Lorenzo	10	M.L. 403	28	**Orama**	5	Relevo	15
Lottie Leask	12	M.L. 421	28	Orcades	14	Remarko	15
Lotusmere	13	M.L. 424	28	Orianda	10	Remembrance	14
Louis	3	M.L. 431	23	Orlando	11	●Remindo	26
Louvain	7	M.L. 474	23	Orphesia	22	Remus	24
Lowdale	17	M.L. 534	23	Orsino	15	Renarro	27
Lowtyne	24	M.L. 540	23	Orthos	21	Repro	21
Lucent	17	M.L. 541	23	Osmanieh	16	Repton	18
Luciston	14	M.L. 561	28	Othello II.	12	Resono	12
●Lucknow	22	Mobile	10	Othonna	21	Resource II.	11
Ludgate	26	●**Moldavia**	6	**Otranto**	7	Responso	12
Ludlow	13	Mona	20	**Otway**	5	Restore	12
●Lullington	17	Monitoria	11			Rewa	24
Lumina	11	Monkstone	18	**P.**		Rhiannon	11
Lundy	12	**Monmouth**	3			Rhodesia	11
Lustring	28	Morning Star	15	●P. 12	6	**Rhododendron**	6
Lydian	12	Morococola	22	●P. 26	5	Ribston	13
●Lydie	24	Mountpark	18	Palmleaf	20	Rio Tiete	13
Lynx	3	Munificent	17	●**Paragon**	5	Riparvo	27
Lynfield	17	Murex	14	Partridge	5	River Forth	17
		Muriel	25	**Pathfinder**	3	Robert Smith	22
		●**Myrmidon**	5	Patia	7	●Roburn	16
				Pecheur	15	Roedean (ex Roebuck)	10
M.		**N.**		**Pegasus**	3	Rohilla	9
M. 15	4			●Pelagia	16	Rolulo	12
M. 21	6			Penshurst	21	Romeo	24
M. 28	6	Nadine	12	Penylan	13	●Romsdalen	17
M. 30	4	Nairn	18	Pera	19	Rondo	11
●Madryn	25	**Narbrough**	6	Persier	19	●Rooke	16
Majestic (B.S.)	3	Narval	15	●Persistive	15	Rosalind	20
Majestic II. (A.P.P.)	13	**Nasturtium**	4	Perugia	14	Rose II.	21
Malta	12	**Natal**	3	Peverill	21	Rosehill	19
Maltby	24	Nathaniel Cole	26	**Pheasant**	5	Rose Lea	17
Mansuri	14	Neath Castle	15	**Phoenix**	6	Rose Marie	24
Manx Hero	11	**Negro**	4	●Picton Castle	21	Rosevine	23
Manx Queen	14	Nellie Nutten	15	**Pincher**	6	Rosie	16
Manzanita	16	Nelson	20	Pinewood	24	Rosy Morn	14
Maori	3	Nepaulin	16	Piscatorial II.	23	Rubio	24
Marcella	4	Neptunian	27	Pitstruan	21	Ruby 1 (Trawler)	12
Margam Abbey	13	Nerissa II.	26	Plantin	23	Ruby 2 (Trawler)	22
Margate	21	**Nessus**	6	Plethos	27	**Russell**	4
Margit	17	**Nestor**	4	Plutus	17	Ruthin Castle	21
Marie Suzanne	25	●Newbrough	22	Pola	17		
Marion	26	New Comet	21	Polar Prince	19	**S.**	
Marmion	5	●New Dawn	27	Poldown	19		
Marmora	7	Newmarket	6	Polruan	13	St. Gothard	13
Marsa	16	New Zealand Transport	18	●Ponus	14	●St. Ives	15
Marsden	11	Nexus	27	Poonah	12	St. Johns	27
Marstonmoor	25	●**Niger**	3	●Porthkerry	18	St. Seiriol	24
Mary	10	Night Hawk	10	Portia	10	**Salvia**	5
Mary Rose	5	●Nina	23	Powhatan	20	Samoset	25
Maston	18	Nita Pita	12	**Primula**	4	Sanda	11
Mavisbrook	25	**Nomad**	4	Princess Alberta	16	Sandsend	19
●Mechanician	24	Norhilda	18	Princess Alice	26	San Onofre	20
Mediator	14	Northfield	24	Princess Beatrice	10	●Sapper	21
Medusa	4	**North Star**	6	**Princess Irene**	3	Sarah Alice	15
Mekong	14	Northumbria	21	Princess Olga	27	Sarah Radcliffe	13
Meldon	17	●Northville	24	Princess Victoria	12	Sardius II.	26
Merse	22						

	Page.		Page.		Page.		Page.
Sarnia	7	Strathgarry	12	**Torpedo Boats**—*cont.*		**W.**	
Satrap	11	Strathmore	28	24	5		
Saxon Prince	14	Strathrannoch	21	90	6	Waltham	22
Scania	27	**Strongbow**	5	96	3	Waneta	26
Schiehallion	12	Strymon	22	117	5	Waitemata	25
Scott (T.B.D.)	6	**Success**	3	Torrent	5	Wapello	20
Scott (Trawler)	12	Sunbeam I.	27	Towneley	24	War Council	25
Seagull	6	**Surprise**	5	Towhee	22	Warner	20
Sealark II.	27	Susanna	12	Transit	23	**Warrior**	4
Sebastian	20	Swallow	27	Trefusis	17	Waterlily	12
Seistan	19	Swift Wings	13	Trevose	17	Waveney II.	16
Selby	23			**Triumph**	3	Weigelia	14
Select	27	**T.**		Trocas	25	Wellholme	26
Senator	22			Trowbridge	19	W. Elliott	27
Serene	23	Taipo	22	Trunkby	13	Westbury	18
Setter	5	Taits	23	Trygon	11	Western Coast	19
Shaitan	3	Taiyabi	24	Tuberose	16	Westphalia	26
Shark	4	Tandil	17	Tugela	15	West Wales	24
Silver Queen	27	**Tara**	4	**Tulip** (Sloop)	4	Westwood	25
Silverton	13	Tatarrax	26	Tulip II. (Drifter)	28	White Head	17
Silvery Harvest	27	Teakwood	20	**Turbulent**	4	White Rose	16
Silvery Wave	12	Teal	21	Turnbridge	20	Whooper	15
Silvia	11	Telena	20	Turquoise	10	William Morrison	12
Simoom	5	Tern	11	Turritella	20	William Tennant	27
Sirius	6	Tervani	15	Tweed	24	Willow Branch	26
Sisters Melville	21	Tettenhall	22	Tynemouth	11	Wilston	13
Snaefell	7	Thames	26			Winlaton	18
Sneaton	13	The Queen	10	**U.**		**Wolverine**	5
Snowdon	25	**The Ramsey**	4			Worsley	12
Snowdonian	18	**Thetis**	6	Ulleswater	6	Wychwood	17
Sophron	22	Thistle IV.	12	Ulysses	6		
Southesk	23	Thos. Collard	26			**X.**	
Southina	18	Thos. Cornwall	26	**V.**		Xerxes	12
Sparrowhawk	4	Thomas Stratten	22	Vala	21		
Speedwell II.	27	Thomas W. Irwin	10	Valentia	18	**Y.**	
Speedwell V.	16	Thorpwood	11	Vale of Leven	22		
Speedy	3	Thuringia	22	Valpa	14	Yesso	21
Speeton	12	**Tipperary**	4	**Vanguard**	4	Young Linnett	23
Spennymoor	10	**Tithonus**	7	**Vehement**	6	Yucca	27
Spider	9	Tokio	22	Vellore	17		
Spotless Prince	16	Tom Tit	10	**Velox**	3	**Z.**	
Standish Hall	24	**Tornado**	5	Venetia	19		
Star of Buchan	12	Torpedo Boats—		Veracity	27	Zafra	13
Star of Freedom	21	046	3	Verona	21	Zaida	14
Staunch	5	064	3	**Viknor**	3	Zambesi	17
Steelville	24	9	4	**Vindictive**	6	Zarefah	21
Stephen Furness	5	10	3	Vitality	22	Zoroaster	14
Stirling Castle	13	11	4	Vivanti	21	**Zulu**	4
Stockforce	26	12	3	Vulture II.	26	Zylpha	20
Strathcarron	10	13	4				

Section II
MERCHANT SHIPPING (LOSSES)

MERCHANT SHIPPING (LOSSES).

RETURN to an Order of the Honourable The House of Commons, dated 1 August 1919 ;—*for,*

RETURN "showing separately, BRITISH MERCHANT and FISHING VESSELS captured or destroyed by the ENEMY; also BRITISH MERCHANT VESSELS damaged or molested by the ENEMY, but not sunk; during the period 4th day of August 1914 to 11th day of November 1918; to show, as far as is known, Name, Gross Tonnage, Date, Position, and Method of Attack, Cause of Loss or Escape, and Number of Lives lost."

Admiralty,
August 1919.

O. A. R. MURRAY,
Secretary.

(*Lieutenant-Colonel Burgoyne.*)

Ordered, by The House of Commons, *to be Printed,*
19 *August* 1919.

CONTENTS.

	Page
List I.—British Merchant Vessels Captured or Destroyed by the Enemy	1
List II.—British Fishing Vessels Captured or Destroyed by the Enemy	99
List III.—British Merchant Vessels Damaged or Molested by the Enemy but not Sunk	125
Table A.—Showing Number and Gross Tonnage of BRITISH MERCHANT VESSELS Lost through Enemy Action during each month since Outbreak of War; and number of Lives Lost	162
Table B.—Showing Number and Gross Tonnage of BRITISH FISHING VESSELS Lost through Enemy Action during each month since Outbreak of War; and number of Lives Lost	163
Table C.—Showing Number and Gross Tonnage of BRITISH MERCHANT VESSELS Damaged or Molested (but not Sunk) by the Enemy during each month since Outbreak of War; and number of Lives Lost	164
Index	165

A † before a vessel's name indicates that she was armed for defensive purposes.

Vessels armed for offensive purposes are not included in these lists. Unless otherwise stated, all bearings given are magnetic. Crew and civilian passengers only are included in column headed "Lives lost."

I.—BRITISH MERCHANT VESSELS CAPTURED OR DESTROYED BY THE ENEMY.

Name.	Tons.	Date.	Position.	Cause of Loss.	How attacked.	How sunk.	Lives lost.
AUGUST 1914.		1914. Aug.					
San Wilfrido	6,458	3	Off Cuxhaven	Mine	Mine	Mine	Crew made prisoners.
City of Winchester.	6,601	6	280 miles E. (true) from Aden.	Konigsberg	Captured	Scuttled	—
Frau Minna Petersen (S.V.).	176	7	5 miles N.W. from Osterems Port Buoy.	Torpedo Boat	Captured	Taken to Emden.	—
Hyades	3,352	15	180 miles N.E. ¼ N. (true) from Pernambuco.	Dresden	Captured	Gunfire	—
Kaipara	7,392	16	170 miles S. by W. (true) from Tenerife.	Kaiser Wilhelm der Grosse.	Captured	Gunfire	—
Nyanga	3,066	16	240 miles S. ¼ E. (true) from Tenerife.	Kaiser Wilhelm der Grosse.	Captured	Scuttled	—
Bowes Castle	4,650	18	350 miles N. by W. ½ W. (true) from Cape Orange.	Karlsruhe	Captured	Scuttled	—
Holmwood	4,223	26	170 miles S. ½ W. (true) from Cape Santa Marta Grande.	Dresden	Captured	Bombs	—
Strathroy	4,336	31	100 miles N.N.E. (true) from Cape St. Roque.	Karlsruhe	Captured	Scuttled	—
SEPTEMBER	1914. Sept.						
Maple Branch	4,338	3	250 miles S.W. ¼ S. (true) from St. Paul Rocks.	Karlsruhe	Captured	Bomb	—
Indian Prince	2,846	4	210 miles E. by N. ½ N. (true) from Pernambuco.	Kronprinz Wilhelm	Captured	Bomb	—
Runo	1,679	5	About 22 miles E. by N. from Tyne.	Mine	Mine	Mine	29
Indus	3,413	10	240 miles S.E. by E. (true) from Madras.	Emden	Captured	Gunfire	—
Lovat	6,102	11	260 miles E. ½ N. (true) from Madras.	Emden	Captured	Gunfire	—
Elsinore	6,542	11	80 miles S.W. by W. (true) from Cape Corrientes.	Leipzig	Captured	Gunfire	—
Killin	3,544	13	410 miles N.E. by E. (true) from Madras.	Emden	Captured	Gunfire	—
Diplomat	7,615	13	480 miles N.E. ½ E. (true) from Madras.	Emden	Captured	Gunfire	—
Trabboch	4,028	14	70 miles S.W. by S. (true) from Pilots Lt., Mouth of Hooghli.	Emden	Captured	Gunfire	—

MERCHANT VESSELS CAPTURED OR SUNK.   2

Name.	Tons.	Date.	Position.	Cause of Loss.	How attacked.	How sunk.	Lives lost.
		1914. Sept.					
Clan Matheson	4,775	14	60 miles S.W. by S. (true) from Pilots Lt., Mouth of Hooghli.	Emden	Captured	Bombs	—
Highland Hope	5,150	14	190 miles S.W. ½ W. (true) from St. Paul Rocks.	Karlsruhe	Captured	Scuttled	—
Indrani	5,706	17	145 miles N. by W. (true) from Cape St. Roque.	Karlsruhe	Captured	Scuttled	—
Cornish City	3,816	21	245 miles S.W. ¼ S. (true) from St. Paul Rocks.	Karlsruhe	Captured	Bombs	—
Rio Iguassu	3,817	22	155 miles S.W. ½ W. (true) from St. Paul Rocks.	Karlsruhe	Captured	Bombs	—
King Lud	3,650	25	25 miles S.S.W. (true) from Point de Galle.	Emden	Captured	Bombs	—
Tymeric	3,314	25	50 miles W. by N. (true) from Colombo.	Emden	Captured	Bombs	—
Bankfields	3,763	25	In Gulf of Guayaquil.	Leipzig	Captured	Gunfire	—
Buresk	4,337	27	180 miles W. by N. ¾ N. (true) from Colombo.	Emden	Captured	By H.M.A.S. "Sydney" on 9th Nov. 1914.	—
Ribera	3,500	27	210 miles W. by N. (true) from Colombo.	Emden	Captured	Gunfire	—
Foyle	4,147	27	300 miles W. ¾ N. (true) from Colombo.	Emden	Captured	Scuttled	—
Selby	2,137	30	34 miles S.E. by S. from Newarp L.V.	Mine	Mine	Mine	—

OCTOBER 1914.

		Oct.					
Dawdon	1,310	3	10 miles N.W. by W. from Wandelaar L.V.	Mine	Mine	Mine	10
Ardmount	3,510	5	3 miles E. by S. ½ S. from Wandelaar L.V.	Mine	Mine	Mine	—
Niceto de Larrinaga.	5,018	6	100 miles S. by W. ¼ W. (true) from St. Paul Rocks.	Karlsruhe	Captured	Bombs	—
Lynrowan	3,384	7	90 miles S.S.W. (true) from St. Paul Rocks.	Karlsruhe	Captured	Bombs	—
La Correntina	8,529	7	320 miles E. ½ N. (true) from Monte Video.	Kronprinz Wilhelm	Captured	Scuttled	—
Cervantes	4,635	8	100 miles S. ¾ W. (true) from St. Paul Rocks.	Karlsruhe	Captured	Bombs	—
Pruth	4,408	9	90 miles S. by W. ¼ W. (true) from St. Paul Rocks.	Karlsruhe	Captured	Bombs	—
Condor	3,053	11	215 miles N. by E. ¾ E. (true) from Cape St. Roque.	Karlsruhe	Captured	Scuttled	—
Clan Grant	3,948	16	150 miles W. ¼ S. (true) from Minikoi.	Emden	Captured	Gunfire	---
Benmohr	4,806	16	65 miles N.W. ½ W. (true) from Minikoi.	Emden	Captured	Scuttled	—

3 MERCHANT VESSELS CAPTURED OR SUNK.

Name.	Tons.	Date.	Position.	Cause of Loss.	How attacked.	How sunk.	Lives lost.
		1914. Oct.					
Ponrabbel (Dredger).	473	16	20 miles N.W. (true) from Minikoi.	Emden	Captured	Gunfire	—
Troilus	7,562	18	170 miles E. (true) from Minikoi.	Emden	Captured	Gunfire	—
Glanton	3,021	18	195 miles S.W. (true) from St. Paul Rocks.	Karlsruhe	Captured	Bomb	—
Chilkana	3,244	19	110 miles E.N.E. (true) from Minikoi.	Emden	Captured	Gunfire	—
Glitra	866	20	14 miles W.S.W. from Skudesnaes, Norway.	Submarine	Captured	Scuttled	—
Cormorant	1,595	21	4 miles E. from West Gabbard L.V.	Mine	Mine	Mine	—
Hurstdale	2,752	23	205 miles S.W. $\frac{1}{4}$ W. (true) from St. Paul Rocks.	Karlsruhe	Captured	Scuttled	—
Vandyk	10,328	26	690 miles W. by S. (true) from St. Paul Rocks.	Karlsruhe	Captured	Not known	—
Manchester Commerce.	5,363	27	20 miles N. $\frac{1}{4}$ E. from Tory Island.	Mine	Mine	Mine	14 including Master.
NOVEMBER 1914.		Nov.					
Ayesha (S.V.)	123	9	Off N. Keeling Island.	Emden *	Captured	Scuttled 15th Dec. 1914.	—
North Wales	3,661	16	360 miles S.W. $\frac{1}{4}$ W. (true) from Valparaiso.	Dresden	Captured	Bombs	—
Malachite	718	23	4 miles N. by W. from Cape la Hève.	Submarine	Captured	Gunfire	—
Primo	1,366	26	6 miles N.W. by N. from Cape Antifer.	Submarine	Captured	Gunfire	—
Khartoum	3,020	27	20 miles E.S.E. from Spurn Point.	Mine	Mine	Mine	—
DECEMBER 1914.		Dec.					
Drummuir (S.V.)	1,844	2	70 miles E. by N. (true) from Cape Horn.	Liepzig	Captured	Bombs	—
Bellevue	3,814	4	460 miles N.E. $\frac{1}{4}$ E. (true) from Pernambuco.	Kronprinz Wilhelm	Captured	Scuttled	—
Charcas	5,067	5	70 miles S. by W. $\frac{1}{2}$ W. (true) from Valparaiso.	Prinz Eitel Friedrich.	Captured	Bombs	—
Kildalton (S.V.)	1,784	12	870 miles S.W. $\frac{3}{4}$ S. (true) from Valparaiso.	Prinz Eitel Friedrich.	Captured	Bombs	—
Elterwater	1,228	16	3 miles E. from Scarborough.	Mine	Mine	Mine	6
Princess Olga	998	16	5 miles E.N.E. from Scarborough.	Mine	Mine	Mine	—
Tritonia	4,272	19	22 miles N.N.E. from Tory Island.	Mine	Mine	Mine	—
Gem	461	25	$3\frac{1}{2}$ miles S.E. by E. $\frac{1}{4}$ E. from Scarborough.	Mine	Mine	Mine	10 including Master.
Linaria	3,081	26	$2\frac{1}{2}$ miles N.N.E. from Filey.	Mine	Mine	Mine	—
Hemisphere	3,486	28	400 miles N.E. by E. (true) from Pernambuco.	Kronprinz Wilhelm	Captured	Scuttled	—

MERCHANT VESSELS CAPTURED OR SUNK. 4

Name.	Tons.	Date.	Position.	Cause of Loss.	How attacked.	How sunk.	Lives lost.
JANUARY 1915.		1915. Jan.					
Elfrida	2,624	7	2 miles E.N.E. from Scarborough.	Mine	Mine	Mine	—
Potaro	4,419	10	560 miles E. by N. ¼ N. (true) from Pernambuco.	Kronprinz Wilhelm	Captured	Scuttled	—
Highland Brae	7,634	14	630 miles N.E. by E. ¼ E. (true) from Pernambuco.	Kronprinz Wilhelm	Captured	Scuttled	—
Wilfrid M. (S.V.)	251	14	625 miles N.E. by E. ¼ E. (true) from Pernambuco.	Kronprinz Wilhelm	Captured	Rammed	—
Durward	1,301	21	22 miles N.W. from Maas L.V.	Submarine	Captured	Bombs	—
Ben Cruachan	3,092	30	15 miles N.W. from Morecambe Lt.	Submarine	Captured	Bombs	—
Linda Blanche	369	30	18 miles N.W. ½ N. from Liverpool Bar L.V.	Submarine	Captured	Bombs	—
Kilcoan	456	30	18 miles N.W. from Liverpool Bar L.V.	Submarine	Captured	Bombs	—
● Tokomaru	6,084	30	7 miles N.W. from Havre L.V.	Submarine	No warning	Torpedo	—
● Ikaria	4,335	30	25 miles N.W. from Havre.	Submarine	No warning	Torpedo	—
● Oriole	1,489	30	English Channel	Submarine (probably).	No warning	Torpedo	21 including Master.
FEBRUARY 1915.		Feb.					
Invercoe (S.V.)	1,421	12	890 miles E. by S. ¼ S. (true) from Cape Frio.	Prinz Eitel Friedrich.	Captured	Bombs	—
Dulwich	3,289	15	27 miles N.N.E. from Cape la Hève.	Submarine	No warning	Torpedo	2
Membland	3,027	15 (?)	North Sea	Mine (?)	Mine (?)	Mine (?)	20 including Master.
Mary Ada Short	3,605	18	400 miles E. by N. ¾ N. (true) from Pernambuco.	Prinz Eitel Friedrich.	Captured	Bombs	—
Willerby	3,630	20	490 miles N.E. by N. (true) from Pernambuco.	Prinz Eitel Friedrich.	Captured	Bombs	—
Cambank	3,112	20	10 miles E. from Point Lynas.	Submarine	No warning	Torpedo	4
Downshire	337	20	8 miles N.W. ½ W. from Calf of Man.	Submarine	Captured	Bomb	—
● Oakby	1,976	23	4 miles E. by N. from Royal Sovereign L.V.	Submarine	No warning	Torpedo	—
● Branksome Chine	2,026	23	6 miles E. by S. ¾ S. from Beachy Head.	Submarine	No warning	Torpedo	—
● Rio Parana	4,015	24	4 miles S.E. from Beachy Head.	Submarine	No warning	Torpedo	—
● Western Coast	1,165	24	8 miles S.E. by E. ½ E. from Beachy Head.	Submarine	No warning	Torpedo	—
Deptford	1,208	24	3 miles off Scarborough.	Mine	Mine	Mine	1

MERCHANT VESSELS CAPTURED OR SUNK.

Name.	Tons.	Date.	Position.	Cause of Loss.	How attacked.	How sunk.	Lives lost.
		1915. Feb.					
● Harpalion	5,867	24	6½ miles W. from Royal Sovereign L.V.	Submarine	No warning	Torpedo	3
Conway Castle (S.V.)	1,694	27	560 miles S.W. by W. ½ W. (true) from Valparaiso.	Dresden	Captured	Scuttled	—
MARCH 1915.		Mar.					
Bengrove	3,840	7	5 miles N.N.E. from Ilfracombe.	Submarine	No warning	Torpedo	—
Princess Victoria	1,108	9	16 miles N.W. by N. from Liverpool Bar L.V.	Submarine	No warning	Torpedo	—
● Blackwood	1,230	9	18 miles S.W. by S. from Dungeness.	Submarine	No warning	Torpedo	—
Tangistan	3,738	9	9 miles N. from Flamborough Head.	Submarine	No warning	Torpedo	38 including Master.
Florazan	4,658	11	53 miles N.E. ½ E. from Longships.	Submarine	No warning	Torpedo	1
Headlands	2,988	12	8 miles S. from Scilly Isles.	Submarine	Chased	Torpedo	—
Indian City	4,645	12	10 miles S. from St. Mary's, Scilly.	Submarine	Captured	Torpedo	—
Andalusian	2,349	12	25 miles W.N.W. from Bishop Rock.	Submarine	Captured	Scuttled	—
Invergyle	1,794	12	12 miles N.N.E. from Tyne.	Submarine	No warning	Torpedo	—
Hartdale	3,839	13	7 miles S.E. by E. from South Rock, Co. Down.	Submarine	Chased	Torpedo	2
Fingal	1,562	15	6 miles E. by S. from Coquet Island.	Submarine	No warning	Torpedo	6
Leeuwarden	990	17	4 miles W. by N. ¼ N. from Maas L.V.	Submarine	Captured	Gunfire	—
● Glenartney	5,201	18	4 miles S. from Royal Sovereign L.V.	Submarine	No warning	Torpedo	1
● Cairntorr	3,588	21	7 miles S. from Beachy Head.	Submarine	No warning	Torpedo	—
● Concord	2,861	22	9 miles S.E. by E. ½ E. from Royal Sovereign L.V.	Submarine	No warning	Torpedo	—
Tamar	3,207	25	500 miles E.N.E. (true) from Pernambuco.	Kronprinz Wilhelm	Captured	Gunfire	—
Vosges	1,295	27	38 miles W. by N. from Trevose Head.	Submarine	Chased	Gunfire	1
South Point	3,837	27	60 miles W. from Lundy Island.	Submarine	Captured	Torpedo	—
Aguila	2,114	27	47 miles S.W. from Smalls L.H.	Submarine	Captured	Torpedo	8
Coleby	3,824	27	460 miles N.E. ½ N. (true) from Pernambuco.	Kronprinz Wilhelm	Captured	Gunfire	—
Falaba	4,806	28	38 miles W. from Smalls L.H.	Submarine	Captured	Torpedo	104 including Master.
Flaminian	3,500	29	50 miles S.W. by W. from Scilly Isles.	Submarine	Captured	Gunfire	—
Crown of Castile	4,505	30	31 miles S.W. from Bishop Rock.	Submarine	Captured	Bombs	—

MERCHANT VESSELS CAPTURED OR SUNK.   6

Name.	Tons.	Date.	Position.	Cause of Loss.	How attacked.	How sunk.	Lives lost.
APRIL 1915.		1915. April					
● Seven Seas	1,194	1	6 miles S. from Beachy Head.	Submarine	No warning	Torpedo	9 including Master.
● Lochwood	2,042	2	25 miles S.W. from Start Point.	Submarine	Captured	Torpedo	—
City of Bremen	1,258	4	20 miles S. ¾ W. from Wolf Rock.	Submarine	No warning	Torpedo	4
● Olivine	634	4	30 miles S. from St. Catherine's Point.	Submarine	Captured	Torpedo	—
● Northlands	2,776	5	24 miles S.W. from Beachy Head.	Submarine	Captured	Torpedo	—
Harpalyce	5,940	10	7 miles E. by S. from N. Hinder L.V.	Submarine	No warning	Torpedo	15 including Master.
● The President	647	10	14 miles S. by W. from Lizard.	Submarine	Captured	Bomb	—
Ptarmigan	784	15	6 miles W. by N. from N. Hinder L.V.	Submarine	No warning	Torpedo	8
Mobile	1,950	28	25 miles N.W. from Butt of Lewis.	Submarine	Captured	Gunfire	—
Cherbury	3,220	29	27 miles W.N.W. from Eagle Island.	Submarine	Captured	Bombs	—
Fulgent	2,008	30	20 miles W.N.W. from Blaskets.	Submarine	Captured	Bombs	2 including Master.
MAY 1915.		May					
Edale	3,110	1	45 miles N.W. by W. from Scilly Isles.	Submarine	No warning	Torpedo	—
Minterne	3,018	3	50 miles S.W. from Wolf Rock.	Submarine	No warning	Torpedo	2
Earl of Lathom (S.V.)	132	5	8 miles S. by W. from Old Head of Kinsale.	Submarine	Captured	Gunfire	—
Candidate	5,858	6	13 miles S. by E. ¼ E. from Coningbeg L.V.	Submarine	Captured	Torpedo	—
Centurion	5,945	6	15 miles S. from Barrel L.V.	Submarine	No warning	Torpedo	—
Truro	836	6	85 miles E.N.E. from St. Abb's Head.	Submarine	Captured	Torpedo	—
Lusitania	30,396	7	15 miles S. from Old Head of Kinsale.	Submarine	No warning	Torpedo	1,198
Queen Wilhelmina	3,590	8	20 miles S. by E. from Longstone.	Submarine	Captured	Torpedo	—
Don	939	8	7 miles E. from Coquet Island.	Submarine	Captured	Torpedo	—
Drumcree	4,052	18	11 miles N. by E. from Trevose Head.	Submarine	No warning	Torpedo	—
Dumfries	4,121	19	13 miles N. from Trevose Head.	Submarine	No warning	Torpedo	2
Glenholm (S.V.)	1,968	21	16 miles W.S.W. from Fastnet.	Submarine	Captured	Torpedo	—
Morwenna	1,414	26	72 miles S. by E. from Fastnet.	Submarine	Captured	Torpedo	1
Cadeby	1,130	27	20 miles S.W. by S. from Wolf Rock.	Submarine	Captured	Gunfire	—
● Spennymoor	2,733	28	50 miles S.W. ¼ W. from Start Point.	Submarine	Captured	Torpedo	5 including Master.

7 Merchant Vessels Captured or Sunk.

Name.	Tons.	Date.	Position.	Cause of Loss.	How attacked.	How sunk.	Lives lost.
Ethiope	3,794	1915. May 28	40 miles S.W. by S. from Start Point.	Submarine	Captured	Torpedo	—
Tullochmoor	3,520	28	52 miles N. from Ushant.	Submarine	Captured	Gunfire	—
Dixiana	3,329	29	40 miles N. from Ushant.	Submarine	Captured	Torpedo	—
Glenlee	4,140	29	67 miles S.S.W. from Wolf Rock.	Submarine	Captured	Torpedo	—
JUNE 1915.		June					
Saidieh	3,303	1	6 miles N.E. from Elbow Buoy.	Submarine	No warning	Torpedo	8
Iona	3,344	3	22 miles S.S.E. from Fair Isle.	Submarine	Captured	Torpedo	—
Inkum	4,747	4	40 miles S.W. from Lizard.	Submarine	No warning	Torpedo	—
George and Mary (S.V.)	100	4	15 miles S.W. from Eagle Island.	Submarine	Captured	Gunfire	—
Dunnet Head	343	4	35 miles E. by S. from Duncansby Head.	Submarine	Captured	Torpedo	—
Sunlight (S.V.)	1,433	6	20 miles S.W. from Galley Head.	Submarine	Captured	Torpedo	—
Strathcarron	4,347	8	60 miles W. from Lundy Island.	Submarine	No warning	Torpedo	—
Express (S.V.)	115	8	44 miles S.S.W. ½ W. from Smalls.	Submarine	Captured	Bomb	—
Susannah (S.V.)	115	8	40 miles S.S.W. from Smalls.	Submarine	Captured	Bombs	—
Lady Salisbury	1,446	9	1 mile N. from Sunk L.V.	Submarine	No warning	Torpedo	3
Erna Boldt	1,731	9	½ mile N.E. by E. from Sunk L.V.	Submarine	No warning	Torpedo	—
Arndale	3,583	11	Entrance to White Sea.	Mine	Mine	Mine	3
Desabla	6,047	12	15 miles E. from Tod Head.	Submarine	Captured	Torpedo	—
Leuctra	3,027	12	1½ miles S.E. by S. from Shipwash L.V.	Submarine	No warning	Torpedo	—
Crown of India (S.V.)	2,034	12	70 miles W.S.W. from St. Ann's Head.	Submarine	Captured	Gunfire	—
Hopemount	3,300	13	70 miles W. by S. from Lundy Island.	Submarine	Captured	Gunfire	—
Pelham	3,534	13	30 miles N.W. from Scilly Isles.	Submarine	Captured	Bombs	—
Strathnairn	4,336	15	25 miles N. by E. from Bishop and Clerks.	Submarine	No warning	Torpedo	21 including Master.
Trafford	215	16	30 miles W.S.W. from Tuskar.	Submarine	Captured	Gunfire	—
Ailsa	876	18	30 miles E. by N. from Bell Rock.	Submarine	Captured	Scuttled	—
Dulcie	2,033	19	6 miles E. from Aldebergh.	Submarine	No warning	Torpedo	1
Carisbrook	2,352	21	70 miles S. ¾ W. from Start Point, Orkneys.	Submarine	Captured	Gunfire	—
Tunisiana	4,220	23	Off Lowestoft	Submarine	No warning	Torpedo	—
Drumloist	3,118	24	Entrance to White Sea.	Mine	Mine	Mine	—
Edith (S.V.)	78	27	10 miles S.E. from Capel Island.	Submarine	Captured	Gunfire	—
Lucena	243	27	4 miles S. from Capel Island.	Submarine	Captured	Gunfire	—
Indrani	3,640	27	40 miles W. from Smalls.	Submarine	Captured	Torpedo	—

MERCHANT VESSELS CAPTURED OR SUNK.

Name.	Tons.	Date.	Position.	Cause of Loss.	How attacked.	How sunk.	Lives lost.
		1915. June					
Dumfriesshire (S.V.).	2,622	28	25 miles S.W. from Smalls.	Submarine	No warning	Torpedo	—
Armenian	8,825	28	20 miles W. from Trevose Head.	Submarine	Captured	Torpedo	29
Scottish Monarch	5,043	29	40 miles S. from Ballycottin Light.	Submarine	Captured	Gunfire	15
Lomas	3,048	30	65 miles W. from Bishop Rock.	Submarine	Captured	Torpedo	1

JULY 1915.

Name.	Tons.	Date.	Position.	Cause of Loss.	How attacked.	How sunk.	Lives lost.
		July					
L. C. Tower (S.V.)	518	1	30 miles S. from Fastnet.	Submarine	Captured	Set on fire	—
Gadsby	3,497	1	33 miles S.S.W. from Wolf Rock.	Submarine	Captured	Torpedo	—
Caucasian	4,656	1	80 miles S. from Lizard.	Submarine	Captured	Gunfire	—
Inglemoor	4,331	1	75 miles S.W. by W. from Lizard.	Submarine	Captured	Torpedo	—
Welbury	3,591	1	40 miles W. from Fastnet.	Submarine	Captured	Gunfire	—
Craigard	3,286	1	50 miles S.W. by S. from Wolf Rock.	Submarine	Captured	Torpedo	—
Richmond	3,214	1	About 54 miles S.W. by S. from Wolf Rock.	Submarine	Captured	Gunfire	—
Renfrew	3,488	3	85 miles S.W. by S. from Wolf Rock.	Submarine	Captured	Gunfire	—
Larchmore	4,355	3	70 miles S.W. ½ S. from Wolf Rock.	Submarine	Captured	Gunfire	1
Sunbeam (S.V.)	132	4	17 miles S. by E. from Wick.	Submarine	Captured	Gunfire	—
African Monarch	4,003	6	Entrance to White Sea.	Mine	Mine	Mine	2
Guido	2,093	8	27 miles N.E. ¼ N. from Rattray Head.	Submarine	Captured	Torpedo	—
Meadowfield	2,750	9	50 miles S.W. from Tuskar.	Submarine	Captured	Gunfire	1
Ellesmere	1,170	9	48 miles S.W. from Smalls.	Submarine	Captured	Torpedo	1
Grangewood	3,422	25	20 miles E.N.E. from Flugga L.H., Shetland.	Submarine	Captured	Torpedo	—
Firth	406	25	4 miles E. by S. from Aldborough Napes Buoy.	Submarine	No warning	Torpedo	4
Mangara	1,821	28	¼ mile E. from Sizewell Buoy, Aldeburgh.	Submarine	No warning	Torpedo	11
Iberian	5,223	30	9 miles S. by W. from Fastnet.	Submarine	Captured	Torpedo	7
Turquoise	486	31	60 miles S.W. from Scilly Isles.	Submarine	Captured	Gunfire	1
Nugget	405	31	45 miles S.W. from Scilly Isles.	Submarine	Captured	Gunfire	—

AUGUST 1915.

Name.	Tons.	Date.	Position.	Cause of Loss.	How attacked.	How sunk.	Lives lost.
		Aug.					
Clintonia	3,830	1	30 miles S.W. by W. from Ushant.	Submarine	Captured	Torpedo	10
Fulgens	2,512	1	1 mile off Palling, Norfolk.	Submarine	No warning	Torpedo	—
Benvorlich	3,381	1	50 miles S.W. from Ushant.	Submarine	Captured	Torpedo	—
Ranza	2,320	1	50 miles S.W. from Ushant.	Submarine	Captured	Torpedo	3
Portia	494	2	70 miles South from Scilly Isles.	Submarine	Captured	Gunfire	—

MERCHANT VESSELS CAPTURED OR SUNK.

Name.	Tons.	Date.	Position.	Cause of Loss.	How attacked.	How sunk.	Lives lost.
		1915. Aug.					
Costello	1,591	3	95 miles W. by S. from Bishop.	Submarine	Captured	Gunfire	1
Midland Queen	1,993	4	70 miles S.W. by W. from Fastnet.	Submarine	Captured	Gunfire	—
Glenravel	1,092	8	25 miles N. from Kinnaird Head.	Submarine	Captured	Bombs	—
Benarthur	2,029	8	8 miles S.E. from Orloff L.H.	Mine	Mine	Beached; wreck.	—
Rosalie	4,243	10	3 miles off Blakeney Buoy.	Submarine	No warning	Torpedo	—
Utopia	155	10	12 miles E. from St. Abb's Hd.	Submarine	Captured	Gunfire	—
Oakwood	4,279	11	45 miles S.S.E. from Old Head of Kinsale.	Submarine	Captured	Gunfire	—
Osprey	310	12	40 miles N.E. by N. from Nush Terragh, Co. Kerry.	Submarine	Captured	Gunfire	—
Jacona	2,969	12	25 miles N.N.W. from Troupe Hd.	Mine	Mine	Mine	29
Grodno	1,955	12	98 miles N.W. from Lofoten Islands.	Submarine	Captured	Torpedo	—
Summerfield	687	13	2 miles East from Lowestoft.	Mine	Mine	Mine	3
Royal Edward	11,117	13	6 miles W. from Kandeliusa, Ægean Sea.	Submarine	No warning	Torpedo	132 including Master.
Cairo	1,671	13	34 miles S.S.W. from Tuskar.	Submarine	Captured	Gunfire	—
Princess Caroline	888	13	14 miles N. by E. ½ E. from Kinnaird Hd.	Mine	Mine	Mine	4
Serbino	2,205	16	Off Worms Lt. Ho., Baltic.	Submarine	No warning	Torpedo	—
Paros	3,596	17	30 miles W. by N. from Bardsey Id.	Submarine	Captured	Torpedo	—
Kirkby	3,034	17	23 miles W. by S. from Bardsey Id.	Submarine	Captured	Torpedo	—
Maggie	269	17	8 miles E. from S. Arklow L.V.	Submarine	Captured	Gunfire	—
Thornfield	488	17	25 miles N.N.E. from Smalls.	Submarine	Captured	Gunfire	—
Glenby	2,196	17	30 miles N. from Smalls.	Submarine	Captured	Gunfire	2
The Queen	557	17	40 miles N.N.E. from Smalls.	Submarine	Captured	Gunfire	—
Bonney	2,702	17	16 miles S. by E. from Tuskar.	Submarine	Captured	Gunfire	—
Dunsley	4,930	19	48 miles S. by W. from Old Hd. of Kinsale.	Submarine	Captured	Gunfire	2
Restormel	2,118	19	28 miles N.N.W. from Bishop Rock.	Submarine	Captured	Torpedo	—
Gladiator	3,359	19	68 miles N. by W. from Bishop Rock.	Submarine	Captured	Gunfire	—
Baron Erskine	5,585	19	25 miles N.N.W. from Bishop Rock.	Submarine	Captured	Torpedo	—
Arabic	15,801	19	50 miles S. by W. ½ W. from Old Hd. of Kinsale.	Submarine	No warning	Torpedo	44
Ben Vrackie	3,908	19	55 miles N.W. by N. from Scilly Is.	Submarine	Captured	Gunfire	—
Samara	3,172	19	35 miles W. from Bishop Rock.	Submarine	Captured	Gunfire	—

MERCHANT VESSELS CAPTURED OR SUNK.

Name.	Tons.	Date.	Position.	Cause of Loss.	How attached.	How sunk.	Lives lost.
		1915. Aug.					
St. Olaf (S.V.)	277	19	58 miles from Galley Hd.	Submarine	Captured	Gunfire	—
New York City	2,970	19	44 miles S.S.E. from Fastnet.	Submarine	Captured	Gunfire	—
Bittern	1,797	20	50 miles N.W. from Ushant.	Submarine	Captured	Gunfire	—
Martha Edmonds (S.V.).	182	20	62 miles W.N.W. from Ushant.	Submarine	Captured	Gunfire	—
Carterswell	4,308	20	65 miles N.W. from Ushant.	Submarine	Captured	Gunfire	—
Windsor	6,055	21	70 miles S.W. ½ S. from Wolf.	Submarine	Captured	Gunfire	—
Cober	3,060	21	45 miles S.S.W. from Scilly Is.	Submarine	Captured	Torpedo	—
William Dawson	284	21	Off Boulogne	Mine	Mine	Mine	5
Ruel	4,029	21	45 miles S.W. from Bishop Rock.	Submarine	Captured	Gunfire	1
Palmgrove	3,100	22	46 miles W. by N. ½ N. from Bishop Rock.	Submarine	Captured	Gunfire	—
Diomed	4,672	22	57 miles W.N.W. from Scilly Is.	Submarine	Captured	Gunfire	10 including Master.
Trafalgar	4,572	23	54 miles S.W. by W. from Fastnet.	Submarine	Captured	Bombs	—
Silvia	5,268	23	47 miles West from Fastnet.	Submarine	Captured	Gunfire	—
Sir William Stephenson.	1,540	29	Off Cockle L.V.	Mine	Mine	Mine	2
Honiton	4,914	30	2½ miles E. from Longsand L.V.	Mine	Mine	Mine	—
SEPTEMBER	**1915.**						
		Sept.					
Whitefield	2,422	1	95 miles N. by W. from Cape Wrath.	Submarine	Captured	Gunfire	—
Savona	1,180	1	½ mile from Shipwash L.V.	Mine	Mine	Mine	3
Roumanie	2,599	2	40 miles N.N.W. from St. Kilda.	Submarine	Captured	Bombs	—
Churston	2,470	3	2½ miles S. from Orfordness.	Mine	Mine	Mine	4
Cymbeline	4,505	4	29 miles W. by S. from Fastnet.	Submarine	Captured	Torpedo	6
Mimosa	3,466	4	137 miles S.W. by W. from Fastnet.	Submarine	Captured	Gunfire	—
Natal Transport	4,107	4	40 miles W. from Gavdo I., Crete.	Submarine	Captured	Gunfire	—
†Hesperian	10,920	4	85 miles S.W. by S. from Fastnet.	Submarine	No warning	Torpedo	32
Dictator	4,116	5	135 miles S. by W. from Fastnet.	Submarine	Captured	Gunfire	—
Douro	1,604	5	79 miles S.W. by W. from Bishop Rock.	Submarine	Captured	Gunfire	—
John Hardie	4,372	6	98 miles W. by S. from C. Finisterre.	Submarine	Captured	Gunfire	1
Caroni	2,652	7	15 miles West from Chassiron.	Submarine	Captured	Torpedo	—
Monarch	1,122	8	2½ miles S. from Folkestone.	Mine	Mine	Mine	3
Mora	3,047	8	68 miles W. by S. from Belle Ile.	Submarine	Captured	Gunfire	—

11 MERCHANT VESSELS CAPTURED OR SUNK.

Name.	Tons.	Date.	Position.	Cause of Loss.	How attacked.	How sunk.	Lives lost.
		1915. Sept.					
Cornubia	1,736	9	75 miles S.E. by S. from Cartagena.	Submarine	Captured	Gunfire	—
Balakani	3,696	9	½ mile S.W. from S. Longsand Buoy.	Mine	Mine	Mine	6
Ashmore	2,519	12	5 miles E. ½ N. from Kentish Knock L.V.	Submarine	No warning	Torpedo	4
Patagonia	6,011	15	10½ miles N.E. from Odessa.	Submarine	No warning	Torpedo	—
Africa	1,038	16	1½ miles off Kingsdown.	Mine	Mine	Mine	2
Ramazan	3,477	19	55 miles S.W. from Cerigotto Island.	Submarine	Captured	Gunfire	1
Linkmoor	4,306	20	50 miles W. from C. Matapan.	Submarine	Captured	Gunfire	—
Horden	1,434	20	½ mile E. from Aldborough Napes Buoy.	Mine	Mine	Mine	—
Groningen	988	23	1½ miles N. by E. from Sunk Head Buoy.	Mine	Mine	Mine	1
Anglo-Colombian	4,792	23	79 miles S.E. from Fastnet.	Submarine	Captured	Gunfire	—
Chancellor	4,586	23	86 miles S. by E. from Fastnet.	Submarine	Captured	Gunfire	—
Hesione	3,663	23	86 miles S by E. from Fastnet.	Submarine	Captured	Gunfire	—
Urbino	6,651	24	67 miles S.W. by W. from Bishop Rock.	Submarine	Captured	Gunfire	—
Vigilant (Pilot Cutter).	69	26	Off Harwich	Mine	Mine	Mine	14 including Master.
H. C. Henry	4,219	28	59 miles S. ½ E. from C. Matapan.	Submarine	Captured	Gunfire	—
Haydn	3,923	29	80 miles S. by E. ½ E. from Gavdo Is., Crete.	Submarine	Captured	Bombs	—
OCTOBER 1915.		Oct.					
Sailor Prince	3,144	2	56 miles S.E. by S. from C. Sidero, Crete.	Submarine	Captured	Gunfire	2
Arabian	2,744	2	15 miles W. ½ S. from Cerigo I.	Submarine	Captured	Gunfire	—
Craigston	2,617	4	35 miles W. from Ovo Is.	Submarine	Captured	Gunfire	—
Bursfield	4,037	5	70 miles W. from C. Matapan.	Submarine	Captured	Gunfire	4 including Master.
Novocastrian	1,151	5	3½ miles S.E. by E. from Lowestoft.	Mine	Mine	Mine	—
Silverash	3,753	6	184 miles E. from Malta.	Submarine	Captured	Gunfire	—
Scawby	3,658	6	220 miles E. from Malta.	Submarine	Captured	Bomb	—
Halizones	5,093	7	122 miles S.S.E.½ E. from C. Martello, Crete.	Submarine	Captured	Gunfire	—
Thorpwood	3,184	8	122 miles S. from C. Martello, Crete.	Submarine	Captured	Gunfire	—
Apollo	3,774	9	63 miles S. from Gavdo I., Crete.	Submarine	Captured	Gunfire	—
Newcastle	3,403	10	4 miles S.W. from Folkestone Pier.	Mine	Mine	Mine	—
Salerno	2,071	14	2½ miles S. from Longsand L.V.	Mine	Mine	Mine	—
Monitoria	1,904	21	1¾ miles N. by E. ¾ E. from Sunk Head Buoy.	Mine	Mine	Mine	—

MERCHANT VESSELS CAPTURED OR SUNK.   12

Name.	Tons.	Date.	Position.	Cause of Loss.	How attacked.	How sunk.	Lives lost.
		1915. Oct.					
Cape Antibes	2,549	21	Entrance to White Sea.	Mine	Mine	Mine	6
Marquette	7,057	23	36 miles S. from Salonica Bay.	Submarine	No warning	Torpedo	29
● Ilaro	2,799	23	4 miles E. from Dungeness.	Mine	Mine	Mine	1
Toward	1,218	31	Off S. Foreland	Mine	Mine	Mine	—
NOVEMBER 1915.		Nov.					
†Woodfield	3,584	3	40 miles E.S.E. from Ceuta.	Submarine	Captured	Gunfire	8
Woolwich	2,936	3	104 miles S. from C. Sidero, Crete.	Submarine	Captured	Gunfire	—
Friargate	264	3	4 miles E. from Orfordness.	Mine	Mine	Mine	2
Moorina	4,994	5	105 miles S. from C. Martello (Crete).[1]	Submarine	Captured	Gunfire	—
Buresk	3,673	5	30 miles N. by W. from C. Bengut (Algiers).	Submarine	Captured	Gunfire	—
Alastair	366	6	4 miles E. from Southwold.	Mine	Mine	Mine	7 including Master.
†Lumina	5,950	6	120 miles S. by E. from C.Martello, (Crete).	Submarine	Captured	Gunfire	—
Caria	3,032	6	120 miles S. by E. from C.Martello, Crete.	Submarine	Captured	Gunfire	—
Clan Macalister	4,835	6	120 miles S. by E. from C.Martello (Crete).	Submarine	Captured	Torpedo	—
Glenmoor	3,075	6	5 miles N.E. from Cap de Fer (Tunis).	Submarine	Captured	Torpedo	—
Den of Crombie	4,949	8	112 miles S. by W.from C. Martello (Crete).	Submarine	Captured	Gunfire	—
Sir Richard Awdry	2,234	8	72 miles S. by E. ½ E. from Gavdo I.	Submarine	Captured	Torpedo	1
Californian	6,223	9	61 miles S.S.W. from C. Matapan.	Submarine	No warning	Torpedo	1
● Irene (Trinity House Yacht).	543	9	1½ miles E.S.E. from Tongue L.V.	Mine	Mine	Mine	21 including Master.
Rhineland	1,501	11	6½ miles S.E. ¼ S. from Southwold.	Mine	Mine	Mine	20 including Master.
Moorside	311	12	Off Boulogne	Mine	Mine	Mine	8 including Master.
Nigel	1,400	12	Off Boulogne	Mine	Mine	Mine	5
†Treneglos	3,886	14	70 miles W.S.W. from Gavdo I.	Submarine	No warning	Torpedo	3
Orange Prince	3,583	15	85 miles S.W. by W. from Gavdo I.	Submarine	No warning	Torpedo	3
● Anglia (Hospital Ship).	1,862	17	1 mile E. from Folkestone Gate.	Mine	Mine	Mine	25
● Lusitania	1,834	17	1 mile E. from Folkestone Gate.	Mine	Mine	Mine	—
Enosis	3,409	18	150 miles E.S.E. from Malta.	Submarine	Captured	Torpedo	1 (Master).
Hallamshire	4,420	19	20 miles S.W.by S. from Cerigotto I.	Submarine	No warning	Torpedo	—

13 MERCHANT VESSELS CAPTURED OR SUNK.

Name.	Tons.	Date.	Position.	Cause of Loss.	How attacked.	How sunk.	Lives lost.
		1915. Nov.					
Merganser	1,905	20	40 miles W.N.W. from Gozo I.	Submarine	Captured	Gunfire	—
Tringa	2,154	26	30 miles N.E. by N. from Galita Is.	Submarine	Captured	Gunfire	3
Tanis	3,655	27	3 miles N. from Zembra I.	Submarine	Captured	Gunfire	—
Kingsway	3,647	27	20 miles E.S.E. from Cape Bon, Tunis.	Submarine	Captured	Gunfire	—
Dotterel	1,596	29	4¾ miles N. by E. from Boulogne Pier.	Mine	Mine	Mine	5
Malinche	1,868	29	50 miles E. from Malta.	Submarine	Captured	Torpedo	—
Middleton	2,506	30	75 miles S.W. by W. from Gavdo I.	Submarine	Captured	Gunfire	4
Colenso	3,861	30	95 miles E.S.E. from Malta.	Submarine	Captured	Gunfire	1
Langton Hall	4,437	30	112 miles E.S.E. from Malta.	Submarine	Captured	Gunfire	—

DECEMBER 1915.

Name.	Tons.	Date.	Position.	Cause of Loss.	How attacked.	How sunk.	Lives lost.
		Dec.					
Clan Macleod	4,796	1	100 miles E.S.E. from Malta.	Submarine	Captured	Gunfire	12
Umeta	5,312	1	112 miles E.S.E. from Malta.	Submarine	Captured	Gunfire	2
Commodore	5,858	2	160 miles E.S.E. from Malta.	Submarine	Captured	Bombs	1
Helmsmuir	4,111	3	66 miles S. by E. from Gavdo I.	Submarine	Captured	Torpedo	—
Veria	3,229	7	24 miles N.W. by W. from Alexandria.	Submarine	Captured	Bombs	—
Ignis	2,042	8	5½ miles N.E. from Aldeburgh.	Mine	Mine	Mine	—
Busiris	2,705	9	190 miles W.N.W. from Alexandria.	Submarine	Captured	Gunfire	—
Orteric	6,535	9	140 miles S. by E. ½ E. from Gavdo I.	Submarine	Captured	Torpedo	2
Pinegrove	2,847	11	8 miles W. ½ S. from C. Grisnez.	Mine	Mine	Mine	2
Huntly	1,153	20	Off Boulogne	Submarine	No warning	Torpedo	2
Belford	516	20	Off Boulogne	Submarine	No warning	Torpedo	—
Knarsdale	1,641	21	2¾ miles E. by S. from Orfordness.	Mine	Mine	Mine	1
Yeddo	4,563	24	122 miles S.W. by S. from C. Matapan.	Submarine	Captured	Bombs	—
Embla	1,172	24	3 miles E.S.E. from Tongue L.V.	Mine	Mine	Mine	—
Van Stirum	3,284	25	8 miles S.S.W. from Smalls.	Submarine	Captured	Torpedo	2
Cottingham	513	26	16 miles S.W. ½ W. from Lundy I.	Submarine	Captured	Gunfire	7
Hadley	1,777	27	3 miles S.E. ½ E. from Shipwash L.V.	Mine	Mine	Mine	—
El Zorro	5,989	28	10 miles S. from Old Head of Kinsale.	Submarine	Captured	Torpedo	2
Abelia	3,650	30	152 miles W. from Gavdo I.	Submarine	Captured	Gunfire	—
†Persia	7,974	30	71 miles S.E. by S. from C. Martello, Crete.	Submarine	No warning	Torpedo	334 including Master.
†Clan Macfarlane	4,823	30	66 miles S.E. by S. from C. Martello, Crete.	Submarine	No warning	Torpedo	52 including Master.

MERCHANT VESSELS CAPTURED OR SUNK.   14

Name.	Tons.	Date.	Position.	Cause of Loss.	How attacked.	How sunk.	Lives lost.
JANUARY 1916.		1916. Jan.					
†Glengyle	9,395	1	240 miles E. by S. from Malta.	Submarine	No warning	Torpedo	10
Coquet	4,396	4	200 miles E. from Malta.	Submarine	Captured	Bombs	17 10 made prisoners by Arabs.
Euterpe	1,522	7	North Sea	Mine (?)	Mine (?)	Mine (?)	19 including Master.
Farringford	3,146	11	150 miles W. by N. ¾ N. (true) from C. Finisterre.	Möwe	Captured	Gunfire	—
Corbridge	3,687	11	140 miles W. by N. ¾ N. (true) from C. Finisterre.	Möwe	Captured	Not known	—
Algerian	3,837	12	2½ miles S.W. from Needles.	Mine	Mine	Mine	—
Traquair	1,067	12	1 mile S.W. from Admiralty Pier, Dover.	Mine	Mine	Mine	—
Dromonby	3,627	13	220 miles W.(true) from Lisbon.	Möwe	Captured	Bombs	—
Author	3,496	13	225 miles W. ½ N. (true) from Lisbon.	Möwe	Captured	Bombs	—
Trader	3,608	13	225 miles W. ½ N. (true) from Lisbon.	Möwe	Captured	Bombs	—
Ariadne	3,035	15	140 miles E. by N. (true) from Funchal.	Möwe	Captured	Torpedo	—
†Clan Mactavish	5,816	16	120 miles S. by W. (true) from Funchal.	Möwe	Captured	Gunfire	17 Master and 2 gunners made prisoners.
Sutherland	3,542	17	192 miles S.E. by E. from Malta.	Submarine	Captured	Gunfire	1
†Marere	6,443	18	236 miles E. from Malta.	Submarine	Captured	Gunfire	—
Trematon	4,198	20	180 miles E. by S. from Malta.	Submarine	Captured	Gunfire	—
Edinburgh (S.V.)	1,473	20	700 miles W. by S. ¾ S. (true) from St. Vincent C.V.	Möwe	Captured	Bombs	—
FEBRUARY 1916.		Feb.					
Belle of France	3,876	1	126 miles N.W. by W. from Alexandria.	Submarine	No warning	Torpedo	19
Franz Fischer	970	1	2 miles S. from Kentish Knock.	Zeppelin	Bomb	Bomb	13 including Master.
Flamenco	4,629	6	310 miles N.E. by N. (true) from Pernambuco.	Möwe	Captured	Bombs	1
Balgownie	1,061	6	1¾ miles E.S.E. from Sunk Head Buoy.	Mine	Mine	Mine	1
Argo	1,720	8	4½ miles N.W. from Boulogne Pier.	Mine	Mine	Mine	1
Westburn	3,300	8	530 miles N.N.E. (true) from Pernambuco.	Möwe	Captured	Scuttled	Master and 2nd officer made prisoners.
Horace	3,335	9	610 miles N.N.E. (true) from Pernambuco,	Möwe	Captured	Bombs	—

15 — Merchant Vessels Captured or Sunk.

Name.	Tons.	Date.	Position.	Cause of Loss.	How attacked.	How sunk.	Lives lost.
		1916. Feb.					
†Springwell	5,593	9	64 miles S.W. by W. from Gavdo Is.	Submarine	No warning	Torpedo	—
Cedarwood	654	12	2½ miles E. from Aldborough Napes.	Mine	Mine	Mine	6
● Leicester	1,001	12	2½ miles S.E. by E. from Folkestone Pier.	Mine	Mine	Mine	17
Tergestea	4,308	13	8 miles E. by S. from Aldeburgh.	Mine	Mine	Mine	—
Wilston	2,611	15	20 miles E.N.E. from Wick.	Mine	Mine	Mine	8 including Master.
● Dingle	593	20	10 miles S. by W. from Kentish Knock.	Mine	Mine	Mine	9 including Master.
Duckbridge	1,491	22	6 miles N. from Straithie Point.	Mine	Mine	Mine	19 including Master.
Diadem	3,752	23	56 miles S.E. by S. from Porquerolles Is.	Submarine	Captured	Gunfire	—
Denaby	2,987	24	40 miles S.S.W. from Planier Island.	Submarine	Captured	Gunfire	1
Fastnet	2,227	24	55 miles S.W. from Planier Island.	Submarine	Captured	Gunfire	—
Tummel	531	24	7 miles S. from Kentish Knock.	Mine	Mine	Mine	9
Saxon Prince	3,471	25	620 miles W.(true) from Fastnet.	Möwe	Captured	Bombs	Crew made prisoners.
Southford	963	25	4 miles E.S.E. from Southwold.	Mine	Mine	Mine	4
Arbonne	672	25(?)	North Sea	Submarine (?)	No warning(?)	Torpedo (?)	14 including Master.
Dido	4,769	26	4 miles N.N.E. from Spurn L.V.	Mine	Mine	Mine	28 including Master.
● †Maloja	12,431	27	2 miles S.W. from Dover Pier.	Mine	Mine	Mine	122
● Empress of Fort William.	2,181	27	2 miles S. from Dover Pier.	Mine	Mine	Mine	—
Thornaby	1,782	28	2 miles N.E. from Shipwash L.V.	Mine	Mine	Mine	19 including Master.
Masunda	4,952	28	106 miles S.W. ½ S. from Cape Matapan.	Submarine	Captured	Gunfire	—
MARCH 1916.		Mar.					
Kilbride	3,712	1	30 miles E. from Galita Is., Tunis.	Submarine	Captured	Gunfire	—
Teutonian	4,824	4	36 miles S.W. by W. from Fastnet.	Submarine	Captured	Torpedo	—
Rothesay	2,007	5	30 miles S.W. from Bishop Rock.	Submarine	Captured	Torpedo	—
Harmatris	6,387	8	¼ mile N.E. by N. from Boulogne Breakwater.	Submarine	No warning	Torpedo	4
Willie (S.V.)	185	16	60 miles N.W. by W. from Fastnet.	Submarine	Captured	Gunfire	—
Lowlands	1,789	18	8 miles N.E. by E. from N. Foreland.	Submarine	No warning	Torpedo	—
Port Dalhousie	1,744	19	2 miles S. ½ W. from Kentish Knock L.V.	Submarine	No warning	Torpedo	12 including Master.

Merchant Vessels Captured or Sunk.

Name.	Tons.	Date.	Position.	Cause of Loss.	How attacked.	How sunk.	Lives lost.
		1916. Mar.					
Aranmore	1,050	21	24 miles E.N.E. from Eagle Island, Co. Mayo.	Submarine	Captured	Torpedo	—
Kelvinbank	4,209	22	Havre Roads	Submarine	No warning	Torpedo	1
⁕ Sea Serpent	902	23	Off Folkestone Pier.	Mine	Mine	Mine	14 including Master.
†Minneapolis	13,543	23	195 miles E. ½ N. from Malta.	Submarine	No warning	Torpedo	12
⁕ Fulmar	1,270	24	7 miles N.E. from N. Foreland.	Mine	Mine	Mine	1 (Master).
Englishman	5,257	24	30 miles N.E. from Malin Head.	Submarine	Captured	Torpedo	10
⁕ Salybia	3,352	24	4 miles S.W. by W. from Dungeness.	Submarine	No warning	Torpedo	—
Fenay Bridge	3,838	24	54 miles W. from Bishop Rock.	Submarine	Captured	Torpedo	—
Saint Cecilia	4,411	26	4 miles from Folkestone L.V.	Mine	Mine	Mine	—
⁕ Cerne	2,579	26	4 miles N.E. from Elbow Buoy.	Mine	Mine	Mine	—
Manchester Engineer.	4,302	27	20 miles W. by S. from Coningbeg L.V.	Submarine	No warning	Torpedo	—
Empress of Midland.	2,224	27	9 miles S. from Kentish Knock L.V.	Mine	Mine	Mine	—
†Eagle Point	5,222	28	100 miles W.N.W. from Bishop Rock.	Submarine	Captured	Torpedo	—
Rio Tiete	7,464	28	140 miles West from Ushant.	Submarine	Captured	Torpedo	—
Lavinia Westoll	3,131	28	33 miles S.E. by S. from Spurn L.V.	Mine	Mine	Mine	—
John Pritchard (S.V.).	118	30	Off Santa Maura Is. (Greece).	Submarine	Captured	Bombs	—
†Goldmouth	7,446	31	60 miles W.N.W. from Ushant.	Submarine	Captured	Torpedo	Master made prisoner.
†Achilles	7,043	31	90 miles W.N.W. from Ushant.	Submarine	No warning	Torpedo	5
Alacrity	1,080	—	North Sea	Mine	Mine	Mine	14 including Master.
APRIL 1916.		April.					
Ashburton	4,445	1	80 miles W.N.W. from Ushant.	Submarine	Captured	Torpedo	—
Perth	653	1	1 mile S.E. by E. from Cross Sand L.V.	Submarine	No warning	Torpedo	6
Bengairn (S.V.)	2,127	1	165 miles W.S.W. from Fastnet.	Submarine	Captured	Gunfire	—
†Simla	5,884	2	45 miles N.W. ½ W. from Gozo Island.	Submarine	No warning	Torpedo	10
Sneaton	3,470	3	35 miles N.N.E. from Cap de Garde, Tunis.	Submarine	Captured	Bombs	—
†Clan Campbell	5,897	3	29 miles S.E. from Cape Bon.	Submarine	No warning	Torpedo	—
Ellaston	3,796	3	65 miles N.W. by W. from Cape Serrat.	Submarine	Captured	Torpedo	—
Bendew	3,681	4	9 miles S. ½ E. from Kentish Knock.	Mine	Mine	Mine	1
†Chantala	4,951	5	15 miles N. from C. Bengut.	Submarine	No warning	Torpedo	9
Zent	3,890	5	28 miles W. by S. ½ S. from Fastnet.	Submarine	No warning	Torpedo	49

17 MERCHANT VESSELS CAPTURED OR SUNK.

Name.	Tons.	Date.	Position.	Cause of Loss.	How attacked.	How sunk.	Lives lost.
		1916. April					
Vesuvio	1,391	6	6 miles E. from Owers L.V.	Mine	Mine	Mine	7 including Master.
Yonne	4,039	6	18 miles N.N.W. from Shershel, Algeria.	Submarine	No warning	Torpedo	—
Halcyon	1,319	7	3½ miles S.W. by S. from Folkestone Pier.	Mine	Mine	Mine	—
Clyde (S.V.)	204	7	32 miles N. from Dieppe.	Submarine	Captured	Bombs	—
Braunton	4,575	7	4½ miles S. by W. from Beachy Head.	Submarine	No warning	Torpedo	—
Zafra	3,578	8	44 miles N. from Oran.	Submarine	Captured	Bombs	—
Adamton	2,304	8	15 miles S. from Skerryvore.	Submarine	Captured	Gunfire	1
Avon	1,574	9	2½ miles S.E. by S. from Tongue L.V.	Mine	Mine	Mine	2
Eastern City	4,341	9	18 miles N. by W. from Ushant.	Submarine	Captured	Gunfire	—
Glenalmond	2,888	9	27 miles N. from Ushant.	Submarine	Captured	Torpedo	—
Silksworth Hall	4,777	10	1¼ miles N.E. from Corton L.V.	Submarine	No warning	Torpedo	3
Margam Abbey	4,471	10	55 miles S.W. ¼ S. from Lizard.	Submarine	Captured	Gunfire	—
Robert Adamson	2,978	10	3 miles N. by E. from Shipwash L.V.	Submarine	No warning	Torpedo	—
Inverlyon (S.V.)	1,827	11	108 miles W.N.W. from Fastnet.	Submarine	Captured	Gunfire	—
Angus	3,619	11	76 miles E. by N. from Valencia.	Submarine	Captured	Gunfire	—
Orlock Head	1,945	12	65 miles S.E. from Barcelona.	Submarine	Captured	Gunfire	—
Chic	3,037	13	45 miles S.W. from Fastnet.	Submarine	Captured	Torpedo	9 including Master.
Shenandoah	3,886	14	1½ miles W. from Folkestone Gate.	Mine	Mine	Mine	2
Fairport	3,838	15	31 miles N. by W. from Bishop Rock.	Submarine	Captured	Torpedo	—
Harrovian	4,309	16	60 miles W. from Bishop Rock.	Submarine	Captured	Gunfire	—
Cardonia (S.V.)	2,169	16	20 miles S. from Fastnet.	Submarine	Captured	Torpedo	—
Ravenhill (S.V.)	1,826	18	78 miles S.E. by S. from Fastnet.	Submarine	Captured	Gunfire	—
Cairngowan	4,017	20	60 miles W. by N. from Fastnet.	Submarine	Captured	Gunfire	—
Sabbia	2,802	20	7 miles S.E. by S. from May Island.	Mine	Mine	Mine	—
Whitgift	4,397	20	Off Ushant	Submarine	No warning	Torpedo	32 including Master.
Feliciana	4,283	21	67 miles W. by N. ½ N. from Fastnet.	Submarine	No warning	Torpedo	—
Tregantle	3,091	22	1½ miles E.S.E. from Corton L.V.	Submarine	No warning	Torpedo	—
Ross	2,666	22	108 miles W. by N. from Bishop Rock.	Submarine	Captured	Torpedo	—
Parisiana	4,763	23	82 miles W. ½ S. from Ushant.	Submarine	Captured	Torpedo	—
Ribston	3,048	23	66 miles W. by S. from Ushant.	Submarine	Captured	Torpedo	—

Merchant Vessels Captured or Sunk.

Name.	Tons.	Date.	Position.	Cause of Loss.	How attacked.	How sunk.	Lives lost.
		1916. April					
Industry	4,044	27	120 miles W. by N. from Fastnet.	Submarine	Captured	Torpedo	—
Teal	716	29	2 miles E. from Seaham Harbour.	Submarine	Captured	Torpedo	—
†City of Lucknow.	3,677	30	60 miles E. from Malta.	Submarine	No warning	Torpedo	—
MAY 1916.		May					
Hendonhall	3,994	1	2 miles S. ½ E. from Inner Gabbard Buoy.	Mine	Mine	Mine	—
Maud (S.V.)	120	1	50 miles S.W. by W. from Ushant.	Submarine	Captured	Gunfire	—
Rochester City	1,239	2	3 miles E. from Southwold.	Mine	Mine	Mine	1
Ruabon	2,004	2	160 miles W. by S. ½ S. from Ushant.	Submarine	Captured	Torpedo	—
Galgate (S.V.)	2,356	6	170 miles W. by N. from Ushant.	Submarine	Captured	Gunfire	—
Cymric	13,370	8	140 miles W.N.W. from Fastnet.	Submarine	No warning	Torpedo	5
Dolcoath	1,706	10	3¼ miles N.N.E. from N. Foreland.	Mine	Mine	Mine	1
Eretria	3,464	13	15 miles S.S.W. from Ile D'Yeu, Bay of Biscay.	Mine	Mine	Mine	—
Rhenass	285	22	Off Aldeburgh	Mine	Mine	Mine	6
†El Argentino	6,809	26	7 miles S.E. by S. from Southwold.	Mine	Mine	Mine	—
Denewood	1,221	26	Off Aldeburgh	Mine	Mine	Mine	—
Lincairn	3,638	27	8 miles N. by E. from Shipwash.	Mine	Mine	Mine	—
Trunkby	2,635	27	50 miles S. by E. from Port Mahon, Minorca.	Submarine	Captured	Gunfire	—
Lady Ninian	4,297	28	106 miles N.E. ½ N. from Algiers.	Submarine	Captured	Gunfire	1
Elmgrove	3,018	29	96 miles N.E. from Algiers.	Submarine	Captured	Gunfire	—
Southgarth	2,414	29	60 miles N.N.E. from Algiers.	Submarine	Captured	Bombs	—
Baron Vernon	1,779	29	56 miles N.E. ½ N. from Algiers.	Submarine	Captured	Gunfire	—
†Dalegarth	2,265	30	12 miles N.E. from Cape Corbelin, Algiers.	Submarine	Captured	Torpedo	—
Julia Park	2,900	30	10 miles N. from Cape Carbon, Algeria.	Submarine	Captured	Torpedo	—
Baron Tweedmouth.	5,007	30	25 miles N.E. by N. from Cape Carbon, Algeria.	Submarine	Captured	Gunfire	—
JUNE 1916.		1916. June					
Dewsland	1,993	1	28 miles N.E. by E. from Cape Carbon, Algeria.	Submarine	Captured	Gunfire	—
Salmonpool	4,905	1	30 miles N.E. by E. from Cape Carbon, Algeria.	Submarine	Captured	Torpedo	—
Golconda	5,874	3	5 miles S.E. by E. from Aldeburgh.	Submarine	No warning	Torpedo	19
Sardinia	1,119	15	38 miles W. ¼ N. from Gorgona Island.	Submarine	Captured	Gunfire	—

19   MERCHANT VESSELS CAPTURED OR SUNK.

Name.	Tons.	Date.	Position.	Cause of Loss.	How attacked.	How sunk.	Lives lost.
		1916. June					
Gafsa	3,922	16	80 miles S.W. by S. from Genoa.	Submarine	Captured	Gunfire	—
Rona	1,312	18	90 miles W. from Cape Falcone, Sardinia.	Submarine	Captured	Gunfire	—
Beachy	4,718	18	98 miles N.E. by E. from Port Mahon.	Submarine	Captured	Torpedo	—
Corton Light Vessel.	—	21	4 miles N.E. by E. from Lowestoft.	Mine	Mine	Mine	5
Burma	706	23	5 miles N. by E. ½ E. from Shipwash L.V.	Mine	Mine	Mine	7
Brussels	1,380	23	Off Dutch Coast	Torpedo boat	Captured	Taken into Zeebrugge.	Crew made prisoners. Master subsequently shot.
Canford Chine	2,398	24	5 miles off Calella, Spain.	Submarine	Captured	Gunfire	
Astrologer	912	26	5 miles S.S.E. from Lowestoft.	Mine	Mine	Mine	11 including Master.
Windermere	2,292	27	58 miles S.S.E. from Port Mahon.	Submarine	Captured	Scuttled	12 including Master.
Mercurius (Dredger).	129	28	3 miles S.E. from Lowestoft.	Mine	Mine	Mine	6
Teano	1,907	29	24 miles N.W. by N. from Marittimo Island, Sicily.	Submarine	Captured	Scuttled	—
†Moeris	3,409	30	46 miles S.E. from Cape Sidero, Crete.	Submarine	No warning	Torpedo	3
JULY 1916.		1916. July					
Rockliffe	3,073	2	Black Sea	Submarine	—	—	—
Lestris	1,384	5	Between Maas L.V. and Schouwenbank.	Torpedo boat and submarine.	Captured	Taken into Zeebrugge.	Crew made prisoners.
Gannet	1,127	7	5 miles E.N.E. from Shipwash L.V.	Mine	Mine	Mine	8
Pendennis	2,123	8	North Sea	Submarine	Captured	Taken to Germany.	Crew made prisoners.
Kara	2,338	10	Near Pakefield Gat Buoy.	Mine	Mine	Mine	—
Calypso	2,876	10	North Sea	Submarine	No warning	Torpedo	30 including Master.
Silverton	2,682	13	14 miles N.E. from Canae Rocks.	Submarine	Captured	Torpedo	—
Ecclesia	3,714	14	11 miles N.W. from Bougaroni Point.	Submarine	Captured	Gunfire	—
Antigua	2,876	14	20 miles E. by N. from Jidjelli, Algeria.	Submarine	Captured	Bombs	—
Sylvie	1,302	15	15 miles from Cape Sigli, Algeria.	Submarine	Captured	Gunfire	—
Alto	2,266	16	4 miles off Kessingland, Suffolk.	Mine	Mine	Mine	—

Merchant Vessels Captured or Sunk. 20

Name.	Tons.	Date.	Position.	Cause of Loss.	How attacked.	How sunk.	Lives lost.
		1916. July					
Virginia	4,279	16	42 miles S.W. by W. from Cape Matapan.	Submarine	Captured	Torpedo	2
Mopsa	885	16	7 miles S. from Lowestoft.	Mine	Mine	Mine	—
Wilton Hall	3,387	16	65 miles N.W. from Algiers.	Submarine	Captured	Bombs	—
†Euphorbia	3,837	16	56 miles N.E. from Algiers.	Submarine	No warning	Torpedo	11
Rosemoor	4,303	17	80 miles N.E. by N. from Algiers.	Submarine	Captured	Bombs	—
Llongwen	4,683	18	90 miles N.E. from Algiers.	Submarine	Captured	Gunfire	14
Grangemoor	3,198	20	75 miles N.W. by W. from Algiers.	Submarine	Captured	Gunfire	—
Yzer	3,538	20	56 miles N.W. ½ N. from Algiers.	Submarine	Captured	Torpedo	1
Karma	3,710	20	68 miles N.N.W. from Algiers.	Submarine	Captured	Gunfire	—
Wolff	2,443	21	75 miles N.N.W. from Algiers.	Submarine	Captured	Gunfire	—
Knutsford	3,842	22	12 miles N.W. by N. from Cape Corbelin, Algeria.	Submarine	Captured	Gunfire	—
†Olive	3,678	22	10 miles N.W. by N. from Cape Corbelin, Algeaia.	Submarine	Captured	Gunfire	—
Badminton	3,847	23	63 miles N.E. by N. from Cape Carbon, Algeria.	Submarine	Captured	Gunfire	—
Eskimo	3,326	26	Off Risoer, in Norwegian territorial waters.	Auxiliary Cruiser	Captured	Taken to Germany.	Crew (except 1) made prisoners.
Claudia	1,144	30	8½ miles S.E. by S. ½ S. from Lowestoft.	Mine	Mine	Mine	3
Ethelbryhta	3,084	30	11 miles W.S.W. from Pantellaria.	Submarine	Captured	Gunfire	—
Britannic	3,487	30	20 miles E.S.E. from Cape Bon.	Submarine	Captured	Gunfire	—
AUGUST 1916.		Aug.					
Aaro	2,603	1	North Sea	Submarine	No warning	Torpedo	3 Remainder of crew made prisoners.
Heighington	2,800	1	40 miles N.E. from Cape Serrat.	Submarine	Captured	Torpedo	—
G. C. Gradwell (S.V.)	156	2	20 miles N.W. from Cape Antifer.	Submarine	Captured	Gunfire	—
S.D. (barge)	131	2	18 miles N.N.W. from Cape Antifer.	Submarine	Captured	Gunfire	—
● Margaret Sutton (S.V.)	197	2	35 miles S.S.E. from St. Catherine's Point.	Submarine	Captured	Bombs	—
● Sphene	740	3	26 miles S.W. from St. Catherine's Point.	Submarine	Captured	Bombs	—
● Badger	89	3	30 miles S.W. ½ S. from St. Catherine's Point.	Submarine	Captured	Gunfire	—

21 MERCHANT VESSELS CAPTURED OR SUNK.

Name.	Tons.	Date.	Position.	Cause of Loss.	How attacked.	How sunk.	Lives lost.
		1916. Aug.					
Fortuna (S.V.)	131	3	15 miles S.S.W. from Portland Bill.	Submarine	Captured	Bombs	—
Ermenilda (S.V.)	94	4	24 miles S.S.W. from Portland Bill.	Submarine	Captured	Bomb	—
Demaris (S.V.)	79	4	20 miles N. from Alderney.	Submarine	Captured	Bomb	—
Spiral	1,342	4	40 miles W.S.W. from St. Catherine's Point.	Submarine	Captured	Bombs	—
Favonian	3,049	4	24 miles S.W. from Planier Island.	Submarine	Captured	Gunfire	—
Tottenham	3,106	4	33 miles S.W. by W. from Marseilles.	Submarine	Captured	Gunfire	—
Stamfordham	921	4	8 miles S. from Longstone.	Submarine	Captured	Gunfire	—
Mount Coniston	3,018	5	7 miles E. by S. from Meda Island, Spain.	Submarine	Captured	Bombs	—
Trident	3,129	7	34 miles N. by E. ¾ E. from Dragonera Is., Majorca.	Submarine	Captured	Torpedo	—
Newburn	3,554	7	34 miles N. by E. ¾ E. from Dragonera Is., Majorca.	Submarine	Captured	Torpedo	—
Imperial	3,818	8	38 miles S.W. by W. from Planier Island.	Submarine	Captured	Gunfire	—
Antiope	2,973	9	88 miles S.W. by W. from Marseilles.	Submarine	Captured	Gunfire	—
San Bernardo	3,803	10	17 miles S.E. from Longstone.	Submarine	Captured	Bombs	—
F. Stobart	801	11	½ mile N. from North Aldborough Napes Buoy.	Mine	Mine	Mine	4
†Swedish Prince	3,712	17	12 miles N.W. by W. from Pantellaria.	Submarine	Captured	Gunfire	1 Master, Chief Engineer and Gunner made prisoners.
Duart	3,108	31	60 miles N. ¾ E. from Shershel, Algeria.	Submarine	Captured	Gunfire	—
SEPTEMBER	**1916.**						
		Sept.					
Baron Yarborough.	1,784	1	27 miles N.W. from Dragonera Island, Majorca.	Submarine	Captured	Bombs	—
†Swift Wings	4,465	1	18 miles E. from Cape Bengut, Algeria.	Submarine	No warning	Torpedo	2 Master made prisoner.
Kelvinia	5,039	2	9 miles S. by W. from Caldy Island, Bristol Channel.	Mine	Mine	Mine	—
Strathallan	4,404	2	20 miles N.E. from Philippeville.	Submarine	Captured	Gunfire	Master made prisoner.
Teesbcrough	308	3	30 miles N.E. by N. from Fecamp.	Submarine	Captured	Bombs	—

MERCHANT VESSELS CAPTURED OR SUNK. 22

Name.	Tons.	Date.	Position.	Cause of Loss.	How attacked.	How sunk.	Lives lost.
		1916. Sept.					
Mascotte	1,097	3	6½ miles S.E. from Southwold.	Mine	Mine	Mine	1
Netta	370	3	35 miles N.E. ½ N. from Cape Antifer.	Submarine	Captured	Bombs	—
Rievaulx Abbey	1,166	3	¾ mile E.N.E. from Rosse Spit Buoy, Humber.	Mine	Mine	Mine	2
Laristan	3,675	4	30 miles W. from Gozo.	Submarine	Captured	Torpedo	Master prisoner.
City of Ghent	199	5	18 miles S.E. from Cape Barfleur.	Submarine	Captured	Bombs	—
Torridge	5,036	6	40 miles S.S.W. from Start Point.	Submarine	Captured	Bombs	—
Tagus	937	6	35 miles N.E. by E. ½ E. from Ushant.	Submarine	Captured	Bombs	—
Britannia (S.V.)	39	6	12 miles N. from Alderney.	Submarine	Captured	Bombs	—
Strathtay	4,428	6	4 miles N. from Pontusval, Finistere.	Submarine	Captured	Torpedo	—
Heathdene	3,541	7	38 miles S.S.W. from the Lizard.	Submarine	Captured	Scuttled	—
†Achaia	2,733	7	300 yards E.N.E. from entrance to Oran Harbour.	Mine	Mine	Mine	—
†Llangorse	3,841	8	48 miles W.S.W. from Cape Matapan.	Submarine	No warning	Torpedo	—
†Butetown	3,789	8	55 miles W.S.W. from Cape Matapan.	Submarine	No warning	Torpedo	—
Lexie	3,778	10	42 miles S.W. from Ushant.	Submarine	Captured	Torpedo	—
†Italiana	2,663	14	112 miles E. from Malta.	Submarine	No warning	Torpedo	—
Counsellor	4,958	14	5 miles W. ½ S. from Galley Head.	Mine	Mine	Mine	—
†Inverbervie	4,309	14	17 miles S. by W. from Cape Rizzuto, Italy.	Submarine	No warning	Torpedo	6
Lord Tredegar	3,856	17	51 miles S.E. by E. from Malta.	Submarine	No warning	Torpedo	4
†Dewa	3,802	17	45 miles E. ¾ N. from Malta.	Submarine	No warning	Torpedo	3
Etton	2,831	20	Entrance to White Sea.	Mine	Mine	Mine	1
Colchester	964	22	North Sea	Torpedo Boats	Captured	Taken into Zeebrugge.	Crew prisoners.
Kennett	1,679	22	Baltic	Submarine	No warning	Torpedo	1 (Master).
†Charterhouse	3,021	23	26 miles E. by S. ½ S. from S.E. point of Formentera.	Submarine	Captured	Bombs	Master and 2 gunners made prisoners.
Dresden	807	23	41 miles S. by E. ¼ E. from the Nab.	Submarine	Captured	Bombs	—
Pearl	613	23	41 miles S. ¼ E. from the Nab.	Submarine	Captured	Bombs	—
†Bronwen	4,250	24	25 miles N. by E. from Dragonera Island.	Submarine	Captured	Gunfire	Master and 2 gunners made prisoners.
Stathe	2,623	26	50 miles E. by S. from Barcelona.	Submarine	Captured	Gunfire	—
Newby	2,168	26	53 miles E. from Barcelona.	Submarine	Captured	Gunfire	—

MERCHANT VESSELS CAPTURED OR SUNK.

Name.	Tons.	Date.	Position.	Cause of Loss.	How attacked.	How sunk.	Lives lost.
		1916. Sept.					
Thelma	1,002	26	24 miles E. from Fair Isle.	Submarine	Captured	Torpedo	—
†Boddam	3,218	26	76 miles E.S.E. from Barcelona.	Submarine	Captured	Gunfire	Master made prisoner.
St. Gothard	2,788	26	12 miles N. by W. from Fair Isle.	Submarine	Captured	Torpedo	—
Thurso	1,244	27	60 miles N.E. by E. from Rattray Head.	Submarine	Captured	Gunfire	Master and Chief Engineer made prisoners.
†Secondo	3,912	27	40 miles N.N.E. from Dragonera Island.	Submarine	No warning	Torpedo	—
†Rallus	1,752	27	45 miles N.E. by N. from Dragonera Island.	Submarine	Captured	Gunfire	—
Maywood	1,188	30	1 mile W. from Whistle Buoy, Havre.	Mine	Mine	Mine	—
Pearl (S.V.)	144	30	6 miles S.S.E. from Lizard.	Submarine	Captured	Bombs	—
William George (S.V.).	151	30	10 miles N.N.E. from Cap la Hague.	Submarine	Captured	Gunfire	—

OCTOBER 1916.

Name.	Tons.	Date.	Position.	Cause of Loss.	How attacked.	How sunk.	Lives lost.
		Oct.					
†Vanellus	1,797	1	Havre Roads	Mine	Mine	Mine	3
Lotusmere	3,911	2	48 miles N.N.E. from Teriberski L.H.	Submarine	Captured	Torpedo	—
†Huntsfall	4,331	2	12 miles S.S.E. from Skyro.	Submarine	No warning	Torpedo	Master made prisoner.
†Franconia	18,150	4	195 miles E. ½ S. from Malta.	Submarine	No warning	Torpedo	12
J. Y. Short	2,193	4	80 miles E. from Vardo.	Submarine	Captured	Gunfire	—
Brantingham	2,617	4	Arctic Ocean	Submarine	No warning (probably).	Torpedo	24 including Master
Isle of Hastings	1,575	5	10 miles S. by W. from Ushant.	Submarine	Captured	Bombs	—
Lanterna	1,685	6	2½ miles N.E. ½ E. from Cromer.	Mine	Mine	Mine	—
Strathdene	4,321	8	20 miles S. by E. from Nantucket L.V.	Submarine	Captured	Torpedo	—
West Point	3,847	8	46 miles S.E. by E. from Nantucket L.V.	Submarine	Captured	Bombs	—
Stephano	3,449	8	2½ miles E.N.E. from Nantucket L.V.	Submarine	Captured	Torpedo	—
Astoria	4,262	9	120 miles N.W. by W. from Vardo.	Submarine	Captured	Torpedo	17
†Elax	3,980	10	70 miles W.S.W. from Cape Matapan.	Submarine	No warning	Torpedo	—
Gardepee	1,633	10	70 miles N.N.E. from North Cape.	Submarine	Captured	Bombs	—
†Crosshill	5,002	11	60 miles W. from Malta.	Submarine	No warning	Torpedo	4
Iolo	3,903	11	153 miles N. from Vardo.	Submarine	Captured	Torpedo	—

Merchant Vessels Captured or Sunk.

Name.	Tons.	Date.	Position.	Cause of Loss.	How attacked.	How sunk.	Lives lost.
		1916. Oct.					
Welsh Prince	4,934	13	33 miles S.W. from Cape Matapan.	Submarine	No warning	Torpedo	2
Ethel Duncan	2,510	18	40 miles W.N.W. from Noop Head, Orkney.	Submarine	Captured	Torpedo	—
†Penylan	3,875	19	5 miles W. by N. from Cape Bougaroni.	Submarine	No warning	Torpedo	—
Alaunia	13,405	19	2 miles S. from Royal Sovereign L.V.	Mine	Mine	Mine	2
Huguenot	1,032	20	4 miles N.E. ½ E. from Sunk L.V.	Mine	Mine	Mine	—
†Mombassa	4,689	20	8 miles N.W. by N. from Cape Corbelin.	Submarine	No warning	Torpedo	1
The Duke	376	20	40 miles N.N.E. from Havre.	Submarine	Captured	Gunfire	—
Cabotia	4,309	20	120 miles W.N.W. from Tory Island.	Submarine	Captured	Gunfire	32 including Master.
The Marchioness	553	20	30 miles N.W. from Fecamp.	Submarine	Captured	Gunfire	—
Cliburn	440	20	30 miles S.S.E. from St. Catherine's Point.	Submarine	Captured	Bombs	—
Barbara	3,740	20	25 miles S. from Isle of Wight.	Submarine	Captured	Gunfire	—
Midland	4,247	20	60 miles E. by N. ½ N. from Ushant.	Submarine	Captured	Bombs	—
Cock o' the Walk (S.V.)	111	21	30 miles N.W. by N. from Hanois, Guernsey.	Submarine	Captured	Gunfire	—
Grit (Motor Barge)	147	21	25 miles S. from Beachy Head.	Submarine	Captured	Gunfire	—
Princess May (S.V.)	104	21	25 miles S. from Beachy Head.	Submarine	Captured	Bomb	—
†Cluden	3,166	22	11 miles W. from Cape Tenez, Algeria.	Submarine	No warning	Torpedo	4
W. Harkess	1,185	22	17 miles W. from Cape Tenez, Algeria.	Submarine	Captured	Bombs	—
Sidmouth	4,045	24	22 miles S. from Wolf.	Submarine	Captured	Torpedo	—
Twig (S.V.)	128	24	15 miles N. from Alderney.	Submarine	Captured	Bomb	—
Framfield	2,510	24	3 miles N.E. from Sunk L.V.	Mine	Mine	Mine	6 including Master.
Rowanmore	10,320	26	128 miles W.N.W. from Fastnet.	Submarine	Captured	Torpedo	Master made prisoner.
The Queen	1,676	26	3 miles N.E. from Varne L.V.	Destroyers	Captured	—	—
Oola	2,494	26	22 miles N.E. by N. from North Cape.	Submarine	Captured	Bombs	—
Rappahannock	3,871	26	70 miles from Scilly Isles.	Submarine	Captured	Not known	37 including Master.
Sparta	480	28	3½ miles E. by N. from Southwold.	Mine	Mine	Mine	4
†Marina	5,204	28	30 miles W. from Fastnet.	Submarine	No warning	Torpedo	18
Rio Pirahy	3,561	28	60 miles S. from Cape St. Vincent.	Submarine	Captured	Bombs	—
Galeka (Hospital Ship)	6,772	28	5 miles N.W. from Cape la Hague.	Mine	Mine	Mine	—

25 MERCHANT VESSELS CAPTURED OR SUNK.

Name.	Tons.	Date.	Position.	Cause of Loss.	How attacked.	How sunk.	Lives lost.
		1916. Oct.					
†Meroë	3,552	29	70 miles W. ½ N. from Cape Trafalgar.	Submarine	Captured	Torpedo	—
†Torino	1,850	29	70 miles W. ½ N. from Cape Trafalgar.	Submarine	Captured	Torpedo	1
†Marquis Bacquehem.	4,396	29	50 miles S. by E. from Cape St. Vincent.	Submarine	No warning	Torpedo	—
†Glenlogan	5,838	31	10 miles S.E. from Stromboli.	Submarine	No warning	Torpedo	—
North Wales	4,072	—	Off Scilly Islands	Submarine (reported).	No warning (probably).	Torpedo	30 including Master.
NOVEMBER 1916.		Nov.					
Brierley Hill	1,168	1	18 miles W.N.W. from Hellisö L.H., Norway.	Submarine	Captured	Torpedo	—
Seatonia	3,533	1	80 miles N.W.½ N. from Fastnet.	Submarine	Captured	Torpedo	—
Spero	1,132	2	95 miles W.S.W. from Hellisö L.H., Norway.	Submarine	Captured	Torpedo	—
Statesman	6,153	3	200 miles E. from Malta.	Submarine	No warning	Torpedo	6
Skerries	4,278	4	15 miles N.N.W. from the Skerries, Anglesea.	Mine	Mine	Mine	2 including Master.
†Clan Leslie	3,937	4	200 miles E. ½ S. from Malta.	Submarine	No warning	Torpedo	3
†Huntsvale	5,398	4	200 miles E. from Malta.	Submarine	No warning	Torpedo	7 including Master.
†Arabia	7,933	6	112 miles W. by S. from Cape Matapan.	Submarine	No warning	Torpedo	2
Suffolk Coast	780	7	14 miles E.S.E. from Cape Barfleur.	Submarine	Captured	Bombs	—
Killellan	1,971	8	17 miles S.W. by S. ¼ S. from Colbart L.V.	Submarine	Captured	Torpedo	—
Sheldrake	2,697	8	20 miles W.S.W. from Marittimo Island.	Submarine	Captured	Gunfire	Master and Chief Engineer made prisoners.
Sunniside	447	9	4 miles E.N.E. from Southwold.	Mine	Mine	Mine	4 including Master.
Bogota	4,577	10	120 miles S.W. ½ W. from Ushant.	Submarine	No warning	Torpedo	—
Marga	674	10	16 miles N. by W. from Ushant.	Submarine	Captured	Gunfire	—
H.M.W. (sailing barge).	75	10	1 mile N. by W. from Boulogne L.V.	Mine	Mine	Mine	1
†Morazan	3,486	11	145 miles S.W. by W. from Ushant.	Submarine	Captured	Torpedo	Master made prisoner.
Sarah Radcliffe	3,333	11	170 miles S.W. from Ushant.	Submarine	Captured	Torpedo	—
†Kapunda	3,383	12	205 miles E.S.E. from Malta.	Submarine	No warning	Torpedo	—
†Lady Carrington	3,269	12	98 miles N. by W. from Cape Ortegal.	Submarine	Captured	Torpedo	—
Caterham	1,777	13	15 miles S.S.E. from Beachy Head.	Submarine	Captured	Bombs	—

Merchant Vessels Captured or Sunk.

Name.	Tons.	Date.	Position.	Cause of Loss.	How attacked.	How sunk.	Lives lost.
		1916. Nov.					
Corinth	3,669	13	28 miles S. $\frac{3}{4}$ E. from Flamborough Head.	Submarine	Captured	Bombs	—
● Bernicia	957	13	20 miles S.S.E. from Beachy Head.	Submarine	Captured	Bombs	—
● Polpedn	1,510	14	20 miles S. from Littlehampton.	Submarine	No warning	Torpedo	—
†F. Matarazzo	2,823	15	26 miles E.N.E. from Linosa Island.	Submarine	No warning	Torpedo	—
Trevarrack	4,199	16	25 miles W. $\frac{1}{2}$ N. from Les Hanois, Guernsey.	Submarine	Captured	Gunfire	—
Vanguard (S.V.)	142	16	18 miles N.W. $\frac{1}{2}$ N. from Cape Antifer.	Submarine	Captured	Bombs	—
● †Vasco	1,914	16	10 miles W. by S. from Beachy Head.	Mine	Mine	Mine	17 (including Master).
Britannic (Hospital ship).	48,158	21	Zea Channel	Mine	Mine	Mine	21
†Brierton	3,255	22	32 miles S.W. from Ushant.	Submarine	No warning	Torpedo	—
● Grenada (S.V.)	2,268	22	32 miles S.W. by S. from Beachy Head.	Submarine	Captured	Gunfire	—
Jerseyman	358	24	30 miles N.W. $\frac{1}{2}$ W. from Dieppe.	Submarine	No warning(?)	Torpedo(?)	—
Emlynverne	544	25	30 miles N.W. by N. from Cape Antifer.	Submarine	Captured	Gunfire	—
†City of Birmingham.	7,498	27	90 miles S.E. from Malta.	Submarine	No warning	Torpedo	4
Maude Larssen	1,222	27	22 miles W.S.W. from Marittimo.	Submarine	Captured	Bombs	—
Rhona	640	27	19 miles N.W. by N. from Guernsey.	Submarine	Captured	Bombs	—
†Reapwell	3,417	27	148 miles N.W. by N. from Alexandria.	Submarine	No warning	Torpedo	Master made prisoner.
● Alison	286	28	8 miles E.S.E. from Owers L.V.	Submarine	Captured	Bombs	—
● Alert	289	28	6 miles E.S.E. from Owers L.V.	Submarine	Captured	Bombs	—
● Ramsgarth	1,553	28	11 miles E. by S. from Owers L.V.	Submarine	Captured	Bomb	—
● Lady of the Lake (S.V.).	79	28	35 miles S.E. from Start Point.	Submarine	Captured	Gunfire	—
†King Malcolm	4,351	28	144 miles N.W. by N. from Alexandria.	Submarine	No warning	Torpedo	Master made prisoner.
†Moresby	1,763	28	120 miles N.W. by N. from Alexandria.	Submarine	No warning	Torpedo	33
†Luciston	2,948	29	4 miles E. from Dellamara Point, Malta.	Mine	Mine	Mine	—
● Grace (S.V.)	135	29	40 miles S.E. by E. from Start Point.	Submarine	Captured	Bomb	—
†Minnewaska	14,317	29	Suda Bay	Mine	Mine	Mine	—
Christabel (S.V.)	175	30	10 miles N. by W. from St. Ives.	Submarine	Captured	Bomb	—
● Behrend (S.V.)	141	30	35 miles S.W. from Portland Bill.	Submarine	Captured	Bomb	—

MERCHANT VESSELS CAPTURED OR SUNK.

Name.	Tons.	Date.	Position.	Cause of Loss.	How attacked.	How sunk.	Lives lost.
		1916. Nov.					
Heinrich (S.V.)	98	30	29 miles S. by E. from Start Point.	Submarine	Captured	Bombs	—
Roma (S.V.)	99	30	Off E. Coast of Sardinia.	Submarine	Captured	Gunfire	—

DECEMBER 1916.

Name.	Tons.	Date.	Position.	Cause of Loss.	How attacked.	How sunk.	Lives lost.
		Dec.					
King Bleddyn	4,387	1	30 miles S. by W. ½ W. from Ushant.	Submarine	Captured	Bombs	—
†Burcombe	3,516	1	100 miles S.E. by E. from Malta.	Submarine	No warning	Torpedo	?
Briardene	2,701	1	12½ miles S.E. by S. from Bishop Rock.	Submarine	Captured	Bombs	—
Palacine	3,286	2	18 miles E.N.E. from Ushant.	Submarine	Captured	Bombs	—
Harpalus	1,445	2	34 miles S.S.W. from Galley Head	Submarine	Captured	Bombs	—
†Istrar	4,582	2	120 miles N.N.W. ½ W. from Alexandria.	Submarine	No warning	Torpedo	1 Chief Engineer made prisoner.
†Voltaire	8,618	2	650 miles W. ¼ N. (true) from Fastnet.	Möwe	Captured	Not known	Crew made prisoners.
Dacia	1,856	3	Funchal Roads	Submarine	No warning	Torpedo	—
Seeker (S.V.)	74	3	30 miles N.W. from Les Hanois.	Submarine	Captured	Bombs	—
Mizpah (S.V.)	57	3	30 miles S.S.E. from Eddystone.	Submarine	Captured	Bombs	—
†Caledonia	9,223	4	125 miles E. by S. from Malta.	Submarine	No warning	Torpedo	1 Master made prisoner.
†Mount Temple	9,792	6	620 miles W. ½ S. (true) from Fastnet.	Möwe	Captured	Bombs	3 Remainder prisoners.
Duchess of Cornwall (S.V.).	152	6	620 miles W. ¾ S. (true) from Fastnet.	Möwe	Captured	Not known	Crew made prisoners.
Avristan	3,818	7	14 miles S. by W. ½ W. from Ushant.	Submarine	No warning	Torpedo	1
†Conch	5,620	7	12 miles S. by W. ½ W. from Anvil Point.	Submarine	No warning	Torpedo	28 (including Master).
†Britannia	1,814	8	70 miles W. by S. from Cape Sines, Portugal.	Submarine	No warning	Torpedo	2 Master made prisoner.
King George	3,852	8	700 miles E. ½ N. (true) from C. Race.	Möwe	Captured	Not known	Crew made prisoners.
Harlington	1,089	9	4 miles S.W. from Shipwash L.V.	Mine	Mine	Mine	7
Harlyn	1,794	9	4 miles S.W. from Shipwash L.V.	Mine	Mine	Mine	2
Forth	1,159	9	4 miles S.W. from Shipwash L.V.	Mine	Mine	Mine	—
Cambrian Range	4,234	9	610 miles E. ½ S. (true) from C. Race.	Möwe	Captured	Bombs	Crew made prisoners.
Strathalbyn	4,331	10	2 miles N.E. by E. from Cherbourg Breakwater.	Mine	Mine	Mine	

Name.	Gross Tons.	Date.	Position.	Cause of Loss.	How attacked.	How sunk.	Lives lost.
		1916. Dec.					
†Georgic	10,077	10	590 miles E.S.E. (true) from C. Race.	Möwe	Captured	Torpedo	1 Remainder prisoners.
Yarrowdale	4,652	11	540 miles S.E. ¾ E. (true) from C. Race.	Möwe	Captured	Taken to Germany.	Crew made prisoners.
Coath	975	12	English Channel	Mine (?)	Mine (?)	Mine (?)	16 including Master.
†St. Ursula	5,011	12	45 miles S.E. by S. from Malta.	Submarine	No warning	Torpedo	4
Conrad (S.V.)	164	12	40 miles S.S.E. from St. Catherines Point.	Submarine	Captured	Bombs	—
Saint Theodore	4,992	12	520 miles W. ½ S. (true) from Flores.	Möwe	Captured	Not known. Sunk 12th Feb. 1917.	—
†Bretwalda	4,037	13	220 miles E by S. from Malta.	Submarine	No warning	Torpedo	—
Glencoe	2,560	14	14 miles N.N.W. from Ile d'Yeu.	Submarine	Captured	Torpedo	—
Burnhope	1,941	14	In Hartlepool Bay	Mine	Mine	Mine	1 (Master).
†Westminster	4,342	14	196 miles E. by S. from Malta.	Submarine	No warning	Torpedo	15 (including Master).
†Russian	8,825	14	210 miles E. by S. from Malta.	Submarine	No warning	Torpedo	28
Naiad (S.V.)	1,907	15	25 miles S.E. by S. from Bishop Rock.	Submarine	Captured	Torpedo	—
Constance Mary (S.V.).	177	15	20 miles N.E. from Cape Barfleur.	Submarine	Captured	Bombs	—
Bayhall	3,898	17	90 miles N. by E. from Cape Ortegal.	Submarine	Captured	Bombs	Master made prisoner.
Pascal	5,587	17	12 miles N. from Casquets.	Submarine	Captured	Torpedo	2 Master made prisoner.
Flimston	5,751	18	21 miles N. by E. ½ E. from Ushant.	Submarine	Captured	Bombs	Master and Chief Engineer made prisoners.
Opal	599	18	Off Isle of Man	Mine	Mine	Mine	12 including Master.
Dramatist	5,415	18	490 miles S.W. ½ S. (true) from Flores.	Möwe	Captured	Bombs	—
Liverpool	686	19	11 miles S.E. by S. from Chicken Rock, Calf of Man.	Mine	Mine	Mine	3
Hildawell	2,494	20	North Sea	Mine	Mine	Mine	22 including Master.
†Itonus	5,340	20	60 miles N.W. by W. ½ W. from Malta.	Submarine	No warning	Torpedo	5 Master made prisoner.
†Murex	3,564	21	94 miles N.W. from Port Said.	Submarine	No warning	Torpedo	1
†Thistleban	4,117	23	5 miles N.N.W. from Alexandria.	Submarine	No warning	Torpedo	—
Harry W. Adams (S.V.).	127	24	46 miles N.W. by N. from C. Villano.	Submarine	Captured	Gunfire	—
Bargany	872	24ᵇ	25 miles N. from Ushant.	Submarine	Captured	Gunfire	—
Agnes (S.V.)	99	26	15 miles S.W. by W. from St. Ann's Head.	Submarine	Captured	Bombs	—

Merchant Vessels Captured or Sunk.

Name.	Gross Tons.	Date.	Position.	Cause of Loss.	How attacked.	How sunk.	Lives lost.
		1916. Dec.					
Spinaway (S.V.)	95	26	About 42 miles N.W. from Cape Villano.	Submarine	Captured	Gunfire	—
Copsewood	599	27	34 miles S. by W. $\frac{3}{4}$ W. from Lizard.	Submarine	Captured	Torpedo	—
Aislaby	2,692	27	10 miles N.E. from Estaca Point.	Submarine	Captured	Bombs	Master made prisoner.
†Oronsay	3,761	28	48 miles S.E. from Malta.	Submarine	No warning	Torpedo	Master made prisoner.
Pitho (S.V.)	150	28	30 miles S.E. from Start Point.	Submarine	Captured	Bombs	—
†Zoroaster	3,803	29	1$\frac{3}{4}$ miles E.N.E. from Sunk L.V.	Mine	Mine	Mine	3
Lonada	1,286	29	5 miles N. by E. $\frac{1}{2}$ E. from Shipwash L.V.	Mine	Mine	Mine	6
†Apsleyhall	3,882	30	28 miles W. by N. from Gozo.	Submarine	No warning	Torpedo	Master made prisoner.
Jean (S.V.)	215	30	60 miles E. (true) from St. Paul Rocks.	St. Theodore, after conversion into raider by Möwe.	Captured	Not known	—
Protector (pilot cutter).	200	31	Off Entrance to River Tyne.	Mine	Mine	Mine	19 (including Master).

JANUARY 1917.

Name.	Gross Tons.	Date.	Position.	Cause of Loss.	How attacked.	How sunk.	Lives lost.
		1917. Jan.					
†Baycraig	3,761	1	84 miles E.S.E. from Malta.	Submarine	No warning	Torpedo	Master made prisoner.
†Ivernia	14,278	1	58 miles S. by E. $\frac{1}{4}$ E. from Cape Matapan.	Submarine	No warning	Torpedo	36
Holly Branch	3,568	1	14 miles N.E. by N. from Ile de Bas.	Submarine	Captured	Bombs	—
Carlyle	466	2	5 miles W.S.W. from Ile de Sein L.H.	Submarine	Captured	Bombs	—
Wragby	3,641	4	45 miles W. by N. from C. Spartel.	Submarine	Captured	Gunfire	—
Lonclara	1,294	4	Off River Wear	Mine	Mine	Mine	4
Allie	1,127	5	10 miles W. by N. from Ile de Re.	Submarine	Captured	Bombs	—
†Lesbian	2,555	5	125 miles E. by S. from Malta.	Submarine	Captured	Gunfire	Master made prisoner.
†Hudworth	3,966	6	94 miles E.S.E. from Malta.	Submarine	No warning	Torpedo	—
Beaufront	1,720	6	76 miles N.W. by W. from Ushant.	Submarine	Captured	Torpedo	—
Brenda (S.V.)	249	7	10 miles S.S.W. from Beachy Head.	Submarine	Captured	Gunfire	—
†Mohacsfield	3,678	7	40 miles S.E. by E. $\frac{1}{4}$ E. from Malta.	Submarine	Captured	Not known	3 Master made prisoner.
†Radnorshire	4,310	7	110 miles E. (true) from Pernambuco.	Möwe	Captured	Bombs	—
†Andoni	3,188	8	46 miles S.E. from Malta.	Submarine	No warning	Torpedo	3 Master made prisoner.
†Lynfield	3,023	8	32 miles S.E. by S. from Malta.	Submarine	Captured	Not known	1 Master made prisoner.

Merchant Vessels Captured or Sunk.

Name.	Gross Tons.	Date.	Position.	Cause of Loss.	How attacked.	How sunk.	Lives lost.
		1917. Jan.					
†Bayuesk	3,286	9	130 miles N. by W. from Alexandria.	Submarine	No warning	Torpedo	7
Excellent	1,944	9	40 miles N.W. from Noop Head, Orkneys.	Submarine	Captured	Gunfire	Master made prisoner.
Minieh	3,806	9	170 miles E.N.E. (true) from Pernambuco.	Möwe	Captured	Bombs	—
Gladys Royle	3,268	9	120 miles S. ¼ W. (true) from Sta Maria, Azores.	Seeadler	Captured	Bombs	—
Brookwood	3,093	10	210 miles N. by W. from C. Finisterre.	Submarine	Captured	Gunfire	2
Netherby Hall	4,461	10	300 miles E. by N. (true) from Pernambuco.	Möwe	Captured	Bombs	—
Lundy Island	3,095	10	190 miles S.E.½E. true from Sta Maria, Azores.	Seeadler	Captured	Gunfire	Steward made prisoner.
Brentwood	1,192	12	4 miles E.N.E. from Whitby.	Mine	Mine	Mine	2
Auchencrag	3,916	12	20 miles W. from Ushant.	Submarine	Captured	Torpedo	4
Toftwood	3,082	13	24 miles N. ½ W. from Sept Iles.	Submarine	Captured	Torpedo	—
Martin	1,904	14	8 miles N. by W. from Ushant.	Submarine	Captured	Gunfire	—
†Port Nicholson	8,418	15	15 miles W. ½ N. from Dunkirk.	Mine	Mine	Mine	2
†Garfield	3,838	15	60 miles N.E. by N. ¼ N. from Alexandria.	Submarine	No warning	Torpedo	Master made prisoner.
Kinpurney (S.V.)	1,944	15	110 miles W. from Bishop Rock.	Submarine	Captured	Torpedo	—
Baron Sempill	1,607	16	180 miles S.W. from Fastnet.	Submarine	Captured	Bombs	—
Manchester Inventor.	4,247	18	50 miles N.W. by W. ½ W. from Fastnet.	Submarine	Captured	Torpedo	—
†Nailsea Court	3,295	19	32 miles W. from the Skelligs.	Submarine	No warning	Torpedo	—
Tremeadow	3,653	19	35 miles N.E. ¾ N. from Ushant.	Submarine	Captured	Gunfire	—
Lilian H. (S.V.)	467	19	15 miles S. by E. from Old Head of Kinsale.	Submarine	Captured	Bombs	—
Neuquen	3,583	20	20 miles N.W. by W. from the Skelligs.	Submarine	Captured	Torpedo	18 including Master.
†Bulgarian	2,515	20	Atlantic	Submarine	No warning (probably).	Torpedo	14 including Master. 9 crew prisoners.
Planudes	542	20 (?)	North Sea	Mine (?)	Mine (?)	Mine (?)	11 including Master.
†Trevean	3,081	22	240 miles S.W. by W. from Fastnet.	Submarine	Captured	Bombs	Master and two gunners made prisoners.
†Clan Shaw	3,943	23	Mouth of the Tay.	Mine	Mine	Mine	2
Jerington	2,747	23	52 miles N.W. ½ W. from Cape Ortegal.	Submarine	No warning	Torpedo	—
Tabasco	2,987	26	55 miles W.N.W. from the Skelligs.	Submarine	Captured	Torpedo	—

31 MERCHANT VESSELS CAPTURED OR SUNK.

Name.	Gross Tons.	Date.	Position.	Cause of Loss.	How attacked.	How sunk.	Lives lost.
		1917. Jan.					
†Matheran	7,654	26	9 miles W. from Dassen Island, Cape of Good Hope.	Mine	Mine	Mine	1
†Artist	3,570	27	58 miles W. ½ S. from the Smalls.	Submarine	No warning	Torpedo	35 including Master.
†Ava	5,076	27 (?)	Off S. Ireland (?)	Submarine (?)	No warning (?)	Torpedo (?)	92 including Master.
Perce (S.V.)	364	28	150 miles N.E. by N. (true) from St. Paul Rocks.	Seeadler	Captured	Gunfire	—
†Ravensbourne	1,226	31	8 miles S.E. from Tyne.	Mine	Mine	Mine	3
†Dundee	2,278	31	10 miles N. by W. from St. Ives Head.	Submarine	No warning	Torpedo	1
Ida Duncan (tug)	139	31	½ mile E. from S. Gare L.H.	Mine	Mine	Mine	6 including Master.
Lux	2,621	(?)	Atlantic	Submarine (?)	No warning (?)	Torpedo (?)	29 including Master.

FEBRUARY 1917.

Name.	Gross Tons.	Date.	Position.	Cause of Loss.	How attacked.	How sunk.	Lives lost.
		Feb.					
Essonite	589	1	3 miles N.N.W. from Trevose Head.	Submarine	No warning	Torpedo	10
Isle of Arran (S.V.)	1,918	2	100 miles S. from Old Head of Kinsale.	Submarine	Captured	Bombs	—
Eavestone	1,858	3	95 miles W. from Fastnet.	Submarine	Captured	Gunfire	5 including Master.
†Port Adelaide	8,181	3	180 miles S.W. from Fastnet.	Submarine	No warning	Torpedo	Master made prisoner.
†Hollinside	2,682	3	115 miles W.S.W. from Fastnet.	Submarine	No warning	Torpedo	1
Belford (S.V.)	1,905	3	110 miles W. from Fastnet.	Submarine	Captured	Bombs	—
Floridian	4,777	4	200 miles W. by N. from Fastnet.	Submarine	Captured	Torpedo	5 Master, chief engineer, and W/T operator made prisoners.
†Palmleaf	5,489	4	230 miles W. from Fastnet.	Submarine	No warning	Torpedo	Master and chief engineer made prisoners.
†Turino	4,241	4	174 miles W. from Fastnet.	Submarine	No warning	Torpedo	4
†Ghazee	5,084	4	2 miles S.S.W. from Galley Head.	Submarine	No warning	Torpedo	—
†Dauntless	2,157	4	10 miles from La Coubre Point.	Submarine	Captured	Bombs	15
Hurstwood	1,229	5	6 miles N.E. from Whitby.	Submarine	No warning	Torpedo	4
†Warley Pickering.	4,196	5	46 miles W. by N. from Fastnet.	Submarine	No warning	Torpedo	—
†Wartenfels	4,511	5	120 miles S.W. from Fastnet.	Submarine	No warning	Torpedo	2 Master made prisoner
Azul	3,074	5	180 miles W. ½ N. from Fastnet.	Submarine	No warning	Torpedo	11
†Cliftonian	4,303	6	4½ miles S. ¾ E. from Galley Head.	Submarine	No warning	Torpedo	—

Name.	Gross Tons.	Date.	Position.	Cause of Loss.	How attacked.	How sunk.	Lives lost.
		1917. Feb.					
†Saxon Briton	1,337	6	3 miles N.N.E. from Gurnard Head.	Submarine	No warning	Torpedo	2
†Vestra	1,021	6	5 miles N.E. from Hartlepool.	Submarine	No warning	Torpedo	2
†Crown Point	5,218	6	55 miles W. from Scilly Isles.	Submarine	No warning	Torpedo	7 including Master.
Corsican Prince	2,776	7	3 miles E. from Whitby.	Submarine	No warning	Torpedo	1
†Saint Ninian	3,026	7	3 miles E. from Whitby.	Submarine	No warning	Torpedo	15 including Master.
†California	8,669	7	38 miles W. by S. from Fastnet.	Submarine	No warning	Torpedo	43
Boyne Castle	245	7	12 miles N. by E. from St. Abb's Head.	Submarine	Captured	Gunfire	—
Saxonian	4,855	7	270 miles W. by N. from Fastnet.	Submarine	Capture	are	1
†Vedamore	6,330	7	20 miles W. from Fastnet.	Submarine	No war...	Torpedo	23
†Gravine	1,242	7	85 miles W. from Fastnet.	Submarine	No warning	Torpedo	7 Master and 14 made prisoners.
Hanna Larsen	1,311	8	20 miles E. ¾ N. from Spurn Point.	Submarine	Captured	Bombs	1
Lullington	2,816	8	3 miles E. from Royal Sovereign L.V.	Mine	Mine	Mine	—
†Mantola	8,253	8	143 miles W.S.W. from Fastnet.	Submarine	No warning	Torpedo	7
Beechtree	1,277	10	11 miles S.E. from Start Point.	Submarine	No warning	Torpedo	—
Japanese Prince	4,876	10	24 miles S.W. from Bishop Rock.	Submarine	No warning	Torpedo	—
Sallagh	325	10	Off Bardsey Island	Submarine	Captured	Bombs	1
Olivia	242	11	21 miles S.W. ½ S. from Bardsey Island.	Submarine	Captured	Bombs	—
Voltaire	409	11	25 miles N.E. by N. from S. Bishop.	Submarine	Captured	Bombs	—
Netherlee	4,227	11	92 miles W. ½ S. from Fastnet.	Submarine	No warning	Torpedo	2
†Lycia	2,715	11	20 miles N.E. by N. from S. Bishop.	Submarine	Captured	Bombs	—
Ada (S.V.)	186	11	8 miles S. from Anvil Point.	Submarine	Captured	Gunfire	—
†Afric	11,999	12	12 miles S.S.W. from Eddystone.	Submarine	No warning	Torpedo	5
Foreland	1,960	12	6 miles S. ¾ W. from Shipwash L.V.	Mine	Mine	Mine	—
Lucent	1,409	12	20 miles E. from Lizard.	Submarine	Captured	Gunfire	—
Cilicia	3,750	12	5 miles S. from Dassen Island, Cape of Good Hope.	Mine	Mine	Mine	—
Norwood	798	11(?)	North Sea	Mine (?)	Mine (?)	Mine (?)	18 including Master.
Percy Roy (S.V.)	110	13	30 miles S.E. from Cabrera Island.	Submarine	Captured	Bombs	—
†F. D. Lambert	2,195	13	1 mile E. from Royal Sovereign L.V.	Submarine	No warning	Torpedo	—

33 MERCHANT VESSELS CAPTURED OR SUNK.

Name.	Gross Tons.	Date.	Position.	Cause of Loss.	How attacked.	How sunk.	Lives lost.
		1917. Feb.					
†Inishowen Head	3,050	14	1¼ miles S. from Skokham Island	Submarine	No warning	Torpedo	1
Ferga	791	14	15 miles S. from Bardsey Island.	Submarine	Captured	Gunfire	—
Margarita	375	14	20 miles S.W. by S. from Bardsey Island.	Submarine	Captured	Bombs	—
Hopemoor	3,740	14	20 miles N.W. from the Skelligs.	Submarine	No warning	Torpedo	—
Marie Leonhardt	1,466	14	2¼ miles E. ½ N. from Sunk L.V.	Mine	Mine	Mine	5
Greenland	1,763	14	20 miles S.W. from Bardsey Island.	Submarine	Captured	Bombs	—
†Longscar	2,777	14	15 miles S.W. from River Gironde.	Submarine	Captured	Bombs	2 gunners made prisoners.
Eudora (S.V.)	1,991	14	30 miles S.S.W. from Fastnet.	Submarine	Captured	Gunfire	—
†Marion Dawson	2,300	14	8 miles S.S.W. from Ile d'Oleron.	Submarine	Captured	Bombs	—
Afton	1,156	15	23 miles N. by E. from Strumble Head.	Submarine	Captured	Bombs	—
Kyanite	564	15	27 miles S.S.W. from Bardsey Island.	Submarine	Captured	Bombs	—
Leven (dredger)	775	15	¾ mile S. by E. ½ E. from Newhaven Breakwater.	Mine	Mine	Mine	—
†Brecknockshire	8,423	15	490 miles E. by N. (true) from Cape Frio, Brazil.	Möwe	Captured	Not known	Crew made prisoners.
French Prince	4,766	15	490 miles E.N.E. (true) from Cape Frio, Brazil.	Möwe	Captured	Not known	Crew made prisoners.
Lady Ann	1,016	16	3 miles E. by S. from Scarborough.	Submarine	No warning	Torpedo	11 including Master.
Queenswood	2,701	16	6 miles S.W. from Hartland Point.	Submarine	Captured	Gunfire	3
Rose Dorothea (S.V.).	147	16	30 miles S.E. by E. from Cape St. Vincent.	Submarine	Captured	Bombs	—
Mayola (S.V.)	146	16	50 miles S.E. by E. from Cape St. Vincent.	Submarine	Captured	Bombs	—
Eddie	2,652	16	550 miles N.E. by E. ¾ E. (true) from Cape Frio, Brazil.	Möwe	Captured	Not known	Crew made prisoners.
†Iolo	3,840	17	40 miles S. by W. from the Fastnet.	Submarine	No warning	Torpedo	2 Master, chief engineer, and 2 gunners made prisoners.
†Romsdalen	2,548	17	10 miles S.W. from Portland Bill.	Submarine	No warning	Torpedo	—
Valdes	2,233	17	7 miles S. from Portland Bill.	Submarine	No warning	Torpedo	11
†Okement	4,349	17	140 miles S.E. by S. from Malta.	Submarine	No warning	Torpedo	11 including Master.
Worcestershire	7,175	17	10 miles S.W. from Colombo.	Mine	Mine	Mine	2
Netherton (S.V.)	199	18	16 miles S. from Anvil Point.	Submarine	Captured	Bombs	—

MERCHANT VESSELS CAPTURED OR SUNK. 34

Name.	Gross Tons.	Date.	Position.	Cause of Loss.	How attacked.	How sunk.	Lives lost.
		1917. Feb.					
Triumph (S.V.)	46	18	45 miles N.N.W. from Roches Douvres.	Submarine -	Captured -	Gunfire -	—
Brigade - -	425	19	12 miles N.W. ½ W. from Cayeux - sur-Somme.	Submarine -	Captured -	Gunfire -	—
†Corso - -	3,242	19	110 miles S. by W. from Malta.	Submarine -	No warning -	Torpedo -	Master, chief engineer, and 2 gunners made prisoners.
Centurion (S.V.)	1,828	19	15 miles S.E. from the Lizard.	Submarine -	Captured -	Bombs -	—
†Headley - -	4,953	19	35 miles S.S.W. from Bishop Rock.	Submarine -	No warning -	Torpedo -	—
Pinmore (S.V.) -	2,431	19	540 miles N.W. ½ N. (true) from St. Paul Rocks.	Seeadler -	Captured -	Bombs -	—
†Rosalie - -	4,237	20	8 miles E. from Jidjelli, Algeria.	Submarine -	No warning -	Torpedo -	21 including Master.
Perseus - -	6,728	21	11 miles W. from Colombo.	Mine - -	Mine - -	Mine -	3
†Wathfield - -	3,012	21	15 miles N. from C. Carbon.	Submarine -	No warning -	Torpedo -	18 including Master.
Tecwyn (motor)	132	21	20 miles S. from Portland Bill.	Submarine -	Captured -	Gunfire -	—
John Miles -	687	22	11 miles S.E. from Hartlepool.	Mine - -	Mine - -	Mine -	10 including Master.
Invercauld (S.V.)	1,416	22	22 miles S.E. from Mine Head, Ireland.	Submarine -	Captured -	Torpedo -	—
Nostra Signora del Porto Salvo (S.V.).	136	22	35 miles N.W. from Marittimo.	Submarine -	Captured -	Bombs -	—
†Trojan Prince -	3,196	23	5 miles N.W. from Point Shershel.	Submarine -	No warning -	Torpedo -	2
Grenadier -	1,004	23	6 miles E.N.E. from Shipwash L.V.	Submarine -	No warning -	Torpedo -	8 including Master.
Belgier - -	4,588	23	30 miles W. from Belle Ile.	Submarine -	Captured -	Gunfire -	—
†Iser - -	2,160	23	14 miles N.W. from Belle Ile.	Submarine -	No warning -	Torpedo -	1
†Longhirst - -	3,053	23	20 miles E. from Cape Bon.	Submarine -	No warning -	Torpedo -	2
Katherine - -	2,926	23	200 miles N.E. by N. ¾ N. (true) from St. Paul Rocks.	Möwe - -	Captured -	Not known	Crew made prisoners.
†Beneficent -	1,963	24	Off Mouth of Tees	Mine - -	Mine - -	Mine -	3
†Falcon - -	2,244	24	190 miles W.N.W. from Fastnet.	Submarine -	Captured -	Gunfire -	—
†Dorothy - -	3,806	24	25 miles S.E. by S. ½ S. from Pantellaria.	Submarine -	No warning -	Torpedo -	6
†Laconia - -	18,099	25	160 miles N.W. by W. from Fastnet.	Submarine -	No warning -	Torpedo -	12
†Aries - -	3,071	25	190 miles N.W. by W. from Fastnet.	Submarine -	Captured -	Gunfire -	Master made prisoner.
†Huntsman -	7,160	25	180 miles N.W. by W. from the Fastnet.	Submarine -	No warning -	Torpedo -	2
†Algiers - -	2,361	26	3 miles S. from Owers L.V.	Submarine -	No warning -	Torpedo -	8

35 MERCHANT VESSELS CAPTURED OR SUNK.

Name.	Gross Tons.	Date.	Position.	Cause of Loss.	How attacked.	How sunk.	Lives lost.
Sea Gull	144	1917. Feb. 26	4 miles off Folkestone.	Mine	Mine	Mine	2
Hannah Crossdell (S.V.).	151	26	4 miles W. ¾ N. from St. Ann's Head.	Mine (?)	Mine (?)	Mine (?)	4 including Master.
†Burnby	3,665	26	20 miles N. from C. Falcone.	Submarine	No warning	Torpedo	Master made prisoner.
†Clan Farquhar	5,858	26	80 miles N. from Ben Ghazi.	Submarine	No warning	Torpedo	49 including Master, 2nd engineer made prisoner.
British Yeoman (S.V.).	1,953	26	230 miles N.W. by N. ¾ N. (true) from St. Paul Rocks.	Seeadler	Captured	—	—
†Tritonia	4,445	27	20 miles N.W. by W. from Tearagh Is.	Submarine	No warning	Torpedo	2
Galgorm Castle (S.V.).	1,596	27	90 miles W. from the Fastnet.	Submarine	Captured	Gunfire	11
†Brodmore	4,071	27	70 miles N.W. by N. from Marsa Susa.	Submarine	No warning	Torpedo	Master made prisoner.
Turritella	5,528	27	600 miles W. ¾ S. (true) from Minikoi.	Wolf	Captured	Scuttled, 4 Mar.	—
Harriet Williams (S.V.).	157	28	15 miles N.N.E from C. Antifer.	Submarine	Captured	Bombs	—

MARCH 1917.

Name.	Gross Tons.	Date.	Position.	Cause of Loss.	How attacked.	How sunk.	Lives lost.
†Drina	11,483	Mar. 1	2 miles W. from Skokham Island.	Submarine	No warning	Torpedo	15
Tillycorthie	382	1	16 miles N. ½ E. from Longstone.	Submarine	Captured	Gunfire	Master made prisoner.
Chatburn	1,942	1	22 miles N.E. ½ E. from Cape Barfleur.	Submarine	No warning	Torpedo	—
†Munificent	3,270	1	3½ miles N.N.W. from Cape Gris Nez.	Submarine	No warning	Torpedo	3
Jumna	4,152	1	650 miles W. (true) from Minikoi.	Wolf	Captured	Bombs	—
Utopia (S.V.)	184	2	20 miles S.S.W. from Dungeness.	Submarine	Captured	Gunfire	—
Gazelle (S.V.)	119	2	20 miles S.S.W. from Dungeness.	Submarine	Captured	Bomb	—
Meldon	2,514	3	Firth of Lorne	Mine	Mine	Mine	—
Connaught	2,646	3	29 miles S. by W. ½ W. from Owers L.V.	Submarine	No warning	Torpedo	3
†River Forth	4,421	3	60 miles S. by E. from Malta.	Submarine	No warning	Torpedo	2
†Kincardine	4,108	3	20 miles N.E. from Tearagh Island.	Submarine	No warning	Torpedo	—
†Craigendoran	2,789	3	6 miles E. from Cape Sigli, Algeria.	Submarine	No warning	Torpedo	3 Master and chief engineer made prisoners.
†Sagamore	5,197	3	150 miles W. from the Fastnet.	Submarine	No warning	Torpedo	52 including Master.

Merchant Vessels Captured or Sunk. 36

Name.	Gross Tons.	Date.	Position.	Cause of Loss.	How attacked.	How sunk.	Lives lost.
		1917. Mar.					
†Newstead	2,836	3	150 miles W.N.W. from the Fastnet.	Submarine	No warning	Torpedo	15
The Macbain (S.V.).	291	4	20 miles S.S.W. from Portland Bill.	Submarine	Captured	Bomb	—
†Rhodanthe	3,061	4	330 miles N.N.W. (true) from St. Vincent (C.V.).	Möwe	Captured	Not known	Crew made prisoners.
Copenhagen	2,570	5	8 miles E. ½ N. from N. Hinder L.V.	Submarine	No warning	Torpedo	6
Cornelia	903	6	9 miles W.N.W. from the Skelligs.	Submarine	Captured	Gunfire	—
†Caldergrove	4,327	6	200 miles W.N.W. from the Fastnet.	Submarine	No warning	Torpedo	19 including Master.
Fenay Lodge	3,323	6	250 miles N.W. by W. ½ W. from the Fastnet.	Submarine	No warning	Torpedo	4 including Master.
Antonio	2,652	7	7 miles from Dartmouth.	Mine (?)	Mine (?)	Mine (?)	11 including Master.
†Baron Wemyss	1,605	7	73 miles N.W. by W. from the Fastnet.	Submarine	Captured	Torpedo	2 including Master.
Westwick	5,694	7	1 mile S. from Roche Point.	Mine	Mine	Mine	—
†Georgian	5,088	8	52 miles N. from C. Sidero.	Submarine	No warning	Torpedo	5
†Dunbarmoor	3,651	8	180 miles W.N.W. from the Fastnet.	Submarine	Captured	Gunfire	12 including Master.
Abeja (S.V.)	174	9	20 miles S.W. ½ S. from Start Point.	Submarine	Captured	Gunfire	—
†East Point	5,234	9	9 miles E. by S. ½ S. from the Eddystone.	Submarine	No warning	Torpedo	—
Inverlogie (S.V.)	2,347	9	15 miles S.W. from the Smalls.	Submarine	Captured	Torpedo	—
Mediterranean (S.V.).	105	10	13 miles S. from Hook Point, Waterford.	Submarine	Captured	Gunfire	—
T. Crowley (S.V.)	97	10	12 miles S. from Hook Point, Waterford.	Submarine	Captured	Gunfire	—
James Burton (Cook S.V.).	133	10	25 miles S.S.E. from Malaga.	Submarine	Captured	Gunfire	—
†Esmeraldas	4,678	10	420 miles W. by N. (true) from Lisbon.	Möwe	Captured	Not known	Crew made prisoners.
†Otaki	9,575	10	420 miles W. ¾ S. (true) from Lisbon.	Möwe	Captured	Torpedoes	6 including Master. Remainder made prisoners.
Wordsworth	3,509	11	680 miles E. (true) from Mahe, Seychelles.	Wolf	Captured	Bombs	—
Kwasind	2,211	11	Off Southwold	Mine	Mine	Mine	12
†Folia	6,705	11	4 miles E.S.E. from Ram Head, Youghal.	Submarine	No warning	Torpedo	7
Horngarth	3,609	11	220 miles E.N.E. (true) from St. Paul Rocks.	Seeadler	Captured	Bombs	1
G. A. Savage	357	11 (?)	Bristol Channel	Submarine (?)	No warning (?)	Torpedo (?)	9 including Master.

MERCHANT VESSELS CAPTURED OR SUNK.

Name.	Gross Tons.	Date.	Position.	Cause of Loss.	How attacked.	How sunk.	Lives lost.
		1917. Mar.					
Tandil	2,897	12	20 miles W. by N. ½ N. from Portland.	Submarine	No warning	Torpedo	4
Ambient	1,517	12	Off Aldeburgh	Mine	Mine	Mine	—
Pontypridd	1,556	12	Off Aldeburgh	Mine	Mine	Mine	3
Memnon	3,203	12	20 miles S.W. from Portland Bill.	Submarine	No warning	Torpedo	6
Glynymel	1,394	12	23 miles S. by W. from St. Catherine's Pt.	Submarine	Captured	Torpedo	1
†Bilswood	3,097	12	8 miles N.W. from Alexandria.	Mine	Mine	Mine	—
Lucy Anderson	1,073	12	55 miles E.S.E. from Noss Head, Wick.	Submarine	Captured	Gunfire	—
Topaz	696	12	27 miles E. by N. ½ N. from Cape Barfleur.	Submarine	No warning	Torpedo	3
†Brika	3,549	13	13 miles S.E. by S. from Coningbeg L.V.	Submarine	No warning	Torpedo	2
†Northwaite	3,626	13	14 miles W.N.W. from the Blaskets.	Submarine	No warning	Torpedo	...
†Norwegian	6,327	13	4 miles S.W. from Seven Heads, Co. Cork.	Submarine	No warning	Torpedo	5
†Coronda	2,733	13	180 miles N.W. from Tory Island.	Submarine	No warning	Torpedo	9
Elizabeth Eleanor (S.V.).	169	13	77 miles N.W. by W. ½ W. from Trevose Head.	Submarine	Captured	Gunfire	—
†Demeterton	6,048	13	730 miles E. by N. (true) from C. Race.	Möwe	Captured	Bombs	Crew made prisoners.
†Paignton	2,017	14	40 miles N.W. from the Skelligs.	Submarine	Captured	Gunfire	1
†Rose Lea	2,830	14	230 miles W. from Bishop Rock.	Submarine	No warning	Torpedo	—
†Bray Head	3,077	14	375 miles N.W. by W. from the Fastnet.	Submarine	Captured	Gunfire	21 including Master.
†Governor	5,524	14	930 miles W. ¼ S. (true) from the Fastnet.	Möwe	Captured	Torpedo	4 Remainder made prisoners.
†Frimaire	1,778	15	21 miles S.S.E. from Belle Ile.	Submarine	No warning	Torpedo	12 including Master.
Norma Pratt	4,416	16	150 miles W. from Bishop Rock.	Submarine	Captured	Torpedo	Chief officer and 3rd engineer made prisoners.
William Martin (S.V.).	104	16	9 miles S. by W. ½ W. from Ram Head, Youghal.	Submarine	Captured	Bombs	—
Sir Joseph (S.V.)	84	16	30 miles S.S.E. from Start Point.	Submarine	Captured	Bombs	—
†Narragansett	9,196	16	Off S.W. Ireland	Submarine	No warning	Torpedo	46 including Master.
Tasso	1,859	17	5 miles S. from Groix Island.	Submarine	No warning	Torpedo	19 including Master.

MERCHANT VESSELS CAPTURED OR SUNK.

Name.	Gross Tons.	Date.	Position.	Cause of Loss.	How attacked.	How sunk.	Lives lost.
		1917. Mar.					
†Antony	6,446	17	19 miles W. by N. from Coningbeg L.V.	Submarine	No warning	Torpedo	55
†Pola	3,061	18	280 miles W.N.W. from Ushant.	Submarine	No warning	Torpedo	5
†Trevose	3,112	18	230 miles W. by N. ½ N. from Ushant.	Submarine	No warning	Torpedo	2
†Joshua Nicholson	1,853	18	Off Wolf Rock	Submarine	No warning	Torpedo	26 including Master.
Greypoint	894	18	2 miles S.E. by E. from Broadstairs Landing.	T.B.D.	No warning	Torpedo	—
†Ainwick Castle	5,900	19	310 miles W. ½ S. from Bishop Rock.	Submarine	No warning	Torpedo	40
†Frinton	4,194	19	320 miles W. by N. ½ N. from Ushant.	Submarine	No warning	Torpedo	4
†Hazelpark	1,964	20	3 miles S. by E. from Start Point.	Submarine	No warning	Torpedo	—
†Stanley	3,987	21	230 miles W. by N. from the Fastnet.	Submarine	No warning	Torpedo	8
Rio Sorocaba	4,307	21	10 miles S. from Eddystone.	Submarine	Captured	Bombs	—
Hindustan	3,692	21	150 miles W.N.W. from the Fastnet.	Submarine	No warning	Torpedo	2
Rio Colorado	3,565	22	Entrance to River Tyne.	Mine	Mine	Mine	10 including Master.
†Providence	2,970	22	1¼ miles S. by W. ½ W. from Barrels L.V.	Submarine	No warning	Torpedo	—
†Rotorua	11,140	22	24 miles E. from Start Point.	Submarine	No warning	Torpedo	1
Chorley	3,828	22	25 miles E. by S. from Start Point.	Submarine	No warning	Torpedo	—
†Stuart Prince	3,597	22	85 miles N. by W. from Broad Haven.	Submarine	No warning	Torpedo	20 including Master.
†C'an Macmillan	4,525	23	5 miles S.W. from Newhaven.	Submarine	No warning	Torpedo	—
†Maine	3,616	23	11 miles S.E. by E. from Start Point.	Submarine	No warning	Torpedo	—
†Eptalofos	4,431	23	47 miles N.W. from Malta.	Submarine	No warning	Torpedo	Master, 2 officers, 4 engineers, 1 gunner made prisoners.
Achille Adam	460	23	31 miles S.E. by S. from Beachy Head.	Submarine	Captured	Bombs	6
Exchange	279	23	30 miles N.W. from Cayeux.	Submarine	Captured	Gunfire	8
Fairearn	592	24	16 miles W.N.W. from S. Stack, Holyhead.	Submarine	Captured	Bombs	—
Ennistown	689	24	10 miles S.E. from S. Arklow L.V.	Submarine	Captured	Bombs	—
Howe (S.V.)	175	24	4 miles N.E. from N. Arklow L.V.	Submarine	Captured	Bombs	—

MERCHANT VESSELS CAPTURED OR SUNK.

Name.	Gross Tons.	Date.	Position.	Cause of Loss.	How attacked.	How sunk.	Lives lost.
		1917. Mar.					
†Queen Eugenie	4,358	25	23 miles N.N.E. from Cani Rocks.	Submarine	No warning	Torpedo	35 (including Master). 1 apprentice and 1 gunner made prisoners.
†Adenwen	3,793	25	6 miles S.E. by E. from N. Arklow L.V.	Submarine	No warning	Torpedo	10
†Vellore	4,926	25	21 miles N.W. by N. from Alexandria.	Submarine	No warning	Torpedo	Master and chief engineer prisoners.
†Berbera	4,352	25	60 miles E. from Catania.	Submarine	No warning	Torpedo	1 2nd officer and 2 cadets made prisoners.
†Baynaen	3,227	25	20 miles N.W. by W. from Belle Ile.	Submarine	No warning	Torpedo	5
Huntleys (S.V.)	186	25	28 miles S.S.W. from Beachy Head.	Submarine	Captured	Bombs	—
Mary Annie (SV.).	154	25	28 miles S.S.W. from Beachy Head.	Submarine	Captured	Bombs	—
Brandon (S.V.)	130	25(?)	Not known	Submarine (reported).	Not known	Not known	4 including Master.
†Ledbury	3,046	26	90 miles N. by E. from Ben Ghazi.	Submarine	No warning	Torpedo	3
†Holgate	2,604	27	10 miles N.W. from the Skelligs.	Submarine	No warning	Torpedo	Master made prisoner.
†Kelvinhead	3,063	27	¾ mile W.S.W. from Liverpool Bar L.V.	Mine	Mine	Mine	—
Neath (auxiliary barque).	5,548	27	28 miles S. by E. from the Fastnet.	Submarine	No warning	Torpedo	Master made prisoner.
†Thracia	2,891	27	12 miles N. from Belle Ile.	Submarine	No warning	Torpedo	36 including Master.
†Glenogle	7,682	27	207 miles S.W. from the Fastnet.	Submarine	No warning	Torpedo	—
Oakwell	248	28	3 miles N.E. from N. Cheek, Robin Hood Bay.	Mine	Mine	Mine	4
†Snowdon Range	4,662	28	25 miles W. from Bardsey Island.	Submarine	No warning	Torpedo	4
Hero (tug)	66	28	Entrance to River Wear.	Mine	Mine	Mine	1 (Master).
†Gafsa	3,974	28	10 miles S.E. ½ S. from Kinsale Head.	Submarine	No warning	Torpedo	7
Ardglass	778	28	4 miles E. from S. Arklow L.V.	Submarine	Captured	Bombs	—
Wychwood	1,985	28	4 miles S.S.W. from S. Arklow L.V.	Submarine	No warning	Torpedo	3
†Cannizaro	6,133	28	145 miles S.S.W. from the Fastnet.	Submarine	No warning	Torpedo	—
Harvest Home (S.V.).	103	28	4 miles N.E. from S. Arklow L.V.	Submarine	Captured	Gunfire	—
Ruby	234	28	2½ miles from Auskerry, Orkney Is.	Mine	Mine	Mine	6 including Master.

Merchant Vessels Captured or Sunk.

Name.	Gross Tons.	Date.	Position.	Cause of Loss.	How attacked.	How sunk.	Lives lost.
		1917. Mar.					
South Arklow Light Vessel.	—	28	10 miles S.E. by S. ½ S. from Arklow.	Submarine	Boarded	Bombs	—
†Mascota	674	29	8 miles E. from Lowestoft.	T.B.D.	Captured	Not known	7 (seven made prisoners).
Kathleen Lily	521	29	2 miles E. from N. Cheek, Robin Hood Bay.	Mine	Mine	Mine	4 including Master.
Lincolnshire	3,965	29	8 miles S.W. by S. from Hook Point, Waterford.	Submarine	No warning	Torpedo	—
†Bywell	1,522	29	3 miles E. from Scarborough.	Submarine	No warning	Torpedo	—
†Crispin	3,965	29	14 miles S. from Hook Point, Waterford.	Submarine	No warning	Torpedo	8
Conoid (S.V.)	165	29	3 miles N. from C. Barfleur.	Submarine	Captured	Gunfire	—
†Somme	1,828	30	20 miles E. by N. from C. Barfleur.	Submarine	No warning	Torpedo	5
Dee (S.V.)	1,169	30	410 miles W. by S. (true) from Cape Leeuwin.	Wolf	Captured	Bombs	—
Harberton	1,443	30 (?)	North Sea	Submarine (?)	No warning (?)	Torpedo (?)	15 including Master.
Endymion (S.V.)	67	30	English Channel	Submarine (reported).	Not known	Not known	4 including Master.
†Brodness	5,736	31	5 miles W.N.W. from Port Anzio.	Submarine	No warning	Torpedo	—
Boaz (S.V.)	111	31	15 miles N.E. from C. Barfleur.	Submarine	Captured	Bombs	—
●Primrose (S.V.)	113	31	35 miles S.E. from Start Point.	Submarine	Gunfire	Gunfire	1
Gippeswic (S.V.)	116	31	15 miles N.E. from C. Barfleur.	Submarine	Captured	Bombs	—
Braefield	427	31 (?)	Bristol Channel	Submarine (?)	No warning (?)	Torpedo (?)	10 including Master.
●Coonagh	1,412	(?)	English Channel	Submarine	Not known	Not known	10 including Master.
●Acton	207	(?)	English Channel	Submarine	Not known	Not known	6 including Master.
APRIL,		**1917.**					
†Warren	3,709	1	20 miles S.W. from Civita Vecchia.	Submarine	No warning	Torpedo	3 (Master made prisoner).
†Kasenga	4,652	1	2 miles from the Hormigas, Cape Palos.	Submarine	No warning	Torpedo	—
●Eastern Belle (S.V.)	97	1	30 miles S.W. from St. Catherine's Point.	Submarine	Captured	Bombs	—
●Silvia (S.V.)	164	1	15 miles S.S.E. from the Owers L.V.	Submarine	Captured	Bombs	—
†Zambesi	3,759	1	15 miles N. by W. from Alexandria.	Submarine	No warning	Torpedo	3
†Britannia	3,129	2	22 miles W.N.W. from Pantellaria.	Submarine	No warning	Torpedo	Master and W/T operator made prisoners.
†Ardgask	4,542	3	15 miles S.W. from C. Rosello, Sicily.	Submarine	No warning	Torpedo	1

41   MERCHANT VESSELS CAPTURED OR SUNK.

Name.	Gross Tons.	Date.	Position.	Cause of Loss.	How attacked.	How sunk.	Lives lost.
		1917. Apr.					
Ellen James (S.V.)	165	3	Bay of Biscay	Submarine	Captured	Gunfire	5 including Master.
†Parkgate	3,232	4	80 miles N.E. from Cap de Fer.	Submarine	Captured	Bombs	16 Master made prisoner.
†Margit	2,490	4	80 miles S.W. ½ W. from C. Matapan.	Submarine	No warning	Torpedo	—
†Hunstanton	4,504	4	36 miles W. from Scilly Islands.	Submarine	No warning	Torpedo	--
†City of Paris	9,239	4	46 miles S. by E. from Cap d'Antibes.	Submarine	No warning	Torpedo	122
†Canadian	9,309	5	47 miles N.W. by W. from the Fastnet.	Submarine	No warning	Torpedo	1 Master.
†Calliope	3,829	5	35 miles S.W. from Ustica.	Submarine	No warning	Torpedo	6 including Master, 1st and 2nd Officers and 3rd Engineer made prisoners.
†Benheather	4,701	5	110 miles W.N.W. from the Fastnet.	Submarine	No warning	Torpedo	—
• Gower Coast	804	5 (?)	English Channel	Mine (?)	Mine (?)	Mine (?)	15 including Master.
†Spithead	4,697	6	12 miles N. by W. from Damietta Lt.	Submarine	No warning	Torpedo	1 Master and Chief Engineer made prisoners.
†Presto	1,143	6	4 miles E. from Roker Point, Sunderland.	Mine	Mine	Mine	6
†Powhatan	6,117	6	25 miles N. by W. from N. Rona.	Submarine	No warning	Torpedo	36 Master made prisoner.
†Rosalind	6,535	6	180 miles W.N.W. from the Fastnet.	Submarine	No warning	Torpedo	2
†Maplewood	3,239	7	47 miles S.W. from C. Sperone, Sardinia.	Submarine	Captured	Torpedo	Master made prisoner.
†Salmo	1,721	7	210 miles N.W. from the Fastnet.	Submarine	No warning	Torpedo	2
†Trefusis	2,642	7	30 miles S.E. from C. Pula, Sardinia.	Submarine	Captured	Bombs	Master, Chief Officer, and Chief Engineer made prisoners.
†Petridge	1,712	8	200 miles W.N.W. from Ushant.	Submarine	No warning	Torpedo	Master and one gunner made prisoners.
Geilan Bahri (S.V.)	19	8	54 miles from Alexandria.	Submarine	Captured	Bomb	—
†Umvoti	2,616	8	200 miles N.W. by W. from Ushant.	Submarine	No warning	Torpedo	4 Master and gunner made prisoners.

MERCHANT VESSELS CAPTURED OR SUNK.   42

Name.	Gross Tons.	Date.	Position.	Cause of Loss.	How attacked.	How sunk.	Lives lost.
†Trrington	5,597	1917. Apr. 8	Not known	Submarine	No warning	Torpedo	34 Master made prisoner.
Kittiwake	1,866	9	25 miles N.W. from the Maas L.V.	Submarine	No warning	Torpedo	7
†Dalton	3,486	10	25 miles S. by W. from C. Matapan.	Submarine	No warning	Torpedo	3 Master made prisoner.
Pluto	1,266	10	32 miles S.E. by E. from Lowestoft.	Submarine	No warning	Torpedo	—
● Salta (Hospital Ship).	7,284	10	½ mile N. from Whistle Buoy, Havre.	Mine	Mine	Mine	79
Miss Morris (S.V.)	156	11	20 miles S.E. from Garrucha, Spain.	Submarine	Captured	Bomb	—
†Vine Branch	3,442	11 (?)	Not known	Submarine	No warning (probably).	Torpedo	44 including Master.
†Quaggy	993	11	3 miles E. from N. Cheek, Robin Hood Bay.	Mine	Mine	Mine	2
†Imperial Transport.	4,648	11	140 miles N.W. by N. ½ N. from Alexandria.	Submarine	No warning	Torpedo	Master made prisoner.
†Cyfarthfa	3,014	11	32 miles W.S.W. from Cerigotto.	Submarine	No warning	Torpedo	Master made prisoner.
†Tremorvah	3,654	11	70 miles N.N.W. from C. Bougaroni.	Submarine	Captured	Gunfire	Master, Chief Engineer, and two gunners made prisoners
†Duchess of Cornwall.	1,706	11	5 miles N. from C. Barfleur.	Submarine	No warning	Torpedo	23 including Master.
†Glencliffe	3,673	12	2¼ miles S.E. from Tabarca Island, Spain.	Submarine	No warning	Torpedo	1 Chief Engineer and two gunners made prisoners.
†Kildale	3,830	12	40 miles E. by S. from Pantellaria.	Submarine	No warning	Torpedo	1
†Toro	3,066	12	200 miles W.N.W. from Ushant.	Submarine	No warning	Torpedo	14 Master and one gunner made prisoners.
● †Lismore	1,305	12	22 miles N.W. by N. ½ N. from Havre.	Submarine	No warning	Torpedo	5
†Argyll	3,547	13	110 miles W. from Bishop Rock.	Submarine	No warning	Torpedo	22
†Bandon	1,456	13	2½ miles S.W. from Mine Head, S. Ireland.	Submarine	No warning	Torpedo	28
● Maria (S.V.)	175	13	25 miles S. by W. from Portland Bill.	Submarine	Captured	Bombs	—

43 MERCHANT VESSELS CAPTURED OR SUNK.

Name.	Gross Tons.	Date.	Position.	Cause of Loss.	How attacked.	How sunk.	Lives lost.
		1917. Apr.					
†Zara	1,331	13	90 miles W. ¾ W. from Helliso Island.	Submarine	No warning	Torpedo	27
†Kariba	3,697	13	260 miles W.N.W. from Ushant.	Submarine	No warning	Torpedo	13
Strathcona	1,881	13	145 miles W.N.W. from Ronaldshay.	Submarine	Captured	Bombs	9 Master, chief and 3rd engineers made prisoners.
Spray	1,072	14	3½ miles N.E. from Tyne Pier.	Mine	Mine	Mine	—
†Hermione	4,011	14	1½ miles S. from Coningbeg L.V.	Mine	Mine	Mine	—
Patagonier	3,832	14	135 miles W. from Gibraltar.	Submarine	Captured	Gunfire	Master made prisoner.
†Mashobra	8,236	15	140 miles S.W. from C. Matapan.	Submarine	No warning	Torpedo	8 Master made prisoner.
Alert	777	15	Off Dover	Mine	Mine	Mine	11
†Cameronia	10,963	15	150 miles E. from Malta.	Submarine	No warning	Torpedo	11
†Arcadian	8,939	15	26 miles N.E. from Milo.	Submarine	No warning	Torpedo	35
†Cairndhu	4,019	15	25 miles W. from Beachy Head.	Submarine	No warning	Torpedo	11
Victoria (S.V.)	165	16	30 miles S.W. from Beachy Head.	Submarine	Captured	Bombs	—
Rochester Castle (S.V.)	102	16	5 miles W.S.W. from C. Grisnez.	Submarine	Captured	Gunfire	—
Eduard (S.V.)	476	16	12 miles S.W. from Beachy Head.	Submarine	Captured	Bombs	—
Marden	297	16	6 miles N.W. from C. Grisnez.	Submarine	Gunfire	Gunfire	1 (Master).
Towergate	3,697	16	250 miles N.W. by W. from the Fastnet.	Submarine	Captured	Torpedo	—
Queen Mary	5,658	16	180 miles N.W. by W. from the Fastnet.	Submarine	No warning	Torpedo	9
Charles Goodanew.	791	17	3½ miles E.N.E. from Rattray Head.	Mine	Mine	Mine	13 including Master.
Brisbane River	4,989	17	140 miles W. from Gibraltar.	Submarine	Captured	Bombs	Master made prisoner.
†Aburi	3,730	17	125 miles N.W. from Tory Island.	Submarine	No warning	Torpedo	25
Cairnhill	4,981	17	160 miles N.W. from the Fastnet.	Submarine	Captured	Bombs	Master made prisoner.
†Kish	4,928	17	160 miles N.W. by W. from the Fastnet.	Submarine	No warning	Torpedo	6
Corfu	3,695	17	160 miles W. from Gibraltar.	Submarine	Captured	Bombs	3
William Shepherd (S.V.)	143	17	30 miles S. by W. from St. Anns Head.	Submarine	Captured	Bombs	—
Dantzic	108	17	30 miles S. by W. from St. Ann's Head.	Submarine	Captured	Bombs	—
Fernmoor	3,098	17	150 miles W. from Gibraltar.	Submarine	Captured	Bombs	—
Lanfranc (Hospital Ship).	6,287	17	42 miles N, ½ E. from Havre.	Submarine	No warning	Torpedo	5

MERCHANT VESSELS CAPTURED OR SUNK.

Name.	Gross Tons.	Date.	Position.	Cause of Loss.	How attacked.	How sunk.	Lives lost.
		1917. Apr.					
†Donegal	1,885	17	19 miles S. from Dean L.V.	Submarine	No warning	Torpedo	11
†Trekieve	3,087	18	100 miles W. from Gibraltar.	Submarine	No warning	Torpedo	3 Master made prisoner.
†Rhydwen	4,799	18	170 miles N.W. by W. ½ W. from the Fastnet.	Submarine	No warning	Torpedo	6
†Rowena	3,017	18	95 miles W. by S. ½ S. from Bishop Rock.	Submarine	No warning	Torpedo	1
†Castillian	1,923	18	110 miles N.W. by N. from Tory Island.	Submarine	No warning	Torpedo	10
Thomas (S.V.)	132	18	40 miles S.E. from C. St. Vincent.	Submarine	Captured	Bombs	—
†Lena	2,463	18 (?)	Not known	Submarine (reported)	No warning (probably).	Torpedo	25 including Master.
†Rinaldo	4,321	18	18 miles W. by N. from C. Shershel.	Submarine	No warning	Torpedo	—
†Scalpa	1,010	18	150 miles N.W. by W. from the Fastnet.	Submarine	No warning	Torpedo	—
†Cragoswald	3,235	18	60 miles W. by S. from Bishop Rock.	Submarine	No warning	Torpedo	2
†Sculptor	3,846	18	120 miles N.W. by W. from the Fastnet.	Submarine	No warning	Torpedo	1
Jewel (S.V.)	195	19	20 miles S.E. from Coningbeg L.V.	Submarine	Captured	Bombs	—
†Sowwell	3,781	19	170 miles W. ½ S. from Gibraltar.	Submarine	No warning	Torpedo	21 including Master.
Bethlehem (motor)	379	19	½ mile E. from S. Holm Buoy.	Mine	Mine	Mine	1
†Avocet	1,219	19	100 miles W.N.W. from the Fastnet.	Submarine	Captured	Torpedo	—
†Caithness	3,500	19	130 miles N.W. by N. from Cape Ortegal.	Submarine	No warning	Torpedo	47 including Master.
Poltava	945	19	3 miles E.N.E. from Souter Point.	Mine	Mine	Mine	—
†Howth Head	4,440	19	158 miles N.W. from the Fastnet.	Submarine	No warning	Torpedo	2
Senator Dantziger (S.V.)	164	19	15 miles S. by E. ½ E. from Newhaven.	Submarine	Captured	Gunfire	—
†Tempus	2,981	19	130 miles N.W. by W. ½ W. from the Fastnet.	Submarine	No warning	Torpedo	1
†Annapolis	4,567	19	74 miles N.W. ½ N. from Eagle Island.	Submarine	No warning	Torpedo	—
†Gold Coast	4,255	19	14 miles S. from Mine Head.	Submarine	No warning	Torpedo	—
†Elswick Manor	3,943	19	180 miles W. from Ushant.	Submarine	No warning	Torpedo	—
†Cilurnum	3,126	19	5 miles S.W. from Penmarch.	Submarine	No warning	Torpedo	1
Lowdaie	2,660	20	90 miles W. by N. from Gibraltar.	Submarine	Captured	Gunfire	—
†San Hilario	10,157	20	270 miles W. by N. from the Fastnet.	Submarine	Captured	Torpedo	Master made prisoner.
†Portloe	3,187	20	160 miles W.N.W. from the Fastnet.	Submarine	No warning	Torpedo	24 including Master.

45 MERCHANT VESSELS CAPTURED OR SUNK.

Name.	Gross Tons.	Date.	Position.	Cause of Loss.	How attacked.	How sunk.	Lives lost.
		1917. Apr.					
†Malakand	7,653	20	145 miles W. ½ N. from Bishop Rock.	Submarine	Captured	Torpedo	1
†Torr Head	5,911	20	160 miles N.W. by W. from the Fastnet.	Submarine	No warning	Torpedo	—
Nentmoor	3,535	20	140 miles W. from Gibraltar.	Submarine	Captured	Gunfire	—
Emma	2,520	20	200 miles S.W. by S. from the Fastnet.	Submarine	No warning	Torpedo	2
Ballochbuie	921	20	7 miles E. from May Island.	Submarine	No warning	Torpedo	3 including Master.
†Pontiac	1,698	21	56 miles S.W. ½ S. from the Fastnet.	Submarine	No warning	Torpedo	2
†Diadem	4,307	21	200 miles S.W. by W. from the Fastnet.	Submarine	No warning	Torpedo	—
†Telena	4,778	21	170 miles W.N.W. from the Fastnet.	Submarine	No warning	Torpedo	—
†Sebek	4,601	21	145 miles N.W. from Tory Island.	Submarine	No warning	Torpedo	1
†Warrior	3,674	21	7 miles N. from Fratelli Rocks.	Mine	Mine	Mine	1
†Neepawah	1,799	22	120 miles W. from Bishop Rock.	Submarine	Captured	Bombs	—
†Capenor	2,536	22	Entrance to La Pallice Roads.	Mine	Mine	Mine	—
†Dykland	4,291	22	200 miles W.N.W. from the Fastnet.	Submarine	No warning	Torpedo	—
†Imataka	1,776	23	15 miles S.S.W. from Daunts Rock.	Submarine	No warning	Torpedo	—
Auriac	871	23	5 miles E.S.E. from St. Abbs Head.	Submarine	Captured	Gunfire	1
Oswald	5,185	23	200 miles S.W. from the Fastnet.	Submarine	No warning	Torpedo	1
†Eptapyrgion	4,307	23	150 miles W. by S. from Scilly Islands.	Submarine	No warning	Torpedo	—
Arethusa (S.V.)	1,279	23	15 miles N.W. from Eagle Island.	Submarine	Captured	Bombs	—
†Anglesea	4,534	24	160 miles W. from Bishop Rock.	Submarine	No warning	Torpedo	—
Plutus	1,189	24	9 miles N.N.W. from Trevose Head.	Submarine	No warning	Torpedo	1
†Thistleard	4,136	24	135 miles WNW. from Tory Island.	Submarine	No warning	Torpedo	—
†Kenilworth	2,735	24	3½ miles S.W. by S. from St. Mathieu Point, Brest.	Mine	Mine	Mine	—
Barnton	1,858	24	40 miles W. by S. from Chassiron Light.	Submarine	No warning	Torpedo	14
Amulree (S.V.)	1,445	24	50 miles N. by E. from Tory Island.	Submarine	Captured	Not known	—
†Ferndene	3,770	24	150 miles W. from Bishop Rock.	Submarine	No warning	Torpedo	9 including Master.
†Abosso	7,782	24	180 miles W. by N. from the Fastnet.	Submarine	No warning	Torpedo	65

Name.	Gross Tons.	Date.	Position.	Cause of Loss.	How attacked.	How sunk.	Lives lost
		1917. Apr.					
Invermay (S.V.)	1,471	25	40 miles N.W. by N. from Eagle Island.	Submarine	Captured	Bombs	—
†Stephanotis (ex "Hackensack.")	4,060	25	180 miles N.W. by W. from the Fastnet.	Submarine	No warning	Torpedo	6
Heathfield (S.V.)	1,643	25	53 miles W. by N. from Eagle Island.	Submarine	Captured	Bombs	—
†Ballarat	11,120	25	24 miles S. by W. from Wolf Rock.	Submarine	No warning	Torpedo	—
Laura (S.V.)	335	25	150 miles W.N.W. from the Fastnet.	Submarine	Captured	Bombs	—
Hesperides	3,393	25	130 miles N.W. ½ W. from the Fastnet.	Submarine	No warning	Torpedo	1
†Hirondelle	1,648	25	13 miles S. by E. from Belle Ile.	Submarine	No warning	Torpedo	—
†Swanmore	6,373	25	230 miles W.N.W. from the Fastnet.	Submarine	No warning	Torpedo	11
†Vauxhall	3,629	25	110 miles N.W. by W. from the Fastnet.	Submarine	No warning	Torpedo	2
†Rio Lages	3,591	26	155 miles N.W. by W. from the Fastnet.	Submarine	No warning	Torpedo	3
†Manchester Citizen.	4,251	26	240 miles N.W. from the Fastnet.	Submarine	No warning	Torpedo	1
●†Alhama	1,744	26	1½ miles N. from Calais.	Mine	Mine	Mine	—
Agnes Cairns (S.V.)	146	26	8 miles N.E. from Alderney.	Submarine	Captured	Bombs	—
†Chertsey	3,264	26	4 miles N. from Algiers.	Submarine	No warning	Torpedo	—
●Athole (motor barge).	150	26	20 miles S. from Owers L.V.	Submarine	Captured	Gunfire	—
†Harflete	4,814	26	200 miles N.W. by W. from the Fastnet.	Submarine	Gunfire	Torpedo	1
Monitor (S.V.)	120	26	20 miles S. by E. from C. Antibes.	Submarine	Captured	Bombs	—
†Beemah	4,750	27	30 miles S.W. by S. from Bishop Rock.	Submarine	No warning	Torpedo	3
†Glencluny	4,812	27	4 miles N.W. from C. Sigli.	Submarine	No warning	Torpedo	4
†Dromore	4,398	27	140 miles N.W. by N. from Tory Island.	Submarine	No warning	Torpedo	—
†Karuma	2,995	27	5 miles N. from C. Sigli.	Submarine	No warning	Torpedo	2
†Dunmore Head	2,293	27	135 miles N.W. from Tory Island.	Submarine	No warning	Torpedo	—
Good Hope (S.V.)	77	27	15 miles N.N.W. from C. Barfleur.	Submarine	Gunfire	Gunfire	—
●Jessie (S.V.)	108	27	7 miles W. ½ S. from Portland Bill.	Submarine	Captured	Bombs	—
Burrowa (S.V.)	2,902	27	60 miles W. from Scilly Islands.	Submarine	Captured	Bombs	—
†Alfalfa	2,993	27 (?)	Not known	Submarine	No warning (probably).	Torpedo	30 including Master.
†Bullmouth	4,018	28	125 miles N.W. by N. from Tory Island.	Submarine	No warning	Torpedo	—

MERCHANT VESSELS CAPTURED OR SUNK.

Name.	Gross Tons.	Date.	Position.	Cause of Loss.	How attacked.	How sunk.	Lives lost.
		1917. Apr.					
†Jose de Larrinaga	5,017	28	150 miles W.N.W. from the Fastnet.	Submarine	No warning	Torpedo	12 including Master.
Port Jackson (S.V.)	2,309	28	180 miles W. by N. from the Fastnet.	Submarine	No warning	Torpedo	14 including Master.
†Pontiac	3,345	28	70 miles N. by E. from Marsa Susa.	Submarine	No warning	Torpedo	1 Master, chief engineer, and 2 gunners made prisoners.
● †Medina	12,350	28	3 miles E.N.E. from Start Point.	Submarine	No warning	Torpedo	6
†Teakwood	5,315	28	26 miles S.W. by W. from Sapienza Island.	Submarine	No warning	Torpedo	—
†Terence	4,309	28	150 miles N.W. by W. from the Fastnet.	Submarine	Gunfire	Torpedo	1
†Karonga	4,665	29	Strait of Messina	Submarine	No warning	Torpedo	18 Master prisoner.
Ellen Harrison (S.V.)	103	29	7 miles N.W. from Cherbourg.	Submarine	Gunfire	Gunfire	—
● Mermaid (S.V.)	76	29	18 miles S.S.W. from Anvil Point.	Submarine	Captured	Bombs	—
†Daleby	3,628	29	180 miles N.W. from the Fastnet.	Submarine	No warning	Torpedo	25 including Master.
Victoria	1,620	29	5 miles N.E. by N. from Scarborough.	Submarine	No warning	Torpedo	1
†Comedian	4,889	29	200 miles W. by S. from Bishop Rock.	Submarine	No warning	Torpedo	3 One gunner made prisoner.
†Ikbal	5,434	29	200 miles W. by S. from Bishop Rock.	Submarine	No warning	Torpedo	Master and 2 gunners made prisoners.
● Little Mystery (S.V.)	114	30	25 miles S.S.E. from Portland Bill.	Submarine	Captured	Bombs	—
†Delamere	1,525	30	110 miles W. by N. from the Fastnet.	Submarine	No warning	Torpedo	10
†Horsa	2,949	30	195 miles S.W. by W. from the Fastnet.	Submarine	No warning	Torpedo	11 including Master, 1 gunner made prisoner.
†Gretaston	3,395	(?)	Atlantic	Submarine (?)	Not known	Not known	29 including Master.
MAY 1917.		May					
†Gena	2,784	1	Off Southwold	Seaplane	No warning	Torpedo	—
C. A. Jaques	2,105	1	26 miles W.S.W. from Boulogne.	Submarine	No warning	Torpedo	3
†British Sun	5,565	1	230 miles E.S.E. from Malta.	Submarine	No warning	Torpedo	—
Ladywood	2,314	1	15 miles S.W. from Wolf Rock.	Submarine	Captured	Bombs	—
†Bagdale	3,045	1	13 miles N. by E. ½ E. from Creac'h Point, Ushant.	Submarine	No warning	Torpedo	23 including Master.

Merchant Vessels Captured or Sunk.

Name.	Gross Tons.	Date.	Position.	Cause of Loss.	How attacked.	How sunk.	Lives lost.
		1917. May					
Firelight	1,143	1	1¾ miles East from N. Tyne Pier.	Submarine	No warning	Torpedo	—
†San Urbano	6,458	1	180 miles N.W. by W. from the Fastnet.	Submarine	No warning	Torpedo	4
W. D. Potts (S.V.)	112	1	10 miles S.W. from Portpatrick.	Submarine	Captured	Gunfire	—
● John W. Pearn (S.V.)	75	1	40 miles S.S.E. from Start Point.	Submarine	Captured	Bombs	—
Helen	322	1	11 miles West from the Mull of Galloway.	Submarine	Captured	Bombs	—
Dora	296	1	11 miles West from Mull of Galloway.	Submarine	Captured	Bombs	—
Juno	1,384	2	17 miles E. ¾ S. from Cape Barfleur.	Submarine	No warning	Torpedo	1
†Tela	7,226	2	16 miles N.E. ½ E. from Cape Barfleur.	Submarine	No warning	Torpedo	—
Warnow	1,593	2	6 miles West from Trevose Head.	Submarine	No warning	Torpedo	14 including Master.
Saint Mungo	402	2	Ballyhalbert Bay, County Down.	Submarine	Captured	Bombs	—
Derrymore	485	2	Ballyhalbert Bay, County Down.	Submarine	Captured	Bombs	—
Amber	401	2	Ballyhalbert Bay, County Down.	Submarine	Captured	Bombs	—
Ernest (S.V.)	111	2	6 miles S.E. from Skulmartin L.V.	Submarine	Captured	Bombs	—
Morion	299	2	Ballyhalbert Bay, County Down.	Submarine	Captured	Bombs	—
†Troilus	7,625	2	140 miles W.N.W. from Malin Head.	Submarine	No warning	Torpedo	—
Beeswing (S.V.)	1,462	2	140 miles W. by N. from the Fastnet.	Submarine	Captured	Gunfire	—
●†Ussa	2,066	3	2½ miles N.W. from W. Entrance, Cherbourg.	Mine	Mine	Mine	—
†Frederick Knight	3,604	3	115 miles N.W. by W. from the Fastnet.	Submarine	No warning	Torpedo	—
Glen Tanar	817	3	1 mile N.E. from Girdleness.	Mine	Mine	Mine	—
Washington	5,080	3	Off Rapallo Bay	Submarine	No warning	Torpedo	—
●†Clodmoor	3,753	3	5 miles S.W. from Newhaven.	Submarine	No warning	Torpedo	—
Herrington	1,258	4	¾ mile E.S.E. from Red Head, Forfar.	Mine	Mine	Mine	—
Joseph (S.V.)	205	4	20 miles W. by N. from Caen Hr.	Submarine	Captured	Bombs	—
†Transylvania	14,315	4	2½ miles South from Cape Vado, Gulf of Genoa.	Submarine	No warning	Torpedo	12 including Master.
New Design, No. 2 (S.V.)	66	4	15 miles E. by S. from Tuskar Rock.	Submarine	Captured	Bombs	—
†Pilar de Larrinaga.	4,136	4	2 miles S.E. by S. from the Tuskar L.V.	Submarine	No warning	Torpedo	20 including Master.
†Harmattan	4,792	5	7 miles N. from Cape Rosa, Algeria.	Mine	Mine	Mine	36 including Master.
Greta	297	5	11 miles S.E. from Mine Head.	Submarine	Captured	Gunfire	—

49   MERCHANT VESSELS CAPTURED OR SUNK.

Name.	Gross Tons.	Date.	Position.	Cause of Loss.	How attacked.	How sunk.	Lives lost.
		1917. May					
Lodes	396	5	4 miles S.E. from Ballycottin.	Mine	Mine	Mine	7 including Master.
Angela (S.V.)	122	5	3 miles S.E. from Tyne.	Mine	Mine	Mine	5
†Feltria	5,254	5	8 miles S.E. from Mine Head.	Submarine	No warning	Torpedo	45 including Master.
†Adansi	2,644	6	80 miles W. ½ N. from the Fastnet.	Submarine	No warning	Torpedo	—
Hebble	904	6	1½ miles E. from Roker Pier, Sunderland.	Mine	Mine	Mine	5
Maude (S.V.)	93	7	Near Bardsey Island.	Submarine	Captured	Bombs	—
†Kinross	4,120	7	10 miles E. from Wolf Rock.	Submarine	No warning	Torpedo	—
†Repton	2,881	7	45 miles S.S.E. from Cape Matapan.	Submarine	No warning	Torpedo	3
†Polamhall	4,010	7	80 miles W.S.W. from Bishop Rock.	Submarine	No warning	Torpedo	—
Lowmount	2,070	7	4 miles S.E. from Nab L.V.	Mine	Mine	Mine	5
Killarney (S.V.)	1,413	8	200 miles W. by N. from the Fastnet.	Submarine	Captured	Gunfire	—
†Petunia	1,749	8	45 miles W. from Bishop Rock.	Submarine	No warning	Torpedo	2 Master and 2 gunners made prisoners.
Iris (S.V.)	75	8 (?)	English Channel	Submarine (?)	Captured (?)	Bombs (?)	4 including Master.
†Harpagus	5,866	9	62 miles S.W. from Planier Island.	Submarine	No warning	Torpedo	3 Master and Chief Engineer made prisoners.
Broomhill	1,392	10	9 miles S.W. from Portland Bill.	Submarine	Captured	Bombs	2
Tarpeia	538	11	9 miles N. from Port en Bessin.	Submarine	Captured	Bombs	—
†Calchas	6,748	11	5 miles W. by S. from Tearaght Island.	Submarine	No warning	Torpedo	—
†Barrister	3,679	11	7 miles S.W. from Mine Head, Waterford.	Submarine	No warning	Torpedo	—
Limasol (S.V.)	100	11	18 miles S.W. by W. from Monte Cristo.	Submarine	Captured	Bombs	—
†San Onofre	9,717	12	64 miles N.W. ½ N. from the Skelligs.	Submarine	No warning	Torpedo	1
†Galicia	5,922	12	3 miles East from Teignmouth.	Mine	Mine	Mine	—
†Refugio	2,642	12	115 miles N.W. ¼ W. from Tory Island.	Submarine	Captured	Gunfire	1
†Egyptian Prince	3,117	12	240 miles S.S.E. from Malta.	Submarine	Captured	Bombs	—
†Locksley Hall	3,635	12	30 miles S.E. by S. from Malta.	Submarine	No warning	Torpedo	6
†Zanoni	3,851	12	12 miles N.E. by E. from Cape Oropesa.	Submarine	Captured	Torpedo	1

Merchant Vessels Captured or Sunk.

Name.	Gross Tons.	Date.	Position.	Cause of Loss.	How attacked.	How sunk.	Lives lost.
		1917. May					
†Wirral	4,207	12	23 miles N.W. from Utvaer Island, Norway.	Submarine	No warning	Torpedo	1
†Jessmore	3,911	13	180 miles W.N.W. from the Fastnet.	Submarine	No warning	Torpedo	—
†Farley	3,692	14	70 miles S.W. ½ W. from the Bishop Rock.	Submarine	No warning	Torpedo	—
Carnmoney (S.V.)	1,299	14	150 miles W. from the Fastnet.	Submarine	Captured	Bombs	—
Elizabeth Hampton (S.V.)	108	14	25 miles S. by W. from St. Catherine's.	Submarine	Captured	Bombs	—
†Lewisham	2,810	14(?)	Atlantic	Submarine	No warning (probably).	Torpedo	24 Master and 2 gunners made prisoners.
†Polymnia	2,426	15	15 miles W. from the Lizard.	Submarine	No warning	Torpedo	8
†Tung Shan	3,999	15	7 miles North from Cape San Antonio.	Submarine	Captured	Bombs	1 Master, Chief Engineer and one gunner prisoners.
Cuba (S.V.)	271	15	18 miles E.S.E. from Owers L.V.	Submarine	Captured	Bombs	—
†Pagenturm	5,000	16	16 miles W. from Beachy Head.	Submarine	No warning	Torpedo	4
Dorothy Duff (S.V.)	186	16	14 miles from Cape Cullera.	Submarine	Captured	Bomb	—
†Highland Corrie	7,583	16	4 miles S. from Owers L.V.	Submarine	No warning	Torpedo	5
†Middlesex	8,364	16	150 miles N.W. from Tory Island.	Submarine	No warning	Torpedo	—
†Kilmaho	2,155	16	10 miles W.N.W. from the Lizard.	Submarine	No warning	Torpedo	21 including Master.
Florence Louisa (S.V.)	115	17	8 miles S. from the Needles.	Submarine	Captured	Bombs	—
†George Pyman	3,859	17	130 miles N.W. from Tearaght Island.	Submarine	No warning	Torpedo	—
Cito	819	17	20 miles E. from North Hinder L.V.	T.B.D.'s	No warning	Gunfire	11 including Master.
Elford	1,739	18	2 miles S. from Nab L.V.	Mine	Mine	Mine	—
†Penhale	3,712	18	72 miles N.W. by N. ½ N. from Tearaght Island.	Submarine	No warning	Torpedo	1 Master made prisoner.
†Camberwell	4,078	18	6 miles S.E. by E. from Dunnose Head.	Mine	Mine	Mine	7
C.E.C.G. (S.V.)	47	18	30 miles S.S.E. from the Start.	Submarine	Captured	Gunfire	—
†Millicent Knight	3,563	18	130 miles E. by S. ¼ S. from Malta.	Submarine	No warning	Torpedo	1
†Llandrindod	3,841	18	165 miles N.W. by W. from the Fastnet.	Submarine	No warning	Torpedo	Master made prisoner.
Dromore	268	18	6 miles South from St. Martin Point, Guernsey.	Submarine	Captured	Gunfire	—
†Mary Baird	1,830	18	2½ miles W. ½ N. from Pendeen Cove.	Mine	Mine	Mine	7

MERCHANT VESSELS CAPTURED OR SUNK.

Name.	Gross Tons.	Date.	Position.	Cause of Loss.	How attacked.	How sunk.	Lives lost.
		1917. May					
†Mordenwood	3,125	19	90 miles S.E. by S. ½ S. from Cape Matapan.	Submarine (?)	No warning	Torpedo (?)	21 including Master.
†Farnham	3,102	19	90 miles N.W. from the Fastnet.	Submarine	No warning	Torpedo	17 including Master.
†Mardinian	3,322	19	4 miles S. by W. from Tabarca Island.	Submarine	No warning	Torpedo	—
†Caspian	3,606	20	3½ miles E. from Cape Cervera, Spain.	Submarine	Captured	Torpedo	25 (including Master). Chief Engineer, 2nd Officer, and 1 gunner made prisoners.
Dana (S.V.)	182	20	25 miles N. from Les Hanois.	Submarine	Captured	Bombs	
Mientji (S.V.)	120	20	25 miles N. from Les Hanois.	Submarine	Captured	Bombs	—
†Tycho	3,216	20	16 miles W. ½ S. from Beachy Head.	Submarine	No warning	Torpedo	15 including Master.
Porthkerry	1,920	20	16 miles W. by S. from Beachy Head.	Submarine	No warning	Torpedo	7 including Master.
†Jupiter	2,124	21	15 miles West from Beachy Head.	Submarine	No warning	Torpedo	19 including Master.
†Don Diégo	3,632	21	40 miles E. by S. from Linosa.	Submarine	Captured	Gunfire	5
†Ampleforth	3,873	21	15 miles W.S.W. from Gozo.	Submarine	No warning	Torpedo	4
†City of Corinth	5,870	21	12 miles S.W. from the Lizard.	Submarine	No warning	Torpedo	
Lanthorn	2,299	22	3 miles East from Whitby.	Submarine	Captured	Bombs	—
†England	3,798	23	40 miles S. by E. from Cape Bon.	Submarine	Captured	Bombs	3 including Master.
†Elmmoor	3,744	23	36 miles E. by S. from Syracuse.	Submarine	No warning	Torpedo	Master made prisoner.
†Lesto	1,940	23	8 miles West from Ile du Pilier.	Submarine	No warning	Torpedo	4
†Jersey City	4,670	24	35 miles N.W. from the Flannan Isles.	Submarine	No warning	Torpedo	Master made prisoner.
†Belgian	3,657	24	50 miles W. ½ S. from the Fastnet.	Submarine	No warning	Torpedo	2
McClure (S.V.)	220	24	30 miles E. by S. from C. Carbonara.	Submarine	Captured	Bombs	—
Sjaelland	1,405	25	18 miles E. by N. from Start Point.	Submarine	Captured	Gunfire	1 (Master.)
†Kohinur	2,265	25	150 miles North from Alexandria.	Submarine	No warning	Torpedo	37 including Master.
Saint Mirren (S.V.)	1,956	26	45 miles N.W. from Inistrahull.	Submarine	Captured	Gunfire	—
†Holmesbank	3,051	26	90 miles N. by W. from Alexandria.	Submarine	Captured	Gunfire	—

MERCHANT VESSELS CAPTURED OR SUNK. 52

Name.	Gross Tons.	Date.	Position.	Cause of Loss.	How attacked.	How sunk.	Lives lost.
		1917. May					
†Umaria	5,317	26	20 miles S.W. by S. from Policastro, Italy.	Submarine	Captured	Torpedo	5 Chief Engineer, 2nd Officer and 1 Cadet made prisoners.
Dover Castle (Hospital Ship)	8,271	26	50 miles North from Bona.	Submarine	No warning	Torpedo	7
†Boldwell	3,118	27	35 miles N.E. from Linosa.	Submarine	No warning	Torpedo	3
†Dartmoor	2,870	27	35 miles S.E. from Fastnet.	Submarine	No warning	Torpedo	25 including Master.
†Antinoe	2,396	28	150 miles W.S.W. from Bishop Rock.	Submarine	No warning	Torpedo	21 including Master.
†Limerick	6,827	28	140 miles W. ½ S. from Bishop Rock.	Submarine	No warning	Torpedo	8
Detlef Wagner (S.V.)	225	28	5 miles W. from Armen Rock.	Submarine	Captured	Bombs	—
†Clan Murray	4,835	29	40 miles W. by S. from Fastnet.	Submarine	No warning	Torpedo	64 (including Master). 3rd Officer and probably 3rd Engineer made prisoners.
†Oswego	5,793	29	175 miles W. ½ S. from Bishop Rock.	Submarine	No warning	Torpedo	—
†Ashleaf	5,768	29	150 miles West from Bishop Rock.	Submarine	No warning	Torpedo	—
†Lisbon	1,203	30	5 miles S. from Royal Sovereign L.V.	Mine	Mine	Mine	1
†Corbet Woodall	917	30	1½ miles E. from the Nab L.V.	Mine	Mine	Mine	—
†Hanley	3,331	30	95 miles W. from Bishop Rock.	Submarine	No warning	Torpedo	1
Bathurst	2,821	30	90 miles W. from Bishop Rock.	Submarine	Captured	Torpedo	—
†Rosebank	3,837	31	120 miles N. from Ben Ghazi.	Submarine	No warning	Torpedo	2 Master made prisoner.
†Esneh	3,247	31	190 miles N.W. by W. from Tory Island.	Submarine	No warning	Torpedo	—
JUNE 191		June					
†Cavina	6,539	1	45 miles W. by S. from the Fastnet.	Submarine	No warning	Torpedo	—
†Cameronian	5,861	2	50 miles N.W. by N. ¼ N. from Alexandria.	Submarine	No warning	Torpedo	11 including Master.
†Hollington	4,221	2	14 miles S. from Faeroe Islands.	Submarine	No warning	Torpedo	30 including Master.
Wairuna	3,947	2	Off Sunday Island, Kermadec Islands.	Wolf	Captured	Bombs	—
†Islandmore	3,046	3	20 miles N.W. from Cape Falcon, Algeria.	Submarine	Captured	Gunfire	2 Master made prisoner.

MERCHANT VESSELS CAPTURED OR SUNK.

Name.	Gross Tons.	Date.	Position.	Cause of Loss.	How attacked.	How sunk.	Lives lost.
		1917. June					
†Greenbank	3,881	3	12 miles north from Cape Falcon, Algeria.	Submarine	Captured	Torpedo	1
†Merioneth	3,004	3	105 miles N. by W. from Tromso.	Submarine	Captured	Gunfire	—
†Southland	11,899	4	140 miles N.W. ½ W. from Tory Island.	Submarine	No warning	Torpedo	4
†City of Baroda	5,541	4	90 miles N.W. ½ N. from Tory Island.	Submarine	No warning	Torpedo	6
†Manchester Trader.	3,938	4	8 miles S.E. from Pantellaria.	Submarine	Captured	Gunfire	1 Second officer made prisoner.
†Phemius	6,699	4	80 miles N.W. ½ N. from Eagle Island.	Submarine	No warning	Torpedo	—
Laura Ann (S.V.)	116	5	20 miles S.S.E. from Beachy Head.	Submarine	Captured	Gunfire	1 (Master).
†Manchester Miller.	4,234	5	190 miles N.W. ½ N. from the Fastnet.	Submarine	No warning	Torpedo	8
†Kallundborg	1,590	5	80 miles S.S.W. from Toulon.	Submarine	Captured	Bombs	1
†Parthenia	5,160	6	140 miles W. by N. from Bishop Rock.	Submarine	No warning	Torpedo	3
† Sir Francis	1,991	7	2 miles N.E. from Scarborough.	Submarine	No warning	Torpedo	10 including Master.
Wilhelm (S.V.)	187	7	20 miles S.E. by S. from the Lizard.	Submarine	Captured	Gunfire	—
†Ikalis	4,329	7	170 miles N.W. ½ W. from the Fastnet.	Submarine	No warning	Torpedo	—
†Jonathan Holt	1,522	7	130 miles N.W. by W. ½ W. from the Fastnet.	Submarine	No warning	Torpedo	—
†Saragossa	3,541	8	178 miles N.W. from the Fastnet.	Submarine	No warning	Torpedo	—
Phantom (S.V.)	251	8	25 miles N.N.W. from Cape La Heve.	Submarine	Captured	Gunfire	3
Enidwen	3,594	8	170 miles N.W. from the Fastnet.	Submarine	No warning	Torpedo	—
†Orator	3,563	8	84 miles W.N.W. from the Fastnet.	Submarine	No warning	Torpedo	5
†Huntstrick	8,151	8	80 miles W.N.W. from Cape Spartel.	Submarine	No warning	Torpedo	15 including Master.
†Cheltonian	4,426	8	54 miles W. by S. from Planier L. Ho.	Submarine	Captured	Gunfire	Master and 1 gunner made prisoners.
†Isle of Jura	3,809	8	15 miles W.S.W. from Cape Spartel.	Submarine	Captured	Bombs	2
†Harbury	4,572	9	170 miles W. ½ N. from Ushant.	Submarine	No warning	Torpedo	12 including Master.
†Egyptiana	3,818	9	120 miles W.S.W. from the Scillies.	Submarine	No warning	Torpedo	—
General Laurie (S.V.).	238	9	70 miles S.W. by S. from Planier L. Ho.	Submarine	Captured	Set on fire	—

Merchant Vessels Captured or Sunk.

Name.	Gross Tons.	Date.	Position.	Cause of Loss.	How attacked.	How sunk.	Lives lost.
		1917. June					
Marjorie (motor)	119	9	30 miles S.E. by S. from the Lizard.	Submarine	Captured	Bombs	—
†Appledore	3,843	9	164 miles S. by W. from the Fastnet.	Submarine	No warning	Torpedo	—
†Achilles	641	9	75 miles W. by S. from the Fastnet.	Submarine	Captured	Gunfire	Master and 1 gunner made prisoners.
†Clan Alpine	3,587	9	40 miles N. by E. ½ E. from Muckle Flugga.	Submarine	No warning	Torpedo	8
†Baron Cawdor	4,316	9	150 miles S.W. by S. ½ S. from the Fastnet.	Submarine	No warning	Torpedo	3
†Haulwen	4,032	9	250 miles N.W. from the Fastnet.	Submarine	No warning	Torpedo	4
†Galicia	1,400	10	140 miles S.W. by S. ½ S. from the Fastnet.	Submarine	No warning	Torpedo	4
†Bay State	6,583	10	250 miles N.W. from the Fastnet.	Submarine	No warning	Torpedo	—
†Scottish Hero	2,205	10	440 miles W. by S. ½ S. from the Fastnet.	Submarine	Captured	Gunfire	1
†Dulwich	1,460	10	7 miles N. by E. ½ E. from the Shipwash L.V.	Mine	Mine	Mine	5
†Marie Elsie	2,615	10	125 miles N. by W. from C. Teriberski, Lapland.	Submarine	No warning	Torpedo	3
†Perla	5,355	10	130 miles N ¾ W. from C. Teriberski, Lapland.	Submarine	Captured	Not known	4
†Ribera	3,511	10	70 miles North from C. Wrath.	Submarine	No warning	Torpedo	—
†Anglian	5,532	10	43 miles S.W. by W. ½ W. from the Bishop Rock.	Submarine	No warning	Torpedo	1
Keeper	572	10(?)	Irish Channel	Submarine (?)	No warning (?)	Torpedo (?)	12 including Master.
†Teviotdale	3,847	11	330 miles N.W. by W. from the Fastnet.	Submarine	No warning	Torpedo	1
†Benha	1,878	11	50 miles N. by E. from Marsa Susa.	Submarine	Captured	Bombs	—
†Polyxena	5,737	11	57 miles West from the Fastnet.	Submarine	No warning	Torpedo	7
†City of Perth	3,427	11	195 miles S.S.W. from the Fastnet.	Submarine	No warning	Torpedo	8
†South Point	4,258	11	30 miles S.W. ½ S. from Bishop Rock.	Submarine	No warning	Torpedo	—
†Huntsolm	2,073	11	4 miles E. by S. from the Owers L.V.	Submarine	No warning	Torpedo	—
†Amakura	2,316	12	180 miles N.W. ½ W. from Tory Island.	Submarine	No warning	Torpedo	2
Alfred (S.V.)	130	12	15 miles S.W. from Boulogne.	Submarine	Captured	Bombs	—
Alwyn (S.V.)	73	12	5 miles S.E. from Girdleness.	Submarine	Captured	Bombs	—

55 MERCHANT VESSELS CAPTURED OR SUNK.

Name.	Gross Tons.	Date.	Position.	Cause of Loss.	How attacked.	How sunk.	Lives lost.
		1917. June					
†St. Andrews	3,613	13	4 miles West from C. Spartivento, Italy.	Submarine	No warning	Torpedo	3
Silverburn	284	13	4 miles S.E. from Cove Bay.	Submarine	Captured	Gunfire	—
†Darius	3,426	13	210 miles S.W. from the Fastnet.	Submarine	No warning	Torpedo	15
†Kelvinbank	4,072	13	100 miles North from C. Wrath.	Submarine	No warning	Torpedo	16 including Master.
†Aysgarth	3,118	14	430 miles W.N.W. from C. Finisterre.	Submarine	Captured	Bombs	3
†New Zealand Transport.	4,481	14	8 miles S.E. from Serpho Pulo, Ægean.	Submarine	No warning	Torpedo	3
†Dart	3,207	14	6 miles S.S.W. from Ballycottin L. Ho.	Submarine	No warning	Torpedo	4
†Kankakee	3,718	14	2 miles N.E. from Sunk L.V.	Seaplane	No warning	Torpedo	2
†Ortolan	1,727	14	100 miles W.S.W. from Bishop Rock.	Submarine	No warning	Torpedo	3
†Carthaginian	4,444	14	2½ miles N.W. from Innistrahul L. Ho.	Mine	Mine	Mine	—
Wega	839	14	20 miles W. by S. from Royal Sovereign L.V.	Submarine	No warning	Torpedo	5
†Pasha	5,930	15	Southern entrance to Straits of Messina.	Submarine	No warning	Torpedo	3
†Westonby	3,795	15	195 miles S.W. by S. from the Fastnet.	Submarine	No warning	Torpedo	—
†Addah	4,397	15	35 miles S.W. from Penmarch.	Submarine	No warning	Torpedo	9
†Wapello	5,576	15	14 miles W.S.W. from Owers L.V.	Submarine	No warning	Torpedo	2
†Jessie	2,256	16	260 miles W. ½ S. from Bishop Rock.	Submarine	No warning	Torpedo	—
Carrie Hervey, (S.V.)	111	16	52 miles S.E. by S. from Armen Rock.	Submarine	Captured	Gunfire	—
†Stanhope	2,854	17	7 miles S.W. by W. from Start Point.	Submarine	No warning	Torpedo	22
†Fornebo	4,259	17	4 miles North from C. Wrath.	Submarine	No warning	Torpedo	—
†Lizzie Westoll	2,855	17	120 miles N.W. by W. from the Fastnet.	Submarine	No warning	Torpedo	—
†Raloo	1,012	17	6 miles S.E. by E. from Coningbeg L.V.	Submarine	No warning	Torpedo	3 including Master.
†Tyne	2,909	17	18 miles S.W. from the Lizard.	Submarine	No warning	Torpedo	—
†English Monarch	4,947	18	300 miles N.W. by W. from the Fastnet.	Submarine	No warning	Torpedo	3
†Thistledhu	4,032	18	218 miles N.W. ½ W. from the Fastnet.	Submarine	No warning	Torpedo	4
†Elele	6,557	18	300 miles N.W. ¾ W. from the Fastnet.	Submarine	No warning	Torpedo	—
Queen Adelaide	4,965	18	13 miles N.N.E. from St. Kilda.	Submarine	No warning	Torpedo	3

Merchant Vessels Captured or Sunk. 56

Name.	Gross Tons.	Date.	Position.	Cause of Loss.	How attacked.	How sunk.	Lives lost.
		1917. June					
Violet (S.V.)	158	18	9 miles S.S.E. from Coningbeg L.V.	Submarine	Captured	Gunfire	—
Kangaroo (S.V.)	76	18	20 miles S. from Tuskar.	Submarine	Captured	Gunfire	4 including Master.
Gauntlet (S.V.)	58	18	30 miles N.W. from Les Hanois.	Submarine	Captured	Bombs	—
†Buffalo	4,106	18	80 miles N.W. by N. ½ N. from C. Wrath.	Submarine	No warning	Torpedo	—
†Batoum	4,054	19	6 miles South from the Fastnet.	Submarine	No warning	Torpedo	1
Kate and Annie (S.V.)	96	19	25 miles N.W. by W. from Les Hanois.	Submarine	Captured	Bombs	—
†Brookby	3,679	19	155 miles S. ½ W. from the Fastnet.	Submarine	Captured	Torpedo	—
†Kelso	1,292	19	33 miles W.S.W. from Bishop Rock.	Submarine	No warning	Torpedo	—
Penpol	2,061	19	Gulf of Bothnia	Submarine	Captured	Taken to Germany.	—
†Ruperra	4,232	20	50 miles E. by S. from Pantellaria.	Submarine	No warning	Torpedo	—
†Bengore Head	2,490	20	150 miles N.W. from the Fastnet.	Submarine	Captured	Torpedo	—
Benita (S.V.)	130	20	15 miles South from Portland Bill.	Submarine	Captured	Bombs	—
Black Head	1,898	21	52 miles E.S.E. from Out Skerries, Shetland.	Submarine	No warning	Torpedo	—
†Lord Roberts	4,166	21	270 miles N.W. by N. from the Fastnet.	Submarine	Captured	Gunfire	—
†Ortona	5,524	21	140 miles S.S.W. from the Fastnet.	Submarine	No warning	Torpedo	1
†Melford Hall	6,339	22	95 miles N. by W. ¾ W. from Tory Island.	Submarine	No warning	Torpedo	—
†Miami	3,762	22	11 miles E.S.E. from the Fastnet.	Submarine	No warning	Torpedo	—
Meggie	1,802	24	Gulf of Bothnia	Submarine	Captured	Taken to Germany.	—
†Clan Davidson	6,486	24	130 miles S.W. by W. ¼ W. from the Scilly Isles.	Submarine	No warning	Torpedo	12
†South Wales	3,668	24	128 miles West from Bishop Rock.	Submarine	No warning	Torpedo	2
†Sylvanian	4,858	24	170 miles N.W. from Tory Island.	Submarine	No warning	Torpedo	2
†Mongolia	9,505	24	50 miles S. by W. from Bombay.	Mine	Mine	Mine	24
†Crown of Arragon	4,500	24	124 miles S.W. ½ W. from Bishop Rock.	Submarine	No warning	Torpedo	1
†Saxon Monarch	4,828	24	140 miles S.W. by W. from Scilly Isles.	Submarine	No warning	Torpedo	2
†Cestrian	8,912	24	4 miles S.E. from Skyro.	Submarine	No warning	Torpedo	3
†Don Arturo	3,680	25(?)	Atlantic	Submarine (reported).	No warning (probably).	Torpedo	34 including Master.

MERCHANT VESSELS CAPTURED OR SUNK.

*Name.	Gross Tons.	Date.	Position.	Cause of Loss.	How attacked.	How sunk.	Lives lost.
		1917. June					
†Guildhall	2,609	25	40 miles S.W. by W. ½ W. from Bishop Rock.	Submarine	No warning	Torpedo	12
†Anatolia	3,847	25	1½ miles off Genoa.	Mine	Mine	Mine	—
Neotsfield (S.V.)	1,875	26	112 miles S.W. by W. from Bishop Rock.	Submarine	Captured	Bombs	—
†Birdoswald	4,013	26	25 miles E. ½ S. from Tarragona.	Submarine	No warning	Torpedo	Master and Chief Engineer prisoners.
†Manistee	3,869	26	86 miles W.S.W. from Bishop Rock.	Submarine	No warning	Torpedo	5
†Cattaro	2,908	26	130 miles W.S.W. from Bishop Rock.	Submarine	No warning	Torpedo	—
Serapis	1,932	26	106 miles N.N W. ½ W. from Tory Island.	Submarine	No warning	Torpedo	19 Master and Chief Officer prisoners.
†Armadale	6,153	27	160 miles N.W. from Tory Island.	Submarine	No warning	Torpedo	3
Solway Prince	317	27	8 miles North from Alderney.	Submarine	Captured	Bombs	—
†Tong Hong	2,184	27	75 miles S.W. from Cape Sicie.	Submarine	Captured	Not known	Master prisoner.
†Ultonia	10,402	27	190 miles S.W. from the Fastnet.	Submarine	No warning	Torpedo	1
Longbenton	924	27	12 miles S. by W. from Flamborough Head.	Submarine	No warning	Torpedo	—
†Baron Ogilvy	4,570	27	172 miles N.W. from Tory Island.	Submarine	No warning	Torpedo	2
Lizzie Ellen (S.V.).	114	28	46 miles South from Start Point.	Submarine	Captured	Bombs	—
Haigh Hall	4,809	30	40 miles East from Malta.	Submarine	No warning	Torpedo	—
Ilston	2,426	30	4 miles S.E. from the Lizard.	Submarine	No warning	Torpedo	6
Lady of the Lake (S.V.).	51	30	15 miles S.S.W. from Hook Point, Waterford.	Submarine	Captured	Bombs	—

JULY 1917.

		July					
Ariel, (S.V.)	86	1	25 miles E.N.E. from Rattray Head.	Submarine	Captured	Bombs	—
Don Emilio	3,651	1	10 miles N.W. by W. from Esha Ness, West Shetland.	Submarine	No warning	Torpedo	1
†Thirlby	2,009	2	122 miles N.W. by W. ¼ W. from the Fastnet.	Submarine	No warning	Torpedo	2
†City of Cambridge.	3,844	3	10 miles N.W. from Jidjelli.	Submarine	No warning	Torpedo	—
†Iceland	1,501	3	10 miles S.W. from Galley Head.	Submarine	No warning	Torpedo	2
†Mongara	8,205	3	1½ miles from Messina Breakwater.	Submarine	No warning	Torpedo	—

MERCHANT VESSELS CAPTURED OR SUNK.   58

Name.	Gross Tons.	Date.	Position.	Cause of Loss.	How attacked.	How sunk.	Lives lost.
		1917. July					
†Matador	3,642	3	115 miles W. by N. ½ N. from the Fastnet.	Submarine	No warning	Torpedo	2
†Goathland	3,044	4	10 miles South from Belle Ile.	Submarine	No warning	Torpedo	21 including Master.
†Hurstside	3,149	4	108 miles N.N.E. ¼ E. from Cape Wrath.	Submarine	No warning	Torpedo	—
†Cuyahoga	4,586	5	130 miles W.N.W. from Tory Island.	Submarine	No warning	Torpedo	—
Ocean Swell (S.V.)	195	5	15 miles S.E. from Start Point.	Submarine	Captured	Gunfire	—
Cumberland	9,471	6	16 miles S.W. from Gabo Island, Australia.	Mine	Mine	Mine	—
Coral Leaf (S.V.)	428	7	18 miles N.W. by N. from Tearaght I.	Submarine	Captured	Gunfire	—
†Southina	3,506	7	6 miles W.N.W. from Cape Sigli, Algeria.	Submarine	No warning	Torpedo	1
†Turquah	3,859	7	10 miles S.W. from Bull Rock.	Submarine	No warning	Torpedo	—
†Bellucia	4,368	7	2 miles S.S.E. from the Lizard.	Submarine	No warning	Torpedo	4
†Wilberforce	3,074	7	25 miles South from Cape de Gata.	Submarine	No warning	Torpedo	1 Master and Chief Engineer prisoners.
†Condesa	8,557	7	105 miles West from Bishop Rock.	Submarine	No warning	Torpedo	—
†Obuasi	4,416	8	290 miles N.W. by W. ¼ W. from the Fastnet.	Submarine	No warning	Torpedo	2 Master made prisoner.
†Vendee	1,295	8	Mouth of River Gironde.	Mine	Mine	Mine	3
†Pegu	6,348	8	7 miles S.E. from Galley Head.	Mine	Mine	Mine	1
†Valetta	5,871	8	118 miles N.W. ¾ W. from the Fastnet.	Submarine	No warning	Torpedo	—
†Prince Abbas	2,030	9	29 miles East from Fair Island.	Submarine	No warning	Torpedo	2
†King David	3,680	10	360 miles N.W. ½ W. from the Fastnet.	Submarine	Captured	Gunfire	2
†Seang Choon	5,807	10	10 miles S.W. from the Fastnet.	Submarine	No warning	Torpedo	19
†Garmoyle	1,229	10	14 miles S.E. from Mine Head.	Submarine	No warning	Torpedo	20 including Master.
†Kioto	6,182	11	20 miles S.W. from the Fastnet.	Submarine	No warning	Torpedo	—
†Anglo-Patagonian.	5,017	11	20 miles W.S.W. from Les Sables d'Olonne.	Submarine	No warning	Torpedo	4
†Brunhilda	2,296	11	7 miles E. by S. from Start Point.	Submarine	No warning	Torpedo	—
†Muirfield	3,086	11	350 miles N.W. from the Fastnet.	Submarine	No warning	Torpedo	2 Chief Officer and W/T operator prisoners.

Merchant Vessels Captured or Sunk.

Name.	Gross Tons.	Date.	Position.	Cause of Loss.	How attacked.	How sunk.	Lives lost.
		1917. July					
†Castleton	2,395	12	60 miles S.S.W. from Bishop Rock.	Submarine	Captured	Gunfire	—
Gibel-Yedid	949	13	150 miles W. ¾ N. from Ushant.	Submarine	Captured	Bombs	—
†Exford	5,886	14	180 miles W. by S. ½ S. from Ushant.	Submarine	No warning	Torpedo	6
†Calliope	2,883	14 (?)	Atlantic	Submarine (?)	No warning(?)	Torpedo (?)	27 including Master.
†Mariston	2,903	15	82 miles West from the Fastnet.	Submarine	No warning	Torpedo	28 including Master.
Dudhope (S.V.)	2,086	15	200 miles West from the Fastnet.	Submarine	Captured	Bombs	—
Dinorwic (S.V.)	124	15	10 miles S. by E. from Hastings.	Submarine	Captured	Bombs	—
†Torcello	2,929	15	160 miles S.W. by W. from Bishop Rock.	Submarine	No warning	Torpedo	1
Ebenezer (S.V.)	177	15	25 miles N.W. from Dieppe.	Submarine	Captured	Bombs	—
†Trelissick	4,168	15	80 miles S.W. by W. ¼ W. from Ushant.	Submarine	No warning	Torpedo	Master and two gunners prisoners.
†Henry R. James	3,146	16	10 miles E. by N. from Ile de Bas.	Mine	Mine	Mine	24
†Ribston	3,372	16	85 miles West from the Fastnet.	Submarine	No warning	Torpedo	25 including Master.
†Valentia	3,242	16	70 miles W. ½ S. from Bishop Rock.	Submarine	No warning	Torpedo	3
†Khephren	2,774	16	178 miles East from Malta.	Submarine	No warning	Torpedo	—
Firfield	4,029	16	10 miles N.W. from Cape Papas, Nikaria.	Submarine	No warning	Torpedo	—
†Tamele	3,932	16	65 miles W. by S. from the Fastnet.	Submarine	No warning	Torpedo	1
†Haworth	4,456	17	94 miles West from the Fastnet.	Submarine	No warning	Torpedo	—
†Bramham	1,978	19	10 miles E. by S. from the Lizard.	Mine	Mine	Mine	1
†Eloby	6,545	19	75 miles S.E. by E. from Malta.	Submarine	No warning	Torpedo	56 including Master.
†Beatrice	712	20	10 miles E. by S. from the Lizard.	Submarine	No warning	Torpedo	11
†City of Florence	5,399	20	188 miles W. ¾ N. from Ushant.	Submarine	No warning	Torpedo	—
†Salsette	5,842	20	15 miles S.W. from Portland Bill.	Submarine	No warning	Torpedo	15
†Nevisbrook	3,140	20	90 miles W. ½ S. from the Fastnet.	Submarine	No warning	Torpedo	—
†Fluent	3,660	20	16 miles South from Anvil Point.	Mine	Mine	Mine	—
†L. H. Carl	1,916	20	14 miles W. ½ S. from Portland Bill.	Submarine	No warning	Torpedo	2
†Ramillies	2,935	21	120 miles W.N.W. from Tory Island.	Submarine	Captured	Gunfire	Master prisoner.
†Coniston Water	3,738	21	70 miles N. by W. from Butt of Lewis.	Submarine	No warning	Torpedo	1 gunner prisoner.

Merchant Vessels Captured or Sunk.

Name.	Gross Tons.	Date.	Position.	Cause of Loss.	How attacked.	How sunk.	Lives lost.
		1917. July					
Willena Gertrude (S.V.)	317	21	120 miles S. by E. ½ E. from Sta. Maria, Azores.	Submarine	Captured	Bombs	—
†Paddington	5,084	21	250 miles West from the Fastnet.	Submarine	No warning	Torpedo	29 including Master.
Harold (S.V.)	1,376	21	65 miles N.N.W. ½ W. from Tory Island.	Submarine	No warning	Torpedo	13 including Master.
†African Prince	4,916	21	60 miles N.N.W. from Tory Island.	Submarine	No warning	Torpedo	—
†Dafila	1,754	21	85 miles W. by S. ¼ S. from the Fastnet.	Submarine	No warning	Torpedo	2
†Trelyon	3,099	21	3 miles N. from Scarborough.	Mine	Mine	Beached, became total wreck.	—
†Cotovia	4,020	22	2 miles S.E. by E. from Auskerry.	Mine	Mine	Mine	—
†Rota	2,171	22	7 miles S. from Berry Head.	Submarine	No warning	Torpedo	5 including Master.
†Glow	1,141	22	4 miles S.E. by E. from S. Cheek, Robin Hood Bay.	Submarine	No warning	Torpedo	1
†Ashleigh	6 985	23	290 miles S.W. from the Fastnet.	Submarine	No warning	Torpedo	—
†Huelva	4,867	23	270 miles S.W. from the Fastnet.	Submarine	No warning	Torpedo	—
Sir Walter	492	24	2½ miles N. from Cape Ortegal.	Submarine	Captured	Bombs	—
†Zermatt	3,767	24	355 miles W. by N. from Ushant.	Submarine	No warning	Torpedo	3
†Blake	3,740	24	30 miles N. by W. ½ W. from Cape Wrath.	Submarine	No warning	Torpedo	5
†Brumaire	2,324	24	265 miles W. by N. from Ushant.	Submarine	No warning	Torpedo	2
†Purley	4,500	25	210 miles S.W. ¼ S. from the Fastnet.	Submarine	No warning	Torpedo	—
†Oakleaf	8,106	25	64 miles N.W. ¼ N. from Butt of Lewis.	Submarine	No warning	Torpedo	—
†Peninsula	1,384	25	235 miles S.W. from the Fastnet.	Submarine	No warning	Torpedo	1
†Monkstone	3,097	25	240 miles W. from Scilly Islands.	Submarine	No warning	Torpedo	1
†Rustington	3,071	25	235 miles W. by S. from Ushant.	Submarine	No warning	Torpedo	—
†Somerset	8,710	26	230 miles W. by S. ½ S. from Ushant.	Submarine	No warning	Torpedo	—
†Ludgate	3,708	26	2 miles S. from Galley Head.	Mine	Mine	Mine	24 including Master.
†Carmarthen	4,262	26	2 miles S.E. from the Lizard.	Submarine	No warning	Torpedo	—
†Mooltan	9,723	26	53 miles N.N.W. ½ W. from Cape Serrat.	Submarine	No warning	Torpedo	2
†Candia	6,482	27	8 miles S. from Owers L.V.	Submarine	No warning	Torpedo	1
†Begona No. 4	2,407	27	70 miles W. by N. ½ N. from the Fastnet.	Submarine	No warning	Torpedo	2
†Belle of England	3,877	27	155 miles W.N.W. from the Fastnet.	Submarine	No warning	Torpedo	—

MERCHANT VESSELS CAPTURED OR SUNK.

Name.	Gross Tons.	Date.	Position.	Cause of Loss.	How attacked.	How sunk.	Lives lost.
		1917. July					
†Whitehall	3,158	28	270 miles W. by N. from the Fastnet.	Submarine	No warning	Torpedo	1
†Glenstrae	4,718	28	66 miles S.W. by S. ¼ S. from Bishop Rock.	Submarine	No warning	Torpedo	1
Okhla	5,288	29	30 miles W. from Bombay.	Mine	Mine	Mine	9 including Master.
†Manchester Commerce.	4,144	29	15 miles W. by N. ½ N. from Cape Spartel.	Submarine	No warning	Torpedo	1
†Adalia	3,847	29	53 miles N.E. from Muckle Flugga.	Submarine	Captured	Gunfire	1
†Manchester Inventor.	4,112	30	80 miles N.N.E. from Muckle Flugga.	Submarine	Captured	Gunfire	—
†Ganges	4,177	30	8 miles S.W. from C. Spartel.	Submarine	No warning	Torpedo	1
†Shimosa	4,221	30	220 miles N.W. ½ W. from Eagle Island.	Submarine	No warning	Torpedo	17 including Master.
†Fremona	3,028	31	10 miles N. by W. from Ile de Bas.	Submarine	No warning	Torpedo	11
†Empress	2,914	31	4½ miles E. by S. ½ S. from Withernsea L. Ho.	Mine	Mine	Mine	5
Ypres	305	31	10 miles N.N.W. ½ W. from Cape Trafalgar.	Submarine	Captured	Gunfire	—
†Orubian	3,876	31	160 miles N.W. ½ W. from Eagle Island.	Submarine	No warning	Torpedo	1
†Belgian Prince	4,765	31	175 miles N.W. by W. from Tory Island.	Submarine	No warning	Torpedo	39 Master made prisoner.
†Snowdonian	3,870	31	245 miles S. by E. from Sta Maria, Azores.	Submarine	Captured	Bombs	—
†Quernmore	7,302	31	160 miles W. by N. ¾ N. from Tory Island.	Submarine	No warning	Torpedo	1

AUGUST 1917.

		Aug.					
†Karina	4,222	1	17 miles S.S.W. ½ W. from Hook Point, Waterford.	Submarine	No warning	Torpedo	11
†Laertes	4,541	1	1¼ miles S.S.W. from Prawle Point.	Submarine	No warning	Torpedo	14
†Llandudno	4,187	1	110 miles S. by W. from Porquerolles Island.	Submarine	Captured	Bombs	1
Alcyone (motor)	149	1	45 miles N.N.W. from Roches Douvres.	Submarine	Captured	Gunfire	—
†Newlyn	4,019	2	2 miles South from Prawle Point.	Submarine	No warning	Torpedo	4
†Beechpark	4,763	2	4 miles South from St. Mary's, Scilly.	Submarine	No warning	Torpedo	—
Hornchurch	2,159	3	3½ miles E.N.E. from Coquet Island.	Mine	Mine	Mine	2
†Aube	1,837	3	3½ miles N. by W. from Ile d'Yeu.	Submarine	No warning	Torpedo	1

Merchant Vessels Captured or Sunk.

Name.	Gross Tons.	Date.	Position.	Cause of Loss.	How attacked.	How sunk.	Lives lost.
		1917. Aug.					
†Cairnstrath	2,128	4	6 miles S.S.W. from Ile du Pilier.	Submarine	No warning	Torpedo	22 including Master.
†British Monarch	5,749	4	2 miles S.S.W. from Porquerolles Lighthouse.	Mine	Mine	Mine	—
Azira	1,144	4	6 miles S.E. from Seaham Harbour.	Submarine	No warning	Torpedo	1
†Countess of Mar	2,234	4	55 miles N. ¼ E. from Bayonne.	Submarine	No warning	Torpedo	20 including Master
†Kathleen	3,915	5	90 miles West from Skelligs.	Submarine	No warning	Torpedo	1 (Master).
Talisman	153	6	7 miles E.S.E. from Hartlepool.	Submarine	Captured	Bombs	—
†Rosemount	3,044	6	45 miles N.E. by N. ½ N. from Muckle Flugga.	Submarine	Captured	Torpedo	1
†Argalia	4,641	6	81 miles N.W. ¾ W. from Tory Island.	Submarine	No warning	Torpedo	3
Matunga	1,608	6	300 miles E. (true) from Riche Island, New Guinea.	Wolf	Captured	Bombs	—
†Polanna	2,345	6	3 miles East from Whitby.	Submarine	No warning	Torpedo	2
†Baysoto	3,082	6	33 miles S.E. by E. from Girdleness.	Submarine	No warning	Torpedo	—
†Port Curtis	4,710	7	70 miles West from Penmarch.	Submarine	Captured	Bombs	—
†Iran	6,250	7	200 miles E.S.E. from Santa Maria, Azores.	Submarine	No warning	Torpedo	—
†Llanishen	3,837	8	8 miles N. by E. from Cape de Creus, Gulf of Lyons.	Submarine	No warning	Torpedo	2
†Blagdon	1,996	9	75 miles E. by S. from Muckle Flugga.	Submarine	No warning	Torpedo	12 including Master.
†War Patrol	2,045	10	1 mile West from Penmarch.	Mine	Mine	Mine	13 including Master.
City of Athens	5,604	10	20 miles N.W. from Cape Town.	Mine	Mine	Mine	19
†Sonnie	2,642	11	5 miles N.W. from Le Four Lighthouse.	Submarine	No warning	Torpedo	11
†Lynorta	3,684	11	102 miles N.W. by N. from Tory Island.	Submarine	No warning	Torpedo	2
†Roanoke	4,803	12	100 miles W.N.W. from the Butt of Lewis.	Submarine	Captured	Bombs	Master made prisoner.
†Akassa	3,919	13	8 miles S.E. from Galley Head.	Submarine	No warning	Torpedo	7
†Turakina	9,920	13	120 miles W.S.W. from Bishop Rock.	Submarine	No warning	Torpedo	2
†Maston	3,881	13	35 miles E.N.E. from Cape Spartivento, Italy.	Submarine	No warning	Torpedo	2
†Wisbech	1,282	14	12 miles N.E. from Trevose Head	Submarine	No warning	Torpedo	2

MERCHANT VESSELS CAPTURED OR SUNK.

Name.	Gross Tons.	Date.	Position.	Cause of Loss.	How attacked.	How sunk.	Lives lost.
		1917. Aug.					
†Brodstone	4,927	15	95 miles W. ¼ S. from Ushant.	Submarine	No warning	Torpedo	5
†Hylas	4,240	15	10 miles East from Butt of Lewis.	Submarine	No warning	Torpedo	—
†Athenia	8,668	16	7 miles North from Inishtrahull.	Submarine	No warning	Torpedo	15
†Palatine	2,110	16	10 miles W.N.W. from Island of Canna.	Submarine	No warning	Torpedo	Master made prisoner.
†Delphic	8,273	16	135 miles S.W. ¾ W. from Bishop Rock.	Submarine	No warning	Torpedo	5
†Manchester Engineer.	4,465	16	4½ miles S.E. from Flamborough Head.	Submarine	No warning	Torpedo	—
Edina	455	17	30 miles S.E. from Store Dimon, Faroë.	Submarine	Captured	Gunfire	—
†Rosario	1,821	18	Atlantic	Submarine	No warning	Torpedo	20 including Master. 1 fireman prisoner.
†Politania	3,133	18	10 miles N.W. by W. from Cape Sigli.	Submarine	No warning	Torpedo	—
†Ardens	1,274	18	2 miles East from Filey Brig.	Submarine	No warning	Torpedo	1
†Monksgarth	1,928	19	17 miles N. by E. ¼ E. from Ushant N.W. Lighthouse.	Submarine	No warning	Torpedo	—
†Spectator	3,808	19	11 miles S.E. from Galley Head.	Submarine	No warning	Torpedo	—
●†Glocliffe	2,211	19	9 miles E.N.E. from Berry Head.	Submarine	No warning	Torpedo	2
Brema	1,537	19	7½ miles S. ½ E. from Flamborough Head.	Submarine	No warning	Torpedo	—
†Gartness	2,422	19	180 miles S.E. by E. ¾ E. from Malta.	Submarine	No warning	Torpedo	13 including Master.
†Claverley	3,829	20	4 miles S.E. from the Eddystone.	Submarine	No warning	Torpedo	10
†Elswick Lodge	3,558	20	260 miles W. by S. from Ushant.	Submarine	No warning	Torpedo	4
†Incemore	3,060	20	52 miles S.E. by E. ½ E. from Pantellaria.	Submarine	No warning	Torpedo	1
†Edernian	3,588	20	6 miles S. by E. from Southwold.	Submarine	No warning	Torpedo	14
†Bulysses	6,127	20	145 miles W.N.W. from the Butt of Lewis.	Submarine	No warning	Torpedo	—
†Volodia	5,689	21	285 miles W. ¼ S. from Ushant.	Submarine	No warning	Torpedo	10
†Goodwood	3,086	21	28 miles N.W. by W. from Cape Bon.	Submarine	No warning	Torpedo	—
†Roscommon	8,238	21	20 miles N.E. from Tory Island.	Submarine	No warning	Torpedo	—
†Devonian	10,435	21	20 miles N.E. from Tory Island.	Submarine	No warning	Torpedo	2
†Oslo	2,296	21	15 miles E. by N. from Out Skerries, Shetland.	Submarine	No warning	Torpedo	3
H.S. 4 (tug) and R.B. 6 (barge).	—	21	130 miles W.S.W. from Ushant.	Submarine	Captured	Bombs	—

MERCHANT VESSELS CAPTURED OR SUNK.

Name.	Gross Tons.	Date.	Position.	Cause of Loss.	How attacked.	How sunk.	Lives lost.
		1917. Aug.					
Norhilda	1,175	21	5 miles S.E. from Scarborough.	Submarine	No warning	Torpedo	1
†Verdi	7,120	22	115 miles N.W. by N. from Eagle Island.	Submarine	No warning	Torpedo	6
Winlaton	3,270	23	25 miles W. from Cape Spartel.	Submarine	No warning	Torpedo	2 Master made prisoner.
†Veghtstroom	1,353	23	7 miles N.W. from Godrevy Lighthouse.	Submarine	No warning	Torpedo	5
†Boniface	3,799	23	7 miles N.E. by N. from Aran Island.	Submarine	No warning	Torpedo	1
Penelope	1,202	24	3 cables from Swalfer Ort Lighthouse, Baltic.	Submarine	No warning	Torpedo	—
†Springhill	1,507	24	4 miles N. by E. ¾ E. from Scarborough.	Mine	Mine	Mine	5
†Kilwinning	3,071	24	94 miles E.S.E. from Malta.	Submarine	No warning	Torpedo	—
†Heatherside	2767	24 (?)	Atlantic	Submarine (?)	No warning(?)	Torpedo (?)	27 including Master.
†Sycamore	6,550	25	125 miles N.W. from Tory Island.	Submarine	No warning	Torpedo	11
†Cymrian	1,014	25	13 miles S.E. by S. from Tuskar Rock.	Submarine	No warning	Torpedo	10
†Malda	7,896	25	130 miles W. ¼ S. from Bishop Rock.	Submarine	No warning	Torpedo	64
†Nascent	4,969	25	27 miles S. from Bishop Rock.	Submarine	No warning	Torpedo	6
†Kenmore	3,919	26	30 miles North from Inishtrahull.	Submarine	No warning	Torpedo	5
†Titian	4,170	26	170 miles S.E. ½ E. from Malta.	Submarine	No warning	Torpedo	—
•†W. H. Dwyer	1,770	26	15 miles E. by N. from Berry Head.	Submarine	No warning	Torpedo	—
Minas Queen (S.V.).	492	26	350 miles N.W. from C. Finisterre.	Submarine	Captured	Gunfire	6 including Master.
†Hathor	3,823	26	3 miles N.W. from Cape Tedles, Algeria.	Submarine	No warning	Torpedo	1 Master made prisoner.
†Assyria	6,370	26	34 miles N.W. by N. ½ N. from Tory Island.	Submarine	No warning	Torpedo	—
†Durango	3,008	26	50 miles N.W. from Barra Head.	Submarine	Captured	Gunfire	—
†Marmion	4,066	26	300 miles W. ¾ S. from Ushant.	Submarine	No warning	Torpedo	17
†Nairn	3,627	27	125 miles N. by W. ¼ W. from Ben Ghazi.	Submarine	No warning	Torpedo	—
†Hidalgo	4,271	28	120 miles N.E. ½ N. from North Cape.	Submarine	No warning	Torpedo	15
†Whitecourt	3,680	28	120 miles N.N.E. from North Cape.	Submarine	Captured	Gunfire	—
†Vronwen	5,714	29	20 miles N.W. by W. from Gozo.	Submarine	No warning	Torpedo	1
†Treloske	3 071	29	145 miles N. by W. ¾ W. from Cape Finisterre.	Submarine	No warning	Torpedo	1

MERCHANT VESSELS CAPTURED OR SUNK.

Name.	Gross Tons.	Date.	Position.	Cause of Loss.	How attacked.	How sunk.	Lives lost.
		1917. Aug.					
†Lynburn	587	29	½ mile S.E. from N. Arklow L.V.	Mine	Mine	Mine	8
Cooroy (S.V.)	2,470	29	10 miles S. by W. ½ W. from Hook Point, Waterford.	Submarine	Captured	Torpedo	—
†Noya	4,282	30	8 miles W.S.W. from the Lizard.	Submarine	No warning	Torpedo	1
†Eastern Prince	2,885	30	30 miles S. ¾ W. from the Eddystone.	Submarine	No warning	Torpedo	5
● †Grelhame	3,740	30	4 miles S.W. from Start Point.	Submarine	No warning	Torpedo	—
● †Miniota	6,422	31	30 miles S.E. ½ E. from Start Point.	Submarine	No warning	Torpedo	3
Westbury	3,097	31	8 miles S.S.E. from the Fastnet.	Submarine	No warning	Torpedo	—
†Vernon	982	31	22 miles S.E. by S. from Spurn Point.	Submarine	No warning	Torpedo	1 (Master.)

SEPTEMBER 1917.

Name.	Gross Tons.	Date.	Position.	Cause of Loss.	How attacked.	How sunk.	Lives lost.
		Sept.					
†Erato	2,041	1	4 miles S.E. from the Lizard.	Mine	Mine	Mine	—
†Rytonhall	4,203	2	105 miles W. ½ S. from Ushant.	Submarine	Captured	Torpedo	—
†Wentworth	3,828	2	36 miles W. ¼ S. from Belle Ile.	Submarine	No warning	Torpedo	1 Master and two gunners prisoners.
†Olive Branch	4,649	2	85 miles N. by E. ½ E. from North Cape.	Submarine	No warning	Torpedo	1
†Treverbyn	4,163	3	2 miles E.S.E. from Ushinish Lighthouse, South Uist.	Mine	Mine	Mine	27 including Master.
†Ragnhild	1,495	3	14 miles S. by E. ¼ E. from Flamborough Head.	Submarine	No warning	Torpedo	15 including Master.
● †La Negra	8,312	3	50 miles S.S.W. from Start Point.	Submarine	No warning	Torpedo	4
†Peerless	3,112	4	60 miles S.W. from Bishop Rock.	Submarine	No warning	Torpedo	2 Master and two gunners prisoners.
● †Bishopston	2,513	4	30 miles S. by E. from St. Catherines.	Submarine	No warning	Torpedo	2
Glynn, S.V.	60	5	32 miles N.W. from Les Hanois.	Submarine	Captured	Gunfire	—
Industry, S.V.	91	5	20 miles N.N.W. from Les Hanois.	Submarine	Captured	Gunfire	—
†Echunga	6,285	5	40 miles N. by E. from Ushant.	Submarine	No warning	Torpedo	9
Theodor, S.V.	230	5	13 miles N. by W. ½ W. from Sept Iles.	Submarine	Captured	Bombs	—
Florence Muspratt, S.V.	79	5	10 miles North from Sept Iles.	Submarine	Captured	Gunfire	1
Emma, S.V.	73	5	8 miles N. by W. from Sept Iles.	Submarine	Captured	Gunfire	—

MERCHANT VESSELS CAPTURED OR SUNK.

Name.	Gross Tons.	Date.	Position.	Cause of Loss.	How attacked.	How sunk.	Lives lost.
		1917. Sept.					
Frances, S.V.	89	5	8 miles N. by W. from Sept Iles.	Submarine	Captured	Bombs	—
†Tuskar	1,159	6	3 miles West from Eagle Island.	Mine	Mine	Mine	10
†Clan Ferguson	4,808	6	15 miles N.W. from Cape Spartel.	Submarine	No warning	Torpedo	10
Hinemoa, S.V.	2,283	7	35 miles W.S.W. from Bishop Rock.	Submarine	Captured	Gunfire	—
†Minnehaha	13,714	7	12 miles S.E. from the Fastnet.	Submarine	No warning	Torpedo	43
†Hunsbridge	3,424	7	60 miles S.W. by W. ¾ W. from Cape Spartel.	Submarine	No warning	Torpedo	2
●†Newholm	3,399	8	1 mile South from Start Point.	Mine	Mine	Mine	20
Ezel, S.V.	163	8	20 miles North from St. Valery (en Caux).	Submarine	Captured	Gunfire	—
Laura, S.V.	86	8	25 miles North from Fecamp.	Submarine	Captured	Bombs	—
†Harrow	1,777	8	4 miles S.E. from Whitby.	Submarine	No warning	Torpedo	2
● Elizabeth, S.V.	49	8	12 miles E. by S. from Start Point.	Submarine	Captured	Bombs	—
Storm	440	9	1 mile S.E. from Sunk L.V.	Seaplane	No warning	Torpedo	3
†Swiftsure	823	9	Shapinsay Sound	Mine	Mine	Mine	1
†Parkmill	1,316	10	1¼ miles from Kirkalister Lighthouse, Bressay.	Mine	Mine	Mine	—
Mary Orr (S.V.)	91	10	8 miles N. by E. from Pendeen Lighthouse.	Submarine	Captured	Bombs	—
Moss Rose (S.V.)	161	10	7 miles N.N.E. from Pendeen Lighthouse.	Submarine	Captured	Gunfire	—
Mary Seymour (S.V.)	150	10	7 miles N.N.E. from Pendeen Lighthouse.	Submarine	Captured	Gunfire	—
Water Lily (S.V.)	111	10	8 miles N. by E. from Pendeen Lighthouse.	Submarine	Captured	Bombs	—
Jane Williamson (S.V.)	197	10	20 miles N.N.E. from St. Ives.	Submarine	Captured	Gunfire	4 including Master.
†Luxembourg	1,417	11	3½ miles N.N.E. from Pendeen Lighthouse.	Mine	Mine	Mine	—
†Vienna	4,170	11	340 miles W. ½ N. from Ushant.	Submarine	No warning	Torpedo	25 Master prisoner.
†Embleton	5,377	11	150 miles W. from Cape Spartel.	Submarine	Captured	Gunfire	—
William (S.V.)	60	11	4 miles N.W. by N. from Crackington Haven, Cornwall.	Submarine	Captured	Bombs	—
†Urd	3,049	11	10 miles N. by E. ½ E. from Cape Palos.	Submarine	No warning	Torpedo	3
H.S. 3 Tug and R.B. 10 Barge	—	12	18 miles W. by N. from Cape Sines.	Submarine	Captured	Bombs	—
†Gibraltar	3,803	12	100 miles S.E. ½ S. from Cape de Creus.	Submarine	No warning	Torpedo	4
†St. Margaret	943	12	30 miles S.E. from Lille Dimon Island, Faroe.	Submarine	No warning	Torpedo	5

MERCHANT VESSELS CAPTURED OR SUNK.

Name.	Gross Tons.	Date.	Position.	Cause of Loss.	How attacked.	How sunk.	Lives lost.
		1917. Sept.					
Agricola (S.V.)	49	12	15 miles W.N.W. from Lundy Island.	Submarine	Captured	Bombs	—
†Chulmleigh	4,911	14	10 miles S.W. by W. from Cape Salou, Spain.	Submarine	No warning	Torpedo	—
†Zeta	2,269	14	8 miles S. by W. from Mine Head	Submarine	No warning	Torpedo	—
†Sommeina	3,317	15	4 miles S.E. from the Manacles.	Mine	Mine	Mine	....
Dependence (S.V.)	120	15	6 miles West from the Lizard.	Submarine	Captured	Bombs	—
†Santaren	4,256	15	40 miles N.E. from Muckle Flugga.	Submarine	No warning	Torpedo	Master and Chief Officer prisoners.
†Rollesby	3,955	15	80 miles E.N.E. from Muckle Flugga.	Submarine	Captured	Torpedo	—
†Arabis	3,928	16	210 miles W. by S. from Ushant.	Submarine	No warning	Torpedo	20 including Master.
†Sandsend	3,814	16	6 miles S.E. by E. from Mine Head.	Submarine	No warning	Torpedo	3
†Queen Amelie	4,278	17	19 miles N.N.E. from Muckle Flugga.	Submarine	Captured	Torpedo	—
Port Kembla	4,700	18	Off Cape Farewell, New Zealand.	Mine	Mine	Mine	—
†Arendal	1,387	18	115 miles W. ½ N. from Cape Spartel.	Submarine	Captured	Gunfire	—
†Joseph Chamberlain.	3,709	18	50 miles N. by W. from Muckle Flugga.	Submarine	No warning	Torpedo	18 Master and one gunner prisoners.
†Polar Prince	3,611	18	8 miles W. by S. from Cape Spartel.	Submarine	No warning	Torpedo	Master made prisoner.
†Saint Ronald	4,387	19	95 miles N.N.W. from Tory Island.	Submarine	No warning	Torpedo	24
Etal Manor	1,875	19	7 miles S. by W. from Hook Point, Waterford.	Submarine	No warning	Torpedo	6 including Master.
†Fabian	2,246	20	30 miles W. ½ N. from Cape Spartel.	Submarine	No warning	Torpedo	3
†Kurdistan	3,720	20	27 miles E.S.E. from Pantellaria.	Submarine	No warning	Torpedo	—
†Greleen	2,286	22	7 miles E. by N. from Berry Head.	Submarine	No warning	Torpedo	19 including Master.
Trongate	2,553	22	5 miles N. from Flamborough Head.	Submarine	No warning	Torpedo	2
Perseverance (S.V.).	118	23	14 miles N.W. by N. from St. Valery (en Caux).	Submarine	Captured	Gunfire	—
St. Dunstan (Dredger.)	—	23	12 miles N.W. by N. from Bill of Portland.	Mine	Mine	Mine	2
†Hornsund	3,646	23	2½ miles E.S.E. from Scarborough.	Submarine	No warning	Torpedo	1

MERCHANT VESSELS CAPTURED OR SUNK.

Name.	Gross Tons.	Date.	Position.	Cause of Loss.	How attacked.	How sunk.	Lives lost.
		1917. Sept.					
†Irthington	2,845	23	3 miles E.N.E. from Cape Vaticano, Italy.	Submarine	No warning	Torpedo	—
●†Rosehill	2,788	23	5 miles S.W. by S. from Fowey.	Submarine	No warning	Torpedo	—
†Iriston	3,221	24	7 miles S. by W. from Cape Camerat.	Submarine	No warning	Torpedo	—
†Boynton	2,578	24	5 miles W.N.W. from Cape Cornwall.	Submarine	No warning	Torpedo	23 including Master.
●†City of Swansea	1,375	25	15 miles E.N.E. from Berry Head.	Submarine	No warning	Torpedo	2
● Acorn (S.V.)	97	26	20 miles S. by E. from Start Point.	Submarine	Captured	Gunfire	—
†Swan River	4,724	27	27 miles N.N.W. from Oran.	Submarine	No warning	Torpedo	—
†Greltoria	5,143	27	3 miles N.W. by N. $\frac{1}{2}$ N. from Flamborough Head.	Submarine	No warning	Torpedo	—
†Sanwen	3,689	29	50 miles E. $\frac{3}{4}$ N. from Cape Bear.	Submarine	No warning	Torpedo	2
Kildonan	2,118	29	2 miles N.N.W. from Pendeen Lighthouse.	Submarine	No warning	Torpedo	14 including Master.
†Elmsgarth	3,503	29	50 miles N.W. $\frac{1}{2}$ W. from Tory Island.	Submarine	No warning	Torpedo	—
Percy B. (S.V.)	330	29	180 miles N. $\frac{3}{4}$ W. from Cape Villano.	Submarine	Captured	Gunfire	—
†Heron	885	30	400 miles West from Ushant. (?)	Submarine	No warning	Torpedo	22 including Master.
†Midlothian	1,321	30	80 miles South from Cape Greco, Cyprus.	Submarine	Captured	Gunfire	Master and 2 Gunners prisoners.
†Drake	2,267	30	340 miles West from Ushant.	Submarine	Captured	Gunfire	Master prisoner.
OCTOBER 1917.		Oct.					
†Normanton	3,862	1	115 miles W. $\frac{1}{2}$ N. from Cape Spartel.	Submarine	No warning	Torpedo	—
Carrabin (S.V.)	2,739	1	10 miles South from Daunts Rock.	Submarine	No warning	Torpedo	—
†Mersario	3,847	1	86 miles W. by N. from Cape Spartel.	Submarine	No warning	Torpedo	3
Ludovicos (S.V.)	50 apprx.	1	Mediterranean	Submarine	Captured	Bomb	—
†Almora	4,385	2	100 miles W. $\frac{1}{2}$ N. from Cape Spartel.	Submarine	No warning	Torpedo	—
†Lugano	3,810	2	2 miles S.W. from Bull Point, Rathlin.	Mine	Mine	Mine	—
†Nuceria	4,702	2	120 miles W. $\frac{1}{2}$ N. from Cape Spartel.	Submarine	No warning	Torpedo	2
†Hurst	4,718	3	2$\frac{1}{4}$ miles W. by N. from Skokham Id.	Submarine	No warning	Torpedo	—
†Memling	7,307	3	Laberildut Channel, near Brest.	Submarine	No warning	Torpedo	—
†Baron Blantyre	1,844	3	60 miles N.W. $\frac{3}{4}$ W. from Cape Finisterre.	Submarine	No warning	Torpedo	1

69. MERCHANT VESSELS CAPTURED OR SUNK.

Name.	Gross Tons.	Date.	Position.	Cause of Loss.	How attacked.	How sunk.	Lives lost.
		1917. Oct.					
†Forestmoor	2,844	5	54 miles W. by N. ¾ N. from Cape Spartel.	Submarine	No warning	Torpedo	22 including Master.
†Boutnewydd	3,296	5	60 miles N.N.E. from Marsa Susa.	Submarine	No warning	Torpedo	3
Toledo	1,159	5 apprx.	Baltic	Reported as destroyed to avoid capture.	—	—	—
†Civilian	7,871	6	15 miles North from Alexandria.	Submarine	No warning	Torpedo	2
†Bedale	2,116	6	25 miles S.E. by S. from Mine Head.	Submarine	No warning	Torpedo	3
Alcyone (S.V.)	116	7	12 miles W.N.W. from Boulogne.	Submarine	Captured	Bombs	—
†Aylevarroo	908	7 (?)	Off S. Ireland	Submarine (?)	No warning(?)	Torpedo (?)	20 including Master.
†Richard de Larrinaga.	5,591	8	15 miles S.E. ½ S. from Ballycottin Id.	Submarine	No warning	Torpedo	35 including Master.
†Memphian	6,305	8	7 miles E.N.E. from N. Arklow L.V.	Submarine	No warning	Torpedo	32
†Greldon	3,322	8	7 miles E.N.E. from N. Arklow L.V.	Submarine	No warning	Torpedo	28 including Master.
†Main	715	9	1½ miles East from Drummore, Luce Bay.	Submarine	Gunfire	Gunfire	12
†Poldown	1,370	9	2 miles W.S.W. from Trevose Head.	Mine	Mine	Mine	18 including Master.
†Peshawur	7,634	9	7 miles S.E. ¼ E. from Ballyquintin Point, Co. Down.	Submarine	No warning	Torpedo	11
Gowrie	1,031	10	14 miles N.E. from Cherbourg.	Submarine	No warning	Torpedo	—
• †Bostonian	5,736	10	34 miles S. by E. ½ E. from Start Point.	Submarine	No warning	Torpedo	4
†Cayo Bonito	3,427	11	4 miles E.N.E. from Savona.	Submarine	No warning	Torpedo	6
†Rhodesia	4,313	11	7 miles S.E. by S. from Coningbeg L.V.	Submarine	No warning	Torpedo	4
• †Baychattan	3,758	11	½ a mile S.S.W. from Prawle Point.	Submarine	No warning	Torpedo	—
• †Mira	3,700	11	4 miles S.W. ½ W. from Beachy Head.	Mine	Mine	Mine	
†W. M. Barkley	569	12	7 miles East from the Kish L.V.	Submarine	No warning	Torpedo	4 including Master.
Joshua (S.V.)	60	12(?)	English Channel	Submarine	Not known	Not known	3 including Master.
†Eskmere	2,293	13	15 miles W.N.W. from South Stack.	Submarine	No warning	Torpedo	20 including Master.
†Alavi	3,627	13	6 miles N.E. from Cape Palos.	Submarine	Captured	Gunfire	13
†Peebles	4,284	13	14 miles S. by E. ½ E. from Flamborough Head.	Submarine	No warning	Torpedo	—
†East Wales	4,321	14	8 miles S. by W. ½ W. from Daunts Rock.	Submarine	Captured	Gunfire	3

MERCHANT VESSELS CAPTURED OR SUNK.

Name.	Gross Tons.	Date.	Position.	Cause of Loss.	How attacked.	How sunk.	Lives lost.
		1917. Oct.					
†Semantha	2,847	14	10 miles N.W. by N. from Cape St. John, Crete.	Submarine	No warning	Torpedo	32 including Master.
†Hartburn	2,367	15	10 miles South from Anvil Point.	Submarine	No warning	Torpedo	3
†White Head	1,172	15	40 miles N.N.E. from Suda Bay.	Submarine	No warning	Torpedo	23
†Garthclyde	2,124	15	12 miles W. ¼ S. from the Lizard.	Submarine	No warning	Torpedo	—
†California	5,629	17	145 miles N.W. by N. ¾ N. from Cape Villano.	Submarine	No warning	Torpedo	4
†Polvena	4,750	17	25 miles N. by E. ¼ E. from Ushant.	Submarine	No warning	Torpedo	3
†Manchuria	2,997	17	60 miles N.W. from Ushant.	Submarine	No warning	Torpedo	26 including Master.
†Adams	2,223	17	6 miles S.E. by E. from the Lizard.	Submarine	No warning	Torpedo	—
†Madura	4,484	18	23 miles W.S.W. from Bishop Rock.	Submarine	No warning	Torpedo	3
†Hazelwood	3,120	18	8 miles S. by E. ½ E. from Anvil Point.	Submarine	No warning	Torpedo	32 including Master.
Sten	928	18	5 miles North from Godrevy Lighthouse.	Submarine	No warning	Torpedo	9 including Master.
†Amsteldam	1,233	18	6 miles North from Flamborough Head.	Submarine	No warning	Torpedo	4
†Togston	1,057	18	20 miles S. by E. ½ E. from Flamborough Head.	Submarine	No warning	Torpedo	5
†Cadmus	1,879	18	20 miles S. by E. ½ E. from Flamborough Head.	Submarine	No warning	Torpedo	—
†War Clover	5,174	19	25 miles E. by N. ¾ N. from Pantellaria.	Submarine	No warning	Torpedo	14
Cupica (Motor)	1,240	19	75 miles W. by S. ½ S. from Bishop Rock.	Submarine	Captured	Gunfire	—
Eldra (S.V.)	227	19	35 miles N.W. from Treport.	Submarine	Captured	Bombs	—
†Waikawa	5,666	19	4 miles East from Start Point.	Submarine	No warning	Torpedo	—
†Pera	7,635	19	105 miles E. ¾ N. from Marsa Susa.	Submarine	No warning	Torpedo	1
†Good Hope	3,618	19	125 miles E. by S. from Malta.	Submarine	No warning	Torpedo	—
†Australdale	4,379	19	165 miles N.W. by N. ¾ N. from Cape Villano.	Submarine	No warning	Torpedo	27
†Gemma	1,385	19	5 miles N. by W. from Flamborough Head.	Submarine	No warning	Torpedo	4
†Elsiston	2,908	19	150 miles E. by S. ½ S. from Malta.	Submarine	No warning	Torpedo	1
†Britannia	765	19 (?)	English Channel	Submarine (?)	No warning (?)	Torpedo (?)	22 including Master.
†Algarve	1,274	20	15 miles W.S.W. from Portland Bill.	Submarine	No warning	Torpedo	21 including Master.
†Collegian	7,520	20	100 miles N.W. by N. ¼ N. from Alexandria.	Submarine	No warning	Torpedo	—
†Colorado	7,165	20	1½ miles East from Start Point.	Submarine	No warning	Torpedo	4

MERCHANT VESSELS CAPTURED OR SUNK.

Name.	Gross Tons.	Date.	Position.	Cause of Loss.	How attacked.	How sunk.	Lives lost.
		1917. Oct.					
†Ionian	8,268	20	2 miles West from St. Govan's Head.	Submarine	No warning	Torpedo	7
†Gryfevale	4,437	21	10 miles N. from Cape Blanco.	Submarine	Chased	Ran ashore	—
● Tom Roper (S.V.)	120	21	20 miles S.S.E. from Start Point.	Submarine	Captured	Bombs	1
Bunty (tug)	73	21	Off Whitby	Mine	Mine	Mine	5 including Master.
†Zillah	3,788	22	25 miles N.E. from Kildin Island, Murmanski Coast.	Submarine	No warning	Torpedo	18
†Tredegar Hall	3,764	23	4½ miles E.S.E. from Flamborough Head.	Submarine	No warning	Torpedo	3
†Seistan	4,238	23	3½ miles N. by W. ¼ W. from Flamborough Head.	Submarine	No warning	Torpedo	5
†Euston	2,841	24	37 miles S.W. from Cape Matapan.	Submarine	No warning	Torpedo	1
†Ilderton	3,125	24	35 miles N.E. from Kildin Island, Murmanski Coast.	Submarine	No warning	Torpedo	—
†Sheaf Blade	2,378	25	13 miles S.E. by S. from Cape de Gata.	Submarine	No warning	Torpedo	2 including Master.
†Ness	3,050	25	10 miles S.E. from Cape de Gata.	Submarine	Captured	Gunfire	2
†Wearside	3,560	25	3 miles W. by S. from Sunk L.V.	Mine	Mine	Mine	—
● Gefion	1,123	25	10 miles N.E. from Berry Head.	Submarine	No warning	Torpedo	2 including Master.
†Sapele	4,366	26	100 miles N.W. from Tory Island.	Submarine	No warning	Torpedo	3
Lady Helen	811	27	½ mile East from S. Cheek, Robin Hood Bay.	Mine	Mine	Mine	7 including Master.
● †Redesmere	2,123	28	6 miles W.S.W. from St. Catherines.	Submarine	No warning	Torpedo	19
†Ferrona	4,591	28	7 miles N.E. from Valencia.	Submarine	Captured	Bombs	1
● †Baron Garioch	1,831	28	5 miles S.E. from Anvil Point.	Submarine	No warning	Torpedo	2
†Baron Balfour	3,991	28	8 miles North from Sem Island, Murmanski Coast.	Submarine	No warning	Torpedo	—
†Namur	6,701	29	55 miles E. by S. ½ S. from Gibraltar.	Submarine	No warning	Torpedo	1
†Cambric	3,403	31	14 miles West from Cape Shershel.	Submarine	No warning	Torpedo	24 including Master. Four prisoners.
†Estrellano	1,161	31	14 miles W. by N. ½ N. from Pilier Island.	Submarine	No warning	Torpedo	3
● North Sea	1,711	31	2½ miles S.W. by S. from Prawle Point.	Submarine	No warning	Torpedo	1
†Phare	1,282	31	2½ miles N. ½ E. from Scarborough.	Submarine	No warning	Torpedo	14

MERCHANT VESSELS CAPTURED OR SUNK.

Name.	Gross Tons.	Date.	Position.	Cause of Loss.	How attacked.	How sunk.	Lives lost.
NOVEMBER 1917.		1917. Nov.					
Jessie - -	332	2	3 miles N.E. from Flamborough Head.	Submarine - -	Gunfire -	Beached; total wreck.	4 including Master.
†Cape Finisterre	4,380	2	1 mile S.S.E. from Manacles Buoy.	Submarine - -	No warning -	Torpedo -	35 including Master.
†Farraline - -	1,226	2	15 miles N.E. ¼ E. from Ushant.	Submarine - -	No warning -	Torpedo -	1
†Antæus - -	3,061	4	42 miles N. by W. ½ W. from Cape Bon.	Submarine - -	No warning -	Torpedo -	Master prisoner.
†Border Knight -	3,724	4	1½ miles E.S.E. from the Lizard.	Submarine - -	No warning -	Torpedo -	1
Hilda R. (S.V.)	100	5	20 miles South from Cape St. Mary.	Submarine - -	Captured -	Bombs -	1
†Suntrap - -	1,353	7	2½ miles East from S. Cheek, Robin Hood Bay.	Submarine - -	No warning -	Torpedo -	—
The Marquis -	373	8	16 miles E.S.E. from Rockabill.	Submarine - -	Captured -	Gunfire -	—
†Ardglamis -	4,540	9	125 miles West from Cape Spartel.	Submarine - -	No warning -	Torpedo -	—
†Ballogie - -	1,207	9	1½ miles N.E. from Filey.	Submarine - -	No warning -	Torpedo -	13 including Master.
Lapwing - -	1,192	11	9 miles S.E. from Southwold.	Mine - -	Mine -	Mine -	—
Morning Star (motor).	129	12	10 miles S.E. ¾ E. from Cape Barfleur.	Submarine - -	Captured -	Bombs -	—
†Barbary - -	4,185	12	56 miles N.W. by N. from Port Said.	Submarine - -	No warning -	Torpedo -	3 including Master.
†Carlo - -	3,040	13	7 miles S. by W. from Coningbeg L.V.	Submarine - -	No warning -	Torpedo -	2
†Atlas - -	989	13	5 miles S.E. from Owers L.V.	Submarine - -	No warning -	Torpedo -	—
†Axwell - -	1,442	13	5 miles N.N.E. from Owers L.V.	Submarine - -	No warning -	Torpedo -	2
†Axminster -	1,905	13	Off Pakefield Gat	Submarine - -	No warning -	Torpedo -	3
†Australbush -	4,398	13	7 miles E. ½ N. from the Eddystone.	Submarine - -	No warning -	Torpedo -	2
†Ardmore - -	1,304	13	13 miles W.S.W. from Coningbeg L.V.	Submarine - -	No warning -	Torpedo -	19
Dolly Varden (S.V.)	202	14	20 miles N.W. from Treport.	Submarine - -	Captured -	Gunfire -	—
†Prophet - -	3,230	14	3 miles S.E. from Antikithera Island.	Submarine - -	No warning -	Torpedo -	—
†Trowbridge -	3,712	14	12 miles S.E. from Cape de Gata.	Submarine - -	No warning -	Torpedo -	—
†Kyno - -	3,034	16	9 miles N. by E. ¾ E. from Shershel.	Submarine - -	No warning -	Torpedo -	5
†Garron Head -	1,933	16	40 miles N. by E. ½ E. from Bayonne.	Mine - -	Mine -	Mine -	28
†Gasconia - -	3,801	16	12 miles N.E. ½ E. from Shershel.	Submarine - -	No warning -	Torpedo -	3
†Western Coast -	1,394	17	10 miles W.S.W. from the Eddystone.	Submarine - -	No warning -	Torpedo -	17
†Victoria - -	974	17	14 miles W. ½ N. from the Eddystone.	Submarine - -	No warning -	Torpedo -	2

Name.	Gross Tons.	Date.	Position.	Cause of Loss.	How attacked.	How sunk.	Lives lost.
		1917. Nov.					
†Clan Maccorquodale.	6,517	17	165 miles N.W. by N. from Alexandria.	Submarine	No warning	Torpedo	—
†Croxteth Hall	5,872	17	25 miles West from Bombay.	Mine	Mine	Mine	9
†Gisella	2,502	18	2 miles S.W. by S. from Skokham Island.	Submarine	No warning	Torpedo	2
†Antwerpen	1,637	18	2 miles S.S.W. from the Runnelstone.	Submarine	No warning	Torpedo	—
●†Aparima	5,704	19	6 miles S.W. ¾ W. from Anvil Point.	Submarine	No warning	Torpedo	56
●†Farn	4,393	19	5 miles E. by N. from Start Point.	Submarine	No warning	Torpedo	—
Minnie Coles (S.V.)	116	19	30 miles N.W. by N. from Les Hanois.	Submarine	Captured	Bombs	—
Robert Brown (S.V.)	119	19	25 miles W.N.W. from Hartland Point.	Submarine	Captured	Bombs	—
†Jutland	2,824	19	18 miles N.E. by N. from Ushant.	Submarine	No warning	Torpedo	26 including Master.
Clangula	1,754	19	4 miles S.W. ¾ W. from Hartland Point.	Submarine	No warning	Torpedo	15 including Master.
Robert Morris (S.V.)	146	20	155 miles W.S.W. from Bishop Rock.	Submarine	Captured	Bombs	—
†Aros Castle	4,460	21	300 miles W. by S. ¼ S. from Bishop Rock.	Submarine	No warning	Torpedo	2
Elsena	335	22	16 miles S.E. ½ S. from S. Arklow L.V.	Submarine	Captured	Gunfire	—
Conovium (S.V.)	86	22	14 miles S.E. ½ S. from S. Arklow L.V.	Submarine	Captured	Gunfire	—
†King Idwal	3,631	22	29 miles S.E. by E. ½ E. from Buchan Ness.	Submarine	No warning	Torpedo	1
†Kohistan	4,732	22	25 miles W. ½ S. from Marittimo.	Submarine	No warning	Torpedo	—
†Westlands	3,112	23	10 miles North from Ile de Vierge.	Submarine	No warning	Torpedo	—
†Ocean	1,442	23	4 miles E. by N. from Hartlepool.	Submarine	No warning	Torpedo	—
●†La Blanca	7,479	23	10 miles S.S.E. from Berry Head.	Submarine	No warning	Torpedo	2
†Dunrobin	3,617	24	49 miles S.W. by S. ½ S. from the Lizard.	Submarine	No warning	Torpedo	31 including Master.
†Sabia	2,807	24	6 miles S.S.E. from the Lizard.	Submarine	No warning	Torpedo	11
†Nyassa	2,579	24	3 miles E.S.E. from the Lizard.	Submarine	No warning	Torpedo	—
French Rose	465	24	6 miles S. by W. from Shipwash L.V.	Mine	Mine	Mine	—
†Ostpreussen	1,779	25	1½ miles East from Shipwash L.V.	Mine	Mine	Mine	1
†Karema	5,285	25	33 miles S.E. by E. from Cape de Gata.	Submarine	No warning	Torpedo	3
†Ovid	4,159	25	65 miles N.E. ½ E. from Suda Bay.	Submarine	No warning	Torpedo	2

MERCHANT VESSELS CAPTURED OR SUNK.   74

Name.	Gross Tons.	Date.	Position.	Cause of Loss.	How attacked.	How sunk.	Lives lost.
†Oriflamme	3,764	1917. Nov. 25	1.4 ST. CATHERINES miles South L.V.	Mine	Mine	Mine	—
†Groeswen	3,570	27	3 miles N.E. ½ E. from Sunk L.V.	Mine	Mine	Mine	—
Gladys	179	27	3 miles S.W. from Cape Gris Nez.	Mine	Mine	Mine	6
†Almond Branch	3,461	27	2 miles S.E. from Dodman Point.	Submarine	No warning	Torpedo	1
†Eastfield	2,145	27	7 miles E.S.E. from Dodman Point.	Submarine	No warning	Torpedo	1
†Bleamoor	3,755	27	4 miles S.S.E. from Berry Head.	Submarine	No warning	Torpedo	8
†Apapa	7,832	28	3 miles N. by E. from Lynas Point.	Submarine	No warning	Torpedo	77
†Jane Radcliffe	4,074	28	2 miles S.W. from Antimilo.	Submarine	No warning	Torpedo	—
†Georgios Antippa	1,960	28	25 miles S. by E. from Flamborough Head.	Submarine	No warning	Torpedo	—
†Derbent	3,178	30	6 miles N.E. by E. from Lynas Point.	Submarine	No warning	Torpedo	—
†Kalibia	4,930	30	29 miles S.W. from the Lizard.	Submarine	No warning	Torpedo	25
DECEMBER 1917.		Dec.					
†Molesey	3,218	1	12 miles S.W. by W. from Brighton L.V.	Submarine	No warning	Torpedo	—
†Euphorbia	3,109	1	14 miles E. by S. from Royal Sovereign L.V.	Submarine	No warning	Torpedo	14
†Rydal Hall	3,314	1	14 miles E. by S. from Royal Sovereign L.V.	Submarine	No warning	Torpedo	23
†Birchgrove	2,821	2	10 miles W. by N. ½ N. from Ile de Groix.	Submarine	No warning	Torpedo	1
†Kintuck	4,639	2	8 miles N.W. by N. ½ N. from Godrevy L.H.	Submarine	No warning	Torpedo	1
†Berwick Law	4,680	2	22 miles West from Cape Tenez.	Submarine	No warning	Torpedo	1 (Master prisoner).
†Copeland	1,184	2	15 miles S.S.W. from the Tuskar.	Submarine	No warning	Torpedo	12
†Wreathier	852	3	1 mile West from Prawle Point.	Submarine	No warning	Torpedo	3
†Livonia	1,879	3	4 miles E. by N. ½ N. from Start Point.	Submarine	No warning	Torpedo	23 including Master.
†Dowlais	3,016	3	Off Cap de Fer	Submarine	No warning	Torpedo	26 including Master.
Eagle	182	4	10 miles South from Start Point.	Submarine	Captured	Bombs	—
†Brigitta	2,084	4	6 miles S.W. from the Nab L.V.	Mine	Mine	Mine	2
†Forfar	3,827	4	115 miles S.W. by W. from the Lizard.	Submarine	No warning	Torpedo	3
†Greenwich	2,938	5	9 miles South from Planier Island.	Submarine	No warning	Torpedo	—
†Aigburth	824	5	2 miles N.E. by E. from S. Cheek, Robin Hood Bay.	Submarine	No warning	Torpedo	11 including Master.

MERCHANT VESSELS CAPTURED OR SUNK.

Name.	Gross Tons.	Date.	Position.	Cause of Loss.	How attacked.	How sunk.	Lives lost.
		1917. Dec.					
†Ilvington Court	4,217	6	8 miles N.W. by N. from Shershel.	Submarine	No warning	Torpedo	8
†Asaba	972	6	2 miles W.S.W. from the Lizard.	Submarine	No warning	Torpedo	16 including Master.
†Wyndhurst	570	6	30 miles South from St. Catherines.	Submarine	No warning	Torpedo	11 including Master.
†Earl of Elgin	4,448	7	10 miles W. ½ S. from Carnarvon Bay L.V.	Submarine	No warning	Torpedo	18 including Master.
Proba (S.V.)	105	7	3 miles S.E. from the Lizard.	Submarine	Captured	Bombs	—
†Highgate	1,780	7	2½ miles East from S. Cheek, Robin Hood Bay.	Submarine	No warning	Torpedo	—
†Maindy Bridge	3,653	8	4 miles E.N.E. from Sunderland.	Submarine	No warning	Torpedo	2
†Lampada	2,220	8	3 miles North from Whitby.	Submarine	No warning	Torpedo	5
†Consols	3,756	8	40 miles N.W. ½ N. from Cape Bon.	Submarine	No warning	Torpedo	3
†War Tune	2,045	9	1½ miles S.S.E. from Black Head.	Submarine	No warning	Torpedo	1
†Venetia	3,596	9	3 miles N.N.W. from Whitby Rock buoy.	Submarine	No warning	Torpedo	—
†Minorca	1,145	11	2 to 3 miles from C. de las Huertas.	Submarine	No warning	Torpedo	15 including Master.
†Persier	3,874	11	50 miles E. from C. Spartivento, Italy.	Submarine	No warning	Torpedo	1
†D.A. Gordon	2,301	11	1¼ miles E.S.E. from C. de las Huertas.	Submarine	No warning	Torpedo	1
†Oldfield Grange	4,653	11	30 miles N.E. from Tory I.	Submarine	No warning	Torpedo	—
†Leonatus	2,099	12	2 miles E. by S. from Kirkabister L.H.	Mine	Mine	Mine	—
†Charleston	1,866	12	30 miles West from the Smalls.	Submarine	Captured	Bombs	Two gunners prisoners.
†Cordova	2,284	12	North Sea	T.B.D.	—	—	—
Britannic (S.V.)	92	13	12 miles N.N.W. from Les Hanois.	Submarine	Captured	Bombs	—
Little Gem (S.V.)	114	13	Off Channel Islands.	Submarine (reported).	Not known	Not known	5 including Master.
†Bangarth	1,872	13	13 miles N.N.E. from the Tyne.	Submarine	No warning	Torpedo	2
†Garthwaite	5,690	13	4 miles East from Whitby.	Submarine	No warning	Torpedo	14 including Master.
†Arnewood	2,259	13	4 miles E.S.E. from Sleat Point, Skye.	Mine	Mine	Mine	—
†Volnay	4,610	14	2 miles E. by S. from Manacles.	Mine	Mine	Mine	—
†Coila	4,135	14	3 miles S.E. by S. from Canet Point, Valencia.	Submarine	No warning	Torpedo	3
†Hare	774	14	7 miles East from the Kish L.V.	Submarine	No warning	Torpedo	12
†Bernard	3,682	15	180 miles W.S.W. from Bishop Rk.	Submarine	No warning	Torpedo	1

Merchant Vessels Captured or Sunk.

Name.	Gross Tons.	Date.	Position.	Cause of Loss.	How attacked.	How sunk.	Lives lost.
		1917. Dec.					
†Bristol City	2,511	16	Atlantic	Submarine (reported).	No warning (probably).	Torpedo (probably).	30 including Master.
Formby	1,282	16(?)	Irish Sea	Submarine (?)	No warning(?)	Torpedo (?)	15 including Master.
†Foylemore	3,831	16	22 miles E. ½ S. from the Lizard.	Submarine	No warning	Torpedo	—
†Riversdale	2,805	18	1 mile South from Prawle Point.	Submarine	No warning	Torpedo	1
Charles (S.V.)	56	18	English Channel	Submarine	Gunfire	Gunfire	1 Master and 2 crew prisoners.
Coningbeg	1,279	18(?)	Irish Sea	Submarine (?)	No warning(?)	Torpedo (?)	15 including Master.
†Vinovia	7,046	19	8 miles South from Wolf Rock.	Submarine	No warning	Torpedo	9
†Alice Marie	2,210	19	6 miles E.N.E. from Start Pt.	Submarine	No warning	Torpedo	—
†Warsaw	608	20	4 miles S.E. by E. from Start Point.	Submarine	No warning	Torpedo	17 including Master.
†Fiscus	4,732	20	10 miles N.N.E. from Cape Ivi.	Submarine	No warning	Torpedo	1
Eveline	2,605	20	9½ miles S. ½ W. from Berry Hd.	Submarine	No warning	Torpedo	—
†Waverley	3,853	20	33 miles N.E. ½ N. from Cape Ivi.	Submarine	No warning	Torpedo	22
†Polvarth	3,146	20	35 miles West from Ushant.	Submarine	No warning	Torpedo	2
†City of Lucknow	8,293	21	50 miles N.E. by N. ½ N. from Cani Rocks.	Submarine	No warning	Torpedo	—
†Mabel Baird	2,500	22	4 miles W.S.W. from the Lizard.	Submarine	No warning	Torpedo	5
†Colemere	2,120	22	35 miles West from the Smalls.	Submarine	No warning	Torpedo	4
†Clan Cameron	3,595	22	23 miles S.W. by S. ½ S. from Portland Bill.	Submarine	No warning	Torpedo	—
†Grantleyhall	4,008	23	5 miles East from Orfordness.	Mine	Mine	Mine	—
†Hilda Lea	1,328	23	24 miles S. by E. from St. Catherines.	Submarine	No warning	Torpedo	1
†Canova	4,637	24	15 miles South from Mine Head.	Submarine	No warning	Torpedo	7
†Daybreak	3,238	24	1 mile East from South Rock L.V.	Submarine	No warning	Torpedo	21 including Master.
†Turnbridge	2,874	24	34 miles N.E. by N. from Cape Ivi.	Submarine	No warning	Torpedo	1
†Argo	3,071	24	18 miles N.W. from Cape Tenez.	Submarine	No warning	Torpedo	—
†Cliftondale	3,811	25	36 miles E. by N. ½ N. from Cape Tenez.	Submarine	No warning	Torpedo	3 Master prisoner.
†Agberi	4,821	25	18 miles N.W. ½ N. from Bardsey Island.	Submarine	No warning	Torpedo	—
†Umballa	5,310	25	8 miles S.W. by W. from Cape Scalea, Gulf of Policastro.	Submarine	No warning	Torpedo	15
†Tregenna	5,772	26	9 miles South from Dodman Point.	Submarine	No warning	Torpedo	—

77 MERCHANT VESSELS CAPTURED OR SUNK.

Name.	Gross Tons.	Date.	Position.	Cause of Loss.	How attacked.	How sunk.	Lives lost.
		1917. Dec.					
†Benito	4,712	26	9 miles South from Dodman Point.	Submarine	No warning	Torpedo	—
†Adela	685	27	12 miles N.W. from the Skerries, Anglesea.	Submarine	No warning	Torpedo	24
†Santa Amalia	4,306	28	30 miles N. by E. $\frac{1}{2}$ E. from Malin Head.	Submarine	No warning	Torpedo	43 including Master.
†Maxton	5,094	28	28 miles N. $\frac{1}{4}$ W. from Malin Head.	Submarine	No warning	Torpedo	1
†Lord Derby	3,757	28	7 miles S.W. by S. from St. Ann's Head.	Submarine	No warning	Torpedo	3
†Chirripo	4,050	28	$\frac{1}{2}$ mile from Black Head, Belfast.	Mine	Mine	Mine	—
†Robert Eggleton	2,274	28	10 miles S.W. from Bardsey Island.	Submarine	No warning	Torpedo	1
†Fallodon	3,012	28	12 miles S.S.E. from St. Catherines.	Submarine	No warning	Torpedo	1
Alfred H. Read	457	28	Entrance to River Mersey.	Mine	Mine	Mine	39 including Master.
†Clara	2,425	28	1$\frac{1}{2}$ miles S.S.W. from the Runnelstone.	Submarine	No warning	Torpedo	—
†Ennismore	1,499	29	23 miles East from Girdleness.	Submarine	No warning	Torpedo	10
†Zone	3,914	30	4 miles North from St. Ives.	Submarine	No warning	Torpedo	—
†Hercules	1,295	30	3 miles E.N.E. from Whitby.	Submarine	No warning	Torpedo	12 including Master.
†Aragon	9,588	30	Entrance to Alexandria.	Submarine	No warning	Torpedo	19 including Master.
†Westville	3,207	31	5 miles W.S.W. from St. Catherines.	Submarine	No warning	Torpedo	—
†Osmanieh	4,041	31	Entrance to Alexandria.	Mine	Mine	Mine	24 including Master.
JANUARY 1918.		1918. Jan.					
†Sandon Hall	5,134	1	22 miles N.N.E. from Linosa.	Submarine	No warning	Torpedo	—
†Boston City	2,711	2	11 miles W. $\frac{1}{2}$ N. from St. Ann's Head.	Submarine	No warning	Torpedo	—
†Gallier	4,592	2	7 miles E.N.E. from Wolf Rock.	Submarine	No warning	Torpedo	—
†Gartland	2,613	3	5 miles E.S.E. from Owers L.V.	Submarine	No warning	Torpedo	2
†Birchwood	2,756	3	25 miles East from Blackwater L.V.	Submarine	No warning	Torpedo	—
†Steelville	3,649	3	20 miles North from Cape Bon.	Submarine	No warning	Torpedo	—
†Allantou	4,253	3	20 miles North from Cape Bon.	Submarine	No warning	Torpedo	—
Otto S.V.	96	4	10 miles S.S.W. from St. John's Point, Co. Down.	Submarine	Captured	Gunfire	—
Rewa (Hospital Ship)	7,308	4	19 miles W. $\frac{1}{4}$ S. from Hartland Point.	Submarine	No warning	Torpedo	4
†Iolanthe	3,081	4	10 miles S.E. by E. from Portland Bill.	Submarine	No warning	Torpedo	—

MERCHANT VESSELS CAPTURED OR SUNK. 78

Name.	Gross Tons.	Date.	Position.	Cause of Loss.	How attacked.	How sunk.	Lives lost.
		1918. Jan.					
•†Glenarm Head	3,908	4	5 miles S.W. by S. from Brighton L.V.	Submarine	No warning	Torpedo	2 including Master.
†Birtley	1,438	4	8 miles N. from Flamboro' Head.	Submarine (?)	No warning(?)	Torpedo (?)	18 including Master.
†Knightsgarth	2,889	5	5 miles W.N.W. from Bull Point, Rathlin Island.	Submarine	No warning	Torpedo	2
†Rio Claro	3,687	5	Rapallo Bay	Submarine	No warning	Torpedo	—
†War Baron	5,730	5	8 miles N.E. from Godrevy L.H.	Submarine	No warning	Torpedo	2
†Rose Marie	2,220	5	13 miles S.E. from N. Arklow L.V.	Submarine	No warning	Torpedo	1
†Spenser	4,186	6	28 miles S.W. by W. ½ W. from Bardsey Island.	Submarine	No warning	Torpedo	—
†Halberdier	1,049	6	27 miles W. by N. from Bardsey Island.	Submarine	No warning	Torpedo	5
•†Gascony	3,133	6	20 miles N.N.E. from Owers L.V.	Submarine	No warning	Torpedo	—
†Arab	4,191	7	18 miles N. by E. from Cape Serrat.	Submarine	No warning	Torpedo	21
Bayvoe	2,979	9	10 miles South from Iles de Glenan.	Submarine	No warning	Torpedo	4
W. C. McKay (S.V.)	145	10(?)	Off the Azores	Submarine	Not known	Not known	6 including Master.
†Rapallo	3,811	13	1¼ miles South from Cape Peloro, Sicily.	Submarine	No warning	Torpedo	1
†Alster	964	14	5 miles E.S.E. from Noss Head, Shetland.	Submarine	No warning	Torpedo	—
†Spital	4,718	15	4 miles S.S.E. from St. Anthony Point.	Submarine	No warning	Torpedo	—
†War Song	2,535	15	12 miles West from Ile de Sein.	Submarine	Captured	Gunfire	16 including Master.
†Kingsdyke	1,710	17	20 miles N.E. ¾ E. from Cape Barfleur.	Submarine	No warning	Torpedo	16 including Master.
†Windsor Hall	3,693	17	45 miles N.W. from Alexandria.	Submarine	No warning	Torpedo	27 Master prisoner.
Maria P. (S.V.)	263	18	75 miles West from Cape Mannu, Sardinia.	Submarine	Captured	Gunfire	—
†Trocas	4,129	19	10 miles N.E. from Skyros L.H.	Submarine	No warning	Torpedo	24
•†Mechanician	9,044	20	8 miles West from St. Catherines.	Submarine	No warning	Torpedo	13
†West Wales	4,331	21	140 miles S.E. ¾ S. from Malta.	Submarine	No warning	Torpedo	2
•†Teelin Head	1,718	21	12 miles S.S.W. from Owers L.V.	Submarine	No warning	Torpedo	13 including Master.
•†Serrana	3,677	22	10 miles West from St. Catherines.	Submarine	No warning	Torpedo	5
•†Greatham	2,338	22	3 miles S.E. from Dartmouth.	Submarine	No warning	Torpedo	7
†Anglo Canadian	4,239	22	33 miles S. ½ E. from Malta.	Submarine	No warning	Torpedo	3

MERCHANT VESSELS CAPTURED OR SUNK.

Name.	Gross Tons.	Date.	Position.	Cause of Loss.	How attacked.	How sunk.	Lives lost.
		1918. Jan.					
†Manchester Spinner.	4,247	22	33 miles S. ½ E. from Malta.	Submarine	No warning	Torpedo	—
†Birkhall	4,541	23	4 miles S.E. from Cape Doro.	Submarine	No warning	Torpedo	2 including Master.
†Normandy	618	25	8 miles E. by N. from Cape La Hague.	Submarine	No warning	Torpedo	14
†Humber	280	25	2 miles East from Sunderland.	Submarine	No warning	Torpedo	7 including Master.
†Eastlands	3,113	25	13 miles N.W. from Ile de Vierge.	Submarine	No warning	Torpedo	1
Apostolos Andreas (S.V.)	50 apprx.	25	Mediterranean	Submarine	Captured	Gunfire	—
†Cork	1,232	26	9 miles N.E. from Lynas Point.	Submarine	No warning	Torpedo	12
†Hartley	1,150	26	2 miles N.E. from Skinningrove.	Submarine	No warning	Torpedo	—
Rob Roy (S.V.)	112	26	20 miles S.W. from St. Catherines.	Submarine	Captured	Gunfire	—
Louie Bell (S.V.)	118	26	15 miles North from Cherbourg.	Submarine	Captured	Bombs	—
†Andania	13,405	27	2 miles N.N.E. from Rathlin Island L.H.	Submarine	No warning	Torpedo	7
W.H.L. (S.V.)	97	28	8 miles S.S.E. from Portland Bill.	Submarine	Captured	Bombs	—
†Ethelinda	3,257	29	15 miles N.W. from the Skerries, Anglesea.	Submarine	No warning	Torpedo	26 including Master.
†Geo	3,048	29	6 miles N. by W. from Cape Peloro, Sicily.	Submarine	No warning	Torpedo	16 including Master.
Taxiarchis (S.V.)	160	29	100 miles S.W. from Cape Gata, Cyprus.	Submarine	Captured	Gunfire	—
Perriton (S.V.)	90	29	20 miles E. ½ S. from Berry Head.	Submarine	Captured	Gunfire	—
†Butetown	1,829	29	1½ miles South from Dodman Point.	Submarine	No warning	Torpedo	2
Ferryhill	411	30	15 miles W. ½ N. from Cape Antifer.	Submarine	Captured	Gunfire	—
†Maizar	7,293	30	38 miles N. by W. ½ W. from Cape Ferrat.	Submarine	No warning	Torpedo	—
†Minnetonka	13,528	30	40 miles E.N.E. from Malta.	Submarine	No warning	Torpedo	4 Ten prisoners.
†Towneley	2,476	31	18 miles N.E. ¼ E. from Trevose Head.	Submarine	No warning	Torpedo	6 including Master.
FEBRUARY 1918.		1918. Feb.					
Kindly Light (S.V.)	116	1	10 miles E.N.E. from Trevose Head.	Submarine	Captured	Gunfire	—
†Arrino	4,484	1	14 miles N.W. by W. from Ile de Vierge.	Submarine	No warning	Torpedo	—
†Cavallo	2,086	1	6 miles N.W. from Trevose Head.	Submarine	No warning	Torpedo	3
†Jaffa	1,383	2	3 miles E. by S. from Owers L.V.	Submarine	No warning	Torpedo	10
†Avanti	2,128	2	4 miles S.E. by E. from St. Albans Head.	Submarine	No warning	Torpedo	22 including Master.

MERCHANT VESSELS CAPTURED OR SUNK.   80

Name.	Gross Tons.	Date.	Position.	Cause of Loss	How attacked.	How sunk.	Lives lost.
		1918. Feb.					
†Newminster Abbey.	3,114	2	44 miles E. by N. ½ N. from Cape de Creus.	Submarine	No warning	Torpedo	—
†Celia	5,004	2	44 miles E. by N. ½ N. from Cape de Creus.	Submarine	No warning	Torpedo	—
Sofie	354	3 (?)	Bristol Channel	Submarine	Not known	Not known	8 including Master.
†Aboukir	3,660	3	20 miles E. by S. from Cape de Creus.	Submarine	Captured	Gunfire	Master prisoner.
†Lofoten	942	3	7 miles S.E. by E. from Start Pt.	Submarine	No warning	Torpedo	17
Maid of Harlech (S.V.)	315	4	46 miles N. by W. from Cape Ivi.	Submarine	Captured	Gunfire	—
†Standish Hall	3,996	4	38 miles W. by N. from Alexandria.	Submarine	No warning	Torpedo	—
Treveal	4,160	4	Off the Skerries, Anglesey.	Submarine	No warning	Torpedo	33 including Master.
†Aurania	13,936	4	15 miles N. ½ W. from Inishtrahull.	Submarine	No warning	Torpedo	8
†Cresswell	2,829	5	18 miles E. by N. ¼ N. from Kish L.V.	Submarine	No warning	Torpedo	—
†Tuscania	14,348	5	7 miles North from Rathlin Island L.H.	Submarine	No warning	Torpedo	44
†Mexico City	5,078	5	15 miles W. by S. ½ S. from S. Stack, Holyhead.	Submarine	No warning	Torpedo	29 including Master.
†Glenartney	7,263	5	30 miles N.E. from Cape Bon.	Submarine	No warning	Torpedo	2
†Beaumaris	2,372	7	2½ miles N. by W. from the Longships.	Submarine	No warning	Torpedo	—
Limesfield	427	7	24 miles S.E. by E. from Douglas, Isle of Man.	Submarine	Captured	Gunfire	—
Ben Rein	212	7	35 miles N. ½ W. from Liverpool.	Submarine	Captured	Gunfire	—
Ardbeg	227	7	32 miles N. ½ E. from Mersey Bar L.V.	Submarine	Captured	Gunfire	—
†Sturton	4,406	7	15 miles S.E. by E. ¼ E. from Porquerolles Id.	Submarine	No warning	Torpedo	—
†Basuta	2,876	8	45 miles S.S.W. from the Lizard.	Submarine	No warning	Torpedo	1
†Artesia	2,762	8	190 miles E. by N. from Madeira.	Submarine	Captured	Bombs	1
Kia Ora (Barge)	77	8	20 miles N. by W. from Dieppe.	Submarine	Captured	Bombs	—
†Lydie	2,559	9	1 mile E. by S. from Manacles buoy.	Submarine	No warning	Torpedo	2
†Romford	3,035	10	2½ miles East from Cape Carthage.	Submarine	No warning	Torpedo	28 including Master.
†Merton Hall	4,327	11	30 miles N. by E. from Ushant.	Submarine	No warning	Torpedo	57 including Master.
†Baku Standard	3,708	11	5 miles S. by W. ½ W. from Tod Head.	Submarine	No warning	Torpedo	24
†Eleanor	1,980	12	9 miles W. by S. ½ S. from St. Catherines.	Submarine	No warning	Torpedo	34 including Master.

MERCHANT VESSELS CAPTURED OR SUNK.

Name.	Gross Tons.	Date.	Position.	Cause of Loss.	How attacked.	How sunk.	Lives lost.
		1918. Feb.					
†St. Magnus	809	12	3 miles N.N.E. from Peterhead.	Submarine	No warning	Torpedo	5
†Polo	2,915	12	6 miles S.E. by E. from St. Catherines.	Submarine	No warning	Torpedo	3
†Atlas	3,090	14	10 miles E.S.E. from Hartlepool.	Submarine	No warning	Torpedo	—
Carlisle Castle	4,325	14	8 miles E. by N. from Royal Sovereign L.V.	Submarine	No warning	Torpedo	1
†Saga	1,143	14	4 miles E.N.E. from Sunderland.	Submarine	No warning	Torpedo	—
†Ventmoor	3,456	14	8 miles S.W. by W. from Skyros L.H.	Submarine	No warning	Torpedo	21 including Master.
†War Monarch	7,887	14	11 miles East from Royal Sovereign L.V.	Submarine	No warning	Torpedo	—
Bessie Stephens (S.V.)	119	14	10 miles W. by S. ½ S. from South L.H., Lundy Island.	Submarine	Captured	Gunfire	—
†San Rito	3,310	15	23 miles S.W by W. ½ W. from Cape Mastiko, Khios.	Submarine	No warning	Torpedo	3
†Northville	2,472	17	3½ miles S.E. by E. from Berry Head.	Submarine	No warning	Torpedo	—
†Pinewood	2,219	17	15 miles South from Mine Head.	Submarine	Captured	Gunfire	2
†Beacon Light	2,768	19	15 miles S.E. from Butt of Lewis.	Submarine	No warning	Torpedo	33 including Master.
†Glencarron	5,117	19	47 miles S. by E. ½ E. from the Lizard.	Submarine	No warning	Torpedo	—
†Philadelphian	5,165	19	47 miles S. by E. ¼ E. from the Lizard.	Submarine	No warning	Torpedo	4
Wheatflower	188	19	10 miles S.E. by S. from Tuskar Rock.	Submarine	Captured	Gunfire	1
†Barrowmore	3,832	19	53 miles N.W. by W. ¼ W. from Bishop Rock.	Submarine	No warning	Torpedo	25 including Master.
†Commonwealth	3,353	19	5 miles N.E. from Flamborough Head.	Submarine	No warning	Torpedo	14
†Balgray	3,603	20	38 miles S.W. by W. from Dellimara Point, Malta.	Submarine	No warning	Torpedo	—
†Djerv	1,527	20	12 miles N.N.W. from the Skerries, Anglesea.	Submarine	No warning	Torpedo	2 including Master.
†Zeno	2,890	20	48 miles S.W. ½ S. from Dellimara Point Malta.	Submarine	No warning	Torpedo	—
†Huntsmoor	4,957	20	23 miles S. ½ W. from Owers L.V.	Submarine	No warning	Torpedo	20 including Master.
†Rio Verde	4,025	21	4 miles West from Crammock Head, Mull of Galloway.	Submarine	No warning	Torpedo	20 including Master.
Cheviot Range	3,691	21	25 miles South from the Lizard.	Submarine	Captured	Gunfire	27 including Master.

Merchant Vessels Captured or Sunk.

Name.	Gross Tons.	Date.	Position.	Cause of Loss.	How attacked.	How sunk.	Lives lost.
		1918. Feb.					
†Haileybury	2,888	22	15 miles S.E. by E. ¾ E. from the Maidens.	Submarine	No warning	Torpedo	2 including Master.
†British Viscount	3,287	23	12 miles N. by W. ½ W. from the Skerries, Anglesey.	Submarine	No warning	Torpedo	6
†Remus	1,079	23	6 miles S.S.W. from Copinsay, Orkney.	Submarine	No warning	Torpedo	5
Amsterdam	806	24	3 miles S.E. by E. from Coquet Island.	Submarine	No warning	Torpedo	4
†Renfrew	3,830	24	8 miles S.W. from St. Ann's Head.	Submarine	No warning	Torpedo	40 including Master.
†Rubio	2,395	25	4 miles N. ½ E. from Shipwash L.V.	Mine	Mine	Mine	—
†Eumaeus	6,696	26	24 miles N.N.E. from Ile de Vierge.	Submarine	No warning	Torpedo	—
Glenart Castle (hospital ship).	6,824	26	10 miles West from Lundy Island.	Submarine	No warning	Torpedo	95 including Master.
†Greavesash	1,263	26	10 miles N.E. from Cape Barfleur.	Submarine	No warning	Torpedo	8
†Romny	1,024	26	10 miles N.N.E. from Cape Barfleur.	Submarine	No warning	Torpedo	9
†Maltby	3,977	26	10 miles S.W. by S. from Pantellaria.	Submarine	No warning	Torpedo	5
†Dalewood	2,420	26	10 miles S.W. from Isle of Man.	Submarine	No warning	Torpedo	19 including Master.
†Tiberia	4,880	26	1½ miles East from Black Head, Belfast Lough.	Submarine	No warning	Torpedo	—
†Machaon	6,738	27	50 miles N.E. ¾ N. from Cani Rocks.	Submarine	No warning	Torpedo	—
†Largo	1,764	27	12 miles West from Calf of Man.	Submarine	No warning	Torpedo	—

MARCH 1918.

Name.	Gross Tons.	Date.	Position.	Cause of Loss.	How attacked.	How sunk.	Lives lost.
		March.					
●†Borga	1,046	1	9 miles S.E. by S. from Beer Head.	Submarine	No warning	Torpedo	5
†Penvearn	3,710	1	15 miles N. ½ W. from S. Stack.	Submarine	No warning	Torpedo	21
Cecil L. Shave (S.V.).	102	1 (?)	Off the Azores	Submarine (reported).	Not known	Not known	
†Carmelite	2,583	2	10 miles S.W. by W. from Calf of Man.	Submarine	No warning	Torpedo	2
†Rockpool	4,502	2	12 miles N.E. by N. from Eagle Island.	Submarine	No warning	Torpedo	Master prisoner.
Bessy (Motor)	60	2	12 miles N.N.W. from Peel.	Submarine	Captured	Gunfire	—
†Kenmare	1,330	2	25 miles N.W. from the Skerries, Anglesey.	Submarine	No warning	Torpedo	29 including Master.
†Romeo	1,730	3	7 miles South from Mull of Galloway.	Submarine	No warning	Torpedo	29 including Master.
†Northfield	2,099	3	25 miles S.W. from Lundy Island.	Submarine	No warning	Torpedo	15 including Master.

MERCHANT VESSELS CAPTURED OR SUNK.

Name.	Gross Tons.	Date.	Position.	Cause of Loss.	How attacked.	How sunk.	Lives lost.
		1918. Feb.					
†Castle Eden	1,949	4	4 miles S.S.E. from Inistrahull L.H.	Submarine	No warning	Torpedo	1
†Clan Macpherson	4,779	4	24 miles North from C. Serrat.	Submarine	No warning	Torpedo	18
†Roxburgh	4,630	4	15 miles E. by N. ½ N. from C. St. John, Crete.	Submarine	No warning	Torpedo	6
Uskmoor	3,189	5	3 miles S.W. from Prawle Point.	Submarine	No warning	Torpedo	—
†Estrella	1,740	5	5 miles S. ½ W. from Shipwash L.V.	Mine	Mine	Mine	20
†Coalgas	2,257	5	5 miles S. by W. from Shipwash L.V.	Mine	Mine	Mine	—
†Kalgan	1,862	6	33 miles S.W. ½ W. from Yafa, Syria.	Submarine	No warning	Torpedo	1
Tarbetness	3,018	7	12 miles S.W. from Carnarvon L.V.	Submarine	No warning	Torpedo	—
Erica (S.V.)	167	8	5 miles S.W. from Bardsey Island.	Submarine	Captured	Gunfire	—
†Intent	1,564	8	4 miles E. by N. from Seaham.	Submarine	No warning	Torpedo	1
†Madeline	2,890	8	14 miles E.N.E. from Pendeen L.H.	Submarine	No warning	Torpedo	3
†Uganda	4,315	8	32 miles N.E. ¾ N. from Linosa.	Submarine	No warning	Torpedo	1
†Corsham	2,760	8	6 miles E.S.E. from entrance to River Tees.	Submarine	No warning	Torpedo	9
†Ayr	3,050	8	31 miles N. ½ W. from Linosa.	Submarine	No warning	Torpedo	—
†Silverdale	3,835	9	28 miles E. by N. ½ N. from Cani Rocks.	Submarine	No warning	Torpedo	—
Nanny Wignall (S.V.).	93	9	14 miles S.E. by S. from Tuskar Rock.	Submarine	Captured	Gunfire	—
†Chagres	5,288	10	62 miles N. by E. ¾ E. from C. Drepano, Crete.	Submarine	No warning	Torpedo	1
Stolt-Nielsen	5,684	11	38 miles S. ½ E. from Dellimara Point, Malta.	Submarine	No warning	Torpedo	—
†Gaupen	622	12	5 miles S.E. by E. ¼ E. from N. Foreland Lt.	Mine	Mine	Mine	—
Tweed	1,025	13	10 miles S. by W. ¼ W. from St. Catherines.	Submarine	No warning	Torpedo	7
†Lisette	895	13	8 miles N.E. by N. from Shipwash L.V.	Submarine	No warning	Torpedo	1
†Crayford	1,209	13	110 miles W. by S. from Skudesnes.	Submarine	No warning	Torpedo	1
Ardandearg	3,237	14	86 miles E. ¼ N. from Malta.	Submarine	No warning	Torpedo	2 including Master.
†Castleford	1,741	14	2 miles E. by N. from S. Cheek, Robin Hood Bay.	Submarine	No warning	Torpedo	—
Tweed	1,777	14	15 miles S.S.E. from Tuskar Rock.	Submarine	No warning	Torpedo	—
†Amazon	10,037	15	30 miles N. by W. from Malin Head.	Submarine	No warning	Torpedo	—

Merchant Vessels Captured or Sunk.

Name.	Gross Tons.	Date.	Position.	Cause of Loss.	How attacked.	How sunk.	Lives lost.
		1918. Mar.					
Sparkling Foam (S.V.)	199	15	9 miles S. by E. from Beer Head.	Submarine	Captured	Bombs	—
†Armonia	5,226	15	38 miles S.E. by S. ¼ S. from Porquerolles Id.	Submarine	No warning	Torpedo	7
†Clan Macdougall	4,710	15	60 miles S.E. by E. ½ E. from C. Carbonara.	Submarine	No warning	Torpedo	33 including Master.
†Lightfoot	1,875	16	2 miles S. from Owers L.V.	Submarine	No warning	Torpedo	—
†Ellaston	3,192	16	180 miles W. by S. (true) from Palma, Canary Islands.	Submarine	Captured	Bombs	Master prisoner.
†South Western	674	16	9 miles S.W. by S. from St. Catherines.	Submarine	No warning	Torpedo	24
†Oilfield	4,000	16	15 miles N.W. from Cape Wrath.	Submarine	Torpedoed	Beached; refloated; wreck.	3
Cressida	157	17	16 miles W. by N. ½ N. from Skerries, Anglesey.	Submarine	No warning	Torpedo	3
†Sea Gull	976	17	7 miles N.E. from Lynas Point.	Submarine	No warning	Torpedo	20 including Master.
†Waihemo	4,283	17	Gulf of Athens	Submarine	No warning	Torpedo	—
Eliza Anne (S.V.)	36	17	33 miles S. by W. ½ W. from the Eddystone.	Submarine	Captured	Bombs	—
†Ivydene	3,541	17	36 miles N.N.E. from C. Bougaroni.	Submarine	No warning	Torpedo	1
†John H. Barry	3,083	18	104 miles N. by W. ¾ W. from C. Bougaroni.	Submarine	No warning	Torpedo	3 including Master.
†Baygitano	3,073	18	1½ miles S.W. from Lyme Regis.	Submarine	No warning	Torpedo	2
†Saldanha	4,594	18	95 miles N. from Algiers.	Submarine	No warning	Torpedo	6
†Luxor	3,571	19	27 miles S.W. by S. from St. Catherines.	Submarine	No warning	Torpedo	—
†Burnstone	2,340	19	44 miles N. from Farn Islands.	Submarine	No warning	Torpedo	5
†Samoset	5,251	20	50 miles N. by E. ¾ E. from Port Said.	Submarine	No warning	Torpedo	3
†Yochow	2,127	20	54 miles N. ¾ E. from Port Said.	Submarine	No warning	Torpedo	50 including Master.
†St. Dimitrios	3,359	20	50 miles N. ¾ E. from Port Said.	Submarine	No warning	Torpedo	—
Glenford	494	20	24 miles E. ½ S. from Rockabill.	Submarine	Captured	Gunfire	—
†Kassanga	3,015	20	23 miles S.E. by S. from S. Arklow L.V.	Submarine	No warning	Torpedo	—
†Begonia	3,070	21	44 miles S. by W. from Wolf Rock.	Submarine	No warning	Torpedo	—
†Ikeda	6,311	21	7 miles W. from Brighton L.V.	Submarine	No warning	Torpedo	—
†Tyrhaug	1,483	22	10 miles N.E. from Pendeen L.H.	Submarine	No warning	Torpedo	2
†Polieon	1,155	22	3 miles E.N.E. from entrance to River Tyne.	Submarine	No warning	Torpedo	4

MERCHANT VESSELS CAPTURED OR SUNK.

Name.	Gross Tons.	Date.	Position.	Cause of Loss.	How attacked.	How sunk.	Lives lost.
		1918. Mar.					
†Trinidad	2,592	22	12 miles East from Codling L.V.	Submarine	No warning	Torpedo	39 including Master.
†Etonian	6,515	23	34 miles S. by E. ½ E. from Old Head of Kinsale.	Submarine	No warning	Torpedo	7
†Madame Midas (ex Duva).	1,203	23	38 miles S. by W. ¾ W. from the Lizard.	Submarine	No warning	Torpedo	—
†Aulton	634	23	9 miles S.E. by E. ½ E. from Berwick Harbour.	Submarine	No warning	Torpedo	2
Jane Gray (S.V.)	124	23	14 miles N. by W. from the Smalls.	Submarine	Captured	Gunfire	—
†Anteros	4,241	24	16 miles W. by N. from South Stack.	Submarine	No warning	Torpedo	2
John G. Walter (S.V.).	258	24	20 miles S.W. from the Smalls.	Submarine	Captured	Became derelict.	—
Jorgina (S.V.)	103	24	320 miles N. by W. (true) from Madeira.	Submarine	Captured	—	—
†Hercules	1,095	25	4 miles N.N.W. from Flamborough Head.	Submarine	No warning	Torpedo	1
†Destro	859	25	5 miles S.W. from Mull of Galloway.	Submarine	No warning	Torpedo	—
†Lady Cory-Wright.	2,516	26	14 miles S.S.W. from the Lizard.	Submarine	No warning	Torpedo	39 including Master.
Watauga (S.V.)	127	27	450 miles W. by N. (true) from Lisbon.	Submarine	Captured	Bombs	5 including Master.
†Allendale	2,153	27	52 miles S. by W. from the Lizard.	Submarine	No warning	Torpedo	1
†Iukosi	3,661	28	14 miles S.E. by E. ½ E. from Mull of Galloway.	Submarine	No warning	Torpedo	3
City of Winchester (S.V.).	83	28	10 miles N.W. by W. from Les Hanois.	Submarine	Captured	Gunfire	—
● †T. R. Thompson	3,538	29	7 miles South from Newhaven.	Submarine	No warning	Torpedo	33 including Master.
†Lough Fisher	418	30	12 miles S.S.E. from Helvick Head.	Submarine (?)	Gunfire (?)	Gunfire (?)	13 including Master.
● †Excellence Pleske	2,059	31	2½ miles S.S.E. from Dungeness.	Submarine	No warning	Torpedo	13
†Conargo	4,312	31	12 miles W. by N. from Calf of Man.	Submarine	No warning	Torpedo	9
†Vianna	401	31	4 miles East from Seaham Harbour.	Submarine	No warning	Torpedo	4
San Nicola (S.V.)	24	31	18 miles E.NE. from Valetta.	Submarine	Captured	Gunfire	—

APRIL 1918.

		Apr.					
Ardglass	4,617	1	6 miles East from the Maidens.	Submarine	No warning	Torpedo	6
Solway Queen	307	2	7 miles West from Black Head, Wigtonshire.	Submarine	No warning	Torpedo	11 including Master.
†Cyrene	2,904	5	15 miles North from Bardsey Island.	Submarine	No warning	Torpedo	24 including Master.

Merchant Vessels Captured or Sunk.

Name.	Gross Tons.	Date.	Position.	Cause of Loss.	How attacked.	How sunk.	Lives lost.
		1918. Apr.					
†Port Campbell	6,230	7	115 miles W.S.W. from Bishop Rock.	Submarine	No warning	Torpedo	—
†Rye	986	7	19 miles N. by W. ½ W. from Cape Antifer.	Submarine	No warning	Torpedo	4
†Highland Brigade	5,669	7	7½ miles E. from St. Catherine's.	Submarine	No warning	Torpedo	—
†Boscastle	2,346	7	14 miles N.N.W. from Strumble Head.	Submarine	No warning	Torpedo	18 including Master.
†Bengali	5,684	8	14 miles North from Alexandria.	Submarine	No warning	Torpedo	—
†Henley	3,249	10	25 miles S.W. ½ W. from the Lizard.	Submarine	No warning	Torpedo	6
†Westfield	3,453	10	45 miles S.W. by S. from Bishop Rock.	Submarine	No warning	Torpedo	—
Cicero	1,834	10 apprx.	Baltic	Reported as sunk to avoid capture.	—	—	—
Emilie	1,635	10 apprx.	Baltic	Reported as sunk to avoid capture.	—	—	—
Obsidian	742	10 apprx.	Baltic	Reported as sunk to avoid capture.	—	—	—
†Myrtle Branch	3,741	11	9 miles N.E. by N. from Inishtrahull.	Submarine	No warning	Torpedo	15 including Master.
†Highland Prince	3,390	11	36 miles N.E. ¼ E. from Cape Bon.	Submarine	No warning	Torpedo	3
†Lonhelen	1,281	12	North End of Shipwash.	Mine	Mine	Mine	—
Moyune	4,935	12	32 miles S.E. by E. from Cape Palos.	Submarine	No warning	Torpedo	—
Autolycus	5,806	12	32 miles S.E. by E. from Cape Palos.	Submarine	No warning	Torpedo	—
Wilson (S V.)	110	12	10 miles N.W. from the Smalls.	Submarine	Captured	Bombs	—
†Luis	4,284	12	3½ miles S.S.E. from St. Catherine's.	Submarine	No warning	Torpedo	4
†Harewood	4,150	13	380 miles W. by S. (true) from Lisbon.	Submarine	Captured	Gunfire	2 including Master.
†Marstonmoor	2,744	14	55 miles N.N.E. from Cape Wrath.	Submarine	No warning	Torpedo	—
†Santa Isabel	2,023	14	15 miles West from Cape Verde.	Submarine	Captured	Gunfire	1
†Chelford	2,995	14	10 miles N.W. by W. from Bardsey Island.	Submarine	No warning	Torpedo	—
†Pomeranian	4,241	15	9 miles N.W. by W. ½ W. from Portland Bill.	Submarine	No warning	Torpedo	55 including Master.
†Ailsa Craig	601	15	13 miles W. by N. from Portland Bill.	Submarine	No warning	Torpedo	—
†Hungerford	5,811	16	9 miles S.S.E. from Owers L.V.	Submarine	No warning	Torpedo	8
†Lake Michigan	9,288	16	93 miles N. by W. from Eagle Island.	Submarine	No warning	Torpedo	1 Master.
†Nirpura	7,640	16	110 miles W.N.W. (true) from Cape Roca.	Submarine	No warning	Torpedo	—

MERCHANT VESSELS CAPTURED OR SUNK.

Name.	Gross Tons.	Date.	Position.	Cause of Loss.	How attacked.	How sunk.	Lives lost.
		1918. Apr.					
†Ladoga	1,917	16	15 miles S.E. from S. Arklow L.V.	Submarine	No warning	Torpedo	29 including Master.
†Bamse	958	17	15 miles W. by N. from Portland Bill.	Submarine	No warning	Torpedo	4
†Gregynog	1,701	18	16 miles S.W. from Hartland Point.	Submarine	No warning	Torpedo	3
†Runswick	3,060	18	3 miles North from Trevose Head.	Submarine	No warning	Torpedo	—
†Dalegarth Force	684	18	12 miles S.W. from Hartland Point.	Submarine	No warning	Torpedo	5
†Pentyrch	3,312	18	5 miles W.N.W. from Brighton L.V.	Submarine	No warning	Torpedo	1
†Lord Charlemont	3,209	19	22 miles North from Alboran Island.	Submarine	No warning	Torpedo	8
†War Helmet	8,184	19	3 miles E. by N. ½ N. from Owers L.V.	Submarine	No warning	Torpedo	—
†Florrieston	3,366	20	6 miles E. ½ N. from South Stack.	Submarine	No warning	Torpedo	19 including Master.
†Lowther Range	3,926	20	20 miles W. by N. ½ N. from S. Stack.	Submarine	No warning	Torpedo	—
†Bellview	3,567	21	16 miles E.N.E. from Cape Bon.	Submarine	No warning	Torpedo	—
†Westergate	1,760	21	22 miles E. ½ S. from Start Point.	Submarine	No warning	Torpedo	24 including Master.
†Normandiet	1,843	21	34 miles S.W. by W. from Calf of Man.	Submarine	No warning	Torpedo	19 including Master.
†Landonia	2,504	21	27 miles N. by W. ½ W. from Strumble Head.	Submarine	No warning	Torpedo	21 Master or gunner prisoner.
†Dronning Maud	2,663	22	65 miles N. by E. ¾ E. from Cape Sigli.	Submarine	No warning	Torpedo	1
Mashalla (Egyptian S.V.).	77	22	50 miles North from Port Said.	Submarine	Captured	Gunfire	—
†Welbeck Hall	5,643	22	75 miles N.E. by N. from Port Said.	Submarine	No warning	Torpedo	4
†Eric Calvert	1,862	22	4 miles S.S.W. from St. Anthony Point.	Submarine	No warning	Torpedo	2
†Baron Herries	1,610	22	43 miles N. by W. ½ W. from Bishop Rock.	Submarine	No warning	Torpedo	3 2nd officer prisoner.
†Fern	444	22	5 miles E. by N. from Kish L.V.	Submarine	No warning	Torpedo	13
†Laurium	582	23	15 miles East from Skegness.	Mine	Mine	Mine	1
Frances (S.V.)	56	23	6 miles S. from the Lizard.	Submarine	Captured	Bomb	2
†Agnete	1,127	24	4 miles S. by W. from Start Point.	Submarine	No warning	Torpedo	12 including Master.
Ethel (S.V.)	100	26	19 miles N. ¾ E. from the Smalls.	Submarine	Captured	Gunfire	—
†Llwyngwair	1,304	26	5 miles S.S.E. from Seaham Harbour.	Submarine	No warning	Torpedo	8 including Master.
†Gresham	3,774	26	18 miles N.W. by N. ½ N. from Strumble Head.	Submarine	No warning	Torpedo	—

MERCHANT VESSELS CAPTURED OR SUNK.

Name.	Gross Tons.	Date.	Position.	Cause of Loss.	How attacked.	How sunk.	Lives lost.
		1918. Apr.					
†Romany	3,983	27	47 miles S.W. by W. ¾ W. from Cape Spartivento, Sardinia.	Submarine	No warning	Torpedo	—
†Oronsa	8,075	28	12 miles W. from Bardsey Island.	Submarine	No warning	Torpedo	3
†Upcerne	2,984	28	4 miles S.E. by S. from Coquet Island.	Submarine	No warning	Torpedo	16
†Elba	1,081	28	6 miles N.W. by N. from Pendeen.	Submarine	No warning	Torpedo	10
●†Australier	3,687	29	6 miles S.W. by S. from Dungeness.	Submarine	No warning	Torpedo	5
●†Broderick	4,321	29	7 miles S.S.E. from Hastings.	Submarine	No warning	Torpedo	—
Johnny Toole (S.V.)	84	29	Off Carnsore Point.	Submarine	Captured	Gunfire	—
Christiana Davis (S.V.)	86	29	8 miles S.E. by S. from Tuskar Rock.	Submarine	Captured	Gunfire	—
†Kut Sang	4,895	29	40 miles E.S.E. from Cape Palos.	Submarine	No warning	Torpedo	59 including Master.
†Kingstonian	6,564	29	Ashore in Carloforte Roadstead.	Submarine	Torpedoed	Total wreck	1
●†Ella Sayer	2,549	29	15 miles E. by N. from Royal Sovereign L.V.	Submarine	No warning	Torpedo	2
†Conway	4,003	30	38 miles S. ½ E. from Cape Palos.	Submarine	No warning	Torpedo	—
†Kafue	6,044	30	11 miles S.W. from Mull of Galloway.	Submarine	No warning	Torpedo	1
●†Isleworth	2,871	30	3 miles S.W. from Ventnor Pier.	Submarine	No warning	Torpedo	29
Elsie Birdett (S.V.)	90	(?)	Off Canary Islands	Submarine	Not known	—	6 including Master.
†Kempock	255	30	6½ miles S.E. by S. from Copeland Is. Lt.	Submarine	Captured	Gunfire	—
●†Umba	2,042	30	1 mile S. from Royal Sovereign L.V.	Submarine	No warning	Torpedo	20 including Master.
MAY 1918.		May					
†Era	2,379	1	18 miles N.E. by E. from Cape Tenez.	Submarine	No warning	Torpedo	12
†Matiana	5,313	1	On Keith Reef	Submarine	No warning	Torpedo	—
●†Unity	1,091	2	3 miles W.S.W. from Varne L.V.	Submarine	No warning	Torpedo	12
†Franklyn	4,919	2	65 miles E. by N. from Port Mahon.	Submarine	No warning	Torpedo	—
†Medora	5,135	2	11 miles W.S.W. from Mull of Galloway.	Submarine	No warning	Torpedo	Master, W/T operator and gunner prisoners
†Flawyl	3,592	2	30 miles E.S.E. from Pantellaria.	Submarine	No warning	Torpedo	1
†Girdleness	3,018	2	18 miles N.E. by E. ½ E. from Trevose Head.	Submarine	No warning	Torpedo	2
†Thorsa	1,319	2	3 miles N.N.W. from Pendeen L.H.	Submarine	No warning	Torpedo	—

Merchant Vessels Captured or Sunk.

Name.	Gross Tons.	Date.	Position.	Cause of Loss.	How attacked.	How sunk.	Lives lost.
		1918. May					
†Polbrae	1,087	4	1¼ miles S.W. from Sharpnose, N. Devon.	Submarine	No warning	Torpedo	2
Tommi (S.V.)	116	5	Between Chicken Rock and Calf of Man.	Submarine	Gunfire	Gunfire	4 including Master.
†Leeds City	4,298	6	5 miles E. by S. ½ S. from Skulmartin L.V.	Submarine	No warning	Torpedo	—
†Sandhurst	3,034	6	6 miles N.W. by W. ¼ W. from Corsewall Point.	Submarine	No warning	Torpedo	20
†Nantes	1,580	7	83 miles E.S.E. from Fair Isle.	Submarine	No warning	Torpedo	—
Saxon	1,595	7	83 miles E.S.E. from Fair Isle.	Submarine	No warning	Torpedo	22
†Princess Dagmar	913	7 (?)	Bristol Channel	Submarine (reported).	No warning	Torpedo	24 including Master.
†Constantia	772	8	2 miles E. from S. Cheek, Robin Hood Bay.	Submarine	No warning	Torpedo	3
†Ingleside	3,736	8	80 miles N. by E. from Algiers.	Submarine	No warning	Torpedo	11
†Dux	1,349	8	7 miles N.W. from Godrevy L.H.	Submarine	No warning	Torpedo	—
†Baron Ailsa	1,836	9	18 miles W.N.W. from the Smalls.	Submarine	No warning	Torpedo	10
†Wileysike	2,501	9	8 miles S.W. from St. Ann's Head.	Submarine	No warning	Torpedo	4
†Amplegarth	3,707	10	1 mile W.S.W. from Dover Harbour.	Mine	Mine	Mine	—
†Itinda	5,251	10	40 miles N. from Marsa Susa.	Submarine	No warning	Torpedo	1
†Szechuen	1,862	10	60 miles N. by E. ½ E. from Port Said.	Submarine	No warning	Torpedo	9
Massouda (S.V.)	240	11	50 miles N. from Marsa Matruh.	Submarine	Captured	Bombs	—
†Inniscarra	1,412	12	10 miles S.E. ½ E. from Ballycottin Island.	Submarine	No warning	Torpedo	28
†Haslingden	1,934	12	7 miles E. from Seaham Harbour.	Submarine	No warning	Torpedo	11 including Master.
†Omrah	8,130	12	40 miles S.W. ¾ S. from Cape Spartivento, Sardinia.	Submarine	No warning	Torpedo	1
†Vimeira	5,884	12	16 miles W.S.W. from Lampedusa.	Submarine	No warning	Torpedo	—
†Woolston	2,986	14	1½ miles from Syracuse Harbour.	Submarine	No warning	Torpedo	19 including Master.
†Tartary	4,181	16	8 miles E.N.E. from Skulmartin L.V.	Submarine	No warning	Torpedo	—
†Heron Bridge	2,420	16	320 miles E. by N. (true) from San Miguel, Azores.	Submarine	No warning	Torpedo	1
†Tagona	2,004	16	5 miles W.S.W. from Trevose Head.	Submarine	No warning	Torpedo	8 including Master.
†Llancarvan	4,749	16	370 miles E. ½ N. (true) from San Miguel, Azores.	Submarine	No warning	Torpedo	—
†Mavisbrook	3,152	17	50 miles S.E. by S. ½ S. from Cape de Gata.	Submarine	No warning	Torpedo	18 including Master.
†Sculptor	4,874	17	60 miles N.W. by W. ¼ W. from Oran.	Submarine	No warning	Torpedo; beached; wreck.	7 including Master.

Name.	Gross Tons.	Date.	Position.	Cause of Loss.	How attacked.	How sunk.	Lives lost.
		1918. May					
†Hurunui	10,644	18	48 miles S. by W. from the Lizard.	Submarine	No warning	Torpedo	1
†Scholar	1,635	18	90 miles W. by S. ¾ S. from Bishop Rock.	Submarine	No warning	Torpedo	2
†Denbigh Hall	4,943	18	90 miles W.S.W. from Bishop Rock.	Submarine	No warning	Torpedo	—
†Chesterfield	1,013	18	42 miles N.E. by E. ½ E. from Malta.	Submarine	No warning	Torpedo	4
Ninetta (S.V.)	7	18	22 miles S.E. by S. from Cape Passero.	Submarine	Captured	Gunfire	—
†Snowdon	3,189	19	84 miles S. ½ W. from Malta.	Submarine	No warning	Torpedo	2 including Master.
†Chatham	3,592	21	80 miles S.W. ¼ S. from Cape Matapan.	Submarine	No warning	Torpedo	—
†Skaraas	1,625	23	1 mile S.W. from Black Head.	Submarine	No warning	Torpedo	19
†Innisfallen	1,405	23	16 miles E. ¾ N. from Kish L.V.	Submarine	No warning	Torpedo	10
Ruth Hickman, S.V.	417	24	60 miles N.N.W. (true) from Graciosa, Azores	Submarine	Captured	Bombs	—
†Princess Royal	1,986	26	3 miles W.N.W. from St. Agnes Head.	Submarine	No warning	Torpedo	19
†Kyarra	6,953	26	2 miles S.S.E. from Anvil Point.	Submarine	No warning	Torpedo	6
†Thames	1,327	26	6 miles S.E. by E. from Seaham Harbour.	Submarine	No warning	Torpedo	4 including Master.
†Leasowe Castle	9,737	26	104 miles W. by N. ½ N. from Alexandria.	Submarine	No warning	Torpedo	9 including Master.
†Cairnross	4,016	27	110 miles N.N.W. (true) from Flores, Azores.	Submarine	No warning	Torpedo	—
†Uganda	5,431	27	90 miles N.E. by N. ¾ N. from Algiers.	Submarine	No warning	Torpedo	—
†Merionethshire	4,308	27	120 miles N. ½ E. (true) from Flores, Azores.	Submarine	No warning	Torpedo	—
†Begum	4,646	29	270 miles W. by S. from Bishop Rock.	Submarine	No warning	Torpedo	15
Missir	786	29	80 miles W. by N. from Alexandria.	Submarine	No warning	Torpedo	34
†Carlton	5,262	29	270 miles W. by S. from Bishop Rock.	Submarine	No warning	Torpedo	—
†Ausonia	8,153	30	620 miles W. by S. ¾ S. (true) from the Fastnet.	Submarine	No warning	Torpedo	44
†Waneta	1,683	30	42 miles S.S.E. from Kinsale Head.	Submarine	No warning	Torpedo	8
†Asiatic Prince	2,887	30	190 miles E. by S. ½ S. from Malta.	Submarine	No warning	Torpedo	—
†Aymeric	4,363	30	145 miles S.W. by W. from Cape Matapan.	Submarine	No warning	Torpedo	—
Alert (S.V.)	59	31	9 miles N.E. by N. ½ N. from Coquet Island.	Submarine	Captured	Bombs	—

MERCHANT VESSELS CAPTURED OR SUNK.

Name.	Gross Tons.	Date.	Position.	Cause of Loss.	How attacked.	How sunk.	Lives lost.
JUNE 1918.		1918. June					
†Nora	3,933	3	205 miles S.E. from Malta.	Submarine	No warning	Torpedo	1
†Glaucus	5,295	3	20 miles W. from Cape Granitola, Sicily.	Submarine	No warning	Torpedo	2
†Polwell	2,013	5	6 miles E. by S. $\frac{1}{2}$ S. from Rockabill.	Submarine	No warning	Torpedo	—
†Harpathian	4,588	5	Off Cape Henry, Virginia.	Submarine	No warning	Torpedo	—
†Archbank	3,767	5	240 miles E.S.E. from Malta.	Submarine	No warning	Torpedo	1
†Menzaleh	1,859	5	230 miles E.S.E. from Malta.	Submarine	No warning	Torpedo	10 Master prisoner.
†Huntsland	2,871	6	23 miles N. by W. from Havre.	Submarine	No warning	Torpedo	—
†Diana	1,119	7	10 miles S.S.E. from Flamborough Head.	Submarine	No warning	Torpedo	—
†Hogarth	1,231	7	10 miles S. $\frac{1}{2}$ E. from the Longstone.	Submarine	No warning	Torpedo	26 including Master
†Saima	1,147	8	10 miles W. from Trevose Head.	Submarine	No warning	Torpedo	16 including Master.
†Hunsgrove	3,063	8	6 miles N.W. from Trevose Head.	Submarine	No warning	Torpedo	3
†Moidart	1,303	9	7 miles S.E. $\frac{1}{2}$ E. from Lyme Regis.	Submarine	No warning	Torpedo	15
Queen Victoria (S.V.).	92	9	6 miles S.E. from Lundy Island.	Submarine	Captured	Bombs	—
†Vandalia	7,333	9	18 miles W.N.W. from the Smalls.	Submarine	No warning	Torpedo	—
†Tewfikieh	2,490	9	115 miles W.N.W. from Alexandria.	Submarine	No warning	Torpedo	5
†Clan Forbes	3,946	9	115 miles W.N.W. from Alexandria.	Submarine	No warning	Torpedo	2
†Pundit	5,917	9	85 miles W.N.W. from Alexandria.	Submarine	No warning	Torpedo	6 including Master.
†Mountby	3,263	10	8 miles E. by S. from the Lizard.	Submarine	No warning	Torpedo	—
†Stryn	2,143	10	5 miles E. from Berry Head.	Submarine	No warning	Torpedo	8
†Princess Maud	1,566	10	5 miles N.E. by N. from Blyth.	Submarine	No warning	Torpedo	3
Lowtyne	3,231	10	$3\frac{1}{2}$ miles E.S.E. from Whitby.	Submarine	No warning	Torpedo	3
†Borg	2,111	10	20 miles S.W. by S. from the Lizard.	Submarine	No warning	Torpedo	24 including Master.
†Lorle	2,686	11	12 miles S.S.W. from the Lizard.	Submarine	No warning	Torpedo	19 including Master.
†Boma	2,694	11	10 miles S.W. $\frac{3}{4}$ W. from Beer Head.	Submarine	No warning	Torpedo	—
†Kul	1,095	12	$3\frac{1}{2}$ miles N.E. $\frac{1}{4}$ N. from Wolf Rock.	Submarine	No warning	Torpedo	4
†Penhallow	4,318	12	52 miles N. by W. from Cape Caxine.	Submarine	No warning	Torpedo	1
†Kennington	1,536	12	15 miles E. from Flamborough Head.	Submarine	No warning	Torpedo	4

MERCHANT VESSELS CAPTURED OR SUNK.   92

Name.	Gross Tons.	Date.	Position.	Cause of Loss.	How attacked.	How sunk.	Lives lost.
		1918. June					
†Kalo	1,957	13	18 miles S. by E. ½ E. from Flamborough Head.	Submarine	No warning	Torpedo	3
†Kieldrecht	1,284	15	21 miles E. by S. from Flamborough Head.	Submarine	No warning	Torpedo	—
†Melanie	2,996	16	2 miles East from S. Cheek, Robin Hood Bay.	Submarine	No warning	Torpedo	5
†Dwinsk	8,173	18	400 miles N.E. by N. ¾ N. (true) from Bermuda.	Submarine	No warning	Torpedo	24
†Norfolk Coast	782	18	23 miles S.E. from Flamborough Head.	Submarine	No warning	Torpedo	8
†Montebello	4,324	21	320 miles W. ½ N. from Ushant.	Submarine	No warning	Torpedo	41 including Master.
†Rhea	1,308	22	Off Etaples	Mine	Mine	Mine	—
†London	1,706	23	4 miles E. by S. from Whitby.	Submarine	No warning	Torpedo	—
†Moorlands	3,602	24	3 miles S.E. by E. from Whitby.	Submarine	No warning	Torpedo	10
†Atlantian	9,399	25	110 miles N. by W. ½ W. from Eagle Island.	Submarine	No warning	Torpedo	Chief Officer and W/T Operator prisoners.
†Orissa	5,358	25	21 miles S.W. by W. ¼ W. from Skerryvore.	Submarine	No warning	Torpedo	6
†African Transport	4,482	25	3 miles North from Whitby.	Submarine	No warning	Torpedo	3
Wimmera	3,022	26	24 miles N.W. ½ W. from Hooper's Point, N.Z.	Mine	Mine	Mine	16 including Master.
†Tortuguero	4,175	26	205 miles N.W. ¼ N. from Eagle Island.	Submarine	No warning	Torpedo	12
†Keelung	6,672	27	110 miles W. ¾ S. from Ushant.	Submarine	No warning	Torpedo	6
Llandovery Castle (Hospital Ship).	11,423	27	116 miles West from the Fastnet.	Submarine	No warning	Torpedo	146
Dictator (S.V.)	99	(?)	Atlantic	Submarine (reported)	Not known	Not known	Crew prisoners.
†Queen	4,956	28	130 miles N. ½ W. from Cape Villano.	Submarine	No warning	Torpedo	20 including Master.
†Sunniva	1,913	28	4 miles East from Sunderland.	Submarine	No warning	Torpedo	2
†Sixty-Six	214	29	3 miles East from Scarborough.	Submarine	No warning	Torpedo	6 including Master.
†Florentia	3,688	29	2 miles E. by N. from S. Cheek, Robin Hood Bay.	Submarine	No warning	Torpedo	3
†Herdis	1,157	29	7 miles S.E. by S. from S. Cheek, Robin Hood Bay.	Submarine	No warning	Torpedo	—
W.M.L. (S.V.)	145	30	400 miles N.N.W. from Cape Finisterre.	Submarine	Captured	Gunfire	4 including Master.
†Origen	3,545	30	115 miles W. ¼ S. from Ushant.	Submarine	No warning	Torpedo	1

93 MERCHANT VESSELS CAPTURED OR SUNK.

Name.	Gross Tons.	Date.	Position.	Cause of Loss.	How attacked.	How sunk.	Lives lost.
JULY 1918.		1918. July					
†Charing Cross	2,534	1	4 miles E. by N. from Flamborough Head.	Submarine	No warning	Torpedo	—
†Westmoor	4,329	1	210 miles N.W. by W. ¾ W. from Casablanca.	Submarine	No warning	Torpedo	2 Master prisoner.
Admiral (Tug)	102	2	2 miles N. from Flamborough Head.	Submarine	Captured	Gunfire	—
Erme (Motor)	116	2	240 miles N.W by W. from the Fastnet.	Submarine	Captured	Bombs	—
†Shirala	5,306	2	4 miles N.E. by E. ½ E. from Owers L.V.	Submarine	No warning	Torpedo	8
†Vera Elizabeth (Motor).	179	5	54 miles S. by E. ½ E. from Sydero, Faeroe Islands.	Submarine	Captured	Gunfire	—
†Bertrand	3,613	6	28 miles E.S.E. from Cape Bon.	Submarine	No warning	Torpedo	—
†Port Hardy	6,533	6	78 miles W. by N. from Cape Spartel.	Submarine	No warning	Torpedo	7
†Ben Lomond	2,814	7	30 miles S.E. from Daunts Rock.	Submarine	No warning	Torpedo	23 including Master.
†Chicago	7,709	8	4 miles N.E. from Flamborough Head.	Submarine	No warning	Torpedo	3
†War Crocus	5,296	8	2½ miles E. by N. from Flamborough Head.	Submarine	No warning	Torpedo	—
†Mars	3,550	8	74 miles W. by N. from Bishop Rock.	Submarine	No warning	Torpedo	—
†Plawsworth	4,724	13	105 miles W. by N. from Bishop Rock.	Submarine	No warning	Torpedo	1
†Badagri	2,956	13	425 miles W.N.W. from Cape St. Vincent.	Submarine	No warning	Torpedo	Chief Officer prisoner.
†Branksome Hall	4,262	14	68 miles N.W. by W. from Marsa Susa.	Submarine	No warning	Torpedo	—
†Waitemata	5,432	14	100 miles E. ¾ N. from Marsa Susa.	Submarine	No warning	Torpedo	—
†Barunga	7,484	15	150 miles W. by S. ½ S. from Bishop Rock.	Submarine	No warning	Torpedo	—
Fisherman (S.V.)	136	16	380 miles N.W. by W. ½ W. from Cape Roca.	Submarine	Captured	Gunfire	—
†War Swallow	5,216	16	72 miles S.W. by S. ½ S. from Malta.	Submarine	No warning	Torpedo	7
†Southborough	3,709	16	5 miles N. by E. ½ E. from Scarborough.	Submarine	No warning	Torpedo	30 including Master.
†Carpathia	13,603	17	170 miles W. by N. from Bishop Rock.	Submarine	No warning	Torpedo	5
Ranger (Motor)	79	19	20 miles N.W. from Barra Head.	Submarine	Captured	Bombs	—
†Justicia	32,234	19	20 miles W. by N. ¾ N. from Skerryvore.	Submarine	No warning	Torpedo	10

MERCHANT VESSELS CAPTURED OR SUNK.

Name.	Gross Tons.	Date.	Position.	Cause of Loss.	How attacked.	How sunk.	Lives lost.
		1918. July					
†Gemini	2,128	20	7 miles N.W. ½ N. from Godrevy L.H.	Submarine	No warning	Torpedo	2
†Orfordness	2,790	20	2½ miles W. by N. from Newquay.	Submarine	No warning	Torpedo	2
†Kosseir	1,855	20	40 miles N.E. by N. ½ N. from Alexandria.	Submarine	No warning	Torpedo	39 including Master.
†Mongolian	4,892	21	5 miles S.E. from Filey Brig.	Submarine	No warning	Torpedo	36
†Anna Sofie	2,577	23	4 miles W. from Trevose Head.	Submarine	No warning	Torpedo	1
†Messidor	3,883	23	73 miles S.E. by S. ¼ S. from Port Mahon.	Submarine	No warning	Torpedo	1
†Rutherglen	4,214	24	50 miles E.S.E. from Port Mahon.	Submarine	No warning	Torpedo	---
†Magellan	3,642	25	53 miles N. ½ E. from Cape Serrat.	Submarine	No warning	Torpedo	1
†Blairhall	2,549	26	3½ miles E.N.E. from Sunderland.	Submarine	No warning	Torpedo	1
Kirkham Abbey	1,166	27	2 miles N.E. by E. from Winterton.	Submarine	No warning	Torpedo	8
†Subadar	4,911	27	112 miles N. by W. from Cape Roca.	Submarine	No warning	Torpedo	3
†Chloris	984	27	17 miles S. by E. from Flamborough Head.	Submarine	No warning	Torpedo	3 including Master.
†Hyperia	3,905	28	84 miles N.W. by N. from Port Said.	Submarine	No warning	Torpedo	7 including Master.
†Rio Pallaresa	4,034	29	62 miles E.N.E. from Malta.	Submarine	No warning	Torpedo	2
AUGUST 1918.		Aug.					
†Malvina	1,244	2	1 mile N.N.E. from Flamborough Head.	Submarine	No warning	Torpedo	14 including Master.
Dornfontein (Motor).	766	2	25 miles W.N.W. from Brier Island, N.S.	Submarine	Captured	Burnt	—
†Warilda	7,713	3	32 miles S.S.W. from Owers L.V.	Submarine	No warning	Torpedo	7
†Clan Macnab	4,675	4	14 miles N.N.W. from Pendeen L.H.	Submarine	No warning	Torpedo	22 including Master.
†Freshfield	3,445	5	4 miles N.E. by N. from Cape Colonne, Italy.	Submarine	No warning	Torpedo	3
†Luz Blanca	4,868	5	35 miles S.W. from Outer Gas Buoy, Halifax, N.S.	Submarine	No warning	Torpedo	2
†Clan Macneil	3,939	6	10 miles North from Alexandria.	Submarine	No warning	Torpedo	—
†Biruta	1,733	6	8 miles N.W. ¾ W. from Calais.	Submarine	No warning	Torpedo	12 including Master.
†Highland Harris	6,032	6	82 miles N. ¾ W. from Eagle Island.	Submarine	No warning	Torpedo	24

MERCHANT VESSELS CAPTURED OR SUNK.

Name.	Gross Tons.	Date.	Position.	Cause of Loss.	How attacked.	How sunk.	Lives lost.
		1918. Aug.					
†Clan Macvey	5,815	8	½ mile S.E. from Anvil Point.	Submarine	No warning	Torpedo	7
†Glenlee	4,915	9	4 miles E. by N. from Owers L.V.	Submarine	No warning	Torpedo	1
†Madam Renee	509	10	1 mile N.N.E. from Scarborough.	Submarine	No warning	Torpedo	10
†City of Adelaide	8,389	11	60 miles E.N.E. from Malta.	Submarine	No warning	Torpedo	4
†Penistone	4,139	11	145 miles S.W. ½ S. from Nantucket Island.	Submarine	No warning	Torpedo	1
†Anhui	2,209	12	2 miles S.E. from Cape Greco, Cyprus.	Submarine	No warning	Torpedo	4
†City of Brisbane	7,094	13	1½ miles S.S.W. from Newhaven.	Submarine	No warning	Torpedo	—
†Wallsend	2,697	14	1 mile S.E. from S. Cheek, Robin Hood Bay.	Submarine	No warning	Torpedo	—
†Escrick	4,151	16	360 miles N.W. by N. from Cape Finisterre.	Submarine	No warning	Torpedo	1 Master prisoner.
†Mirlo	6,978	16	½ mile S. by E. from Wimble Shoal Buoy, Cape Hatteras.	Submarine	No warning	Torpedo	9
†Eros	1,122	17	2 miles N.E. by N. from Filey Brig.	Submarine	No warning	Torpedo	7 including Master.
†Denebola	1,481	17	2 miles N. by W. from Gurnard Head.	Submarine	No warning	Torpedo	2
†Zinal	4,037	17	360 miles N. by E. (true) from Terceira, Azores.	Submarine	No warning	Torpedo	2
†Idaho	3,023	19	120 miles N. by W. ½ W. from Cape Villano.	Submarine	No warning	Torpedo	11
†Marie Suzanne	3,106	19	47 miles W. ¾ S. from Mudros Bay.	Submarine	No warning	Torpedo	—
†Boltonhall	3,535	20	34 miles S.W. by W. ¼ W. from Bardsey Island.	Submarine	No warning	Torpedo	5
†Otis Tetrax	996	20	28 miles S. ¼ E. from Flamborough Head.	Submarine	No warning	Torpedo	—
†The Stewart's Court.	813	21	4 miles S.S.E. from Seaham Harbour.	Submarine	No warning	Torpedo	1
†Diomed	7,523	21	195 miles E.S.E. from Nantucket Island.	Submarine	Captured	Gunfire	2
†Boscawen	1,936	21	23 miles W.N.W. from Bardsey Island.	Submarine	No warning	Torpedo	1
†Palmella	1,352	22	25 miles N.W. ½ W. from South Stack.	Submarine	No warning	Torpedo	28 including Master.
Abbasieh (Egyptian S.V.).	140	22	100 miles N.E. from Alexandria.	Submarine	Captured	Gunfire	—
†Prunelle	578	22	2 miles S.E. from Blyth.	Submarine	No warning	Torpedo	12 including Master.
†Australian Transport.	4,784	23	40 miles W.N.W. from Marittimo.	Submarine	No warning	Torpedo	1
†Flavia	9,291	24	30 miles N.W. by W. from Tory Island.	Submarine	No warning	Torpedo	1

Merchant Vessels Captured or Sunk. 96

Name.	Gross Tons.	Date.	Position.	Cause of Loss.	How attacked.	How sunk.	Lives lost.
		1918. Aug.					
†Virent	3,771	24	38 miles W. by S. from the Smalls.	Submarine	No warning	Torpedo	—
†Auckland Castle	1,084	24	5 miles E. by S. ½ S. from Farn Island.	Submarine	No warning	Torpedo	12 including Master.
†Willingtonia	3,228	25	13 miles S.W. by W. from Marittimo.	Submarine	No warning	Torpedo	4
Erik	583	25	70 miles N.W. by W. from St. Pierre, N.F.L.	Submarine	Captured	Bombs	—
†Ant Cassar	3,544	27	30 miles N.N.W. from Strumble Head.	Submarine	No warning	Torpedo	—
†Giralda	1,100	28	5 miles N.N.W. from Whitby.	Submarine	No warning	Torpedo	6
†Milwaukee	7,323	31	260 miles S.W. from the Fastnet.	Submarine	No warning	Torpedo	1
SEPTEMBER 1918.		Sept.					
†Mesaba	6,833	1	21 miles E. ¼ N. from Tuskar Rock.	Submarine	No warning	Torpedo	20 including Master.
†City of Glasgow	6,545	1	21 miles E. ¼ N. from Tuskar Rock.	Submarine	No warning	Torpedo	12
†San Andres	3,314	2	40 miles N. by W. from Port Said.	Submarine	No warning	Torpedo	—
†Highcliffe	3,238	3	13 miles S.E. from Tuskar Rock.	Submarine	No warning	Torpedo	1
†War Firth	3,112	4	33 miles S. ¾ W. from the Lizard.	Submarine	No warning	Torpedo	11
†Arum	3,681	4	40 miles E. from Pantellaria.	Submarine	No warning	Torpedo	—
†Audax	975	6	6½ miles E. by N. from N. Cheek, Robin Hood Bay.	Submarine	No warning	Torpedo	3
†Milly	2,964	6	2¼ miles W. ¾ S. from Tintagell Head.	Submarine	No warning	Torpedo	2
†Bellbank	3,250	7	25 miles S.S.W. from Planier Island.	Submarine	No warning	Torpedo	1
†Ruysdael	3,478	7	228 miles W. ¾ S. from Ushant.	Submarine	No warning	Torpedo	12 including Master.
†Missanabie	12,469	9	52 miles S. by E. ½ E. from Daunts Rock.	Submarine	No warning	Torpedo	45
†War Arabis	5,183	9	88 miles N. by E. ¼ E. from Cape Sigli.	Submarine	No warning	Torpedo	—
†Galway Castle	7,988	12	160 miles S.W. ½ S. from the Fastnet.	Submarine	No warning	Torpedo	143
†Setter	956	13	6 miles N.W. by N. from Corsewall Point.	Submarine	No warning	Torpedo	9 including Master.
†Buffalo	286	13	Off Corsewall Point.	Submarine	No warning	Torpedo	10 including Master.
†M. J. Craig	691	13	7 miles N.E. ½ E. from Black Head, Belfast.	Submarine	No warning	Torpedo	4
Aghios Nicolaos (S.V.).	113	14	10 miles S.E. from Paphos.	Submarine	Captured	Bomb	—

MERCHANT VESSELS CAPTURED OR SUNK.

Name.	Gross Tons.	Date.	Position.	Cause of Loss.	How attacked.	How sunk.	Lives lost.
		1918. Sept.					
†Neotsfield	3,821	14	1½ miles South from Skulmartin L.V.	Submarine	No warning	Torpedo	—
●†Gibel-Hamam	647	14	Off Abbotsbury, Dorset.	Submarine	No warning	Torpedo	21 including Master.
●†Kendal Castle	3,885	15	4 miles S.E. from Berry Head.	Submarine	No warning	Torpedo	18 including Master.
Joseph Fisher (S.V.).	79	15	16 miles E. by N. from Codling L.V.	Submarine	Captured	Gunfire	—
Energy (S.V.)	89	15	18 miles E. by N. from Codling L.V.	Submarine	Captured	Gunfire	—
●†Ethel	2,336	16	8 miles S.E. from Berry Head.	Submarine	No warning	Torpedo	—
†Madryn	2,244	16	5 miles N.N.E. from Trevose Head.	Submarine	No warning	Torpedo	—
†Wellington	5,600	16	175 miles N. by W. from Cape Villano.	Submarine	No warning	Torpedo	5 including Master.
†Serula	1,388	16	13½ miles N.E ½ N. from Strumble Head.	Submarine	No warning	Torpedo	17 including Master.
†Tasman	5,023	16	220 miles N. by W. ¼ W. from Cape Villano.	Submarine	No warning	Torpedo	14 including Master.
†Philomel	3,050	16	12 miles S.E. by E. from Glenan Island.	Submarine	No warning	Torpedo	—
●†Lord Stewart	1,445	16	6 miles E. ½ N. from Hope's Nose.	Submarine	No warning	Torpedo	1
†Acadian	2,305	16	11 miles S.W. by W. from Trevose Head.	Submarine	No warning	Torpedo	25 including Master.
†Lavernock	2,406	17	5 miles S.W. from Trevose Head.	Submarine	No warning	Torpedo	25 including Master.
†Muriel	1,831	17	3⅔ miles N.E. from Peterhead.	Submarine	No warning	Torpedo	—
Cairo (Egyptian S.V.).	254	17	110 miles N. by E. from Alexandria.	Submarine	Captured	Gunfire	—
†John O. Scott	1,235	18	9 miles W. by N. from Trevose Head.	Submarine	No warning	Torpedo	18 including Master.
†Primo	1,037	18	3½ miles N.N.W. from Godrevy L.H.	Submarine	No warning	Torpedo	—
†Barrister	4,952	19	9 miles W. ½ N. from Chicken Rock.	Submarine	No warning	Torpedo	30
Staithes	336	21	1½ miles S.E. by S. ½ S. from Sunderland.	Submarine	No warning	Torpedo	4 including Master.
†Downshire	368	21	8 miles E.S.E. from Rockabill.	Submarine	Captured	Gunfire	—
†Polesley	4,221	21	1 mile North from Pendeen L.H.	Submarine	No warning	Torpedo	43 including Master.
†Gorsemore	3,079	22	44 miles S.E. ½ E. from Cape Colonne.	Submarine	No warning	Torpedo	—
†Edlington	3,864	23	70 miles E. by S. from Cape Passero.	Submarine	No warning	Torpedo	—
●†Aldershot	2,177	23	5 miles E.S.E. from Dartmouth.	Submarine	No warning	Torpedo	1
†Hebburn	1,938	25	14 miles South from Mine Head.	Submarine	No warning	Torpedo	6

MERCHANT VESSELS CAPTURED OR SUNK.   98

Name.	Gross Tons.	Date.	Position.	Cause of Loss.	How attacked.	How sunk.	Lives lost.
		1918. Sept.					
†Hatasu - -	3,193	27	50 miles N. ¾ W. from Oran.	Submarine -	No warning -	Torpedo -	2
†Baldersby -	3,613	28	9 miles E. ½ S. from Codling L.V.	Submarine -	No warning -	Torpedo -	2
Benha (Egyptian S.V.).	95	28	Off Ras el Dabaa	Submarine -	Captured -	Gunfire -	—
†Nyanza - -	4,053	29	14 miles N.E. by E. from the Maidens.	Submarine -	No warning -	Torpedo -	13 including Master.
†Libourne - -	1,219	29	10 miles South from the Lizard.	Submarine -	No warning -	Torpedo -	3

OCTOBER 1918.

Name.	Gross Tons.	Date.	Position.	Cause of Loss.	How attacked.	How sunk.	Lives lost.
		Oct.					
†Bylands - -	3,309	1	150 miles N.N.W. from Cape Villano.	Submarine -	Captured -	Gunfire -	—
†Montfort - -	6,578	1	170 miles W. by S. ¾ S. from Bishop Rock.	Submarine -	No warning -	Torpedo -	5
†Bamse - -	1,001	2	5½ miles E. ¾ N. from the Lizard.	Submarine -	No warning -	Torpedo -	11
†Poljames - -	856	2	6 miles South from the Lizard.	Submarine -	No warning -	Torpedo -	13
†Arca - -	4,839	2	40 miles N.W. by W. from Tory Island.	Submarine -	No warning -	Torpedo -	52 including Master.
†Westwood -	1,968	3	5 miles S.W. ½ W. from the Lizard.	Submarine -	No warning -	Torpedo -	1
†Ariel - -	3,428	3	54 miles North from Cape Tenez.	Submarine -	No warning -	Torpedo -	—
†Eupion - -	3,575	3	10 miles West from Loop Head.	Submarine -	No warning -	Torpedo -	11
†Oopack - -	3,883	4	110 miles East from Malta.	Submarine -	No warning -	Torpedo -	—
Kassid Karim (Egyptian S.V.)	103	4	75 miles N. from Alexandria.	Submarine -	Captured -	Gunfire -	—
Industrial (S.V.)	330	4	250 miles S.E. ½ S. (true) from Nantucket Island.	Submarine -	Captured -	Bombs -	—
†Reventazon -	4,050	5	14 miles W. by S. from Kassandra Point, Gulf of Salonika.	Submarine -	No warning -	Torpedo -	15 including Master.
†Thalia - -	1,308	8	4 miles E.S.E. from Filey Brig.	Submarine -	No warning -	Torpedo -	3
Hawanee (S.V.)	124	8	350 miles West (true) from Cape Finisterre.	Submarine -	Captured -	Bombs -	—
†Leinster - -	2,646	10	7 miles E.S.E. from Kish L.V.	Submarine -	No warning -	Torpedo -	176 including Master.
Hamidieh (Egyptian S.V.).	85	13	50 miles N.W. from Alexandria.	Submarine -	Captured -	Gunfire -	—
†Dundalk - -	794	14	5 miles N.N.W. from Skerries, Anglesey.	Submarine -	No warning -	Torpedo -	21 including Master.
†Pentwyn - -	3,587	16	20 miles N.E. by N. ¼ N. from the Smalls.	Submarine -	No warning -	Torpedo -	1
†War Council -	5,875	16	85 miles W.S.W. from Cape Matapan.	Submarine -	No warning -	Torpedo -	—
†Bonvilston -	2,866	17	9½ miles N.W. by W. from Corsewall Point.	Submarine -	No warning -	Torpedo -	—

MERCHANT VESSELS CAPTURED OR SUNK.

Name.	Gross Tons.	Date.	Position.	Cause of Loss.	How attacked.	How sunk.	Lives lost.
		1918. Oct.					
†Hunsdon	2,899	18	1 mile S. from Strangford Light Buoy.	Submarine	No warning	Torpedo	1
†Almerian	3,030	19	13 miles W. by S. from Licata, Sicily.	Mine	Mine	Mine	—
Emily Millington (S.V.)	111	20	13 miles N.N.E. from South Bishop.	Submarine	Captured	Gunfire	—
†Saint Barchan	362	21	4 miles from St. John's Point, Co. Down.	Submarine	No warning	Torpedo	8 including Master.
Moscow	1,622	21	Petrograd	Bolsheviks	—	Scuttled	—

NOVEMBER 1918.

†Surada	5,324	2	Port Said swept channel.	Submarine	No warning	Torpedo	—
†Murcia	4,871	2	12 miles North from Port Said.	Submarine	No warning	Torpedo	1

II.—BRITISH FISHING VESSELS CAPTURED OR DESTROYED BY THE ENEMY.

Name.	Tons.	Date.	Position.	Cause of Loss.	How attacked.	How sunk.	Lives lost.
AUGUST 1914.		1914. Aug.					
Tubal Cain	227	7	50 miles W.N.W. from Stalberg, Iceland.	Kaiser Wilhelm der Grosse.	Captured	Gunfire	—
Marnay	153	22	85 miles E. by N. from Spurn.	Torpedo Boat	Captured	Bomb	Crew made prisoners.
Capricornus	194	22	85 miles E. by N. from Spurn.	Torpedo Boat	Captured	Not known	Crew made prisoners.
Skirbeck	171	22	North Sea	Cruiser	Captured	Gunfire	Crew made prisoners.
Wigtoft	155	22	North Sea	Cruiser	Captured	Gunfire	Crew made prisoners.
Walrus	159	22	North Sea	Cruiser	Captured	Gunfire	Crew made prisoners.
Flavian	186	22	North Sea	Torpedo Boat	Captured	Not known	Crew made prisoners.
Julian	185	22	North Sea	Torpedo Boat	Captured	Not known	Crew made prisoners.
Indian	185	22	North Sea	Torpedo Boat	Captured	Not known	Crew made prisoners.
Pegasus	155	24–26	North Sea	Torpedo Boat	Captured	Not known	Crew made prisoners.
Chameleon	132	24–26	North Sea	Torpedo Boat	Captured	Not known	Crew made prisoners.
Rideo	230	24–26	North Sea	Torpedo Boat	Captured	Not known	Crew made prisoners.

FISHING VESSELS CAPTURED OR SUNK.

Name.	Tons.	Date.	Position.	Cause of Loss.	How attacked.	How sunk.	Lives lost.
		1914. Aug.					
Argonaut	225	24–26	North Sea	Torpedo Boat	Captured	Not known	Crew made prisoners.
Lobelia	147	24–26	North Sea	Torpedo Boat	Captured	Not known	Crew made prisoners.
Harrier	208	24–26	North Sea	Torpedo Boat	Captured	Not known	Crew made prisoners.
Pollux	182	24–26	North Sea	Torpedo Boat	Captured	Not known	Crew made prisoners.
Porpoise	159	25	70 miles E.N.E. from Inner Dowsing L.V.	Torpedo Boat	Captured	Bomb	Crew made prisoners.
Lindsey	144	25	70 miles E.N.E. from Inner Dowsing L.V.	Torpedo Boat	Captured	Bomb	Crew made prisoners.
Kesteven	150	25	69 miles E. by N. from Inner Dowsing L.V.	Torpedo Boat	Captured	Bomb	Crew made prisoners.
Rhine	117	25	North Sea	Torpedo Boat	Captured	Not known	Crew made prisoners.
Zenobia	152	25	North Sea	Torpedo Boat	Captured	Not known	Crew made prisoners.
Valiant	198	25	Off Whitby	Torpedo Boat	Captured	Not known	Crew made prisoners.
Mersey	196	25	North Sea	Torpedo Boat	Captured	Not known	Crew made prisoners.
Seti	169	26	North Sea	Torpedo Boat	Captured	Not known	Crew made prisoners.
St. Cuthbert	189	24–26	70 miles E.N.E. from Spurn.	Torpedo Boat	Captured	Not known	Crew made prisoners.
Barley Rig	70	27	Off Tyne	Mine	Mine	Mine	5
SEPTEMBER		**1914.**					
		Sept.					
Ajax	120	2	Off the mouth of the Humber.	Mine	Mine	Mine	9 including Skipper.
Fittonia	146	2	27 miles E. by S. from Spurn.	Mine	Mine	Mine	7
Imperialist	195	6	40 miles E.N.E. from Tyne	Mine	Mine	Mine	2
Revigo	230	7	25 miles E. ½ N. from Spurn.	Mine	Mine	Mine	—
Kilmarnock	165	22	31 miles E. from Spurn.	Mine	Mine	Mine	6
Rebono	176	23	25 miles E. by N. from Spurn L.V.	Mine	Mine	Mine	1
OCTOBER 1914.							
		Oct.					
Rosella	243	29	25 miles S.E. from Tyne.	Mine	Mine	Mine	2
Our Tom	40	29	45 miles S.E. from Southwold.	Mine	Mine	Mine	3
NOVEMBER 1914.							
		Nov.					
Fraternal	100	3	16 miles N.E. by N from Lowestoft.	Mine	Mine	Mine	3
Will and Maggie	100	3	17 miles E. by N. from Lowestoft.	Mine	Mine	Mine	6

FISHING VESSELS CAPTURED OR SUNK.

Name.	Tons.	Date.	Position.	Cause of Loss.	How attacked.	How sunk.	Lives lost.
		1914. Nov.					
Copious	100	3	15 miles E. by S. from Yarmouth.	Mine	Mine	Mine	9 including Skipper.
Speculator (Smack).	60	10	Near Smith's Knoll	Mine	Mine	Mine	5
Seymolicus	50	18	12 miles E. by N. ½ N. from Smith's Knoll.	Mine	Mine	Mine	9 including Skipper.
Lord Carnarvon	50	20	Off Yarmouth	Mine	Mine	Mine	10 including Skipper.
DECEMBER 1914.		Dec.					
Earl Howard	226	11	90 miles N.E. by N. from Spurn L.V.	Mine (?)	Mine (?)	Mine (?)	9 including Skipper.
Wayside Flower (Motor)	35	16	Off Hartlepool	German bombarding squadron.	Gunfire	Gunfire	
Constance (Motor)	40	16	Off Hartlepool	German bombarding squadron.	Gunfire	Gunfire	
Manx Queen	219	16	North Sea	Torpedo boat	Captured	Not known	Crew made prisoners.
Ocana	260	23	75 miles N.E. by E. from Flamborough Head.	Mine	Mine	Mine	9
JANUARY 1915.		1915. Jan.					
Windsor	172	22	55 miles E. from Spurn Point.	Mine	Mine	Mine	—
Golden Oriole	50	22	37 miles E. by N. from Lowestoft.	Mine	Mine	Mine	—
MARCH 1915.		Mar.					
Sapphire	289	1	Off Filey	Mine	Mine	Mine	1
APRIL 1915.		April					
Jason	176	1	40 miles N.E. by E. from Tyne.	Submarine	Captured	Bomb	—
Gloxinia	145	1	40 miles N.E. by E. from Tyne.	Submarine	Captured	Bomb	—
Nellie	109	1	35 miles N.E. by E. from Tyne.	Submarine	Captured	Bomb	—
Acantha	322	5	25 miles E. by N. from Longstone.	Submarine	Captured	Torpedo	—
Zarina	154	7	72 miles E. by N. from Spurn L.V.	Submarine	No warning	Torpedo	9 including Skipper.
Vanilla	158	18	53 miles E. by S. from Inner Dowsing L.V.	Submarine	No warning	Torpedo	9 including Skipper.
Glencarse	188	18–20	Between Shetlands and Aberdeen.	Submarine	Captured	Reported taken to Germany.	Crew made prisoners.
St. Lawrence	196	22	88 miles E. ½ N. from Spurn L.V.	Submarine	Captured	Bomb	2
Cancer	183	22	North Sea	Probably T.B.	Captured	Not known	Crew made prisoners.
Recolo	170	26	60 miles E. by N. from Spurn Point.	Mine	Mine	Mine	2
Lilydale	129	28	37 miles E. from St. Abbs Head.	Submarine	Captured	Bomb	—

FISHING VESSELS CAPTURED OR SUNK.

Name.	Tons.	Date.	Position.	Cause of Loss.	How attacked.	How sunk.	Lives lost.
MAY 1915.		1915. May					
St. George	215	2	65 miles E. ½ N. from Aberdeen.	Submarine	Gunfire	Gunfire	Crew made prisoners.
Martaban	148	2	22 miles E. ½ N. from Aberdeen.	Submarine	Captured	Gunfire	—
Cruiser	146	2	50 miles S.E. from Aberdeen.	Submarine	Gunfire	Gunfire	4 including Skipper.
Sunray	167	2	56 miles N.N.E. from Longstone.	Submarine	Captured	Gunfire	—
Mercury	222	2	14 miles E. ½ N. from Aberdeen.	Submarine	Captured	Gunfire	—
St. Louis No. 1	211	2	60 miles E. by N. ½ N. from May Is.	Submarine	Captured	Gunfire	—
Iolanthe	179	3	140 miles E.N.E. from Hornsea.	Submarine	Captured	Bomb	—
Hero	173	3	150 miles E.N.E. from Hornsea.	Submarine	Captured	Bomb	—
Northward Ho!	180	3	145 miles E.N.E. from Hornsea.	Submarine	Captured	Bomb	—
Scottish Queen	125	3	50 miles E.S.E. from Aberdeen.	Submarine	Captured	Gunfire	—
Coquet	176	3	160 miles E.N.E. from Spurn.	Submarine	Captured	Bomb	—
Progress	273	3	160 miles E.N.E. from Spurn.	Submarine	Captured	Bomb	—
Hector	179	3	160 miles E.N.E. from Spurn.	Submarine	Captured	Gunfire	—
Bob White	192	3	155 miles N.E. by E. ½ E. from Spurn.	Submarine	Captured	Gunfire	—
Uxbridge	164	3	North Sea	Mine	Mine	Mine	—
Rugby	205	4	100 miles N.E. from Spurn.	Submarine	Captured	Bomb	—
Sceptre	166	5	40 miles S.E. by S. from Peterhead.	Submarine	Captured	Gunfire	—
Straton	198	5	40 miles E. from Hartlepool.	Submarine	Captured	Gunfire	—
Merrie Islington	147	6	6 miles N.N.E. from Whitby Rock Buoy.	Submarine	Captured	Bomb	—
Don	151	6	100 miles E. by S. from Spurn.	Mine	Mine	Mine	7
Benington	131	7	10 miles S.E. from Peterhead.	Submarine	Captured	Gunfire	—
Hellenic	159	8	98 miles E. by S. from Spurn.	Mine	Mine	Mine	3
King Charles	163	17	N.W. corner of Dogger Bank.	Torpedo boat	Captured	Not known	Crew made prisoners.
Euclid	165	18	N.W. corner of Dogger Bank.	Torpedo boat	Captured	Not known	Crew made prisoners.
Duke of Wellington.	182	18	N.W. corner of Dogger Bank.	Torpedo boat	Captured	Not known	Crew made prisoners.
Titania	179	18	N.W. corner of Dogger Bank.	Torpedo boat	Captured	Not known	Crew made prisoners.
Crimond	173	19	60 miles E. from Wick.	Submarine	Captured	Bomb	—
Lucerne	154	19	50 miles N.E. by N. from Rattray Hd.	Submarine	Captured	Bomb	—
Chrysolite	222	19	25 miles S.W. by S. from Lerwick.	Submarine	Captured	Bomb	—
Angelo	173	21	Dogger Bank	Mine	Mine	Mine	—

FISHING VESSELS CAPTURED OR SUNK.

Name.	Tons.	Date.	Position.	Cause of Loss.	How attacked.	How sunk.	Lives lost.
		1915. May					
Sabrina	179	21	160 miles E.N.E. from Spurn L.V.	Mine	Mine	Mine	9 including Skipper.
Condor	151	29	30 miles N.E. from Scarborough.	Mine	Mine	Mine	9 including Skipper.

JUNE 1915.

Name.	Tons.	Date.	Position.	Cause of Loss.	How attacked.	How sunk.	Lives lost.
		June					
Victoria	155	1	145 miles W. by S. from St. Ann's Head.	Submarine	Captured	Bomb	6 including Skipper.
Hirose	274	2	130 miles W. by S. ½ S. from Lundy Island.	Submarine	Captured	Bomb	—
Ena May	90	3	60 miles S.W. by S. ½ S. from Sumburgh Head.	Submarine	Captured	Gunfire	—
Chrysoprasus	119	3	45 miles E. by S. from Papa, Stronsay.	Submarine	Captured	Gunfire	—
Dogberry	214	3	120 miles N.N.E. from Aberdeen.	Submarine	Captured	Bomb	—
Kathleen	92	3	40 miles E.S.E. from Start Point, Orkney.	Submarine	Captured	Bomb	—
E. & C. (Smack)	60	3	40 miles S.E. by E. from Lowestoft.	Submarine	Captured	Bomb	—
Boy Horace (Smack).	69	3	50 miles S.E. from Lowestoft.	Submarine	Captured	Bomb	—
Strathbran	163	3	35 miles E.S.E. from Pentland Skerries.	Submarine	Captured	Gunfire	—
Economy (Smack)	69	4	50 miles S.E. from Lowestoft.	Submarine	Captured	Bomb	—
Petrel	187	4	55 miles N.N.E. ½ E. from Buchanness.	Submarine	Captured	Gunfire	—
Cortes	174	4	50 miles E.S.E. from Copinsay.	Submarine	Captured	Bomb	—
Evening Star	120	4	50 miles E.S.E. from Copinsay.	Submarine	Captured	Gunfire	—
Ebenezer	113	4	117 miles S.W. by S. ½ S. from Out Skerries.	Submarine	Captured	Gunfire	—
Explorer	156	4	73 miles N.E. by N. from Buchanness.	Submarine	Captured	Gunfire	—
Persimon	255	5	50 miles N.E. from Buchanness.	Submarine	Captured	Gunfire	—
Gazehound	138	5	50 miles E. by N. from Aberdeen.	Submarine	Captured	Gunfire	—
Curlew	134	5	50 miles E. by N. from Aberdeen.	Submarine	Captured	Gunfire	—
Bardolph	215	5	115 miles S. by W. from Sumburgh Head.	Submarine	Captured	Gunfire	—
Star of the West	197	5	55 miles N.E. ½ N. from Buchanness.	Submarine	Captured	Gunfire	—
Japonica	145	5	45 miles E. from Kinnaird Head.	Submarine	Captured	Gunfire	—
Arctic	169	5	65 miles E.S.E. from Spurn.	Submarine	Gunfire	Gunfire	4 including Skipper.
Dromio	208	6	35 miles N.E. by E. from Buchanness.	Submarine	Captured	Scuttled	—
Pentland	204	7	75 miles E.N.E. from Hornsea.	Submarine	Captured	Gunfire	—
Nottingham	165	7	70 miles N.E. from Spurn.	Submarine	Captured	Gunfire	—

Fishing Vessels Captured or Sunk.

Name.	Tons.	Date.	Position.	Cause of Loss.	How attacked.	How sunk.	Lives lost.
		1915. June					
Velocity	186	7	75 miles N.E. from Spurn.	Submarine	Captured	Gunfire	—
Saturn	183	7	86 miles N.E. from Spurn.	Submarine	Captured	Gunfire	—
Castor	182	9	85 miles N.E. by E. from Spurn.	Submarine	Captured	Gunfire	—
Tunisian	211	9	95 miles N.E. by N. from Spurn.	Submarine	Captured	Gunfire	—
J. Leyman	197	9	100 miles E. by N. from Spurn.	Submarine	Captured	Gunfire	—
Cardiff	163	9	90 miles N.E. by E. from Spurn.	Submarine	Captured	Gunfire	—
Edward (Smack)	52	9	48 miles E. by S. from Lowestoft.	Submarine	Captured	Bomb	—
Qui Vive (Smack)	50	9	48 miles E. by S. from Lowestoft.	Submarine	Captured	Bomb	—
Britannia (Smack)	43	9	55 miles E. from Lowestoft.	Submarine	Captured	Bomb	—
Welfare (Smack)	45	9	50 miles E.S.E. from Lowestoft.	Submarine	Captured	Bomb	—
Laurestina (Smack).	48	9	30 miles N.N.W. from Maas L.V.	Submarine	Captured	Bomb	—
Intrepid (Smack)	59	10	60 miles S.E. from Lowestoft.	Submarine	Captured	Bomb	—
Waago	154	11	80 miles N.E. by N. from Spurn.	Submarine	Captured	Bomb	—
Plymouth	165	11	67 miles N.E. ½ N. from Spurn.	Submarine	Captured	Gunfire	—
Dovey	160	11	50 miles E. by S. from Spurn.	Mine	Mine	Mine	9 including Skipper.
Queen Alexandra	208	13	8 miles E. by S. ½ S. from Tod Head.	Mine	Mine	Mine	—
Argyll	280	15	¼ mile from Sunk L.V.	Submarine	No warning	Torpedo	7 including Skipper.
Premier	169	20	75 miles N. by W. from Troup Head.	Submarine	Captured	Gunfire	—
Ugiebrae	79	23	35 miles E.N.E. from Out Skerries.	Submarine	Captured	Gunfire	—
Elizabeth	94	23	40 miles E.N.E. from Out Skerries.	Submarine	Captured	Gunfire	—
Lebanon	111	23	30 miles E. ½ N. from Muckle Flugga.	Submarine	Captured	Gunfire	—
Quiet Waters	63	23	35 miles E. by N. from Balta Sound.	Submarine	Captured	Gunfire	—
Josephine	85	23	40 miles N.E. by E. ½ E. from Out Skerries.	Submarine	Captured	Gunfire	—
Uffa	79	23	45 miles E.N.E. from Out Skerries.	Submarine	Captured	Gunfire	—
Viceroy	150	23	50 miles E.N.E. from Out Skerries.	Submarine	Captured	Gunfire	—
Research	89	23	42 miles N.E. from Out Skerries.	Submarine	Captured	Gunfire	—
Primrose	91	23	40 miles N.E. by E. from Out Skerries.	Submarine	Captured	Gunfire	—
Piscatorial	84	23	41 miles E.N.E. from Out Skerries.	Submarine	Captured	Gunfire	—

FISHING VESSELS CAPTURED OR SUNK.

Name.	Tons.	Date.	Position.	Cause of Loss.	How attacked.	How sunk.	Lives lost.
		1915. June					
Four	84	23	45 miles N.E. by E. ½E. from Out Skerries.	Submarine	Captured	Gunfire	—
J. M. & S.	78	23	42 miles E.N.E. from Out Skerries.	Submarine	Captured	Gunfire	—
Star of Bethlehem	77	23	40 miles E.N.E. from Out Skerries.	Submarine	Captured	Gunfire	—
Vine	110	24	30 miles N.E. by E. from Out Skerries.	Submarine	Captured	Gunfire	—
Monarda	87	24	41 miles E.N.E. from Out Skerries.	Submarine	Captured	Gunfire	—
Commander	149	24	49 miles E. from Balta Sound.	Submarine	Captured	Gunfire	—
Campania	167	26	60 miles N. by W. from Hoy Head.	Submarine	Captured	Gunfire	—

JULY 1915.

Name.	Tons.	Date.	Position.	Cause of Loss.	How attacked.	How sunk.	Lives lost.
		July					
Cheshire	148	7	50 miles E. by S. from Spurn.	Mine	Mine	Mine	8
Syrian	176	11	45 miles E.N.E. from Hornsea.	Submarine	Captured	Gunfire	—
Hainton	156	11	45 miles N.E. by E. from Hornsea.	Submarine	Captured	Gunfire	—
Purple Heather (Smack).	42	12	23 miles S.E. by S. from Lowestoft.	Submarine	Captured	Bomb	—
Merlin (Smack)	47	12	20 miles E.S.E. from Lowestoft.	Submarine	Captured	Bomb	—
Speedwell (Smack)	38	12	19 miles S.E. by E. from Lowestoft.	Submarine	Captured	Bomb	—
Woodbine (Smack)	29	12	18 miles S.E. from Lowestoft.	Submarine	Captured	Burnt	—
Star of Peace	180	22	114 miles N. ½ W. from Hoy Head.	Submarine	Captured	Gunfire	—
King Athelstan	159	22	100 miles N. by W. from Hoy Head.	Submarine	Captured	Bomb	—
Sutton	332	23	130 miles N.N.W. from Cape Wrath.	Submarine	Captured	Gunfire	—
Hermione	210	23	135 miles N.N.W. from Cape Wrath.	Submarine	Captured	Gunfire	—
Honoria	207	23	35 miles N.N.W. from Cape Wrath.	Submarine	Captured	Gunfire	—
Roslin	128	24	60 miles N. by W. from Butt of Lewis.	Submarine	Captured	Gunfire	—
Strathmore	163	24	60 miles N. by W. from Butt of Lewis.	Submarine	Captured	Gunfire	—
Anglia	107	24	25 miles N.W. from Sulisker.	Submarine	Captured	Gunfire	—
Cassio	172	24	123 miles N.W. by W. from Hoy Head.	Submarine	Captured	Gunfire	—
Perseus	155	24	60 miles E. from Spurn.	Mine	Mine	Mine	10 including Skipper.
Henry Charles (Smack).	41	24	30 miles E.N.E. from Lowestoft.	Submarine	Captured	Bomb	—
Kathleen (Smack)	46	24	30 miles E.N.E. from Lowestoft.	Submarine	Captured	Bomb	—

Fishing Vessels Captured or Sunk.

Name.	Tons.	Date.	Position.	Cause of Loss.	How attacked.	How sunk.	Lives lost.
		1915. July					
Activity (Smack)	56	24	30 miles E.N.E. from Lowestoft.	Submarine	Captured	Bomb	—
Prosper (Smack)	45	24	30 miles E.N.E. from Lowestoft.	Submarine	Captured	Bomb	—
Emblem	157	25	60 miles N. by W. from Hoy Head.	Submarine	Captured	Gunfire	—
Honoria	179	25	100 miles W.N.W. from N. Ronaldshay.	Submarine	Captured	Gunfire	—
Cydonia	259	25	70 miles N. by W. from Hoy Head.	Submarine	Captured	Gunfire	—
Gadwall	192	25	70 miles N. by W. from Hoy Head.	Submarine	Captured	Gunfire	—
Celtic	264	25	70 miles N. by W. from Hoy Head.	Submarine	Captured	Gunfire	—
Westward Ho! (Smack).	47	27	25 miles S.E. from Lowestoft.	Submarine	Captured	Bomb	—
Salacia (Smack)	48	27	15 miles E. from Lowestoft.	Submarine	Captured	Bomb	—
Iceni (Smack)	44	27	15 miles E. from Lowestoft.	Submarine	Captured	Bomb	—
Young Percy (Smack).	45	28	30 miles E. by N. from Lowestoft.	Submarine	Captured	Bomb	—
Coriander (Smack).	46	30	20 miles E.S.E. from Lowestoft.	Submarine	Captured	Bomb	—
Fitzgerald (Smack).	51	30	30 miles E.S.E from Lowestoft.	Submarine	Captured	Bomb	—
Achieve (Smack)	43	30	35 miles E. by N. from Lowestoft.	Submarine	Captured	Bomb	—
Quest (Smack)	46	30	35 miles E. by N. from Lowestoft.	Submarine	Captured	Bomb	—
Prospector (Smack).	59	30	28 miles E.N.E. from Lowestoft.	Submarine	Captured	Bomb	—
Strive (Smack)	63	30	35 miles E. by N. from Lowestoft.	Submarine	Captured	Bomb	—
Athena (Smack)	45	30	35 miles E. by N. from Lowestoft.	Submarine	Captured	Bomb	—
Venture (Smack)	44	30	27 miles E.N.E. from Lowestoft.	Submarine	Captured	Bomb	—
Tors	158	30	43 miles E. from Spurn.	Mine	Mine	Mine	8

AUGUST 1915.

		Aug.					
Alert (Smack)	59	1	18 miles N.E. from Lowestoft.	Submarine	Captured	Burnt	—
Lark (Fishing Boat).	—	1	Off Lowestoft	Submarine	—	—	—
Grimbarian	146	4	56 miles E. by N. from Spurn.	Mine	Mine	Mine	6
Challenger (Smack).	50	4	23 miles E. by N. from Lowestoft.	Submarine	Captured	Bomb	—
Heliotrope (Smack).	28	4	23 miles E. by N. from Lowestoft.	Submarine	Captured	Bomb	—
Hesperus (Smack)	57	6	37 miles E.N.E. from Lowestoft.	Submarine	Captured	Bomb	—
Fisherman (Smack).	24	6	37 miles E.N.E. from Lowestoft.	Submarine	Captured	Bomb	—
C. E. S. (Smack)	47	6	42 miles E. from Lowestoft.	Submarine	Captured	Bomb	—
Ivan (Smack)	44	6	42 miles E.N.E. from Lowestoft.	Submarine	Captured	Bomb	—
Ocean Queen	185	6	23 miles N. by W. from Muckle Flugga.	Submarine	Captured	Bomb	—
Westminster	252	6	20 miles E.S.E. from Muckle Flugga.	Submarine	Captured	Bomb	—
Xmas Rose (Smack).	27	6	Off Lowestoft	Submarine	Captured	Bomb	—
Arbor Vitæ (Smack)	26	8	35 miles N.E. by N. from Lowestoft.	Submarine	Captured	Bomb	—

FISHING VESSELS CAPTURED OR SUNK.

Name.	Tons.	Date.	Position.	Cause of Loss.	How attacked.	How sunk.	Lives lost.
		1915. Aug.					
Thrush	264	9	50 miles W. from Eagle Island.	Submarine	Captured	Bomb	—
Esperance (Smack).	46	10	17 miles N.E. by E. from Cromer.	Submarine	Captured	Gunfire	—
Young Admiral (Smack).	60	11	17 miles E. by N. from Cromer.	Submarine	Captured	Bomb	—
Trevear (Smack)	47	11	17 miles E. by N. from Cromer.	Submarine	Captured	Bomb	—
Welcome (Smack)	56	11	17 miles E. by N. from Cromer.	Submarine	Captured	Bomb	—
Palm (Smack)	47	11	17 miles E. by N. from Cromer.	Submarine	Captured	Bomb	—
Illustrious (Smack).	59	11	17 miles E. by N. from Cromer.	Submarine	Captured	Bomb	—
George Crabbe (Smack).	42	11	16 miles E. by N. from Cromer.	Submarine	Captured	Bomb	—
George Borrow (Smack).	62	11	15 miles E.N.E. from Cromer.	Submarine	Captured	Bomb	—
Ocean's Gift (Smack).	60	11	36 miles E. from Cromer.	Submarine	Captured	Bomb	—
Humphrey (Smack).	41	11	48 miles E. $\tfrac{3}{4}$ S. from Cromer.	Submarine	Captured	Bomb	—
Leader (Smack)	57	11	20 miles E. by N. from Lowestoft.	Submarine	Captured	Bomb	—
Sunflower (Smack)	60	12	30 miles E. by N. from Lowestoft.	Submarine	Captured	Bomb	—
Amethyst (Smack)	57	13	7 miles E.S.E. from Lowestoft.	Submarine	Captured	Bomb	—
E. M. W. (Smack)	47	13	29 miles N.E. by N. from Cromer.	Submarine	Captured	Bomb	—
J. W. F. T. (Smack).	60	13	29 miles N.E. by N. from Cromer.	Submarine	Captured	Bomb	—
Gloria	130	14	55 miles E. by N. from Aberdeen.	Submarine	Captured	Gunfire	—
White City (Smack).	45	14	At Cromer Knoll	Submarine	Captured	Bomb	—
Bona Fide (Smack)	59	14	35 miles E.N.E. from Lowestoft.	Submarine	Captured	Bomb	—
Repeat	107	17	18 miles W. by S. from Bardsey Island.	Submarine	Captured	Gunfire	—
George Baker	91	17	45 miles N. from Bishop Rock.	Submarine	Captured	Gunfire	—
Commander Boyle	290	23	40 miles N. by W. from Rattray Head.	Mine	Mine	Mine	3
Boy Bert (Smack)	57	23	50 miles E. from Lowestoft.	Submarine	Captured	Bomb	—
Integrity (Smack)	52	23	24 miles E.S.E. from Cromer.	Submarine	Captured	Bomb	—
Young Frank (Smack).	49	23	58 miles N.E. by E. $\tfrac{1}{2}$ E. from Lowestoft.	Submarine	Captured	Bomb	—
SEPTEMBER		1915. Sept.					
Emblem (Smack)	50	7	44 miles E.S.E. from Lowestoft.	Submarine	Captured	Bomb	—
Victorious (Smack)	43	7	44 miles from Lowestoft.	Submarine	Captured	Bomb	—
Constance (Smack)	57	7	44 miles E.S.E. from Lowestoft.	Submarine	Captured	Bomb	—
Emmanuel (Smack).	44	7	44 miles E.S.E. from Lowestoft.	Submarine	Captured	Bomb	—
Devonian	128	9	30 miles N.E. $\tfrac{1}{2}$ N. from Spurn L.V.	Mine (?)	Mine (?)	Mine (?)	9 including Skipper.
Boy Ernie (Smack)	47	10	58 miles E. from Cromer.	Submarine	Captured	Bomb	—
Nimrod (Smack)	51	10	45 miles E. by S. from Lowestoft.	Submarine	Captured	Bomb	—
Albion (Smack)	25	30	8 miles S. by W. from Berry Head.	Mine	Mine	Mine	3 including Skipper.

FISHING VESSELS CAPTURED OR SUNK.

Name.	Tons.	Date.	Position.	Cause of Loss.	How attacked.	How sunk.	Lives lost.
NOVEMBER 1915.		1915. Nov.					
King William	162	5	125 miles E. by N. from Spurn L.V.	Mine	Mine	Mine	2 including Skipper.
JANUARY 1916.		1916. Jan.					
Foam Crest (Smack).	46	18	25 miles S.E. by E. from Lowestoft.	Submarine	Captured	Bomb	—
Evelyn (Smack)	55	18	35 miles S.E. by E. from Lowestoft.	Submarine	Captured	Bomb	—
Sunshine (Smack)	52	18	28 miles S.E. from Lowestoft.	Submarine	Captured	Bomb	—
Crystal (Smack)	57	27	25 miles E.S.E. from Southwold.	Submarine	Captured	Bomb	—
Radium (Smack)	59	31	25 miles S.E. by E. from Lowestoft.	Submarine	Captured	Bomb	—
Arthur William (Smack).	44	31	24 miles S.E. from Lowestoft.	Submarine	Captured	Bomb	—
Hilda (Smack)	44	31	25 miles E.S.E. from Southwold.	Submarine	Captured	Bomb	—
FEBRUARY 1916.		Feb.					
W. E. Brown (Smack).	34	21	20 miles S.E. from Lowestoft.	Submarine	Captured	Bomb	—
Oleander (Smack)	34	21	28 miles S.E. from Lowestoft.	Submarine	Captured	Bomb	—
MARCH 1916.		Mar.					
Reliance (Smack)	54	1	25 miles E. by S. from Lowestoft.	Submarine	Captured	Bomb	—
Try On (Smack)	46	1	26 miles E. by S. from Lowestoft.	Submarine	Captured	Bomb	—
Harold (Smack)	56	1	18 miles E. from Lowestoft.	Submarine	Captured	Bomb	—
Trevose (Smack)	46	1	18 miles E. by N. from Lowestoft.	Submarine	Captured	Bomb	—
Springflower (Smack).	59	6	28 miles East from Lowestoft.	Submarine	Captured	Bomb	—
Young Harry (Smack).	43	6	35 miles E. from Lowestoft.	Submarine	Captured	Bomb	—
Khartoum	303	26	6 miles N.E. from Longstone L.V.	Mine	Mine	Mine	9
APRIL 1916.		April					
Alfred (Smack)	24	25	27 miles E. by S. from Lowestoft.	Submarine	Captured	Bomb	—
Horus	173	25	North Sea	Enemy Squadron	Captured	Not known	Crew prisoners.
Blessing (Motor)	19	28	16 miles E. by N. from Tyne.	Submarine	Captured	Bomb	—
MAY 1916.		May					
Research (Smack)	44	17	35 miles East from Cromer.	Submarine	Captured	Bomb	1
Wanderer (Smack).	47	17	North Sea	Submarine	Captured	Bomb	—
Boy Percy (Smack).	46	17	North Sea	Submarine	Captured	Bomb	—
Boy Sam (Smack).	46	17	North Sea	Submarine	Captured	Bomb	—
Osprey (Motor)	18	18	13 miles E.N.E. from Spurn L.V.	Submarine	Captured	Bomb	—

FISHING VESSELS CAPTURED OR SUNK.

Name.	Tons.	Date.	Position.	Cause of Loss.	How attacked.	How sunk.	Lives lost.
JULY 1916.		1916. July					
Queen Bee (Smack).	34	4	28 miles N.E. from Scarborough.	Submarine	Captured	Bomb	1 (Skipper)
Annie Anderson (Motor).	77	5	16 miles E. by S. from the Tyne.	Submarine	Captured	Bomb	—
Peep o' Day	52	5	25 miles E.N.E. from the Tyne.	Submarine	Captured	Bomb	—
Petunia	58	6	18 miles E.S.E. from the Tyne.	Submarine	Captured	Bomb	1
Nancy Hunnam	58	6	24 miles E. by S. from the Tyne.	Submarine	Captured	Bomb	—
Watchful (Motor)	52	6	23 miles S.E. by S. from the Tyne.	Submarine	Captured	Bomb	—
Newark Castle	85	6	23 miles S.E. from the Tyne.	Submarine	Captured	Bomb	—
Girl Bessie	62	6	23 miles S.E. by E. from the Tyne.	Submarine	Captured	Bomb	—
Staffa	176	10	45 miles E. by N. from the Tyne.	Submarine	Captured	Bomb	—
Florence	149	13	10 miles N.E. from Scarborough.	Submarine	Captured	Bomb	—
Dalhousie	89	13	10 miles N.N.E. from Whitby.	Submarine	Captured	Bomb	—
Mary Ann (Fishing Boat).	5	13	13 miles N. by F. from Whitby.	Submarine	Captured	Scuttled	—
Success (Fishing Boat).	6	13	13 miles N. by E. from Whitby.	Submarine	Captured	Scuttled	—
Recorder	149	14	16 miles N.E. by E. from the Tyne.	Submarine	Captured	Bomb	—
Langley Castle	93	14	18 miles N.E. by E. from the Tyne.	Submarine	Captured	Bomb	—
Bute	176	14	25 miles S.E. from the Tyne.	Submarine	Captured	Bomb	—
Ben Aden	176	14	15 miles E. from Hartlepool.	Submarine	Captured	Bomb	—
Girl's Friend	55	14	21 miles E. from Hartlepool.	Submarine	Captured	Bomb	—
Loch Tay (Smack)	44	17	10 miles N.N.E. from N. Haisboro L.V.	Submarine	Captured	Bomb	—
Waverley (Smack)	59	17	10 miles N.N.E. from N. Haisboro L.V.	Submarine	Captured	Bomb	—
V. M. G. (Smack)	59	17	6 miles N.E. from N. Haisboro L.V.	Submarine	Captured	Bomb	—
Glance (Smack)	60	17	10 miles E.N.E. from N. Haisboro L.V.	Submarine	Captured	Bomb	—
Gertrude (Smack)	57	17	10 miles E.N.E. from N. Haisboro L.V.	Submarine	Captured	Bomb	—
Loch Nevis (Smack).	58	17	Near Smith's Knoll.	Submarine	Captured	Bomb	—
Volunteer (Motor)	15	27	15 miles N.E. from the Tyne.	Submarine	Captured	Bomb	—
Jane Stewart (Motor).	15	27	15 miles N.E. from the Tyne.	Submarine	Captured	Bomb	—
Speedwell (Motor)	11	27	12 miles N.E. from the Tyne.	Submarine	Captured	Bomb	—
Renown	61	28	15 miles N.E. from the Tyne.	Submarine	Captured	Bomb	—
Andrewina (Motor)	50	28	12 miles N.E. from the Tyne.	Submarine	Captured	Bomb	—
Good Design (Motor).	40	28	15 miles N.E. by E. from the Tyne.	Submarine	Captured	Bomb	—
Spero Meliora (Motor).	11	28	15 miles N.E. from the Tyne.	Submarine	Captured	Bomb	—
Johan (Motor)	49	28	15 miles N.E. by E. from the Tyne.	Submarine	Captured	Bomb	—

Fishing Vessels Captured or Sunk.

Name.	Tons.	Date.	Position.	Cause of Loss.	How attacked.	How sunk.	Lives lost.
		1916. July					
Janet Ovenstone (Motor).	15	28	13 miles E.N.E. from the Tyne.	Submarine	Rammed	Rammed	—
King James	163	31	15 miles S.E. from the Tyne.	Submarine	Captured	Bomb	—
Braconash	192	31	18 miles S.E. from the Tyne.	Submarine	Captured	Bomb	—
Tatiana	285	31	19 miles S.E. from the Tyne.	Submarine	Captured	Bomb	—
AUGUST 1916.		Aug.					
Helvetia	167	1	5 miles E. from Seaham.	Submarine	Captured	Bomb	—
Rnodesia	110	1	14 miles E.S.E. from Tyne.	Submarine	Captured	Bomb	—
Smiling Morn	126	2	10 miles E. from Coquet Island.	Submarine	Captured	Bomb	—
Twiddler	99	2	8 miles E. from Coquet Island.	Submarine	Captured	Bomb	—
Olympia	221	3	3 miles E. from Coquet Island.	Submarine	Captured	Gunfire	—
Lucania	92	3	7½ miles E.N.E. from Coquet Island.	Submarine	Captured	Bomb	—
Trawler Prince	126	3	12 miles S.S.E. from Longstone Light.	Submarine	Captured	Bomb	—
Merchant Prince	130	3	14 miles S.E. by E. from Farne Islands.	Submarine	Captured	Bomb	—
Egyptian Prince	129	5	12 miles S.S.E. from Longstone Light.	Submarine	Captured	Bomb	—
St. Olive	202	5	11 miles E. from Coquet Island.	Submarine	Captured	Bomb	—
Loch Lomond (Smack).	42	6	18 miles E. from Yarmouth.	Submarine	Captured	Gunfire	—
Dragoon (smack)	30	20	36 miles N.E. by N. from Cromer.	Submarine	Captured	Bomb	—
Equinox	198	25	39 miles S.E. by E. from Humber L.V.	Mine	Mine	Mine	9 including Skipper.
SEPTEMBER 1916.		1916. Sept.					
Dorado (Smack)	36	9	20 miles S.S.E. from Start Point.	Submarine	Captured	Bomb	—
Muriel Franklin (Smack).	29	9	20 miles S.E. from Start Point.	Submarine	Captured	Gunfire	—
Consolation (Smack).	47	9	15 miles S.E. from Start Point.	Submarine	Captured	Gunfire	—
Favourite (Smack)	38	9	20 miles S.E. from Start Point.	Submarine	Captured	Gunfire	—
Mercury	183	23	65 miles S.E. by E. ½ E. from Spurn L.V.	Submarine	Captured	Bomb	—
Viella	144	23	38 miles S.E. by E. from Spurn L.V.	Submarine	Captured	Bomb	—
Restless	125	23	40 miles S.E. by E. from Spurn L.V.	Submarine	Captured	Gunfire	—
Beechwold	129	23	40 miles S.E. by E. from Spurn L.V.	Submarine	Gunfire	Gunfire	—
Weelsby	112	23	40 miles S.E. by E. from Spurn L.V.	Submarine	Captured	Bomb	—

111 Fishing Vessels Captured or Sunk.

Name.	Tons.	Date.	Position.	Cause of Loss.	How attacked.	How sunk.	Lives lost.
		1916. Sept					
Britannia III.	138	23	40 miles S.E. by E. from Spurn L.V.	Submarine	Captured	Gunfire	—
Refino	182	23	39 miles S.E. by E. from Spurn L.V.	Submarine	Captured	Gunfire	—
Andromeda	149	23	39 miles S.E. by E. from Spurn L.V.	Submarine	Captured	Gunfire	—
Rego	176	23	40 miles S.E. by E. from Spurn L.V.	Submarine	Captured	Gunfire	—
Cockatrice	115	23	40 miles S.E. by E. from Spurn L.V.	Submarine	Captured	Gunfire	—
Phœnix	117	23	45 miles E.S.E. from Spurn L.V.	Submarine	Captured	Gunfire	—
Devonshire	148	24	33 miles N.E. ½ N. from Spurn L.V.	Submarine	Captured	Gunfire	—
Briton	134	24	18 miles S.E. by S. from Flamborough Head.	Submarine	Captured	Gunfire	—
Albatross	158	24	20 miles E. from Flamborough Head.	Submarine	Captured	Gunfire	—
Aphelion	197	24	20 miles E. from Flamborough Head.	Submarine	Captured	Gunfire	—
Fisher Prince	125	24	20 miles N.E. from Scarborough.	Submarine	Captured	Gunfire	—
Otterhound	150	24	20 miles N.E. from Scarborough.	Submarine	Captured	Gunfire	—
Otter	123	24	20 miles N.E. from Scarborough.	Submarine	Captured	Gunfire	—
Harrier	162	24	20 miles N.E. from Scarborough.	Submarine	Captured	Gunfire	—
Tarantula	155	24	20 miles N.E. from Scarborough.	Submarine	Captured	Gunfire	—
Marguerite	151	24	20 miles N.E. from Scarborough.	Submarine	Captured	Gunfire	—
Sunshine	74	24	20 miles N.E. from Scarborough.	Submarine	Captured	Gunfire	—
Loch Ness	176	25	20 miles N.E. from Scarborough.	Submarine	Captured	Gunfire	—
Gamecock	151	25	20 miles N.E. from Scarborough.	Submarine	Captured	Gunfire	—
Nil Desperandum	148	25	20 miles N.E. from Scarborough.	Submarine	Captured	Bomb	—
Quebec	133	25	16 miles E. by N. from Whitby.	Submarine	Captured	Gunfire	—
St. Hilda	94	25	20 miles N.E. from Scarborough.	Submarine	Captured	Gunfire	—
Trinidad	147	25	23 miles N.E. from Whitby.	Submarine	Captured	Gunfire	—
Seal	135	25	33 miles E. by S. from Hartlepool.	Submarine	Captured	Gunfire	—
Cynthia	133	25	23 miles E. by S. ½ S. from Flamborough Head.	Submarine	Captured	Gunfire	—
Bella (Motor)	11	25	Off Tod Head	Submarine	Captured	Not known	Crew made prisoners.

Fishing Vessels Captured or Sunk.

Name.	Tons.	Date.	Position.	Cause of Loss.	How attacked.	How sunk.	Lives lost.
		1916. Sept.					
Marjorie (Smack)	55	28	Off Smith's Knoll	Submarine	Captured	Bomb	—
Loch Ryan	186	28	North Sea	Submarine	Reported captured.	Taken to Germany.	Crew made prisoners.
Fuchsia	145	—	North Sea	Submarine	Captured	Not known	Crew made prisoners.

OCTOBER 1916.

		Oct.					
Rado	182	4	15 miles N.E. by E. from Spurn L.V.	Submarine	Captured	Bomb	—
Jersey	162	4	16 miles N.E. by E. from Spurn L.V.	Submarine	Captured	Bomb	—
Jennie Bullas (Motor).	26	4	14 miles E.N.E. from Spurn L.V.	Submarine	Captured	Bomb	—
Rover	42	5	10 miles E.N.E. from Spurn L.V.	Submarine	Captured	Bomb	—
Magnus	154	8	40 miles E.N.E. from Longstone.	Submarine	Captured	Bomb	—
Effort	159	22	30 miles E.N.E. from Buchanness.	Submarine	Captured	Gunfire	—
Titan	171	26	56 miles S.E. from Girdleness.	Submarine	Captured	Gunfire	—
Nellie Bruce	79	30	Off Beru Fiord, Iceland.	Submarine	Gunfire	Gunfire	—
Floreal	163	30	20 miles N. by W. from Flannan Islands.	Submarine	Captured	Bomb	—

NOVEMBER 1916.

		Nov.					
Kyoto	282	2	90 miles S.W. by W. from Fastnet.	Submarine	Captured	Gunfire	—
Caswell	245	2	90 miles S.W. by W. from Fastnet.	Submarine	Captured	Bombs	—
Harfat Castle	274	2	90 miles S.W. by W. from Fastnet.	Submarine	Captured	Bombs	—
Vineyard	126	8	13 miles S. by E. $\frac{3}{4}$ E. from Aberdeen.	Mine	Mine	Mine	8 including Skipper.
Veronica (Smack)	27	11	9 miles from Start Point.	Submarine	Captured	Bombs	—
Superb (Smack)	50	13	5 miles N.E. by E. from Smith's Knoll Spar Buoy.	Submarine	Captured	Gunfire	—
Our Boys (Smack)	63	13	4 miles N. by E. from Smith's Knoll Spar Buoy.	Submarine	Captured	Gunfire	—
Hatsuse	282	14	86 miles S.W. by W. from Fastnet.	Submarine	Captured	Gunfire	—
Clematis (Smack)	22	28	35 miles S.E. from Start Point.	Submarine	Captured	Bombs	—
Vulcan (Smack)	27	28	28 miles S.E. by E. from Berry Head.	Submarine	Captured	Bombs	—
Provident (Smack)	38	28	24 miles W. by S. from Portland Bill.	Submarine	Captured	Bombs	—
Amphitrite (Smack).	44	28	24 miles W. by S. from Portland Bill.	Submarine	Captured	Gunfire	—
Catena (Smack)	36	28	25 miles S.W. by S. from Berry Head.	Submarine	Captured	Gunfire	—

FISHING VESSELS CAPTURED OR SUNK.

Name.	Tons.	Date.	Position.	Cause of Loss.	How attacked.	How sunk.	Lives lost.
Sea Lark (Smack)	42	1916. Nov. 28	24 miles S.E. by S. from Berry Head.	Submarine	Captured	Gunfire	—
Concord (Smack)	42	30	28 miles S.E. by S. from Start Point.	Submarine	Captured	Bombs	—
DECEMBER 1916.							
E.L.G. (Smack)	25	Dec. 1	25 miles N.W. from Trevose Head.	Submarine	Captured	Bombs	—
T. and A. C. (Smack).	23	1	20 miles N.N.W. from Trevose Head.	Submarine	Captured	Bombs	—
Camellia (Smack)	46	1	Off Eddystone	Mine	Mine	Mine	3 (including Skipper).
Margaret	54	17	Between Hastings and Dungeness.	Mine	Mine	Mine	6 (including Skipper).
Athole	112	17	8 miles E. by S. from Tod Head.	Mine	Mine	Mine	—
Arran	176	18	110 miles E. from Longstone.	Submarine	Captured	Gunfire	—
JANUARY 1917.							
Gladys	275	Jan. 21	40 miles N.W. by N. from Inishtrahull.	Submarine	Captured	Gunfire	—
Star of the Sea	197	21	43 miles N.W. by N. ½ N. from Inishtrahull.	Submarine	Captured	Gunfire	—
Lucy	280	21	42 miles N.W. by N. from Inishtrahull.	Submarine	Captured	Gunfire	—
Ethel (smack)	23	22	30 miles S.S.E. from Start Point.	Submarine	Captured	Gunfire	—
George E. Benson.	155	—	North Sea	Submarine	Captured	-	Crew made prisoners.
Alexandra	179	28	60 miles E. from Longstone.	Submarine	Captured	Bombs	Skipper made prisoner
Shamrock	173	29	115 miles N.N.E. from Longstone.	Submarine	Captured	Gunfire	—
Wetherill (smack)	46	30	25 miles N.N.W. from Trevose Head.	Submarine	Captured	Gunfire	—
Merit (smack)	39	30	20 miles N. by E. from Trevose Head.	Submarine	Captured	Gunfire	—
W. A. H. (smack)	47	30	32 miles N.W. from Trevose Head.	Submarine	Captured	Gunfire	—
Trevone (smack)	46	30	30 miles N.W. by N. from Trevose Head.	Submarine	Captured	Gunfire	2 including Skipper.
Helena and Samuel (smack).	59	30	30 miles N.N.W. from Trevose Head.	Submarine	Captured	Gunfire	—
Thistle	167	29	140 miles N.E. by E. ½ E. from the Tyne.	Submarine	Captured	Gunfire	—
Euonymous (smack).	59	30	34 miles N.W. from Trevose Head.	Submarine	Captured	Gunfire	—

Fishing Vessels Captured or Sunk.

Name.	Tons.	Date.	Position.	Cause of Loss.	How attacked.	How sunk.	Lives lost.
Vera	150	1917. Jan. —	North Sea	Submarine (?)	Reported captured.	Not known	Crew prisoners.
Agnes	125	—	North Sea	Submarine (?)	Reported captured.	Not known	Crew prisoners.
FEBRUARY 1917.		Feb.					
Inverlyon (smack)	59	1	15 miles N. by W. from Trevose Head.	Submarine	Captured	Gunfire	—
Ada (smack)	24	1	40 miles N.N.W. from Trevose Head.	Submarine	Captured	Bombs	—
Primrose	136	5	17 miles S.S.W. from Tod Head.	Mine	Mine	Mine	9 including Skipper.
Resolute	125	5	64 miles E. by S. from St. Abb's Head.	Submarine	Captured	Gunfire	—
Emerald (smack)	57	5	32 miles N.E. ¾ E. from Lowestoft.	Submarine	Captured	Gunfire	—
Adelaide	133	6	30 miles E.N.E. from the Tyne.	Submarine	Captured	Bombs	—
Romeo	114	6	70 miles E. from Berwick.	Submarine	Captured	Scuttled	—
Rupert	114	6	42 miles E.N.E. from the Tyne.	Submarine	Captured	Bombs	—
Mary Ann (smack)	17	8	18 miles N.N.E. from St. Ives Head.	Submarine	Captured	Bombs	—
Duke of York	150	9	34 miles E. by S. from Girdleness.	Submarine	Captured	Bombs	—
Benbow	172	9	25 miles E. by S. from Bell Rock.	Submarine	Captured	Bombs	—
Ostrich	148	10	135 miles N.E. from Longstone.	Submarine	Captured	Gunfire	—
Athenian	171	10	105 miles E. by S. ¼ S. from Aberdeen.	Submarine	Captured	Scuttled	—
Ireland	152	10	105 miles E.S.E. from Girdleness.	Submarine	Captured	Gunfire	—
Ashwold	129	11	130 miles N.E. by N. from Shields.	Submarine	Captured	Gunfire	Skipper made prisoner.
Brissons (smack)	60	12	9 miles W. from Trevose Head.	Submarine	Captured	Bomb	—
Dale	198	12	42 miles S. by E. ¼ E. from N. Ronaldshay.	Submarine	Captured	Bombs	Skipper made prisoner.
Barnsley	144	13	13 miles N. from Inishtrahull.	Submarine	Captured	Bombs	Skipper and chief engineer made prisoners.
King Alfred	159	13	75 miles S. from Fair Isle.	Submarine	Captured	Bomb	Skipper made prisoner.
Friendship (smack)	37	13	Off Smalls	Submarine	Captured	Not known	4 including Skipper.
Zircon (smack)	48	13	26 miles S.W. from Smalls.	Submarine	Captured	Bombs	—
Belvoir Castle	221	14	15 miles S.E. ½ E. from Buchan Ness.	Submarine	Captured	Bomb	Skipper made prisoner.
Mary Bell	144	14	50 miles E. by N. from Aberdeen.	Submarine	Captured	Bomb	Skipper made prisoner.
Excel	157	17	53 miles N.E. from the Tyne.	Submarine	Captured	Gunfire	—
Halcyon	190	19	Off Butt of Lewis	Mine	Mine	Mine	10 including Skipper.

115 FISHING VESSELS CAPTURED OR SUNK.

Name.	Tons.	Date.	Position.	Cause of Loss.	How attacked.	How sunk.	Lives lost.
K. L. M. (smack)	28	1917. Feb. 21	8 miles N.W. by W. from Eddystone.	Submarine	Captured	Gunfire	—
Monarch (smack)	35	21	14 miles S.E. by S. from Eddystone.	Submarine	Captured	Bomb	—
Energy (smack)	25	21	11 miles S.S.E. $\frac{1}{2}$ S. from Eddystone.	Submarine	Captured	Gunfire	—
Frolic	183	22	90 miles E. by S. from Aberdeen.	Submarine	Captured	Gunfire	—
Lord Collingwood.	148	22	129 miles N.E. $\frac{1}{4}$ E. from Longstone.	Submarine	Captured	Not known	—

MARCH 1917.

Name.	Tons.	Date.	Position.	Cause of Loss.	How attacked.	How sunk.	Lives lost.
Herbert Ingram	142	Mar. 1	70 miles E. from Longstone.	Submarine	Captured	Bomb	—
Redcap	199	1	97 miles E. from Longstone.	Submarine	Gunfire	Gunfire	1
Vulcana	219	7	40 miles E.S.E. from Auskerry L.H.	Submarine	Gunfire	Gunfire	2 including Skipper.
Naamah	269	7	35 miles S. by E. from N. Ronaldshay.	Submarine	Captured	Gunfire	—
Thrift (smack)	40	11	15 miles W. from Trevose Head.	Submarine	Gunfire	Gunfire	—
Inter-nos (smack).	59	12	12 miles N.N.W. from Trevose Head.	Submarine	Captured	Bomb	—
Rivina (smack)	22	12	15 miles N.N.W. from Trevose Head.	Submarine	Captured	Bomb	—
Lent Lily (smack).	23	12	13 miles N.N.W. from Trevose Head.	Submarine	Captured	Bomb	—
Gracia (smack)	25	12	12 miles N. by W. from Trevose Head.	Submarine	Captured	Bomb	—
Nellie (smack)	60	12	13 miles N. by W. from Trevose Head.	Submarine	Captured	Bomb	—
C.A.S. (smack)	56	12	12 miles N.N.W. from Trevose Head.	Submarine	Captured	Bomb	—
Jessamine (smack).	56	12	14 miles N.N.W. from Trevose Head.	Submarine	Captured	Bomb	—
Hyacinth (smack).	61	12	15 miles N. by W. from Trevose Head.	Submarine	Captured	Bomb	—
● Reindeer (smack).	52	12	15 miles S.E. from Berry Head.	Submarine	Captured	Not known	—
● Forget-me-not (smack).	40	12	12 miles S.W. by W. from Portland Bill.	Submarine	Captured	Not known	—
Ena (smack)	56	12	10 miles N. by W. from Trevose Head.	Submarine	Captured	Bomb	—
Provero (smack)	24	12	25 miles N.W. from Trevose Head.	Submarine	Captured	Bomb	—
Try (smack)	34	13	10 miles S. from Wolf Rock.	Submarine	Captured	Gunfire	—
Gold Seeker (smack).	62	13	4 miles from Smith's Knoll Spar Buoy.	Submarine	Captured	Gunfire	—
Comrades (smack).	58	13	2$\frac{1}{2}$ miles W. from Smith's Knoll Middle Buoy.	Submarine	Captured	Gunfire	—

Fishing Vessels Captured or Sunk.

Name.	Tons.	Date.	Position.	Cause of Loss.	How attacked.	How sunk.	Lives lost.
		1917. Mar.					
Navenby	167	13	85 miles E. by S. ½ S. from Rattray Head.	Submarine	Captured	Bomb	—
Pencaer (smack)	46	16	8 miles S.E. from Mine Head L.H.	Submarine	Captured	Bomb	—
Gowan (motor)	25	17	15 miles E.S.E. from Longstone.	Submarine	Captured	Gunfire	—
Kestrel	181	17	20 miles E. by S. from Longstone.	Submarine	Captured	Gunfire	—
Guard (smack)	38	17	8 miles S.W. from Coningbeg L.V.	Submarine	Captured	Gunfire	—
∗ Avance (smack)	60	21	25 miles W.S.W. from Portland Bill.	Submarine	Captured	Gunfire	—
● Curlew (smack)	51	22	14 miles S. from Berry Head.	Submarine	Captured	Bomb	—
Qui Vive (smack).	22	24	15 miles S.E. from Eddystone.	Submarine	Captured	Bomb	—
Boy Walter (smack).	43	24	15 miles S.E. from Eddystone.	Submarine	Captured	Bomb	—
Mayflower (smack).	38	24	15 miles S.E. from Eddystone.	Submarine	Captured	Bomb	—
Endeavour (smack).	25	24	15 miles S.E. from Eddystone.	Submarine	Captured	Bomb	—
H.C.G. (smack)	24	24	15 miles S.E. from Eddystone.	Submarine	Captured	Bomb	—
Enigma (smack)	24	24	15 miles S.E. from Eddystone.	Submarine	Captured	Bomb	—
Reindeer (smack)	28	24	15 miles S. from Eddystone.	Submarine	Captured	Bomb	—
Alice (smack)	61	24	12 miles S.S.W. from Eddystone.	Submarine	Captured	Bomb	—
Satanita (smack)	30	24	12 miles S.S.W. from Eddystone.	Submarine	Captured	Bomb	—
Median	214	25	30 miles E. by S. from Aberdeen.	Submarine	Captured	Bomb	—
Prince of Wales	158	25	17 miles E. by S. from Girdleness.	Submarine	Captured	Bomb	—.
Rosslyn	113	25	54 miles E. ¼ S. from Girdleness.	Submarine	Captured	Bomb	—
Galatia	150	28	30 miles S.S.W. from Buchan Ness.	Submarine	Captured	Bomb	—
Moulmein	151	28	25 miles N.E. from Longstone.	Submarine	Captured	Scuttled	—
Petrel	151	30	120 miles E. from Aberdeen.	Submarine	Captured	Gunfire	—
Nuttalia	229	—	North Sea	Submarine (?)	Captured	Reported taken to Germany.	—
APRIL	**1917.**	April					
Lord Scarborough	158	2	100 miles E. from May Island.	Submarine	Captured	Scuttled	—
Maggie Ross	183	4	70 miles N.E. from Aberdeen.	Submarine	Captured	Gunfire	—
Gibraltar	188	4	20 miles E.N.E. from Rattray Head.	Submarine	Captured	Bomb	—
Lord Kitchener	158	6	45 miles N. by E. from Kinnaird Head.	Submarine	Captured	Bomb	—
Recto	177	6	45 miles N. by E. from Kinnaird Head.	Submarine	Captured	Bomb	—
Narberth Castle	168	6	30 miles N.N.W. from Dennis Head.	Submarine	Captured	Gunfire	—
Nestor	176	6	20 miles N.W. by N. ½ N. from N. Ronaldshay.	Submarine	Captured	Gunfire	—

Fishing Vessels Captured or Sunk.

Name.	Tons.	Date.	Position.	Cause of Loss.	How attacked.	How sunk.	Lives lost
Precedent (smack)	36	1917. April 11	12 miles E.S.E. from Berry Head.	Submarine	Captured	Bombs	—
Equerry	168	12	35 miles N.E. from Kinnaird Head.	Submarine	Captured	Gunfire	—
Chinkiang	125	12	30 miles N.E. from Buchan Ness.	Submarine	Captured	Gunfire	—
Caliban	215	12	45 miles N.E. by N. from Rattray Head.	Submarine	Captured	Gunfire	—
Crown Prince	103	12	45 miles N.E. by E. from Girdleness.	Submarine	Captured	Gunfire	—
Lillian	120	12	45 miles N.E. by E. from Girdleness.	Submarine	Captured	Gunfire	—
Fife Ness	123	12	23 miles E.N.E. from Fraserburgh.	Submarine	Captured	Gunfire	—
Largo Bay	125	12	30 miles N.E. by E. from Buchan Ness.	Submarine	Captured	Gunfire	—
Osprey	106	12	45 miles N.E. by E. from Girdleness.	Submarine	Captured	Gunfire	—
Stork	152	13	20 miles E. ½ S. from St. Abb's Head.	Submarine	Captured	Bombs	—
Sutterton	160	15	65 miles E.S.E. from St. Abb's Head.	Submarine	Captured	Bomb	1
Dalmatian	186	15	North Sea	Submarine	Captured	Bombs	9 including Skipper.
Lord Chancellor	135	16	50 miles N.E. from Longstone.	Submarine	Captured	Bombs	—
U.S.A.	182	17	16 miles E.N.E. from Longstone.	Submarine	Captured	Bombs	—
John S. Boyle	143	18	25 miles E. by S. from St. Abb's Head.	Submarine	Captured	Bombs	—
Rameses	155	18	60 miles N.E. from Blyth.	Submarine	Captured	Bombs	—
Witham	144	18	125 miles E. by S. ½ S. from St. Abb's Head.	Submarine	Captured	Gunfire	—
Erith	168	20	40 miles S. ½ W. from Girdleness.	Submarine	Captured	Bombs	—
Grecian	119	20	22 miles N.E. by E. from Longstone.	Submarine	Captured	Bomb	—
Jedburgh	165	21	35 miles N.N.W. from Foula Island.	Submarine	Captured	Bomb	—
Yeovil	164	21	35 miles N.N.W. from Foula Island.	Submarine	Captured	Bomb	1
Nightingale	91	22	26 miles S. from Aberdeen.	Submarine	Captured	Bomb	—
Mayfly	191	24	70 miles N.E. by N. from Spurn L.V.	Submarine	Gunfire	Gunfire	2 including Skipper.
Heather	58	24	14 miles W. by N. from Bishop Rock.	Submarine	Captured	Bombs	—
Upton Castle	145	24	60 miles E. from Longstone.	Submarine	Captured	Bomb	—
Boy Denis (smack).	41	26	12 miles S.S.W. from Start Point.	Submarine	Captured	Bomb	—
Active	149	26	80 miles E.S.E. from St. Abb's Head.	Submarine	Captured	Bomb	—

FISHING VESSELS CAPTURED OR SUNK.   118

Name.	Tons.	Date.	Position.	Cause of Loss.	How attacked.	How sunk.	Lives lost.
		1917. Apr.					
Pursue (smack)	37	28	12 miles S.W. from Bolt Head.	Submarine	Captured	Bomb	—
Dilston Castle	129	29	16 miles E. by S. from Aberdeen.	Submarine	Captured	Bombs	—
Argo	131	30	15 miles E. ½ S. from Buchan Ness.	Submarine	Captured	Gunfire	—
Andromache	313	—	North Sea	Submarine	Captured	Not known	Skipper made prisoner.
Brothertoft	155	—	North Sea	Submarine (reported).	Captured	Not known	
Expedient	145	—	North Sea	Submarine (reported).	Captured	Not known	
Industria	133	—	North Sea	Submarine (reported).	Captured	Not known	

MAY 1917.

Name.	Tons.	Date.	Position.	Cause of Loss.	How attacked.	How sunk.	Lives lost.
		May					
United (smack)	61	2	5 miles N.W. from Godrevy L.H.	Submarine	Captured	Bomb	—
Sir Edward Birkbeck (smack)	23	3	16 miles S.E. from Stags.	Submarine	Captured	Bomb	—
Hibernia (smack)	21	3	14 miles S.E. from Baltimore Harbour.	Submarine	Captured	Bomb	
Eleanor (smack)	31	3	13 miles S. from Stags.	Submarine	Captured	Bomb	—
Fastnet (smack)	31	3	13 miles S. from Stags.	Submarine	Captured	Bomb	—
Lucky Lass (smack).	10	3	15 miles S. from Stags.	Sumbarine	Captured	Scuttled	
North Star (smack).	15	3	13 miles S. from Stags.	Submarine	Captured	Bomb	—
Carbery King (smack).	21	3	14 miles S. from Stags.	Submarine	Captured	Bomb	—
Strumble (smack)	45	4	10 miles N.N.E. from Strumble Head.	Submarine	Captured	Bomb	—
Victorious (smack)	39	4	10 miles N.N.E. from Strumble Head.	Submarine	Captured	Bomb	—
Edith Cavell (motor).	20	5	7½ miles E. from Robin Hood Bay.	Submarine	Captured	Bomb	—
Kitty	181	9	25 miles E.N.E. from St. Abb's Head.	Submarine	Captured	Bomb	Skipper and Chief Engineer made prisoners.
Windward Ho!	226	9	3 miles S. from Peterhead.	Mine	Mine	Mine	8 including Skipper.
G. L. C. (smack)	24	12	6 miles S.E. from Eddystone.	Submarine	Captured	Bomb	—
Bel Lily	168	14	1½ miles E. by N. from Peterhead.	Mine	Mine	Mine	10 including Skipper.
Primrose	62	18	22 miles W. by S. ¼ S. from Bishop Rock.	Submarine	Captured	Gunfire	—
Adventure	50	18	49 miles W. by S. from Wolf.	Submarine	Captured	Gunfire	—
Sisapon	211	23	Faroe Banks	Submarine	Captured		—
Olearia	209	23	Faroe Banks	Submarine	Captured	Bombs	—

FISHING VESSELS CAPTURED OR SUNK.

Name.	Tons.	Date.	Position.	Cause of Loss.	How attacked.	How sunk.	Lives lost.
JUNE 1917.		June					
Teal	141	1	57 miles N.W. by N. from Sule Skerry Light.	Submarine	Captured	Gunfire	—
Shamrock	170	2	66 miles N.N.E. from Sule Skerry.	Submarine	Captured	Gunfire	—
St. Bernard	186	2	65 miles N. by W. from Noup Head.	Submarine	Captured	Gunfire	—
Prudence (smack)	25	3	15 miles W.S.W. from Eddystone.	Submarine	Captured	Gunfire	—
Geralda (smack)	46	3	22 miles N.E. ½ E. from Cromer.	Mine	Mine	Mine	—
Virgilia	209	3	5 miles E. from Girdleness.	Submarine	Captured	Bombs	Skipper made prisoner.
Golden Hope	22	7	30 miles E. from Kinnaird Head.	Submarine	Captured	Bombs	—
Cariad (smack)	38	8	6 miles E. by S. from Start Point.	Submarine	Captured	Bombs	—
Torbay Lass (smack).	38	8	9 miles E. by S. from Start Point.	Submarine	Captured	Bombs	—
Onward (smack)	39	8	9 miles E. by S. from Start Point.	Submarine	Captured	Bombs	—
Ocean's Pride (smack).	42	8	9 miles E. by S. from Start Point.	Submarine	Captured	Bombs	—
Frances (motor)	20	28	10 miles N.E. from Spurn Point.	Submarine	Captured	Bombs	—
Rose of June (motor).	20	28	10 miles N.E. from Spurn Point.	Submarine	Captured	Bombs	—
William and Betty (motor).	21	28	10 miles N.E. from Spurn Point.	Submarine	Captured	Bombs	—
Elsie (motor)	20	28	10 miles N.E. from Spurn Point.	Submarine	Captured	Bombs	—
Glenelg	32	28	10 miles N.E. from Spurn Point.	Submarine	Captured	Bombs	—
Harbinger	39	28	10 miles N.E. from Spurn Point.	Submarine	Captured	Bombs	—
Corona	48	28	65 miles E. from Sumburgh Head.	Submarine	Captured	Gunfire	—
Frigate Bird (motor).	20	28	North Sea	Submarine (?)	Captured (?)	Not known	
Gem	79	29	18 miles E. by S. from Rattray Head.	Submarine	Captured	Gunfire	—
Manx Princess	87	29	18 miles E. by S. from Rattray Head.	Submarine	Captured	Gunfire	—
JULY 1917.		1917. July					
Gleam (Smack)	54	1	½ mile E.N.E. from S. Owers Buoy.	Submarine	Captured	Gunfire	—
Advance (Smack)	44	1	5 miles S.E. from S. Owers Buoy.	Submarine	Captured	Gunfire	—
Radiance (Smack)	57	1	3 miles N. by E. from North Leman Buoy.	Submarine	Captured	Bombs	—

Fishing Vessels Captured or Sunk.

Name.	Tons.	Date.	Position.	Cause of Loss.	How attacked.	How sunk.	Lives lost.
		1917. July					
Eclipse	185	1	100 miles N. by W. from Brough of Birsa, Orkney.	Submarine	Captured	Gunfire	—
General Buller	72	2	26 miles E.S.E. from Sumburgh Head.	Submarine	Captured	Gunfire	—
Hamnavoe	57	2	26 miles E.S.E. from Sumburgh Head.	Submarine	Captured	Gunfire	—
Chrysolite (Smack)	57	4	4 miles North from Haisbro L.V.	Mine	Mine	Mine	5
Loch Katrine	151	4	85 miles S.S.E from Sando, Faeroe Islands.	Submarine	Captured	Gunfire	—
†Stoic	200	10	60 miles S. by E. from Sydero.	Submarine	Captured	Gunfire	—
†Pretoria	283	10	60 miles S. by E. from Sydero.	Submarine	Captured	Gunfire	—
Romantic	197	10	60 miles S. by E. from Sydero.	Submarine	Captured	Gunfire	—
Mabel	205	10	60 miles S. by E. from Sydero.	Submarine	Captured	Bombs	—
Pacific	235	10	60 miles S. by E. from Sydero.	Submarine	Captured	Gunfire	—
Cedric	197	10	60 miles S. by E. from Sydero.	Submarine	Captured	Bombs	—
Sea King	185	10	60 miles S. by E. from Sydero.	Submarine	Captured	Bombs	—
Peridot	214	10	60 miles S. by E. from Sydero.	Submarine	Captured	Bombs	—
†Asama	284	16	160 miles S.W. by S. from the Fastnet.	Submarine	Captured	Gunfire	1
Young Bert (smack).	59	31 (?)	North Sea	Submarine (reported).	Captured	Not known	

AUGUST 1917.

Name.	Tons.	Date.	Position.	Cause of Loss.	How attacked.	How sunk.	Lives lost.
		Aug.					
Narcissus	58	6	12 miles S.E. from the Tyne.	Submarine	Captured	Bombs	—
Gloriosa (smack)	23	11	12 miles S. by W. from Caldy Island.	Submarine	Captured	Bombs	—
Eleazar	111	12	25 miles S.W. by W. from St. Ann's Head.	Submarine	Captured	Gunfire	—
Jane S. (motor)	12	14	11 miles S.E. from St. Abb's Head.	Mine	Mine	Mine	5
Susie (smack)	38	17	10 miles N.E. by E. from Scarborough.	Submarine	Captured	Gunfire	1

SEPTEMBER 1917.

Name.	Tons.	Date.	Position.	Cause of Loss.	How attacked.	How sunk.	Lives lost.
		Sept.					
Unity (smack)	56	5	8 miles East from Cross Sand L.V.	Submarine	Captured	Bombs	—
Margaret (motor)	12	5	Near Wick	Mine	Mine	Mine	5
Rosary (smack)	37	6	6 miles W. by N. from Smith's Knoll Spar Buoy.	Submarine	Captured	Bombs	—
Family's Pride (motor).	39	8	28 miles E. by S. from Peterhead.	Submarine	Captured	Bombs	—
Rosy Cross (smack).	25	11	4 miles N W. by W. from Crackington Haven, Cornwall.	Submarine	Captured	Bombs	—
Ronald (smack)	38	17	25 miles S.W. from Coningbeg L.V.	Submarine	Captured	Gunfire	—
Our Bairns (smack).	38	17	25 miles S.W. from Coningbeg L.V.	Submarine	Captured	Gunfire	—

FISHING VESSELS CAPTURED OR SUNK.

Name.	Tons.	Date.	Position.	Cause of Loss.	How attacked.	How sunk.	Lives lost.
OCTOBER 1917.		1917. Oct.					
Willing Boys (smack).	51	2	10 miles N.W. from Smith's Knoll Spar Buoy.	Mine - - -	Mine - -	Mine - -	5
Perseverance (smack).	30	4	15 miles S. by W. from the Eddystone.	Submarine - -	Captured -	Gunfire -	—
Rupee (smack)	39	4	12 miles North from Lundy Island.	Submarine - -	Captured -	Gunfire -	4 including Skipper.
Young Clifford (smack).	47	4	12 miles North from Lundy Island.	Submarine - -	Captured -	Gunfire -	—
Reliance - -	60	7 (?)	North Sea - -	Mine (?) - -	Mine (?) -	Mine (?) -	10 including Skipper.
NOVEMBER 1917.		Nov.					
Premier (smack)	23	27	16 miles S.E. from Start Point.	Submarine - -	Captured -	Gunfire -	—.
Courage (smack)	39	30	6 miles W. by N. from Lundy, North Lighthouse.	Submarine - -	Captured -	Gunfire -	—
Gazelle (smack)	41	30	6 miles W. by N. from Lundy, North Lighthouse.	Submarine - -	Captured -	Gunfire -	—
DECEMBER 1917.		Dec.					
Rion (smack) -	39	1	8 miles N.E. from Start Point.	Submarine - -	Captured -	Bombs -	—
Forward (smack)	40	10	Off Aldeburgh -	Submarine - -	Captured -	Bombs -	—
John M. Smart -	113	12	10 miles East from the Tyne.	T.B.D. - -	Gunfire -	Gunfire -	4
Amadavat -	171	12	East Coast of Shetlands.	Mine (?) - -	Mine (?) -	Mine (?) -	9 including Skipper.
Neptune (smack).	50	17	Galway Bay -	Mine - - -	Mine - -	Mine - -	4
JANUARY 1918.		1918. Jan.					
Veda (smack) -	25	2	30 miles S.S.W. from Eddystone.	Submarine - -	Captured -	Gunfire -	—
Gratitude (smack).	40	4	8 miles S.E. by E. from Berry Head.	Submarine - -	Captured -	Bombs -	—
Day Spring (smack).	39	4	8 miles S.E. from Berry Head.	Submarine - -	Captured -	Bombs -	—
Varuna (smack)	40	4	15 miles S.E. by E. from Berry Head.	Submarine - -	Captured -	Bombs -	—
Premier - -	89	7	3 miles West from L. Eynort, Skye.	Submarine - -	Captured -	Gunfire -	1
May (smack) -	24	26	18 miles S.E. ½ E. from Berry Head.	Submarine - -	Captured -	Bombs -	—
Ibex (smack) -	42	29	14 miles S.E. by E. from Berry Head.	Submarine - -	Captured -	Gunfire -	—
Addax (smack) -	40	29	14 miles S.E. by E. from Berry Head.	Submarine - -	Captured -	Gunfire -	—
General Leman (smack).	45	29	14 miles S.E. by E. from Berry Head.	Submarine - -	Captured -	Gunfire -	—
Perseverance (smack).	40	29	14 miles S.E. by E. from Berry Head.	Submarine - -	Captured -	Gunfire -	—

FISHING VESSELS CAPTURED OR SUNK.

Name.	Tons.	Date.	Position.	Cause of Loss.	How attacked.	How sunk.	Lives lost.
FEBRUARY 1918.		1918. Feb.					
Holkar (smack)	48	6	8 miles North from Trevose Head.	Submarine	Captured	Gunfire	—
Straton	197	8	26 miles East from Humber L.V.	Mine	Mine	Mine	—
Maggie Smith (motor).	24	9	3 miles North from Bell Rock.	Submarine	Captured	Bomb (?)	3
Commander (smack).	47	16	8 miles S.W. from Beer Head.	Submarine	Captured	Bombs	—
Snowdrop (smack).	40	20	8 miles S.W. ½ S. from the Eddystone.	Submarine	Captured	Gunfire	—
Irex (smack)	16	21	10 miles E. by S. from Hopes Nose.	Submarine	Captured	Bomb	—
Leonora (smack)	26	21	11 miles East from Hopes Nose.	Submarine	Captured	Gunfire	—
Rosebud (smack)	44	21	10 miles S.S.E. from Hopes Nose.	Submarine	Captured	Bomb	—
Idalia (smack)	23	21	10 miles S.E. by S. from Berry Head.	Submarine	Captured	Bomb	—
Oryx (smack)	38	21	10 miles S.E. by S. from Berry Head.	Submarine	Captured	Gunfire	—
Reaper	91	21	2 miles N.E. from Tynemouth.	Mine	Mine	Mine	8 including Skipper.
†Rambler	92	26	4 miles E. from Blyth.	Mine	Mine	Mine	9 including Skipper.
MARCH 1918.		Mar.					
Marguerite (smack).	10	9	25 miles N. ¼ E. from Beaumaris Point.	Submarine	Captured	Bombs	—
Sunrise (smack)	24	10	18 miles S.E. from Maughold Head, I. of Man.	Submarine	Captured	Bombs	—
Wave (smack)	23	10	10 miles S.W. by W. from St. Bees Head.	Submarine	Captured	Bombs	—
W. A. Massey	84	11	4 miles W. by N. from Handa Id., Minch.	Mine	Mine	Mine	10 including Skipper.
Honora (motor)	29	28	6 miles E.N.E. from Whitby.	Submarine	Captured	Gunfire	—
Botha (motor)	17	28	3 miles East from Whitby.	Submarine	Captured	Bombs	—
Noel (motor)	21	28	6 miles N.E. by E. from Whitby.	Submarine	Captured	Gunfire	—
Brotherly Love (motor).	19	28	6 miles N.E. by E. from Whitby.	Submarine	Captured	Gunfire	—
St. Michan	43	30	10 miles E. from Lambay Island.	Submarine	Captured	Gunfire	—
Geraldine (Smack.)	23	30	10 miles E. from Lambay Island.	Submarine	Not known	Not known	5 including Skipper.
APRIL 191 .		Apr.					
Ruth (Smack)	44	13	1½ miles E.S.E. from S. Cross Sand buoy.	Submarine	Captured	Bombs	—
Tyne Wave	121	23	20 miles W.N.W. from Ramna Stacks, Shetland.	Submarine	Captured	Gunfire	—

123 FISHING VESSELS CAPTURED OR SUNK.

Name.	Tons.	Date.	Position.	Cause of Loss.	How attacked.	How sunk.	Lives lost.
Peregrine	76	1918. Apr. 23	15 miles N.N.W. from Ramna Stacks, Shetland.	Submarine	Captured	Gunfire	—
MAY 1918.		May					
Eclipse (smack)	47	26	10 miles N.E. by N. from Smith's Knoll Spar Buoy.	Submarine	Captured	Gunfire	—
Dayspring (smack).	57	26	10 miles N.E. by N. from Smith's Knoll Spar Buoy.	Submarine	Captured	Gunfire	—
Fortuna (smack)	61	26	10 miles N.E. by N. from Smith's Knoll Spar Buoy.	Submarine	Captured	Bombs	—
Wayside Flower (motor).	21	27	20 miles N.E. by N. from the Humber.	Submarine	Captured	Bombs	—
Coronation (motor).	19	28	13 miles E.S.E. from Flamborough Head.	Submarine	Captured	Gunfire	—
Seabird (motor)	15	30	26 miles W.N.W. from Calf of Man.	Submarine	Captured	Bombs	—
Glad Tidings (smack).	15	30	26 miles W.N.W. from Calf of Man.	Submarine	Captured	Bombs	—
Never Can Tell (smack).	31	30	26 miles W.N.W. from Calf of Man.	Submarine	Captured	Bombs	—
Sparkling Wave (smack).	29	30	26 miles W.N.W. from Calf of Man.	Submarine	Captured	Bombs	—
St. Mary (smack)	29	30	26 miles W.N.W. from Calf of Man.	Submarine	Captured	Bombs	—
Cyprus (smack)	35	30	26 miles W.N.W. from Calf of Man.	Submarine	Captured	Bombs	—
Honey Bee (motor).	34	30	26 miles W.N.W. from Calf of Man.	Submarine	Captured	Bombs	—
Jane Gordon (smack).	27	30	26 miles W.N.W. from Calf of Man.	Submarine	Captured	Bombs	—
Lloyd (smack)	35	30	26 miles W.N.W. from Calf of Man.	Submarine	Captured	Bombs	—
Marianne McCrum (smack).	30	30	26 miles W.N.W. from Calf of Man.	Submarine	Captured	Bombs	—
Pretty Polly (smack).	19	31	Off Roundstone Bay, W. of Ireland.	Submarine	Gunfire	Gunfire	7
JUNE 1918.		June					
†Egret	169	1	2 miles E. by N. from Humber L.V.	Submarine	No warning	Torpedo	11 including Skipper.
Dianthus (smack)	40	6	5 miles N. ½ E. from Smith's Knoll Spar Buoy.	Submarine	Captured	Bombs	—
Active (smack)	46	6	5 miles N. ½ E. from Smith's Knoll Spar Buoy.	Submarine	Captured	Gunfire	—

FISHING VESSELS CAPTURED OR SUNK.

Name.	Tons.	Date.	Position.	Cause of Loss.	How attacked.	How sunk.	Lives lost.
Beryl (smack)	57	1918. June 6	5 miles N. ½ E. from Smith's Knoll Spar Buoy.	Submarine	Captured	Bombs	—
Eros	181	8	North Sea	Mine	Mine	Mine	6 including Skipper.
Pochard	146	28	North Sea	Mine	Mine	Mine	—
JULY 1918.							
Aby (Motor)	25	July 7	25 miles E. ¾ N. from Spurn Point.	Submarine	Captured	Bombs	—
Albion (Motor)	22	7	25 miles E. ¾ N. from Spurn Point.	Submarine	Captured	Bombs	—
Boy Jack (Smack).	57	26	4 miles East from Cross Sand L.V.	Submarine	Captured	Bombs	3
Fear Not (Smack).	59	27	14 miles N.N.E. from Haisborough L.V.	Submarine	Captured	Bombs	—
Passion Flower (Smack).	46	27	14 miles N.N.E. from Haisborough L.V.	Submarine	Captured	Bombs	—
I'll Try (Smack)	51	27	14 miles N.N.E. from Haisborough L.V.	Submarine	Captured	Bombs	—
Valour (Smack)	39	27	14 miles N.N.E. from Haisborough L.V.	Submarine	Captured	Bombs	—
Paragon (Smack)	56	27	8 miles N.E. by E. from Haisborough L.V.	Submarine	Captured	Bombs	—
Le Bijou (Smack).	46	27	9 miles N.E. from Haisborough L.V.	Submarine	Captured	Bombs	—
Success (Smack)	54	27	7 miles N.E. by E. from Haisborough L.V.	Submarine	Captured	Gunfire	—
Counsellor (Smack).	56	27	2½ miles North from Haisborough L.V.	Submarine	Captured	Bombs	—
Francis Robert (Smack).	44	28	8 miles N.E. from Haisborough L.V.	Submarine	Captured	Gunfire	—
AUGUST 1918.							
Nelson A. (S.V.).	72	Aug. 4	25 miles from Shelburne, N.S.	Submarine	Captured	Bomb	—
Triumph	239	20	60 miles S.W. by S. from Cape Canso, N.S.	Submarine	Captured	Converted into a raider.	—
Uda A. Saunders (S.V.).	125	20	52 miles South from Cape Canso, N.S.	Submarine (Triumph.)	Captured	Bombs	—
Lucille M. Schnare (S.V.).	121	20	52 miles South from Cape Canso, N.S.	Submarine (Triumph.)	Captured	Bombs	—
Pasadena (S.V.).	91	21	70 miles S.S.E. from Cape Canso, N.S.	Submarine	Captured	Bomb	—
E. B. Walters (S.V.).	98	25	35 miles W. by S. from Little Miquelon, N.F.L.	Submarine	Captured	Bombs	—
C. M. Walters (S.V.).	107	25	35 miles W. by S. from Little Miquelon, N.F.L.	Submarine	Captured	Bombs	—
Verna D. Adams (S.V.).	132	25	35 miles W. by S. from Little Miquelon, N.F.L.	Submarine (Triumph.)	Captured	Bombs	—

FISHING VESSELS CAPTURED OR SUNK.

Name.	Tons.	Date.	Position.	Cause of Loss.	How attacked.	How sunk.	Lives lost.
		1918. Aug.					
Clayton W. Walters (S.V.)	80	25	Off St. Pierre, N.F.L.	Submarine	Captured	Bombs	—
Marion Adams (S.V.).	99	25	Off St. Pierre, N.F.L.	Submarine	Captured	Bombs	—
Gloaming (S.V.)	100	26	70 miles S.S.W. from St. Pierre, N.F.L.	Submarine	Captured	Bombs	—
Elsie Porter (S.V.).	136	30	290 miles E. ½ N. from St. John's, N.F.L.	Submarine	Captured	Bombs	—
Potentate (S.V.).	136	30	290 miles E. ½ N. from St. John's, N.F.L.	Submarine	Captured	Bombs	—
SEPTEMBER 1918.		Sept.					
†Euthamia	142	22	65 miles E. by N. ½ N. from Humber L.V.	Mine	Mine	Mine	—
NOVEMBER 1918.		Nov.					
Conster (Smack)	25.	7	Off Rye	Mine	Mine	Mine	—

III.—BRITISH MERCHANT VESSELS DAMAGED OR MOLESTED BY THE ENEMY BUT NOT SUNK.

Name.	Tons.	Date.	Position.	Attacked by	How attacked.	How saved.	Lives lost.
AUGUST 1914.		1914. Aug.					
Craigforth	2,900	5	In Bosphorus	Mine	Mine	Beached	—
Lynton Grange	4,252	6	N. Atlantic	Dresden	Captured	Released	—
Drumcliffe	4,072	6	N. Atlantic	Dresden	Captured	Released	—
Hostilius	3,325	6	N. Atlantic	Dresden	Captured	Released	—
Galician	6,762	15	N. Atlantic	Kaiser Wilhelm der Grosse.	Captured	Released	—
Arlanza	15,044	16	N. Atlantic	Kaiser Wilhelm der Grosse.	Captured	Released	—
Siamese Prince	4,847	16	S. Atlantic	Dresden	Captured	Released	—
Isle of Hastings	1,575	20	Philippeville	Goeben and Breslau	Gunfire	Damaged	—
Katharine Park	4,854	26	S. Atlantic	Dresden	Captured	Released	—
Holtby	3,675	30	2½ miles from Seaham.	Mine	Mine	Arrived Tyne.	—
SEPTEMBER 1914.		Sept.					
Southport	3,588	4	Caroline Is.	Geier	Captured	Escaped	—
Kabinga	4,657	12	Bay of Bengal	Emden	Captured	Released	—
Ortega	8,075	19	S. Atlantic	Dresden	Chased	Speed	—
Chupra	6,175	22	Madras	Emden	Gunfire	Damaged	1
Gryfevale	4,437	26	Indian Ocean	Emden	Captured	Released	—
OCTOBER 1914.		Oct.					
Farn	4,393	5	140 miles S.W. ¾ S. (true) from St. Paul Rocks.	Karlsruhe	Captured	Interned at San Juan P.R. Released Feb. 1917.	—
St. Egbert	5,596	18	Indian Ocean	Emden	Captured	Released	—
Exford	4,542	19	Indian Ocean	Emden	Captured	Recaptured	—

MERCHANT VESSELS ATTACKED.   126

Name.	Tons.	Date.	Position.	Attacked by	How attacked.	How saved.	Lives lost.
		1915. Oct.					
Royal Sceptre	3,838	27	530 miles W. (true) from St. Paul Rocks.	Karlsruhe	Captured	Released	—
Glenturret	4,696	28	Malacca Strait	Emden	Captured	Released	—
Friederike	3,574	30	Novorossisk	Turkish warships	Gunfire	Damaged	—
Newburn	3,554	30	Indian Ocean	Emden	Captured	Released	—
NOVEMBER	**1914.**						
Colusa	5,732	1	Pacific	Prinz Eitel Friedrich.	Chased	Escaped	—
DECEMBER	**1914.**	Dec.					
Colchester	1,209	11	North Sea	Submarine	Chased	Speed	—
Munificent	3,270	16	West Hartlepool	German warships	Gunfire	Damaged	1
Phœbe	2,754	16	East Hartlepool	German warships	Gunfire	Damaged	1
Gallier	4,592	25	Off Scarborough	Mine	Mine	Arrived Scarborough.	—
JANUARY 1915.		1915. Jan.					
Westergate	1,742	1	North Sea	Mine	Mine	Towed in	—
Graphic	1,871	30	22 miles N.W. from Liverpool Bar L.V.	Submarine	Chased	Speed	—
FEBRUARY 1915.		Feb.					
Asturias (Hospital Ship).	12,002	1	15 miles N.N.E. from Havre L.V.	Submarine	Torpedo	Missed	—
Laertes	4,541	10	12 miles N.E. by E. from Schowen L.V.	Submarine	Gunfire and torpedo.	Speed	—
Torquay	870	12	Off Filey	Mine	Mine	Towed in	1
Wavelet	2,992	13	11 miles N.E. by N. from N. Goodwin.	Mine	Mine	Beached	12
Kirkham Abbey	1,166	14	North Sea	Submarine	Chased	Speed	—
Colchester	1,209	17	North Sea	Submarine	Chased	Speed	—
Penhale	3,712	21	3 miles W. from Holyhead.	Submarine	Chased	Speed	—
Victoria	1,689	22	6 miles from Boulogne.	Submarine	Torpedo	Missed	—
Chasehill	4,583	22	S. Atlantic	Kronprinz Wilhelm	Captured	Released	—
Kalibia	4,930	23	Off Dungeness	Submarine	Chased	Speed	—
Hungarian Prince	4,765	24	Off Beachy Head	Submarine	Chased	Speed	—
Surrey	5,987	25	Off Calais	Mine	Mine	Towed in	—
St. Andrew (Hospital Ship).	2,528	25	10 miles N.W. by W. from Boulogne.	Submarine	Chased	Speed	—
Thordis	501	28	English Channel	Submarine	Torpedo	Missed	—
MARCH 1915.		1915. Mar.					
Wrexham	1,414	2	North Sea	Submarine	Chased	Speed	—
Ningchow	9,021	4	Bristol Channel	Submarine	Chased	Speed	—
Lydia	1,133	5	English Channel	Submarine	Torpedo	Missed	—
Clan Macrae	5,058	9	Off Liverpool Bar L.V.	Submarine	Chased	Speed	—
Adenwen	3,798	11	20 miles N.W. from Casquets.	Submarine	Bombs after capture.	Towed in	—
Helen	322	11	8 miles N.N.W. from Liverpool Bar L.V.	Submarine	Torpedo	Missed	—
Atlantic City	4,707	12	6 miles E. from South Rock.	Submarine	Chased	Speed	—
Umtata	2,655	14	English Channel	Submarine	Torpedo	Missed	—

Name.	Tons.	Date.	Position.	Attacked by	How attacked.	How saved.	Lives lost.
		1915. Mar.					
Sutton Hall (Belgian Relief).	4,460	14	English Channel	Submarine	Torpedo	Missed	—
Quentin	1,274	14	5 miles N.N.W. from Maas L.V.	Submarine	Chased	Speed	—
†Atalanta	519	14	12 miles W.S.W. from Inishturk Island.	Submarine	Set on fire after capture.	Towed in	—
Blonde	613	15	3 miles off N. Foreland.	Aircraft	Bomb	Missed	—
Hyndford	4,286	15	12 miles S. from Beachy Head.	Submarine	Torpedoed	Beached	1
Highland Scot	7,604	16	English Channel	Submarine	Chased	Speed	—
Wolverton	3,868	16	5 miles E. by S. from Fontana L.H., Odessa.	Mine	Mine	Towed in	1
Blue Jacket	3,515	18	15 miles E. from Owers L.V.	Submarine	Torpedoed	Arrived Southampton Water.	—
Strathfillan (Belgian Relief).	4,353	18	Off Beachy Head	Submarine	Chased	Speed	—
Colchester	1,209	18	Off Hook of Holland.	Submarine	Chased	Speed	—
San Dunstano	6,220	19	English Channel	Submarine	Chased	Speed	—
John Duncan	1,832	20	Near Royal Sovereign L.V.	Submarine	Chased	Speed	—
Dorset Coast	672	20	English Channel	Submarine	Chased	Speed	—
Elfland (Belgian Relief).	4,190	21	Off North Hinder L.V.	Aircraft	Bomb	Missed	—
Ennismore	1,499	21	10 miles N.E. by N. from Coquet Island.	Submarine	Torpedo	Missed	—
Lestris	1,384	21	14 miles E. from Galloper.	Aircraft	Bombs	Missed	—
Tycho	3,216	21	In the Downs	Submarine	Torpedo	Missed	—
Pandion	1,279	21	Between N. Hinder and Galloper.	Aircraft	Bombs	Missed	—
Osceola	393	22	North Sea	Aircraft	Bombs	Missed	—
Teal	764	23	North Sea	Aircraft	Bombs and darts.	Missed	—
Delmira	3,459	25	23 miles N.N.E. from Cape Antifer.	Submarine	Bomb after capture.	Beached	—
Tewfikieh	2,490	25	Off Ailsa Craig	Submarine	Chased	Speed	—
Lizzie	802	25	English Channel	Submarine	Chased	Speed	—
Groningen	988	25	North Sea	Submarine	Chased	Speed	—
Ousel	1,284	27	Between N. Hinder and Galloper.	Aircraft	Bombs	Missed	—
Dunedin	4,796	28	St. George's Channel.	Submarine	Chased	Speed	—
Brussels	1,380	28	8 miles W. from Maas L.V.	Submarine	Chased	Speed	—
City of Cambridge	3,844	28	25 miles N.W. by N. from Bishop Rock.	Submarine	Gunfire	Speed	—
Theseus	6,724	29	40 miles S.W. from Scilly Islands.	Submarine	Gunfire	Speed	—
Staffa	1,008	30	Off N. Galloper Buoy.	Aircraft	Bombs	Missed	—

APRIL 1915.

		1915 April					
San Silvestre	6,233	2	21 miles S. from Eddystone.	Submarine	Chased	Speed	—
Homer (tug)	150	8	25 miles S.W. from Owers L.V.	Submarine	Gunfire and torpedo.	Speed	—
Denaby	2,987	8	Off St. Catherine's Point.	Submarine	Torpedo	Missed	—
Wayfarer	9,599	11	60 miles W.N.W. from Scilly Isles.	Submarine	Torpedoed	Towed in	2

MERCHANT VESSELS ATTACKED   128

Name.	Tons.	Date.	Position.	Attacked by.	How attacked.	How saved.	Lives lost.
Serula	1,388	1915. April. 11	Off N. Hinder L.V.	Aircraft	Bombs	Missed	—
Imber	2,154	12	3 miles W. from N. Hinder L.V.	Aircraft	Bombs	Missed	—
Manitou	6,849	16	Mediterranean	Turkish T.B.	3 torpedoes	Missed	8
†La Rosarina	8,332	17	Off S. of Ireland	Submarine	Chased	By gun	—
Lestris	1,384	19	2 miles E. from N. Hinder L.V.	Submarine	Chased	Speed	—
Arvonian	2,794	22	English Channel	Submarine	Torpedo	Missed	—
MAY 1915.		May					
Cayo Romano	3,675	4	Off the Fastnet	Submarine	Torpedo	Missed	—
Etonian	6,438	7	Off Queenstown	Submarine	Chased	Speed	—
Narragansett	9,196	7	Off S. Ireland	Submarine	Torpedo	Missed	—
City of Exeter	9,300	7	Off Queenstown	Submarine	Chased	Speed	—
†Arabia	7,933	9	English Channel	Submarine	Chased	Speed	—
City of Dortmund (Belgian Relief).	803	10	8 miles E. ½ N. from N. Hinder L.V.	Submarine	Torpedo	Missed	—
Poona	7,626	10	40 miles S.W. from Portland.	Submarine	Chased	Speed	—
Comeric (Belgian Relief).	3,980	20	Near N. Hinder L.V.	Submarine	Torpedo	Missed	—
Marquette	7,057	25	English Channel	Submarine	Chased	Speed	—
Ousel	1,284	27	2 miles E. from Elbow Buoy.	Submarine	Chased	Speed	—
†Argyllshire	12,097	27	Off Havre	Submarine	Two torpedoes	Missed	—
†Ping Suey	6,458	29	English Channel	Submarine	Gunfire	By gun	—
Megantic	14,878	30	Off S. of Ireland	Submarine	Chased	Speed	—
Colchester	1,209	30	North Sea	Submarine	Chased	Speed	—
†Demerara	11,484	31	Off S. of Ireland	Submarine	Chased	By gun	—
Kelvinia	5,039	31	Bristol Channel	Submarine	Chased	Rescued	—
Highland Laird	4,223	31	St. George's Channel.	Submarine	Chased	Speed	—
†Garmoyle	1,229	31	Bristol Channel	Submarine	Chased	By gun	—
Hambleton Range	3,682	31	English Channel	Submarine	Chased	Speed	—
JUNE 1915.							
†Pontypridd	1,556	1	40 miles S. ½ W. from Wolf Rock.	Submarine	Chased	By gun	—
Ballycotton	1,273	6	30 miles S. from Waterford.	Submarine	Torpedo	Missed	—
Llandovery Castle	11,423	8	Off Cape Finisterre.	Submarine	Chased	Speed	—
Teespool	1,577	9	Bristol Channel	Submarine	Gunfire	Speed	—
Tenasserim	5,089	9	Off S. of Ireland	Submarine	Chased	Speed	—
Orthia	4,225	10	Bristol Channel	Submarine	Chased	Speed	—
Brussels	1,380	11	North Sea	Submarine	Chased	Speed	—
Alt	1,004	15	St. George's Channel.	Submarine	Torpedo	Missed	—
Cromer	812	15	Near Galloper	Submarine	Chased	Speed	—
Brussels	1,380	15	Near Sunk L.V.	Submarine	Chased	Speed	—
Turnwell	4,264	16	35 miles S.W. from Tuskar.	Submarine	Bombs after capture.	Arrived Milford Haven.	—
Cameronia	10,963	20	23 miles W. from Skerries, Anglesey.	Submarine	Chased	Speed	—
Clan Robertson	4,826	20	St. George's Chan.	Submarine	Chased	Speed	—
Twilight	3,100	20	White Sea	Mine	Mine	Arrived Archangel.	—
Sachem	5,354	21	23 miles W. from Liverpool Bar L.V.	Submarine	Chased	Speed	—
Herbert Fischer	938	22	2 miles S.E. from Southwold.	Submarine	Torpedo	Missed	—
Kenmare	1,330	27	Between Ardmore and Capel Island.	Submarine	Gunfire	Speed	—
Orduna	15,499	28	20 miles S.W. from Smalls.	Submarine	Chased	Speed	—

MERCHANT VESSELS ATTACKED.

Name.	Tons.	Date.	Position.	Attacked by	How attacked.	How saved.	Lives lost.
		1915. June					
Brussels	1,380	29	56 miles E. from Sunk L.V.	Submarine	Chased	Speed	—
Teiresias	7,606	30	Small Bitter Lake	Mine	Mine	Towed in	—
JULY 1915.		July					
City of Edinburgh	6,255	2	English Channel	Submarine	Torpedo; gunfire.	Torpedo missed.	4
†Zealandic	8,090	2	English Channel	Submarine	Chased	Speed	—
†Arabia	7,933	3	English Channel	Submarine	Chased	Speed	—
Guido	2,093	3	North Sea	Submarine	Gunfire	Speed	—
Anglo Californian	7,333	4	90 miles S. from Queenstown.	Submarine	Gunfire	Rescued	21 including Master.
Groningen	988	6	4 miles from Galloper.	Aircraft	Bombs	Missed	—
Traquair	1,067	8	Knock Deep	Submarine	Chased	Speed	—
Orduna	15,499	9	30 miles S. from Queenstown.	Submarine	Torpedo; gunfire.	Torpedo missed.	—
Etonian	6,438	9	Off S. of Ireland	Submarine	Chased	Speed	—
Panama	5,981	10	11 miles S. from Lizard.	Submarine	Chased	Speed	—
Warri	2,493	14	3 miles S.W. from Shipwash.	Submarine	Torpedo	Missed	—
†Corso	1,178	15	English Channel	Submarine	Chased	By gun	—
Batoum	4,054	18	North Sea	Submarine	Torpedoed	Beached	6
Brussels	1,380	20	20 miles E. ½ S. from S. Inner Gabbard Buoy.	Submarine	Torpedo	Missed	—
†Sheerness	1,274	20	North Sea	Submarine	Chased	By gun	—
Madura	4,484	26	Entrance to White Sea.	Mine	Mine	Arrived Archangel.	—
Canto	1,202	28	North Sea	Submarine	Torpedo	Missed	—
Chinkoa	5,222	31	Off the Tagus	Submarine	Chased	Speed	—
Galicia	5,922	31	In the Downs	Mine	Mine	Beached	—
AUGUST 1915.		Aug.					
Como	1,246	4	Near N. Ronaldshay.	Submarine	Chased	Rescued	—
Cito	819	5	2½ miles E. by S. from Aldborough Napes.	Submarine	Chased	Speed	—
Highland Harris	6,023	6	North from Scilly Is.	Submarine	Chased	Speed	—
Edenside	322	8	Off Rattray Head	Submarine	Chased	Speed	—
Moto	1,941	10	Bristol Channel	Submarine	Torpedo	Missed	—
†Woodfield	3,584	12	Bristol Channel	Submarine	Torpedo	Missed	—
Start Point	3,840	14	10 miles S.E. from Tuskar.	Submarine	Chased	Speed	—
Highland Corrie	7,583	14	3 miles E.N.E. from N. Foreland.	Mine	Mine	Arrived Tilbury.	—
Eimstad	689	17	1 mile N. of Cross Sand L.V.	Submarines	Gunfire	Darkness	—
Matje	278	17	43 miles N. by E. from S. Bishops.	Submarine	Gunfire	Rescued	—
Cromer	812	17	North Sea	Submarine	Torpedo	Missed	—
City of Liverpool	1,101	18	40 miles S.S.W. from Smalls.	Submarine	Gunfire	Rescued	—
†Lady Wolseley	1,424	18	55 miles N.E. ¼ E. from Longships.	Submarine	Gunfire	By gun	—
Nicosian	6,369	19	73 miles S. by W. from Old Head of Kinsale.	Submarine	Gunfire after capture.	Rescued	—
Bovic	6,583	19	Off S. of Ireland	Submarine	Chased	Speed	—

MERCHANT VESSELS ATTACKED.

Name.	Tons.	Date.	Position.	Attacked by	How attacked.	How saved.	Lives lost.
		1915. Aug.					
San Melito	10,160	21	70 miles S.W. from Lizard.	Submarine	Gunfire	Rescued	—
Westbury	3,097	21	50 miles S. from Wolf.	Submarine	Gunfire	Rescued	—
Avocet	1,219	22	Off S. of Ireland	Submarine	Gunfire	Speed	—
Avocet	1,219	22	Off S. of Ireland	Submarine	Chased	Speed	—
Baron Polwarth	4,913	30	West from Scilly Is.	Submarine	Chased	Speed	—
Bretwalda	4,037	30	3 miles E. from Longsand L.V.	Mine	Mine	Towed in	—

SEPTEMBER 1915.

		Sept.					
†Southland	11,899	2	Ægean Sea	Submarine	Torpedoed	Since arrived.	—
W. T. Lewis (S.V.)	2,166	2	95 miles W. by N. from Fastnet.	Submarine	Gunfire after capture.	Towed in	—
Crossby	3,893	4	200 miles W. from Bishop.	Submarine	Chased	Speed	—
Fulmar	1,270	6	9 miles W. from N. Hinder.	Aircraft	Bombs	Missed	—
Leicestershire	8,059	7	Bay of Biscay	Submarine	Chased	Speed	—
†Antilochus	9,039	10	Mediterranean	Submarine	Gunfire	By gun	—
San Zeferino	6,430	18	2 miles N.N.W. from S. Goodwin L.V.	Mine	Mine	Beached	2
Nigretia	3,187	18	Off S. Foreland	Mine	Mine	Beached	—

OCTOBER 1915.

		Oct.					
†Olympic	46,359	1	40 miles W. from C. Matapan.	Submarine	Chased	Speed	—
Enfield	2,124	4	4 miles S.S.W. from Folkestone Pier.	Mine	Mine	Beached	—
Ajax	7,040	10	Mediterranean	Submarine	Gunfire	Rescued	—
Oslo	2,296	11	5 miles E. by N. ½ N. from Holy Island.	Submarine	Chased	Speed	—
Volscian	570	16	2½ miles S. by E. ½ E. from Longsand L.V.	Mine	Mine	Beached	—
Aleppo	3,870	18	1½ miles E. from Sunk Head Buoy.	Mine	Mine	Beached	—
Glenroy	2,755	29	20 miles E.N.E. from Peterhead.	Submarine	Chased	Speed	—
Avocet	1,408	30	8 miles W. from N. Hinder.	Aircraft	Bombs and machine gun.	Bombs missed.	—

NOVEMBER 1915.

		Nov.					
Japanese Prince	4,876	3	Mediterranean	Submarine	Chased	Speed	—
Dotterel	1,596	4	14 miles W. ½ N. from N. Hinder.	Aircraft	Bombs and machine guns.	Bombs missed.	—
Mercian	6,305	4	Mediterranean	Submarine	Gunfire	Speed	—
†City of York	7,834	5	Mediterranean	Submarine	Chased	By gun	—
†Huntsman	7,460	5	Mediterranean	Submarine	Chased	By gun	—
Lady Plymouth	3,521	5	Off Algiers	Submarine	Chased	Speed	—
Lady Plymouth	3,521	6	Off Algiers	Submarine	Gunfire	Speed	—
Pola	3,061	6	Off Tukush Is., Algeria.	Submarine	Chased	Speed	—
City of Cambridge	3,844	8	Mediterranean	Submarine	Chased	Speed	—
†Kashgar	8,840	9	Mediterranean	Submarine	Chased	By gun	—
Ballater	2,286	21	In S. Edinburgh Channel.	Mine	Mine	Towed in	—
†City of Marseilles	8,250	23	Mediterranean	Submarine	Gunfire	By gun	

MERCHANT VESSELS ATTACKED.

Name.	Tons.	Date.	Position.	Attacked by	How attacked.	How saved.	Lives lost.
		1915. Nov.					
†City of Lahore	6,948	24	10 miles E. from Cape de Gata.	Submarine	Chased	By gun	—
Balgownie	1,061	27	Near N. Hinder	Aircraft	Bombs and machine guns.	Bombs missed.	—

DECEMBER 1915.

		Dec.					
†Benalla	11,118	3	Mediterranean	Submarine	Gunfire	By gun	—
†Torilla	5,205	3	Mediterranean	Submarine	Gunfire	Rescued	—
Andania	13,405	3	Mediterranean	Submarine	Chased	Rescued	—
†Tintoretto	4,181	8	70 miles N.W. from Alexandria.	Submarine	Torpedo; gunfire.	Missed; gun	—
Southgarth	2.414	12	Off La Panne, Belgium.	Aircraft	Bombs	Missed	—
†Cawdor Castle	6,243	13	Mediterranean	Submarine	Gunfire	By gun	—
Teucer	9,045	16	Mediterranean	Submarine	Chased	Speed	—
Levenpool	4,844	16	North Sea	Mine	Mine	Beached	—
Huronian	8,766	28	8 miles S. by E. from Fastnet.	Submarine	Torpedoed	Arrived Bantry Bay.	—
†Ionic	12,332	31	Mediterranean	Submarine	Torpedo	Missed	—

JANUARY 1916.

		1916. Jan.					
San Tirso	6,236	1	Mediterranean	Submarine	Chased	Speed	—
Glociiffe	2,211	2	North Sea	Mine	Mine	Beached	—
Breslau	1,339	14	6 miles N.W. from Boulogne.	Mine	Mine	Beached	—
†Appam	7,781	15	135 miles E. ½ N. (true) from Madeira.	Möwe	Captured	Released by order of U.S. Court.	2 gunners made prisoners.
†Baron Napier	4,943	17	Mediterranean	Submarine	Gunfire	By gun	—
†Esneh	3,247	17	Mediterranean	Submarine	Gunfire	By gun	—
Gemma	1,385	22	Off Deal	Aircraft	Bombs	Missed	—
†Norseman	9,542	22	Gulf of Salonica	Submarine	Torpedoed	Beached	—
Falls City	4,729	22	South from Kentish Knock.	Mine	Mine	Beached	—
Carlo	1,987	23	North Sea	Aircraft	Bombs	Missed	—
Esneh	3,247	23	Mediterranean	Submarine	Torpedo	Missed	—
Astræa	3,229	26	Mediterranean	Submarine	Captured	Rescued	—
†Trewellard	4,202	27	Mediterranean	Submarine	Chased	By gun	—
†Malta	6,064	28	Mediterranean	Submarine	Gunfire	By gun	—
†Ingoma	5,686	30	Mediterranean	Submarine	Gunfire	By gun	—
†Sebek	4,601	30	Mediterranean	Submarine	Chased	By gun	—

FEBRUARY 1916.

		Feb.					
†Professor	3,580	8	Mediterranean	Submarine	Chased	By gun	—
Elswick Manor	3,943	8	North Sea	Mine	Mine	Towed in	—
†Demerara	11,484	17	N. Atlantic	Möwe	Chased	Escaped	—
Glenfoyle	1,680	20	North Sea	Aircraft	Bombs	Missed	—
†Olympic	46,359	23	Mediterranean	Submarine	Torpedo	Missed	—
†Hunsworth	3,038	28	Mediterranean	Submarine	Gunfire	By gun	—
†Olympic	46,359	28	Mediterranean	Submarine	Torpedo	Missed	—
†Benedict	3,378	28	Mediterranean	Submarine	Gunfire	By gun	—
Malvina	1,244	29	North Sea	Mine	Mine	Towed in	—
Den of Ogil	5,689	29	North Sea	Mine	Mine	Towed in	—
†Nyanza	6,695	29	Mediterranean	Submarine	Chased	By gun	—
†Sebek	4,601	29	Mediterranean	Submarine	Torpedo	Missed	—

MARCH 1916.

		March					
†Turbo	4,782	1	Mediterranean	Submarine	Gunfire	By gun	—
Arracan	5,520	5	Entrance to English Channel.	Submarine	Gunfire	Speed	—
Foreland	1,960	8	Off Islay	Submarine	Torpedo	Missed	—

MERCHANT VESSELS ATTACKED. 132

Name.	Tons	Date.	Position.	Attacked by	How attacked.	How saved.	Lives lost.
		1916. March					
Falcon	675	16	10 miles N.W. by W. ½ W. from N. Hinder.	Submarine	Torpedo	Missed	—
Berwindvale	5,242	16	30 miles W. from Fastnet.	Submarine	Torpedoed and captured.	Rescued	—
Lutterworth	994	18	21 miles N. from C. Antifer.	Submarine	Torpedo	Missed	—
†Kaisar-i-Hind	11,430	23	Mediterranean	Submarine	Torpedo	Missed	—
Eveline	2,605	23	85 miles S.W. by S. from Tuskar.	Submarine	Torpedo	Missed	—
†Phrygia	3,353	24	110 miles West from Fastnet.	Submarine	Gunfire	By gun	—
Duendes	4,602	25	70 miles West from Scilly Islands.	Submarine	Gunfire	Speed	—
†Inkonka	3,430	25	160 miles West from Scilly Islands.	Submarine	Torpedo	Missed	—
Musician	4,764	26	St. George's Channel.	Submarine	Chased	Speed	—
Mallard	1,300	30	15 miles E. ¾ S. from Inner Gabbard Buoy.	Submarine	Chased	Speed	—
Clinton	3,381	31	1½ miles S. by E. from Pakefield Gat Buoy.	Mine	Mine	Beached	—
APRIL 1916.		April					
†Megantic	14,878	2	Mediterranean	Submarine	Gunfire	By gun	—
†Laomedon	6,693	2	Mediterranean	Submarine	Gunfire	By gun	—
Brema	1,537	3	Between Shipwash and Longsand L.V.	Submarine	Torpedo	Missed	—
Ganges	4,177	5	Mediterranean	Submarine	Gunfire	Speed	—
Vennacher	4,700	6	28 miles W.N.W. from Skerryvore.	Submarine	Torpedoed	Arrived Lough Swilly.	—
Danubian	5,064	7	West of Scotland	Submarine	Gunfire	Speed	—
†Polyxena	5,737	9	Mediterranean	Submarine	Gunfire	By gun	—
†Sydney Reid	2,852	19	30 miles off Ushant	Submarine	Gunfire	By gun	—
†Norman Prince	3,464	22	90 miles South from the Fastnet.	Submarine	Gunfire	By gun	—
†Bonvilston	2,866	23	Mediterranean	Submarine	Torpedo	Missed	—
F. D. Lambert	2,195	25	5 miles E.S.E. from Gorleston Pier.	German warship	Gunfire	Damaged	—
‡Wandle	889	29	15 miles S.S.E. from Souter Point, Durham.	Submarine	Gunfire	By gun	—
Sussex	5,686	29	100 miles West from Ushant.	Submarine	Gunfire	Speed	—
MAY 1916.		May					
†Phrygia	3,353	1	Bay of Biscay	Submarine	Chased	By gun	—
†Clan MacFadyen	2,816	2	Bay of Biscay	Submarine	Gunfire	By gun	—
†Port Augusta	4,063	2	Bay of Biscay	Submarine	Gunfire	By gun	—
†Clan Lindsay	3,937	3	Bay of Biscay	Submarine	Gunfire	By gun	—
Lestris	1,384	6	8 miles E. from N. Hinder.	Submarine	Chased	Speed	—
†Ramore Head	4,444	9	Mediterranean	Submarine	Chased	By gun	—
†Pagenturm	5,000	12	Bay of Biscay	Submarine	Chased	Speed	—
East Wales	4,331	13	Off Cape Finisterre.	Submarine	Gunfire	Speed	—
†Rooke	3,391	17	Mediterranean	Submarine	Gunfire	By gun	—
Seattle	5,133	19	Dunkirk Dock	Aircraft	Bombs	Damaged	1
Ernst	653	19	Dunkirk Dock	Aircraft	Machine gun	Slight damage.	—
Lord Strathcona	7,335	20	Dunkirk Dock	Aircraft	Bomb	Slight damage.	1

MERCHANT VESSELS ATTACKED.

Name.	Tons.	Date.	Position.	Attacked by	How attacked.	How saved.	Lives lost.
		1916. May					
Valentia	3,242	21	Dunkirk Dock	Aircraft	Bomb	Slight damage.	—
Ernst	653	21	Dunkirk Dock	Aircraft	Bomb	Slight damage.	—
†Media	5,437	27	Mediterranean	Submarine	Chased	By gun	—

JUNE 1916.

		June					
†Maryland	4,731	1	Mediterranean	Submarine	Torpedo	Missed	—
Parkgate	3,232	1	2 miles E.N.E. from Sunk Buoy.	Mine	Mine	Beached	—
†Cypria	2,950	2	Mediterranean	Submarine	Gunfire	By gun	—
†Malakand	7,653	9	Mediterranean	Submarine	Torpedo	Missed	—
†Clodmoor	3,753	16	Mediterranean	Submarine	Gunfire	By gun	—
†Uganda	5,431	17	Mediterranean	Submarine	Gunfire	By gun	—
Thurso	1,244	18	3 miles N.N.W. from Longstone.	Submarine	Chased	Speed	—
₁Le Coq	3,419	18	Mediterranean	Submarine	Gunfire	By gun	—
†Malda	7,884	20	Mediterranean	Submarine	Chased	By gun	—
†Ashby	1,947	24	Mediterranean	Submarine	Gunfire	Rescued	—
†Mexico City	5,078	25	Mediterranean	Submarine	Gunfire	By gun	—
†Eloby	6,545	26	Mediterranean	Submarine	Torpedo	Missed	—

JULY 1916.

		July					
†Reynolds	3,264	5	Mediterranean	Submarine	Chased	By gun	—
†Strathness	4,353	15	Mediterranean	Submarine	Gunfire	By gun	—
†Kingsmere	5,476	17	Mediterranean	Submarine	Gunfire	By gun	—
†Anglesea	4,534	18	Mediterranean	Submarine	Gunfire	By gun	—
Rubio	2,395	24	Mediterranean	Submarine	Gunfire	Rescued	—
Frodingham	1,081	29	Off Bridlington	Aircraft	Bombs	Missed	—
†Bosnian	2,506	30	Mediterranean	Submarine	Gunfire	By gun	—

AUGUST 1916.

		Aug.					
†Kalimba	4,982	1	Mediterranean	Submarine	Gunfire	By gun	—
Destro	859	3	10 miles N.E. by E. from Coquet Island.	Submarine	Gunfire	Speed	—
Galway Castle	7,988	3	Near Gull L.V.	Aircraft	Bombs	Missed	—
Ivo (S.V.)	56	3	19 miles S.S.W. from Portland Bill.	Submarine	Bomb after capture.	Towed in	—
Oruro	1,919	8	East Coast of Scotland.	Submarine	Chased	Speed	—
Hessle	952	10	Off Cape Barfleur	Submarine	Chased	Rescued	—
†Pacuare	3,891	18	Mediterranean	Submarine	Gunfire	By gun	—
†Kineardine	4,108	25	Mediterranean	Submarine	Torpedo	Missed	—
Rio Tinto	2,165	26	Mediterranean	Submarine	Chased	Speed	—
†Devian	3,689	26	Mediterranean	Submarine	Gunfire	By gun	—
Katharine Park	4,854	26	Bay of Biscay	Mine	Mine	Beached	—
†Italiana	2,663	27	Mediterranean	Submarine	Gunfire	By gun	—
†Strathness	4,354	29	Mediterranean	Submarine	Gunfire	By gun	—
†Polo	1,906	31	Mediterranean	Submarine	Gunfire	By gun	—
†Regent	3,281	31	Mediterranean	Submarine	Gunfire	By gun	—

SEPTEMBER 1916.

		Sept.					
†Antinous	3,682	1	Mediterranean	Submarine	Gunfire	By gun	—
†Glenogle	7,682	2	Mediterranean	Submarine	Gunfire	By gun	—
Spen	900	3	English Channel	Submarine	Gunfire	Speed	—
†Hunstanton	4,504	5	Mediterranean	Submarine	Gunfire	By gun	—
†San Dunstano	6,220	6	English Channel	Submarine	Gunfire	By gun	—
Ancona	1,168	6	English Channel	Submarine	Gunfire	Rescued	—
†Bengali	5,684	6	English Channel	Submarine	Gunfire	By gun	—
†Atalanta	519	11	English Channel	Submarine	Gunfire	By gun	—
†Kyarra	6,953	11	Mediterranean	Submarine	Chased	Speed	—
†Avocet	1,219	12	Off Ushant	Submarine	Chased	By gun	—

MERCHANT VESSELS ATTACKED. 134

Name.	Tons.	Date.	Position.	Attacked by	How attacked.	How saved.	Lives lost.
		1916. Sept.					
†Tahiti	7,586	12	Mediterranean	Submarine	Torpedo	Missed	—
†Irthington	3,845	12	Mediterranean	Submarine	Torpedo	Missed	—
†Cilurnum	3,126	13	Mediterranean	Submarine	Torpedo	Failed to explode.	—
†Eptalofos	4,431	14	Mediterranean	Submarine	Gunfire	Rescued	—
†Aysgarth	3,118	14	Mediterranean	Submarine	Torpedo	Missed	—
†Highcliffe	3,238	14	Mediterranean	Submarine	Gunfire	By gun	—
†Bellview	3,567	17	Mediterranean	Submarine	Gunfire	By gun	—
†Dunbar	3,672	17	Mediterranean	Submarine	Torpedo	Missed	—
†Martaban	5,106	18	Mediterranean	Submarine	Gunfire	By gun	—
†Katuna	4,641	18	Mediterranean	Submarine	Chased	By gun	—
†Clan Chisholm	2,647	18	Mediterranean	Submarine	Gunfire	By gun	—
†Persic	12,042	20	Mediterranean	Submarine	Torpedo	Missed	—
Pembroke	918	24	22 miles N. from Casquets.	Submarine	Gunfire	Speed	—
†Strathness	4,354	24	Mediterranean	Submarine	Gunfire	By gun	—
†Dunrobin	3,617	26	Mediterranean	Submarine	Gunfire	By gun	—
Princess Victoria	1,687	28	English Channel	Submarine	Torpedo	Missed	—
†Nellore	6,853	29	Mediterranean	Submarine	Gunfire	By gun	—
†Pentyrch	3,382	30	Mediterranean	Submarine	Torpedo; gunfire.	Torpedo missed. By gun	—
†Califol	6,572	30	West of Shetland	Submarine	Chased	Rescued	—
OCTOBER 1916.		Oct.					
†Carlo	1,987	1	Mediterranean	Submarine	Gunfire	By gun	—
†Jutland	2,824	2	Mediterranean	Submarine	Gunfire	By gun	—
†Melania	5,824	2	Mediterranean	Submarine	Torpedo	Missed	—
Camlake	3,230	5	Mediterranean	Submarine	Gunfire	Rescued	—
†Hyndford	4,286	6	Arctic Sea	Submarine	Gunfire	By gun	—
Coronilla	1,312	7	English Channel	Submarine	Chased	Weather	—
Jupiter	2,124	7	40 miles N.E. by E. from Longstone.	Submarine	Damaged by bomb after capture.	Towed in	—
†Somali	6,712	8	Mediterranean	Submarine	Torpedo	Missed	—
†Sebek	4,601	12	Mediterranean	Submarine	Torpedoed	Beached	—
†Malda	7,884	16	Mediterranean	Submarine	Chased	By gun	—
†Royal Sceptre	3,838	19	Mediterranean	Submarine	Gunfire	By gun	—
†Glenmay	2,485	20	English Channel	Submarine	Gunfire	By gun	—
Glenmorag	3,535	20	English Channel	Submarine	Gunfire	Speed	—
†Matiana	5,313	21	English Channel	Submarine	Gunfire	By gun	—
†Stork	2,029	21	English Channel	Submarine	Gunfire	By gun	—
†Australia	7,526	21	English Channel	Submarine	Chased	By gun	—
†Cyrene	2,904	22	Off Ushant	Submarine	Gunfire	By gun	—
†Lady Plymouth	3,521	22	Mediterranean	Submarine	Torpedo	Missed	—
†Russian	8,825	22	Mediterranean	Submarine	Torpedo	Missed	—
Trevorian	4,144	22	Black Sea	Submarine	Torpedo	Missed	—
†Kandy	4,921	23	Off South of Ireland.	Submarine	Chased	By gun	—
Alexandrian	4,467	23	Off S.W. of Ireland.	Submarine	Torpedo	Missed	—
†Izaston	3,060	24	English Channel	Submarine	Chased	By gun	—
Bagdale	3,045	24	English Channel	Submarine	Captured	Rescued	—
†Venetia	3,596	24	English Channel	Submarine	Gunfire	By gun	—
Joseph Davis	2,243	24	English Channel	Submarine	Gunfire	Rescued	—
†Queen	4,956	25	Mediterranean	Submarine	Torpedo	Missed	—
†City of Edinburgh	6,255	26	English Channel	Submarine	Gunfire	By gun	—
†Fabian	2,246	26	St. George's Channel.	Submarine	Gunfire	By gun	1
Morlais	950	26	English Channel	Submarine	Gunfire	Rescued	—
Princess Thyra	781	29	English Channel	Submarine	Gunfire	Speed	—
†Mantola	8,253	30	North Sea	Mine	Mine	Arrived London.	—
†Arlington Court	4,346	30	50 miles S.W. from Cape St. Vincent.	Submarine	Chased	By gun	—
NOVEMBER 1916.		Nov.					
†Lindenhall	4,003	1	Mediterranean	Submarine	Gunfire	By gun	—
†Daybreak	3,238	1	Arctic Sea	Submarine	Gunfire	By gun	—
†Huntspill	5,440	1	Arctic Sea	Submarine	Torpedoes	Missed	—

MERCHANT VESSELS ATTACKED.

Name.	Tons.	Date.	Position.	Attacked by	How attacked.	How saved.	Lives lost.
		1916. Nov.					
†Polo	1,906	2	Mediterranean	Submarine	Torpedo	Missed	—
Siamese Prince	4,847	4	210 miles S.W. from Scilly Isles.	Submarine	Gunfire	Speed	—
Ryhope	1,334	7	English Channel	Submarine	Gunfire	Speed	—
†Carlo	1,987	9	Bay of Biscay	Submarine	Gunfire	By gun	—
†City of Cairo	7,672	11	Off Cape Ortegal	Submarine	Gunfire	By gun	—
†Malda	7,884	11	English Channel	Submarine	Gunfire	Weather	—
†Clan Buchanan	5,212	12	Off Cape Ortegal	Submarine	Gunfire	By gun	—
†Islandia	2,069	13	Mediterranean	Submarine	Gunfire	By gun	—
†Clan Chisholm	2,647	13	Off Cape Finisterre.	Submarine	Gunfire	By gun	—
Idaho	4,887	14	190 miles W. by N. from Ushant.	Submarine	Torpedoes	Missed; rescued.	—
Bayhowel	4,343	14	Off Ushant	Submarine	Chased	Rescued	—
Serbistan	2,934	14	Off Ushant	Submarine	Chased	Rescued	—
†Esneh	3,247	14	English Channel	Submarine	Gunfire	By gun	—
†Lake Michigan	9,288	15	9 miles from Brest	Mine	Mine	Reached Brest.	—
Saint Leonards	4,574	15	Off Havre	Mine	Mine	Reached Havre.	—
†Kintail	3,537	15	Off Ushant	Submarine	Gunfire	By gun	—
†Monmouth	4,078	17	Off Cherbourg	Mine	Mine	Towed in	—
†Kintail	3,537	17	English Channel	Submarine	Chased	By gun	—
†Tanfield	4,300	18	English Channel	Submarine	Chased	Weather	—
Palm Branch	3,891	21	English Channel	Submarine	Gunfire	Speed	—
Errington Court	4,461	21	Off S.W. Ireland	Submarine	Gunfire	Speed	—
†Peshawur	7,634	22	Off Ushant	Submarine	Chased	By gun	—
Braemar Castle (hospital ship).	6,318	23	Mykoni Channel	Mine (?)	Mine (?)	Beached	4
†Egyptiana	3,818	24	Off Cape Finisterre	Submarine	Gunfire	By gun	—
†Clan Colquhoun	5,856	25	Mediterranean	Submarine	Gunfire	By gun	—
†Arum	3,681	25	Mediterranean	Submarine	Gunfire	By gun	—
†Highland Heather	6,036	26	Mediterranean	Submarine	Torpedoed	Arrived	—
†Huntscape	2,933	27	English Channel	Submarine	Gunfire	By gun	—
†Ballater	2,286	28	English Channel	Submarine	Gunfire	By gun	—
†Pikepool	3,683	28	Mediterranean	Submarine	Torpedo	Missed	—
†Megantic	14,878	28	Mediterranean	Submarine	Chased	Speed	—
†Polanna	2,345	29	English Channel	Submarine	Gunfire	By gun	—
Swazi	4,941	29	Entrance to English Channel.	Submarine	Chased	Rescued	—
†Kandy	4,921	29	English Channel	Submarine	Gunfire	By gun	—
†Ibex	951	30	English Channel	Submarine	Chased	Speed	—
Verdala	5,880	30	Off Ushant	Submarine	Gunfire	Rescued	—
Eggesford	4,414	30	30 miles N. from Ushant.	Submarine	Damaged after capture.	Towed in	—
DECEMBER 1916.		1916. Dec.					
†Dykland	4,291	1	Off Ushant	Submarine	Gunfire	By gun	—
†Dunachton	5,201	1	Mediterranean	Submarine	Gunfire	By gun	—
†Kintuck	4,616	2	Off S.W. Ireland	Submarine	Gunfire	By gun	—
†Nagoya	6,854	2	Mediterranean	Submarine	Gunfire	By gun	—
†Umona	3,753	2	Arctic Sea	Submarine	Gunfire	By gun	—
†Reims	3,717	2	Mediterranean	Submarine	Chased	Speed	—
†Tapton	3,569	3	Off Ushant	Submarine	Gunfire	By gun	—
†Lucellum	5,184	3	Mediterranean	Submarine	Torpedoed	Arrived Villefranche.	—
†Sutherland Grange.	6,852	4	Off Ushant	Submarine	Gunfire	Speed	—
Taxandrier	4,231	4	Off Ushant	Submarine	Gunfire	Rescued	—
Rossia	4,576	4	Off Ushant	Submarine	Chased	Speed	—
†Castalia	6,396	5	Mediterranean	Submarine	Gunfire	By gun	—
†Camberwell	4,078	5	Mediterranean	Submarine	Gunfire	By gun	—
†Poona	7,626	6	English Channel	Mine	Mine	Towed in	—
†John Sanderson	3,274	6	Entrance to English Channel.	Submarine	Gunfire	By gun	—
†Usher	3,594	7	Off Scilly Is.	Submarine	Chased	By gun	—
†Usher	3,594	8	W. from Ushant	Submarine	Chased	By gun	—
†Antar	3,580	8	Off Coast of Portugal.	Submarine	Chased	By gun	—

MERCHANT VESSELS ATTACKED.

Name.	Tons.	Date.	Position.	Attacked by	How attacked.	How saved.	Lives lost.
		1916. Dec.					
†Astyanax	4,872	9	Off S. Ireland	Submarine	Chased	Speed	—
†Rosefield	3,089	10	Mediterranean	Submarine	2 torpedoes	Missed	—
†Caledonia	7,572	14	3 miles E. from Planier Island Light.	Mine	Mine	Arrived Marseilles.	1
Hildawell	2,494	14	Off Ushant	Submarine	Chased	Rescued	—
†Queen	4,956	15	Off S. Ireland	Submarine	Gunfire	By gun	—
Vancouver	4,419	15	Bay of Biscay	Submarine	Gunfire	Rescued	—
†Rio Tinto	2,165	15	150 miles S.W. by S. from Fastnet.	Submarine	Gunfire	By gun	—
†Maryland	4,731	16	W. from Gibraltar	Submarine	Gunfire	By gun	—
Red Rose	401	16	English Channel	Submarine	Captured	Rescued	—
Englishman (S.V.)	144	16	N. from Scillies	Submarine	Gunfire	Rescued	—
†Petrograd	1,713	17	Mediterranean	Submarine	Chased	By gun	—
†Dartmoor	2,870	19	Mediterranean	Submarine	Gunfire	By gun	—
†Griqua	3,344	20	Mediterranean	Submarine	Gunfire	By gun	—
Arracan	5,520	21	Off S.W. Ireland	Submarine	Chased	Speed	—
†Clan Stuart	5,775	22	Mediterranean	Submarine	Torpedo	Missed	—
William Middleton.	2,543	23	Bristol Channel	Submarine	Captured	Rescued	—
Bertrand	3,613	23	Bristol Channel	Submarine	Gunfire	Rescued	—
†Benalder	3,044	23	Mediterranean	Submarine	Torpedoed	Arrived Alexandria.	—
†Wisbech	1,282	23	Bay of Biscay	Submarine	Gunfire	By gun	—
†Paul Paix	4,196	24	Bristol Channel	Mine	Mine	Towed in	—
†Newstead	2,836	24	W. from Gibraltar	Submarine	Chased	Speed	—
†Cameronian	5,861	24	Mediterranean	Submarine	Torpedo	Missed	—
†Suffolk	7,573	28	English Channel	Mine	Mine	Arrived Portsmouth.	—
†Polesley	4,221	28	Mediterranean	Submarine	Chased	By gun	—
†Oxonian	6,306	28	Mediterranean	Submarine	Torpedo	Missed	—
†Malda	7,884	30	Mediterranean	Submarine	Torpedo	Missed	—
†Aspenleaf	7,535	30	English Channel	Mine	Mine	Towed in	—
†City of Oran	7,395	31	English Channel	Submarine	Gunfire	By gun	—
JANUARY 1917.		1917. Jan.					
†Sussex	5,686	1	Off Calais	Mine	Mine	Beached	—
†Bengali	5,684	2	Mediterranean	Submarine	Gunfire	By gun	—
Luga	1,988	2	Bay of Biscay	Submarine	Gunfire	Speed	—
†Cromarty	2,742	2	Bay of Biscay	Submarine	Chased	By gun	—
†Huntsend	8,826	3	Mediterranean	Submarine	Torpedoed	Towed in	1
Eastgate	4,277	5	Bay of Biscay	Submarine	Captured	Brought in	—
†La Rosarina	8,332	6	Off Ushant	Submarine	Gunfire	By gun	—
†Bampton	4,496	7	Off Coast of Portugal.	Submarine	Chased	Speed	—
Alexandrian	4,467	9	20 miles S.W. from Fastnet.	Submarine	Gunfire and torpedo.	Beached Berehaven.	—
†Inventor	7,679	10	W. from Scillies	Submarine	Gunfire	By gun	—
†Knight Companion.	7,241	10	Off C. Finisterre	Submarine	Gunfire	By gun	—
†Amazon	10,037	13	Off C. Finisterre	Submarine	Torpedo	Missed	—
Fernley	3,820	13	English Channel	Submarine	Gunfire	Rescued	—
Ussa	2,066	14	English Channel	Submarine	Gunfire	Speed	—
†Cardiganshire	9,426	14	Mediterranean	Submarine	Chased	Speed	—
†Comeric	3,980	15	Mediterranean	Submarine	Torpedo	Missed	—
†Caithness	3,500	18	Bay of Biscay	Submarine	Gunfire	By gun	—
†Deseado	11,477	19	Off S.W. Ireland	Submarine	Gunfire	By gun	—
†Trevaylor	4,249	19	Off S.W. Ireland	Submarine	Gunfire	By gun	—
†Bendoran	4,074	22	225 miles S.W. by W. from Fastnet.	Submarine	Gunfire	Rescued	—
Argo	1,102	22	North Sea	Submarine	Gunfire	Speed	—
†Messina	4,271	23	Entrance to English Channel.	Submarine	Chased	Speed	—
†Clumberhall	3,599	25	Off S.W. Ireland	Submarine	Chased	Speed	—
Valentia	3,242	26	114 miles N.W. by W. from the Skelligs.	Submarine	Gunfire	Speed	—

MERCHANT VESSELS ATTACKED.

Name.	Gross Tons.	Date.	Position.	Attacked by	How attacked.	How saved.	Lives lost.
		1917. Jan.					
†Liddesdale	4,403	26	65 miles W. by N. from the Skelligs.	Submarine	Gunfire	By gun	—
†Ingleby	3,815	27	Mediterranean	Submarine	Torpedo	Missed	—
†Miniota	4,928	31	Off S. Ireland	Submarine	Gunfire	By gun	—
Baron Garioch	1,831	31	North Sea	Submarine	Torpedo	Missed	—
†Foyle	4,703	31	Entrance to English Channel.	Submarine	Gunfire	By gun	—

FEBRUARY 1917.

Name.	Gross Tons.	Date.	Position.	Attacked by	How attacked.	How saved.	Lives lost.
		Feb.					
Wellholme (S.V.)	89	1	English Channel	Submarine	Gunfire	Rescued	—
†Malta	2,236	2	Off S. Ireland	Submarine	Gunfire	Speed	—
†Saturnia	8,611	3	Off S.W. Ireland	Submarine	Torpedo ; gunfire.	Missed ; by gun.	—
†Tiverton	3,825	3	Mediterranean	Submarine	Torpedo	Missed	—
†Tresillian	3,585	4	Off S.W. Ireland	Submarine	Torpedo ; gunfire.	Missed ; by gun.	—
Manchester Hero	5,738	5	Off S.W. Ireland	Submarine	Gunfire	Rescued	—
Ambassador	2,578	5	Off S.W. Ireland	Submarine	Gunfire	Rescued	—
Ainsdale (S.V.)	1,825	5	Off S.W. Ireland	Submarine	Gunfire	Towed in	—
†Kaffir Prince	2,228	5	Off S.W. Ireland	Submarine	Gunfire	By gun	—
†Argyllshire	12,097	5	3 miles S.W. from Start Point.	Submarine	Torpedoed	Arrived	—
Dorothy	3,806	6	Mediterranean	Submarine	Torpedo	Missed	—
Mona's Queen	1,559	6	English Channel	Submarine	Torpedo	Missed	—
†Explorer	7,608	6	Off S. Ireland	Submarine	Torpedoed	Arrived	—
Tyndareus	11,000	6	10 miles off Cape Agulhas.	Mine	Mine	Towed in	—
Wallace	3,930	7	Off S. Ireland	Submarine	Gunfire	Rescued	1 Chief Officer made prisoner.
†Cranley	4,644	7	Off S. Ireland	Submarine	Chased	Speed	—
Etal Manor	1,875	7	North Sea	Submarine	Torpedo	Missed	—
Hotham Newton	2,648	8	Entrance to English Channel.	Submarine	Gunfire	Rescued	—
Peregrine	1,681	8	English Channel	Submarine	Gunfire	Speed	—
Hornsey	1,803	8	North Sea	Submarine	Gunfire	Rescued	—
†Jumna	4,152	8	Mediterranean	Submarine	Chased	Speed	—
†San Fraterno	9,587	10	Entrance to Firth of Forth.	Mine	Mine	Beached	—
†Roanoke	3,755	11	4 miles S.E. from Girdleness.	Submarine	Torpedoed	Towed in	1
†Woodfield	4,300	11	6 miles S.S.E. from Beachy Head.	Submarine	Torpedoed	Beached	—
†Ariadne Christine.	3,550	11	Off Scilly Isles	Submarine	Gunfire	By gun	—
†Cyclops	9,033	11	Off S.W. Ireland	Submarine	Chased	Speed	—
†Geddington Court.	3,989	11	Mediterranean	Submarine	Two torpedoes	Missed	—
Portuguese Prince	4,981	11	Bay of Biscay	Submarine	Gunfire	Speed	—
Pinna	6,288	12	7½ miles S.S.E. from S. Bishop.	Submarine	Torpedoed	Beached	—
†Gleneden	4,735	12	St. George's Channel.	Submarine	Gunfire	By gun	—
Kamouraska	4,903	12	Off S.W. Ireland	Submarine	Torpedo	Missed	—
†Chenab	3,549	12	Mediterranean	Submarine	Gunfire	Speed	—
†Sequoya	5,263	13	Bristol Channel	Submarine	Gunfire	By gun	1
†Anteros	4,241	13	Off S. Ireland	Submarine	Torpedo	Missed	—
†Trowbridge	3,712	14	Mediterranean	Submarine	Torpedoed	Towed in	1
Millicent Knight	3,563	14	In the Downs	Aircraft	Bombs	Missed	—
Harrow	1,777	15	North Sea	Submarine	Torpedo	Missed	—
Kittiwake	1,866	15	St. George's Channel.	Submarine	Torpedo	Missed	—
†Celtic	20,904	15	Irish Sea	Mine	Mine	Arrived Liverpool.	—
Pollcrea	1,209	16	Bay of Biscay	Submarine	Gunfire	Arrived Bayonne.	—
†The Princess	623	16	Bristol Channel	Submarine	Gunfire	By gun	—
†Delphic	8,273	16	Off S.W. Ireland	Submarine	Torpedo	Missed	—

MERCHANT VESSELS ATTACKED.   138

Name.	Gross Tons.	Date.	Position.	Attacked by	How attacked.	How saved.	Lives lost.
		1917. Feb.					
†Grelford	2,823	16	Bay of Biscay	Submarine	Gunfire	By gun	—
†Sheerness	1,274	16	Bristol Channel	Submarine	Gunfire	By gun	—
Buranda	3,651	16	Mediterranean	Submarine	Gunfire	Arrived Alicante.	—
†Grelford	2,823	17	Off Ushant	Submarine	Gunfire	By gun	—
Gwent	5,754	17	Entrance to English Channel.	Submarine Submarine	Chased	Speed	—
†Cambrian	5,626	18	English Channel	Submarine	Chased	Gunfire	—
†Hunsworth	2,991	18	English Channel	Submarine	Torpedoed	Towed in	2
†Asturian	3,193	18	Mediterranean	Submarine	Gunfire	Rescued	2
†Berrima	11,137	18	English Channel	Submarine	Torpedoed	Towed in	4
†Janeta	4,271	18	Mediterranean	Submarine	Gunfire	By gun	—
†Kovno	1,985	18	North Sea	Submarine	Chased	Speed	—
†Araguaya	10,537	19	Off S.W. Ireland	Submarine	Chased	Speed	—
†Northwaite	3,626	19	Mediterranean	Submarine	Gunfire	By gun	—
†Carperby	2,104	20	Off St. Ives	Submarine	Torpedo	Missed	—
†Tahiti	7,585	20	English Channel	Submarine	Chased	Gunfire	—
†Nascent	3,720	21	Off S. Ireland	Submarine	Gunfire	By gun	—
†Cameronian	5,861	21	Mediterranean	Submarine	Torpedo	Missed	—
†Canadian	9,309	22	Off S.W. Ireland	Submarine	Chased	Speed	—
†Gambia	3,296	22	English Channel	Submarine	Chased	Speed	—
†Ashtabula	7,025	22	North Sea	Mine	Mine	Arrived London.	—
Largo Law	3,974	24	English Channel	Submarine	Torpedo; gunfire.	Missed; fog	—
†Somme	1,828	24	English Channel	Submarine	Gunfire	By gun	—
†Megantic	14,878	24	Mediterranean	Submarine	Torpedo	Missed	—
†Silverdale	3,835	24	Off S.W. Ireland	Submarine	Torpedo	Missed	—
†Gleneden	4,735	24	Mediterranean	Submarine	Torpedo	Missed	—
†Hooton	1,892	25	Bristol Channel	Submarines	Chased	By gun	—
†Novington	3,442	25	Mediterranean	Submarine	Torpedo	Missed	—
†Venus	3,152	25	Mediterranean	Submarine	Gunfire	By gun	—
†Cameron	3,044	26	Off W. Ireland	Submarine	Gunfire	Rescued	—
Lydia	1,133	27	English Channel	Submarine	Gunfire	Rescued	—
†San Patricio	9,712	27	Off Orkney Islands.	Submarine	Chased	By gun	—
†Polzeath	882	27	English Channel	Submarine	Gunfire	By gun	—
†Bellorado	4,649	27	Mediterranean	Submarine	Gunfire	By gun	3 including Master.
†Ayr	3,050	27	Off S.W. Ireland	Submarine	Gunfire	By gun	—
†Huntscape	2,933	28	English Channel	Submarine	Gunfire	By gun	—
†Lynorta	3,684	28	Mediterranean	Submarine	Chased	Speed	—
†Rowena	3,017	28	Mediterranean	Submarine	Gunfire	By gun	—

MARCH 1917.

		March					
Glenart Castle (hospital ship).	6,807	1	English Channel	Mine (?)	Mine (?)	Towed in	—
†Euterpe	3,540	1	Mediterranean	Submarine	Torpedoed	Arrived	2
†Tabarka	3,933	1	Mediterranean	Submarine	Torpedo	Missed	—
†Birchgrove	2,821	1	North Sea	Submarine	Gunfire	By gun	—
Sarus (crane barge).	819	1	Off Boulogne	Submarine	Gunfire	Rescued	—
Donegal	1,885	1	English Channel	Submarine	Chased	Speed	—
Trojan	4,017	2	Off S.W. Ireland	Submarine	Torpedo	Missed	—
†Argyll	3,547	3	Off S.W. Ireland	Submarine	Gunfire	By gun	—
Adelaide (S.V.)	180	4	English Channel	Submarine	Gunfire after capture.	Towed in	—
†Princess Melita	1,094	5	North Sea	Submarine	Torpedo	Missed	—
†Syndic	2,727	6	Off S.W. Ireland	Submarine	Gunfire	By gun	—
†Zambesi	3,759	7	English Channel	Submarine	Chased	Speed	—
†Pagenturm	5,000	7	Mediterranean	Submarine	Torpedo	Failed to explode.	—
Salvus	2,259	10	Off S. Ireland	Submarine	Two torpedoes.	Missed	—
†Aracataca	4,154	10	250 miles W.N.W. from Fastnet.	Submarine	Gunfire	By gun	1

MERCHANT VESSELS ATTACKED.

Name.	Gross Tons.	Date.	Position.	Attacked by	How attacked.	How saved.	Lives lost.
		1917. March					
†Boonah	5,926	10	Off W. Ireland	Submarine	Chased	Gun	—
Pylades	681	10	North Sea	Submarine	Torpedo	Missed	—
†San Eduardo	6,225	10	8 miles S.S.E. from Stornoway.	Submarine	Torpedoed	Arrived	—
†Ambassador	2,578	10	Entrance to English Channel.	Submarine	Gunfire	By gun	—
†Spectator	3,808	11	Off S.W. Ireland	Submarine	Gunfire	By gun	—
†Eddystone	853	11	Bristol Channel	Submarine	Gunfire	By gun	—
†Semantha	2,847	12	Off S. Ireland	Submarine	Gunfire	By smoke	—
†Port Chalmers	6,534	12	Off S.W. Ireland	Submarine	Chased	By gun	—
†Winnebago	4,666	12	Off Scilly Islands	Submarine	Torpedoed	Towed in	—
Ravelston	2,085	12	North Sea	Submarine	Torpedo	Missed	-
†Raphael	4,699	12	Off S. Ireland	Submarine	Chased	Speed	—
Luciline	3,765	13	40 miles W.N.W. from Tearaght Island.	Submarine	Torpedoed	Beached	15
†Glencliffe	3,673	13	St. George's Channel.	Submarine	Gunfire	By gun	—
†Trecarne	4,196	13	W. from Scilly Islands.	Submarine	Gunfire	By gun	—
†Burgundy	3,364	13	Off S.W. Ireland	Submarine	Gunfire	By gun	—
†Orsova	12,036	14	3 miles E. by S. ½ S. from Eddystone.	Submarine	Torpedoed	Reached port.	8
†Ranella	5,583	14	Off S. Ireland	Submarine	Torpedo	Missed	—
†Tortuguero	4,175	14	Off N.W. Ireland	Submarine	Gunfire	Speed	—
†Fallodon	3,012	14	English Channel	Submarine	Gunfire	By gun	—
†Polescar	5,832	14	Off N.W. Ireland	Submarine	Chased	Speed	—
†Lepanto	6,389	15	English Channel	Submarine	Gunfire	By gun	—
†Willaston	5,658	15	Entrance to English Channel.	Submarine	Gunfire	By gun	—
Raymond (S.V.)	200	16	Off Ushant	Submarine	Gunfire	Rescued	—
†Ruahine	10,758	17	167 miles S.W. by S. from Fastnet.	Submarine	Torpedo	Missed	—
†Anglo-Egyptian	7,379	17	Mediterranean	Submarine	Chased	Speed	—
†Karmala	8,983	17	Mediterranean	Submarine	Torpedo; gunfire.	Missed; by gun.	—
†Laurel Leaf	5,631	17	Off S. Ireland	Submarine	Torpedo	Missed	—
†Baygitano	3,073	17	W. from Ushant	Submarine	Torpedo	Missed	—
Danubian	5,064	20	11 miles S. by W. from Asses Ears, Aden.	Mine	Mine	Arrived	—
†Huntscape	2,933	21	English Channel	Submarine	Torpedoed	Arrived	—
Asturias (hospital ship).	12,002	21	5 miles S. from Start Point.	Submarine	Torpedoed	Beached	35
†South Pacific	3,661	22	Mediterranean	Submarine	Chased	By gun	—
†Mexico	5,549	23	English Channel	Submarine	Torpedoed	Arrived	—
Genesee	2,892	23	North Sea	Submarine	Torpedo	Missed	—
Sagenite	712	23	North Sea	Submarine	Torpedo	Missed	—
†Crown of Granada.	2,746	23	Atlantic	Submarine	Gunfire	By gun	—
†Coronado	6,539	24	Off S.W. Ireland	Submarine	Gunfire	By gun	—
†Shimosa	4,221	24	Atlantic	Submarine	Gunfire	By gun	—
†Ionian	8,268	24	English Channel	Submarine	Torpedo	Missed	—
†Manhattan	8,004	25	W. from Scilly Islands.	Submarine	Gunfire	By gun	—
†Thessalia	3,691	25	Mediterranean	Submarine	Torpedo	Missed	—
†Tremorvah	3,654	26	Mediterranean	Submarine	Torpedo	Missed	—
†Loos	2,787	26	Mediterranean	Submarine	Gunfire	By gun and smoke.	—
Kelsomoor	3,174	26	Off S.W. Ireland	Submarine	Torpedo	Missed	—
†Trecarne	1,196	26	Mediterranean	Submarine	Chased	Speed	—
†Ventura de Larrinaga.	4,648	27	Off S.W. Ireland	Submarine	Gunfire	Speed	—
†Baron Napier	4,943	27	Off S.W. Ireland	Submarine	Torpedo	Missed	—
Andree	3,689	27	Off Ushant	Submarine	Torpedo	Missed	—
†Kurmark	5,137	27	Mediterranean	Submarine	Torpedo	Missed	—
Le Coq	3,419	27	Bay of Biscay	Submarine	Torpedo	Missed	—
†Borderer	4,372	28	St. George's Channel.	Submarine	Gunfire	Nightfall	—
†Kurdistan	3,720	28	Off S. Ireland	Submarine	Two torpedoes	Missed	—

MERCHANT VESSELS ATTACKED.

Name.	Gross Tons.	Date.	Position.	Attacked by	How attacked.	How saved.	Lives lost.
		1917. March					
†Geo	3,048	29	Mediterranean	Submarine	Torpedo	Missed	—
†Khiva	8,947	29	Mediterranean	Submarine	Torpedo	Missed	—
Amsterdam	1,777	30	North Sea	Submarine	Torpedo	Missed	—
†Edernian	3,588	30	English Channel	Mine	Mine	Reached Dieppe.	—
†Parklands	1,607	30	English Channel	Submarine	Chased	By gun	—
Penmorvah	4,323	31	English Channel	Submarine	Torpedo	Missed	—
Amulet	1,018	31	North Sea	Aircraft	Bombs	Missed	—
Quentin	1,274	31	North Sea	Aircraft	Bombs	Missed	—
Gloucester Castle (Hospital Ship).	7,999	31	English Channel	Submarine	Torpedoed	Towed in	3
†Valacia	6,526	31	English Channel	Submarine	Torpedoed	Towed in	—
†Queen Louise	4,879	31	English Channel	Submarine	Torpedoed	Reached Havre.	—
Sofie	354	31	English Channel	Submarine	Gunfire	Weather	—
†Ocean Monarch	4,511	31	Off S. Ireland	Submarine	Torpedo	Failed to explode.	—
†Parklands	1,607	31	English Channel	Submarine	Gunfire	By gun	—
†Ariosto	4,313	31	Mediterranean	Submarine	Torpedo	Missed	—
APRIL 1917.		April					
†Wandby	3,981	2	Bay of Biscay	Submarine	Gunfire	By gun	—
†Brodliffe	5,893	3	Mediterranean	Submarine	Torpedo	Missed	—
†Oberon	5,142	3	Mediterranean	Submarine	Torpedoed	Arrived	—
†Cloughton	4,221	3	Mediterranean	Mine	Mine	Towed in	—
†Queensland Transport.	4,663	4	Mediterranean	Submarine	Torpedo	Missed	—
Southerndown	4,431	4	Atlantic	Submarine	Chased	Speed	—
†Dundrennan	4,248	4	Mediterranean	Submarine	Gunfire	By gun	—
†Kanawha	3,884	4	Off Ushant	Submarine	Gunfire	Speed	—
†Hyacinthus	5,756	4	Off N.W. Ireland	Submarine	Torpedo	Missed	—
†Kangaroo	4,348	5	Mediterranean	Submarine	Gunfire	By gun	—
†Ethelaric	3,232	6	Off S.W. Ireland	Submarine	Torpedo	Missed	—
Lime Branch	5,379	6	Off Canary Islands	Submarine	Chased	Speed	—
†Hillhouse	3,049	6	Off S.W. Ireland	Submarine	Torpedo; gunfire.	Missed; by gun.	—
†Lapland	18,565	7	Off Liverpool Bar L.V.	Mine	Mine	Arrived	2
†Carmarthenshire	7,823	8	Off entrance to English Channel.	Submarine	Gunfire	By gun	—
†Lord Derby	3,757	9	Mediterranean	Submarine	Torpedo	Missed	—
†Neto	1,696	9	English Channel	Submarine	Torpedo	Missed	—
†Cyclops	9,033	11	W. from Scilly Islands.	Submarine	Torpedo	Missed	—
†Troilus	7,625	11	North Sea	Submarine	Chased	Speed	—
†Monsaldale	2,805	11	Mediterranean	Submarine	Gunfire	By gun and smoke.	—
†Branksome Hall	4,262	11	English Channel	Submarine	Torpedoed	Towed in	—
†Echunga	4,589	13	Off N.W. Scotland.	Submarine	Gunfire	Rescued	—
Lime Branch	5,379	13	W. from Ushant	Submarine	Torpedoed	Arrived	—
†Ajana	7,759	14	English Channel	Submarine	Torpedo	Missed	—
†Tarantia	4,754	14	W. from Ushant	Submarine	Torpedo	Missed	—
†Boveric	4,445	14	Mediterranean	Submarine	Torpedo	Missed	—
†Adala	3,847	15	North Sea	Submarine	Gunfire	Weather	—
†Highcliffe	3,238	16	English Channel	Submarine	Gunfire	By gun	—
†City	2,893	16	English Channel	Submarine	Torpedo	Missed	—
†Benguela	5,520	17	Off W. Ireland	Submarine	Torpedo	Missed	—
†Khephren	2,774	17	Mediterranean	Submarine	Torpedo	Missed	—
†Ryton	3,991	17	Mediterranean	Submarine	Torpedo	Missed	—
†Nirvana	6,021	17	English Channel	Mine	Mine	Arrived	—
†Gisella	2,502	17	Off Island of Lewis.	Mine	Mine	Arrived	1
†Winifredian	10,422	17	North Sea	Mine	Mine	Arrived	—
†Clan Sutherland	2,820	17	English Channel	Submarine	Torpedoed	Beached	12
†Lanuvium	4,417	17	Mediterranean	Submarine	Chased	By gun	—

MERCHANT VESSELS ATTACKED

Name.	Gross Tons.	Date.	Position.	Attacked by	How attacked.	How saved	Lives lost.
		1917. April					
†Nigaristan	4,345	18	Bristol Channel	Submarine	Gunfire	By gun	—
†Hurst	4,718	18	W. from Gibraltar	Submarine	Gunfire	By gun	—
†Clan Sinclair	5,215	18	Atlantic	Submarine	Torpedo; gunfire.	Missed; by gun.	—
†Frankier	3,836	18	Entrance to English Channel.	Submarine	Torpedo	Missed	
†Thermidor	3,788	19	Off W. Ireland	Submarine	Chased	Speed	—
Old Head (S.V.)	105	19	Off Coningbeg L.V.	Submarine	Gunfire after capture.	Towed in	—
†Bristol City	2,511	19	Off S.W. Ireland	Submarine	Torpedo	Missed	—
†Limeleaf	7,339	19	English Channel	Submarine	Torpedoed	Towed in	7
†Lumina	5,856	19	North Sea	Mine	Mine	Towed in	—
†Suwanee	2,748	20	Atlantic	Submarine	Gunfire	By gun	—
†Terek	3,710	20	Off W. Ireland	Submarine	Torpedo	Missed	—
†Oriflamme	3,764	20	Off W. Ireland	Submarine	Torpedo	Missed	—
†Ikalis	4,329	20	Mediterranean	Submarine	Torpedo	Missed	—
†Inverness	3,734	20	W. from Gibraltar	Submarine	Gunfire	By gun	—
†Leasowe Castle	9,737	20	W. from Gibraltar	Submarine	Torpedoed	Arrived	—
†Roumanian Prince	4,147	21	Off S.W. Ireland	Submarine	Gunfire	Speed	—
†Crown of Toledo	5,806	21	Off S.W. Ireland	Submarine	Chased	Speed	—
†Elysia	6,368	21	Off S.W. Ireland	Submarine	Torpedo	Missed	—
†Wapello	5,576	21	Off S.W. Ireland	Submarine	Gunfire	By gun	—
†Valeria	5,865	22	Off S.W. Ireland	Submarine	Chased	By gun	—
†Austrian	3,127	22	Off S.W. Ireland	Submarine	Chased	Rescued	—
†Karroo	6,127	22	W. from Scilly Islands.	Submarine	2 torpedoes; gunfire.	Missed; rescued.	—
†Izaston	3,060	22	Bay of Biscay	Submarine	Torpedo	Missed	—
Tommi (S.V.)	138	23	Off St. Ives	Submarine	Gunfire after capture.	Towed in	—
†Normanby	4,219	23	W. from Gibraltar	Submarine	Gunfire	By smoke	—
†Nephrite	673	23	Bristol Channel	Submarine	Gunfire	By gun	—
†Drumcliffe	4,073	24	Atlantic	Submarine	Chased	Rescued	—
†Thirlby	2,009	24	Atlantic	Submarine	Torpedo	Missed	—
Huntsholm	2,073	24	English Channel	Submarine	Torpedo	Missed	—
†Martaban	5,106	25	Off S.W. Ireland	Submarine	Gunfire	By gun	—
†Baltic	23,876	25	Off W. Ireland	Submarine	Torpedo	Missed	—
†Bideford	3,562	25	Off Dunkirk	T.B.D.'s	Gunfire	Slightly damaged.	—
†Lynorta	3,684	25	Off entrance to English Channel.	Submarine	Gunfire	By gun	—
†Flaxmere	1,525	25	Off S.W. Ireland	Submarine	Chased	By gun	—
†Florrieston	3,366	25	Mediterranean	Submarine	Torpedo	Missed	—
†Ascania	9,121	26	W. from Scilly Islands.	Submarine	Chased	Gunfire	—
†Pontwen	4,796	26	Off W. Ireland	Submarine	Gunfire	By gun and smoke.	—
†Knight of the Thistle.	6,675	26	Off S.W. Ireland	Submarine	Chased	Speed	—
†Baltic	23,876	26	Off S. Ireland	Submarine	Torpedo	Missed	—
Karnak	3,171	26	English-Channel	Submarine	Gunfire	Speed	—
†Polzeath	882	26	English Channel	Submarine	Gunfire	By gun	—
Quantock	4,470	26	Off Fastnet	Submarine	Torpedoed	Towed in	2
†Roseleaf	6,572	27	Off N.W. Ireland	Submarine	Gunfire	By gun	—
†Headcliffe	3,654	27	Off S. Ireland	Submarine	Gunfire	By gun	—
Amelia and Jane (S.V.).	62	27	English Channel	Submarine	Gunfire after capture.	Towed in	—
†Clan Macarthur	7,382	27	Off Scilly Isles	Submarine	Chased	Speed	—
†Bernard	3,682	28	Entrance to English Channel.	Submarine	Chased	By gun	—
†Sheaf Blade	2,378	28	Entrance to English Channel.	Submarine	Gunfire	By gun	—
Rob Roy (S.V.)	93	28	St. George's Channel.	Submarine	Captured	Rescued	—
Freighter	297	28	English Channel	Submarine	Torpedo	Missed	—
Highgate	1,780	29	North Sea	Aeroplane	Bombs	Missed	—
†Palma	7,632	29	W. from Scilly Islands.	Submarine	Gunfire	By gun	—
†Gena	2,784	29	North Sea	Submarine	Gunfire	By gun	—
†Princess Helena	677	29	North Sea	Submarine	Gunfire	By gun	—
†Nantes	1,640	29	North Sea	Submarine	Chased	By gun	—
†Lord Downshire	4,808	29	W. from Ushant	Submarine	Chased	Speed	—

MERCHANT VESSELS ATTACKED. 142

Name.	Gross Tons.	Date.	Position.	Attacked by	How attacked.	How saved.	Lives lost.
		1917. April					
†Pretorian	6,948	30	Off S.W. Ireland	Submarine	Chased	Speed	—
†Arranmoor	4,008	30	Bristol Channel	Submarine	Gunfire	Speed	—
†Sutlej	3,549	30	Off S.W. Ireland	Submarines	Torpedo	Missed	—
†Huntsmoor	4,957	30	W. from Scilly Islands.	Submarine	Gunfire	By gun	—
Oilfield	4,005	30	English Channel	Submarine	Gunfire	Rescued	—
†Kamouraska	4,903	30	Off Ushant	Submarine	Gunfire	By gun	—
†Vestalia	5,528	30	English Channel	Submarine	Chased	By gun	—
MAY 1917.		May					
†Haslingden	1,934	1	English Channel	Submarine	Torpedo	Missed	—
*Querida	1,175	1	English Channel	Submarine	Chased	Gunfire	—
†Cordova	2,284	1	Off Entrance to English Channel.	Submarine	Torpedo	Missed	—
†Quarrydene	2,883	1	Off W. Ireland	Submarine	Gunfire	By gun	—
†Nellore	6,853	1	Mediterranean	Submarine	Chased	Speed	—
†Devonshire	500	1	Irish Sea	Submarine	Gunfire	By gun	—
†Dorie	3,264	1	Off S.W. Ireland	Submarine	Torpedoed	Towed in	—
†Camerata	3,723	2	Mediterranean	Submarine	Torpedoed	Beached	—
†Hambleton Range.	3,682	2	North Sea	Submarine	Chased	Speed	—
†San Melito	10,160	2	Off Orkney Islands.	Submarine	Chased	By gun	—
†Gorsemore	3,079	2	Bristol Channel	Submarine	Torpedo	Missed	—
†Isla	222	2	Irish Sea	Submarine	Gunfire	By escort	—
†Archbank	3,767	2	English Channel	Submarine	Gunfire	Rescued	—
City of London	225	3	North Sea	Submarine	Gunfire	Missed	—
†Palm Branch	3,891	3	Arctic Sea	Submarines	Torpedo ; gunfire.	Missed ; by gun.	—
Yorkshire	394	4	St. George's Channel.	Submarine	Gunfire	Rescued	—
†Ben Lomond	2,814	4	Mediterranean	Submarine	Torpedo	Missed	—
†Maidan	8,205	4	St. George's Channel.	Submarine	Chased	By gun	—
†Monmouthshire	5,097	4	Atlantic	Submarine	Chased	By gun	—
†Talawa	3,834	5	Mediterranean	Submarine	Torpedoed	Beached	—
†Mahanada	7,196	5	Off Scilly Islands	Submarine	Chased	By gun	—
†Bengore Head	2,490	5	Off S. Ireland	Submarine	Gunfire	By gun	—
†Photinia	4,583	5	W. from Ushant	Submarine	Torpedo	Missed	—
†Norton	1,825	5	Off S. Ireland	Submarine	Chased	Speed	—
Katie Cluett (S.V.).	136	6	English Channel	Submarine	Gunfire	Towed in	—
†New Abbotshall	783	7	North Sea	Submarine	Gunfire	By gun	—
†Griqua	3,344	7	Mediterranean	Submarine	Gunfire	By gun	—
†Southwaite	3,618	7	Off entrance to English Channel.	Submarine	Torpedo	Missed	—
†Crown of Leon	3,391	7	Mediterranean	Submarine	Torpedoed	Beached	1
†San Patricio	9,712	8	Bristol Channel	Submarine	Torpedoed	Arrived	—
†Astyanax	4,872	9	Off S.W. Ireland	Submarine	Chased	Speed	—
*Malda	7,884	9	North Sea	Submarine	Torpedo	Missed	—
†Kassanga	3,015	10	Mediterranean	Submarine	Gunfire	By gun and smoke.	—
*Treverbyn	4,163	10	English Channel	Submarine	Gunfire	By gun	—
†Hessle	952	10	North Sea	Submarine	Torpedo	Missed	—
†Putney	3,232	10	Mediterranean	Submarine	Torpedo	Missed	—
†Clan MacNab	4,675	10	Mediterranean	Submarine	Torpedo	Missed	—
†Hindoo	4,915	11	Mediterranean	Submarine	Torpedoed	Beached	—
Waterville	1,968	12	Off Elbow Light Buoy.	Mine	Mine	Beached	—
†Cuthbert	3,834	12	Off S.W. Ireland	Submarine	Torpedo	Missed	—
†Calabria	4,376	12	Mediterranean	Submarine	Chased	Speed	—
†Rio Claro	3,687	12	Mediterranean	Submarine	Torpedo	Missed	—
†Cliffside	4,850	12	Mediterranean	Submarine	Torpedo	Missed	—
†Ismailia	3,704	12	Mediterranean	Submarine	Torpedo	Missed	—
†Anglo Chilean	6,900	13	Mediterranean	Submarine	Gunfire	By gun	—
†Neilrose	3,568	13	Off S.W. Ireland	Submarine	Torpedo	Missed	—
Galtee	565	13	English Channel	Submarine	Torpedo	Missed	—
Trevaylor	4,249	13	Mediterranean	Submarine	Gunfire	Rescued	—
†Fiscus	4,170	13	North Sea	Submarine	Torpedo	Missed	—
†Canara	6,012	14	Mediterranean	Submarine	Torpedo	Missed	—

MERCHANT VESSELS ATTACKED.

Name.	Gross Tons.	Date.	Position.	Attacked by	How attacked.	How saved.	Lives lost.
		1917. May					
†Volga	4,404	14	Mediterranean	Submarine	Torpedoed	Beached	—
†Arlington Court	4,346	14	Off S.W. Ireland	Submarine	Torpedoed	Towed in	—
†Grelhame	3,740	14	Off Entrance to English Channel.	Submarine	Chased	Gun	—
†Upcerne	2,984	14	Off Entrance to English Channel.	Submarine	Chased	Weather	—
†Baychattan	3,758	15	English Channel	Submarine	Gunfire	By gun	—
†Ibex	951	15	English Channel	Submarine	Torpedo	Missed	—
†Nellore	6,853	15	Mediterranean	Submarines	Gunfire	By gun	—
†Pancras	4,436	15	Mediterranean	Submarine	Gunfire	Beached; refloated.	—
†Huntsholm	2,073	17	English Channel	Submarine	Torpedo	Missed	—
†Chiswick	3,246	17	North Sea	Submarine	Chased	Gun	—
†Denetown	653	18	English Channel	Submarine	Gunfire	Rescued	—
†Celtic	20,904	19	Off S.W. Ireland	Submarine	Torpedo	Missed	—
†Karagola	7,000	19	W. from Gibraltar	Submarine	Chased	Gunfire and smoke.	—
†Kwarra	4,441	19	Atlantic	Submarine	Chased	Gunfire	—
†Southwestern Miller.	6,514	20	English Channel	Submarines	Chased	Escort	—
†Birchgrove	2,821	20	North Sea	Seaplanes	Torpedoes; machine gun.	Missed; by gun.	—
†Karroo	6,127	21	English Channel	Submarine	Gunfire	By gun	—
†Medora	5,135	21	Off the Lizard	Submarine	Torpedo	Missed	—
†Austrian	3,127	21	Off N.W. Ireland	Submarine	Torpedo	Missed	—
Highgate	1,780	21	North Sea	Submarine	Torpedo	Missed	—
†Ioanna	3,459	22	English Channel	Submarine	Chased	Rescued	—
†Myrtle Branch	3,741	22	Atlantic	Submarine	Torpedo	Missed	—
†Marie Suzanne	3,106	22	Mediterranean	Submarine	Torpedo	Missed	—
†Chicago City	2,324	23	Off S. Ireland	Submarine	Torpedoed	Towed in; beached.	2
†Nellore	6,853	23	Entrance to English Channel.	Submarine	Torpedo	Missed	—
†Carperby	2,104	23	English Channel	Submarine	Torpedo	Missed	—
†Madura	4,484	24	Entrance to English Channel.	Submarine	2 torpedoes	One missed; one failed to explode.	—
New Pioneer	722	25	English Channel	Submarine	Chased	Speed	—
†Rabymere	1,776	25	Off S. Ireland	Submarine	Torpedo	Missed	—
†Myrtle Branch	3,741	25	Off W. Ireland	Submarine	Torpedo	Missed	—
†Atlas	3,090	25	Mediterranean	Submarine	Torpedo	Missed	—
Manchester Inventor.	4,112	25	Off W. Ireland	Submarine	Chased	Speed	—
†Clan Graham	5,213	26	Mediterranean	Submarine	Gunfire	By gun	—
†Inca	3,593	26	Off S.W. Ireland	Submarine	Torpedo	Missed	—
†Inverness	3,734	26	Off Scilly Isles	Submarine	Torpepo	Missed	—
Baku Standard	3,708	26	North Sea	Submarine	Chased	By escort	—
†Indian Transport	4,111	27	English Channel	Submarine	Gunfire	By gun	—
†Meaford	1,889	27	Off entrance to English Channel.	Submarine	Chased	By gun	—
†Cymric Vale	3,580	27	Bay of Biscay	Submarine	Gunfire	By gun	—
†Cresswell	2,829	28	Off S.W. Ireland	Submarine	Gunfire	By gun	—
†Peebles	4,284	29	English Channel	Submarine	Gunfire	By gun	—
†Hyson	6,608	29	English Channel	Submarine	Chased	By gun	—
†Pavia	2,945	29	Off S.W. Ireland	Submarine	Torpedo	Missed	—
†Grangetown	1,640	29	North Sea	Submarine	Torpedo	Missed	—
†Cairnross	4,016	30	Mediterranean	Submarine	Torpedo	Missed	—
†San Ricardo	6,465	30	Off N.W. Ireland	Submarine	Gunfire	By escort	—
†El Uruguayo	8,361	30	Off N.W. Ireland	Submarine	Chased	Speed	—
†Fernley	3,820	30	Off S.W. Ireland	Submarine	Torpedoed	Arrived	—
†Ozarda	4,791	31	Mediterranean	Submarine	Torpedoed	Beached	—
JUNE 1917.		June					
†Turnbridge	2,874	1	Off S.W. Ireland	Submarine	Gunfire	Speed	—
†Antinous	3,682	1	Off the Lizard	Submarine	Torpedo	Missed	—
†Cymric Vale	3,580	1	Atlantic	Submarine	Chased	Speed	—
†Kingstonian	6,564	1	Ashore near Cape Granitola, Sicily.	Submarine	Torpedo	Missed	—

Merchant Vessels Attacked.

Name.	Gross Tons.	Date.	Position.	Attacked by	How attacked.	How saved.	Lives lost.
		1917. June					
†Cotovia	4,020	1	Arctic	Submarine	Gunfire	By gun	—
†Waiwera	6,237	2	Off the Lizard	Submarine	Torpedo	Missed	—
†Hypatia	5,663	2	Atlantic	Submarine	Torpedo	Missed	—
†Snowdonian	3,870	2	Mediterranean	Submarine	Gunfire	Smoke	—
†Tonawanda	3,421	2	English Channel	Submarine	Torpedoed	Reached port.	—
†Dockleaf	5,311	3	Mediterranean	Mine	Mine	Reached port.	—
†San Lorenzo	9,607	3	Off N.W. Ireland	Submarine	Torpedoed	Reached port.	—
Cornhill	900	4	Off Cape Wrath	Submarine	Gunfire	Rescued	—
†Manchester Port	4,093	4	Atlantic	Submarine	Gunfire	By gun	—
†Miniota	4,928	4	Atlantic	Submarine	Gunfire	By gun	—
†Graciana	3,536	5	Off N.W. Ireland	Submarine	Gunfire	By gun	—
†Tuskar	1,159	6	Off N.W. Ireland	Submarine	Gunfire	By gun	—
†Mitra	5,592	6	Mediterranean	Submarine	Torpedoed	Reached port	—
†Imani	4,590	7	W. from Ushant	Submarine	Gunfire	By gun	—
†Cape Transport	4,109	7	Bay of Biscay	Submarine	Gunfire	Gun	—
†Jerseymoor	5,662	7	Bay of Biscay	Submarine	Gunfire	By gun	—
†Oldfield Grange	4,653	7	English Channel	Submarine	Torpedoed	Beached	—
†Mahopac	2,216	7	English Channel	Submarine	Torpedoed	Beached	—
†Cranmore	3,157	7	Off W. Ireland	Submarine	Torpedoed	Beached	—
†Errington Court	4,461	7	Mediterranean	Mine	Mine	Beached	—
†Chevington	3,876	8	English Channel	Submarine	Chased	Speed	—
†Addington	1,613	8	English Channel	Submarine	Gunfire	By gun and smoke.	—
†Manchester Engineer.	4,465	8	Arctic	Submarine	Chased	Rescued	—
†Freshfield	3,445	8	Mediterranean	Submarine	Gunfire	By gun	—
†Russian Prince	4,158	8	Off S.W. Ireland	Submarine	Torpedoed	Reached port	—
†Gaboon	3,297	9	Atlantic	Submarine	Gunfire	By gun	—
†Akabo	3,814	9	Off S.W. Ireland	Submarine	3 torpedoes	Missed	—
†Sapele	3,152	9	Off S.W. Ireland	Submarine	Chased	Speed	—
†Itola	5,257	9	Mediterranean	Submarine	Torpedo	Missed	—
†Ceramic	18,481	9	Entrance to English Channel.	Submarine	Torpedo	Missed	—
†Fernleaf	5,838	10	Off S.W. Ireland	Submarine	Chased	By gun	—
†Loch Lomond	2,619	10	W. from Gibraltar	Submarine	Gunfire	By gun and smoke.	—
†Lautaro	3,476	10	Mediterranean	Submarine	Chased	By gun	—
†Harpathian	4,588	10	English Channel	Submarine	Torpedo	Missed	—
†Acadian	2,305	10	West from Gibraltar.	Submarine	Gunfire	Gun	—
†Athenia	8,668	11	N.W. Ireland	Submarine	Chased	Speed	—
†Pathan	4,956	11	Off S.W. Ireland	Submarine	Chased	Rescued	—
†Kerry Range	5,856	11	Off N.W. Ireland	Submarine	Torpedo	Missed	—
†Mackinaw	3,204	11	W. from Scilly Isles.	Submarine	Torpedo	Missed	—
†Minnie de Larrinaga.	5,046	11	Atlantic	Submarine	Gunfire	Gun	—
†Leafield	2,539	11	Entrance to English Channel.	Submarine	Torpedo	Missed	—
†Pentwyn	3,587	11	Atlantic	Submarine	Torpedo; gunfire.	Missed; by gun.	—
†Thessaly	3,128	11	Atlantic	Submarine	Gunfire	By gun	1
†Metagama	12,420	11	Off S.W. Ireland	Submarine	Torpedo	Missed	—
†Holywell	4,867	11	Off S.W. Ireland	Submarine	Gunfire	Rescued	—
†Eurymachus	4,995	11	Atlantic	Submarine	Chased	Speed	—
†Dominic	2,966	11	Off N.W. Ireland	Submarine	Chased	By gun and smoke.	—
†Ausonia	8,153	11	Off S. Ireland	Submarine	Torpedoed	Reached port	1
†City of Exeter	9,373	11	Off Bombay	Mine	Mine	Reached port	—
†Knight Companion.	7,241	11	Atlantic	Submarine	Torpedoed	Towed in	—
†Margarita	2,788	11	English Channel	Submarine	Torpedoed	Reached port	—
†Eustace	3,995	11	English Channel	Submarine	Torpedoed	Reached port	—
†Coronado	6,539	12	Off S. Ireland	Submarine	Torpedoed	Reached port	—
†Haverford	11,635	12	Off S. Ireland	Submarine	Torpedo	Missed	—
†Indian	9,121	12	Off S.W. Ireland	Submarine	Torpedo	Missed	—
†Quillota	3,692	12	Atlantic	Submarine	Gunfire	By gun	—
†Bonvilston	2,866	12	W. from Gibraltar	Submarine	Gunfire	By gun	—
†Paris	599	13	Entrance to English Channel.	Submarine	Torpedo	Missed	—

MERCHANT VESSELS ATTACKED.

Name.	Gross Tons.	Date.	Position.	Attacked by	How attacked.	How saved.	Lives lost.
		1917. June					
†Kintuck	4,639	13	Atlantic	Submarine	Gunfire	Gun	—
†Lorle	2,686	13	Off Ushant	Submarine	Torpedo	Missed	—
†Collegian	7,237	14	Off S. Ireland	Submarine	Torpedo	Missed	—
†Ramore Head	4,444	14	Atlantic	Submarine	Torpedo	Missed	—
†Canto	1,243	14	North Sea	Seaplanes	3 torpedoes; machine gun.	Missed	—
†Lowther Castle	4,439	14	Mediterranean	Mine	Mine	Reached port.	—
†Nascopie	1,870	14	Arctic Sea	Submarine	Gunfire	Gun	—
†Winamac	5,767	15	Off S. Ireland	Submarine	Torpedo	Missed	—
Scartho	569	15	North Sea	Submarine	Torpedo	Missed	—
†Branksome Hall	4,262	15	English Channel	Submarine	Torpedo	Missed	—
†Crane	2,033	15	Off entrance to English Channel.	Submarine	Torpedo	Missed	—
†Queen Alexandra	785	15	English Channel	Submarine	Chased	By gun	—
†Camito	6,611	15	Off entrance to English Channel.	Submarine	Gunfire	Gun	—
†Teesdale	2,470	15	English Channel	Submarine	Torpedoed	Beached	—
†Elvaston	4,130	15	Mediterranean	Submarine	Torpedoed	Reached port.	3
†Deddington	2,827	15	Bay of Biscay	Submarine	Chased	Gun	—
†Fallodon	3,012	16	Off S. Ireland	Submarine	Torpedoed	Towed in	—
†Bayford	4,113	16	Atlantic	Submarine	Torpedo	Missed	—
†Rutherglen	4,214	16	Atlantic	Submarine	Gunfire	Gun	—
†Elysia	6,397	16	Off S. Ireland	Submarine	Torpedo	Missed	—
Ardmore	1,304	16	Off S. Ireland	Submarine	Chased	Rescued	—
†Claveresk	3,829	17	Off Casablanca	Submarine	Torpedo	Missed	—
†Kaiser-i-Hind	11,430	17	W. from Gibraltar	Submarine	Torpedo	Missed	—
†Alban	5,223	17	Off W. Ireland	Submarine	Torpedo	Missed	—
†Kathlamba	6,382	18	Off entrance to English Channel.	Submarine	Torpedoed	Reached port.	—
†Marie Suzanne	3,106	18	Atlantic	Submarine	Gunfire	Rescued	—
†Palma	7,632	18	Atlantic	Submarine	3 torpedoes	Missed	—
†Trevanion	4,267	18	Mediterranean	Submarine	2 torpedoes	Missed	—
†Whateley Hall	3,712	18	W. from Gibraltar	Submarine	Gunfire	By gun and smoke.	—
†Minnie Coles (S.V.)	116	18	Irish Channel	Submarine	Gunfire	Towed in	—
†Hazelwood	3,120	18	Mediterranean	Submarine	Torpedo	Missed	—
†Hurst	4,718	19	Mediterranean	Submarine	Torpedo	Missed	—
†Ganges	3,497	19	Atlantic	Submarine	Torpedo	Missed	—
†Morinier	3,804	19	Bay of Biscay	Submarine	Gunfire	By gun	—
†Wonganella	3,998	19	Atlantic	Submarine	Gunfire	Gun	—
†Great City	5,525	19	Off Scilly Isles	Submarine	Torpedoed	Towed in	4
Mary Ann (S.V.)	164	19	English Channel	Submarine	Set on fire after capture.	Towed in	—
†Aylestone	3,400	19	Atlantic	Submarine	Gunfire	Gun	—
†Devona	3,779	20	Bay of Biscay	Submarine	Gunfire	By gun	—
†Valeria	5,865	20	Off S.W. Ireland	Submarine	Chased	By gun	—
†Lancastrian	5,120	20	Off entrance to English Channel.	Submarine	Chased	Speed	—
†Nitonian	6,381	20	Off W. Ireland	Submarine	Gunfire	By gun	—
†Buranda	3,651	20	Off Ushant	Submarine	Gunfire	Gun	—
†Charing Cross	2,534	22	Off N.W. Ireland	Submarine	Gunfire	Gun	—
†Osmanieh	4,041	23	Mediterranean	Submarine	2 torpedoes	Missed	—
†Celia	5,004	24	Atlantic	Submarine	Chased	Gun	—
†Lackenby	2,108	25	Bristol Channel	Submarine	Torpedo	Missed	—
†Fernleaf	5,838	25	Atlantic	Submarine	Gunfire	Gun	—
†Southern	5,694	25	Mediterranean	Mine	Mine	Beached	—
†Gorsemore	3,079	26	Entrance to English Channel.	Submarine	Gunfire	Gun	1
†Swindon	5,084	26	Off N.W. Ireland	Submarine	2 torpedoes	Missed	—
†Haverford	11,635	26	Off W. Scotland	Submarine	Torpedoed	Beached	8
†Aurania	13,936	26	N.W. Ireland	Submarine	Chased	Gun	—
†Elysia	6,397	26	N.W. Ireland	Submarine	Gunfire	Gun	—
†Skipton Castle	3,823	26	Mediterranean	Submarine	Gunfire	Gun	—
†City of Hankow	7,369	27	N.W. Scotland	Submarine	Torpedo	Missed	—
†Claveresk	3,829	27	W. Ireland	Submarine	Gunfire	Gun	—
†Elsie (S.V.)	165	28	English Channel	Submarine	Gunfire	Weather	—

MERCHANT VESSELS ATTACKED. 146

Name.	Gross Tons.	Date.	Position.	Attacked by	How attacked.	How saved.	Lives lost.
		1917. June					
Northfield	2,099	28	English Channel	Submarine	Torpedoed	Reached port	—
†Cheyenne	4,987	29	English Channel	Submarine	Torpedo	Missed	—
†Morocco	3,783	29	Off Cape Wrath	Submarine	Gunfire	Gun	—
Fairmuir	593	30	Arctic Sea	Submarine	Chased	Speed	—
†Purley	4,500	30	Atlantic	Submarine	Torpedo	Missed	—
†Ardens	1,274	30	North Sea	Submarine	Torpedo	Missed	—
†Normandiet	1,843	30	English Channel	Submarine	Torpedo	Missed	—
†Poldennis	3,539	30	Mediterranean	Submarine	Chased	Speed	—
JULY 1917.		July					
†Tintoretto	4,181	1	Atlantic	Submarine	Torpedo	Missed	—
†Demerara	11,484	1	Bay of Biscay	Submarine	Torpedoed	Beached	1
†Bayvoe	2,979	3	English Channel	Submarine	Torpedo	Missed	—
†Lingneld	4,065	4	English Channel	Submarine	Gunfire	Gun and weather.	—
†Miniota	4,928	4	N.W. Ireland	Submarine	Gunfire	Gun	—
†Gladstone (Tug)	214	4	N.W. of Ireland	Submarine	Chased	Gun	—
†Cowrie	4,893	4	S.W. Ireland	Submarine	Torpedo	Missed	—
†Clan Macintosh	4,774	5	Entrance to English Channel.	Submarine	Gunfire	Gun	—
†Eburna	4,735	5	Mediterranean	Submarine	Torpedoed	Arrived	—
†Karroo	6,127	6	English Channel	Submarine	Torpedo	Missed	—
†Ariadne Christine	3,550	6	English Channel	Submarine	Torpedoed	Beached	—
†Wabasha	5,864	6	English Channel	Submarine	Torpedoed	Arrived	2
†Glenturret	4,696	6	Atlantic	Submarine	Gunfire	Gun	—
†Siamese Prince	4,847	6	Atlantic	Submarine	Chased	Gun	—
†Hero	1,812	7	W. Ireland	Submarine	Chased	Gun	—
†Coblenz	1,338	7	Atlantic	Submarine	Torpedo; Gunfire.	Missed; gun	1
Onitsha	3,921	8	West of Ireland	Submarine	Torpedo	Missed	—
†Plutarch	5,613	8	N.W. Ireland	Submarine	Torpedo	Missed	—
†Clifftower	3,509	8	English Channel	Submarine	Torpedo	Missed	—
†Cuthbert	3,834	8	S.W. Ireland	Submarine	Chased	Gun	—
†Manitou	6,849	8	Mediterranean	Submarine	Torpedo	Missed	—
†Clan Chisholm	2,647	8	Atlantic	Submarine	Chased	Gun	—
†Peebles	4,284	8	Off Ushant	Submarine	Gunfire	Gun	—
Jarrix	429	9	North Sea	Seaplanes	Torpedo	Missed	—
Largo	1,764	9	N. Scotland	Submarine	Chased	Smoke apparatus.	—
†Haslingden	1,934	9	North Sea	Seaplane	Torpedo	Missed	—
†Battersea	860	9	North Sea	Seaplane	Torpedo	Missed	—
†Hartley	1,150	9	North Sea	Seaplane	Torpedo	Missed	—
†Flamma	1,920	10	North Sea	Mine	Mine	Beached	—
Grosvenor	267	11	Dunkirk Harbour	Aircraft	Bombs	Missed	—
†Mercian	6,305	12	S. Ireland	Submarine	Torpedo	Missed	—
†Tredegar Hall	3,764	12	Off Ushant	Submarine	Torpedo; Gunfire.	Missed; Gun.	—
†Mile End	859	12	North Sea	Submarine	Chased	Gunfire	—
†Dunrobin	3,617	12	Channel	Submarine	Torpedo; Gunfire.	Missed; gun.	—
†Nellore	6,853	13	Mediterranean	Submarine	Torpedo	Missed	—
†Elstree Grange	3,930	13	Atlantic	Submarine	Chased	Gun	—
†Pentwyn	3,587	13	S. Ireland	Submarine	Torpedo	Missed	—
†Rhesus	6,704	14	S.W. Ireland	Submarine	Torpedo	Missed	—
†Kelbergen	4,751	14	Atlantic	Submarine	Gunfire	Gun	—
†Westmeath	9,179	15	English Channel	Submarine	Torpedoed	Arrived	—
†Incemore	3,060	15	Mediterranean	Submarine	Torpedoed	Arrived	—
†Abinsi	6,365	15	S.W. Ireland	Submarine	Torpedo	Missed	—
†Leeds City	4,298	15	Off Ushant	Submarine	Torpedo	Missed	—
†Agamemnon	7,011	16	S.W. Ireland	Submarine	Chased	Gun	—
†Benguela	5,520	16	N.W. Ireland	Submarine	Torpedo; gunfire.	Missed; gun.	—
†Saturnia	8,611	16	S.W. Ireland	Submarine	Torpedo	Missed	—
†Khiva	8,947	16	Mediterranean	Submarine	Torpedo	Missed	—
†Virent	3,771	17	Mediterranean	Submarine	Torpedoed	Beached	—
†Kaiser-i-Hind	11,430	17	S.W. Scilly	Submarine	Torpedo	Missed	—
†City of Canton	6,692	18	N.W. Scotland	Submarine	Gunfire	Gun	—
†Blakemoor	3,752	19	S.W. Ireland	Submarine	Torpedo	Missed	—
†Loch Lomond	2,619	19	Mediterranean	Submarine	Torpedoes	Missed	—
†Polyphemus	4,968	20	W. Scotland	Submarine	Torpedo	Missed	—
†Hurtsend	8,826	20	Entrance to English Channel.	Submarine	Chased	Speed	—
†Ceramic	18,481	21	Bristol Channel	Submarine	Chased	Rescued	—

MERCHANT VESSELS ATTACKED.

Name.	Gross Tons.	Date.	Position.	Attacked by	How attacked.	How saved.	Lives lost.
		1917. July.					
†Polyphemus	4,968	21	W. Scotland	Submarine	Torpedo	Missed	—
†Volodia	5,689	21	W. Scilly Is.	Submarine	Chased	Gun	—
†Highland Monarch.	3,931	22	Mediterranean	Submarine	Torpedo	Missed	—
†Yearby	2,639	22	English Channel	Submarine	Torpedo	Missed	—
†Corinthic	12,343	22	English Channel	Submarine	Chased	Speed	—
†Waipara	6,393	23	S.W. Ireland	Submarine	Torpedo	Missed	—
†Paul Paix	4,196	25	Off S. Ireland	Submarine	Torpedo	Missed	—
†Effra	1,325	25	North Sea	Submarine	Torpedo	Missed	—
Stettin	876	25	North Sea	Submarine	Torpedo	Missed	—
†Baynyassa	4,937	25	Atlantic	Submarine	Gunfire	Gun	—
†Ryde	3,556	26	Atlantic	Submarine	Gunfire	Gun	—
†Ethelwynne	3,230	26	North Sea	Mine	Mine	Towed in	—
†Khiva	8,947	27	Atlantic	Submarine	Chased	Speed	—
†Bellagio	3,919	27	English Channel	Submarine	Torpedoed	Beached	1
†Ocamo	1,910	27	Atlantic	Submarine	Torpedo	Missed	—
†Ardgryfe	4,897	27	Atlantic	Submarine	Gunfire	Gun	—
†Comanchee	5,588	28	N.W. Ireland	Submarine	Torpedoed	Arrived	—
†Tabchee	6,508	28	N.W. Ireland	Submarine	Torpedo	Missed	—
†Alexandra	3,865	28	W. from Ushant	Submarine	Gunfire	Gun	—
†Livonia	1,879	28	W. from Ushant	Submarine	Gunfire	Gun	—
†Saturnia	8,611	29	Atlantic	Submarine	Torpedo	Missed	—
†Ajana	7,759	29	N.W. Ireland	Submarine	Chased	Speed	—
†Devona	3,779	30	Atlantic	Submarine	Gunfire	Gun	—
†Karina	4,222	30	W. Ireland	Submarine	Torpedo	Missed	—
†Excellence Pleske.	2,059	30	Mediterranean	Submarine	Torpedo	Missed	—
†Beacon Grange	4,237	31	W. Ireland	Submarine	Gunfire	Gun	1
†Hunsbrook	4,463	31	W. Ireland	Submarine	Torpedo Gunfire	Missed Gun.	—
†Worsley Hall	3,489	31	Atlantic	Submarine	Torpedo; Gunfire.	Missed; gun and smoke.	—
†Hannah	3,697	31	Dunkirk Harbour	Aircraft	Bomb	Slightly damaged.	—
AUGUST 1917.		Aug.					
†Rokeby	3,786	1	Mediterranean	Mine	Mine	Towed in	—
†Glamorgan	3,539	1	West from Gibraltar.	Submarine	Torpedo	Missed	—
†City of Colombo	6,000	1	Atlantic	Submarine	Gunfire	Gun	—
†Tarantia	4,754	2	Off Ushant	Submarine	Gunfire	Gun	—
†El Cordobes	5,683	2	Atlantic	Submarine	Chased	Speed	—
†Newby Hall	4,391	3	West Ireland	Submarine	Chased	Rescued	—
†City of Colombo	6,000	4	Atlantic	Submarine	Chased	Gun	—
†Mahronda	7,630	4	Atlantic	Submarine	Gunfire	Gun	—
†Eda	2,525	5	North Sea	Submarine	Chased	Gun	—
†Welshman	5,730	6	Off Ushant	Submarine	Torpedo	Missed	—
†Zamora	3,639	6	North Sea	Submarine	Torpedoed	Towed in	1
†Scarlet Tower	3,187	6	Atlantic	2 Submarines	Gunfire	Gun	—
†Inveric	4,789	6	Atlantic	Submarine	Gunfire	Gun	—
†Naukin	6,853	7	English Channel	Submarine	Torpedo	Missed	—
Emlyn	370	7	North Sea	Submarine	Gunfire	Attack abandoned.	—
†Morinier	3,804	8	Mediterranean	Submarine	Torpedo	Failed to explode.	—
†Alster	964	8	North Sea	Submarine	Torpedo	Missed	—
†Canara	6,012	9	Mediterranean	Submarine	Torpedoed	Towed in	9
†Oakfield	3,618	9	South of Ireland	Submarine	Torpedoed	Reached port	—
†Belgic	24,540	11	South of Ireland	Submarine	Torpedo	Missed	—
†Lowther Range	3,926	11	N.W. Scotland	Submarine	Torpedo	Missed	—
†Parattah	4,196	11	Atlantic	Submarine	Chased	Attack abandoned.	—
†Camito	6,611	13	N.W. Ireland	Mine	Mine	Reached port	—
†Leafield	2,539	14	English Channel	Submarine	Torpedo	Missed	—
†Ardeola	3,140	14	West of Ireland	Submarine	Torpedo	Missed	—
†Normandiet	1,858	14	Bristol Channel	Submarine	Gunfire	Gun	—
†Natica	5,579	14	Bristol Channel	Submarine	Torpedo	Missed	—
†Induna	4,426	14	Off N.W. Ireland	Submarine	Torpedo	Missed	—
†Manchuria	2,997	15	S.W. from Scilly	Submarine	Chased	Speed and weather.	—
†Rapallo	3,810	15	Atlantic	Submarine	Chased	Attack abandoned.	—
†Flaminian	3,227	15	Mediterranean	Submarine	Torpedo	Missed	—
†Blakemoor	3,752	15	Atlantic	Submarine	Torpedo	Missed	—

MERCHANT VESSELS ATTACKED. 148

Name.	Gross Tons.	Date.	Position.	Attacked by	How attacked.	How saved.	Lives lost.
		1917. Aug.					
†Eastgate	4,277	16	Atlantic	Submarine	Torpedoed	Reached port	—
†Horseferry	1,812	17	North Sea	Submarine	Chased	Gun	—
†Ricardo A. Mestres.	4,468	17	Atlantic	Submarine	Torpedo	Missed	—
†Ovid	4,159	18	S.W. from Cape Spartel.	Submarine	Torpedo	Missed	—
†Cliftonhall	3,900	19	Atlantic	Submarine	Torpedo ; gunfire.	Missed ; gun	—
†Waimana	7,852	19	Atlantic	Submarine	Chased	Gun	—
†Winifredian	10,422	19	North of Ireland	Submarine	Torpedo	Missed	—
†Canopic	12,097	19	Mediterranean	Submarine	Chased	Gun	—
†Vasari	10,117	21	N.W. Ireland	Submarine	Torpedo	Missed	—
†Trongate	2,553	22	Atlantic	Submarine	Torpedo	Missed	—
†Lundy	2,857	23	Mediterranean	Submarine	Torpedo	Missed	—
†Manxman	4,827	23	W. from Gibraltar	Submarine	Torpedo	Missed	—
†Baron Fairlie	3,593	25	Atlantic	Submarine	Chased	Gun	—
†Glenturret	4,696	25	Atlantic	Submarine	2 Torpedoes	Missed	—
†Polwell	2,013	25	Atlantic	Submarine	Torpedo	Missed	—
†Cherryleaf	5,896	25	English Channel	Submarine	Torpedo	Missed	—
†Hercules	1,095	26	North Sea	Submarine	Torpedo	Missed	—
Bhamo	5,244	26	Off Cape Agulhas	Mine	Mine	Reached port.	—
†Luga	1,988	26	North Sea	Submarine	Chased	Rescued	—
†Kurdistan	3,720	27	North Sea	Submarine	Torpedo	Missed	—
†Devon City	4,316	29	English Channel	Submarine	2 torpedoes	Missed	—
†Clifftower	3,509	29	Mediterranean	Submarine	Torpedoed	Towed in	—
†Ardendearg	3,237	29	Atlantic	Submarine	Gunfire	Gun	—
†Novington	3,442	29	E. from Shetlands	Submarine	Torpedo	Failed to explode.	—
†Haslemere	2,180	31	Mediterranean	Submarine	Chased	Gun	—
SEPTEMBER 1917.		Sept.					
†Arrino	4,484	1	Atlantic	Submarine	Gunfire	Gun	—
†Orangemoor	4,134	2	Dunkirk Harbour	Aircraft	Bombs	Damaged	—
†Umgeni	2,622	3	North of Shetland	2 Submarines	Gunfire	Gun	—
†Datchet	3,076	3	Mediterranean	Submarine	Chased	Gun	—
†Siamese Prince	4,847	4	Bay of Biscay	Submarine	Torpedo	Missed	—
†Lady Cloe	1,581	4	English Channel	Submarine	Chased	Speed	—
†San Dunstano	6,220	5	English Channel	Submarine	Torpedoed	Reached port.	1
†Colin Stuart	659	6	English Channel	Submarine	Torpedo	Missed	—
†Aldershot	2,177	6	Bay of Biscay	Submarine	Torpedo	Missed	—
†Pearleaf	5,919	6	N.W. Scotland	Submarine	Chased	Gun	—
†Brodmead	5,646	7	West from Gibraltar.	Submarine	Torpedoed	Reached port.	12 including Master.
†St. Edmund	1,223	7	Off Scilly Islands	Submarine	Chased	Gun	—
†Grelfryda	5,136	7	North Sea	Submarine	Torpedoed	Beached	—
†Scottish Prince	2,897	7	English Channel	Submarine	Torpedoed	Reached port.	—
Brunla	750	7	English Channel	Submarine	Torpedo	Missed	—
†Myrmidon	4,965	7	Mediterranean	Submarine	Torpedoed	Beached	2
†Tropic	8,230	7	English Channel	Submarine	Torpedo	Missed	—
†Huntsclyde	2,705	8	English Channel	Submarine	Chased	Gun	—
†Nina	1,082	8	North Sea	Submarine	Gunfire	Gun	—
†Tuscarora	7,106	9	Atlantic	Submarine	Torpedoed	Reached port.	3
†Knowsley Hall	4,190	10	West from Gibraltar.	Submarine	Gunfire	Rescued	—
†Parana	4,182	10	Atlantic	Submarine	Torpedo ; Gunfire.	Missed ; Rescued.	—
†Ioanna	3,459	10	Bristol Channel	Submarine	Torpedoed	Reached port.	—
†Margarita	2,788	10	East Shetland	Mine	Mine	Towed in	—
†Cento	3,708	11	South Ireland	Submarine	Torpedoed	Reached	2
†British Transport.	4,143	11	Atlantic	Submarine	2 torpedoes ; gunfire.	Missed ; gun	—
†Johan Siem	1,660	12	Bristol Channel	Submarine	Gunfire	Gun	—
†Glenelg	4,160	12	East Shetland	Mine	Mine	Towed in	1
†Usher	3,594	12	Mediterranean	Submarine	Gunfire	Gun	—
†Hyndford	4,286	13	West from Gibraltar.	Submarine	Gunfire	Speed and darkness.	—

MERCHANT VESSELS ATTACKED.

Name.	Gross Tons.	Date.	Position.	Attacked by	How attacked.	How saved.	Lives lost.
		1917. Sept.					
†Rossia	4,576	13	North Scotland	Submarine	Gunfire	Gun	—
†Bengali	5,684	13	Mediterranean	Submarine	Torpedoed	Reached port.	1
†Thetis	649	13	English Channel	Submarine	Chased	Gun	—
†Ada	3,821	13	Mediterranean	Submarine	Chased	Gun	—
†Iolanthe	3,081	14	North Shetlands	Submarine	Torpedo; Chased.	Missed; Gun.	—
†Idomeneus	6,692	15	West Scotland	Submarine	Torpedoed	Beached	4
†Orangemoor	4,134	17	South Ireland	Submarine	Torpedo	Missed	—
†City of Lincoln	5,867	18	S.W. Scilly	Submarine	Torpedoed	Towed in	9
†Admiral Cochrane.	6,600	18	North Sea	Submarine	Torpedo	Missed	—
†Isleworth	2,871	18	North Scotland	Submarine	Chased	Weather and darkness.	—
†Monkshaven	3,357	19	North Sea	Submarine	Torpedo	Missed	—
†Roumanian Prince.	4,147	19	N.W. Ireland	Submarine	Torpedo	Missed	—
†Greldon	3,322	20	English Channel	Submarine	Torpedo	Missed	—
†Taywood	505	21	South Ireland	Submarine	Gunfire	Gun	—
†Aldworth	3,369	22	Atlantic	Submarine	Torpedo	Missed	—
†North Britain	3,679	22	Atlantic	Submarine	Gunfire	Gun	—
†Empire	4,496	23	Mediterranean	Submarine	Chased	Gun	—
†Mary Maud (S.V.).	85	23	St. George's Channel.	Submarine	Gunfire	Attack abandoned.	—
†Petersham	3,381	24	N. Ireland	Submarine	Gunfire	Gun	—
†Auricula	815	24	Bay of Biscay	Submarine	Torpedo	Missed	—
Mary Grace (S.V.).	58	24	South Ireland	Submarine	Gunfire	Towed in	—
†Paliki	1,578	24	North Sea	Submarine	Torpedo	Missed	—
†Elve	899	24	Atlantic	Submarine	Chased	Attack abandoned.	—
†Elve	899	25	Atlantic	Submarine	Chased	Attack abandoned.	—
†Polescar	5,832	25	Dunkirk Harbour	Aircraft	Bombs	Damaged	2
†Craonne	4,264	25	Atlantic	Submarine	Gunfire	Gun and smoke.	—
†San Zeferino	6,430	26	St. George's Channel.	Submarine	Torpedoed	Reached port.	3
†Port Victor	7,280	26	English Channel	Submarine	Torpedoed	Reached port	—
†Barima	1,498	26	S.W. Scilly Ids.	Submarine	Chased	Speed	—
Portaferry	236	26	North Sea	Submarine	Torpedo	Missed	—
†Chao Chow Fu	1,909	27	Mediterranean	Submarine	Torpedo	Missed	—
†Genesee	2,892	27	North Sea	Submarine	Torpedo	Missed	—
†William Middleton.	2,543	28	St. George's Channel.	Mine	Mine	Reached port.	2
†North Britain	3,679	29	West from Gibraltar.	Submarine	Torpedo	Missed	—
†Benavon	3,996	30	Atlantic	Submarine	Gunfire	Gun	—
†Cronstadt	1,674	30	Atlantic	Submarine	Gunfire	Gun	—
†Vigo	4,224	30	Atlantic	Submarine	Gunfire	Gun	—
OCTOBER 1917.		Oct.					
†Copenhagen	4,540	1	Atlantic	Submarine	Gunfire	Gun	—
†Clydebrae	502	2	North Sea	Submarine	Torpedoed	Beached	5 including Master.
†Devereux	1,371	2	North Sea	Submarine	Chased	Gun	—
†Verdun	5,691	4	English Channel	Submarine	Torpedo	Missed	—
†Kaffir Prince	2,228	4	Atlantic	Submarine	Chased	Darkness	—
†Le Coq	3,419	6	Bay of Biscay	Mine	Mine	Towed in	—
Harborne	1,278	7	English Channel	Submarine	Torpedo	Missed	—
H.S. 48 (Tug)	—	9	West from Gibraltar.	Submarine	Torpedo	Missed	—
†Boston City	2,711	11	Off N. Ireland	Submarine	Torpedo	Missed	—
†Cape Corso	3,890	12	Bristol Channel	Submarine	Torpedoed	Towed in	13
†Fleswick	648	13	St. George's Channel.	Submarine	Torpedo	Missed	—
†Newquay	4,191	13	North Sea	Submarine	Torpedoed	Towed in	—
Woodburn	2,360	13	English Channel	Submarine	Torpedoed	Arrived in port.	—
†Andorinha	2,548	13	South Ireland	Submarine	Torpedo	Failed to explode.	—
†Daghild	8,000	14	English Channel	Submarine	Torpedo	Missed	—
†Ethyl	3,082	14	Atlantic	Submarine	Gunfire	Gun	—

Merchant Vessels Attacked.

Name.	Gross Tons.	Date.	Position.	Attacked by	How attacked.	How saved.	Lives lost.
		1917. Oct.					
†Carmelite	2,583	15	Off Land's End	Submarine	Torpedo	Missed	—
†San Nazario	10,064	15	S.W. from Scilly	Submarine	Torpedoed	Reached port.	—
†Sealda	5,382	15	W. from Ushant	Submarine	Torpedo	Missed	—
†Leander	2,793	15	English Channel	Submarine	Torpedoed	Towed in	—
†Netherpark	4,362	15	W. from Ushant	Submarine	Torpedo	Missed	—
†Sealda	5,382	16	Atlantic	Submarine	Torpedo; Gunfire.	Missed; Gun.	—
Goorkha (hospital ship).	6,335	17	Mediterranean	Mine	Mine	Arrived in port.	—
†Domino	1,120	17	North Sea	Submarine	Torpedo	Missed	—
†Dallington	2,534	18	English Channel	Submarine	Torpedo	Missed	—
†Wellington	5,600	19	English Channel	Submarine	Torpedoed	Arrived in port.	—
†Orna	4,783	19	Atlantic	Submarine	Torpedo; gunfire.	Missed	—
†Teespool	4,577	19	English Channel	Submarine	Torpedoed	Beached	4
†Wearside	3,560	19	North Sea	Submarine	Torpedo	Missed	—
†Frank Parish	2,893	20	North Sea	Submarine	Torpedo	Failed to explode.	—
†Maidan	8,205	20	Mediterranean	Submarine	Torpedo	Missed	—
†Domino	1,120	20	North Sea	Submarine	Torpedo	Missed	—
†Burma	7,470	20	Mediterranean	Submarine	Torpedo	Missed	—
†St. Fillans	4,622	21	English Channel	Submarine	Torpedo	Missed	—
†Sportsman	572	21	North Sea	Submarine	Torpedo	Missed	—
†Silverlip	9,718	21	N W. Scotland	Submarine	Torpedo	Missed	—
†Mapleleaf	8,039	21	Atlantic	Submarine	Torpedo	Missed	—
Comeric	3,979	22	Atlantic	Submarine	Torpedo	Missed	—
†Lepanto	6,389	23	English Channel	Submarine	Torpedoed	Arrived in port.	2
†Novington	3,442	24	East Shetlands	Submarine	Torpedoed	Beached	—
†Kalo	1,957	25	Mediterranean	Submarine	Torpedo; Gunfire	Missed; Gun.	—
†Clermiston	1,282	26	Mediterranean	Submarine	Torpedo	Missed	—
†Lightfoot	1,875	26	North Sea	Submarine	Chased	Weather	—
†Canadian	2,214	27	Mediterranean	Submarine	Torpedo	Missed	—
†Denebola	1,481	28	North Sea	Submarine	Torpedo	Missed	—
Elwick	1,717	28	English Channel	Submarine	Torpedo	Missed	—

NOVEMBER 1917.

Name.	Gross Tons.	Date.	Position.	Attacked by	How attacked.	How saved.	Lives lost.
		Nov.					
†Margam Abbey	4,367	1	Mediterranean	Submarine	Torpedoed	Beached	2
†Branksome Hall	4,262	2	English Channel	Submarine	Torpedoed	Beached	—
†St. Agnes	1,195	2	North Sea	Submarine	Chased	Fog	—
†Atlantian	9,399	3	Irish Channel	Submarine	Torpedoed	Reached port	—
†Rodskjaer	2,724	3	English Channel	Submarine	Gunfire	Gun	—
†Lucida	1,477	4	North Sea	Submarine	Torpedoed	Beached	4
†Clan Cumming	4,808	5	English Channel	Submarine	Torpedoed	Towed in	13
†Amberton	4,556	5	Mediterranean	Submarine	Torpedoed	Beached	—
†Eider	1,236	5	North Sea	Submarine	Torpedo	Missed	—
†Benledi	3,931	8	W. from Gibraltar	Submarine	Torpedo; gunfire.	Missed; gun	1
†Derwent River	4,724	8	W. from Gibraltar	Submarine	Chased	Gun	—
†Clan Macneil	3,939	9	W. from Gibraltar	Submarine	Torpedo	Missed	—
†Appleleaf	5,891	10	North Sea	Mine	Mine	Towed in	—
†Inniscarra	1,412	11	St. George's Chan.	Submarine	Torpedo	Missed	—
†Southgate	3,661	11	Mediterranean	Mine	Mine	Reached port	—
†Cavallo	2,086	12	English Channel	Submarine	Chased	Gun	—
†Southgare	818	12	North Sea	Submarine	Chased	Gun	—
†Baysarua	4,986	15	Mediterranean	Submarine	Torpedo	Missed	—
†Glenfruin	3,097	16	Mediterranean	Submarine	Torpedo	Missed	—
†Abaris	2,892	17	English Channel	Submarine	Torpedoed	Towed in	5
†David Lloyd George.	4,764	17	English Channel	Submarine	Torpedoed	Reached port	—
†Huntsgulf	3,185	18	Mediterranean	Submarine	Torpedoed	Reached port	—
†Marie Suzanne	3,106	19	Atlantic	Submarine	Gunfire	Gun	—
†City of Chester	5,413	19	English Channel	Submarine	Torpedo	Missed	—
					Torpedo	Failed to explode.	
†Carpentaria	7,755	19	English Channel	Submarine	Torpedo	Missed	—
†Rathlin	1,321	19	St. George's Chan.	Submarine	Chased	Speed	—
†Breynton	4,240	21	St. George's Chan.	Submarine	Torpedoed	Reached port	—

MERCHANT VESSELS ATTACKED.

Name.	Gross Tons.	Date.	Position.	Attacked by	How attacked.	How saved.	Lives lost.
		1917. Nov.					
†Kenmare	1,330	21	Irish Channel	Submarine	Torpedo	Missed	—
†Ubbergen	1,877	21	Mediterranean	Submarine	Torpedo	Missed	—
†Sardinia	6,580	21	Mediterranean	Submarine	Torpedo	Missed	—
†Redbridge	3,834	22	St. George's Chan.	Submarine	Torpedoed	Reached port	—
†Hartland	4,785	22	St. George's Chan.	Submarine	Torpedoed	Reached port	2
†Canonesa	5,583	22	English Channel	Submarine	Torpedo	Missed	—
†Boma	2,694	23	English Channel	Submarine	Chased	Speed	—
†Benue	4,408	23	Irish Channel	Submarine	Torpedo	Missed	—
†Rutherglen	4,214	24	Atlantic	Submarine	Chased	Speed	—
†Quaysider	595	26	English Channel	Submarines	Gunfire	Gun	—
†Crenella	7,035	26	S.W. Ireland	Submarine	Torpedoed	Reached port	—
†Flavia	9,291	26	S.W. Ireland	Submarine	Torpedo	Missed	—
†Thornhill	3,848	27	Mediterranean	Submarine	Torpedoed	Beached	1
†Glenbridge	3,845	27	Mediterranean	Submarine	Torpedoed	Beached	—
†Upcerne	2,984	27	Irish Sea	Submarine	Torpedo	Missed	—
†Herschel	6,293	27	Mediterranean	Submarine	Torpedo	Missed	—
†Glenrazan	4,044	27	English Channel	Submarine	Torpedo	Missed	—
†Kirkholm	4,753	28	English Channel	Submarine	Torpedo	Missed	—
†Agenoria	2,977	28	Irish Channel	Submarine	Torpedoed	Beached	1
†Madeline	2,890	29	Bay of Biscay	Submarine	Torpedo	Missed	—
†Exmouth	3,923	29	Mediterranean	Submarine	Torpedo	Failed to explode.	—
†Linhope	1,339	29	North Sea	Submarine	Chased	Gun	—
†Carrigan Head	4,201	29	English Channel	Submarine	Torpedo	Missed	—
†Somersby	3,647	30	Bristol Channel	Submarine	Gunfire	Gun	—
†Nunima	2,938	30	Bristol Channel	Submarine	Torpedo	Missed	—
DECEMBER 1917.		Dec.					
†Helenus	7,555	1	English Channel	Submarine	Torpedoed	Towed in	—
†Cretic	13,518	1	West from Gibraltar.	Submarine	Chased	Speed	—
†Bonvilston	2,866	1	English Channel	Submarine	Torpedo	Missed	—
†El Uruguayo	8,361	2	English Channel	Submarine	Torpedo	Missed	—
†The Countess	624	3	South Ireland	Submarine	Torpedo	Missed	—
†Leafield	2,539	3	Irish Channel	Submarine	Chased	Speed	—
†Lord Dufferin	4,664	3	Mediterranean	Submarine	Torpedo; Gunfire.	Missed. Gun.	—
†Milton	3,267	4	St. George's Channel.	Submarine	Torpedo	Reached port	1
†Manchester Mariner.	4,106	4	English Channel	Mine	Mine	Mine defence.	—
Dolphin	353	5	Calais	Aircraft	Bomb	Slightly damaged.	—
†Earlswood	2,353	5	English Channel	Submarine	Torpedoed	Reached port	2
†Oneida	698	5	English Channel	Submarine	Torpedo	Missed	—
†Excellence Pleske.	2,059	5	Mediterranean	Submarine	Torpedo	Missed	—
†Llangorse	4,703	5	Mediterranean	Submarine	Torpedo	Missed	—
†Dundalk	794	6	Irish Channel	Submarine	Gunfire	Gun	—
†Linhope	1,339	7	North Sea	Submarine	Torpedo	Missed	—
†Benlawers	3,949	7	North Sea	Submarine	Torpedo	Missed	—
†Chyebassa	6,249	8	Mediterranean	Submarine	Torpedoed	Reached port	—
†Sedbergh	4,230	9	English Channel	Submarine	Torpedoed	Towed in	1
†Nyanza	6,695	9	English Channel	Submarine	Torpedoed	Reached port	49
†Eros	1,843	9	English Channel	Submarine	Torpedo	Failed to explode.	—
†Darino	1,359	9	North Sea	Submarine	2 torpedoes	Missed	—
†Aureole	3,998	10	West Scotland	Mine	Mine	Reached port	—
†Bayusona	986	10	English Channel	Submarine	Gunfire	Gun	—
†Penmount	2,314	10	English Channel	Submarine	Torpedo	Missed	—
†Gwynwood	1,084	10	North Sea	Submarine	Torpedo	Missed	—
†Eastern City	5,992	11	Mediterranean	Submarine	Gunfire	Gun	—
†Occident	813	13	North Sea	Submarine	Torpedo	Failed to explode.	—
†Torquay	870	14	North Sea	Submarine	Torpedo	Missed	—
†Newhailes	1,423	14	North Sea	Submarine	Torpedo	Missed	—
†Sachem	5,354	15	English Channel	Submarine	Torpedoed	Reached port	—
†Ninian	6,385	15	English Channel	Submarine	Torpedo	Missed	—
†Australpeak	4,432	15	Atlantic	Submarine	Torpedo	Missed	—
†North Britain	3,679	15	Atlantic	Submarine	Torpedo	Missed	—
†Hungerford	5,811	16	Mediterranean	Submarine	2 torpedoes	Missed	—
†Novian	6,368	17	Atlantic	Submarine	Torpedo	Missed	—
†Kenmare	1,330	18	Irish Channel	Submarine	Chased	Gun	—
†Kaisar-i-Hind	11,430	18	W. from Gibraltar	Submarine	Torpedo	Missed	—

MERCHANT VESSELS ATTACKED.

Name.	Gross Tons.	Date.	Position.	Attacked by	How attacked.	How saved.	Lives lost.
		1917. Dec.					
†Trevelyan	3,066	19	English Channel	Submarine	Torpedoed	Beached	—
†Baron Cathcart	1,860	19	Irish Channel	Submarine	Torpedo	Missed	—
†Teesbridge	3,898	19	Atlantic	Submarine	Gunfire	Gun	—
†Seattle	5,133	20	Mediterranean	Submarine	Gunfire Torpedo	Gun - Missed.	—
†Polaria	3,546	20	Mediterranean	Submarine	Gunfire	Gun	—
†Sorrento	2,892	20	Mediterranean	Submarine	Gunfire	Gun	—
†Yang-Tsze	6,457	21	Irish Channel	Submarine	Torpedo	Missed	—
†Relillio	2,398	21	English Channel	Submarine	Torpedo	Missed	—
†Mabel Baird	2,500	21	Bristol Channel	Submarine	Torpedo	Missed	—
†Hunsbrook	4,463	22	Bristol Channel	Submarine	Torpedoed	Beached	3
†Cypria	2,950	22	Irish Channel	Submarine	Torpedo	Missed	—
Elwick	1,717	23	Bristol Channel	Submarine	2 torpedoes	Missed	—
†Dunedin	4,796	23	Mediterranean	Mine	Mine	Towed in	—
†Dorie	3,264	23	Irish Channel	Submarine	Chased	Attack abandoned.	—
†Elmleaf	5,948	24	N.W. Scotland	Submarine	Torpedoed	Reached port	—
†Luciston	2,877	24	English Channel	Submarine	Torpedoed	Beached	—
†Hyacinthus	5,756	25	English Channel	Submarine	Torpedoed	Reached port	—
†Modesta	3,832	25	English Channel	Submarine	Torpedo	Missed	—
†Asiatic Prince	2,887	26	English Channel	Submarine	Torpedo	Missed	—
Leinster	2,646	27	Irish Channel	Submarine	Torpedo	Missed	—
†Battersea	860	28	North Sea	Submarine	Chased	Gun	—
†Inverness	3,734	29	North Sea	Submarine	Torpedoed	Reached port	—
†Broompark	2,126	30	English Channel	Submarine	Torpedo	Missed	—
†Baron Inchcape	7,005	30	Mediterranean	Submarine	Torpedo	Missed	—
†Bathampton	3,282	31	English Channel	Submarine	Torpedo	Missed	—
†Devonshire	500	31	St. George's Channel.	Submarine	Torpedo	Missed	—

JANUARY 1918.

Name.	Gross Tons.	Date.	Position.	Attacked by	How attacked.	How saved.	Lives lost.
		Jan.					
†Genesee	2,892	1	North Sea	Submarine	Torpedoed	Reached port	—
†Egyptian Transport.	4,648	1	Mediterranean	Submarine	Torpedoed	Beached	5
†Fleswick	648	1	Irish Channel	Submarine	Gunfire	Gun	—
†Kingsley	633	2	English Channel	Submarine	Gunfire	Gun	5
†El Paraguayo	8,508	2	Bristol Channel	Submarine	Torpedo	Missed	—
†Enda	842	2	Irish Channel	Submarine	Torpedo; Gunfire.	Missed; Gun.	—
†Deneb	1,230	2	Bristol Channel	Submarine	Torpedo	Missed	—
†Beechleaf	5,861	3	Mediterranean	Submarine	Torpedo	Missed	—
Victor (S.V.)	163	4	Bristol Channel	Submarine	Gunfire	Rescued	—
†Newlands	3,012	5	Irish Channel	Submarine	Torpedo	Missed	—
Hong Moh	3,910	5	S.E. Arabia	Mine	Mine	Slight damage.	—
†Arca	4,839	6	English Channel	Submarine	Torpedoed	Reached port	—
†Portwood	2,241	9	English Channel	Submarine	Torpedo	Missed	—
†Cardiff	2,808	10	Bay of Biscay	Submarine	Torpedoed	Beached	8
†Gregynog	1,701	11	English Channel	Submarine	Torpedo	Missed	—
†Ramore Head	4,585	11	St. George's Channel.	Submarine	Chased	Gun	—
†Horsham	401	14	Great Yarmouth	T.B.D.	Gunfire	Damaged	1
†Hova	4,264	15	Mediterranean	Submarine	Torpedo	Missed	—
†Messidor	3,883	17	Bay of Biscay	Submarine	Torpedoed	Reached port	—
†War Thistle	5,166	17	English Channel	Submarine	Torpedoed	Reached port	—
†Izaston	3,060	17	North Sea	Submarine	Gunfire	Gun	—
†Hampstead	3,447	18	Mediterranean	Submarine	Gunfire	Gun	—
†War Anemone	5,214	18	English Channel	Submarine	Chased	Speed	—
†Dux	1,349	19	English Channel	Submarine	Torpedo	Missed	—
†Hunsgrove	3,063	19	English Channel	Submarine	Chased	Speed	—
†Saint Clair	621	19	North Sea	Submarine	Gunfire	Smoke and gun.	2
†Cumbrian	1,131	19	English Channel	Submarine	2 torpedoes	Failed to explode.	—
†Highland Loch	7,493	20	English Channel	Submarine	Torpedo	Missed	—
†Harmonides	3,521	20	English Channel	Submarine	Torpedoed	Reached port	—
†Isleworth	2,871	20	Bristol Channel	Submarine	Torpedo	Missed	—
†Queen Margaret	4,972	20	English Channel	Mine	Mine	Reached port	—
†Admiral Cochrane.	6,565	22	English Channel	Submarine	Torpedoed	Towed in	—
†Corton	3,405	22	English Channel	Submarine	Torpedoed	Towed in	3
†Chinkoa	5,222	22	English Channel	Submarine	Torpedo	Missed	—

MERCHANT VESSELS ATTACKED.

Name.	Gross Tons.	Date.	Position.	Attacked by	How attacked.	How saved.	Lives lost.
		1918. Jan.					
†Knight of the Garter.	6,689	22	Mediterranean	Submarine	Torpedo	Missed	—
†Nembe	3,855	23	Off Scilly Isles	Submarine	Chased	Weather	—
†Justicia	32,234	23	Irish Channel	Submarine	Torpedo	Missed	—
†Lackenby	2,108	25	English Channel	Submarine	Torpedo	Missed	—
†Alice M. Craig	916	25	North Sea	Submarine	Torpedo	Missed	—
†Manhattan	8,115	26	English Channel	Submarine	Torpedoed	Reached port	—
†Vestris	10,494	26	English Channel	Submarine	Torpedo	Missed	—
†Remus	1,079	26	North Sea	Submarine	Torpedo	Missed	—
†Sea Gull	976	27	Irish Channel	Submarine	Torpedo	Missed	—
†Dublin	711	28	Irish Channel	Submarine	Chased	Weather	—
†Ravonia	703	29	North Sea	Submarine	Torpedo	Missed	—
†Normannia	1,567	29	English Channel	Submarine	Torpedo	Missed	—
†Slieve Bawn	1,061	30	Irish Channel	Submarine	Torpedo	Missed	—
†Findhorn	1,122	30	Irish Channel	Submarine	Gunfire	Gun	—
†Brighton	3,463	30	Mediterranean	Submarine	2 Torpedoes	Missed	—
†Eggesford	4,414	31	Mediterranean	Submarine	Torpedoed	Reached port	—
†Starling	804	31	English Channel	Submarine	Chased	Gun	—
†Commonwealth	3,353	31	Mediterranean	Submarine	Torpedo	Missed	—

FEBRUARY 1918.

Name.	Gross Tons.	Date.	Position.	Attacked by	How attacked.	How saved.	Lives lost.
		Feb.					
†Glenamoy	7,269	1	Mediterranean	Submarine	Torpedoed	Reached port	—
†Chertsey	3,264	1	English Channel	Submarine	Torpedo	Missed	—
†Mourino	1,819	1	Bristol Channel	Submarine	Torpedo	Missed	—
†Levensau	2,155	3	North Sea	Submarine	Gunfire	Weather	—
†Petrograd	1,713	3	Bristol Channel	Submarine	2 Torpedoes	Failed to explode.	—
†Longertie	1,126	3	North Sea	Submarine	Torpedo	Missed	—
†Holmpark	1,468	3	North Sea	Submarine	Torpedo	Missed	—
†Ravenshoe	3,592	4	Mediterranean	Submarine	Torpedoed	Reached port.	—
†Euryades	5,713	4	Irish Channel	Submarine	Torpedo	Missed	—
Sardinia	6,580	4	Mediterranean	Submarine	Torpedoed	Reached port.	—
†General Church	6,600	4	Mediterranean	Submarine	Torpedoed	Reached port.	2
†Herefordshire	7,198	4	Mediterranean	Submarine	Torpedo	Missed	—
†Franklyn	4,919	5	Mediterranean	Submarine	Torpedo	Missed	—
†Westmoreland	9,512	6	Irish Channel	Submarine	Torpedoed	Beached	1
†Eda	2.525	7	Irish Channel	Submarine	Chased	Gun	—
†Sandhurst	3,034	8	Mediterranean	Submarine	Torpedo	Missed	—
Scotsman	181	8	Irish Channel	Submarine	Chased	Speed	—
†Oakdale	1,340	8	Irish Channel	Submarine	Gunfire	Gun	—
†Cimbrier	3,905	8	Mediterranean	Submarine	Torpedoed	Reached port.	—
†Sphynx	1,569	8	English Channel	Submarine	Torpedo	Missed	—
†Antenor	5,319	9	Mediterranean	Submarine	Torpedoed	Reached port.	—
†Pomaron	1,809	9	Irish Channel	Submarine	Torpedo	Missed	—
†Knight of the Garter.	6,689	11	English Channel	Submarine	2 Torpedoes	Missed	—
†Helenes	3,332	11	W. from Gibraltar	Submarine	Gunfire	Gun	—
†Swansea Vale	1,310	12	North Sea	Submarine	2 Torpedoes	1 missed; 1 failed to explode.	—
†Syndic	2,727	12	North Sea	Submarine	2 torpedoes	Missed	—
†Farnworth	5,896	12	Atlantic	Submarine	Gunfire	Gun	—
†Sarpen	1,864	13	Bristol Channel	Submarine	Torpedo	Missed	—
†Lackawanna	4,125	13	North Sea	Submarine	Torpedoed	Reached port.	—
Clarecastle	627	14	St. George's Chan.	Submarine	Torpedo	Missed	—
†Skaraas	1,625	14	English Channel	Submarine	Torpedo	Missed	—
†Skegness	2,801	15	North Sea	Submarine	2 torpedoes	Missed	—
†Thames	1,327	15	North Sea	Submarine	Torpedo	Missed	—
†Pikepool	3,683	16	English Channel	Submarine	Torpedoed	Reached port.	—
†Mountby	3,263	16	W. from Gibraltar	Submarine	Chased	Smoke	—
†Craonne	4,264	16	W. from Gibraltar	Submarine	Gunfire	Gun	—
†Lady Tennant	452	19	Bristol Channel	Submarine	Torpedo	Missed	—
†Athenic	4,078	19	North Sea	Submarine	Torpedoed	Towed in	—
†Elleric	3,559	20	Mediterranean	Submarine	Chased	Gun	—

MERCHANT VESSELS ATTACKED.   154

Name.	Gross Tons.	Date.	Position.	Attacked by	How attacked.	How saved.	Lives lost.
		1918. Feb.					
†Largo	1,764	22	English Channel	Submarine	Torpedo	Missed	—
†Birchleaf	5,873	23	Irish Channel	Submarine	Torpedoed	Beached	3 Master prisoner.
†Bellerby	3,089	23	English Channel	Submarine	Torpedo	Missed	—
†Courtfield	4,592	23	English Channel	Submarine	Torpedo	Missed	—
†Mirita	5,830	23	Atlantic	Submarine	Gunfire	Gun	—
†Nyanza	6,695	24	English Channel	Submarine	Torpedoed	Towed in	4
†Duke of Cumberland.	2,036	24	Irish Channel	Submarine	Torpedo	Missed	—
†Slieve Bawn	1,061	25	Irish Channel	Submarine	2 torpedoes	Missed	—
†Appalachee	3,767	25	North Ireland	Submarine	Torpedoed	Towed in	—
†Berwen	3,752	26	North Sea	Mine	Mine	Towed in	—
†Kerman	4,397	27	Mediterranean	Submarine	Torpedoed	Reached port.	—
†Marconi	7,402	27	Mediterranean	Submarine	Torpedoed	Reached port.	2
†Aulton	634	27	North Sea	Submarine	Torpedo	Missed	—
†Sheaf Field	1,533	27	Irish Channel	Submarine	2 torpedoes	Missed	—
†Benedict	3,378	27	Irish Channel	Submarine	Gunfire	Gun	—
Princess Irma	1,520	27	Off Hook of Holland.	Aircraft	Bomb	Missed	—
Kirkham Abbey	1,166	27	Off Hook of Holland.	Aircraft	Bomb	Missed	—
Lady Carmichael (tug).	—	27	Off Hook of Holland.	Aircraft	Bomb; machine gun.	Missed : slightly damaged.	—
MARCH 1918.		Mar.					
†Petroleine	4,217	2	Atlantic	Submarine	Gunfire	Gun	—
†Spey	470	2	Mediterranean	Submarine	Gunfire	Gun	—
†Dundarg (S.V.)	145	2	Irish Sea	Submarine	Gunfire	Gun	—
†Clan Graham	5,213	4	Mediterranean	Submarine	Torpedoed	Reached port	3
†British Princess	7,034	4	North Ireland	Submarine	Torpedoed	Reached port	1
†Silvia	2,035	4	North Sea	Submarine	2 torpedoes	Missed	—
†Clan Mackenzie	6,544	5	English Channel	Submarine	Torpedoed	Reached port	6
Blush Rose	645	5	North Sea	Submarine	2 torpedoes	Missed	—
†Kosseir	1,855	5	Mediterranean	Aircraft	—	—	—
†Gibel-Derif	804	5	English Channel	Submarine	Chased	Gun	—
Favorita Clara	512	6	Bay of Biscay	Submarine	Torpedo	Missed	—
†Bruse	1,711	6	North Sea	Submarine	Torpedo	Missed	—
†Lord Charlemont	3,209	6	English Channel	Submarine	Torpedo	Missed	—
†Cliffside	4,969	7	English Channel	Submarine	Torpedoed	Beached	—
†Volpone	531	7	English Channel	Submarine	Torpedo	Missed	—
†Saba	4,257	8	English Channel	Mine	Mine	Reached port	—
†Mitra	5,592	8	Mediterranean	Submarine	Torpedoed	Reached port	—
†Flixton	4,286	10	English Channel	Submarine	Torpedo	Missed	—
Guildford Castle (hospital ship).	8,036	10	Bristol Channel	Submarine	2 torpedoes	1 failed to explode, 1 missed.	—
†Nellore	6,853	11	W. from Gibraltar	Submarine	Gunfire	Speed	—
†Atlantic	3,016	11	Mediterranean	Submarine	Chased	Gun	—
†Clarissa Radcliffe	5,754	12	English Channel	Submarine	Torpedoed	Reached port	—
†Kerry	1,199	12	Irish Channel	Submarine	Torpedo	Missed	—
†Savan	4,264	12	English Channel	Submarine	Torpedoed	Reached port	1
†Herbert Fischer	938	13	North Sea	Submarine	Torpedo	Missed	—
†Umta	5,422	14	Mediterranean	Submarine	Torpedoed	Reached port	8
†Comrie Castle	5,173	14	English Channel	Submarine	Torpedoed	Beached	9
Silvia	2,035	15	North Sea	Submarine	Gunfire	Gun	—
†Portsea	3,283	15	S.W. from Madeira	Submarine	Chased	Speed	—
†Sheaf Brook	3,544	15	Mediterranean	Submarine	Torpedo	Missed	—
†Meissonier	7,206	16	W. from Gibraltar	Submarine	Gunfire	Speed	—
†Author	5,596	16	English Channel	Submarine	Torpedo	Slight damage.	—
Corbiere (motor)	22	17	English Channel	Submarine	Torpedo	Missed	—
†Lady Charlotte	3,593	17	Irish Channel	Submarine	Chased	Attack abandoned.	—
†Garryvale	3,917	17	Mediterranean	Submarine	2 torpedoes	Missed	—
†Navigator	3,803	18	English Channel	Submarine	Torpedo	Slight damage.	—
†Ibex	951	18	English Channel	Submarine	Chased	Gun	—
†Grainton	6,042	18	Irish Sea	Submarine	Torpedoed	Reached port	—

MERCHANT VESSELS ATTACKED.

Name.	Gross Tons.	Date.	Position.	Attacked by	How attacked.	How saved.	Lives lost.
		1918. Mar.					
†Longnewton	1,878	19	English Channel	Submarine	Torpedo	Missed	—
†Elysia	6,397	19	Mediterranean	Submarine	Torpedo	Missed	—
†Boorara	6,570	20	English Channel	Submarine	Torpedoed	Reached port	5
†Dunaff Head	5,877	20	Irish Chan..el	Submarine	Chased	Gun	—
†Custodian	9,214	20	Irish Channel	Submarine	Torpedoed	Reached port	3
†Lord Ormonde	3,914	20	Mediterranean	Submarine	Torpedoed	Reached port	—
†Western Australia.	2,937	20	English Channel	Submarine	Torpedo	Missed	—
†Hunsdon	2,899	21	English Channel	Submarine	Chased	Gun	—
†Morocco	3,783	21	English Channel	Submarine	Gunfire	Gun	—
†Stanja	1,845	21	English Channel	Submarine	Torpedo	Missed	—
†Ulster	2,641	22	Irish Channel	Submarine	Torpedo	Missed	—
†Lady Tennant	452	22	Irish Channel	Submarine	Gunfire	Gun	—
†Llanelly	369	22	St. George's Chan.	Submarine	Torpedo	Missed	—
†Chupra	6,175	22	East of the Azores	Submarine	Gunfire	Gun	—
†Demodocus	6,689	23	Mediterranean	Submarine	Torpedoed	Reached port	6
†Meline	6,970	23	North Sea	Submarine	Torpedoed	Reached port	—
†Mary Ann Mandal (S.V.).	112	23	English Channel	2 Submarines	Gunfire	Gun	—
†Mary Sinclair (S.V.).	118	23	English Channel	2 Submarines	Gunfire	Gun	—
†Sequoya	5,263	23	English Channel	Submarine	Torpedoed	Reached port	—
†Lucerna	3,247	23	Irish Channel	Submarine	Torpedo	Missed	—
†Morvada	8,193	23	Mediterranean	Submarine	Torpedo	Missed	—
†Shadwell	4,091	23	Mediterranean	Submarine	Torpedoed	Reached port	13
†War Knight	7,951	24	English Channel	Mine after collision.	Fire and Mine.	Beached	32 including Master.
†Anchoria	5,430	24	North Ireland	Submarine	Torpedoed	Reached port	—
†Mirlo	6,978	24	English Channel	Submarine	Torpedo	Missed	—
†Austrian	3,127	24	Irish Channel	Submarine	Chased	Gun	—
†Emma Minlos	1,286	25	North Sea	Submarine	Torpedo	Missed	—
†Norseman	352	25	Little Minch	Submarine	Gunfire	Gun	—
†Warturm	4,965	25	Mediterranean	Submarine	Torpedoed	Reached port	2
†British Star	6,888	26	North Sea	Submarine	Torpedoed	Reached port	—
†Patriotic	2,254	27	Irish Channel	Submarine	Torpedo	Missed	—
†Glenbrook	251	27	North Sea	Submarine	Rifle fire	Gun	—
†Bovic	6,583	27	Irish Channel	Submarine	Torpedo	Missed	—
†Poplar Branch	5,391	28	Irish Channel	Submarine	Torpedo	Missed	—
*Dryden	5,839	28	River Mersey	Mine	Mine	Reached port	—
†Nairung	4,478	28	Mediterranean	Submarine	Torpedo	Missed	—
†Leafield	2,539	28	Irish Channel	Submarine	Gunfire	Gun	—
†Henry Fürst	1,500	29	North Sea	Submarine	Torpedo	Missed	—
†Kul	1,095	29	English Channel	Submarine	Torpedo	Missed	—
†Kentucky	7,169	29	English Channel	Submarine	Torpedo	Missed	—
†Linmere	1,579	29	Irish Channel	Submarine	Chased	Attack abandoned.	—
†Oranian	3,942	29	Irish Sea	Submarine	Torpedo	Missed	—
†Gracefield	2,733	30	English Channel	Submarine	Torpedo	Missed	—
†Westerham	531	30	North Sea	Submarine	Torpedo	Missed	—
†Milwaukee	7,323	31	Irish Channel	Submarine	Torpedo	Missed	—
†Alcinous	6,743	31	English Channel	Submarine	Torpedoed	Reached port	—
†Celtic	20,904	31	Irish Channel	Submarine	Torpedoed	Reached port	6
APRIL 1918.		Apr.					
†Mongolian	4,892	1	English Channel	Submarine	Chased	Speed	—
†Sunik	5,017	1	Mediterranean	Submarine	Torpedo	Missed	—
†Clapham	763	4	English Channel	Submarine	Torpedo	Missed	—
†Zingara	3,463	5	St. George's Chan.	Submarine	Torpedo	Missed	—
†Clam	3,552	5	Irish Channel	Submarine	Torpedoed	Reached port	—
Saint Barchan	362	5	Irish Channel	Submarine	Torpedo	Missed	—
†Ulster	2,641	6	Irish Channel	Submarine	Torpedo	Missed	—
†Fagerton	851	6	North Sea	Submarine	3 Torpedoes	Missed	—
†Headcliffe	3,654	6	Off Gambia River	Submarine	Gunfire	Gun	—
Galacum	585	6	English Channel	Submarine	2 Torpedoes	Missed	—
†Cadillac	11,106	7	W. from Scilly Is.	Submarine	Torpedoed	Reached port	—
†Knight Templar	7,175	7	S.W.from Scilly Is.	Submarine	Torpedoed	Reached port	—
†Kumara	6,063	7	Atlantic	Submarine	Torpedo	Missed; gun	—
Eboe	4,866	7	Off Sierra Leone	Submarine	Gunfire	Speed	—
†Ormiston	4,843	7	Atlantic	Submarine	3 torpedoes	Missed	—
†Tainui	9,965	8	English Channel	Submarine	Torpedoed	Reached port	—
Genesee (Tug)	—	8	W. from Scilly Is.	Submarine	Gunfire	Speed	—
†Northland	11,905	8	English Channel	Submarine	Torpedo	Missed	—

MERCHANT VESSELS ATTACKED.   156

Name.	Gross Tons.	Date.	Position.	Attacked by	How attacked.	How saved.	Lives lost.
		1918. Apr.					
†Asian -	5,614	8	English Channel -	Submarine - -	Torpedo -	Missed -	---
†Uskside -	2,209	8	North Sea - -	Submarine - -	Torpedo -	Missed -	—
†Sunik - -	5,017	9	Mediterranean -	Submarine - -	Torpedoed -	Beached -	—
†Warwickshire -	8,012	10	Mediterranean -	Submarine - -	Torpedoed -	Reached port	—
†Airedale -	3,044	10	Mediterranean -	Submarine - -	Torpedoed -	Beached -	—
†Hunsworth -	2,991	10	English Channel -	Submarine - -	Torpedo -	Missed -	—
†Burutu -	3,902	10	Off Monrovia -	Submarine - -	Torpedo ; Gunfire.	Missed ; gun.	2
†Paul Paix -	4,196	10	English Channel -	Submarine - -	Torpedoed -	Reached port	—
†Kingstonian -	6,564	11	Mediterranean -	Submarine - -	Torpedoed -	Beached -	1
†Eupion -	3,575	12	St. George's Chan.	Submarine - -	2 Torpedoes	Missed -	—
Munster -	2,646	13	Irish Channel -	Submarine - -	Torpedo -	Missed -	—
Bassam -	3,040	13	Off Sierra Leone	Submarine - -	Chased -	Speed -	---
†Norton -	1,825	13	Off Ailsa Craig -	Submarine - -	Torpedo -	Missed -	—
†Boma -	2,694	14	Bristol Channel -	Submarine - -	Torpedo -	Undamaged	—
†Kathlamba -	6,382	14	Irish Channel -	Submarine - -	Torpedo -	Missed -	---
†Ausonia -	8,153	14	Atlantic - -	Submarine - -	Torpedo -	Missed -	—
†Erivan -	2,419	15	North Sea - -	Submarine - -	2 Torpedoes	Missed -	—
†Tanfield -	4,538	15	English Channel -	Submarine - -	Torpedoed -	Reached port	—
†City of Winchester.	7,981	15	English Channel -	Submarine - -	Torpedoed -	Reached port	—
†Vulture -	1,168	15	North Sea - -	Submarine - -	Torpedo -	Missed -	—
George Harper -	1,613	16	English Channel -	Submarine - -	Torpedoed -	Reached port	2
†Kursk -	7,869	17	Mediterranean -	Submarine - -	Torpedo -	Missed -	—
†Haverford -	11,635	17	Atlantic - -	Submarine - -	2 Torpedoes	Missed -	—
†Eupion -	3,575	18	English Channel -	Submarine - -	Torpedo -	Failed to explode.	—
†Malpas Belle (S.V.).	179	18	English Channel	Submarine - -	Gunfire -	Weather -	—
†Southern Coast -	1,872	18	Irish Channel -	Submarine - -	Torpedo -	Missed -	—
†Thomas Holt -	1,521	20	Irish Channel -	Submarine - -	Gunfire -	—	—
†Cumbria -	627	20	Irish Channel -	Submarine - -	Gunfire -	Gun - -	—
†Coya -	3,040	20	Irish Channel -	Submarine - -	Torpedo -	Missed -	—
†Priestfield -	4,033	20	Irish Channel -	Submarine - -	Torpedo -	Failed to explode.	---
†Megantic -	14,878	20	St. George's Chan.	Submarine - -	Torpedo -	Missed -	—
†Lompoc -	7,270	21	North Sea - -	Submarine - -	Torpedoed -	Reached port	—
†Drammenseren -	3,188	21	St. George's Chan.	Submarine - -	Torpedo -	Missed -	—
†Kaisar-I-Hind -	11,430	22	Mediterranean -	Submarine - -	Torpedo -	Missed -	—
†Hitchin -	1,933	25	English Channel	Submarine - -	Torpedo -	Missed -	—
†Yang-Tsze -	6,457	25	W. from Gibraltar	Submarine - -	Torpedo -	Missed -	—
†Traveller -	3,042	26	N.W. Ireland -	Submarine - -	Torpedo -	Missed -	—
†Broom -	576	26	Irish Channel -	Submarine - -	Torpedo -	Missed -	—
Mango -	341	26	Irish Channel -	Submarine - -	Torpedo -	Missed -	—
†Upada -	5,257	27	Mediterranean -	Submarine - -	Torpedoed -	Reached port	1
†Ramsay -	4,318	27	Off S. Cape Blanco	Submarine - -	2 Torpedoes ; Gunfire.	Missed ; gun.	—
†Orion -	851	28	Bristol Channel -	Submarine - -	Torpedo -	Missed -	—
†Libourne -	1,219	28	Bristol Channel -	Submarine - -	Torpedo -	Missed -	—
†Comic -	878	28	Irish Channel -	Submarine - -	Chased -	Speed -	—
†Alert (S.V.) -	163	28	Bristol Channel -	Submarine - -	Gunfire -	Gun - -	—
†Oxonian -	6,383	29	Irish Channel -	Submarine - -	2 Torpedoes	Missed -	—
†Nidd -	996	30	English Channel	Submarine - -	Torpedo -	Missed -	—
†Hollyleaf -	5,167	30	Mediterranean -	Submarine - -	Torpedo -	Missed -	—
MAY 1918.		May					
†Toromeo -	4,149	1	English Channel -	Submarine - -	Torpedo -	Missed -	—
†Canonesa -	5,583	1	English Channel -	Submarine - -	Torpedoed -	Reached port	8
†Ravenstone -	3,049	1	Mediterranean -	Submarine - -	3 Torpedoes	Missed -	—
†Lexington -	5,287	2	W. from Gibraltar	Submarine - -	Gunfire -	Speed -	—
†Magdeburg -	1,451	2	North Sea - -	Submarine - -	Torpedo -	Missed -	—
†Lady Plymouth	3,521	2	Mediterranean -	Submarine - -	Torpedo -	Missed -	---
Prosper -	1,075	2	English Channel -	Submarine - -	Torpedo -	Missed -	—
†Highland Watch	6,031	2	W. from Gibraltar	Submarine - -	2 torpedoes -	Missed -	—
†Chiverstone -	2,946	3	Atlantic - -	Submarine - -	Torpedo -	Missed -	—
†Rosstrevor -	805	3	Irish Channel -	Submarine - -	Torpedo -	Missed -	—
†Pancras -	4,436	3	Mediterranean -	Submarine - -	Torpedoed -	Reached port	2
†Sphynx -	1,569	4	Irish Channel -	Submarine - -	2 torpedoes -	Missed -	—
†M. J. Hedley -	449	4	Irish Channel -	Submarine - -	Gunfire -	Rescued -	1

MERCHANT VESSELS ATTACKED.

Name.	Gross Tons.	Date.	Position.	Attacked by	How attacked.	How saved.	Lives lost.
		1918. May					
†Sunniva	1,913	4	North Sea	Submarine	Torpedo	Missed	—
†Pensilva	4,316	4	Irish Channel	Submarine	Gunfire	Gun	—
†Clan Ross	5,971	5	Mediterranean	Submarine	Torpedoed	Reached port	9
Pandora (S.V.)	86	5	Irish Channel	Submarine	Gunfire	Towed in	—
†Wheatear	383	5	Irish Channel	Submarine	Gunfire	Gun	—
†Claddagh	640	5	St. George's Chan.	Submarine	Torpedo	Missed	—
†Lowther Castle	4,439	7	Mediterranean	Submarine	Torpedo	Missed	—
†Southern Coast	1,872	7	English Channel	Submarine	Torpedo	Missed	—
†Quito	3,358	8	Irish Channel	Submarine	Torpedoed	Reached port	—
†Southern Coast	1,872	8	St. George's Channel.	Submarine	Gunfire	Smoke; rescued.	—
†Elizabetta	335	8	Irish Channel	Submarine	Gunfire	Gun and smoke.	5 Crew prisoners.
†Camborne (S.V.)	118	8	Bristol Channel	Submarine	Gunfire	Gun	—
Cairnvalona (in tow).	4,840	8	North Sea	Submarine	Torpedo	Missed	—
†Venus	3,152	8	Mediterranean	Submarine	Torpedo	Missed	—
†Blackheath	4,868	9	Mediterranean	Submarine	Torpedo	Missed	—
†Alban	5,223	11	Irish Channel	Submarine	Torpedo	Missed	—
†Ainsdale	1,905	12	North Sea	Submarine	Torpedo	Missed	—
†Beulawers	3,949	12	Irish Channel	Mine	Mine	Reached port	5
†Esperanza de Larrinaga.	4,981	13	N. Ireland	Submarine	Torpedoed	Reached port	1
†Huntress	4,997	13	Atlantic	Submarine	Torpedo	Missed	—
†Inverness	3,734	14	Mediterranean	Submarine	Torpedo	Missed	—
†Egret	1,394	14	English Channel	Submarine	Torpedo	Missed	—
†Clifftower	3,509	14	S. Ireland	Submarine	Torpedo	Missed	—
†Pennyworth	5,388	15	English Channel	Submarine	Torpedoed	Reached port	1
†War Grange	3,100	15	Bristol Channel	Submarine	Torpedoed	Beached	5
†Priestfield	4,033	15	Irish Channel	Submarine	Torpedo	Missed	—
†Cremyil (S.V.)	141	15	English Channel	Submarine	Chased	Gun	—
†Elswick Grange	3,926	17	Mediterranean	Submarine	Torpedoed	Reached port	1
†Media	5,437	18	Mediterranean	Submarine	Torpedoed	Reached port	—
†Thomas Holt	1,521	18	St. George's Chan.	Submarine	Torpedo	Missed	—
†Courtfield	4,592	19	English Channel	Submarine	Torpedo	Failed to explode.	—
†Cambrian King	3,601	19	Mediterranean	Submarine	Chased	Attack abandoned.	—
†Saxilby	3,630	19	Mediterranean	Submarine	Torpedoed	Reached port	—
†Manchester Importer.	4,028	20	English Channel	Submarine	Torpedoed	Reached port	—
†Cressington Court.	4,396	21	English Channel	Submarine	Torpedo	Missed	—
†Grebe	761	21	English Channel	Submarine	Torpedo	Missed	—
†Trelawny	3,877	22	Bristol Channel	Submarine	Torpedo	Missed	—
†Crosshands	716	22	Bristol Channel	Submarine	Gunfire	Gun	—
†Arzila	2,737	23	English Channel	Submarine	Torpedo	Missed	—
†Olive	1,047	23	Irish Channel	Submarine	Torpedo	Missed	—
†Parana	4,182	23	S.W. from Scilly Islands.	Submarine	2 torpedoes	Missed	—
†Hubert	3,930	24	Irish Channel	Submarine	Torpedo	Missed	—
†Elysia	6,397	24	Mediterranean	Submarine	Torpedoed	Reached port	13
†Anne	4,083	25	English Channel	Submarine	Torpedoed	Reached port	1
†Rathlin Head	7,378	25	S.W. Ireland	Submarine	Torpedoed	Reached port	3
†Jabiru	1,703	26	English Channel	Submarine	Torpedo	Failed to explode.	—
†Wyncote	4,937	26	English Channel	Submarine	Torpedo	Missed	—
†Pembroke Coast	809	27	Bristol Channel	Submarine	Torpedo	Missed	—
†Grinkle	322	27	North Sea	Submarine	Chased	Gun	—
†Walton Hall	4,932	27	Atlantic	Submarine	Torpedo	Missed	—
†War Angler	5,210	28	S.W. Ireland	Submarine	2 torpedoes	Missed	—
†Ewell	1,036	28	North Sea	Submarine	Torpedo	Missed	—
†Antinous	3,682	29	Mediterranean	Submarine	Torpedoed	Reached port	—
†Teviot	3,271	29	English Channel	Submarine	Torpedo	Missed	—
†Nirvana	6,021	29	English Channel	Submarine	Torpedo	Missed	—
†Elswick Hall	3,797	29	Mediterranean	Submarine	Torpedo	Missed	—
†War Panther	5,260	30	English Channel	Submarine	Torpedoed	Reached port	—
†Dungeness	2,748	30	North Sea	Submarine	Torpedoed	Reached port	4
†Squadron	362	30	Irish Channel	Submarine	Torpedo	Missed	—
†Denbighshire	3,844	30	Mediterranean	Submarine	Torpedo	Missed	—
†Galileo	6,287	31	English Channel	Submarine	Torpedoed	Beached	—
Verbena (S.V.)	41	31	English Channel	Submarine	Gunfire	Rescued	—

Merchant Vessels Attacked.

Name.	Gross Tons.	Date.	Position.	Attacked by	How attacked.	How saved	Lives lost.
JUNE 1918.		1918. June					
†Busk	367	1	Irish Channel	Submarine	Gunfire	Gun	—
†Dunaff Head	5,877	2	Entrance to Clyde	Submarine	Torpedo	Missed	—
†Antiope	3,004	3	North Sea	Submarine	Torpedoed	Reached port	—
†Roquelle	4,364	3	Irish Channel	Submarine	2 Torpedoes	Missed	—
†Cento	3,708	4	North Sea	Submarine	Torpedoed	Reached port	3
†Strombus	6,163	4	Mediterranean	Submarine	Torpedoed	Reached port	2
†Kansas	6,074	4	Irish Channel	Submarine	2 Torpedoes	Missed	—
†Southville	3,518	4	Mediterranean	Submarine	Torpedo	Missed	—
†Clematis	3,406	5	Mediterranean	Submarine	2 torpedoes	Missed	—
†Mantilla	5,660	6	Atlantic	Submarine	Chased	Speed	—
†Highlander	975	8	North Sea	Submarine	Torpedo	Missed	—
†Eastern Coast	1,607	9	St. George's Chan.	Submarine	Torpedo	Missed	—
†Henzada	5,829	9	St. George's Chan.	Submarine	Torpedo	Missed	—
†Essex	8,722	9	St. George's Chan.	Submarine	Torpedo	Missed	—
†Brodholme	5,747	10	Mediterranean	Submarine	Torpedoed	Beached	4
†Gala	1,015	12	North Sea	Submarine	Torpedo	Failed to explode.	—
†Herbert Fischer	938	13	North Sea	Submarine	Torpedo	Missed	—
†Hans Jost	934	13	North Sea	Submarine	Torpedo	Missed	—
†Keemun	9,074	13	Atlantic	Submarine	Gunfire	Gun	—
†Rugbeian	4,042	13	Mediterranean	Submarine	Torpedo	Missed	—
†Gregory	2,030	13	North Sea	Submarine	Torpedo	Missed	—
†Cairnmona	4,666	15	North Sea	Submarine	Torpedoed	Reached port	3
†Sikh	5,150	16	Mediterranean	Submarine	Torpedo	Missed	—
†Rossia	4,576	16	Mediterranean	Submarine	Torpedo	Missed	—
*Kandy	4,921	17	Mediterranean	Submarine	Torpedoed	Reached port	—
*City of Manchester.	5,556	17	Mediterranean	Submarine	Torpedo	Missed	—
●†Sea Serpent	2,424	20	English Channel	Submarine	Torpedo	Missed	—
†Clan Maclaren	2,832	20	Atlantic	Submarine	Torpedo	Missed	—
†Malancha	10,572	21	Atlantic	Submarine	Chased	Speed	—
†Malwa	10,883	21	Mediterranean	Submarine	Torpedo	Missed	—
†Glenlee	4,915	25	Atlantic	Submarine	Gunfire	Gun	—
†Khiva	9,017	25	Atlantic	Submarine	Chased	Gun	—
†Raranga	10,040	26	English Channel	Submarine	Torpedoed	Reached port	—
†Exmoor	4,329	28	English Channel	Submarine	2 Torpedoes	Missed	—
†Noord-Holland	1,006	28	North Sea	Submarine	Torpedo	Missed	—
†Poltolia	1,831	29	English Channel	Submarine	Torpedo	Missed	—
†Kwang-ping	1,999	29	Mediterranean	Submarine	Torpedo	Missed	—
†Helenus	7,555	30	North Sea	Submarine	Torpedo	Missed	—
†Clumberhall	3,599	30	Bay of Biscay	Submarine	Torpedo	Missed	—
†Wilton	4,281	30	English Channel	Submarine	Torpedoed	Reached port	—
JULY 1918.		July					
†Thames	1,079	1	English Channel	Submarine	Torpedo	Missed	—
†Tregarthen	4,263	1	Mediterranean	Submarine	Torpedo	Missed	—
†Magdala	4,814	1	Mediterranean	Submarine	2 torpedoes	Missed	—
†Royal Sceptre	3,838	2	English Channel	Submarine	Torpedoed	Reached port	—
†Copenhagen	4,540	2	W. from Gibraltar	Submarine	Torpedo	Missed	—
†Hornby Grange	2,356	3	English Channel	Submarine	Torpedo	Missed	—
†Hosanger	1,620	3	North Sea	Submarine	Torpedo	Missed	—
†Baron Inchcape	7,005	4	English Channel	Submarine	Torpedo	Missed	—
†Merida	5,951	4	Mediterranean	Submarine	Torpedoed	Reached port	1
†Huntscraft	5,113	6	English Channel	Submarine	Torpedoed	Reached port	6
†Nevasa	9,071	6	Atlantic	Submarine	Gunfire	Gun	—
†Salieut	3,879	7	W. from Scilly I.	Submarine	Torpedo	Missed	—
†Barunga	7,484	7	English Channel	Submarine	Torpedo	Missed	—
†Stockwell	5,643	8	North Sea	Submarine	Torpedo	Missed	—
†Baysarnia	3,458	8	W. from Gibraltar	Submarine	Torpedo	Missed	—
†Luga	1,988	9	North Sea	Submarine	Chased	Gun	—
†Charles Theriault (S.V.)	339	10	Atlantic	Submarine	Set on fire	Towed in	—
Katherine Ellen (S.V.)	111	11	St. George's Chan.	Submarine	Gunfire	Towed in	—
†Rion	2,186	13	North Sea	Submarine	Torpedo	Failed to explode.	—
Trebiskin (S.V.)	59	13	St. George's Chan.	Submarine	Gunfire	Towed in	—
†Imber	2,154	13	Mediterranean	Submarine	Torpedoed	Reached port	—
†Trevisa	1,813	14	Bristol Channel	Submarine	2 torpedoes	Missed	—
†San Tirso	6,236	14	N. Ireland	Submarine	Torpedo	Missed	—
Medway	929	15	Irish Channel	Submarine	Torpedo	Missed	—

MERCHANT VESSELS ATTACKED.

Name.	Gross Tons.	Date.	Position.	Attacked by	How attacked.	How saved.	Lives lost.
		1918. July					
†Niceto de Larrinaga.	5,591	15	Irish Channel	Submarine	Torpedo	Missed	—
†Tudor Prince	4,292	16	English Channel	Submarine	Torpedo	Missed	—
†Patriotic	2,254	17	Irish Channel	Submarine	Torpedo	Missed	—
†Harlseywood	2,701	17	Bristol Channel	Submarine	Torpedoed	Beached	1
†War Spray	3,100	17	Bay of Biscay	Submarine	2 torpedoes	Missed	—
†Polperro	3,365	19	Mediterranean	Submarine	Torpedoed	Reached port	3
†Genesee	2,830	21	North Sea	Submarine	Torpedoed	Reached port	—
†Upada	5,257	21	Mediterranean	Submarine	Torpedoed	Reached port	3
†Athena	250	21	North Sea	Submarine	Torpedo; gunfire.	Missed; by gun.	—
†Eurylochus	5,723	22	Off Madeira	Submarine	Chased	Speed	—
†City of Cork	1,301	23	Bristol Channel	Submarine	2 torpedoes	Missed	—
Boorara	6,570	23	North Sea	Submarine	Torpedoed	Reached port	—
†Defender	8,520	24	S. Ireland	Submarine	Torpedoed	Reached port	—
†Indore	7,300	25	N. Ireland	Submarine	Torpedoed	Beached	2
†British Major	4,147	26	Atlantic	Submarine	Gunfire	Gun	—
†Melita	13,967	26	Atlantic	Submarine	Gunfire	Gun	—
†City of Bombay	5,186	26	Atlantic	Submarine	Gunfire	Gun	—
†Baron Napier	4,943	26	Atlantic	Submarine	Gunfire	Gun	—
†Lombok	5,934	26	English Channel	Submarine	Torpedo	Missed	—
†Zamora	3,639	26	Atlantic	Submarine	Gunfire	Gun	—
†Olive	1,047	27	Irish Channel	Submarine	Torpedo	Missed	—
†Lady Gwendolen	2,163	29	North Sea	Submarine	Torpedo	Missed	—
†Savan	4,264	29	North Sea	Submarine	Torpedo	Missed	—
†Mary Annie (S.V.)	196	29	North Sea	Submarine	Gunfire	Slightly damaged.	—
Englishman (Tug).	62	29	North Sea	Submarine	Gunfire	Speed	—
†Plover	187	29	North Ireland	Submarine	Gunfire	Gun	—
†Bayronto	6,045	30	English Channel	Submarine	Torpedoed	Reached port	2
†War Deer	5,323	30	North Sea	Submarine	Torpedoed	Reached port	—
†Wallsend	2,697	31	North Sea	Submarine	Torpedo	Missed	—
†Freshfield	3,445	31	Mediterranean	Submarine	2 torpedoes	Missed	—
AUGUST 1918.		Aug.					
†Crenella	7,082	1	S.W. of Ireland	Submarine	Torpedo	Missed	—
†Neto	1,696	1	Bristol Channel	Submarine	Torpedo	Missed	—
†Kirkwood	1,674	1	Bristol Channel	Submarine	Torpedo	Missed	—
†War Rambler	5,495	2	Bristol Channel	Submarine	2 torpedoes	Missed	—
†Spermina	3,355	2	Mediterranean	Submarine	Torpedo	Missed	—
†Wyvisbrook	3,158	2	North Sea	Submarine	Torpedo	Missed	—
†Everilda	3,080	3	Bay of Biscay	Submarine	Torpedo	Missed	—
†Mendocino	6,973	3	Atlantic	Submarine	Chased	Gun	—
†Waipara	6,994	4	English Channel	Submarine	Torpedoed	Reached port	1
†Thrift	506	4	North Sea	Submarine	Torpedo	Missed	—
†Dallington	2,542	5	English Channel	Submarine	Torpedo	Missed	—
†Fernley	3,820	5	Atlantic	Submarine	Torpedo	Missed	—
†Polescar	5,832	5	English Channel	Submarine	Torpedoed	Reached port	—
†Tuscan Prince	5,275	5	English Channel	Submarine	Torpedoed	Reached port	2
†Rhodesian Transport.	4,986	5	Atlantic	Submarine	Chased	Gun	—
Gladys M. Hoilett (S.V.).	203	5	W. Atlantic	Submarine	Bombs	Towed in	—
†Bencleuch	4,159	6	Off Cape Hatteras	Submarine			—
†Tasmanian Transport.	4,491	7	English Channel	Submarine	Torpedo	Missed	—
†Clan Macvey	5,815	7	English Channel	Submarine	Torpedo	Missed	—
†Portwood	2,241	8	English Channel	Submarine	Torpedoed	Reached port	3
†Anselma de Larrinaga.	4,090	9	English Channel	Submarine	Torpedoed	Reached port	—
†Kent	8,678	12	North Sea	Submarine	Torpedo	Missed	—
†Wad Lukkus	206	12	English Channel	Submarine	Torpedo	Missed	—
†Scottish Prince	2,897	12	Mediterranean	Submarine	Torpedo	Missed	—
†Exmouth	3,923	12	Mediterranean	Submarine	Torpedo	Missed	—
†Yarrow	908	12	Irish Channel	Submarine	Torpedo	Missed	—
†Desna	11,483	14	W. from Ushant	Submarine	2 torpedoes	Missed	—
†Slieve Gallion	1,071	15	Irish Channel	Submarine	Torpedo	Missed	—
†Snowdon	1,021	15	Irish Channel	Submarine	Torpedo	Missed	—
†Islandia	2,069	16	Bristol Channel	Submarine	Torpedo	Missed	—
†Lackawanna	4,125	16	East from New York.	Submarine	2 torpedoes; gunfire.	Missed; gun	—
†Australpeak	4,432	16	Irish Sea	Submarine	Torpedo	Missed	—

MERCHANT VESSELS ATTACKED.

Name.	Gross Tons.	Date.	Position.	Attacked by	How attacked.	How saved.	Lives lost.
		1918. Aug.					
†Fylde (tug, towing 4 S.V.).	256	16	St. George's Chan.	Submarine	Gunfire	Gun	—
†Liddesdale	4,403	18	Mediterranean	Submarine	Torpedo	Failed to explode.	—
†Charity	1,735	19	Bristol Channel	Submarine	Torpedoed	Reached port	—
Umvolosi	2,980	19	Indian Ocean	Mine	Mine	Reached port	—
†Indian	9,121	21	West of Ireland	Submarine	Torpedo	Missed	—
†Thespis	4,343	21	E. from New York	Submarine	Torpedo	Missed	—
†Greenore	1,488	22	Irish Channel	Submarine	2 Torpedoes	Missed	—
†Sheerness	1,274	22	Irish Channel	Submarine	Torpedo	Missed	—
†Helenus	7,555	22	Atlantic	Submarine	Gunfire	Speed	—
†Brandenburg	1,578	24	North Sea	Submarine	Torpedo	Missed	—
†Delphinula	5,238	24	Mediterranean	Submarine	Torpedoed	Reached port	—
Bianca (Aux.)	408	24	W. Atlantic	Submarine	Gunfire; bombs.	Towed in	—
†Vane Tempest	687	25	North Sea	Submarine	Torpedo	Missed	—
†Highlander	975	25	North Sea	Submarine	Torpedo	Missed	—
†Grace	354	25	North Sea	Submarine	Torpedo	Missed	—
†Pelican	638	26	S.W. Ireland	Submarine	Gunfire	Gun	—
†Archimedes	5,364	27	English Channel	Submarine	Torpedo	Missed	—
†Lompoc	7,270	28	North Sea	Submarine	Torpedoed	Reached port	1
†Henzada	5,829	29	Mediterranean	Submarine	Torpedo	Missed	—
†Andree	3,689	29	St. George's Chan.	Submarine	Torpedo	Missed	—
†Tambov	4,361	31	Atlantic	Submarine			—
†Baron Polwarth	4,913	31	Atlantic	Submarine	Torpedo	Missed	—
†Largo Law	4,005	31	Atlantic	Submarine	Torpedo	Missed	—

SEPTEMBER 1918.

		Sept.					
†Actor	6,082	1	Irish Channel	Submarine	Torpedoed	Reached port	—
†Rose	1,098	1	Mediterranean	Submarine	Chased	Speed	—
†British Star	6,976	1	W. Atlantic	Submarine	Chased	Speed	—
†Baron Minto	4,537	1	Mediterranean	Submarine	Torpedoed	Reached port	—
†Ariadne Christine	3,550	2	Arctic Ocean	Mine	Mine	Towed in	—
†Alcinous	6,743	2	W. Atlantic	Submarine	Gunfire	Gun	—
†Huntsend	8,826	3	N.W. Ireland	Submarine	Torpedo	Missed	—
†Bechuana	4,148	4	Atlantic	Submarine	2 torpedoes	Missed	—
†Islandia	2,069	4	English Channel	Submarine	Torpedo	Missed	—
†War Ranee	5,500	5	Atlantic	Submarine	Torpedo	Missed	—
†Persic	12,042	7	N.W. Scilly Isles	Submarine	Torpedoed	Reached port	—
†Monmouth	4,078	7	W. Atlantic	Submarine	Gunfire	Gun	—
†P.L.A. 17	1,126	8	North Sea	Submarine	Torpedo	Missed	—
†Juliston	2,459	9	Mediterranean	Submarine	Torpedo	Missed	—
†Policastra	4,594	9	Mediterranean	Submarine	Torpedoed	Reached port	—
†Pearleaf	5,911	11	North Sea	Submarine	Torpedo	Missed	—
†Chao Chow Fu	1,909	12	Mediterranean	Submarine	Torpedoed	Reached port	—
†Newby Hall	4,391	13	W. Atlantic	Submarine	Torpedo : Gunfire.	Missed ; gun.	—
†Bondicar	1,441	15	Bristol Channel	Submarine	Torpedo	Missed	—
†Huntscliffe	5,442	15	W. Atlantic	Submarine	Chased	Gun	—
†Dipton	3,811	16	Atlantic	Submarine	2 torpedoes	Missed	—
†Holmpark	1,468	18	Bristol Channel	Submarine	Torpedo	Missed	—
†Cognac	814	19	Bristol Channel	Submarine	Torpedo	Missed	—
†Lackawanna	4,125	20	Irish Channel	Submarine	Torpedo	Missed	—
†Orient	739	20	North Sea	Submarine	Torpedo	Failed to explode.	—
†Lancastrian	5,134	20	English Channel	Submarine	Torpedo	Missed	—
†Henry Furst	1,500	20	North Sea	Submarine	Torpedo	Missed	—
†Minia	2,061	21	Atlantic	Submarine	Torpedo	Missed	—
†Islandia	2,069	21	Irish Channel	Submarine	Torpedo	Missed	—
†Anchises	10,046	23	Atlantic	Submarine	Gunfire	Gun	—
†Alban	5,223	24	Atlantic	Submarine	Gunfire	Gun	—
†Roselands	4,383	25	Bristol Channel	Submarine	Chased	Gun	—
†Malwa	10,883	26	Mediterranean	Submarine	Torpedo	Failed to explode.	—
†Algores	342	28	Irish Channel	Submarine	Torpedo	Missed	—
†Reginolite	2,631	29	W. Atlantic	Submarine	Gunfire	Gun	—

OCTOBER 1918.

		Oct.					
†Karmala	8,983	1	N.W. Ireland	Submarine	Torpedo	Missed	—
†Magdala	4,814	2	Atlantic	Submarine	Chased	Gun	—

MERCHANT VESSELS ATTACKED.

Name.	Gross Tons.	Date.	Position.	Attacked by	How attacked.	How saved.	Lives lost.
		1918. Oct.					
†A. E. McKinstry	1,964	2	English Channel	Submarine	Torpedo	Missed	—
†Nevasa	9,071	2	W. Atlantic	Submarine	Gunfire	Speed	—
†Chindwara	5,192	2	Atlantic	Submarine	Torpedo; gunfire.	Missed; gun	—
†Nizam	5,322	2	Atlantic	Submarine	Chased	Speed	—
†Benrinnes	4,798	2	Atlantic	Submarine	2 torpedoes	Missed	—
†Kingfield	3,028	8	Mediterranean	Submarine	Torpedo	Missed	—
†Waimarino	4,204	9	Mediterranean	Submarine	Torpedo	Missed	—
†Sheerness	1,274	10	Irish Channel	Submarine	Torpedo	Missed	—
†War Crag	3,120	12	Mediterranean	Submarine	Torpedo	Missed	—
†Darro	11,484	13	Irish Channel	Submarine	Torpedo	Missed	—
†Chimu	4,259	14	Mediterranean	Submarine	2 torpedoes	Missed	—
†Messina	4,271	15	Atlantic	Submarine	Gunfire	Gun	—
†Harperley	3,990	17	Atlantic	Submarine	Torpedo	Missed	—
†Briarleaf	5,822	17	Atlantic	Submarine	Torpedo; gunfire.	Exploded prematurely; gun.	—
†Duke of Cumberland.	2,036	22	Irish Channel	Submarine	Torpedo	Missed	—
†Duke of Connaught.	1,564	22	Irish Channel	Submarine	Chased	Speed	—
NOVEMBER 1918.							
†War Roach	5,215	2	Port Said swept channel.	Submarine	Torpedo	Reached port	—
†Sarpedon	4,393	7	Mediterranean	Submarine	Torpedo	Missed	—

TABLE "A."

Showing Number and Gross Tonnage of BRITISH MERCHANT VESSELS Lost through Enemy Action during each Month since the Outbreak of War; and Number of Lives Lost.

Month	By Cruisers, T.B.'s, &c. No.	Gross Tonnage	Lives lost	By Submarines No.	Gross Tonnage	Lives lost	By Mines No.	Gross Tonnage	Lives lost	By Aircraft No.	Gross Tonnage	Lives lost	Total No.	Gross Tonnage	Lives lost
1914.															
August	8	33,796	–	–	–	–	1	6,458	–	–	–	–	9	40,254	–
September	19	84,403	–	–	–	–	2	3,816	29	–	–	–	21	88,219	29
October	14	65,161	–	1	866	–	4	11,778	24	–	–	–	19	77,805	24
November	2	3,784	–	2	2,084	–	1	3,020	–	–	–	–	5	8,888	–
December	5	15,995	–	–	–	–	5	10,040	16	–	–	–	10	26,035	16
1915.															
January	3	12,304	–	7	17,126	21	1	2,624	–	–	–	–	11	32,054	21
February	4	10,350	–	8	21,787	9	2	4,235	21	–	–	–	14	36,372	30
March	2	7,031	–	21	64,448	161	–	–	–	–	–	–	23	71,479	161
April	–	–	–	11	22,453	38	–	–	–	–	–	–	11	22,453	38
May	–	–	–	19	84,025	1,208	–	–	–	–	–	–	19	84,025	1,208
June	–	–	–	29	76,497	78	2	6,701	3	–	–	–	31	83,198	81
July	–	–	–	19	48,844	26	1	4,003	2	–	–	–	20	52,847	28
August	–	–	–	42	135,153	205	7	13,311	43	–	–	–	49	148,464	248
September	–	–	–	22	89,693	44	8	11,997	33	–	–	–	30	101,690	77
October	–	–	–	10	39,061	35	7	15,095	7	–	–	–	17	54,156	42
November	–	–	–	23	84,816	25	9	9,677	93	–	–	–	32	94,493	118
December	–	–	–	16	65,011	416	5	9,479	3	–	–	–	21	74,490	419
1916.															
January	8	27,888	17	5	27,974	28	3	6,426	19	–	–	–	16	62,288	64
February	4	14,735	1	7	24,059	34	14	36,096	243	1	970	13	26	75,860	291
March	–	–	–	19	83,492	44	7	15,597	29	–	–	–	26	99,089	73
April	–	–	–	37	126,540	119	6	14,653	12	–	–	–	43	141,193	131
May	–	–	–	12	42,165	6	8	22,356	8	–	–	–	20	64,521	14
June	1	1,380	1	11	33,849	34	4	1,747	29	–	–	–	16	36,976	64
July	2	4,710	–	21	69,962	58	5	7,760	11	–	–	–	28	82,432	69
August	–	–	–	22	42,553	4	1	801	4	–	–	–	23	43,354	8
September	1	964	–	34	84,596	16	7	19,012	4	–	–	–	42	104,572	20
October	1	1,676	–	41	146,891	182	7	27,681	15	–	–	–	49	176,248	197
November	–	–	–	42	96,672	55	7	72,137	45	–	–	–	49	168,809	100
December	10	51,999	4	36	109,936	91	12	20,357	91	–	–	–	58	182,292	186
1917.															
January	6	19,304	–	35	109,954	245	8	24,408	31	–	–	–	49	153,666	276
February	7	28,679	–	86	256,394	355	12	28,413	47	–	–	–	105	313,486	402
March	11	42,893	18	103	283,647	630	13	26,938	51	–	–	–	127	353,478	699
April	–	–	–	155	516,394	997	14	28,888	128	–	–	–	169	545,282	1,125
May	1	819	11	106	320,572	507	14	28,114	73	1	2,784	–	122	352,289	591
June	1	3,947	–	116	391,004	384	4	19,256	29	1	3,718	3	122	417,925	416
July	–	–	–	88	319,931	401	11	44,927	67	–	–	–	99	364,858	468
August	1	1,608	–	84	310,551	415	6	17,651	47	–	–	–	91	329,810	462
September	–	–	–	68	173,437	293	9	22,335	60	1	440	3	78	196,212	356
October	1	1,159	–	79	261,649	578	6	13,324	30	–	–	–	86	276,132	608
November	–	–	–	56	154,806	376	8	18,754	44	–	–	–	64	173,560	420
December	1	2,284	–	76	227,195	520	8	23,608	65	–	–	–	85	253,087	585
1918.															
January	–	–	–	57	179,973	291	–	–	–	–	–	–	57	179,973	291
February	–	–	–	68	224,501	697	1	2,395	–	–	–	–	69	226,896	697
March	–	–	–	79	194,889	490	3	4,619	20	–	–	–	82	199,458	510
April	3	4,211	–	67	209,469	488	2	1,863	1	–	–	–	72	215,543	489
May	–	–	–	59	188,729	407	1	3,707	–	–	–	–	60	192,436	407
June	–	–	–	49	158,660	453	2	4,330	16	–	–	–	51	162,990	469
July	–	–	–	37	165,449	202	–	–	–	–	–	–	37	165,449	202
August	–	–	–	41	145,721	217	–	–	–	–	–	–	41	145,721	217
September	–	–	–	48	136,859	521	–	–	–	–	–	–	48	136,859	521
October	1	1,622	–	23	54,577	318	1	3,030	–	–	–	–	25	59,229	318
To November 11	–	–	–	2	10,195	1	–	–	–	–	–	–	2	10,195	1
TOTAL to 11th November 1918	117	442,702	52	2099	6,635,059	12723	259	673,417	1493	4	7,912	19	2479	7,759,090	14287

TABLE "B."

Showing Number and Gross Tonnage of BRITISH FISHING VESSELS Lost through Enemy Action during each Month since the Outbreak of War; and Number of Lives Lost.

Month.	By Cruisers, T.B.'s, &c. No.	Gross Tonnage.	Lives lost.	By Submarines. No.	Gross Tonnage.	Lives lost.	By Mines. No.	Gross Tonnage.	Lives lost.	Total. No.	Gross Tonnage.	Lives lost.
1914.												
August	25	4,368	–	–	–	–	1	70	5	26	4,438	5
September	–	–	–	–	–	–	6	1,032	25	6	1,032	25
October	–	–	–	–	–	–	2	283	5	2	283	5
November	–	–	–	–	–	–	6	460	42	6	460	42
December	3	294	–	–	–	–	2	486	18	5	780	18
1915.												
January	–	–	–	–	–	–	2	222	–	2	222	–
February	–	–	–	–	–	–	–	–	–	–	–	–
March	–	–	–	–	–	–	1	289	1	1	289	1
April	–	–	–	10	1,760	20	1	170	2	11	1,930	22
May	4	689	–	22	3,982	4	6	977	28	32	5,648	32
June	–	–	–	58	7,749	17	2	368	9	60	8,117	26
July	–	–	–	36	3,966	–	3	461	26	39	4,427	26
August	–	–	–	36	2,454	–	2	436	9	38	2,890	9
September	–	–	–	6	292	–	2	153	12	8	445	12
October	–	–	–	–	–	–	–	–	–	–	–	–
November	–	–	–	–	–	–	1	162	2	1	162	2
December	–	–	–	–	–	–	–	–	–	–	–	–
1916.												
January	–	–	–	7	357	–	–	–	–	7	357	–
February	–	–	–	2	68	–	–	–	–	2	68	–
March	–	–	–	6	304	–	1	303	9	7	607	9
April	1	173	–	2	43	–	–	–	–	3	216	–
May	–	–	–	5	201	1	–	–	–	5	201	1
June	–	–	–	–	–	–	–	–	–	–	–	–
July	–	–	–	36	2,796	2	–	–	–	36	2,796	2
August	–	–	–	12	1,474	–	1	198	9	13	1,672	9
September	–	–	–	38	4,811	–	–	–	–	38	4,811	–
October	–	–	–	9	1,138	–	–	–	–	9	1,138	–
November	–	–	–	14	1,474	–	1	126	8	15	1,600	8
December	–	–	–	3	224	–	3	212	9	6	436	9
1917.												
January	–	–	–	16	2,020	2	–	–	–	16	2,020	2
February	–	–	–	28	3,152	4	2	326	19	30	3,478	23
March	–	–	–	43	3,586	3	–	–	–	43	3,586	3
April	–	–	–	41	5,920	14	–	–	–	41	5,920	14
May	–	–	–	17	1,054	–	2	394	18	19	1,448	18
June	–	–	–	20	1,296	–	1	46	–	21	1,342	–
July	–	–	–	17	2,679	1	1	57	5	18	2,736	6
August	–	–	–	4	230	1	1	12	5	5	242	6
September	–	–	–	6	233	–	1	12	5	7	245	5
October	–	–	–	3	116	4	2	111	15	5	227	19
November	–	–	–	3	87	–	–	–	–	3	87	–
December	1	113	4	2	79	–	2	221	13	5	413	17
1918.												
January	–	–	–	10	375	1	–	–	–	10	375	1
February	–	–	–	9	306	3	3	380	17	12	686	20
March	–	–	–	9	209	–	1	84	10	10	293	10
April	–	–	–	3	241	–	–	–	–	3	241	–
May	–	–	–	16	504	7	–	–	–	16	504	7
June	–	–	–	4	312	11	2	327	6	6	639	17
July	–	–	–	12	555	3	–	–	–	12	555	3
August	–	–	–	13	1,536	–	–	–	–	13	1,536	–
September	–	–	–	–	–	–	1	142	–	1	142	–
October	–	–	–	–	–	–	–	–	–	–	–	–
To November 11	–	–	–	–	–	–	1	25	–	1	25	–
Total to 11th November 1918	34	5,637	4	578	57,583	98	63	8,545	332	675	71,765	434

TABLE "C."

Showing Number and Gross Tonnage of BRITISH MERCHANT VESSELS DAMAGED or MOLESTED (but not Sunk) by the Enemy during each Month since the Outbreak of War; and Number of Lives Lost.

Month.	By Cruisers. No.	Gross Tonnage	Lives lost.	By Submarines. No.	Gross Tonnage	Lives lost.	By Mines. No.	Gross Tonnage	Lives lost.	By Aircraft. No.	Gross Tonnage	Lives lost.	Total. No.	Gross Tonnage	Lives lost.
1914.															
August	8	44,731	–	–	–	–	2	6,575	–	–	–	–	10	51,306	–
September	5	26,932	1	–	–	–	–	–	–	–	–	–	5	26,932	1
October	7	30,193	–	–	–	–	–	–	–	–	–	–	7	30,193	–
November	1	5,732	–	–	–	–	–	–	–	–	–	–	1	5,732	–
December	2	6,024	2	1	1,209	–	1	4,592	–	–	–	–	4	11,825	2
1915.															
January	–	–	–	1	1,871	–	1	1,742	–	–	–	–	2	3,613	–
February	1	4,583	–	10	37,043	–	3	9,849	13	–	–	–	14	51,475	13
March	–	–	–	29	93,250	1	1	3,868	1	8	10,915	–	38	108,033	2
April	1	6,849	8	7	31,479	2	–	–	–	2	3,542	–	10	41,870	10
May	–	–	–	19	117,591	–	–	–	–	–	–	–	19	117,591	–
June	–	–	–	18	77,273	–	2	10,706	–	–	–	–	20	87,979	–
July	–	–	–	16	77,492	31	2	10,406	–	1	988	–	19	88,886	31
August	–	–	–	19	55,639	–	2	11,620	–	–	–	–	21	67,259	–
September	–	–	–	5	35,056	–	2	9,617	2	1	1,270	–	8	45,943	2
October	–	–	–	4	58,450	–	3	6,564	–	1	1,408	–	8	66,422	–
November	–	–	–	11	64,460	–	1	2,286	–	2	2,657	–	14	69,403	–
December	–	–	–	8	70,295	–	1	4,844	–	1	2,414	–	10	77,553	–
1916.															
January	1	7,781	–	10	50,997	–	3	8,279	–	2	3,372	–	16	70,429	–
February	1	11,484	–	7	114,010	–	3	10,876	–	1	1,680	–	12	138,050	–
March	–	–	–	13	50,657	–	1	3,381	–	–	–	–	14	54,038	–
April	1	2,195	–	12	58,543	–	–	–	–	–	–	–	13	60,738	–
May	–	–	–	10	38,156	–	–	–	–	5	17,016	2	15	55,172	2
June	–	–	–	11	50,635	–	1	3,232	–	–	–	–	12	53,867	–
July	–	–	–	6	22,528	–	–	–	–	1	1,081	–	7	23,609	–
August	–	–	–	13	34,825	–	1	4,854	–	1	7,988	–	15	47,667	–
September	–	–	–	29	122,933	–	–	–	–	–	–	–	29	122,933	–
October	–	–	–	32	125,770	1	1	8,253	–	–	–	–	33	134,023	1
November	–	–	–	36	157,633	–	4	24,258	4	–	–	–	40	181,891	4
December	–	–	–	41	168,838	–	5	34,502	1	–	–	–	46	203,340	1
1917.															
January	–	–	–	29	140,722	1	1	5,686	–	–	–	–	30	146,408	1
February	–	–	–	74	313,971	15	4	48,516	–	1	3,563	–	79	366,050	15
March	–	–	–	77	329,192	64	3	15,459	–	2	2,292	–	82	346,943	64
April	1	3,562	–	92	426,680	21	6	47,587	3	1	1,780	–	100	479,609	24
May	–	–	–	97	388,258	3	1	1,968	–	1	2,821	–	99	393,047	3
June	–	–	–	122	549,907	18	5	29,278	–	1	1,243	–	128	580,428	18
July	–	–	–	76	383,793	6	2	5,150	–	6	8,337	–	84	397,280	6
August	–	–	–	54	252,504	10	3	15,641	–	–	–	–	57	268,145	10
September	–	–	–	61	213,199	37	3	9,491	3	2	9,966	2	66	232,656	42
October	–	–	–	43	162,755	24	2	9,754	–	–	–	–	45	172,509	24
November	–	–	–	50	191,601	27	2	9,552	–	–	–	–	52	201,153	27
December	–	–	–	60	223,533	56	3	12,900	–	1	353	–	64	236,786	56
1918.															
January	1	401	1	49	188,550	23	2	8,882	–	–	–	–	52	197,833	24
February	–	–	–	53	186,283	12	1	3,752	–	2	2,686	–	56	192,721	12
March	–	–	–	81	322,239	63	3	18,047	32	1	1,855	–	85	342,141	95
April	–	–	–	65	277,984	6	–	–	–	–	–	–	65	277,984	6
May	–	–	–	74	237,420	54	1	3,949	5	–	–	–	75	241,369	59
June	–	–	–	40	183,206	12	–	–	–	–	–	–	40	183,206	12
July	–	–	–	54	208,228	18	–	–	–	–	–	–	54	208,228	18
August	–	–	–	54	199,764	7	1	2,980	–	–	–	–	55	202,744	7
September	–	–	–	34	144,601	–	1	3,550	–	–	–	–	35	148,151	–
October	–	–	–	18	85,196	–	–	–	–	–	–	–	18	85,196	–
To November 11	–	–	–	2	9,608	–	–	–	–	–	–	–	2	9,608	–
TOTAL to 11th November 1918	30	150,467	12	1,727	7,335,827	512	84	432,446	64	44	89,227	4	1,885	8,007,967	592

INDEX.

A.	Page.		Page.		Page.
Aaro	20	Alavi	69	Angelo (trawler)	102
A. E. McKinstry	161	Alban	145, 157, 160	Anglesea (attacked)	133
Abaris	150	Albatross (trawler)	111	Anglesea (sunk)	45
Abbasieh (s.v.)	95	Albion (smack)	107	Anglia	12
Abeja (s.v.)	36	Albion (motor)	124	Anglia (trawler)	105
Abelia	13	Alcinous	155, 160	Anglian	54
Abinsi	146	Alcyone (motor 149)	61	Anglo-Californian	129
Abosso	45	Alcyone (s.v. 116)	69	Anglo-Canadian	78
Aboukir	80	Aldershot (attacked)	148	Anglo-Chilean	142
Aburi	43	Aldershot (sunk)	97	Anglo-Colombian	11
Aby (motor)	124	Aldworth	149	Anglo-Egyptian	139
Acadian (attacked)	144	Aleppo	130	Anglo-Patagonian	58
Acadian (sunk)	55	Alert (289)	26	Angus	17
Acantha (trawler)	101	Alert (777)	43	Anhui	95
Achaia	22	Alert (smack)	106	Annapolis	44
Achieve (smack)	106	Alert (s.v.—59) (sunk)	90	Anna Sofie	94
Achille Adam	38	Alert (s.v.—163) (attacked)	156	Anne	157
Achilles (7,043)	16	Alexandra	147	Annie Anderson (motor)	109
Achilles (641)	54	Alexandra (trawler)	113	Anselma de Larrinaga	159
Acorn (s.v.)	68	Alexandrian	134, 136	Antæus	72
Active (trawler)	117	Alfalfa	46	Antar	135
Active (smack)	123	Alfred (smack)	108	Ant Cassar	96
Activity (smack)	106	Alfred (s.v.)	54	Antenor	153
Acton	40	Alfred H. Read	77	Anteros (attacked)	137
Actor	160	Algarve	70	Anteros (sunk)	85
Ada (s.v.)	32	Algerian	14	Antigua	19
Ada (smack)	114	Algiers	34	Antilochus	130
Ada	149	Algores	160	Antinoe	52
Adala	140	Alhama	46	Antinous	133, 143, 157
Adalia	60	Alice (smack)	116	Antiope (2,973)	21
Adams	70	Alice Marie	76	Antiope (3,004)	158
Adamton	17	Alice M. Craig	153	Antonio	36
Adansi	49	Alison	26	Antony	38
Addah	55	Allanton	77	Antwerpen	73
Addax (smack)	121	Allendale	85	Apapa	74
Addington	144	Almerian	99	Aparima	73
Adela	77	Almond Branch	74	Aphelion (trawler)	111
Adelaide (s.v.)	138	Almora	68	Apollo	11
Adelaide (trawler)	114	Allie	29	Apostolos Andreas (s.v.)	79
Adenwen (attacked)	126	Alnwick Castle	38	Appalachee	154
Adenwen (sunk)	39	Alster (attacked)	147	Appam	131
Admiral (tug)	93	Alster (sunk)	78	Appledore	54
Admiral Cochrane	149, 152	Alt	128	Appleleaf	150
Advance (smack)	119	Alto	19	Apsleyhall	29
Adventure (trawler)	118	Alwyn (s.v.)	54	Arab	78
Afric	32	Amadavat (trawler)	121	Arabia (attacked)	128, 129
Africa	11	Amakura	54	Arabia (sunk)	25
African Monarch	8	Amazon (attacked)	136	Arabian	11
African Prince	60	Amazon (sunk)	83	Arabic	9
African Transport	92	Ambassador	137, 139	Arabis	67
Afton	33	Amber	48	Aracataca	138
Agamemnon	146	Amberton	150	Aragon	77
Agberi	76	Ambient	36	Araguaya	138
Agenoria	151	Amelia and Jane (s.v.)	141	Aranmore	16
Aghios Nicolaos (s.v.)	96	Amethyst (smack)	107	Arbonne	15
Agnes (s.v.)	28	Amphitrite (smack)	112	Arbor Vitæ (smack)	106
Agnes (trawler)	114	Ampleforth	51	Arca (attacked)	152
Agnes Cairns (s.v.)	46	Amplegarth	89	Arca (sunk)	98
Agnete	87	Amsteldam	70	Arcadian (8939)	43
Agricola (s.v.)	67	Amsterdam (1777)	140	Arcadian (2,305)	97
Aguila	5	Amsterdam (806)	82	Archbank (attacked)	142
Aigburth	74	Amulet	140	Archbank (sunk)	91
Ailsa	7	Amulree (s.v.)	45	Archimedes	160
Ailsa Craig	86	Anatolia	57	Arctic (trawler)	103
Ainsdale (s.v.)	137	Anchises	160	Ardandearg (attacked)	148
Ainsdale	157	Anchoria	155	Ardandearg (sunk)	83
Airedale	156	Ancona	133	Ardbeg	80
Aislaby	29	Andalusian	5	Ardens (attacked)	146
Ajana	140, 147	Andania (attacked)	131	Ardens (sunk)	63
Ajax	130	Andania (sunk)	79	Ardeola	147
Ajax (trawler)	100	Andoni	29	Ardgask	40
Akabo	144	Andorinha	149	Ardglamis	72
Akassa	62	Andree	139, 160	Ardglass (778)	39
Alacrity	16	Andrewina (motor)	109	Ardglass (4,617)	85
Alastair	12	Andromache (trawler)	118	Ardgryfe	147
Alaunia	24	Andromeda (trawler)	111	Ardmore (attacked)	145
		Angela (s.v.)	49	Ardmore (sunk)	72

Name	Page	Name	Page	Name	Page
Ardmount	2	Aureole	151	Baron Ogilvy	57
Arendal	67	Auriac	45	Baron Polwarth	130, 160
Arethusa (s.v.)	45	Auricula	149	Baron Sempill	30
Argalia	62	Ausonia (attacked)	144, 156	Baron Tweedmouth	18
Argo (1,720)	14	Ausonia (sunk)	90	Baron Vernon	18
Argo (1,102)	136	Australbush	72	Baron Wemyss	36
Argo (3,071)	76	Australdale	70	Baron Yarborough	21
Argo (trawler)	118	Australia	135	Barrister (3,679)	49
Argonaut (trawler)	100	Australian Transport	95	Barrister (4,952)	97
Argyll (attacked)	138	Australier	88	Barrowmore	81
Argyll (sunk)	42	Australpeak	151, 159	Barunga (attacked)	158
Argyll (trawler)	104	Austrian	141, 143, 155	Barunga (sunk)	93
Argyllshire	128, 137	Author (3,496)	14	Bassam	156
Ariadne	14	Author (5,596)	154	Basuta	80
Ariadne Christine	137, 146, 160	Autolycus	86	Bathampton	152
Ariel	98	Ava	31	Bathurst	52
Ariel (s.v.)	57	Avance (smack)	116	Batoum (attacked)	129
Aries	34	Avanti	79	Batoum (sunk)	56
Ariosto	140	Avocet (1,408)	130	Battersea	146, 152
Arlanza	125	Avocet (1,219) (attacked)	130 (2), 133	Baychattan (attacked)	143
Arlington Court	134, 143	Avocet (1,219) (sunk)	44	Baychattan (sunk)	69
Armadale	57	Avon	17	Baycraig	29
Armenian	8	Avristan	27	Bayford	145
Armonia	84	Axminster	72	Baygitano (attacked)	139
Arndale	7	Axwell	72	Baygitano (sunk)	84
Arnewood	75	Ayesha (s.v.)	3	Bayhall	28
Aros Castle	73	Aylestone	145	Bayhowel	135
Arracan	131, 136	Aylevarroo	69	Baynaen	39
Arran (trawler)	113	Aymeric	90	Baynesk	30
Arranmoor	142	Ayr (attacked)	138	Baynyassa	147
Arrino (attacked)	148	Ayr (sunk)	83	Bayronto	159
Arrino (sunk)	79	Aysgarth (attacked)	134	Baysarnia	158
Artesia	80	Aysgarth (sunk)	55	Baysarua	150
Arthur William (smack)	108	Azira	62	Baysoto	62
Artist	31	Azul	31	Bay State	54
Arum (attacked)	135			Bayusona	151
Arum (sunk)	96			Bayvoe (attacked)	146
Arvonian	128	**B.**		Bayvoe (sunk)	78
Arzila	157			Beachy	19
Asaba	75	Badagri	93	Beacon Grange	147
Asama (trawler)	120	Badger	20	Beacon Light	81
Ascania	141	Badminton	20	Beatrice	59
Ashburton	16	Bagdale (attacked)	134	Beaufront	29
Ashby	133	Bagdale (sunk)	47	Beaumaris	80
Ashleaf	52	Baku Standard (attacked)	143	Bechuana	160
Ashleigh	60	Baku Standard (sunk)	80	Bedale	69
Ashmore	11	Balakani	11	Beechleaf	152
Ashtabula	138	Baldersby	98	Beechpark	61
Ashwold (trawler)	114	Balgownie (attacked)	131	Beechtree	32
Asian	156	Balgownie (sunk)	14	Beechwold (trawler)	110
Asiatic Prince (attacked)	152	Balgray	81	Beemah	46
Asiatic Prince (sunk)	90	Ballarat	46	Beeswing (s.v.)	48
Aspenleaf	136	Ballater	130, 135	Begona No. 4	60
Assyria	64	Ballochbuie	45	Begonia	84
Astoria	23	Ballogie	72	Begum	90
Astræa	131	Baltic	141 (2)	Behrend (s.v.)	26
Astrologer	19	Ballycotton	128	Belford	13
Asturian	138	Bampton	136	Belford (s.v.)	31
Asturias	126, 139	Bamse (958)	87	Belgian	51
Astyanax	136, 142	Bamse (1,001)	98	Belgian Prince	61
Atalanta	127, 133	Bandon	42	Belgic	147
Athena	159	Bankfields	2	Belgier	34
Athena (smack)	106	Bangarth	75	Bel Lily (trawler)	118
Athenia (attacked)	144	Barbara	24	Bella (motor)	111
Athenia (sunk)	63	Barbary	72	Bellagio	147
Athenian (trawler)	114	Bardolph (trawler)	103	Bellbank	96
Athenic	153	Bargany	28	Belle of England	60
Athole (motor barge)	46	Barima	149	Belle of France	14
Athole (trawler)	113	Barley Rig (trawler)	100	Bellerby	154
Atlantian (attacked)	150	Barnsley (trawler)	114	Bellevue	3
Atlantian (sunk)	92	Barnton	45	Bellorado	138
Atlantic	154	Baron Ailsa	89	Bellucia	58
Atlantic City	126	Baron Balfour	71	Bellview (sunk)	87
Atlas (3,090) (attacked)	143	Baron Blantyre	68	Bellview (attacked)	134
Atlas (989)	72	Baron Cathcart	152	Belvoir Castle (trawler)	114
Atlas (3,090) (sunk)	81	Baron Cawdor	54	Ben Aden (trawler)	109
Aube	61	Baron Erskine	9	Benalder	136
Auchencrag	30	Baron Fairlie	148	Benalla	131
Auckland Castle	96	Baron Garioch (attacked)	137	Benarthur	9
Audax	96	Baron Garioch (sunk)	71	Benavon	149
Aulton (attacked)	154	Baron Herries	87	Benbow (trawler)	114
Aulton (sunk)	85	Baron Inchcape	152, 158	Bencleuch	159
Aurania (attacked)	145	Baron Minto	160	Ben Cruachan	4
Aurania (sunk)	80	Baron Napier	131, 139, 159	Bendew	16

	Page.		Page.		Page.
Bendoran	136	Borderer	139	Brookby	56
Benedict	131, 154	Border Knight	72	Brookwood	30
Beneficent	34	Borg	91	Broom	156
Bengairn (s.v.)	16	Borga	82	Broomhill	49
Bengali (attacked)	133, 136	Boscastle	86	Broompark	152
Bengali (sunk)	86	Boscawen	95	Brotherly Love (motor f.v.)	122
Bengore Head (attacked)	142	Bosnian	133	Brothertoft (trawler)	118
Bengore Head (sunk)	56	Boston City (attacked)	149	Brumaire	60
Bengrove	5	Boston City (sunk)	77	Brunhilda	58
Benguela	140, 146	Bostonian	69	Brunla	148
Benha	54	Botha (motor f.v.)	122	Bruse	154
Benha (s.v.)	98	Boveric	140	Brussels (attacked) 127,128(2), 129(2)	
Benheather	41	Bovic	129, 155	Brussels (captured)	19
Benington (trawler)	102	Bowes Castle	1	Buffalo (286)	96
Benita (s.v.)	56	Boy Bert (smack)	107	Buffalo (4,106)	56
Benito	77	Boy Denis (smack)	117	Bulgarian	30
Benlawers	151, 157	Boy Ernie (smack)	107	Bullmouth	46
Benledi	150	Boy Horace (smack)	103	Bulysses	63
Ben Arthur	4	Boy Jack (smack)	124	Bunty (tug)	70
Ben Lomond (attacked)	142	Boy Percy (smack)	108	Buranda	138, 145
Ben Lomond (sunk)	93	Boy Sam (smack)	108	Burcombe	27
Benmohr	2	Boy Walter (smack)	116	Buresk (4,337)	2
Ben Rein	80	Boyne Castle	32	Buresk (3,673)	12
Benrinnes	161	Boynton	68	Burgundy	139
Benue	151	Braconash (trawler)	110	Burma (706)	19
Benvorlich	8	Braefield	40	Burma (7470)	150
Ben Vrackie	9	Braemar Castle	135	Burnby	35
Berbera	39	Bramham	59	Burnhope	28
Bernard (attacked)	141	Brandenburg	160	Burnstone	84
Bernard (sunk)	75	Brandon (s.v.)	39	Burrowa (s.v.)	46
Bernicia	26	Branksome Chine	4	Burrsfield	11
Berrima	138	Branksome Hall (attacked) 141, 145,		Burutu	156
Bertrand (attacked)	136		150	Busiris	13
Bertrand (sunk)	93	Branksome Hall (sunk)	93	Busk	158
Berwen	154	Brantingham	23	Bute (trawler)	109
Berwick Law	74	Braunton	17	Butetown (3,789)	22
Berwindvale	132	Bray Head	37	Butetown (1,829)	79
Beryl (smack)	124	Brecknockshire	33	Bylands	98
Bessie Stephens (s.v.)	81	Brema (attacked)	132	Bywell	40
Bessy (motor)	82	Brema (sunk)	63		
Bethlehem (motor)	44	Brenda (s.v.)	29		
Bhamo	148	Brentwood	30		
Bianca (aux.)	160	Breslau	131	**C.**	
Bideford	141	Bretwalda (attacked)	130		
Bilswood	37	Bretwalda (sunk)	28	Cabotia	24
Birchgrove (attacked)	138, 143	Breynton	150	Cadeby	6
Birchgrove (sunk)	74	Briardene	27	Cadillac	155
Birchleaf	154	Briarleaf	161	Cadmus	70
Birchwood	77	Brierley Hill	25	Cairngowan	17
Birdoswald	57	Brierton	26	Cairndhu	43
Birkhall	79	Brigade	34	Cairnhill	43
Birtley	78	Brighton	153	Cairnross	90, 143
Biruta	94	Brigitta	74	Cairntorr	5
Bishopston	65	Brika	37	Cairo	9
Bittern	10	Brisbane River	43	Cairo (s.v.)	97
Black Head	56	Brissons (smack)	114	Cairnmona	158
Blackheath	157	Bristol City (attacked)	141	Cairnross	49
Blackwood	5	Bristol City (sunk)	76	Cairnstrath	62
Blagdon	62	Britannia (765)	70	Cairnvalona	157
Blairhall	94	Britannia (1,814)	27	Caithness (attacked)	136
Blake	60	Britannia (3,129)	40	Caithness (sunk)	44
Blakemoor	146, 147	Britannia (smack)	22	C. A. Jaques	47
Bleamoor	74	Britannia (smack)	104	Calabria	142
Blessing (motor)	108	Britannia III. (trawler)	111	Calchas	49
Blonde	127	Britannic (3,487)	20	Caldergrove	36
Blue Jacket	127	Britannic (48,158)	26	Caledonia (9,223)	27
Blush Rose	154	Britannic (s.v.)	75	Caledonia (7,572)	136
Boaz (s.v.)	40	British Major	159	Caliban (trawler)	117
Bob White (trawler)	102	British Monarch	62	Califol	134
Boddam	23	British Princess	154	California (8,669)	32
Bogota	25	British Star	155, 160	California (5,629)	70
Boldwell	52	British Sun	47	Californian	12
Boltonhall	95	British Transport	148	Calliope (3,829)	41
Boma (attacked)	151, 156	British Viscount	82	Calliope (2,883)	59
Boma (sunk)	91	British Yeoman (s.v.)	35	Calypso	19
Bona Fide (smack)	107	Briton (trawler)	111	Cambank	4
Bondicar	160	Broderick	88	Camberwell (attacked)	135
Boniface	64	Brodholme	158	Camberwell (sunk)	50
Bonney	9	Brodliffe	140	Camborne (s.v.)	157
Bontnewydd	69	Brodmead	148	Cambrian	138
Bonvilston (attacked)	132, 144, 151	Brodmore	35	Cambrian King	157
Bonvilston (sunk)	98	Brodness	40	Cambrian Range	27
Boonah	139	Brodstone	63	Cambric	71
Boorara	155, 159	Bronwen	22	Camellia (smack)	113

Name	Page	Name	Page	Name	Page
Camerata	142	Centurion	6	City of Exeter	128, 144
Cameron	138	Centurion (s.v.)	34	City of Florence	59
Cameronia (attacked)	128	Ceramic	144, 146	City of Ghent	22
Cameronia (sunk)	43	Cerne	16	City of Glasgow	96
Cameronian (attacked)	136, 138	Cervantes	2	City of Hankow	145
Cameronian (sunk)	52	C. E. S. (smack)	106	City of Lahore	131
Camito	145, 147	Cestrian	56	City of Lincoln	149
Camlake	134	Chagres	83	City of Liverpool	129
Campania (trawler)	105	Challenger (smack)	106	City of London	142
Canadian (9,309) (attacked)	138	Chameleon (trawler)	99	City of Lucknow (3,677)	18
Canadian (9,309) (sunk)	41	Chancellor	11	City of Lucknow (8,293)	76
Canadian (2,214)	150	Chantala	16	City of Manchester	158
Canara	142, 147	Chao Chow Fu	149, 160	City of Marseilles	130
Cancer (trawler)	101	Charcas	3	City of Oran	136
Candia	60	Charing Cross (attacked)	145	City of Paris	41
Candidate	6	Charing Cross (sunk)	93	City of Perth	54
Canford Chine	19	Charity	160	City of Swansea	68
Cannizaro	39	Charles (s.v.)	76	City of Winchester (6,601)	1
Canonesa	151, 156	Charles Goodanew	43	City of Winchester (7,981)	156
Canopic	148	Charles Theriault (s.v.)	158	City of Winchester (s.v.)	85
Canova	76	Charleston	75	City of York	130
Canto	129, 145	Charterhouse	22	Civilian	69
Cape Antibes	12	Chasehill	126	Claddagh	157
Cape Corso	149	Chatburn	35	Clam	155
Cape Finisterre	72	Chatham	90	Clan Alpine	54
Capenor	45	Chelford	86	Clan Buchanan	135
Cape Transport	146	Cheltonian	53	Clan Cameron	76
Capricornus (trawler)	99	Chenab	137	Clan Campbell	16
Carbery King (smack)	118	Cherbury	6	Clan Chisholm	134, 135, 146
Cardiff	152	Cherryleaf	148	Clan Colquhoun	135
Cardiff (trawler)	104	Chertsey (sunk)	46	Clan Cumming	150
Cardiganshire	136	Chertsey (attacked)	153	Clan Davidson	56
Cardonia (s.v.)	17	Cheshire (trawler)	105	Clan Farquhar	35
Caria	12	Chesterfield	90	Clan Ferguson	66
Cariad (smack)	119	Chevington	146	Clan Forbes	91
Carisbrook	7	Cheviot Range	81	Clan Graham	143, 154
Carlisle Castle	81	Cheyenne	146	Clan Grant	2
Carlo (3,040)	72	Chic	17	Clangula	73
Carlo (1,987)	131, 134, 135	Chicago	93	Clan Leslie	25
Carlton	90	Chicago City	143	Clan Lindsay	132
Carlyle	29	Chilkana	3	Clan Macalister	12
Carmarthen	60	Chimu	161	Clan Macarthur	141
Carmarthenshire	140	Chindwara	161	Clan Maccorquodale	73
Carmelite (attacked)	150	Chinkiang (trawler)	117	Clan Macdougall	84
Carmelite (sunk)	82	Chinkoa	129, 152	Clan Macfadyen	132
Carnmoney (s.v.)	50	Chirripo	77	Clan Macfarlane	13
Caroni	10	Chiswick	143	Clan Macintosh	146
Carpathia	93	Chiverstone	156	Clan Mackenzie	154
Carpentaria	150	Chloris	94	Clan Maclaren	158
Carperby	138, 143	Chorley	38	Clan Macleod	13
Carrabin (s.v.)	68	Christabel (s.v.)	26	Clan Macmillan	38
Carrie Hervey (s.v.)	55	Christiana Davis (s.v.)	88	Clan MacNab (attacked)	142
Carrigan Head	151	Chrysolite (trawler)	102	Clan Macnab (sunk)	94
Carterswell	10	Chrysolite (smack)	120	Clan Macneil (attacked)	150
Carthaginian	55	Chrysoprasus (trawler)	103	Clan Macneil (sunk)	94
C.A.S. (smack)	115	Chulmleigh	67	Clan Macpherson	83
Caspian	51	Chupra	125, 155	Clan Macrae	126
Cassio (trawler)	105	Churston	10	Clan Mactavish	14
Castalia	135	Chyebassa	151	Clan Macvey (attacked)	159
Castillian	44	Cicero	86	Clan Macvey (sunk)	95
Castle Eden	83	Cilicia	32	Clan Matheson	2
Castleford	83	Cilurnum (attacked)	134	Clan Murray	52
Castleton	59	Cilurnum (sunk)	44	Clan Robertson	128
Castor (trawler)	104	Cimbrier	153	Clan Ross	157
Caswell (trawler)	112	Cito (attacked)	129	Clan Shaw	30
Catena (smack)	112	Cito (sunk)	50	Clan Sinclair	141
Caterham	25	City	140	Clan Stuart	136
Cattaro	57	City of Adelaide	95	Clan Sutherland	140
Caucasian	8	City of Athens	62	Clapham	155
Cavallo (attacked)	150	City of Baroda	53	Clara	77
Cavallo (sunk)	79	City of Birmingham	26	Clarecastle	153
Cavina	52	City of Bombay	159	Clarissa Radcliffe	154
Cawdor Castle	131	City of Bremen	6	Claudia	20
Cayo Bonito	69	City of Brisbane	95	Claveresk	145 (2)
Cayo Romano	128	City of Cairo	135	Claverley	63
C.E.C.G. (s.v.)	50	City of Cambridge (attacked)	127, 130	Clayton W. Walters (f.v.)	124
Cecil L. Shave (s.v.)	82	City of Cambridge (sunk)	57	Clematis	158
Cedarmore	15	City of Canton	146	Clematis (smack)	112
Cedric (trawler)	120	City of Chester	150	Clermiston	150
Celia (attacked)	145	City of Colombo	147 (2)	Cliburn	24
Celia (sunk)	80	City of Corinth	51	Cliffside	142, 154
Celtic	137, 143, 155	City of Cork	159	Clifftower	146, 148, 157
Celtic (trawler)	106	City of Dortmund	128	Cliftondale	76
Cento	148, 158	City of Edinburgh	129, 134	Cliftonhall	148

Name	Page	Name	Page	Name	Page
Cliftonian	31	Corinthic	147	Cyprus (smack)	123
Clinton	132	Cork	79	Cyrene (attacked)	134
Clintonia	8	Cormorant	3	Cyrene (sunk)	85
Clodmoor (attacked)	133	Cornelia	36	Cynthia (trawler)	111
Clodmoor (sunk)	48	Cornhill	146	Cypria	133
Cloughton	140	Cornish City	2		
Cluden	24	Cornubia	11		
Clumberhall (attacked)	136	Corona (trawler)	119		
Clumberhall (sunk)	158	Coronado	139, 144	**D.**	
Clyde (s.v.)	17	Coronation (motor f.v.)	123		
Clydebrae	149	Coronda	37	Dacia	27
C. M. Walters (f.v.)	124	Coronilla	134	Dafila	60
Coalgas	83	Corsham	83	Daghild	149
Coath	28	Corsican Prince	32	D. A. Gordon	75
Cober	10	Corso (attacked)	129	Dale (trawler)	114
Coblenz	146	Corso (sunk)	34	Daleby	47
Cockatrice (trawler)	111	Cortes (trawler)	103	Dalegarth	18
Cock o' the Walk (s.v.)	24	Corton	152	Dalegarth Force	87
Cognac	160	Corton L. V.	19	Dalewood	82
Coila	75	Costello	9	Dalhousie (trawler)	109
Colchester (attacked)	126 (2), 127, 128	Cotovia (attacked)	144	Dallington	150, 159
		Cotovia (sunk)	60	Dalmatian (trawler)	117
Colchester (captured)	22	Cottingham	13	Dalton	42
Coleby	5	Counsellor	22	Dana (s.v.)	51
Colemere	76	Counsellor (smack)	124	Dantzic	43
Colenso	13	Countess of Mar	62	Danubian	132, 139
Colin Stuart	148	Courage (smack)	121	Darino	151
Collegian (attacked)	145	Courtfield	154, 157	Darius	55
Collegian (sunk)	70	Cowrie	146	Darro	161
Colorado	70	Coya	156	Dart	55
Colusa	126	Cragoswald	44	Dartmoor (attacked)	136
Comanchee	147	Craigard	8	Dartmoor (sunk)	52
Comedian	47	Craigendoran	35	Datchet	148
Comeric	128, 136, 150	Craigforth	125	Dauntless	31
Comic	156	Craigston	11	David Lloyd George	150
Commander (smack)	122	Crane	145	Dawdon	2
Commander (trawler)	105	Cranley	137	Daybreak (attacked)	134
Commander Boyle (trawler)	107	Cranmore	149	Daybreak (sunk)	76
Commodore	13	Craonne	149, 153	Dayspring (smack)	123
Commonwealth (attacked)	153	Crayford	83	Day Spring (smack)	121
Commonwealth (sunk)	81	Cremyll (s.v.)	157	Deddington	145
Como	129	Crenella	151, 159	Dee (s.v.)	40
Comrades (smack)	115	Cressida	84	Defender	159
Comrie Castle	154	Cressington Court	157	Delamere	47
Conargo	85	Cresswell (attacked)	144	Delmira	127
Conch	27	Cresswell (sunk)	80	Delphic (attacked)	137
Concord	5	Cretic	151	Delphic (sunk)	63
Concord (smack)	113	Crimond (trawler)	102	Delphinula	160
Condesa	58	Crispin	40	Demaris (s.v.)	21
Condor	2	Cromarty	136	Demerara	128, 131, 146
Condor (trawler)	103	Cromer	128, 129	Demeterton	37
Coningbeg	76	Cronstadt	149	Demodocus	155
Coniston Water	59	Crossby	130	Denaby (attacked)	127
Connaught	35	Crosshands	157	Denaby (sunk)	15
Conoid (s.v.)	40	Crosshill	23	Denbigh Hall	90
Conovium (s.v.)	73	Crown of Arragon	56	Denbighshire	157
Conrad (s.v.)	28	Crown of Castile	5	Deneb	152
Consolation (smack)	110	Crown of Granada	139	Denebola (attacked)	150
Consols	75	Crown of India (s.v.)	7	Denebola (sunk)	95
Constance (motor)	101	Crown of Leon	142	Denetown	143
Constance (smack)	107	Crown of Toledo	141	Denewood	18
Constance Mary (s.v.)	28	Crown Point	32	Den of Crombie	12
Constantia	89	Crown Prince (trawler)	117	Den of Ogil	131
Conster (smack)	125	Croxteth Hall	73	Dependence (s.v.)	67
Conway	88	Cruiser (trawler)	102	Deptford	4
Conway Castle (s.v.)	5	Crystal (smack)	108	Derbent	74
Coonagh	40	Cuba (s.v.)	50	Derrymore	48
Cooroy (s.v.)	65	Cumberland	58	Derwent River	150
Copeland	74	Cumbria	156	Desabla	7
Copenhagen (2,570)	36	Cumbrian	152	Deseado	136
Copenhagen (4,540)	149, 158	Cupica (motor)	70	Desna	159
Copious (trawler)	101	Curlew (smack)	116	Destro (attacked)	133
Copsewood	29	Curlew (trawler)	103	Destro (sunk)	85
Coquet	14	Custodian	155	Detlef Wagner (s.v.)	52
Coquet (trawler)	102	Cuthbert	142, 146	Devereux	149
Coral Leaf (s.v.)	58	Cuyahoga	58	Devian	133
Corbet Woodall	52	Cyclops	137, 140	Devona	145, 147
Corbiere (motor)	154	Cydonia (trawler)	106	Devon City	148
Corbridge	14	Cyfarthfa	42	Devonian	63
Cordova (attacked)	142	Cymbeline	10	Devonian (trawler)	107
Cordova (sunk)	75	Cymrian	64	Devonshire (trawler)	111
Corfu	43	Cymric	18	Devonshire	142, 152
Coriander (smack)	106	Cymric Vale	143 (2)	Dewa	22
Corinth	26	Cypria	152	Dewsland	18

Name	Page.	Name	Page.	Name	Page.
Diadem (3,752)	15	Dundarg (s.v.)	154	Eleanor	80
Diadem (4,307)	45	Dundee	31	Eleanor (smack)	118
Diana	91	Dundrennan	140	Eleazar (trawler)	120
Dianthus (smack)	123	Dunedin	127, 152	Elele	55
Dictator	10	Dungeness	157	Elfland	127
Dictator (s.v.)	92	Dunmore Head	46	Elford	50
Dido	15	Dunnet Head	7	Elfrida	4
Dilston Castle (trawler)	118	Dunrobin (attacked)	134, 146	E. L. G. (smack)	113
Dingle	15	Dunrobin (sunk)	73	Eliza Anne (s.v.)	84
Dinorwic (s.v.)	59	Dunsley	9	Elizabeth (trawler)	104
Diomed (4,672)	10	Durango	64	Elizabeth (s.v.)	66
Diomed (7,523)	95	Durward	4	Elizabeth Eleanor (s.v.)	37
Diplomat	1	Dux (attacked)	152	Elizabeth Hampton (s.v.)	50
Dipton	160	Dux (sunk)	89	Elizabetta	157
Dixiana	7	Dwinsk	92	Ella Sayer	88
Djerv	81	Dykland (attacked)	135	Ellaston (3,796)	16
Dockleaf	144	Dykland (sunk)	45	Ellaston (3,192)	84
Dogberry (trawler)	103			Ellen Harrison (s.v.)	47
Dolcoath	18			Ellen James (s.v.)	41
Dolly Varden (s.v.)	72			Elleric	153
Dolphin	151			Ellesmere	8
Dominic	144	**E.**		Elmgrove	18
Domino	150(2)			Elmleaf	152
Don	6	E. & C. (smack)	103	Elmmoor	51
Don (trawler)	102	Eagle	74	Elmsgarth	68
Don Arturo	56	Eagle Point	16	Eloby (attacked)	133
Don Diego	51	Earl Howard (trawler)	101	Eloby (sunk)	59
Donegal (attacked)	138	Earl of Elgin	75	El Paraguayo	152
Donegal (sunk)	44	Earl of Lathom (s.v.)	6	Elsena	73
Don Emilio	57	Earlswood	151	Elsie (motor)	119
Dora	48	East Point	36	Elsie (s.v.)	145
Dorado (smack)	110	East Wales	132	Elsie Birdett (s.v.)	88
Dorie	142, 152	Eastern Belle (s.v.)	40	Elsie Porter (f.v.)	125
Dornfontein (motor)	94	Eastern City (4,341)	17	Elsinore	1
Dorothy (attacked)	137	Eastern City (5,992)	151	Elsiston	70
Dorothy (sunk)	34	Eastern Coast	158	Elstree Grange	146
Dorothy Duff (s.v.)	50	Eastern Prince	65	Elswick Grange	157
Dorset Coast	127	Eastfield	74	Elswick Hall	157
Dotterel (attacked)	130	Eastgate	136, 148	Elswick Lodge	63
Dotterel (sunk)	13	Eastlands	79	Elswick Manor (attacked)	131
Douro	10	East Wales	69	Elswick Manor (sunk)	44
Dover Castle	52	Eavestone	31	Elterwater	3
Dovey (trawler)	104	Ebenezer (trawler)	103	El Uruguayo	143, 151
Dowlais	74	Ebenezer (s.v.)	59	Elvaston	145
Downshire (337)	4	Eboe	155	Elve	149(2)
Downshire (368)	97	Eburna (trawler)	146	Elwick	150, 152
Drake	68	E. B. Walters (f.v.)	124	Elysia	141, 145(2), 155, 157
Dragoon (smack)	110	Ecclesia	19	El Zorro	13
Dramatist	28	Echunga (attacked)	140	Embla	13
Drammeseren	156	Echunga (sunk)	65	Emblem (trawler)	106
Dresden	22	Eclipse (trawler)	120	Emblem (smack)	107
Drina	35	Eclipse (smack)	123	Embleton	66
Dromio (trawler)	103	Economy (smack)	103	Emerald (smack)	114
Dromonby	14	Eda	147, 153	Emilie	86
Dromore (4,398)	46	Edale	6	Emily Millington (s.v.)	99
Dromore (268)	50	Eddie	33	Emlyn	147
Dronning Maud	87	Eddystone	139	Emlynverne	26
Drumcliffe	125, 141	Edenside	129	Emma	45
Drumcree	6	Edernian (attacked)	140	Emma (s.v.)	65
Drumloist	7	Edernian (sunk)	63	Emma Minlos	155
Drummuir (s.v.)	3	Edina	63	Emmanuel (smack)	107
Dryden	155	Edinburgh (s.v.)	14	Empire	149
Duart	21	Edith Cavell (motor)	118	Empress	61
Dublin	152	Edith (s.v.)	7	Empress of Fort William	15
Duchess of Cornwall (s.v.)	27	Edlington	97	Empress of Midland	16
Duchess of Cornwall	42	Eduard (s.v.)	43	E. M. W. (smack)	107
Duckbridge	15	Edward (smack)	104	Ena (smack)	115
Dudhope (s.v.)	59	Effort (trawler)	112	Ena May (trawler)	103
Duendes	132	Effra	147	Enda	152
Duke of Connaught	161	Eggesford	135, 153	Endeavour (smack)	116
Duke of Cumberland	154, 161	Egret	157	Endymion (s.v.)	40
Duke of Wellington (trawler)	102	Egret (trawler)	123	Energy (smack)	115
Duke of York (trawler)	114	Egyptiana (attacked)	135	Energy (s.v.)	97
Dulcie	7	Egyptiana (sunk)	53	Enfield	130
Dulwich (1,460)	54	Egyptian Prince (trawler)	110	England	51
Dulwich (3,289)	4	Egyptian Prince	49	Englishman	16
Dumfries	6	Egyptian Transport	152	Englishman (s.v.)	136
Dumfriesshire (s.v.)	8	Eider	150	Englishman (tug)	159
Dunachton	135	Eimstad	129	English Monarch	55
Dunaff Head	155, 158	El Argentino	18	Enidwen	53
Dunbar	134	Elax	23	Enigma (smack)	116
Dunbarmoor	36	Elba	88	Ennismore (attacked)	127
Dundalk (attacked)	151	El Cordobes	147	Ennismore (sunk)	77
Dundalk (sunk)	98	Eldra	70	Ennistown	38

Name	Page	Name	Page	Name	Page
Enosis	12	Express (s.v.)	7	Folia	36
Eptalofos (attacked)	134	Ezel (s.v.)	66	Foreland (attacked)	131
Eptalofos (sunk)	38			Foreland (sunk)	32
Eptapyrgion	45			Forestmoor	69
Equerry (trawler)	117			Forfar	74
Equinox (trawler)	110	**F.**		Forget-me-not (smack)	115
Era	88			Formby	76
Erato	65	Fabian (attacked)	134	Fornebo	55
Eretria	18	Fabian (sunk)	67	Forth	27
Eric Calvert	87	Fagerton	155	Fortuna (s.v.)	21
Erica (s.v.)	83	Fairearn	38	Fortuna (smack)	123
Erik	96	Fairmuir	146	Forward (smack)	121
Erivan	156	Fairport	17	Four (trawler)	105
Erith (trawler)	117	Falaba	5	Foyle (4,147)	2
Erme (motor)	93	Falcon (attacked)	132	Foyle (4,703)	136
Ermenilda (s.v.)	21	Falcon (sunk)	34	Foylemore	76
Erna Boldt	7	Fallodon (attacked)	139, 145	Framfield	24
Ernest (s.v.)	48	Fallodon (sunk)	77	Frances (motor)	119
Ernst	132, 133	Falls City	131	Frances (s.v.—56)	87
Eros (attacked)	151	Family's Pride (motor f.v.)	120	Frances (s.v.—89)	66
Eros (sunk)	95	Farley	50	Francis Robert (smack)	124
Eros (trawler)	124	Farn (captured)	125	Franconia	23
Errington Court	135, 144	Farn (sunk)	73	Frankier	141
Escrick	95	Farnham	51	Franklyn (attacked)	153
Eskmere	69	Farnworth	153	Franklyn (sunk)	88
Eskimo	20	Farraline	72	Frank Parish	150
Esmeraldas	36	Farringford	144	Franz Fischer	14
Esperance (smack)	107	Fastnet	15	Fraternal (trawler)	100
Esperanza de Larrinaga	157	Fastnet (smack)	118	Frau Minna Petersen (s.v.)	1
Esneh (attacked)	131 (2), 135	Favonian	21	Frederick Knight	48
Esneh (sunk)	52	Favourite (smack)	110	Freighter	141
Essex	158	Favorita Clara	154	Fremona	61
Essonite	31	F. D. Lambert (attacked)	132	French Prince	33
Estrella	83	F. D. Lambert (sunk)	32	French Rose	73
Estrellano	71	Fear Not (smack)	124	Freshfield (attacked)	144, 159
Etal Manor (attacked)	137	Feliciana	17	Freshfield (sunk)	94
Etal Manor (sunk)	67	Feltria	49	Friargate	12
Ethel	97	Fenay Bridge	16	Friederike	126
Ethel (s.v.)	87	Fenay Lodge	36	Friendship (smack)	114
Ethel (smack)	113	Ferga	33	Frigate Bird (motor)	119
Ethelaric	140	Fern	87	Frimaire	37
Ethelbryhta	20	Ferndene	45	Frinton	38
Ethel Duncan	24	Fernleaf	144, 145	Frodingham	133
Ethelinda	79	Fernley	136, 143, 159	Frolic (trawler)	115
Ethelwynne	147	Fernmoor	43	F. Stobart	21
Ethiope	7	Ferrona	71	Fuchsia (trawler)	112
Ethyl	149	Ferryhill	79	Fulgens	8
Etonian (attacked)	128, 129	Fife Ness (trawler)	117	Fulgent	6
Etonian (sunk)	85	Findhorn	153	Fulmar (attacked)	130
Etton	22	Fingal	5	Fulmar (sunk)	16
Euclid (trawler)	102	Firelight	48	Fylde (tug)	160
Eudora	33	Firfield	59		
Eumaeus	82	Firth	8		
Euonymous (smack)	113	Fiscus (attacked)	142	**G.**	
Euphorbia (3,837)	20	Fiscus (sunk)	76		
Euphorbia (3,109)	74	Fisherman (s.v.)	93	Gaboon	144
Eupion (attacked)	156 (2)	Fisherman (smack)	106	Gadsby	8
Eupion (sunk)	98	Fisher Prince (trawler)	111	Gadwall (trawler)	106
Euryades	153	Fittonia (trawler)	100	Gafsa (3922)	19
Eurylochus	159	Fitzgerald (smack)	106	Gafsa (3,974)	39
Eurymachus	144	Flamenco	14	Gala	158
Eustace	144	Flaminian (3,500)	5	Galacum	155
Euston	70	Flaminian (3,227)	147	Galatia (trawler)	116
Euterpe (1522)	14	Flamma	146	Galeka	24
Euterpe (3540)	138	Flavia (attacked)	151	Galgate (s.v.)	18
Euthamia (trawler)	125	Flavia (sunk)	95	Galgorm Castle (s.v.)	35
Eveline (attacked)	132	Flavian (trawler)	99	Galicia (5922—attacked)	129
Eveline (sunk)	76	Flawyl	88	Galicia (5,922—sunk)	49
Evelyn (smack)	108	Flaxmere	141	Galicia (1,400)	54
Evening Star (trawler)	103	Fleswick	149, 152	Galician	125
Everilda	159	Flimston	28	Galileo	157
Ewell	157	Flixton	154	Gallier (attacked)	126
Excel (trawler)	114	Florazan	5	Gallier (sunk)	77
Excellence Pleske (attacked)	147, 151	Floreal (trawler)	112	Galtee	142
Excellence Pleske (sunk)	85	Florence (trawler)	109	Galway Castle (attacked)	133
Excellent	30	Florence Louisa (s.v.)	50	Galway Castle (sunk)	96
Exchange	38	Florence Muspratt (s.v.)	65	Gambia	138
Exford (attacked)	125	Florentia	92	Gamecock (trawler)	111
Exford (sunk)	59	Floridian	31	Ganges (3,497)	145
Exmoor	158	Florrieston (attacked)	141	Ganges (4,177—attacked)	132
Exmouth	151, 159	Florrieston (sunk)	87	Ganges (4,177—sunk)	61
Expedient (trawler)	118	Fluent	59	Gannet	19
Explorer	137	F. Matarazzo	26	Gardepee	23
Explorer (trawler)	103	Foam Crest (smack)	108	Garfield	30

Name	Page
Garmoyle (attacked)	128
Garmoyle (sunk)	58
Garron Head	72
Garryvale	154
Garthclyde	70
Garthwaite	75
Gartland	77
Gartness	63
G. A. Savage	36
Gasconia	72
Gascony	78
Gauntlet (s.v.)	56
Gaupen	83
Gazehound (trawler)	103
Gazelle (s.v.)	35
Gazelle (smack)	121
G. C. Gradwell (s.v.)	20
Geddington Court	137
Gefion	71
Geilan Bahri (s.v.)	41
Gem	3
Gem (trawler)	119
Gemini	94
Gemma (attacked)	131
Gemma (sunk)	70
Gena (attacked)	141
Gena (sunk)	47
General Buller (trawler)	120
General Church	153
General Laurie (s.v.)	53
General Leman (smack)	121
Genesee (2830)	159
Genesee (2,892)	139, 149, 152
Genesee (tug)	155
Geo (attacked)	140
Geo (sunk)	79
George and Mary (s.v.)	7
George Baker (trawler)	107
George Borrow (smack)	107
George Crabbe (smack)	107
George E. Benson (trawler)	113
George Harper	156
George Pyman	50
Georgian	36
Georgic	28
Georgios Antippa	74
Geraldine (smack)	122
Geralda (smack)	119
Gertrude (smack)	109
Ghazee	31
Gibel Derif	154
Gibel-Hamam	97
Gibel-Yedid	59
Gibraltar	66
Gibraltar (trawler)	116
Gippeswic (s.v.)	40
Giralda	96
Girdleness	88
Girl Bessie (trawler)	109
Girl's Friend (trawler)	109
Gisella (attacked)	140
Gisella (sunk)	73
Gladiator	9
Gladstone (tug)	146
Glad Tidings (smack)	123
Gladys	74
Gladys (trawler)	113
Gladys M. Hollett	159
Gladys Royle	30
Glamorgan	147
Glance (smack)	109
Glanton	3
Glaucus	91
G.L.C. (smack)	118
Gleam (smack)	119
Glenalmond	17
Glenamoy	153
Glenarm Head	78
Glenart Castle (attacked)	138
Glenart Castle (sunk)	82
Glenartney (5,201)	5
Glenartney (7,263)	80
Glenbridge	151
Glenbrook	155

Name	Page
Glenby	9
Glencarron	81
Glencarse (trawler)	101
Glencliffe (attacked)	139
Glencliffe (sunk)	42
Glencluny	46
Glencoe	28
Gleneden	137, 138
Glenelg	148
Glenelg (trawler)	119
Glenford	84
Glenfoyle	131
Glenfruin	150
Glengyle	14
Glenholm (s.v.)	6
Glenlee (4,140)	7
Glenlee (4,915) (attacked)	158
Glenlee (4,915) (sunk)	95
Glenlogan	25
Glenmay	134
Glenmoor	12
Glenmorag	134
Glenogle (attacked)	133
Glenogle (sunk)	39
Glenravel	9
Glenrazan	151
Glenroy	130
Glenstrae	61
Glen Tanar	48
Glenturret	126, 146, 148
Glitra	3
Gloaming (f.v.)	125
Glocliffe (attacked)	131
Glocliffe (sunk)	63
Gloria (trawler)	107
Gloriosa (smack)	120
Gloucester Castle	140
Glow	60
Gloxinia (trawler)	101
Glynn (s.v.)	65
Glynymel	37
Goathland	58
Golconda	18
Gold Coast	44
Golden Hope (trawler)	119
Golden Oriole (trawler)	101
Goldmouth	16
Gold Seeker (smack)	115
Good Design (motor)	109
Good Hope	70
Good Hope (s.v.)	46
Goodwood	63
Goorkha	150
Gorsemore (attacked)	142, 145
Gorsemore (sunk)	97
Governor	37
Gowan (motor)	116
Gower Coast	41
Gowrie	69
Grace	160
Grace (s.v.)	26
Gracefield	155
Gracia (smack)	115
Graciana	144
Grainton	154
Grangemoor	20
Grangetown	143
Grangewood	8
Grantleyhall	76
Graphic	126
Gratitude (smack)	121
Gravina	32
Great City	145
Greatham	78
Greavesash	82
Grebe	157
Grecian (trawler)	117
Greenbank	53
Greenland	33
Greenore	160
Greenwich	74
Gregory	158
Gregynog (attacked)	152
Gregynog (sunk)	87

Name	Page
Greldon (attacked)	149, 152
Greldon (sunk)	69
Greleen	67
Grelford	138 (2)
Grelfryda	148
Grelhame (attacked)	143
Grelhame (sunk)	65
Greltoria	68
Grenada (s.v.)	26
Grenadier	34
Gresham	87
Greta	48
Gretaston	47
Greypoint	38
Grimbarian (trawler)	106
Grinkle	157
Griqua	136, 142
Grit (motor barge)	24
Grodno	9
Groeswen	74
Groningen (attacked)	127, 129
Groningen (sunk)	11
Grosvenor	146
Gryfevale (attacked)	125
Gryfevale (sunk)	71
Guard (smack)	116
Guido (attacked)	129
Guido (sunk)	8
Guildford Castle	154
Guildhall	57
Gwent	138
Gwynwood	151

H.

Name	Page
Hackensack (see Stephanotis)	46
Hadley	13
Haigh Hall	57
Haileybury	82
Hainton (trawler)	105
Halberdier	78
Halcyon	17
Halcyon (trawler)	114
Halizones	11
Hallamshire	12
Hambleton Range	128, 142
Hamidieh (s.v.)	98
Hamnavoe (trawler)	120
Hampstead	152
Hanley	52
Hanna Larsen	32
Hannah	147
Hannah Croasdell (s.v.)	35
Hans Jost	158
Harberton	40
Harbinger (trawler)	119
Harborne	149
Harbury	53
Hare	75
Harewood	86
Harfat Castle (trawler)	112
Harflete	46
Harlington	27
Harlseywood	159
Harlyn	27
Harmattan	48
Harmatris	15
Harmonides	152
Harold (s.v.)	60
Harold (smack)	108
Harpagus	49
Harpalion	5
Harpalus	27
Harpalyce	6
Harpathian (attacked)	144
Harpathian (sunk)	91
Harperley	161
Harrier (trawler—208)	100
Harrier (trawler—162)	111
Harriet Williams (s.v.)	35
Harrovian	17

	Page.		Page.		Page.
Harrow (attacked) -	137	Highland Harris (attacked) -	129	Huntleys (s.v.) - -	39
Harrow (sunk) - -	66	Highland Harris (sunk) -	94	Huntly - - -	13
Harry W. Adams (s.v.) -	28	Highland Heather -	135	Huntress - -	157
Hartburn - - -	70	Highland Hope - -	2	Huntscape - -	135, 138, 139
Hartdale - - -	5	Highland Laird - -	121	Huntscliff - -	160
Hartland - - -	151	Highland Loch - -	152	Huntsclyde - -	148
Hartley (attacked) -	146	Highland Monarch -	147	Huntscraft - -	158
Hartley (sunk) - -	79	Highland Prince - -	86	Huntsend - -	136, 146, 160
Harvest Home (s.v.) -	39	Highland Scot - -	127	Huntsfall - -	23
Haslemere - -	148	Highland Watch - -	156	Huntsgulf - -	150
Haslingden (attacked) -	142, 146	Highlander - -	158, 160	Huntsholm (attacked) -	141, 143
Haslingden (sunk) -	89	Hilda (smack) - -	108	Huntsholm (sunk) -	54
Hatasu - - -	98	Hilda Lea - -	76	Huntsland - -	91
Hathor - - -	64	Hilda R. (s.v.) - -	72	Huntsman (attacked) -	130
Hatsuse (trawler) - -	112	Hildawell (attacked) -	136	Huntsman (sunk) -	34
Haulwen - - -	54	Hildawell (sunk) - -	28	Huntsmoor (attacked) -	142
Haverford - -	145, 146, 156	Hillhouse - -	140	Huntsmoor (sunk) -	81
Hawanee (s.v.) - -	98	Hindoo - - -	142	Huntspill - -	134
Haworth - - -	59	Hindustan - -	38	Huntstrick - -	53
Haydn - - -	11	Hinemona (s.v.) - -	66	Huntsvale - -	25
Hazelpark - -	38	Hirondelle - -	46	Huronian - -	131
Hazelwood (attacked) -	145	Hirose (trawler) - -	103	Hurst (attacked) -	141, 145
Hazelwood (sunk) -	70	Hitchin - - -	156	Hurst (sunk) - -	68
H. C. G. (smack) -	116	H.M.W. (barge) - -	25	Hurstdale - -	3
H. C. Henry - -	11	Hogarth - -	91	Hurstside - -	58
Headcliffe - -	141, 155	Holgate - - -	39	Hurstwood - -	31
Headlands - -	5	Holkar (smack) - -	122	Hurunui - -	90
Headley - - -	34	Hollington - -	52	Hyacinth (smack) -	115
Heathdene - -	22	Hollinside - -	31	Hyacinthus - -	140, 152
Heather (trawler) -	117	Holly Branch - -	29	Hyades - - -	1
Heatherside - -	64	Hollyleaf - -	156	Hylas - - -	63
Heathfield (s.v.) -	46	Holmesbank - -	51	Hyndford - -	127, 134, 148
Hebble - - -	49	Holmpark - -	153, 160	Hypatia - -	144
Hebburn - - -	97	Holmwood - -	1	Hyperia - - -	94
Hector (trawler) - -	102	Holtby - - -	125	Hyson - - -	143
Heighington - -	20	Holywell - -	144		
Heinrich (s.v.) - -	27	Homer (tug) - -	127		
Helen (attacked) - -	126	Honey Bee (motor f.v.) -	123		
Helen (sunk) - -	48	Hong Moh - -	152	**I.**	
Helena and Samuel (smack) -	113	Honora (motor f.v.) -	122		
Helenes - - -	153	Honiton - - -	10		
Helenus - -	151, 158, 160	Honoria (trawler—207) -	105	Iberian - - -	8
Heliotrope (smack) -	106	Honoria (trawler—179) -	106	Ibex - - -	135, 143, 154
Hellenic (trawler) -	102	Hooton - - -	138	Ibex (smack) - -	121
Helmsmuir - -	13	Hopemoor - -	33	Iceland - - -	57
Helvetia (trawler) -	110	Hopemount - -	7	Iceni (smack) - -	106
Hemisphere - -	3	Horace - - -	14	Ida Duncan (tug) -	31
Hendonhall - -	18	Horden - - -	11	Idaho (4,887) - -	135
Henley - - -	86	Hornby Grange - -	158	Idaho (3,023) - -	95
Henry Charles (smack) -	105	Hornchurch - -	61	Idalia (smack) - -	122
Henry Fürst - -	155, 160	Horngarth - -	36	Idomeneus - -	149
Henry R. James - -	59	Hornsey - - -	137	Ignis - - -	13
Henzada - -	158, 160	Hornsund - -	67	Ikalis (attacked) -	141
Herbert Fischer -	128, 154, 158	Horsa - - -	47	Ikalis (sunk) - -	53
Herbert Ingram (trawler) -	115	Horseferry - -	148	Ikaria - - -	4
Hercules (1 095) (attacked) -	148	Horsham - -	152	Ikbal - - -	47
Hercules (1,095) (sunk) -	84	Horus (trawler) - -	108	Ikeda - - -	84
Hercules (1,295) - -	77	Hosanger - -	158	Ilaro - - -	12
Herdis - - -	92	Hostilius - -	125	Ilderton - -	71
Herefordshire - -	153	Hotham Newton -	137	I'll Try (smack) -	124
Hermione (trawler) -	105	Hova - - -	152	Illustrious (smack) -	107
Hermione - -	43	Howe (s.v.) - -	38	Ilston - - -	57
Hero - - -	146	Howth Head - -	44	Ilvington Court -	75
Hero (trawler) - -	102	H.S. 3 (tug) - -	66	Imani - - -	144
Hero (tug) - -	39	H.S. 4 (tug) - -	63	Imataka - - -	45
Heron - - -	68	H.S. 48 (tug) - -	149	Imber - - -	128, 158
Heron Bridge - -	89	Hubert - - -	157	Imperial - - -	21
Herrington - -	48	Hudworth - -	29	Imperialist (trawler) -	100
Herschel - -	151	Huelva - - -	60	Imperial Transport -	42
Hesione - - -	11	Huguenot - -	24	Inca - - -	143
Hesperian - -	10	Humber - - -	79	Incemore (attacked) -	146
Hesperides - -	46	Humphrey (smack) -	107	Incemore (sunk) -	63
Hesperus (smack) -	106	Hungarian Prince -	126	Indian (trawler) -	99
Hessle - -	133, 142	Hungerford (attacked) -	151	Indian - - -	144, 160
Hibernia (smack) -	118	Hungerford (sunk) -	86	Indian City - -	5
Hidalgo - - -	64	Hunsbridge - -	66	Indian Prince -	1
Highcliffe (attacked) -	134, 140	Hunsbrook - -	147, 152	Indian Transport -	143
Highcliffe (sunk) -	96	Hunsdon (attacked) -	155	Indore - - -	159
Highgate (attacked) -	141, 143	Hunsdon (sunk) -	99	Indrani (5,706) - -	2
Highgate (sunk) -	75	Hunsgrove (attacked) -	152	Indrani (3,640) - -	7
Highland Brae - -	4	Hunsgrove (sunk) -	91	Induna - - -	147
Highland Brigade -	86	Hunstanton (attacked) -	133	Indus - - -	1
Highland Corrie (attacked) -	129	Hunstanton (sunk) -	41		
Highland Corrie (sunk) -	50	Hunsworth - -	131, 138, 156	Industria (trawler) -	118

Name	Page	Name	Page	Name	Page
Industrial (s.v.)	98	Jane Williamson (s.v.)	66	Kankakee	55
Industry	18	Janeta	138	Kansas	158
Industry (s.v.)	65	Janet Ovenstone (motor)	110	Kapunda	25
Ingleby	137	Japanese Prince (attacked)	130	Kara	19
Inglemoor	8	Japanese Prince (sunk)	32	Karagola	143
Ingleside	89	Japonica (trawler)	103	Karema	73
Ingoma	131	Jarrix	146	Kariba	43
Inishowen Head	32	Jason (trawler)	101	Karina (attacked)	147
Inkonka	132	Jean (s.v.)	29	Karina (sunk)	61
Inkosi	85	Jedburgh (trawler)	117	Karma	20
Inkum	7	Jennie Bullas (motor)	112	Karmala	139, 160
Inniscarra (attacked)	150	Jersey (trawler)	112	Karnak	141
Inniscarra (sunk)	89	Jersey City	51	Karonga	47
Innisfallen	90	Jerseyman	26	Karroo	141, 143, 146
Integrity (smack)	107	Jerseymoor	144	Karuma	46
Intent	83	Jessamine (smack)	115	Kasenga	40
Inter-Nos (smack)	115	Jessie (2256)	55	Kashgar	130
Intrepid (smack)	104	Jessie (332)	72	Kassanga (attacked)	142
Inventor	136	Jessie (s.v.)	46	Kassanga (sunk)	84
Inverbervie	22	Jessmore	50	Kassid Karim (s.v.)	98
Invercauld (s.v.)	34	Jevington	30	Kate and Annie (s.v.)	56
Invercoe (s.v.)	4	Jewel (s.v.)	44	Katharine Park	125, 133
Invergyle	5	J. Leyman (trawler)	104	Katherine	34
Inveric	147	J. M. & S. (trawler)	105	Katherine Ellen (s.v.)	158
Inverlogie (s.v.)	36	Johan (motor)	109	Kathlamba	145
Inverlyon (s.v.)	17	Johan Siem	148	Kathleen	62
Inverlyon (smack)	114	John Duncan	127	Kathleen (trawler)	103
Invermay (s.v.)	46	John G. Walter (s.v.)	84	Kathleen (smack)	105
Inverness	157, 141, 143, 152	John Hardie	10	Kathleen Lily	40
Ioanna	143, 148	John H. Barry	84	Katie Cluett (s.v.)	142
Iolanthe (attacked)	149	John Miles	34	Katuna	134
Iolanthe (sunk)	77	John M. Smart (trawler)	121	Keelung	92
Iolanthe (trawler)	102	John O. Scott	97	Keemun	158
Iolo (3,903)	23	John Pritchard (s.v.)	16	Keeper	54
Iolo (3,840)	33	John S. Boyle (trawler)	117	Kelbergen	146
Iona	7	John W. Pearn (s.v.)	48	Kelso	56
Ionian (attacked)	139	John Sanderson	135	Kelsomoor	139
Ionian (sunk)	71	Johnny Toole (s.v.)	88	Kelvinbank (4209)	16
Ionic	131	Jonathan Holt	53	Kelvinbank (4072)	55
Iran	62	Jorgina (s.v.)	84	Kelvinhead	39
Ireland (trawler)	114	Jose de Larrinaga	47	Kelvinia (attacked)	128
Irene (yacht)	12	Joseph (s.v.)	48	Kelvinia (sunk)	21
Irex (smack)	122	Joseph Chamberlain	67	Kempock	88
Iris (s.v.)	49	Joseph Davis	134	Kendal Castle	97
Iriston	68	Joseph Fisher (s.v.)	97	Kenilworth	45
Irthington (attacked)	134	Josephine (trawler)	104	Kenmare (attacked)	128, 151 (2)
Irthington (sunk)	68	Joshua (s.v.)	69	Kenmare (sunk)	82
Iser	34	Joshua Nicholson	38	Kenmore	64
Isla	142	Julia Park	18	Kennett	22
Islandia	135, 159, 160 (2)	Julian (trawler)	99	Kennington	91
Islandmore	52	Juliston	160	Kent	159
Isle of Arran (s.v.)	31	Jumna (attacked)	137	Kentucky	155
Isle of Hastings (attacked)	125	Jumna (sunk)	35	Kerman	154
Isle of Hastings (sunk)	23	Juno	48	Kerry	154
Isle of Jura	53	Jupiter (attacked)	134	Kerry Range	144
Isleworth (attacked)	149, 152	Jupiter (sunk)	51	Kesteven (trawler)	100
Isleworth (sunk)	88	Justicia (attacked)	153	Kestrel (trawler)	116
Ismailia	142	Justicia (sunk)	93	Khartoum	3
Istrar	27	Jutland (attacked)	134	Khartoum (trawler)	108
Italiana (attacked)	133	Jutland (sunk)	73	Khephren (attacked)	140
Italiana (sunk)	22	J. W. F. T. (smack)	107	Khephren (sunk)	59
Itinda	89	J. Y. Short	23	Khiva	140, 146, 147, 158
Itola	144			Kia Ora (barge)	80
Itonus	28			Kieldrecht	92
Ivan (smack)	106			Kilbride	15
Ivernia	29	**K.**		Kilcoan	4
Ivo (s.v.)	133			Kildale	42
Ivydene	84	Kabinga	125	Kildalton (s.v.)	3
Izaston	134, 141, 152	Kaffir Prince	137, 149	Kildonan	68
		Kafue	88	Killarney (s.v.)	49
		Kaipara	1	Killellan	25
		Kaiser-i-Hind	132, 145, 146, 151, 156	Killin	1
		Kalgan	83	Kilmaho	50
J.		Kalibia (attacked)	126	Kilmarnock (trawler)	100
		Kalibia (sunk)	74	Kilwinning	64
Jabiru	157	Kalimba	133	Kincardine (attacked)	133
Jacona	9	Kallundborg	53	Kincardine (sunk)	35
Jaffa	79	Kalo (attacked)	150	Kindly Light (s.v.)	79
James Burton Cook (s.v.)	36	Kalo (sunk)	92	King Alfred (trawler)	114
Jane Gordon (smack)	123	Kamouraska	137, 142	King Athelstan (trawler)	105
Jane Gray (s.v.)	84	Kanawha	140	King Bleddyn	27
Jane Radcliffe	74	Kandy	134, 135, 158	King Charles (trawler)	102
Jane S. (motor f.v.)	120	Kangaroo	140	King David	58
Jane Stewart (motor)	109	Kangaroo (s.v.)	56	Kingfield	161

Name	Page	Name	Page	Name	Page
King George	27	Laertes (sunk)	61	Lindenhall	134
King Idwal	73	Lake Michigan (attacked)	135	Lindsey (trawler)	100
King James (trawler)	110	Lake Michigan (sunk)	86	Lingfield	146
King Lud	2	Lampada	75	Linhope	151 (2)
King Malcolm	26	Lancastrian	145, 160	Linkmoor	11
King William (trawler)	108	Landonia	87	Linmere	155
Kingsdyke	78	La Negra	65	Lisbon	52
Kingsley	152	Lanfranc	43	Lisette	83
Kingsmere	133	Langley Castle (trawler)	109	Lismore	42
Kingstonian (attacked)	143, 156	Langton Hall	13	Little Gem (s.v.)	75
Kingstonian (wreck)	88	Lanterna	23	Little Mystery (s.v.)	47
Kingsway	13	Lanthorn	51	Liverpool	28
Kinpurney	30	Lanuvium	140	Livonia (attacked)	147
Kinross	49	Laomedon	132	Livonia (sunk)	74
Kintail	135 (2)	Lapland	140	Lizzie	127
Kintuck (attacked)	135, 145	Lapwing	72	Lizzie Ellen (s.v.)	57
Kintuck (sunk)	74	Larchmore	8	Lizzie Westoll	55
Kioto	58	Largo (attacked)	146, 154	Llancarvan	89
Kirkby	9	Largo (sunk)	82	Llandovery Castle (attacked)	128
Kirkham Abbey (attacked)	126, 154	Largo Bay (trawler)	117	Llandovery Castle (sunk)	92
Kirkham Abbey (sunk)	94	Largo Law	138, 160	Llandrindod	50
Kirkholm	151	Laristan	22	Llandudno	61
Kirkwood	159	Lark (fishing boat)	106	Llanelly	155
Kish	43	La Rosarina	128, 136	Llangorse (3,841)	22
Kittiwake (attacked)	137	Laura (s.v.) (335)	46	Llangorse (4,703)	151
Kittiwake (sunk)	42	Laura (s.v.) (86)	66	Llanishen	62
Kitty (trawler)	118	Laura Ann (s.v.)	53	Llongwen	20
K. L. M. (smack)	115	Laurel Leaf	139	Lloyd (smack)	123
Knarsdale	13	Laurestina (smack)	104	Llwyngwair	87
Knight Companion	136, 144	Laurium	87	Lobelia (trawler)	100
Knight of the Garter	153 (2)	Lautaro	144	Loch Katrine (trawler)	120
Knight of the Thistle	141	Lavinia Westoll	16	Loch Lomond (smack)	110
Knightsgarth	78	Lavernock	97	Loch Lomond	144, 146
Knight Templar	155	L. C. Tower (s.v.)	8	Loch Ness (trawler)	111
Knowsley Hall	148	Leader (smack)	107	Loch Nevis (smack)	109
Knutsford	20	Leafield	144, 147, 151, 155	Loch Ryan (trawler)	112
Kohinur	51	Leander	150	Loch Tay (smack)	109
Kohistan	73	Leasowe Castle (attacked)	141	Lochwood	6
Kosseir (attacked)	154	Leasowe Castle (sunk)	90	Locksley Hall	49
Kosseir (sunk)	94	Lebanon (trawler)	104	Lodes	49
Kovno	138	Le Bijou (smack)	124	Lofoten	80
Kul (attacked)	155	Le Coq	133, 139, 149	Lomas	8
Kul (sunk)	91	Ledbury	39	Lombok	159
Kumara	155	Leeds City (attacked)	146	Lompoc	156, 160
Kurdistan (attacked)	139, 148	Leeds City (sunk)	89	Lonada	29
Kurdistan (sunk)	67	Leeuwarden	5	Lonclara	29
Kurmark	139	Leicester	15	London	92
Kursk	156	Leicestershire	130	Longbenton	57
Kut Sang	88	Leinster (attacked)	152	Longertie	153
Kwang-Ping	158	Leinster (sunk)	98	Longhirst	34
Kwarra	143	Lena	44	Longnewton	155
Kwasind	36	Lent Lily (smack)	115	Longscar	33
Kyanite	33	Leonatus	75	Lonhelen	86
Kyarra (attacked)	133	Leonora (smack)	122	Loos	139
Kyarra (sunk)	90	Lepanto	139, 150	Lord Carnarvon (trawler)	101
Kyno	72	Lesbian	29	Lord Chancellor (trawler)	117
Kyoto (trawler)	112	Lesto	51	Lord Charlemont (attacked)	154
		Lestris (attacked)	126, 128, 132	Lord Charlemont (sunk)	87
		Lestris (captured)	19	Lord Collingwood (trawler)	115
L.		Leuctra	7	Lord Derby (attacked)	140
		Leven (dredger)	33	Lord Derby (sunk)	77
La Blanca	73	Levenpool	131	Lord Downshire	141
Lackawanna	153, 159, 160	Levensau	153	Lord Dufferin	151
Lackenby	145, 153	Lewisham	50	Lord Kitchener (trawler)	116
Laconia	34	Lexie	22	Lord Ormonde	155
La Correntina	2	Lexington	156	Lord Roberts	56
Ladoga	87	L. H. Carl	59	Lord Scarborough (trawler)	116
Lady Ann	33	Libourne (attacked)	156	Lord Stewart	97
Lady Carrington	25	Libourne (sunk)	98	Lord Strathcona	132
Lady Carmichael	154	Liddesdale	136, 160	Lord Tredegar	22
Lady Charlotte	154	Lightfoot (attacked)	150	Lorle (attacked)	145
Lady Cloe	148	Lightfoot (sunk)	84	Lorle (sunk)	91
Lady Cory-Wright	85	Lilian H. (s.v.)	30	Lotusmere	23
Lady Gwendolen	159	Lillian (trawler)	117	Lough Fisher	84
Lady Helen	70	Lilydale (trawler)	101	Louie Bell (s.v.)	79
Lady Ninian	18	Limasol (s.v.)	49	Lovat	1
Lady of the Lake (s.v.) (51)	57	Lime Branch	140 (2)	Lowdale	44
Lady of the Lake (s.v.) (79)	26	Limeleaf	141	Lowlands	15
Lady Plymouth	130 (2), 134, 156	Limerick	52	Lowmount	49
Lady Salisbury	7	Limesfield	80	Lowther Castle	145, 157
Lady Tennant	153, 155	Linaria	3	Lowther Range (attacked)	147
Lady Wolseley	129	Lincairn	18	Lowther Range (sunk)	87
Ladywood	47	Lincolnshire	40	Lowtyne	91
Laertes (attacked)	126	Linda Blanche	4	Lucania (trawler)	110

Name	Page	Name	Page	Name	Page
Lucellum	135	Malpas Belle (s.v.)	156	Mary Ann (smack)	114
Lucena	7	Malta (6,064)	131	Mary Ann (s.v.)	145
Lucent	32	Malta (2,236)	137	Mary Ann (fishing boat)	109
Lucerna	155	Maltby	82	Mary Annie (s.v.)	39
Lucerne (trawler)	102	Malvina (attacked)	131	Mary Annie (s.v.)	159
Lucida	150	Malvina (sunk)	94	Mary Ann Mandal (s.v.)	155
Luciline	139	Malwa	158, 160	Mary Baird	50
Lucille M. Schnare (f.v.)	124	Manchester Citizen	46	Mary Bell (trawler)	114
Luciston (2,948)	26	Manchester Commerce (5,363)	3	Mary Grace (s.v.)	149
Luciston (2,877)	152	Manchester Commerce (4,144)	61	Maryland	133, 136
Lucky Lass (smack)	118	Manchester Engineer (4,302)	16	Mary Maud (s.v.)	149
Lucy (trawler)	113	Manchester Engineer (4,465— attacked)	37	Mary Orr (s.v.)	66
Lucy Anderson	37			Mary Seymour (s.v.)	66
Ludgate	60	Manchester Engineer (4,465— sunk)	68	Mary Sinclair (s.v.)	155
Ludovicos (s.v.)	68			Mascota	40
Luga	136, 148, 158	Manchester Hero	137	Mascotte	22
Lugano	68	Manchester Importer	157	Mashalla (s.v.)	87
Luis	86	Manchester Inventor (4,247)	30	Mashobra	43
Lullington	32	Manchester Inventor (4,112— attacked)	143	Massouda (s.v.)	89
Lumina (5,950)	12			Maston	62
Lumina (5,856)	141	Manchester Inventor (4,112— sunk)	61	Masunda	15
Lundy	148			Matador	58
Lundy Island	30	Manchester Mariner	151	Matheran	31
Lusitania (30,396)	6	Manchester Miller	53	Matiana (attacked)	134
Lusitania (1,834)	12	Manchester Port	144	Matiana (sunk)	88
Lutterworth	132	Manchester Spinner	79	Matje	129
Lux	31	Manchester Trader	53	Matunga	62
Luxembourg	66	Manchuria (attacked)	147	Maud (s.v.)	18
Luxor	84	Manchuria (sunk)	70	Maude (s.v.)	49
Luz Blanca	94	Mangara	8	Maude Larssen	26
Lycia	32	Mango	156	Mavisbrook	89
Lydia	126, 138	Manhattan (8004)	139	Maxton	77
Lydie	80	„ (8115)	153	May (smack)	121
Lynburn	65	Manistee	57	Mayflower (smack)	116
Lynfield	29	Manitou	128, 146	Mayfly (trawler)	117
Lynorta (attacked)	138, 141	Mantilla	158	Mayola (s.v.)	33
Lynorta (sunk)	62	Mantola (attacked)	134	Maywood	23
Lynrowan	2	Mantola (sunk)	32	McClure (s.v.)	51
Lynton Grange	125	Manxman	148	Meadowfield	8
		Manx Princess (trawler)	119	Meaford	143
		Manx Queen (trawler)	101	Mechanician	78
		Maple Branch	1	Media	133, 157
		Mapleleaf	150	Median (trawler)	116
		Maplewood	41	Medina	47
M.		Marconi	154	Mediterranean (s.v.)	36
		Marden	43	Medora (attacked)	143
Mabel (trawler)	120	Mardinian	51	Medora (sunk)	88
Mabel Baird (attacked)	152	Marere	14	Medway	158
Mabel Baird (sunk)	76	Marga	25	Megantic	128, 132, 135, 138, 156
Machaon	82	Margam Abbey (4,471)	17	Meggie	56
Mackinaw	144	Margam Abbey (4,367)	150	Meissonier	154
Madam Renee	95	Margaret (trawler)	113	Melania	134
Madame Midas	84	Margaret (motor f.v.)	120	Melanie	92
Madeline (attacked)	151	Margaret Sutton (s.v.)	20	Meldon	35
Madeline (sunk)	83	Margarita (375)	33	Melford Hall	56
Madryn	97	Margarita (2,788)	144, 148	Meline	155
Madura (attacked)	129, 143	Margit	41	Melita	159
Madura (sunk)	70	Marguerite (trawler)	111	Membland	4
Magdala	158, 160	Marguerite (smack)	122	Memling	68
Magdeburg	156	Maria (s.v.)	42	Memnon	37
Magellan	94	Marianne McCrum (smack)	123	Memphian	69
Maggie	9	Maria P. (s.v.)	78	Mendocino	159
Maggie Ross (trawler)	116	Marie Elsie	54	Menzaleh	91
Maggie Smith (motor f.v.)	122	Marie Leonhardt	33	Merchant Prince (trawler)	110
Magnus (trawler)	112	Marie Suzanne(attacked)	143, 145, 150	Mercian	130, 146
Mahanada	142	Marie Suzanne (sunk)	95	Mercurius (dredger)	19
Mahopac	144	Marina	24	Mercury (trawler—222)	102
Mahronda	147	Marion Adams (f.v.)	125	Mercury (trawler—183)	110
Maidan	142, 150	Marion Dawson	33	Merganser	13
Maid of Harlech (s.v.)	80	Mariston	59	Merida	158
Main	69	Marjorie (smack)	112	Merioneth	53
Maindy Bridge	74	Marjorie (motor ketch)	54	Merionethshire	90
Maine	38	Marmion	64	Merit (smack)	113
Maizar	79	Marnay (trawler)	99	Merlin (smack)	105
Malachite	3	Marquette (attacked)	128	Mermaid (s.v.)	47
Malakand (attacked)	133	Marquette (sunk)	12	Meroë	25
Malakand (sunk)	45	Marquis Bacquehem	25	Merrie Islington (trawler)	102
Malancha	158	Mars	93	Mersario	68
Malda (attacked)	133, 134, 135, 136, 142	Marstonmoor	86	Mersey (trawler)	100
		Martaban	134, 141	Merton Hall	80
Malda (sunk)	64	Martaban (trawler)	102	Mesaba	96
Malinche	13	Martha Edmonds (s.v.)	10	Messidor (attacked)	152
Mallard	132	Martin	30	Messidor (sunk)	94
Maloja	15	Mary Ada Short	4	Messina	136, 161

177

Name	Page	Name	Page	Name	Page
Metagama	144	Morwenna	6	Newcastle	11
Mexico	139	Moscow	99	New Design No. 2 (s.v.)	48
Mexico City (attacked)	133	Moss Rose (s.v.)	66	Newhailes	151
Mexico City (sunk)	80	Moto	129	Newholm	66
Miami	56	Moulmein (trawler)	116	Newlands	152
Middlesex	50	Mountby (attacked)	153	Newlyn	61
Middleton	13	Mountby (sunk)	91	Newminster Abbey	80
Midland	24	Mount Coniston	21	New Pioneer	143
Midland Queen	9	Mount Temple	27	Newquay	149
Midlothian	68	Mourino	153	Newstead (attacked)	136
Mientji (s.v.)	51	Moyune	86	Newstead (sunk)	36
Mile End	146	Muirfield	58	New York City	10
Millicent Knight (attacked)	137	Munificent (attacked)	126	New Zealand Transport	55
Millicent Knight (sunk)	50	Munificent (sunk)	35	Niceto de Larrinaga (5,018)	2
Milly	96	Munster	156	Niceto de Larrinaga (5,591)	159
Milton	151	Murcia	99	Nicosian	129
Milwaukee (attacked)	155	Murex	28	Nidd	156
Milwaukee (sunk)	96	Muriel	97	Nigaristan	141
Mimosa	10	Muriel Franklin (smack)	110	Nigel	12
Minas Queen (s.v.)	64	Musician	132	Nightingale (trawler)	117
Minia	160	Myrmidon	148	Nigretia	130
Minieh	30	Myrtle Branch (attacked)	143 (2)	Nil Desperandum (trawler)	111
Miniota (attacked)	137, 144, 146	Myrtle Branch (sunk)	86	Nimrod (smack)	107
Miniota (sunk)	65			Nina	148
Minneapolis	16			Ninetta (s.v.)	90
Minnehaha	66			Ningchow	126
Minnetonka	79			Ninian	151
Minnewaska	26	**N.**		Nirpura	86
Minnie Coles (s.v.) (attacked)	145			Nirvana	140, 157
Minnie Coles (s.v.) (sunk)	73	Naamah (trawler)	115	Nitonian	145
Minnie de Larrinaga	144	Nagoya	135	Nizam	161
Minorca	75	Naiad (s.v.)	28	Noel (motor f.v.)	122
Minterne	6	Nailsea Court	30	Noord-Holland	158
Mira	69	Nairn	64	Nora	91
Mirita	154	Nairung	155	Norfolk Coast	92
Mirlo (attacked)	155	Namur	71	Norhilda	64
Mirlo (sunk)	95	Nancy Hunnam (trawler)	109	Normanby	141
Missanabie	96	Nankin	147	Normandiet (1843) (attacked)	146
Missir	90	Nanny Wignall (s.v.)	83	Normandiet (1858) (attacked)	147
Miss Morris (s.v.)	42	Nantes (attacked)	141	Normandiet (sunk)	87
Mitra	144, 154	Nantes (sunk)	89	Normandy	79
Mizpah (s.v.)	27	Narberth Castle (trawler)	116	Normannia	153
M. J. Craig	96	Narcissus (trawler)	120	Norman Prince	132
M. J. Hedley	156	Narragansett (attacked)	128	Normanton	68
Mobile	6	Narragansett (sunk)	37	Norma Pratt	37
Modesta	152	Nascent (attacked)	138	Norseman (9,542)	131
Moeris	19	Nascent (sunk)	64	Norseman (352)	155
Mohacsfield	29	Nascopie	145	North Britain	149 (2), 151
Moidart	91	Natal Transport	10	Northfield (attacked)	146
Molesey	74	Natica	147	Northfield (sunk)	82
Mombassa	24	Navenby (trawler)	116	Northlands (2,776)	6
Monarch	10	Navigator	154	Northland (11,905)	155
Monarch (smack)	115	Neath (Aux. bq.)	39	North Sea	71
Monarda (trawler)	105	Neepawah	45	North Star (smack)	118
Mona's Queen	137	Neilrose	142	Northville	81
Mongara	57	Nellie (trawler)	101	Northwaite (attacked)	138
Mongolia	56	Nellie (smack)	115	Northwaite (sunk)	37
Mongolian (attacked)	155	Nellie Bruce (trawler)	112	North Wales (3,661)	3
Mongolian (sunk)	94	Nellore	134, 142, 143 (2), 146, 154	North Wales (4,072)	25
Monitor (s.v.)	46	Nelson A. (f.v.)	124	Northward Ho! (trawler)	102
Monitoria	11	Nembe	153	Norton	142, 156
Monksgarth	63	Nentmoor	45	Norwegian	37
Monkshaven	149	Neotsfield	97	Norwood	32
Monkstone	60	Neotsfield (s.v.)	57	Nostra Signora del Porto Salvo (s.v.)	34
Monmouth	135, 160	Nephrite	141	Nottingham (trawler)	103
Monmouthshire	142	Neptune (smack)	121	Novian	151
Monsaldale	140	Ness	70	Novington	138, 148, 150
Montebello	92	Nestor (trawler)	116	Novocastrian	11
Montfort	98	Netherby Hall	30	Noya	65
Mooltan	60	Netherpark	150	Nuceria	68
Moorina	12	Netherlee	32	Nugget	8
Moorlands	92	Netherton (s.v.)	33	Nunima	151
Moorside	12	Neto	140, 159	Nuttallia (trawler)	116
Mopsa	20	Netta	22	Nyanga	1
Mora	10	Neuquen	30	Nyanza (6,695)	131, 151, 154
Morazan	25	Nevasa	158, 161	Nyanza (4,053)	98
Mordenwood	51	Never Can Tell (smack)	123	Nyassa	73
Moresby	26	Nevisbrook	59		
Morinier	145, 147	New Abbotshall	142		
Morion	48	Newark Castle (trawler)	109	**O.**	
Morlais	134	Newburn (attacked)	126		
Morning Star (motor)	72	Newburn (sunk)	21		
Morocco	146, 155	Newby	22	Oakby	4
Morvada	155	Newby Hall	147, 160	Oakdale	153

	Page.		Page.		Page.
Oakfield	147	Our Boys (smack)	112	Penvearn	82
Oakleaf	60	Our Tom (trawler)	100	Penylan	24
Oakwell	39	Ousel	127, 128	Pera	70
Oakwood	9	Ovid (attacked)	148	Perce (s.v.)	31
Oberon	140	Ovid (sunk)	73	Percy B. (s.v.)	68
Obsidian	86	Oxonian	136, 156	Percy Roy (s.v.)	32
Obuasi	58	Ozarda	143	Peregrine	137
Ocamo	146			Peregrine (trawler)	123
Ocana (trawler)	101			Peridot (trawler)	120
Occident	151			Perla	54
Ocean	73			Perriton (s.v.)	79
Ocean Queen (trawler)	106	**P.**		Perseus	34
Ocean's Gift (smack)	107			Perseus (trawler)	105
Ocean Monarch	140	Pacific (trawler)	120	Perseverance (smack—30)	121
Ocean's Pride (smack)	119	Pacuare	133	Perseverance (smack—40)	121
Ocean Swell (s.v.)	58	Paddington	60	Perseverance (s.v.)	67
Oilfield (attacked)	142	Pagenturm (attacked)	132, 138	Persia	13
Oilfield (wreck)	84	Pagenturm (sunk)	50	Persic	134, 160
Okement	33	Paignton	37	Persier	75
Okhla	60	Palacine	27	Persimon (trawler)	103
Oldfield Grange (attacked)	144	Palatine	63	Perth	16
Oldfield Grange (sunk)	75	Paliki	149	Peshawur (attacked)	135
Old Head (s.v.)	141	Palm (smack)	107	Peshawur (sunk)	69
Oleander (smack)	108	Palma	141, 145	Petersham	149
Olearia (trawler)	118	Palm Branch	135, 142	Petrel (trawler—151)	116
Olive (3,678)	20	Palmella	95	Petrel (trawler—187)	103
Olive (1,047)	157, 159	Palmgrove	10	Petridge	41
Olive Branch	65	Palmleaf	31	Petrograd	136, 153
Olivia	32	Panama	129	Petroleine	154
Olivine	6	Pancras	143, 156	Petunia (trawler)	109
Olympia (trawler)	110	Pandion	127	Petunia	49
Olympic	130, 131 (2)	Pandora (s.v.)	157	Phantom (s.v.)	53
Omrah	89	Paragon (smack)	124	Phare	71
Oneida	151	Parana	148, 157	Phemius	53
Onitsha	146	Parattah	147	Philadelphian	81
Onward (smack)	119	Paris	144	Philomel	97
Oola	24	Parisiana	17	Phœbe	126
Oopack	98	Parkgate (attacked)	133	Phœnix (trawler)	111
Opal	28	Parkgate (sunk)	41	Photinia	142
Orangemoor	148, 149	Parklands	140 (2)	Phrygia	132 (2)
Orange Prince	12	Parkmill	66	Pikepool	135, 153
Oranian	155	Paros	9	Pilar de Larrinaga	48
Orator	53	Parthenia	53	Pinegrove	13
Orduna	128, 129	Pasadena (s.v.)	124	Pinewood	81
Orfordness	94	Pascal	28	Ping Suey	128
Orient	160	Pasha	55	Pinmore (s.v.)	34
Oriflamme (attacked)	141	Passion Flower (smack)	124	Pinna	137
Oriflamme (sunk)	74	Patagonia	11	Piscatorial (trawler)	104
Origen	92	Patagonier	43	Pitho (s.v.)	29
Oriole	4	Pathan	144	P. L. A. 17	160
Orion	156	Patriotic	155, 159	Planudes	30
Orissa	92	Paul Paix	136, 147, 156	Plawsworth	93
Orlock Head	17	Pavia	143	Plover	158
Ormiston	155	Pearl	22	Plutarch	146
Orna	150	Pearl (s.v.)	23	Pluto	42
Oronsa	88	Pearleaf	148, 160	Plutus	45
Oronsay	29	Peebles (attacked)	143, 146	Plymouth (trawler)	104
Orsova	139	Peebles (sunk)	69	Pochard (trawler)	124
Ortega	125	Peep o' Day (trawler)	109	Pola (attacked)	130
Orteric	13	Peerless	65	Pola (sunk)	38
Orthia	128	Pegasus (trawler)	99	Polamhall	49
Ortolan	55	Pegu	58	Polanna (attacked)	135
Ortona	56	Pelham	7	Polanna (sunk)	62
Orubian	61	Pelican	160	Polaria	152
Oruro	133	Pembroke	134	Polar Prince	67
Oryx (smack)	122	Pembroke Coast	157	Polbrae	89
Osceola	127	Pencaer (smack)	116	Poldennis	146
Oslo (attacked)	130	Pendennis	19	Poldown	69
Oslo (sunk)	63	Penelope	66	Polescar	139, 149, 159
Osmanieh (attacked)	145	Penhale (attacked)	126	Polesley (attacked)	136
Osmanieh (sunk)	77	Penhale (sunk)	50	Polesley (sunk)	97
Osprey	9	Penhallow	91	Policastra	160
Osprey (trawler)	117	Peninsula	60	Politania	63
Osprey (motor)	108	Penistone	95	Poljames	98
Ostpreussen	73	Penmorvah	140	Pollcrea	137
Ostrich (trawler)	114	Penmount	151	Polleon	84
Oswald	45	Pennyworth	157	Pollux (trawler)	100
Oswego	52	Penpol	56	Polo (attacked)	133, 135
Otaki	36	Pensilva	157	Polo (sunk)	81
Otis Tetrax	95	Pentland (trawler)	103	Polpedn	26
Otter (trawler)	111	Pentwyn (attacked)	144, 146	Polperro	159
Otterhound (trawler)	111	Pentwyn (sunk)	98	Poltava	44
Otto (s.v.)	77	Pentyrch (attacked)	134	Poltolia	158
Our Bairns (smack)	120	Pentyrch (sunk)	87	Polvarth	76

	Page.		Page.		Page.
Polvena	70	Pundit	91	Rebono (trawler)	100
Polwell (attacked)	148	Purley (attacked)	146	Recolo (trawler)	101
Polwell (sunk)	91	Purley (sunk)	60	Recorder (trawler)	109
Polymnia	50	Purple Heather (smack)	105	Recto (trawler)	116
Polyphemus	146, 147	Pursue (smack)	118	Redbridge	151
Polyxena (attacked)	132	Putney	142	Redcap (trawler)	115
Polyxena (sunk)	54	Pylades	139	Redesmere	91
Polzeath	138, 141			Red Rose	136
Pomaron	153			Refino (trawler)	111
Pomeranian	86			Refugio	49
Ponrabbel (dredger)	3			Regent	133
Pontiac (1,698)	45	**Q.**		Reginolite	160
Pontiac (3,345)	47			Rego (trawler)	111
Pontwen	141	Quaggy	42	Reims	135
Pontypridd (attacked)	128	Quantock	141	Reindeer (smack) (52)	115
Pontypridd (sunk)	37	Quarrydene	142	Reindeer (smack) (28)	116
Poona	128, 135	Quaysider	151	Reliance (smack)	108
Poplar Branch	155	Quebec (trawler)	111	Reliance (trawler)	121
Porpoise (trawler)	100	Queen (attacked)	134, 136	Relillio	152
Port Adelaide	31	Queen (sunk)	92	Remus (attacked)	153
Portaferry	149	Queen Adelaide	55	Remus (sunk)	82
Port Augusta	132	Queen Alexandra (trawler)	104	Renfrew (3,488)	8
Port Campbell	86	Queen Alexandra	145	Renfrew (3,830)	82
Port Chalmers	139	Queen Amelie	67	Renown (trawler)	109
Port Curtis	62	Queen Bee (smack)	109	Repeat (trawler)	107
Port Dalhousie	15	Queen Eugenie	39	Repton	49
Port Hardy	93	Queen Louise	140	Research (trawler)	104
Porthkerry	51	Queen Margaret	152	Research (smack)	108
Port Jackson (s.v.)	47	Queen Mary	43	Resolute (trawler)	114
Port Kembla	67	Queensland Transport	140	Restless (trawler)	110
Portloe	44	Queen Victoria (s.v.)	91	Restormel	9
Port Nicholson	30	Queen Wilhelmina	6	Reventazon	98
Port Victor	149	Queenswood	33	Revigo (trawler)	100
Portia	8	Quentin	127, 140	Rewa	77
Portsea	154	Querida	142	Reynolds	133
Portuguese Prince	137	Quermore	61	Rhea	92
Portwood	152, 159	Quest (smack)	106	Rhenass	18
Potaro	4	Quiet Waters (trawler)	104	Rhesus	146
Potentate (f.v.)	125	Quillota	144	Rhine (trawler)	100
Powhatan	41	Quito	157	Rhineland	12
Precedent (smack)	117	Qui Vive (smack—50)	104	Rhodanthe	36
Premier (trawler) (169)	104	Qui Vive (smack—22)	116	Rhodesia	69
Premier (trawler) (89)	121			Rhodesia (trawler)	110
Premier (smack)	121			Rhodesian Transport	159
Presto	41			Rhona	26
Pretoria (trawler)	120			Rhydwen	44
Pretorian	142	**R.**		Ribera (3,500)	2
Pretty Polly (smack)	123			Ribera (3,511)	54
Priestfield	156, 157	Rabymere	143	Ribston (3,048)	17
Primo (1,366)	3	Radiance (smack)	119	Ribston (3,372)	59
Primo (1,037)	97	Radium (smack)	108	Ricardo A. Mestres	148
Primrose (s.v.)	40	Radnorshire	29	Richard de Larrinaga	69
Primrose (trawler—62)	118	Rado (trawler)	112	Richmond	8
Primrose (trawler—91)	104	Ragnhild	65	Rideo (trawler)	99
Primrose (trawler—136)	114	Raloo	55	Rievaulx Abbey	22
Prince Abbas	58	Rallus	23	Rinaldo	44
Prince of Wales (trawler)	116	Ramazan	11	Rio Claro (attacked)	142
Princess Caroline	9	Rameses (trawler)	117	Rio Claro (sunk)	78
Princess Dagmar	89	Rambler (trawler)	122	Rio Colorado	38
Princess Helena	141	Ramillies	59	Rio Iguassu	2
Princess Irma	154	Ramore Head	132, 145, 152	Rio Lages	46
Princess May (s.v.)	24	Ramsay	156	Rion	158
Princess Maud	91	Ramsgarth	26	Rion (smack)	121
Princess Melita	138	Ranella	139	Rio Pallaresa	94
Princess Olga	3	Ranger (motor)	93	Rio Parana	4
Princess Royal	90	Ranza	8	Rio Pirahy	24
Princess Thyra	134	Rapallo (attacked)	147	Rio Sorocaba	38
Princess Victoria (1687)	134	Rapallo (sunk)	78	Rio Tiete	16
Princess Victoria (1108)	5	Raphael	139	Rio Tinto	133, 136
Proba (s.v.)	75	Rappahannock	24	Rio Verde	81
Professor	131	Raranga	158	Riversdale	76
Progress (trawler)	102	Rathlin	150	River Forth	35
Prophet	72	Rathlin Head	157	Rivina (smack)	115
Prospector (smack)	106	Ravelston	139	Roanoke (3,755)	137
Prosper	156	Ravenhill (s.v.)	17	Roanoke (4,803)	62
Prosper (smack)	106	Ravensbourne	31	Robert Adamson	17
Protector	29	Ravenshoe	153	Robert Brown (s.v.)	73
Proverb (smack)	115	Ravenstone	156	Robert Eggleton	77
Providence	38	Ravonia	153	Robert Morris (s.v.)	73
Provident (smack)	112	Raymond (s.v.)	139	Rob Roy (s.v.) (93)	141
Prudence (smack)	119	Reapwell	26	Rob Roy (s.v.) (112)	79
Prunelle	95	R.B. 6 (barge)	63	Rochester Castle (s.v.)	43
Pruth	2	R.B. 10 (barge)	66	Rochester City	18
Ptarmigan	6	Reaper (trawler)	122	Rockliffe	19

Name	Page.	Name	Page.	Name	Page.
Rockpool	82			San Urbano	48
Roddam	23			Sanwen	68
Rodskjaer	150			San Wilfrido	1
Rokeby	147	**S.**		San Zeferino	130, 149
Rollesby	67			Sapele (attacked)	144
Roma (s.v.)	27	Saba	154	Sapele (sunk)	71
Romantic (trawler)	120	Sabia	73	Sapphire (trawler) (289)	101
Romany	88	Sabbia	17	Saragossa	53
Romeo	82	Sabrina (trawler)	103	Sarah Radcliffe	25
Romeo (trawler)	114	Sachem	128, 151	Sardinia (1,119)	18
Romford	80	Saga	81	Sardinia (6,580)	151, 153
Romny	82	Sagamore	35	Sarpedon	161
Romsdalen	33	Sagenite	139	Sarpen	153
Rona	19	Saidieh	7	Sarus (crane)	138
Ronald (smack)	120	Sailor Prince	11	Satanita (smack)	116
Rooke	132	Saima	91	Saturn (trawler)	104
Roquelle	158	St. Agnes	150	Saturnia	137, 146, 147
Rosalind	41	Saint Andrew	126	Savan	154, 159
Rosalie (4,237)	34	Saint Andrews	55	Savona	10
Rosalie (4,243)	9	Saint Barchan (attacked)	155	Saxilby	157
Rosario	63	Saint Barchan (sunk)	99	Saxon	89
Rosary (smack)	120	Saint Bernard (trawler)	119	Saxon Briton	31
Roscommon	63	Saint Cecilia	16	Saxonian	32
Rose	160	Saint Clair	152	Saxon Monarch	56
Rosebank	52	Saint Cuthbert (trawler)	100	Saxon Prince	32
Rosebud (smack)	122	Saint Dimitrios	84	Scalpa	44
Rose Dorothea (s.v.)	33	St. Dunstan (dredger)	67	Scarlet Tower	147
Rosefield	136	Saint Edmund	148	Scartho	145
Rosehill	68	Saint Egbert	125	Scawby	11
Roselands	160	Saint Fillans	150	Sceptre (trawler)	102
Roseleaf	141	Saint George (trawler)	102	Scholar	90
Rose Lea	37	Saint Gothard	23	Scotsman	153
Rosella (trawler)	100	Saint Hilda (trawler)	82	Scottish Hero	54
Rose Marie	78	Saint Lawrence (trawler)	101	Scottish Monarch	8
Rosemoor	20	Saint Leonards	135	Scottish Prince	148, 159
Rosemount	62	Saint Louis No. 1 (trawler)	102	Scottish Queen (trawler)	102
Rose of June (motor)	119	Saint Mirren (s.v.)	51	Sculptor (3,846)	44
Roslin (trawler)	105	St. Magnus	81	Sculptor (4,874)	89
Ross	17	St. Margaret	66	S. D. (barge)	20
Rossia	135, 149, 158	St. Mary (smack)	123	Seabird (motor f.v.)	123
Rosslyn (trawler)	116	St. Michan (trawler)	122	Sea Gull (144)	35
Rosstrevor	156	Saint Mungo	48	Sea Gull (976) (attacked)	153
Rosy Cross (smack)	120	Saint Ninian	32	Sea Gull (976) (sunk)	84
Rota	60	Saint Olaf (s.v.)	10	Seal (trawler)	111
Rothesay	15	Saint Olive (trawler)	110	Sea King (trawler)	120
Rotorua	38	Saint Ronald	67	Sea Lark (smack)	113
Roumanian Prince	141, 149	Saint Theodore	28	Sealda	150(2)
Roumanie	10	Saint Ursula	28	Seang Choon	58
Rover (trawler)	112	Salacia (smack)	166	Sea Serpent (902)	16
Rowanmore	24	Saldanha	84	Sea Serpent (2,424)	158
Rowena (attacked)	138	Salerno	11	Seatonia	25
Rowena (sunk)	44	Salient	158	Seattle	132, 152
Roxburgh	83	Sallagh	32	Sebek (attacked)	131(2), 134
Royal Edward	9	Salmo	41	Sebek (sunk)	45
Royal Sceptre	126, 134, 158	Salmonpool	13	Secondo	23
Ruabon	18	Salsette	59	Sedbergh	151
Ruahine	139	Salta	42	Seeker (s.v.)	27
Rubio (attacked)	133	Salvus	138	Seistan	71
Rubio (sunk)	82	Salybia	16	Selby	2
Ruby	39	Samara	9	Semantha (attacked)	139
Ruel	10	Samoset	84	Semantha (sunk)	70
Rugbeian	158	San Andres	96	Senator Dantziger (s.v.)	44
Rugby (trawler)	72	San Bernardo	21	Sequoya	137, 155
Runswick	87	Sandhurst (attacked)	153	Serapis	57
Runo	1	Sandhurst (sunk)	47	Serbino	9
Rupee (smack)	121	Sandon Hall	77	Serbistan	135
Ruperra	56	Sandsend	67	Serrana	78
Rupert (trawler)	114	San Dunstano	127, 133, 148	Serula (attacked)	128
Russian (attacked)	134	San Eduardo	139	Serula (sunk)	97
Russian (sunk)	28	San Fraterno	137	Seti (trawler)	100
Russian Prince	144	San Hilario	44	Setter	96
Rustington	60	San Lorenzo	144	Seven Seas	6
Ruth (smack)	122	San Melito	130, 142	Seymolicus (trawler)	101
Ruth Hickman (s.v.)	90	San Nazario	150	Shadwell	155
Rutherglen (attacked)	145, 151	San Nicola (s.v.)	85	Shamrock (trawler—173)	113
Rutherglen (sunk)	94	San Onofre	49	Shamrock (trawler—170)	119
Ruysdael	96	San Patricio	138, 142	Sheaf Blade (attacked)	141
Rydal Hall	74	San Ricardo	143	Sheaf Blade (sunk)	71
Ryde	147	San Rito	81	Sheaf Brook	154
Rye	86	San Silvestre	127	Sheaf Field	154
Ryhope	135	Santa Amalia	77	Sheldrake	25
Ryton	140	Santa Isabel	86	Shenandoah	17
Rytonhall	65	Santaren	67	Sheerness	129, 138, 160, 161
		San Tirso	131, 158	Shimosa (attacked)	139

		Page.			Page.			Page.
Shimosa (sunk)	- - -	61	Spen	- - -	133	Superb (smack)	- -	112
Shirala -	- - -	93	Spennymoor -	- -	6	Surada	- - -	99
Siamese Prince	- 125, 135, 146, 148		Spenser	- - -	78	Surrey -	- - -	126
Sidmouth	- - -	24	Spermina	- - -	159	Susannah (s.v.)	- -	7
Sikh -	- - -	158	Spero -	- - -	25	Susie (smack)	- -	120
Silksworth Hall	- -	17	Spero Meliora (motor) -		109	Sussex -	- -	132, 136
Silverash	- - -	11	Spey -	- - -	154	Sutherland	- - -	14
Silverburn -	- - -	55	Sphene -	- - -	20	Sutherland Grange	-	135
Silverdale (attacked)	- -	138	Sphynx	- -	153, 156	Sutlej -	- - -	142
Silverdale (sunk) -	- -	83	Spinaway (s.v.)	- -	29	Sutterton (trawler)	- -	117
Silverlip	- - -	150	Spiral -	- - -	21	Sutton (trawler)	- -	105
Silverton	- - -	19	Spital -	- - -	78	Sutton Hall -	- -	127
Silvia (5,268)	- - -	10	Spithead -	- - -	41	Suwanee -	- -	141
Silvia (2,035)	- -	154(2)	Sportsman -	- -	150	Swanmore -	- -	46
Silvia (s.v.)	- - -	40	Spray -	- - -	43	Swan River -	- -	68
Simla -	- - -	16	Springflower (smack) -		108	Swansea Vale	- -	153
Sir Edward Birkbeck (smack)		118	Springhill	- - -	64	Swazi -	- - -	135
Sir Francis -	- -	53	Springwell -	- -	15	Swedish Prince	- -	21
Sir Joseph (s.v.)	- -	37	Squadron -	- -	157	Swiftsure -	- -	66
Sir Richard Awdry	- -	12	Staffa -	- - -	127	Swift Wings -	- -	21
Sir Walter -	- -	60	Staffa (trawler)	- -	109	Swindon -	- -	145
Sir William Stephenson	- -	10	Staithes -	- -	97	Sycamore -	- -	64
Sisapon (trawler) -	- -	118	Stamfordham	- -	21	Sydney Reid	- -	132
Sixty-six	- - -	92	Standish Hall -	- -	80	Sylvanian -	- -	56
Sjaelland	- - -	51	Stanhope -	- -	55	Sylvie -	- - -	19
Skaraas (attacked)	- -	153	Stanja -	- - -	155	Syndic -	- -	138, 153
Skaraas (sunk)	- -	90	Stanley -	- - -	38	Syrian (trawler)	- -	105
Skegness -	- -	153	Starling -	- - -	153	Szechuen -	- -	89
Skerries -	- -	25	Star of Bethlehem (trawler) -		105			
Skipton Castle	- -	145	Star of Peace (trawler) -		105			
Skirbeck (trawler)	- -	99	Star of the Sea (trawler)		113			
Slieve Bawn -	-	153, 154	Star of the West (trawler)		103	**T.**		
Slieve Gallion	- -	159	Start Point -	- -	129			
Smiling Morn (trawler) -	-	110	Statesman	- - -	25	Tabarka -	- -	138
Sneaton -	- -	16	Stathe -	- - -	22	Tabasco -	- -	30
Snowdon (3,189)	- -	90	Steelville -	- -	77	Tagona -	- -	89
Snowdon (1,021)	- -	159	Sten -	- - -	70	Tagus -	- - -	22
Snowdonian (attacked)	- -	144	Stephano -	- -	23	Tahchee -	- -	147
Snowdonian (sunk)	- -	61	Stephanotis -	- -	48	Tahiti -	- -	134, 138
Snowdon Range -	- -	39	Stettin -	- - -	147	Tainui -	- - -	155
Snowdrop (smack)	- -	122	Stockwell -	- -	158	Talawa -	- - -	142
Sofie (attacked)	- -	140	Stoic (trawler)	- -	120	Talisman -	- -	62
Sofie (sunk) -	- -	80	Stolt Nielsen -	- -	83	Tamar -	- - -	5
Solway Prince	- -	57	Stork -	- - -	134	Tambov -	- -	160
Solway Queen	- -	85	Stork (trawler)	- -	117	Tamele -	- -	59
Somali -	- - -	134	Storm -	- - -	66	T. & A. C. (smack)	- -	113
Somersby -	- -	151	Strathalbyn -	- -	27	Tandil -	- - -	37
Somerset -	- -	60	Strathallan -	- -	21	Tanfield -	- -	135, 156
Somme (attacked) -	- -	138	Strathbran (trawler) -		103	Tangistan -	- -	5
Somme (sunk) -	- -	40	Strathcarron -	- -	7	Tanis -	- - -	13
Sommeina -	- -	67	Strathcona -	- -	43	Tapton -	- - -	135
Sonnie -	- - -	62	Strathdene -	- -	23	Tarantia -	- -	140, 147
Sorrento -	- -	152	Strathfillan -	- -	127	Tarantula (trawler)	- -	111
South Arklow L.V.	- -	40	Strathmore (trawler)	-	105	Tarbetness -	- -	83
Southborough	- -	93	Strathnairn -	- -	7	Tarpeia -	- -	49
Southern -	- -	145	Strathness -	- 133 (2), 134		Tarquah -	- -	58
Southern Coast -	- 156, 157(2)		Strathroy -	- -	1	Tartary -	- -	89
Southerndown -	- -	140	Strathtay -	- -	22	Tasman -	- -	97
Southford -	- -	15	Straton (trawler) (198) -		102	Tasmanian Transport	-	159
Southgare -	- -	150	Straton (trawler) (197) -		122	Tasso -	- - -	37
Southgarth (attacked) -	-	131	Strombus -	- -	158	Tatiana (trawler)	- -	110
Southgarth (sunk)	- -	18	Strive (smack) -	- -	106	Taxandrier -	- -	135
Southgate -	- -	150	Strumble (smack) -	-	118	Taxiarchis (s.v.)	- -	79
Southina -	- -	58	Stryn -	- - -	91	Taywood -	- -	149
Southland (attacked) -	-	130	Stuart Prince -	- -	38	T. Crowley (s.v.)	- -	36
Southland (sunk) -	- -	53	Sturton -	- - -	80	Teakwood -	- -	47
South Pacific -	- -	139	Subadar -	- - -	94	Teal (attacked)	- -	127
South Point (3337)	- -	5	Success (smack) -	-	124	Teal (sunk) -	- -	18
South Point (4258)	- -	54	Success (fishing boat) -		109	Teal (trawler) -	- -	119
Southport -	- -	125	Suffolk -	- - -	136	Teano -	- - -	19
Southville -	- -	158	Suffolk Coast -	- -	25	Tecwyn (motor)	- -	34
Southwaite -	- -	142	Summerfield -	- -	9	Teelin Head -	- -	78
South Wales -	- -	56	Sunbeam (s.v.) -	- -	8	Teesborough -	- -	21
South-Western	- -	84	Sunflower (smack) -	-	107	Teesbridge -	- -	151
Southwestern Miller	- -	143	Sunik -	- -	155, 156	Teesdale -	- -	145
Sowwell -	- -	44	Sunlight (s.v.) -	- -	7	Teespool -	- -	128, 150
Sparkling Foam (s.v.)	- -	84	Sunniside -	- -	25	Teiresias -	- -	129
Sparkling Wave (smack)	- -	123	Sunniva (attacked) -		157	Tela -	- - -	48
Sparta -	- - -	24	Sunniva (sunk) -	-	92	Telena -	- - -	45
Spectator (attacked) -	-	139	Sunray (trawler) -	-	102	Tempus -	- -	44
Spectator (sunk) -	- -	63	Sunrise (smack) -	-	122	Tenasserim -	- -	128
Speculator (smack)	- -	101	Sunshine (smack) -	-	108	Terek -	- - -	141
Speedwell (smack)	- -	105	Sunshine (trawler)	- -	111	Tergestea -	- -	15
Speedwell (motor)	- -	109	Suntrap -	- -	72	Terence -	- -	47

	Page.		Page.		Page.
Teucer - - - -	131	Trader - - -	14	Tuskar (sunk) - -	66
Teutonian - - -	15	Trafalgar - - -	10	Tweed (1,777) - -	83
Teviot - - - -	157	Trafford - - -	76	Tweed (1,025) - -	83
Teviotdale - - -	54	Transylvania - -	48	Twiddler (trawler) -	110
Tewfikieh (attacked) -	127	Traquair (attacked) -	129	Twig (s.v.) - -	24
Tewfikieh (sunk) - -	91	Traquair (sunk) - -	14	Twilight - - -	128
Thalia - - -	98	Traveller - - -	156	Tycho (attacked) -	127
Thames (1,327—attacked)	153	Trebiskin (s.v.) - -	158	Tycho (sunk) - -	51
Thames (1,327—sunk) -	90	Trawler Prince (trawler)	110	Tymeric - - -	2
Thames (1,079—attacked)	158	Trecarne - - -	139 (2)	Tyndareus - -	137
The Countess - -	151	Tredegar Hall (attacked)	146	Tyne - - -	55
The Duke - - -	24	Tredegar Hall (sunk) -	71	Tyne Wave (trawler) -	122
Thelma - - -	23	Trefusis - - -	41	Tyrhaug - - -	84
The MacBain (s.v.) -	36	Tregantle - - -	17		
The Marchioness - -	24	Tregarthen - -	158		
The Marquis - -	72	Tregenna - - -	76		
Theodor (s.v.) - -	65	Trekieve - - -	44	**U.**	
The President - -	6	Trelawny - - -	157		
The Princess - -	137	Trelissick - - -	59	Ubbergen - - -	151
The Queen (557) - -	9	Treloske - - -	64	Uda A. Saunders (f.v.) -	124
The Queen (1,676) -	24	Trelyon - - -	60	Uffa - - -	104
Thermidor - - -	141	Trematon - - -	14	Uganda (5,431) (attacked)	133
Theseus - - -	127	Tremeadow - -	30	Uganda (4,315) - -	83
Thespis - - -	160	Tremorvah (attacked) -	139	Uganda (5,431) (sunk) -	90
Thessalia - - -	139	Tremorvah (sunk) -	42	Ugiebrae (trawler) -	104
Thessaly - - -	144	Treneglos - - -	12	Ulster - - -	155 (2)
The Stewart's Court -	95	Tresillian - - -	137	Ultonia - - -	57
Thetis - - -	149	Trevanion - - -	145	Umaria - - -	52
Thirlby (attacked) -	141	Trevarrack - -	26	Umba - - -	88
Thirlby (sunk) - -	57	Trevaylor - - -	136, 142	Umballa - - -	76
Thistle (trawler) - -	113	Treveal - - -	80	Umeta - - -	13
Thistleard - - -	45	Trevean - - -	30	Umgeni - - -	148
Thistleban - - -	28	Trevear (smack) - -	107	Umona - - -	135
Thistledhu - - -	55	Trevelyan - - -	152	Umta - - -	154
Thomas (s.v.) - -	44	Treverbyn (attacked) -	142	Umtata - - -	126
Thomas Holt - -	156, 157	Treverbyn (sunk) -	65	Umvolosi - - -	160
Thordis - - -	126	Trevisa - - -	158	Umvoti - - -	41
Thornaby - - -	15	Trevone (smack) - -	113	United (smack) - -	118
Thornfield - - -	9	Trevorian - - -	134	Unity - - -	88
Thornhill - - -	151	Trevose - - -	38	Unity (smack) - -	120
Thorpwood - -	11	Trevose (smack) - -	108	Upada - - -	156, 159
Thorsa - - -	88	Trewellard - - -	131	Upcerne (attacked) -	143, 151
Thracia - - -	39	Trident - - -	21	Upcerne (sunk) - -	88
Thrift - - -	159	Tringa - - -	13	Upton Castle (trawler) -	117
Thrift (smack) - -	115	Trinidad - - -	55	Urbino - - -	11
Thrush (trawler) - -	107	Trinidad (trawler) -	111	Urd - - -	66
Thurso (attacked) -	133	Tritonia (4,445) - -	35	U.S.A. (trawler) - -	117
Thurso (sunk) - -	23	Tritonia (4,272) - -	3	Usher - - -	135 (2), 148
Tiberia - - -	82	Triumph (s.v.) - -	34	Uskmoor - - -	83
Tillycorthie - - -	35	Triumph (trawler) -	124	Uskside - - -	156
Tintoretto - - -	131, 146	Trocas - - -	78	Ussa (attacked) - -	136
Titan (trawler) - -	112	Troilus (7,625) (attacked)	140	Ussa (sunk) - -	48
Titania (trawler) - -	102	Troilus (7,625) (sunk) -	48	Utopia - - -	9
Titian - - -	64	Troilus (7,562) (sunk) -	3	Utopia (s.v.) - -	35
Tiverton - - -	137	Trojan - - -	138	Uxbridge (trawler) -	102
Toftwood - - -	30	Trojan Prince - -	34		
Togston - - -	70	Trongate (attacked) -	148		
Tokomaru - - -	4	Trongate (sunk) - -	67	**V.**	
Toledo - - -	69	Tropic - - -	148		
Tommi (s.v.) (138) -	141	Trowbridge (attacked) -	137	Valacia - - -	140
Tommi (s.v.) (116) -	89	Trowbridge (sunk) -	72	Valdes - - -	33
Tom Roper (s.v.) -	71	Trunkby - - -	18	Valentia (attacked) -	133, 136
Tonawanda - -	146	Truro - - -	6	Valentia (sunk) - -	59
Tong Hong - - -	57	Try (smack) - -	115	Valeria - - -	141, 145
Topaz - - -	37	Try On (smack) - -	108	Valetta - - -	58
Torbay Lass (smack) -	119	Tubal Cain (trawler) -	99	Valiant (trawler) -	100
Torcello - - -	59	Tudor Prince - -	159	Valour (smack) - -	124
Torilla - - -	131	Tullochmoor - -	7	Vancouver - -	136
Torino - - -	25	Tummel - - -	15	Vandalia - - -	91
Toro - - -	42	Tung Shan - -	50	Vandyck - - -	3
Toromeo - - -	156	Tunisian (trawler) -	104	Vanellus - - -	23
Torquay - - -	126, 151	Tunisiana - - -	7	Vane Tempest - -	160
Torr Head - - -	45	Turakina - - -	62	Vanguard (s.v.) -	26
Torridge - - -	22	Turbo - - -	131	Vanilla (trawler) -	101
Torrington - - -	42	Turino - - -	31	Van Stirum - - -	13
Tors (trawler) - -	106	Turnbridge (attacked) -	143	Varuna (smack) - -	121
Tortuguero (attacked) -	130	Turnbridge (sunk) -	76	Vasari - - -	148
Tortuguero (sunk) -	92	Turnwell - - -	128	Vasco - - -	26
Tottenham - - -	21	Turquoise - - -	8	Vauxhall - - -	46
Toward - - -	12	Turritella - - -	35	Veda (smack) - -	121
Towergate - - -	43	Tuscania - - -	80	Vedamore - - -	32
Towneley - - -	79	Tuscan Prince - -	159	Veghtstroom - -	64
T. R. Thompson - -	85	Tuscarora - - -	148	Vellore - - -	39
Trabboch - - -	1	Tuskar (attacked) -	144	Velocity (trawler) -	104

	Page.		Page.		Page.
Vendee - - - -	58	Wallsend (sunk) - -	95	Western Coast (1,394) -	72
Venetia (attacked) -	134	Walrus (trawler) - -	99	Westfield - - -	86
Venetia (sunk) - -	75	Walton Hall - -	157	Westlands - - -	73
Ventmoor - - -	81	W. A. Massey (trawler) -	122	Westmeath - - -	146
Vennacher - - -	132	Wandby - - -	140	Westminster - -	28
Ventura de Larrinaga -	139	Wanderer (smack) -	108	Westminster (trawler) -	106
Venture (smack) - -	106	Wandle - - -	132	Westmoor - - -	93
Venus - - -	138, 157	Waneta - - -	90	Westmoreland - -	153
Vera (trawler) - -	114	Wapello (attacked) -	141	Westonby - - -	55
Vera Elizabeth (motor) -	93	Wapello (sunk) - -	55	West Point - - -	23
Verbena (s.v.) - -	157	War Anemone - -	152	Westward Ho! (smack) -	106
Verdala - - -	135	War Angler - -	157	Westville - - -	77
Verdi - - - -	64	War Arabis - -	96	West Wales - - -	78
Verdun - - -	149	War Baron - -	78	Westwick - - -	36
Veria - - - -	13	War Clover - -	70	Westwood - - -	98
Verna D. Adams (f.v.) -	124	War Council - -	98	Wetherill (smack) -	113
Vernon - - -	65	War Crag - - -	161	Whateley Hall - -	145
Veronica (smack) - -	112	War Crocus - -	93	W. H. Dwyer - -	64
Vestalia - - -	142	War Deer - - -	159	Wheatear - - -	157
Vestra - - - -	32	War Firth - -	96	Wheatflower - -	81
Vestris - - - -	153	War Grange - -	157	White City (smack) -	107
Vesuvio - - -	17	War Helmet - -	87	Whitecourt - - -	64
Vianna - - - -	85	War Knight - -	155	Whitefield - - -	10
Viceroy (trawler) - -	104	War Monarch - -	81	Whitehall - - -	61
Victor (s.v.) - -	152	War Panther - -	157	White Head - -	70
Victoria (974) - -	72	War Patrol - -	62	Whitgift - - -	17
Victoria (1,689) - -	126	War Rambler - -	159	W. H. L. (s.v.) - -	79
Victoria (1,620) - -	47	War Ranee - -	160	Wigtoft (trawler) - -	99
Victoria (s.v.) - -	43	War Roach - -	161	Wilberforce - - -	58
Victoria (trawler) -	103	War Song - - -	78	Wileysike - - -	89
Victorious (smack—43) -	107	War Spray - -	159	Wilfrid M. (s.v.) - -	4
Victorious (smack—39) -	118	War Swallow - -	93	Wilhelm (s.v.) - -	53
Viella (trawler) - -	110	War Thistle - -	152	Will and Maggie (trawler)	100
Vienna - - - -	66	War Tune - - -	75	Willaston - - -	139
Vigilant - - -	11	Warilda - - -	94	Willena Gertrude (s.v.) -	60
Vigo - - - -	149	Warley Pickering -	31	Willerby - - -	4
Vimeira - - - -	89	Warnow - - -	48	William (s.v.) - -	66
Vine (trawler) - -	105	Warren - - -	40	William and Betty (motor)	119
Vine Branch - -	42	Warri - - -	129	William Dawson - -	10
Vineyard (trawler) -	112	Warrior - - -	45	William George (s.v.) -	23
Vinovia - - - -	74	Warsaw - - -	76	William Martyn (s.v.) -	37
Violet (s.v.) - -	56	Wartenfels - -	31	William Middleton -	136, 149
Virent (attacked) -	146	Warturm - - -	155	William Shepherd (s.v.) -	43
Virent (sunk) - -	96	Warwickshire - -	156	Willie (s.v.) - - -	15
Virgilia (trawler) - -	119	Washington - -	48	Willing Boys (smack) -	121
Virginia - - -	20	Watauga (s.v.) - -	84	Willingtonia - -	96
V. M. G. (smack) - -	109	Watchful (motor) -	109	Wilson (s.v.) - -	86
Volga - - - -	143	Water Lily (s.v.) -	66	Wilston - - -	15
Volnay - - - -	75	Waterville - - -	142	Wilton - - - -	158
Volodia (attacked) -	147	Wathfield - - -	34	Wilton Hall - -	20
Volodia (sunk) - -	63	Wave (smack) - -	122	Wimmera - - -	92
Volpone - - - -	154	Wavelet - - -	126	Winamac - - -	145
Volscian - - -	130	Waverley - - -	76	Windermere - -	19
Voltaire (8,618) - -	27	Waverley (smack) -	109	Windsor - - -	10
Voltaire (409) - -	32	Wayfarer - - -	127	Windsor (trawler) -	101
Volunteer (motor) -	109	Wayside Flower (35) (motor)	101	Windsor Hall - -	78
Vosges - - - -	5	Wayside Flower (21) (motor		Windward Ho! (trawler) -	118
Vronwen - - -	64	f.v.) - - - -	123	Winifredian - -	140, 148
Vulcan (smack) - -	112	W. C. McKay (s.v.) -	78	Winlaton - - -	64
Vulcana (trawler) -	115	W. D. Potts (s.v.) -	48	Winnebago - - -	139
Vulture - - - -	156	W. E. Brown (smack) -	108	Wirral - - - -	50
		Wearside (attacked) -	150	Wisbech (attacked) -	136
		Wearside (sunk) - -	71	Wisbech (sunk) - -	62
		Weelsby (trawler) - -	110	Witham (trawler) - -	117
		Wega - - - -	55	W. M. Barkley - -	69
		W. Harkess - -	24	W. M. L. (s.v.) - -	92
		Welbeck Hall - -	87	Wolf - - - -	20
		Welbury - - -	8	Wolverton - - -	127
W.		Welcome (smack) -	107	Wonganella - -	145
		Welfare (smack) - -	104	Woodbine (smack) -	105
Waago (trawler) - -	104	Wellholme (s.v.) - -	137	Woodburn - - -	149
Wabasha - - -	146	Wellington (attacked) -	150	Woodfield (4,300) - -	137
Wad Lukkus - -	159	Wellington (sunk) -	97	Woodfield (3,584) (attacked) -	129
W. A. H. (smack) - -	113	Welshman - - -	147	Woodfield (3,584) (sunk) -	12
Waihemo - - -	84	Welsh Prince - -	24	Woolston - - -	89
Waikawa - - -	70	Wentworth - -	65	Woolwich - - -	12
Waimana - - -	148	Westburn - - -	14	Worcestershire - -	33
Waimarino - - -	161	Westbury (attacked) -	130	Wordsworth - -	36
Waipara - - -	147, 159	Westbury (sunk) - -	65	Worsley Hall - -	147
Wairuna - - -	52	Westergate (attacked) -	126	Wragby - - -	29
Waitemata - - -	93	Westergate (sunk) -	87	Wreathier - - -	74
Waiwera - - -	144	Westerham - - -	155	Wrexham - - -	126
Wallace - - -	137	Western Australia -	155	W. T. Lewis (s.v.) -	130
Wallsend (attacked) -	159	Western Coast (1,165) -	4	Wychwood - - -	39

	Page.		Page.		Page
Wyncote	157	Yeovil (trawler)	117	Zambesi (sunk)	40
Wyndhurst	75	Yochow	84	Zamora	147, 159
Wyvisbrook	159	Yonne	17	Zanoni	49
		Yorkshire	142	Zara	43
X.		Young Admiral (smack)	107	Zarina (trawler)	101
		Young Bert (smack)	120	Zealandic	129
		Young Clifford (smack)	121	Zeno	81
Xmas Rose (smack)	106	Young Frank (smack)	107	Zenobia (trawler)	100
		Young Harry (smack)	108	Zent	16
		Young Percy (smack)	106	Zermatt	60
		Ypres	61	Zeta	67
Y.		Yzer	20	Zillah	70
				Zinal	95
Yang-Tsze	152, 156			Zingara	155
Yarrow	159	**Z.**		Zircon (smack)	114
Yarrowdale	28			Zone	77
Yearby	147	Zafra	17	Zoroaster	29
Yeddo	13	Zambesi (attacked)	138		